Real Estate

Principles and Practices

11th edition

Real Estate
Principles and Practices

Jerome Dasso Alfred A. Ring

H. T. Miner Chairholder in Real Estate
University of Oregon

Professor Emeritus
University of Florida

PRENTICE HALL, *Englewood Cliffs, New Jersey* 07632

Library of Congress Cataloging-in-Publication Data

Dasso, Jerome J.
    Real estate principles and practices / Jerome Dasso, Alfred A.
Ring. -- 11th ed.
        p.   cm.
    Ring's name appears first in earlier editions.
    Includes index.
    ISBN 0-13-766015-4
    1. Real estate business. 2. Real property. 3. Real estate
investment.   I. Ring, Alfred A. II. Title.
HD1375.R5 1989
346.7304'37--dc19   88-7693
[347.306437]   CIP

Editorial/production supervision: Linda Zuk
Interior design: Andrew Zutis
Cover design: Dawn Stanley
Manufacturing buyer: Margaret Rizzi

® 1989, 1985, 1981, 1977, 1972, 1967, 1960, 1954, 1947, 1938, 1922 by Prentice-Hall, Inc.
A Division of Simon & Schuster
Englewood Cliffs, New Jersey 07632

Printed in the United States of America
10 9 8 7 6 5 4 3 2 1

ISBN 0-13-766015-4

Prentice-Hall International (UK) Limited, *London*
Prentice-Hall of Australia Pty. Limited, *Sydney*
Prentice-Hall Canada Inc., *Toronto*
Prentice-Hall Hispanoamericana, S.A., *Mexico*
Prentice-Hall of India Private Limited, *New Delhi*
Prentice-Hall of Japan, Inc., *Tokyo*
Simon & Schuster Asia Pte. Ltd., *Singapore*
Editora Prentice-Hall do Brasil, Ltda, *Rio de Janeiro*

*Dedicated to the reader's success
in the field of real estate
and to the wise use of our land resources.*

Contents

Preface

This book is written and designed for anyone seeking a clear understanding of the many decisions involved in acquiring, owning, and disposing of real estate. The intent is to create a mind set that will make it easier for the reader to understand the world of real estate and how change affects values. The real estate ownership cycle used herein provides an integrated, continuing frame of reference for this decision-making and action process. Some call this continuing cycle "the real estate process." Using and administering realty to maximize the self-interest of the investor—usually taken to mean maximizing wealth—is the assumed motivation or driving force in the cycle.

Using this book you will learn about brokerage, finance, contracts, valuation, closings, and investing—with a balanced perspective. Hence, you will have a sound foundation for further involvement in real estate. The format also provides an investor or practitioner with a continuing awareness of the decisions to be made in any particular situation or transaction.

As in the tenth edition, the material is divided into major parts, each of which takes up important components of the decision-making cycle. The parts are: (1) defining property rights, (2) acquiring ownership rights, (3) finance, (4) markets, and (5) value analysis and investment. Also, in a few instances, chapter sequences have been changed to improve the flow of presentation.

Each chapter begins with a summary outline of topics and types of decisions to be discussed. Key terms, references, and discussion questions continue to be provided, along with case problems. Also, more illustrations have been added to make the material more easily understood. Note that while some topics, such as taxation and deed restrictions, may be mentioned in several places, treatment in depth is provided only once at the most appropriate place.

Great effort has been made to provide accurate, up-to-date, authoritative information. However, the reader should recognize that this material is not meant to replace accounting, legal, real estate, or other professional advice. If expert assistance is needed, the services of a competent professional should be obtained.

As you use *Real Estate*, please note items that you think would improve the material, and send them to the authors at this address:

> Jerome Dasso
> c/o Real Estate Editor
> Prentice Hall
> Englewood Cliffs, NJ 07632

Your help in improving past editions is greatly appreciated.

Jerome Dasso
Eugene, Oregon

Alfred A. Ring
Gainesville, Florida

Real Estate

Principles and Practices

1

Real Estate: The Business

Our main ability is that we know how to win at this game of business. Society can make any rules it wants, as long as they are clear cut, the same for everyone. We can win at any game society can invent.

Michael Maccoby, *The Gamesman*

Many consider real estate to be a market-oriented game in the sense that players, rules, and a way to determine winners and losers is present. They have the same attitude as Michael Maccoby's gamesman, quoted at the beginning of this chapter. In fact, real estate is more than a game because it involves the very setting of life itself. Everyone must play because we all need space in which to live. After all, "under all is the land."

Further, the world of real estate is very pragmatic and very dynamic. The ventures of major players in recent years, such as Trammel Crow, Donald Trump, and Olympia & York, are examples. More recent examples may include the sizable acquisitions of Japanese, British, and German investors. In any event, providing proper preparation for maneuvering in the world is the overall purpose of this book. With mastery of the content, a reader will be able to make an informed decision as to whether to enter, and the best way to enter. To aid the reader, the "rules of play" are set forth throughout. This chapter takes up the several broad topics as outlined. Subsequent chapters also begin with such an outline. Terms introduced in each chapter are defined at the end of the book.

Important Topics or Decision Areas Covered in this Chapter

Real Estate and the Economy
Land Ownership and Land Use
Real Estate as Wealth
Real Estate Employment

History of the Game

Career Opportunities in Real Estate
Brokerage Services
Finance and Investment
Property Development
Specialized Nonbrokerage Services
Professional Organizations
Compensation

Practitioner Ethics
Fair Housing Laws
State/Province Regulation of Licensees

Questions for Review and Discussion

Key Concepts Introduced in this Chapter

Agent

Blockbusting

Broker

Client

Customer

Equity

Escrow

Fair housing laws

Principal

Realtor®

Steering

Real Estate and the Economy

The activities and interaction of people involved in the buying, selling, exchanging, using, and improving of realty make up the real estate market. The commodity is rights in real property. Extending the game analogy, each community constitutes a separate field of play, a distinct market. Each person keeps his or her own score. To win is to maximize self-interest, whatever that may be. Winning usually means ending up with the most money, but it may take the form of earning fees from services rendered or satisfactions from homeownership. The rules of play come from several sources, including contract and real estate law, accounting and finance, management and marketing theory, licensure regulations, and professional and personal ethics. The setting for the community, in turn, is the United States and the world economy. So, a brief look at real estate and the economy seems an appropriate place to begin our discussion.

Type	Land Area (million acres)	Percent Distribution
Land Ownership		
Private	1,380	60.93
Public	885	39.05
Federal	730	32.23
State and Local	155	6.84
Totals	2,265	100.00
Land Use		
Cropland	469	20.71
Grassland	597	26.36
Forest	655	28.92
Special Uses[a]	270	11.92
Other	274	12.10
Totals	2,265	100.00

[a]Urban, transportation, recreation, wildlife, farmstead, national defense, and industrial areas.
SOURCE: *Statistical Abstract of the United States 1986*, Table 336.

FIGURE 1-1
U.S. land ownership and land use, 1982

2.3 billion acres   640 acres scare mile
43,650 square feet = acre

LAND OWNERSHIP AND LAND USE

To begin with, just how much land is there in the United States? The answer is about 2.3 billion acres, 2.265 billion to be exact. An acre contains 43,560 square feet, which is the equivalent of a square parcel, about 209 feet on a side. A typical single family lot contains about one-sixth of an acre. There are 640 acres in a square mile, which means the United States contains about 3.539 million square miles. A regional shopping center requires about 160 acres or one-fourth of a square mile.

Who owns this land? Public lands account for 39.1 percent of the total, leaving 60.9 percent in private ownership. See Figures 1-1 and 1-2. The government controls almost one-third (32.1 percent) of the land area.

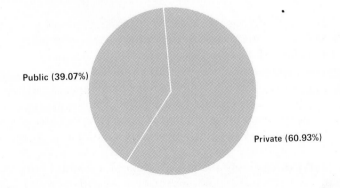

Public (39.07%)

Private (60.93%)

SOURCE: Data in Figure 1-1.

FIGURE 1-2
Percentage distribution of land ownership in the U.S., 1982

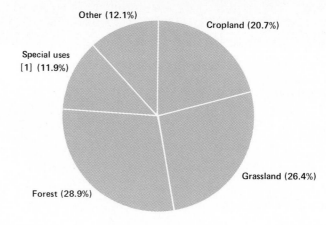

Other (12.1%)

Cropland (20.7%)

Special uses
[1] (11.9%)

Grassland (26.4%)

Forest (28.9%)

SOURCE: Data in Figure 1-1.

FIGURE 1-3
Land use in the U.S., 1982

How do we use or employ the land? Of the total, 11.9 percent is employed for urban areas, transportation, recreation and wildlife, national defense and industrial uses, and farmsteads. The balance is devoted to agricultural purposes and other. See Figure 1-3. Somewhat less than 2 percent is devoted to urban uses.

In the overall, we really have no absolute shortage of land. We do often have a shortage of well-located urban land, however, just as we may have a shortage of highly productive agricultural land. Still, there is no shortage of land that may legally be farmed. Understanding the characteristics that make land productive and valuable for urban purposes is an essential part of understanding the real estate industry.

REAL ESTATE AS WEALTH

Real estate occupies a dominant position in the United States insofar as real wealth is concerned. It accounts for nearly three-fourths of the fixed tangible or nonhuman wealth of the United States. See Figures 1-4 and 1-5. Stocks, bonds, and mortgages are often obvious in investment portfolios. But a substantial portion of the worth of stocks and bonds actually reflects a claim on the earning power of business real estate. The total amount of mortgage loans outstanding, representing a direct claim on real estate, approaches the national debt in size. As may be noted in the figures, real estate as wealth is about evenly split between residential and nonresidential real estate.

Personal property was not taken into account as wealth by the data sources used. At the same time, this lack would certainly be more than offset by the worth of governmental lands, the value of which also was not reported. Governmental lands, as was mentioned earlier, account for 39.1 percent of the total land area of the United States.

	Sub Totals	Class Totals	Percent Distribution
Non-Real Estate Assets			
Household Durables		$ 1,095	10.42
Nonresidential Equipment		1,779	16.92
Private	$1,396		
Public	383		
Real Estate Assets			
Nonresidential Structures		3,076	29.26
Private	$1,591		
Public	1,485		
Residential Structures		2,761	26.27
Private	$2,694		
Public	67		
Private Agricultural Land		730	6.94
Private Nonagricultural Land[a]		1,071	10.19
Public (Values not available)			
Total		10,512	100.00

SOURCE: *Statistical Abstract of the U.S., 1986;*Tables 537, 775, and 1134.
NOTE: Miscellaneous personal property not included. Human capital regarded as intangible wealth.
[a]Value calculated to be 20 percent of value of privately owned, nonagricultural real estate.

FIGURE 1-4
Fixed tangible wealth in the United States, 1982, with percentage distribution by type of asset (billions of dollars)

REAL ESTATE EMPLOYMENT

Employment in real estate and construction typically account for about 5.5–7 percent of total employment in the United States. See Figure 1-6. The value of new construction approximates 10 percent of our gross national product each year. This construction includes from 1.0 to 3.0 million new dwelling units each year.

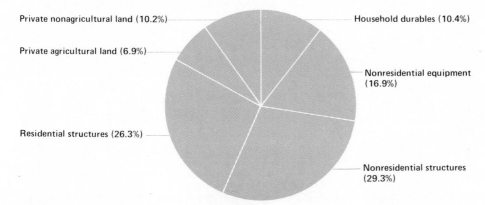

Private nonagricultural land (10.2%)
Household durables (10.4%)
Private agricultural land (6.9%)
Nonresidential equipment (16.9%)
Residential structures (26.3%)
Nonresidential structures (29.3%)

SOURCE: Data in Figure 1-4.

FIGURE 1-5
Percentage distribution, by type of asset, of the fixed tangible wealth in the United States, 1982

Meanings of Real Estate

"Real estate" means different things to different people. It has three common meanings, which are interrelated. For clarification, consider the following definitions.

A field of study. Real estate as a field of study concerns the description and analysis of the occupational, physical, legal, and economic aspects of land and permanent improvements on or to land. The purpose is greater knowledge and understanding for decisions and actions. Books, magazines, courses, and other educational activities focusing on real estate as a business or commodity fit into this definition. This entire book concerns real estate as a field of study.

A form of business activity. Those who look to real estate as their occupation, profession, or line of business activity are considered to be "in real estate." Appraisers, brokers, builders, lenders, planners, housing analysts, and in-

vestors are in real estate in this sense. In other words, real estate as a business activity focuses on human activities concerned with land and its use or improvement. This chapter explains the meaning further.

A financial asset. Real estate as a form of property or financial asset begins with the land and includes all "permanent" improvements on or to the land. As a financial asset, real estate is a national resource, whether publicly or privately owned. It accounts for one-half to two-thirds of the tangible wealth of the United States. This asset or property concept is the most common meaning of real estate and is also the object or focus of all other meanings. The remainder of this book is devoted to real estate as a financial asset. Unless otherwise indicated, the terms "real estate," "realty," and "real property" are used interchangeably in referring to real estate as an asset or commodity.

History of the Game

Real estate transactions date back to the Old Testament. Jeremiah tells of buying a field from his cousin, Hanamel, for 17 shekels of silver.

Land subdivision and promotion is part of our heritage in the United States as well. George Washington and Robert Morris actively engaged in land speculation in the newly laid-out Washington, D.C. Morris, a signer of the Declaration of Indepen-

Year	Employment in Real Estate and Construction	Total Employment	Percentage of Total in Real Estate and Construction
1940	2,517,155	44,888,083	5.61
1950	4,014,790	56,239,449	7.14
1960	4,415,057	64,639,256	6.83
1970	5,003,049	77,308,792	7.04
1980	7,249,000	102,315,000	7.05
1990P	8,603,000	118,315,000	7.27

SOURCE: U.S. Census of Population, 1940–1970; 1980 and 1990 projection from *Statistical Abstract of the United States 1986*, Table 683. Owing to estimation procedures and classification of components, data for 1980 and 1990 may not be exactly comparable to those from other sources. Calculations by authors.

FIGURE 1-6

Employment in real estate and construction compared to U.S. total employment, selected years, 1940–1980, with 1990 projected

dence, died in poverty after serving over 3 years in prison as a result of his speculation.

Until the twentieth century, most buy-sell transactions took place directly between owners and purchasers. After an agreement was made, lawyers were often called in to draw up the contract and to look after the details of the transaction.

In the early 1900s, the real estate business was largely unorganized and fiercely competitive. An attitude of *caveat emptor* (let the buyer beware) generally prevailed. But the use of **brokers** and **agents** soon became established practice. The need for standardized brokerage practices, in turn, led to trade organizations known as real estate boards. The boards proved so successful that the National Association of Real Estate Boards (NAREB) was organized in 1908. The association changed its name to the National Association of **Realtors**® in 1974. Membership of the association has since grown as shown in Figure 1-7.

In 1917 both California and Oregon passed legislation requiring brokers and salespersons to be licensed. All states and provinces now require brokerage personnel to be licensed. In many states, contractors, appraisers, managers, and other real estate specialists must also be licensed.

Career Opportunities in Real Estate

Specialization in real estate has developed rapidly because no one person can master all the knowledge available. Recognizing four broad occupational areas (investment, development, brokerage, and nonbrokerage services) helps greatly in knowing who does what and why. See Figure 1-8. Specializations within each area are discussed here as career opportunities. Some players can and do perform in more than one area.

BROKERAGE SERVICES

Brokers act as catalysts or stimulants to the real estate market in that they earn fees or commissions by bringing buyers and sellers together. With investors and lenders,

Year	Number of Boards	Membership Brokers
1911	43	3,000
1920	225	10,077
1930	608	18,916
1940	458	14,162
1950	1,100	43,990
1960	1,370	68,818
1970	1,590	98,400
1980	1,806	284,654
1988	1,860	N.A.

SOURCE: National Association of Realtors®.

FIGURE 1-7
National Association of Realtors®: boards and membership for selected years, 1911–1985

REAL ESTATE			
Capital investment	Property development	Brokerage services	Nonbrokerage services
— Equity investment	— General development	— Residential	— Appraisal
			— Architecture
		— Commercial investment	— Counseling
— Mortgage lending	— Land subdivision		— Education
			— Escrows
— Syndication investment	— Construction	— Syndication	— Insurance
			— Legal
		— Industrial	— Management
— Leasehold investment			— Planning
		— Farm and land	— Title analysis

FIGURE 1-8
Career areas in real estate

brokers are instrumental in carrying out the exchange function of the real estate market.

Brokerage is most generally thought of first when discussing careers in real estate because of its prominent image. The image comes about because brokers advertise widely and sales people move about freely in search of listings and sales. With their extensive professional expertise and business contacts, brokers save *clients* much time, trouble, and money.

To protect the public, brokers are required to be licensed in all states and provinces. Those interested may obtain appropriate information about becoming licensed by contacting the real estate regulatory agency of their home state or province.

Briefly, obtaining a license requires an application and then an examination. An examination fee must usually be sent in with the application, along with other required documentation. In general, a person must be a high school graduate or equivalent, be at least 18 years of age (in some states, 21), and be a citizen to qualify to take the exam.

Upon applying, a notice will be sent to you stating when and where the exam may be taken, plus any additional response expected of you. Exam results will be sent to you after the exam is taken. If you pass, a license will be sent to you once you send the license fee. If you do not pass, depending on state or provincial requirements, you may usually take a second examination later. Several weeks are usually required for a license application to be processed. Anyone proposing to take the exam upon finishing this book is advised to request application information and materials immediately.

Residential. Most new licensees enter the real estate business through residential brokerage, and this is where most licensees earn their living. A broad understanding of personal psychology and of real estate finance, law, and economics is needed. In addition, the work requires a good understanding of the community, that is, an awareness of income levels and life styles by neighborhood, plus a working knowledge of local tax rates and zoning ordinances. Knowing the location and quality of schools, shopping facilities, and transportation routes is also important. The product is mainly single family houses, condominiums, and vacant residential lots.

Commercial. Arranging the sale and exchange of properties such as apartment buildings, office buildings, stores, and warehouses is the essence of commercial brokerage. The emphasis is on commercial- or investment-type properties. Leasing and/or development of these properties may also be undertaken. Management of these property types for wealthy clients, engaged in other lines of work, may be necessary.

Current knowledge of population, income, and other economic trends, finance, and tax law are all necessary to structure transactions for greatest advantage to the parties involved. High income and great personal satisfaction may be derived from solving these high value problems. Commercial practitioners have considerable prestige, independence, and numerous opportunities for personal investing.

Syndication. An outgrowth of commercial brokerage is securities and syndication brokerage. The work often requires changing the physical form (development) and the legal form (creating a corporation or limited partnership) of real estate to make a more marketable package and, in turn, enhance value. Mainly large and high value properties are involved because the overhead of the syndication process must be absorbed.

Industrial. Knowledge of a community's economic base, transportation system, sources of raw materials, and factors of production such as water, power, and labor is very important for industrial brokers. An engineering or industrial management background is helpful because the work is frequently highly technical. Facts and figures must be collected, analyzed, and presented in a useful form to sophisticated industrial clients. The work is satisfying because complex problems are solved and prestige and high incomes may be gained.

Farm and Land. Farm and land brokers specialize in the sale, leasing, and management of farms and ranches and in the sale and development of raw land. Properties handled may run from a 5 acre "ranchette" to a 160 acre farm to a 12,000 acre corporate spread. Obviously, a thorough knowledge of farming and ranching, and a rural background, are helpful. Specifically, knowledge of soils, crops, seeds, fertilizers, seasons, machinery, government subsidies, and livestock is needed, which in turn must be related to production costs and market prices of the products involved. Capable farm and land brokers have considerable independence, high earning capacity, and opportunities for personal investment.

FINANCE AND INVESTMENT

Investors and lenders are the primary decision makers in the real estate business. They put up the money and take the risks. They account for all major financial interests in the use and operation of real estate. Career specializations are usually as follows.

Equity Investment. Real estate investors lay out money today for uncertain payments to be received in the future; they usually borrow to help finance the purchase of the investment properties and to realize positive financial leverage in the process. The *equity* investor then owns the property but is responsible for keeping the property operational, for debt-service payments, and for any other risks and obligations that may develop.

Most owner-users and owner-investors hold property for long-term benefits. Some even develop or improve property to realize these benefits. On the other hand, some owner-investors, termed speculators, specialize in holding property for short periods in seeking quick gains. A license is not required to become an equity investor, although money and willingness to take risks are necessary.

Investors have many different modes of operation. Some investors regularly follow classified advertisements, visit brokerage offices, and maintain contacts with "cooperative" brokers in search of underpriced properties. Some investors develop properties for themselves. Others are particularly creative in adapting properties to changing local conditions to their own advantage. No license is needed by an investor handling his or her own properties.

Mortgage Lending. The investment of most lenders is in the loan to the owner, which is secured by the property. The lender's main concerns are that the property be kept operational and well maintained and that the loan be repaid on schedule. Banks, savings and loan associations, and insurance companies are the traditional lenders on real estate. These institutions typically use salaried personnel to initiate and administer the loans.

Syndication. Investors familiar with stock and bond investments are increasingly investing in real estate by buying shares in syndicated properties. The portion of all real estate that is syndicated is relatively small, but this type of ownership promises to be increasingly more important.

Leasehold Investment. Renters obtain use of property in return for rental payments to the owner. The renter may develop a leasehold investment or interest because the market value of the space is greater than the capitalized value of the rent. However, most leasehold investors begin by renting an improved property, modernizing it, subdividing it, and subleasing portions at much higher rents; the eventual result is a lease position that involves little or no cash equity investment but still yields a high cash flow.

PROPERTY DEVELOPMENT

In the overall, developers, subdividers, and builders add to or modify the supply of real estate. They specialize in adjusting the quality and quantity of space, a major and very necessary function of the real estate market. A more detailed discussion of each function follows.

Developer. A developer converts raw land into a complete operating property by adding roads, utilities, buildings, landscaping, financing, promotion, and other creative ingredients. Thus, a developer combines the functions of a subdivider and building contractor. A developer coordinates the activities of architects, engineers, planners, attorneys, contractors, lenders, and others toward the completed project. A sound working knowledge of construction, building materials and methods, business matters, the law, and finance are necessary. The work is creative and satisfying, and considerable prestige and financial gain accrue to a successful developer. In many ways, a developer is the epitome of a decision maker and risk taker.

Subdivider. Subdividing is the splitting of a large parcel of land into lots for sale to builders or the general public. Much management skill, negotiating ability, and marketing ability are required. Also, a sound knowledge of financing and local government regulations is needed.

Contractor. Contractors add or modify improvements to real estate, for profit, within the limits of local codes and ordinances. Close accounting and control of material and labor costs are particularly important if a profit is to be realized. Engineering and business education is particularly helpful. Investment and speculative opportunities are many.

SPECIALIZED NONBROKERAGE SERVICES

Technical expertise is available to the finance and investment group on a fee or salary basis, as follows.

Appraising. A professional appraiser must have an analytical mind, practical experience, technical knowledge, and good judgment. Capability in accounting, mathematics, computers, and writing is important for success in this line of activity. Poise is also necessary because appraisers are frequently called on as expert witnesses concerning value in court cases. Beginning appraisers usually gain experience by valuing one-family residences and later broaden their abilities so they can value a wide range of properties. Appraising is one of the more respected specialties in real estate.

Architecture. Architecture involves designing and overseeing the construction of improvements to land. The services of an architect are most used for complex and expensive buildings that must meet both aesthetic and economic standards. Considerable desire and talent is necessary to become an architect. The work is highly creative, prestigious, and community building.

Community Planning. Planners relate development and land use to a community's economic and social needs. Planners usually work for local governments, civic groups, corporations, or developers or as consultants. Thus, planners coordinate the use of land and water resources in providing for new streets and highways, schools, parks, and libraries as well as for residential, commercial, and industrial neighborhoods.

Counseling. A counselor gives expert advice on real estate problems, based on broad knowledge and considerable experience in the areas of brokerage, appraisal, development, financing, leasing, and investment. Needless to say, to maintain a reputation and a practice, the advice given must usually lead to success. Counseling is usually combined with some other specialty, such as appraising, research, education, or market analysis. Counseling, while a relatively young specialization, is growing rapidly.

Property Management. A property manager supervises real estate for an owner, usually to achieve the maximum financial return. Rents are collected, space is leased, and the property must be repaired and maintained. Many corporations have a vice president for real asset management, recognizing that real estate constitutes nearly one-half, or more, of the firm's total assets.

Teaching. The demand for real estate education is considerable at the licensure, professional, and college and university levels. Practitioners often teach short courses (2 or 3 days) in subject areas in which they are expert; many also teach at community colleges. Teaching helps them keep current in their specialty and exposes them to new clients.

Title Analyst, Title Insurance, and Escrow Services. Title search and examination and title insurance are involved in almost every real estate transaction; and escrow closings are increasingly being used. The purpose is to help people achieve secure ownership.

PROFESSIONAL ORGANIZATIONS

Specialization developed in real estate because the field is too broad for any one person to master all its aspects. Professionalism has developed hand in hand with specialization, because the specialists want and need public recognition to maintain themselves. Professional recognition carries with it (1) prestige and distinction, (2) easier acceptance in marketing services, and (3) social responsibility. Those just entering the industry must develop expertise and gain professional recognition to compete. Knowing specializations and professional organizations is, therefore, a great advantage to newcomers. The main specializations and their related professional organizations are shown in Figure 1-9.

COMPENSATION

Income for real estate specialists is competitive with incomes in other professional specialties. Income tends to vary with personal ability, size and type of operation, and section of the country. Figure 1-10 gives an indication of possible income. The highest incomes were earned by those in sales, leasing, and executive positions, for the most part. Huntress Real Estate Executive Search, Inc., compiled the data. The middle range of compensation is probably representative of incomes by specialty; the extremes merely show what is possible. The lowest pay, $12,000, was for an on-site apartment building manager; the highest, $240,000, occurred in office building sales.

Practitioner Ethics

Real estate is a high-value asset, the buying, selling, and financing of which involves large amounts of money. And people tend to act in strange ways and do bizarre things when large amounts of money are involved. Also, discrimination enters into the play at times.

Specialization	Professional Organization
Appraising	American Institute of Real Estate Appraisers[a]
	American Society of Appraisers
	International Association of Assessing Officers
	Society of Real Estate Appraisers
Architecture	American Institute of Architects
Brokerage	Farm and Land Institute[a]
	International Real Estate Federation, American Chapter[a]
	National Association of Realtors®[a]
	Real Estate Securities and Syndication Institute[a]
	Realtors National Marketing Institute[a]
	Society of Industrial Realtors[a]
Building/Contracting	Associated General Contractors of America
	National Association of Home Builders
Counseling	American Society of Real Estate Counselors[a]
Developing	Urban Land Institute
Educating	American Association of Housing Educators
	American Real Estate and Urban Economics Association
	American Real Estate Society
	Real Estate Educators Association
Financing	American Bankers Association
	Mortgage Bankers of America
	National Association of Mutual Savings Banks
	U.S. League of Savings Associations
Insuring	American Institute for Property and Liability Underwriters
Managing	Institute of Real Estate Management[a]
	American Institute of Corporate Asset Management
Owning	National Apartment Owners Association
	National Association of Building Owners and Managers
Planning	American Planning Association

[a]Affiliates of the National Association of Realtors®, 430 N. Michigan, Chicago, IL 60611.

FIGURE 1-9
Real estate specializations and professional organizations

To protect the public, to avoid legal problems, and to preserve professional reputations, government regulators and established practitioners increasingly demand high ethical behavior in real estate transactions. Licensed practitioners, particularly brokerage personnel, are closely scrutinized in their daily business activities for violations of ethical behavior; a breach may result in loss of license. Included here is a summary of the more prominent ethical issues that bind real estate practitioners.

FAIR HOUSING LAWS

Real estate is a "public interest" commodity, and real estate brokerage is a "public service" industry. The average person uses the services of a real estate broker only once every 5 or 10 years and, consequently, is not usually knowledgeable about the services of brokers and the treatment to be expected from brokers. The U.S. government and some state governments, therefore, have laws, known as open or *fair*

Category/Position	Compensation		
	Low	Mid-Range	High
Appraisal, executive manager	$33,000	$64,100	$ 96,000
Appraiser	21,000	45,000	82,000
Architect	23,000	47,200	100,000
Apartment manager, on-site	12,000	23,400	48,000
Brokerage operations manager	30,000	51,800	110,000
Leasing manager, office building	27,000	70,700	225,000
Sales, commercial-investment	32,000	70,200	225,000
Corporate VP, real estate	45,000	74,400	140,000
Manager, office building	27,000	59,200	100,000
Market research manager, apparel chain	24,000	39,600	75,000
VP, Real estate, apparel chain	40,000	70,000	105,000
Property manager, regional mall	24,000	50,300	75,000
Sales, industrial	28,000	70,800	150,000
Sales, residential	16,000	37,600	130,000
Sales, office buildings	36,000	84,100	240,000

SOURCE: "Huntress 1986 Real Estate Compensation Report," *National Real Estate Investor*, June 15, 1986, pp. 6–26.

FIGURE 1-10
Annual income by real estate specialization

housing laws, to ensure equality of treatment of the public by brokers and, in some cases, by owners. Title VIII of the Civil Rights Act of 1968 is of greatest concern to brokers. Owners are subject to both the Civil Rights Act of 1968 and the Civil Rights Act of 1866, as upheld by the U.S. Supreme Court.

The Civil Rights Act of 1968. The Civil Rights Act of 1968 with its amendments requires that real estate agents (brokers) in their business dealings on behalf of principals (clients) must consider their product (real estate) as "open" and for sale, lease, mortgage, and so forth to all legally competent persons. The 1968 act, therefore, prohibits discrimination because of an individual's sex, race, color, religion, or national origin. This act applies particularly to housing transactions; that is, one-family dwellings, apartment buildings, and even vacant residential parcels.

The following acts are specifically prohibited or unlawful if they are based on an individual's sex, race, color, religion, or national origin:

1. Refusing to sell, rent, or negotiate or to otherwise make a dwelling unavailable to any person
2. Using terms, conditions, or privileges of sale or rental to deny or to discriminate against any person
3. Discriminating in the provision of services or facilities against any person
4. Using advertising or oral statements to limit the sale or rental of any dwelling
5. Falsely representing, as a means of discrimination, that a dwelling is not available for inspection, sale, or rental
6. Inducing for profit, or attempting to induce for profit, the sale or rental of housing because of entry, or prospective entry, into a neighborhood of persons of a particular sex, race, color, religion, or national origin

In addition, denying access to, membership in, or participation in any multiple listing service, real estate brokers' organization, or other service or organization relating to the sale or rental of dwellings as a means of discrimination is unlawful.

Almost all the unlawful acts listed relate specifically to discrimination in sale or rental transactions. Steering and blockbusting are also prohibited. *Blockbusting* means using scare tactics (of neighborhood invasion by a minority group) to induce panic sales of houses by owners at below-market prices. The blockbuster buys the homes at the reduced prices and later sells them at inflated prices to minority persons. *Steering* is channeling home seekers to specific areas to create a blockbusting situation or to maintain the homogeneous makeup of a neighborhood.

Individual owners are exempt from the 1968 Civil Rights Act if

1. A sale or lease is arranged without the aid of real estate agents
2. A sale or lease is arranged without discriminating advertising
3. Fewer than three houses or fewer than four apartment units (one of which is owner occupied) are owned by the seller

For enforcement of the law, violations of and complaints about the 1968 Civil Rights Act must be reported to the Fair Housing section of any Housing and Urban Development (HUD) office within 180 days of an infraction.

The Civil Rights Act of 1866. Fair housing had a banner year in 1968. A U.S. Supreme Court decision in June 1968 upheld the constitutionality of the Civil Rights Act of 1866. Under the 1866 act, owners of property are barred from discriminating in the sale or rental of real or personal property to anyone on racial grounds. This 1968 landmark decision derived from a lawsuit brought by a Mr. Jones against the Mayer Company, the builder of a community near St. Louis, Missouri. The Mayer Company had refused to sell Jones a home solely because Jones was black.

Jones' attorney centered the case on the almost forgotten Civil Rights Act of 1866. The district court dismissed the complaint, and the court of appeals affirmed. The Supreme Court, however, reversed, holding that the statute does cover discrimination on racial grounds and that the statute is constitutional under the Thirteenth Amendment to the U.S. Constitution.

In effect, this decision voids the exemptions given individual property owners, under the open housing law of 1968, who sell their homes without assistance from real estate brokers. Those seeking protection under the reaffirmed Civil Rights Act of 1866, however, must bring legal action personally. Support from government agencies is not provided for in the law. Aside from an injunction ordering sale, when a lawsuit is successful, the property owner faces no statutory penalty for damages and no fine under the Civil Rights Act of 1866.

STATE/PROVINCE REGULATION OF LICENSEES

The Code of Ethics of the National Association of Realtors®, first adopted in 1913, contains detailed standards of professional conduct for brokerage personnel. However, it is not comprehensive for other areas of specialization. Thus, the discussion of ethics here is somewhat broader. Licensure examinations for both broker and salesperson in some states include questions on the Realtor's Code. If this applies, copies may usually be obtained from your local realty board or the National Association of Realtors® headquarters in Chicago.

Relations with Customers. The public, as buyers or potential buyers of real estate, looks to practitioners, as specialists and experts in real estate, for reliable information upon which to make decisions on buying, selling, building, and leasing property. Beyond this, certain other ethics are expected of practitioners.

1. There is to be no discrimination by reason of race, creed, sex, or place of national origin.
2. General knowledge possessed in such areas as planning, zoning, or economic trends is to be current and reliable.
3. All pertinent facts provided about a parcel of real estate shall be clearly and accurately stated; none shall be concealed, exaggerated, misrepresented, or otherwise caused to be misleading.
4. An appraiser may not have employment or size of fee contingent on the value to be estimated. Such a contingency leads to biased value estimates and destroys the professional image of appraisers.
5. Any written estimate of the value of a property shall include the following items (to avoid misuse of the estimate):
   a. Estimate of value
   b. Date of estimate
   c. Interest appraised
   d. Limiting conditions
   e. Description of entire property

Relations with Clients. Some ethical guidelines to be expected by clients (principals) from practitioner-specialists (as agents) are as follows:

1. Market value shall not be misrepresented to an owner, as in trying to list a property.
2. Upon accepting an agency agreement, a practitioner owes complete fidelity to the principal. Full disclosure must be made of any personal interest in the client's property or of other conflicts of interest.
3. Compensation must not be accepted from more than one party in a transaction without full and prior disclosure to all parties in the transactions.
4. Owner-principals must be shown all offers as soon as they are received, whether from a prospective purchaser or another broker.
5. Any monies of principals or clients must be placed in special trust accounts until the transaction is completed or terminated.

Relations with Fellow Practitioners. Agents, to be effective, must build and maintain high levels of cooperation and communications with fellow personnel to further the principal's purposes. Sensitive areas of cooperation and communication among brokerage personnel are as follows:

1. Brokerage personnel must willingly and fully disclose the nature of any listing to fellow sales personnel: open listing, exclusive right to sell, and so on.
2. All pertinent facts, negotiations, and communications must be promptly transmitted to an owner through the listing broker.

1. Is ownership by the federal government of about one-third of the land in the United States desirable?
2. How might the value of governmental lands be estimated?
3. Name the four main classes or groups of participants in the real estate business and briefly explain the function of each.
4. What are the purposes of real estate licensing laws? Of real estate ethics? Are the purposes achieved?
5. Explain the effect of the 1968 Civil Rights Act on real estate brokerage operations.
6. Give three reasons for belonging to a profession. Are these reasons valid in real estate?
7. Do real estate investors have a responsibility to society?
8. Are higher or special educational requirements desirable for entry into the real estate business? What are the requirements in your state or province, if any?
9. List and distinguish among the three most common meanings of real estate.
10. Most owners and potential owners are not well prepared to buy and sell property. Do you agree? Explain.
11. What are the main concerns and goals of a real estate specialist? Is the rational investor approach likely to be useful to someone interested in offering specialized real estate services? How?

Case Problems

1. Ascertain the current totals of real estate debt and of the federal debt. How do they compare?
2. Identify a real estate specialization that interests you greatly. Arrange an interview with a prominent local practitioner in this specialty. Ask about necessary preparation, everyday duties and activities, possible risks, and compensation levels. Report to class.

2

Real Estate: The Commodity

The first man, who, having enclosed a piece of ground, bethought himself of saying, "This is mine," and found people willing to believe him, was the real founder of civil society.

Rousseau

Real estate has a myth and reality much like the myth and reality of the sirens of Greek mythology. Where the sirens, with their seductive singing, lured unwary sailors and adventurers to their deaths on rocky coasts, real estate, with its promise of exciting careers and quick riches, may entice many aspiring practitioners and unwary investors to their ruin on the reefs of ignorance and inexperience. Ulysses, with proper preparation, was able to hear the songs of the sirens while escaping the reality of their rocky coasts. In like manner, a newcomer to real estate, with proper preparation, may realize substantial financial rewards and/or career goals while avoiding its hidden reefs.

Real estate, as a business or occupation, was discussed in chapter one. In this chapter, real estate is taken up as a commodity with value.

As a commodity, real estate is extremely complex. Each parcel has distinct physical characteristics. Depending on the culture or society in which each parcel is located, specific institutional and economic characteristics apply. In addition, most urban real estate is man-made space that will be used over a long time. Builders and subdividers, investors and lenders, other professionals, local government officials, and users jointly create this space. Each parcel has a distinct space and time utility, benefit, or advantage. It is this distinct space-time utility that provides the basis for

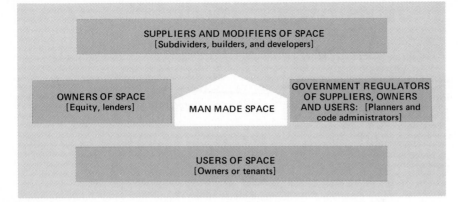

FIGURE 2-1

Real estate as space and market participants (Brokerage and nonbrokerage professional services used by all)

individual decisions, for differing values, and, in the end, for driving the real estate market. See Figure 2-1. James Graaskamp of the University of Wisconsin was the prime initiator of this space-time concept of real estate.[1]

Important Topics or Decision Areas Covered in this Chapter

Real Property Characteristics
Physical Attributes
Institutional Attributes
Economic Attributes

Market Characteristics
Classes of Property Traded
Market Attributes

Book Organization and Decision Analysis
The Decision-Making Cycle
Rational Investor Versus Economic Being Assumption
Investor versus Practitioner Viewpoint

Investor Goals and Constraints
Case Examples
Motivations, Goals, Constraints
Some Applications

Decision-Making and Administrative Processes
The Decision-Making Process
The Administrative Process

Questions for Review and Discussion

Key Concepts Introduced in this Chapter

Accessibility
Durability or fixity of
investment

Economic person
Externality
Heterogeneity

[1]See James A. Graaskamp, *Fundamentals of Real Estate Development* (Washington, D.C.: Urban Land Institute, 1981).

Highest and best use	Land use
Indestructibility	Market value
Infrastructure, urban	Rational investor
Immobility	Scarcity
Institution	Situs
Interdependence	Specific performance
Investment value	

Real Property Characteristics

Real property has distinct attributes or characteristics as a market commodity, which can be classified as physical, economic, and institutional. In practice, the distinction among the classes is sometimes uncertain. Figure 2-2 summarizes these attributes.

PHYSICAL ATTRIBUTES

Immobility. Land is physically immobile; that is, not movable in a geographic sense. Some of the substance of land—soil, minerals, oil—may be removed and transported, but the geographic location of a site remains fixed. A nuclear weapon might destroy an entire city, but the geographic location of each parcel would be determinable by its latitude and longitude. It is **immobility** or *fixity* that causes land to be classed as real estate. Because of immobility, too, the market for land tends to be local in character; demand must come to the site. Immobility results in the value of each parcel changing in direct response to changes in its environment, for better or for worse. Immobility also means that taxes may be levied against a parcel and collected, in one way or another; the parcel cannot escape.

Buildings and other realty improvements are not necessarily immobile. But, considerable expense must be incurred to move a house or other structure. This means that if the value of a site becomes great enough in a use inconsistent with the site's improvements, the improvements may be moved. In turn, the value of the improvements in a different location must exceed the cost of moving them.

Physical	Economic	Institutional
Immobility or fixity	Situs	Real property law
Indestructibility	Scarcity	Public regulation
Heterogeneity	Interdependence	Local and regional custom
	Durability or fixity of investment	Associations and organizations

FIGURE 2-2
Physical, economic, and institutional characteristics of real estate

Indestructibility. Land, as space, cannot be destroyed; it goes on forever; it is indestructible. The *indestructibility* of land tends to popularize it as an investment. A sophisticated investor, of course, distinguishes between physical indestructibility and economic (value) durability. Physically, land may go on forever, but its value may be destroyed by changing conditions. For example, the value of certain locations may disappear almost completely, as has happened in "ghost towns." On the other hand, the permanence of land and space means that it may be used to support buildings and other improvements with extremely long lives. The buildings themselves, however, tend not to be indestructible in a physical or a value sense.

Heterogeneity. No two parcels of land are exactly alike, an attribute called *heterogeneity*, nonhomogeneity, or unlikeness. At the very least, parcels have unique locations. Differences between parcels usually extend to size, shape, and topography. In addition, public *infrastructure* (roads and utilities) are location specific and, not being uniform throughout a community, cause parcels to be unlike. Finally, *externalities,* positive and negative influences from other parcels, cause parcels to differ. Zoning ordinances and title restrictions are efforts to limit negative external influences.

Heterogeneity has caused land to be legally declared a "nonfungible" (not substitutable) commodity requiring specific performance in contracts involving use or sale. In contrast, grain or stock would be considered fungible or legally substitutable. *Specific performance* means that the terms of a contract must be exactly complied with; for example, a particular property must be conveyed and not a similar or substitute property.

Heterogeneity is the basis of problems in pricing or valuing realty because comparison of a site or property with similar but different properties is often a very complex undertaking. Heterogeneity economically means that real estate is not homogeneous as a product, that the market is not perfectly competitive, and that the allocation of resources may not be efficient.

Heterogeneity extends to buildings and other realty improvements. Structures usually differ in size, appearance, and complexity. Even if built to the same plan, workmanship and materials might differ slightly. At the very least, location and orientation are slightly different. In addition, differing owners and occupants lead to differing levels of use and maintenance.

INSTITUTIONAL ATTRIBUTES

An *institution* is an accepted and established part of society, as an organization, a belief, law, or custom. Institutions shape the way we think and act and, in turn, may exert a profound influence on values.

Real Property Law. Real property has its own laws for the most part. Real estate is owned as real property rather than as personal property. This means that the laws affecting real estate ownership and financing differ from laws affecting the ownership and financing of personal property. This difference is so great that several subsequent chapters are devoted to real property law.

Public Regulation. In a fashion similar to real property law, public regulation also affects real estate as a commodity or a product. Community plans and zoning ordinances, rent controls, subdivision regulations, laws pertaining to mortgage finance, and building codes all go to shape the development and use of our realty. Chapter 6, "Governmental Limitations to Ownership," looks at the nature and effects of public regulation of real estate in some detail.

Local and Regional Custom. Custom is a way of thinking or acting that is specific to a local area; it is similar to the habit of an individual. Custom results in Cape Cod houses being prevalent in one community, almost nonexistent in another. New York City is relatively compact, whereas Los Angeles has been described as "17 suburbs in search of a city." Bicycles are an accepted mode of transportation in some areas and firmly rejected in others. Subtle local attitudes and customs do influence the nature, appearance, and use of real estate.

Associations and Organizations. The National Association of Realtors®, the National Association of Homebuilders (NAHB), and the Urban Land Institute all greatly influence the nature of the real estate business and the development of communities. Homebuilders change their methods of construction in response to manuals published by the NAHB. The Urban Land Institute did much of the pioneer work to get planned unit developments, shopping centers, and curvilinear street systems accepted across the country. The National Association of Realtors® emphasizes higher ethics and promotes multiple listing systems to improve the real estate business. In another direction, the Federal National Mortgage Association cooperates with other organizations to create and maintain a secondary mortgage market, an institution developed specifically to benefit real estate.

ECONOMIC ATTRIBUTES

Economic attributes are beyond the physical and institutional characteristics of real estate. Economic attributes may be a result of physical or institutional attributes. In any event, situs, relative scarcity, and interdependence all clearly affect real estate values.

Situs. The location of a parcel relative to other external land-use activities is called *situs.* Both physical and economic location are involved, with the economic relationships being the more important. Situs is the result of choices and preferences of individuals and groups in selecting sites. Differences in situs cause otherwise similar parcels to have different uses and different values.

A major factor affecting locational choice is *accessibility:* the relative costs (in time, money, and effort) of getting to and from a property. When the relative costs of movement to and from are low, a property is said to have high accessibility. In turn, the property's value is likely to be high. Alternatively, poor or difficult accessibility generally leads to low values. The use of, and the improvements or buildings added to, a parcel are largely the result of its situs or relative accessibility. Other situs factors influencing locational decisions include direction of population growth, availability of services and utilities, shifts in centers of trade and manufacture, direction of prevailing winds, sun orientation, and changing life styles.

Scarcity. Certain types of land may be in comparatively short supply, termed *scarcity.* The physical supply of land is fixed for all practical purposes. But there is only relative scarcity of space as such. With money, time, and effort, the supply of space can be increased in response to demand. Even so, the fear of an ever-increasing population outrunning a limited physical supply of land has caused periodic land booms and busts.

Interdependence or Modification. The mutual interaction of uses, improvements, and values of parcels is called *interdependence.* The development of a shopping center across the street strongly influences how we use our site. Or we may have a restaurant along a major highway that depends heavily on nearby motels for customers. Development of a bypass route may severely cut business of both the motels and our restaurant, with a consequent sharp drop in value of all properties. Thus, the use and value of a given property is subject to modification by decisions and changes made about other properties. In net, the value relationship between properties tends to be synergistic, both positively and negatively.

Durability of Investment. The long time required to recover costs of a site and its improvements is termed *durability of investment.* Once a site is purchased and labor and capital committed to build a structure, the investment is "set" or "fixed" for many years from the viewpoint of the community or of society. Drainage, sewage, electric, water and gas facilities, or buildings cannot as a rule be dismantled and shifted economically to locations in which they would be in greater demand. The investment is "sunk" in the realty and must be recovered during the economic life of the improvements. Further, the immobility and fixity of land and land improvements make real estate vulnerable to taxation and other social or political controls.

At the same time, fixity of investment does not preclude disposition of the property by one investor and acquisition by another. That is, the investment is not "set" or "fixed" for a specific owner.

Market Characteristics

The function of any market, by definition, is trade or exchange. Beyond trade, the market gives signals to change the quantity and quality of the product. Finally, markets provide price and value information to participants and others.

The real estate market appears disorganized and inefficient when compared with the stock and bond markets. This difference is partially due to greater government intervention in real estate markets, which takes the form of regulations, several types of taxes (property, sales, and income) and tax incentives, as depreciation allowances. Further, unit values tend to be high. In addition, differences flow from the physical and economic characteristics of real estate, discussed earlier, and from the classes of property traded. Thus, all things considered, real estate markets are undoubtedly less efficient than stock, bond, and grain markets.

To help clarify the discussion, classes of property traded are taken up before discussing the distinct characteristics of real estate markets.

CLASSES OF PROPERTY TRADED

Each class of real property represents stratified demand and constitutes a submarket that is often the basis of specialization by real estate practitioners.

Residential. Residential real estate is generally considered to include one-family and multifamily residences up to six units plus vacant land or lots that might be improved for anything up to six dwelling units, whether located in a city, a suburb, or a rural area. Technically, larger multifamily properties are also residential, but because of their higher value and greater complexity, they are more frequently classified as commercial investment properties.

Commercial Investment. Large apartment buildings, stores, shopping centers, office buildings, theaters, hotels and motels, vacant commercial sites, and other business properties are termed commercial investment real estate. Most commercial-investment properties are rental or income producing and are usually located in urban areas.

Industrial. Industrial real estate includes factories, warehouses, utilities, mines, and vacant industrial sites. Large industrial properties are usually located in or near urban areas because of their dependence on an adequate labor supply. Industrial plants may sometimes be located and developed in rural areas if the availability of raw materials and power so dictates. Labor will be drawn to the plant, and eventually an urban area will grow up around or near the plant.

Rural (Farm and Land). Farms and ranches make up the bulk of the rural properties that are bought and sold. Recreational properties are often included, but they seem likely eventually to become a distinct class. Raw, vacant land near urban areas, though ripe for conversion to residential, commercial, or industrial use, is also typically included in this category.

Special Purpose. Churches, colleges, and other educational institutions, hospitals, cemeteries, nursing homes, and golf courses are collectively termed special-purpose properties. These properties are bought and sold only infrequently, and no specialization has developed around them. They tend, for the most part, to be located in or near urban areas.

Public. Public agencies need real estate for highways, post offices, parks, administration buildings, schools, and numerous other public uses. Public properties are generally held for a long time and are sold only if considered excess property. For the most part, public properties are not considered as being bought and sold in a free market.

MARKET ATTRIBUTES

The physical, institutional, and economic characteristics of real estate, along with its market attributes, all work in concert to make real estate markets relatively inefficient. Stated another way, the time and money costs of overcoming space and of collecting and analyzing data all work to make real estate markets less efficient than most other markets. Let us look at these market attributes in more detail.

Localized Competition. Immobility, heterogeneity, and durability cause competition for real estate to be area specific. Inability to move real estate in response to changes in supply and demand conditions and lack of similarity and standardization means that a potential buyer must inspect each property of interest to understand fully its merits. Without easy means for buyers to compare one property with another, competition between properties is limited. Localized competition is more true of residential properties than of commercial-investment and industrial properties. Investors and industrialists are usually more knowledgeable and have greater reason to look around carefully before buying a property.

Stratified Demand. People generally seek and use real estate for a specific purpose. For example, a family looking for a detached home limits its search to one-family houses. A merchant seeking a property from which to sell furniture looks only at store buildings. An investor for dollar income looks only at income properties. The market responds accordingly. The market for apartments may be very active while the market for one-family residences may be very slow. Specializations develop, and properties are classified according to this stratified demand; thus, brokers, appraisers, and managers may limit their activities to income or industrial real estate only.

Confidential Transactions. Buyers and sellers usually meet in private, and their offering and agreed prices are not freely disseminated as a rule. Moreover, transactions are not made in a central marketplace but rather in homes, offices, restaurants, cars, planes, and dozens of other such locations. Decentralized and confidential transactions make market information difficult to collect and, therefore, costly.

Why Real Estate Decisions are Different

High value. Real estate has relatively high value. This high value tends to be a market-limiting factor; that is, the ability of most people to own real estate is limited because of their relatively low wealth or earning capacity.

Long economic life. Real estate has a long life. Land goes on forever; buildings last for decades. It generates services and income over an extended time. During this period, its services must be used as produced. They cannot be stored, to be used later, like toys, wheat, or cars. Each time period must stand on its own. If an apartment remains vacant during one month, the loss of rent cannot be made up in the next.

Debt financing. Debt financing is usually necessary as well as desirable. It is (1) necessary because most people cannot afford to purchase real estate outright, and (2) desirable because the use of credit provides the opportunity for financial leverage and the possibility of a higher rate of return on the money invested. *Leverage*, or "trading on the equity," results from borrowing money on a property at an interest rate lower than the rate at which the property earns. Leverage is illustrated, by example, in the chapters on real estate finance and investment.

High transaction costs. In both time and money, costs of buying and selling real estate are high. At a minimum, several days are required to complete a simple closing and transfer of ownership. Several weeks is usual, and several months is not uncommon for large expensive properties. A dollar transaction cost of 6 or 7 percent of the sale price of a property is also usual.

Relatively Uninformed Participants. Most buyers and sellers lack adequate price and value information in making their decisions because having information collected and analyzed is costly. Business firms increasingly use real estate specialists—negotiators—in buying and selling properties to overcome information limitations. But owners and potential purchasers often make less than optimal decisions in their real property dealings. Only those who are closely associated with the market have relatively easy access to price and value information. Nevertheless, sellers and buyers increasingly seek, and pay for, price information to maximize self-interest. Of course, this means higher transaction costs.

Supply Fixed in Short Run. Supply, in the real estate market, is fixed for periods of a few years. If demand falls, it remains. If demand increases, several weeks to several months or longer are required to build new structures. Conversion of existing properties is no less time consuming. In any given year, the total supply of space is increased by only 2–3 percent.

Demand in a specific area or community can be quite volatile in the short run. Thus, demand could advance sharply. The consequence is sharp price increases for space if demand runs too far ahead of supply. On the other hand, prices decrease only slowly if demand drops because owners resist taking losses on high value, durable assets.

Book Organization and Decision Analysis

The decision-making cycle of a person making choices about owning, managing, and eventually disposing of real estate provides the framework for explaining real estate as a commodity.

The material is presented in modules. The modules are presented in a sequence that parallels a sales transaction but includes, in addition, ownership, administration, and disposition concerns. The modules are (1) defining ownership rights, (2) conveying ownership rights, (3) financing, (4) markets and the investment climate, and (5) value analysis. It is our belief that this approach facilitates reading, discussion, and understanding and makes us much more aware of the decisions and actions needed to become a successful participant in the real estate market.

The cycle approach also makes it easier to take risk into account. Risk is the chance that reality will differ from assumption about reality. Every day, suppliers of space, investors, lenders, and users must make assumptions about future personal, political, financial, and technological conditions.

Following discussion of the decision-making cycle, a brief explanation is given for the use of a "rational investor" viewpoint.

THE DECISION-MAKING CYCLE

Real estate ownership decisions are best divided into three broad phases: (1) *acquisition* or *purchase*, (2) *administration and management*, and (3) *alienation* or *disposition*. The one commonality to all these decisions is the person making the choices. Almost every aspect of real estate is touched on in this *decision-making cycle*. Every investor-owner goes through these phases. As one investor passes ownership on, another takes it up. The three phases may also be called the investment or ownership cycle. The cycle, with an indication of decisions to be made in each cycle, is shown in Figure 2-3.

The cycle is more easily understood if looked at in its entirety. Better investment decisions and results are likely if all aspects of ownership are looked at prior to actual acquisition because the phases are interrelated. For example, understanding property rights involved should precede any considerations of financing or investment analysis. Assuming a purchase contract, clear title has to be established at the same time that financing is being obtained. Failure of an investor to give proper attention to any one of these areas may mean less than optimal results.

In looking at Figure 2-3, note that a major portion of the analysis and decision making connected with ownership takes place in the acquisition phase. Once a prop-

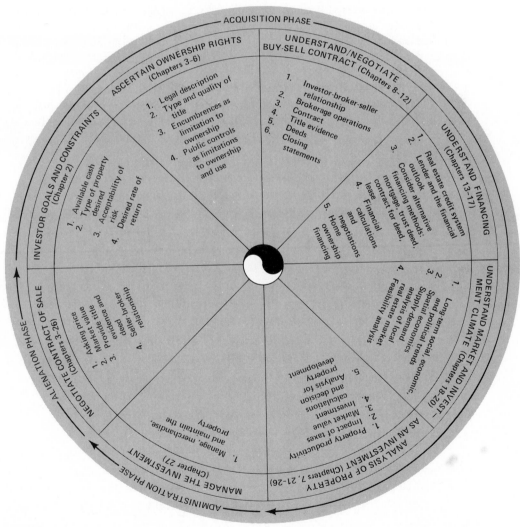

FIGURE 2-3
The real estate decision-making cycle (Numbers in parenthesis are chapters in which the topic is discussed)

erty is acquired (a contract signed, financing arranged, and title closed), an investor is locked in and may have a proverbial tiger by the tail. Even so, acquisition takes only a relatively short time, typically from 2 to 3 months. On the other hand, ownership administration requires only occasional major decisions, even though it may last for 5 to 10 years, or longer. Disposition may take several months or longer, measuring from the initial offering of the property to the closing of the sale. The main difference between acquisition and alienation decisions is that a specific investor is on the opposite side of the transaction.

RATIONAL INVESTOR VERSUS ECONOMIC BEING ASSUMPTION

The person making the decisions in the decision-making cycle is assumed to be a "rational investor." The assumptions about this rational investor are generally consistent with the "economic person" orientation commonly found in economic theory.[2] Each acts in self-interest. Each is strongly influenced by the institutional environment. But there are differences.

An *economic person,* by way of review, is used in economic literature as a primary decision maker motivated to maximize his or her economic returns. But the economic person has an uncanny knowledge of the alternatives and of what to expect under varying production, cost, and pricing situations. The economic person looks at the use of land resources from the viewpoint of the typical investor.

A *rational investor* operates under slightly different assumptions than does the economic person. Knowledge is less than total, which means that risk and uncertainty are present. Also, institutional considerations (laws and taxes, mainly) affect investors individually and specifically. These differences are the major reasons that the viewpoint of an individual, rational investor is preferred in making decisions about real estate as a financial asset.

The goal of maximizing self-interest (wealth) is an important assumption for our rational investor. The concept of a rational being was developed shortly after World War II by Herbert A. Simon, who won a Nobel Prize for his work in economic and decision theory in 1978.[3] Acting in self-interest, a rational being always selects the choice or alternative, within his or her range of knowledge, that gives the greatest personal advantage. This selection process is called "making a trade-off."

Self-interest is realistic as a supporting assumption, as evidenced by workers seeking to maximize wages and businesses seeking to maximize profits. Self-interest is neither good nor bad, desirable nor undesirable, per se. In a sense, self-interest is to people as gravity is to the earth. We can curse gravity for keeping us from flying at will and requiring us to exert energy to conquer distance or elevation. But gravity also works to our advantage. It causes rain to fall and rivers to flow downhill. It keeps us on earth under predictable conditions and maintains our atmosphere. We even turn gravity to our advantage in our work and play when we irrigate gardens, ski, skydive, or play ball.

Self-interest is a force or motivation that causes us to try to maximize our satisfactions in life. We seek leisure, self-expression, travel, company of loved ones, thrills from skydiving, or social change out of self-interest. Most of us seek money (rents, profits, interest, wages) only as an intermediate goal. In our complex society, an in-

[2]See Raleigh Barlowe, *Land Resource Economics*, 3rd ed. (Englewood Cliffs, N.J.: Prentice Hall, 1986), p. 101.
[3]See Herbert A. Simon, *Administrative Behavior* (New York: Macmillan, 1947).

vestor seeking profits may be making a contribution to society as great as, or even greater than, a doctor seeking fees or a politician seeking power.

Self-interest acts to push real estate to its highest and best use. ***Highest and best use*** is that legal and possible employment of land that gives it its greatest present value while preserving its utility. A ***land use*** is that activity in which a parcel of real estate is made productive (generates services of value), as a residential, commercial, or industrial use.

Highest and best use of a parcel to the typical investor in the market may well differ from the highest and best use to a specific investor because of differences in what each is seeking to maximize. In turn, the market value of a parcel may not equal its value to the individual investor. A quick definition of ***market value*** is "most probable selling price, in cash to the seller" and represents the worth of the property to a typical investor. ***Investment value,*** on the other hand, is the worth of the property to a specific investor. This difference is the major reason a financial approach to real estate investment is needed rather than an economic approach. The effect is to provide us with a highly useful model for numerous investment decisions about real estate as a financial asset.

INVESTOR VERSUS PRACTITIONER VIEWPOINT

A practitioner benefits greatly from a knowledge of the investor viewpoint, be his or her specialty salesperson, broker, appraiser, building contractor, counselor, lender, planner, manager, housing analyst, escrow agent, or title analyst. As was mentioned, investor decisions and actions serve as the one commonality to all these specialties. For example, an architect must know a client's needs and life style to design a suitable house. In a similar sense, each practitioner must know his or her client's needs and goals to render the best possible service. Further, a practitioner aware of an investor's perspective should more easily and quickly grasp an investor-client's needs. Mastery of the investor's perspective and of the decision-making cycle should also provide a better understanding of investment property, enabling a practitioner to convey a better image to clients, render a higher quality of services, and, in turn, earn higher fees.

Discussion centers on an investment property for two major reasons. The first is that the laws concerning ownership, conveyancing of ownership, and financing are essentially the same whether for a one-family residence or for an investment property. Therefore, the reader mastering this material has basic preparation for either residential or commercial-investment real estate. Second, readers are assumed to be interested in investing on their own or in rendering competent, professional investment services to others.

Investor Goals and Constraints

Investors have varying goals depending on available resources (mainly money), age, and decision-making horizon. A recent college graduate with $5,000 to invest differs from an established family with investment experience and $50,000 to reinvest. An elderly person with $500,000 looking for opportunity would be in a different class yet. Three case examples are presented here, for later referencing, to reflect the implications of these differences. Background is given first, followed by goals and motivations.

CASE EXAMPLES

1. John Burgoyne graduated last June from East Coast University. He earns $24,000 a year in his new job. But, after all deductions, his take-home pay is just over $1,200 per month. John likes the work and feels secure and wants to do some investing in real estate. Combining graduation gifts and savings, John has $7,800 available. After living expenses, including payments on a recently purchased Ford Escort, John usually is able to save about $300 per month. He is considering what issues or concerns should be important to him in starting his investment program.

2. Gerald and Nancy Investor, in their early thirties, have two children, Kelly in first grade and Ulysses in second grade. Gerald is a financial executive with the Diamond Distributing Company, the operations of which are limited to his state. Nancy works part-time for the county as a biologist. Together they earn after-tax income of $48,000 per year. After purchasing a home several years ago, they began investing small amounts in other real estate, most of which has done well. They spend considerable time managing the several properties involved and would like some relief from this chore. They have gained considerable knowledge and experience but now wish to adopt a less demanding approach.

3. Wendy Welloff, an elderly and wealthy widow, owns several quality pieces of real estate. She recognizes the need to begin changing her investment strategy because of her age. Also, she wants to arrange her affairs so as to pass on as much of her estate to her children and grandchildren as possible. Wendy is selling a property and will soon have nearly $500,000 to invest. She is considering what overall strategy would be best for her situation.

MOTIVATIONS, GOALS, CONSTRAINTS

Self-interest is equated with wealth maximization in economic and financial theory. In life, however, self-interest takes other forms as well. Several of the more common human motivations and the implied goals for investment purposes are shown in Figure 2-4.

Thus, one investor may want the comfort and convenience of owning a personal residence free and clear of any debt. A second investor may seek to own real estate as protection against inflation. A third enters real estate as a way of building prestige and maximizing wealth. In short, investors have different needs, wants, and resources as time, money, and personal capability. Even so, real estate is such a large field that each may find a niche with search and analysis. On balance, a real estate investment strategy makes sense only if it is related to an individual's overall situation and desired lifestyle.

Investors also operate subject to constraints or limitations. Age, analytical ability, executive ability, energy level, work preferences, and time availability all act as

Motivation	Goal or Objective
Gain/economy	Increasing rate of return, net present value, and wealth
Protection/safety	Protecting purchasing power, hedging against inflation
Comfort/convenience	Avoiding undue risk, personal effort, or personal stress
Personal identity/ prestige	Exhibiting power to control property and others; acquiring showpiece properties for ego satisfaction
Concern for welfare of others	Assisting or helping others, including relatives, by passing wealth on to them

FIGURE 2-4
Investor motivations and goals

constraints on an investor. See Figure 2-5. A young person can afford a longer time horizon than can an elderly person. A person with limited time or energy is probably best advised to invest in a medium requiring little effort. Likewise, a person with limited ability to analyze and administer investments is better off avoiding active investments, meaning most real estate investments. Locational preferences are self-explanatory as personal constraints.

Risk preferences are also very personal; some may seek risk and opportunity, others avoid risk with a vengeance. Certainly, anyone interested in real estate should weigh the risks against the expected rates of return. What type of risks? Risks in real estate are discussed at some length later on. But a brief overview is appropriate here.

Certainly, owning any type of real estate contains the possibility of value decreases because of lags in local economic activity or extremely high interest rates. Further, expected revenues may fluctuate owing to variability in economic activity. These same conditions and the very nature of real estate itself tend to make it a relatively nonliquid asset. Many people borrow to own real estate and to realize financial leverage; but this borrowing gives others prior claim should debt service on the loan not be met. Owners are also subject to having managers unable to operate the property efficiently or to adapting it to changing competition. Finally, owning real estate always involves the possibility of new legislation that affects the property adversely such as rent controls, rezoning, or increased taxes. Certainly, anyone should take these types of risk into account when embarking on a real estate investment program.

Factor or Consideration	Constraint
Financial/economic	Wealth
	Income level
	Risk of alternative investments
Personal	Age (time horizon)
	Energy level and work preferences
	Time availability
	Investment analysis ability
	Executive ability
	Risk preference
	Location/mobility preferences

FIGURE 2-5
Investor constraints

SOME APPLICATIONS

How are these motivations and constraints likely to affect our cast of characters?

John Burgoyne is primarily interested in gaining investment experience to increase his wealth and protect it against inflation. He is willing to take on extra risk, effort, and stress toward this end. His time horizon is quite long, whereas his cash resources are somewhat limited. The idea of being able to talk about "his" investment property excites him. John is willing to remain in this community if he can find a suitable investment, such as a duplex. He plans to work extra hard in his job to earn a promotion and a raise.

Gerald and Nancy Investor have adequate income for their present needs, by their own standards. They do not have great wealth and, therefore, are not able to get into very large properties. They have experience in real estate investing and are willing to undertake reasonable risks in investing. At the same time, they want to avoid extreme risks. They have adequate capital to acquire a moderate-sized property because of successful investments in the past. Both are satisfied with their work and the community; therefore, their preference is to limit their investing to the local area. Gerry has adequate ability to analyze and administer active investments for a financial management viewpoint. Neither has adequate time, energy, or desire personally to manage property on an everyday basis. Their goals are, as for many people, greater wealth, protection against inflation, and adequate time and money to travel. They do not feel the need for greater personal identity through development and management of property or control of people.

Wendy Welloff has considerable wealth, from which she obtains a comfortable income. She does not have or want a steady job. Wendy has adequate analytical and administrative ability to manage her own investments quite successfully. She takes great pride in owning good properties and exercising power. At the same time, she likes to travel and does not wish to be tied down with day-to-day details of property management. In short, she wants to continue enjoying the comforts and pleasures of life. She is well established in her community, having lived there most of her life. Wendy, in her late fifties, is beginning to shorten her time horizon; more and more she's thinking of ways to pass on as much of her wealth as possible to her children and grandchildren. Thus, she increasingly wants to preserve what she has rather than reach out and take high risks for greater gains.

Decision-Making and Administrative Processes

We make simple, everyday decisions about what to eat or wear or do, about whom to see or where to go, by feel, habit, hunch, or intuition. Actions generally flow out of the decisions in a very natural manner. As situations become more complex, it becomes worthwhile to devote more time to identifying alternatives and their implications prior to making a decision and taking action. It also becomes worthwhile to devote more time to administering or implementing the decision. The benefits of a good decision or the costs of a bad decision, at some point, become great enough to warrant spending extra time, money, and effort to reach the best choice. Choosing a career, a spouse, or a home are examples.

Higher costs of decision making are also justified in making real estate investments because of the high values involved. Investing in real estate is certainly an appropriate place in which to use these processes for a variety of reasons. Real estate is complex and relatively unique as a commodity. It has physical, legal, locational, and financial facets, which must all be analyzed prior to making decisions or taking actions about its use, purchase, sale, financing, and management.

THE DECISION-MAKING PROCESS

The decision-making process has five steps as identified by a number of scholars.[4]

1. *Recognize decision or problem situation.* Based on objectives or experience, the need for choice or some action becomes evident. For example, John Burgoyne, our novice investor, recognizes that real estate usually offers greater returns than do stocks and bonds. The objective, stated or unstated, is to maximize rate of return or wealth.

2. *Collect data.* All pertinent data or facts within reasonable limits are collected, based on the importance of the problem and the time available to reach a decision. Our investor obtains data from securities dealers, real estate brokers, *The Wall Street Journal,* and other sources about various investment opportunities.

3. *Identify problems.* The collected information is studied, key issues or problems are identified, and, possibly, subproblems are recognized. Our investor determines, for example, that real estate really does offer better rates of return and is, therefore, worth pursuing. Important subproblems recognized are (1) getting more background in real estate ownership and investment, (2) learning about ownership and acquisition of titles, (3) finding out value trends in the community, (4) learning real estate finance because not enough money for 100 percent personal ownership is available, (5) learning tax implications of real estate ownership, (6) determining investment value of available properties, and (7) figuring out management needs, assuming acquisition.

4. *Pose alternatives.* Possible solutions or modes of action are listed, and the probable implications of each are considered. For example, our investor now has the alternative of not going into real estate at all, going in part way, or going in with all available assets. In short, it is a portfolio-management and estate-building situation.

5. *Make decision.* The entire situation is reviewed, and a choice is made of that action likely to give the best result. In our example, John decides to get his feet wet by going after duplex ownership. It's time for action.

The decision-making process is not as clear or as clean-cut in practice as presented here. Much going back and forth, or interweaving, between the steps is likely. Except for the last step, the sequence is likely to vary from situation to situation. The

[4]For a complete discussion of decision-making and administrative processes, see Herbert A. Simon, *The New Science of Management Decisions* (Englewood Cliffs, N.J.: Prentice Hall, 1977). For early discussions, see the following sources: Peter F. Drucker, *The Practice of Management* (New York: Harper & Row, 1954); Chester I. Bernard, *The Functions of the Executive* (Cambridge, Mass.: Harvard University Press, 1953); and Herbert A. Simon, *Administrative Behavior* (New York: Macmillan, 1947).

important consideration is the decision. The steps ultimately boil down to answering three questions: (1) What problem is to be solved? (2) What are the alternative solutions? (3) Which of the alternatives solutions is the best?

THE ADMINISTRATIVE PROCESS

The administrative process is an extension of the decision-making process; it is action oriented rather than analysis oriented. It usually involves achieving objectives through people and also has five steps.

1. *Decide to achieve an objective.* In deciding to achieve an objective or desired result, much effort and study, termed the decision-making process, are often necessary. For our example, the objective decided upon is to invest in a duplex.
2. *Organize resources.* Money and people must be mobilized to accomplish an objective. In our example, our investor must now plan to learn about real estate ownership, investment analysis, and property management. Ability to work with brokers, lenders, counselors, and appraisers must also be developed.
3. *Exert leadership.* Action must be sparked to put a plan into action. A real estate broker must be informed of the need for a duplex, a counselor or appraiser may be engaged, and a loan arranged with a bank or savings and loan association.
4. *Control operation.* Efforts to achieve the desired objective must be coordinated and monitored on a continuing basis to assure conformance with the plan and achievement of the objective. Eventually, an appropriate property is located, financed, and purchased. Also, suitable arrangements must be made for the management of the property.
5. *Reevaluate periodically.* On a long-term basis, the investment must be reviewed periodically to determine if the past choices and actions are working out. In our example, this means comparing the risks and rates of return from stocks and bonds with the risks and rates of return from real estate and is a portfolio-management strategy concern. More or larger real estate investments may eventually be desirable. Investment in different types of properties may become advantageous.

For greater depth into the decision-making and administrative processes, the reader is referred to the sources cited. Successful investment does depend on selecting properties offering the greatest returns and on following through with a sound management system.

Questions for Review and Discussion

1. List at least three physical attributes of realty, and briefly give the implications of each.
2. What is situs, and why is it important in real estate?

3. List at least two economic attributes of real estate, in addition to situs, and briefly give the implications of each.

4. Identify and explain briefly the implications of at least five characteristics of the real estate market.

5. Do the various classes of real estate (residential, commercial investment, etc.) have different-sized areas of market influence? If so, why? Discuss.

6. What are the stated goals and assumptions of a rational investor? How can the approach of the rational investor be helpful to anyone interested in making real-world investments in real estate?

7. State and explain briefly at least three ways in which real estate decisions tend to be unique.

8. Indicate briefly some risks involved when investing in real estate. Might an investor avoid these risks?

9. In 150 words or less, write your main objectives in studying real estate. Discuss your objectives with others, and revise as desired. Then save it until your immediate study or term is completed as an administrative check on yourself.

3

Property Descriptions and Public Records

But that land—it is one thing that will still be there when I come back—land is always there.

Pearl S. Buck, *A House Divided*

An accurate, clear, and complete system of descriptions is necessary for packaging real estate as a commodity because it involves both ownership and value. Physical descriptions provide for the establishment of boundaries, for the calculation of area, and for noting location relative to other properties. Legal descriptions allow for the identification of rights owned, as, for example, air, water, and mineral rights, and for transfer of ownership from one person to another. Both physical and legal descriptions are used extensively in real estate.

Real property is a legal and somewhat abstract legal concept that means the ownership of rights in real estate. The rights are to control, to use, to exclude, to dispose of, and to otherwise capture the benefits of real estate. This term, real property, is what makes the physical real estate flexible as a commodity; real property can be split up in many ways, as we shall see in the next chapter. Real property, as a term, is often used interchangeably with land, real estate, and realty; yet each is a distinct concept. *Land*, of course, really means the solid part of the earth not covered by water. *Realty* and *real estate* are essentially identical concepts that include land, land improvements, and the natural assets of land, such as oil, water, and minerals. Except in this immediate discussion, the four terms will continue to be used interchangeably.

Important Topics or Decision Areas Covered in this Chapter

From Earth to Real Property
Real Versus Personal Property
Land and Land "Improvements"
Fixtures

Legal Descriptions of Real Property
Elements of Surveying
Metes and Bounds Descriptions
Rectangular or Government Survey Descriptions
Recorded Plat Descriptions
The State Plane Coordinate System
Description by Rights

Public Records
Real Property Title Records
Mortgagor-Mortgagee Records
Plat and Plan Records
Secured Personal Property Records

Questions for Review and Discussion

Case Problems

Key Concepts Introduced in this Chapter

Acre	**Plat**
Actual notice	**Principal meridian**
Base line	**Range**
Bench mark	**Real estate, realty**
Constructive notice	**Real property**
Fixture	**Rectangular survey system**
Grantor/grantee	**Riparian rights**
Grantor-grantee index	**Section**
Guide meridian	**Standard parallel**
Legal description	**Tier**
Metes and bounds	**Township**
Monument	**Tract index**
Personalty, personal property	**Uniform Commercial Code**

From Earth to Real Property

To understand modern property descriptions, we must go back to when the earth was only land and water, and there were few people relative to the amount of land. As the population increased and crowded more closely on the land, a system of physical property descriptions gradually came into use.

Current legal description of most real property begins with physical boundaries. Initially, only surface descriptions were of concern. The surface description was considered to extend in the shape of an inverted pyramid from the center of the earth to the limits of the sky, as portrayed in Figure 3-1. Thus, the surface description was adequate, whether the land were used for farming or for an apartment building.

Later, real estate came to include both the land and "permanent improvements" to the land. These improvements might be above or below the surface of the earth or something that affects the utility of a given parcel, as the fertilizer added to enrich the soil.

Today, even more complicated descriptions are necessary because real property is more than three-dimensional space, though we might begin with a physical description, as for a condominium unit. Property rights came to be described as air rights, surface rights, and subsurface rights. And, more difficult to describe, are water and mineral rights. Today, a "right to light" (sunshine) appears to be evolving with our increasing dependence on solar power.

Thus, real property, as the object of ownership, may be described in many ways. Before going further in our effort to describe real property, we need to distinguish between real and personal property.

REAL VERSUS PERSONAL PROPERTY

We begin with a basic relationship: "personalty is to personal property as realty is to real property," based on our earlier discussion of realty. That is, if realty is the object of ownership for real property, then personalty is the object of ownership for personal property. **Personalty** means physical objects that are movable and not attached to the land. **Personal property** refers to ownership rights and privileges in these movable things, such as cars, typewriters, and furniture. Personal property, in addition to being easily moved, is sometimes consumed or destroyed and is usually considered as something temporary or transient. Real property, on the other hand, refers to something that is fixed and permanent, which is probably the basis of its being considered "real." Also, a deed is used to transfer ownership of real property, whereas a bill of sale is used to transfer ownership of personal property.

But the actual distinction is sometimes more subtle. Invariably, in specific situations, a line must be drawn between the two. So, in a specific situation, how do we

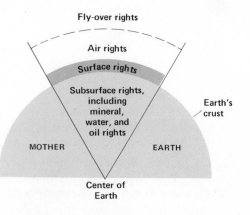

FIGURE 3-1

Real estate extends from the center of the earth to the tops of the highest created improvements, above which common fly-over rights exist

determine whether an object is personal or real property? We begin by defining real estate more fully and then move on to a discussion of fixtures.

LAND AND LAND "IMPROVEMENTS"

Real estate includes "permanent improvements" to a site as well as the land itself. Houses, stores, factories, office buildings, schools, outbuildings, fences, and landscaping, as permanent improvements, are clearly included. By law and tradition, conveying ownership of a parcel of land to another also conveys ownership of any improvements thereon. In a similar sense, trees, natural vegetation, and assorted perennial plants, which do not require annual cultivation, are considered real estate. The term for them is *fructus naturales* (fruit of nature). On the other hand, annual cultivation crops (e.g., corn, potatoes, and cotton) are considered personal property even though they are attached to the earth. They are called *fructus industriales* (fruit of industry) or emblements.

FIXTURES

But, still, a "movable" item under one set of circumstances is considered to be personal property, or chattel, and under another set as real property, or a *fixture*. The bricks and windows in a building, for example, are usually taken to be part of the real estate and are termed fixtures. That is, an item of movable personal property annexed, affixed, or installed so as to be considered real estate is a fixture. But, when such items are not part of a building, they are considered personal property. A bathroom sink is personal property, a chattel, in a plumber's shop; it becomes real property, a fixture, when installed in a house.

The determination is particularly important at the time of sale and conveyance, of mortgaging, of lease termination, and of assessment for property tax purposes. A sales contract and deed convey ownership of land and fixtures but not of chattels. A fixture is part of the security for a mortgage loan, while a chattel is not. A tenant installation, if a fixture, may not be removed at the end of a lease. During the lease, an owner usually pays real property taxes on fixtures while the tenant pays personal property taxes on chattels.

Several tests are used to determine whether an article is a fixture. Meeting or passing the tests makes the item at issue a fixture and therefore real property.

1. *Manner of attachment*. Generally, if the article is annexed to the land or building, and to remove it would leave the building or land incomplete, it is a fixture. Thus, installed electrical wiring, water pipes, a furnace, and wood siding are fixtures.
2. *Manner of adaption*. An article specially constructed or fitted to a particular structure, or designed and installed to carry out the purposes of the property, is usually considered a fixture. In other words, the article is essential to the ordinary and convenient use of the property. Thus, drapes cut and sewn for particular windows, screens and storm windows fitted to a house, and a front door key are almost certainly fixtures.

3. *Intent, relationship, or agreement of parties.* The reasonably presumable intent of the person placing the article is probably most important in making the determination of an item as a fixture. Kratovil and Werner say that tests 1 and 2 are important, but "once the intention is determined, it must govern."[1] The test is based on the nature of the article, the manner of adaption, the manner of annexation, and all pertinent circumstances. Thus, an owner's statements to neighbors may show whether or not an article was intended to become a fixture. An agreement between parties before an item is annexed would make intent clear and avoid later differences and a possible legal suit.

The relation between parties is often such that a presumable intention is inferred by the courts. For example, an owner may be presumed to be permanently annexing the article. A tenant is ordinarily bound to leave articles fastened to the building. Even so, if a property is leased for business, it is a general rule that trade fixtures, such as shelves, counters, and showcases, do not become real fixtures. But such equipment must be removed before the lease expires. A renewal that fails to state that the equipment is to remain the tenant's property may deprive the tenant of ownership.

Legal Descriptions of Real Property

For most legal purposes, real estate must be identifiable with reference only to documents. Courts consider a description adequate if a competent surveyor can exactly locate the parcel of concern from it. In other words, a ***legal description*** is a specific and unique identification of a property that is recognized and acceptable in a court of law.

A street address is the simplest form of property description, but a street address is not specific enough for most legal documents or for court purposes. Other methods of legally describing real estate are therefore needed.

The three accepted methods of legally describing real estate are (1) metes and bounds, (2) rectangular or government survey, and (3) recorded plat. A fourth method, the state plane coordinate system, is gradually being accepted as a supplement to the foregoing three methods.

Each of these methods provides for a description suitable for use in a sales contract, mortgage, deed, or court of law. Description by recorded plat is used mostly in urban areas. Metes and bounds descriptions are also frequently used in urban areas for describing parcels that have been split off and developed individually; that is, the parcels were not part of a larger recorded plat. The governmental survey system is used mainly in rural areas for large acreages; it is too crude for smaller urban parcels. Except for condominium descriptions, these methods describe land only and do not describe improvements to a parcel.

A brief description of the elements of surveying is appropriate before taking up the methods themselves.

[1]Robert Kratovil and Raymond J. Werner, *Real Estate Law*, 8th ed. (Englewood Cliffs, N.J.: Prentice Hall, 1983).

ELEMENTS OF SURVEYING

Several considerations are common to all systems of describing real estate. To begin, any land description should contain (1) a definite point of beginning (P.O.B.); (2) definite corners or turning points; (3) specific directions and distances for borders or boundaries; (4) closure, or return to point of beginning; and (5) the area enclosed in accepted units of measurement.

A point of beginning is the point of takeoff in describing real estate. Ideally, P.O.B. ties into a larger system of property descriptions so that the resulting legal description relates the subject parcel to other parcels and to the rest of the world. In addition, a basic knowledge of units of measurement for angles or bearings, distances, and areas is needed to understand fully legal descriptions.

Angle Measurement. The full circle about a turning point contains 360 degrees. A bearing is a direction of measurement from an imaginary north-south line passing through a corner or turning point on a property. A bearing or angle of measurement is measured east or west of the imaginary line and cannot exceed 90 degrees. For example, assume a circular compass properly oriented and set exactly over the corner point of a property, as in Figure 3-2. A line running just slightly north of due east might have a bearing of "north, 89 degrees east." A 3-degree more southerly line would have a bearing "south 88 degrees east." A minute, in angle measurement, equals one-sixtieth of a degree.

Distance Measurement. Distance measurements in surveying have traditionally been in miles, rods, feet, and inches. A mile equals 5,280 feet, or 320 rods. A rod, or stick 16.5 feet in length, was a convenient unit of measurement in centuries past; it is not used much now because steel tapes and other new methods of measurement are faster and more accurate.

Area Measurement. Areas are most commonly measured in square feet, acres, and square miles or sections. An *acre* is a measure of land that contains 43,560 square feet. A square mile covers 640 acres.

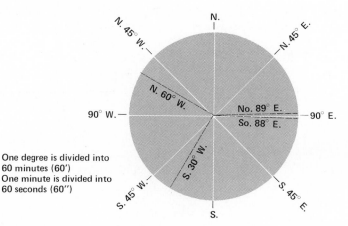

One degree is divided into
60 minutes (60')
One minute is divided into
60 seconds (60")

FIGURE 3-2
Illustration of angle measurements

Elevation Measurement.   A final element of surveying is elevation. Elevations are usually measured from mean sea level in New York Harbor, which is the basic elevation datum or point of reference for the United States. Elevations are important in establishing limits on heights of buildings and other structures and in setting grades for streets and highways. Condominium developments also depend on accurate elevation data.

Permanent reference points, called *bench marks,* have been created and are located throughout the country to aid surveyors in work involving elevations. That is, a surveyor may take an elevation from a local bench mark and need not measure from a basic bench mark in the city or area that is miles from the parcel under survey. Bench mark locations may be obtained from the U.S. Geodetic Survey, if needed.

METES AND BOUNDS DESCRIPTIONS

Metes and bounds descriptions are widely used in the eastern United States. They are also used throughout the country to describe irregular or unplatted tracts in conjunction with the rectangular survey system. *Metes and bounds* means measures and boundaries; the edges of a property are, of course, its limits and boundaries. A metes and bounds description can be highly accurate when it is developed and written by a competent surveyor using precision equipment; it can also be quite complex. A metes and bounds description for parcel Z, shown in Figure 3-3, might be as follows:

All that tract or parcel of land situated in the Town of East Hampton, County of Suffolk and State of New York, bounded and described as follows: BEGINNING at the

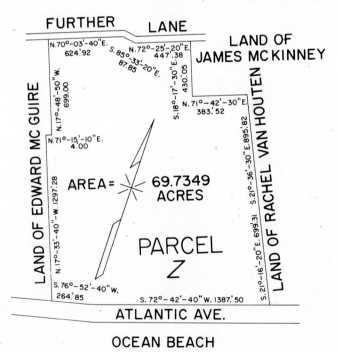

FIGURE 3-3

Parcel Z based on metes and bounds description

junction of the westerly line of land of James McKinney and the southerly side of Further Land, and running thence along the land of said James McKinney, south 18 degrees 17 minutes 30 seconds east 430 and 5/100 feet; thence along the land of said James McKinney north 71 degrees 42 minutes 30 seconds east, 383 and 52/100 feet to land of Rachel Van Houten; thence along the land of said Rachel Van Houten south 21 degrees 36 minutes 30 seconds east 895 and 82/100 feet to a point; thence still along the land of Rachel Van Houten south 21 degrees 16 minutes 20 seconds east 699 and 31/100 feet to the proposed Atlantic Avenue Highway, thence along said Atlantic Avenue south 72 degrees 42 minutes 40 seconds west 1387 and 50/100 feet; thence continuing along said Atlantic Avenue south 76 degrees 52 minutes 40 seconds west 264 and 85/100 feet to land of Edward J. McGuire; thence along the lands of said Edward J. McGuire north 17 degrees 33 minutes 40 seconds west 1297 and 28/100 feet, thence north 71 degrees 15 minutes 10 seconds east 4 feet; thence continuing along the land of said Edward J. McGuire north 17 degrees 48 minutes 50 seconds west 699 feet to Further Land Highway; thence along said Further Lane Highway north 70 degrees 3 minutes 40 seconds east 624 and 92/100 feet, thence continuing along said Further Lane Highway south 85 degrees 33 minutes 20 seconds east 87 and 85/100 feet; thence continuing along said Further Lane Highway north 72 degrees 25 minutes 20 seconds east 447 and 38/100 feet to the point or place of beginning.

Containing by actual measurement as per survey dated April 10, 1971, of Nathan F. Tiffany 69.7349 acres. Atlantic Beach, New Jersey.

A simple variation of the metes and bounds system of identifying real estate is based on monuments. A *monument* is an identifiable landmark that serves as a corner of a property. A monument description, which does not require exact measurements or directions, is acceptable whenever land is not too valuable and the expense of a detailed, accurate survey would be out of proportion to the value. Monument descriptions are not widely used today, although at one time they were prevalent.

Monuments may be tangible or intangible. If tangible, they are either natural or artificial. Rivers, lakes, streams, trees, creeks, springs, and the like are natural monuments. Fences, walls, houses, canals, streets, stakes, and posts are artificial monuments. The center line of a street is an example of an intangible monument. Since all monuments are susceptible to destruction, removal, or shifting, they should be used only when necessary, and then every available identifying fact should be stated, for example, not merely "a tree" but "an old oak tree." Thus, even after the tree has become a stump, it may still be identified as oak and distinct from other trees.

RECTANGULAR OR GOVERNMENT SURVEY DESCRIPTIONS

The *rectangular survey system,* or government survey system, was approved by the U.S. Congress in 1785 to establish a standardized system of property descriptions. It is relatively simple in operation, at least for rural lands, is easily the most general survey system, and is used in 30 states. The New England states, the Atlantic coast states, southeastern Ohio, and Texas are not covered.

The General Framework. This system is based on surveying lines that run north and south, called *principal meridians,* and east and west, called *base lines.* Principal meridians and base lines, created in pairs, were established and given a name and number by the land office in Washington, D.C. A map showing the location of the several principal meridians and their base lines in the United States is in Figure 3-4.

FIGURE 3-4

Principal meridians and their base lines within the United States

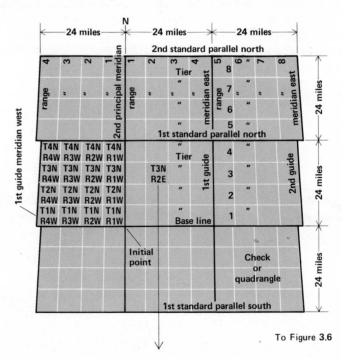

FIGURE 3-5

Designation of townships by tiers and ranges

Guide meridians were established by the surveyors to minimize errors in measurement caused by the curvature of the earth. Guide meridians run parallel to the principal meridian at 24-mile intervals and converge as one goes north. In a comparable manner, *standard parallels* run east and west at 24 mile intervals north and south of the base lines. Thus, surveyors created areas called checks or quadrangles, 24 miles on each side.

These checks are further subdivided into 16 areas each measuring 6 miles by 6 miles (36 square miles) called *townships.* The townships are again subdivided into *sections,* each a mile square and containing 640 acres. In turn, the sections were further split up into halves, quarters, or smaller parcels as needed to describe individual land holdings.

To identify the exact location of a given 36-square-mile township, the east-west rows of townships, parallel to the base line, are numbered as *tiers* 1, 2, 3, and so forth, north or south, of a given base line. The north-south columns of townships, parallel to the meridians, are called *ranges* and are numbered 1, 2, 3, and so forth, east or west of a principal meridian. The general system is illustrated in Figure 3-5.

Sections in a township are identified by number and are related to adjoining sections, as is indicated in Figure 3-6.

In describing a section, as in Figure 3-6, it is customary to state first the number of the section, then tier and range: "Section 12, Tier 3 North, Range 2 East of the principal named meridian." It may be abbreviated: "Sect. 12, T.3 N., R. 2 E., . . . County, State of . . . ."

Specific Description. The description of a specific parcel is relatively simple. For example, the parcel designated as parcel X in Figure 3-7 is northeast one-fourth of the northwest one-fourth of Section 12, and so on. Parcel Y's description is "west one-half of the southwest one-fourth of Section 12," and so on.

The acreage of each parcel can be determined quickly by working backward in the legal description from the section area of 640 acres. For example, areas of parcels X and Y are calculated as follows:

Parcel X: NE ¼ of NW ¼ of Section 12
$$\tfrac{1}{4} \times \tfrac{1}{4} \times 640 \text{ acres} = 40 \text{ acres}$$

Parcel Y: W ½ of SW ¼ of Section 12
$$\tfrac{1}{2} \times \tfrac{1}{4} \times 640 \text{ acres} = 80 \text{ acres}$$

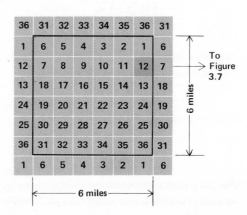

FIGURE 3-6
Designation of Section 12 by Tier 3 North, Range 2 East, and location relative to other sections

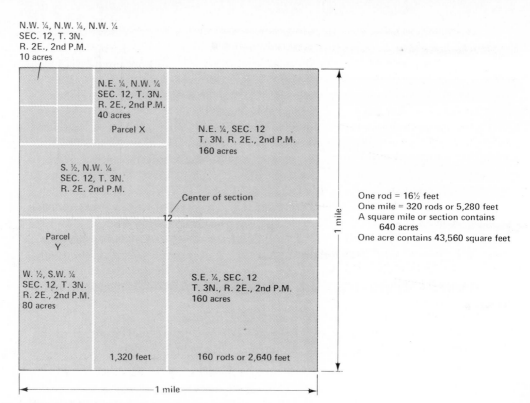

N.W. ¼, N.W. ¼, N.W. ¼
SEC. 12, T. 3N.
R. 2E., 2nd P.M.
10 acres

N.E. ¼, N.W. ¼
SEC. 12, T. 3N.
R. 2E., 2nd P.M.
40 acres

Parcel X

N.E. ¼, SEC. 12
T. 3N. R. 2E., 2nd P.M.
160 acres

S. ½, N.W. ¼
SEC. 12, T. 3N.
R. 2E. 2nd P.M.

Center of section

12

Parcel
Y

W. ½, S.W. ¼
SEC. 12, T. 3N.
R. 2E., 2nd P.M.
80 acres

S.E. ¼, SEC. 12
T. 3N., R. 2E., 2nd P.M.
160 acres

1,320 feet

160 rods or 2,640 feet

1 mile

1 mile

One rod = 16½ feet
One mile = 320 rods or 5,280 feet
A square mile or section contains
640 acres
One acre contains 43,560 square feet

FIGURE 3-7
Measurements and subdivisions of a section

Occasionally, a section is incomplete because it extends into the ocean, a lake, or a river. Since some parcels in the section are irregular in shape, a standard legal description based on the government survey system is not suitable for them. These incomplete lots are called government lots or irregular lots. In these situations, a metes and bounds description is made up for the irregular parcel and tied back to a point of beginning based on the rectangular survey system.

RECORDED PLAT DESCRIPTIONS

The government survey system is extremely cumbersome for describing the small parcels commonly found in urban areas. The descriptions become much too involved. A more efficient and widely accepted way of describing property is by recorded plat, as a subdivision or a condominium. A *plat* is a drawing or map showing actual or proposed property lines, buildings' setback lines, and so on entered into the public record, as for a subdivision.

Subdivision Plat. Subdividing requires a very accurate initial survey map of a tract of land. The land is then divided into streets and lots and blocks. Easements and deed restrictions are also often either included on the subdivision map or filed with it. The map, easements, and deed restrictions are all entered into the public record as a plat. The map assigns numbers to the various blocks and lots for convenience of identification, and the map usually bears a subdivision title, the owner's and surveyor's names, the date of survey, and the date of approval by community or county officials. Figure 3-8 is a simplified illustration of a small tract that the owner subdivided into lots.

The subdivision plat map describes exactly the size and location of each lot by the metes and bounds property description system. Once the subdivision plat map has been recorded, only the plat name need be referred to insofar as lots and blocks in the subdivision are concerned. "Lot 8, Block 3 in Green Acres Subdivision, Rustic County, Wisconsin," would therefore constitute a complete and adequate legal description. Reference to the plat map would show the exact location, shape, size and dimensions of the lot and would give considerable additional information about it.

Condominium Plat. Condominium ownership is created by a special condominium law that permits individual interests and estates to be established within a total and larger property estate. The individual estates are technically established by use of vertical and horizontal planes (surfaces) that are usually identified vertically, such as the walls (not room partitions) of the unit, and horizontally, such as the floors and ceilings of the unit. It is here that elevations above sea level become critical.

The exact location of the building or buildings on the site and the exact location of the unit within the buildings are described in the plat (location map) and in the architectural plans. Each is also described in legal language in a master deed. After all the individual unit estates have been described in the total property estate, all of what remains such as the land and the structural parts of the buildings becomes a common estate to be owned jointly by the owners of the individual unit estates. Thus, each condominium owner owns his or her individual unit estate and an undivided interest in the common estate.

Recording of the master deed extends the condominium laws of the state in which the condominium is located to the individual units of ownership. The master deed also establishes an association to look after the use and maintenance of the common estate. The association is governed by a board of directors, elected from among the owners of the individual units. Membership, with its attendant rights and responsibilities, applies to each unit in much the same sense that easements and deed restrictions apply to lots in a subdivision plat.

After recording, condominium units may be legally identified by reference to the plat or master deed. The complex three-dimensional descriptions need not be repeated in deeds, mortgages, or contracts.

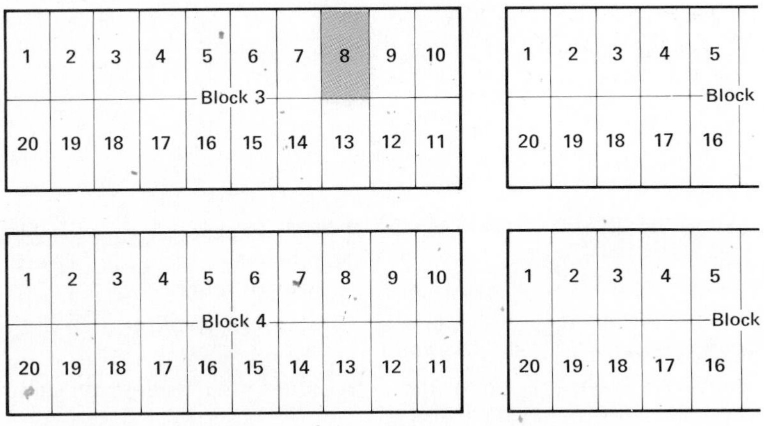

FIGURE 3-8
Green Acres subdivision, Rustic County, Wisconsin

THE STATE PLANE COORDINATE SYSTEM

The state plane coordinate system is intended to supplement other methods of describing real estate. The system provides a definite and very accurate means of identifying parcels, even if landmarks, monuments, and other points of origin are destroyed, moved, or otherwise obliterated.

The coordinate system is based on a system of coordinate grids for each state, with the state flattened mathematically into a level plane. Points in each grid are identified by longitude and latitude, much as a ship's navigator might do at sea; thus, the need for physical landmarks is avoided. Because of the complexity of the state plane coordinate system, property owners and lawyers are likely to continue to rely on traditional methods of describing realty. The system simply provides a certain means of locating critical points of beginning from which other methods of describing parcels may take off.

DESCRIPTION BY RIGHTS

Ownership may sometimes involve only air rights or riparian rights. Air rights are described in a similar manner to condominium rights. For example, rights of development over railroad tracks and cemeteries have been sold off in many larger cities. A legal description of air rights in a deed might convey all development rights 280 feet above mean sea level and up. To be useful, the description must also provide for the location and placement of footings and pillars among the railroad tracks, grave sites, and other surface uses, to support any structure built in the air space.

Riparian rights are the rights of use and enjoyment of the waters of a stream or lake by the owner of land bordering the body of water. Riparian rights are usually not subject to physical survey per se. If they are, the survey is only incidental to more complex legal considerations involving interaction with other property owners, relocation of streams, and the rights to shut off or restrict the flow of water. These rights should be clearly set forth in any legal document.

A seller must use care to convey only what is owned. Generally, this can best be accomplished by using the identical description under which the property was acquired.

Public Records

Anyone who has an interest in realty must give notice to the world to protect that interest. Notice may be actual or constructive. Possession of realty is legally considered *actual notice* to the world of an interest in the property. Entering a legal instrument that evidences an interest in real estate into the public records is considered *constructive notice.* In turn, the public record serves as a source of information to anyone about to enter into a transaction concerning real estate, such as lenders, potential tenants, or interested buyers.

Public records are maintained by local government in all states in accordance with recording acts. Public records provide a central repository or storehouse for certain kinds of information. Recording acts provide for the registration of every legal instrument creating, transferring, mortgaging, assigning, or otherwise affecting title to realty. Public records thus are designed to protect against fraud and to reinforce the Statute of Frauds. The records are maintained by city, town, and county officials under titles such as clerk, recorder, treasurer, or tax collector. Public records include many documents affecting title to real and personal property, taxes, special assessments, ordinances, and building and zoning codes. See Figure 3-9 for an overview of the public records system.

Historically, possession of realty served as actual notice of an interest in realty and was adequate for almost all purposes. Modern society is complex, however, and a more efficient and effective system of notice became necessary. For example, owner A might sell property to B, conveying title with a deed. But, if B does not take possession, A might also sell to C, who upon moving into occupancy acquires a claim of title superior to that of B. Owner A might also obtain cash under a mortgage from D, after the sale to B, and subsequently leave the area. Either situation involves fraud and many legal problems. Recording deeds and mortgages gives constructive notice of the interest to all parties and is recognized as notice equal to actual possession. As a general rule, recording acts give legal priority to interests according to the sequence in which they are recorded.

REAL PROPERTY PUBLIC RECORDS

Recording of a deed is highly recommended to give constructive notice to all of the grantee's interest in the property. The obligation and the benefit of recording both go to the new owner. Recording is doubly important when vacant land is involved or when the new owner does not take immediate possession. Failure to record or to occupy gives a seller an opportunity to sell a second time to another buyer. If the second buyer records or occupies first, a claim of ownership superior to the first buyer's is realized. The first buyer's only recourse, for all practical purposes, would

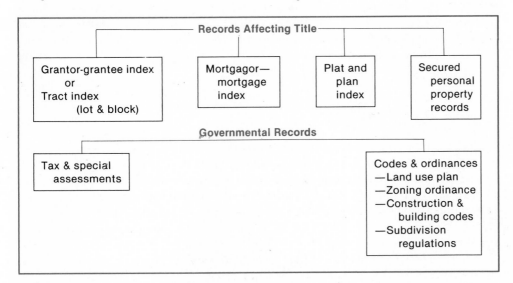

FIGURE 3-9
Real property public records

be against the fraudulent grantor. Two systems are used to maintain title records: The first is a grantor-grantee index; the second is a tract or lot and block index.

Grantor-Grantee Index. A *grantor* is the party conveying property ownership by way of a deed; a *grantee* is the party receiving title or ownership. A *grantor-grantee index* lists deeds according to the last name of the previous owner (grantor) and of the new owner (grantee). Thus, a title search can be initiated and a chain of title can be run if the name of either is known. In running a chain of title, the grantor is regarded as a grantee in a previous transaction. When located in the grantee index, the previous grantor's name then becomes immediately available.

Tract Index (Lot and Block). A *tract index* lists deeds and other documents affecting specific properties according to their legal descriptions rather than by grantor-grantee. In urban areas, the name of the subdivision in which the property is located will often serve as the key to entering the index. Alternatively, maps of the area will include a distinct number for each block. Transactions involving individual lots on the block can then be ascertained by looking in the index itself.

Entry into a tract index is more difficult in rural areas because the classification system is more involved in that property has a distinct legal description. The general system of the tract index in rural areas is based on identifying properties by township and by section. A chain of title can be run more easily with a tract index because all transactions involving a specific property are recorded on the same page. A tract index, however, is considered more difficult and more expensive to maintain than is a grantor-grantee index.

MORTGAGOR-MORTGAGEE RECORDS

In nearly every state, mortgages are accepted for recording in, and constructive notice is given by, a mortgagor-mortgagee index. A mortgagor is the party receiving money in exchange for a claim against property; a mortgagee advances the money. A mortgagor-mortgagee index functions in a manner very similar to a grantor-grantee index; that is, the index may be entered with either the name of the borrower-mortgagor or the lender-mortgagee. When a mortgage lien has been satisfied, this also is entered in the index. In some states, mortgages are filed and recorded in the same grantor-grantee index that is used for deeds.

PLAT AND PLAN RECORDS

Maps, restrictions, architectural plans, and other pertinent information on subdivision and condominium plats are maintained as a part of the public record. The plats are a particularly excellent source of information on easements and restrictions on a specific plat. Parcel and building dimensions and building layout can also be readily determined from this source.

SECURED PERSONAL PROPERTY RECORDS

The *Uniform Commercial Code* is a set of laws governing the sale, financing, and use as security of personal property. The code provides that items of personal property may be purchased on a conditional sales contract, which is also termed a secu-rity agreement. Legally, purchase by conditional sales contract means that title does not pass until full payment is made. In the meantime, a short version of the security agreement, termed a financing statement, is entered into the public record to give constructive notice of a collateral lien on the property. For owners of real estate, this notice is of considerable importance when items such as water heaters, boilers, ap-pliances, draperies, and other equipment frequently classed as fixtures are involved. The items do not become fixtures, or part of the real estate, until the security agree-ment is satisfied. That is, important components of a property may not actually be a part of the realty. Notice of the financing statement is usually entered in the mortga-gor-mortgagee index.

Questions for Review and Discussion

1. What is a fixture? When is the identification of a fixture important? Not impor-tant? When are the following things fixtures: key, storm windows, hot-water heater?
2. Explain the following methods of describing realty in detail.
   a. Metes and bounds
   b. The government survey system
   c. The recorded plat
3. Are there occasions where the methods or systems in question 2 are not ade-quate to describe realty? Explain.
4. What effects will adoption of the metric system have on legal descriptions of real estate, if any? Discuss.
5. The rectangular survey system is obsolete for describing real estate and should be replaced. Discuss.
6. Explain briefly the nature and use of the following public record indexes.
   a. Grantor-grantee
   b. Tract
   c. Mortgagor-mortgagee
   d. Secured personal property
7. Why should a deed be recorded from a grantee's viewpoint? A lender's? A lessee's?

Case Problems

Wendy Welloff asks you to help her identify and otherwise describe some properties she just bought.

1. Begin by making a square approximately 2 inches, or 5 centimeters, on each side on a sheet of paper to represent Section 31, T2N, R5W, which is where the parcels are located. Sketch the parcels of land within the section: (a) N.E.1/4;

(b) S.E.1/4 of the S.E.1/4; (c) W.1/2 of the N.W.1/4 of the S.W./1/4; (d) S.W.1/4 of the N.W.1/4 of the N.W.1/4; and (e) W.1/2 of the N.E.1/4 of the N.E.1/4 of the N.W.1/4.

2. How many acres in each parcel of case problem 1 (a)–(e)?

3. How many miles from the eastern edge of Sect. 31, T.2N, R.5W to the western edge of Sect. 36, T.2N, R.3W?

4. How far is it from the northern edge of Sect. 31 T.2N., R.5W to the northern border of Sect. 6, T.1N, R.5W?

5. Gerald and Nancy Investor receive a deed to property they just bought from Wendy Welloff. They move into the property but do not record the deed. To what extent are their rights in the property protected?

6. The Investors obtain a mortgage loan for $500,000 from Wendy Welloff to help finance the purchase. Wendy fails to record the mortgage. To what extent is the mortgage valid?

4

Real Property Rights and Interests

Property has its duties as well as its rights.
Thomas Drummond (Letter to the Tipperary Magistrates, 1838)

Property rights are the true commodity in the real estate market, even though attention is usually focused on the physical realty. The main ownership rights are control, possession and use (enjoyment), exclusion, and disposition. Control means the right to build or remove buildings, to grant easements, to impose covenants or conditions, to lease, to agree to a lien, or to act in any other way that allows an encumbrance to be placed against the property. Occupying the property as a home or using it as a place of business are ways of enjoying ownership. Keeping others off of a property for privacy is exclusion. Rights of disposition include selling or refusing to sell, giving the property to others by gift or will, and even abandonment.

Fee ownership of real estate is commonly considered as a bundle of rights. See Figure 4-1. Law and order provided by a government serves to preserve, protect, and enforce the rights. When any of the rights are given up, as when an easement is granted or a mortgage lien is placed against the property, the value of the bundle is reduced. The purpose of this chapter is to explain the bundle of rights, the forms of ownership of the bundle, and the ways in which the bundle may be reduced.

Knowledge of property rights is extremely important because decisions and actions an owner may take are implied in the rights owned. Lack of complete or clear ownership translates directly into risk of loss of ownership because of poor title. *Title* is another way of saying ownership of real property. Having high-quality title of the right type reduces investor risks, enhances value, and increases owner flexibility in administering the property.

Right or Benefit	Stick in Bundle
Control	Mortgage
	Lease
	Impose covenants or conditions
	Grant easements
	Grant license
	Build or remove structures
Use and enjoy	Occupy as residence
	Use as place of business
	Farm
	Mine/drill for oil, etc.
	Place of recreation
Exclusion	Maintain privacy
	Nontrespass
Disposition	Sell or refuse to sell
	Gift
	Will
	Abandon

FIGURE 4-1
Real property is a bundle of rights

Important Topics or Decision Areas Covered in this Chapter

Freehold Ownership Interests
Completeness of Ownership
Time When Active
Number and Relationship of Owners
Condominium
Nonfreehold or Leasehold Interests

Owning Real Estate as Personal Property
Corporation
Trust
Cooperative
Syndicates and Joint Ventures

Encumbrances to Ownership
Lien
Easement
Title Restriction
Encroachment
Licenses

Questions for Review and Discussion

Case Problems

Key Concepts Introduced in this Chapter

Community property   **Deed restriction**
Condominium   **Easement**
Cooperative   **Lien**

Encroachment	Life estate
Encumbrance	Separate property
Estate	Statute of Frauds
Fee, fee simple, fee simple absolute	Tenancy by the entirety
Homestead	Tenancy in common
Joint tenancy	Tenancy in partnership
Lease	Tenancy in severalty
License	Title

Freehold Ownership Interests

An ownership interest in real property is termed an *estate.* Estates are basically classified according to the time of enjoyment, with two major classes: (1) freehold and (2) nonfreehold. The term freehold has its origins in the holding of land by a freeman in the English feudal system. A freehold estate continues for an indeterminate period and is considered real property. Title to most freehold estates is held for the lifetime of the owner (unless sold or otherwise disposed of) and then passed on to an heir. Title may be held for the lifetime of some other designated person whose life expectancy is uncertain. The time of possession may be now or in the future. The most common freehold estates are fee simple, qualified fees, life estates, and remainders.

A nonfreehold estate, also termed a leasehold estate or less than freehold estate, on the other hand, endures for a determinate time only; that is, for a period measured in years, months, weeks, or days. Leasehold estates are personal rather than real property.

Transactions involving real property interests are subject to a set of laws, called the *Statute of Frauds,* in every state. These laws require, among other things, that any contract creating or transferring an interest in land or realty be in writing to be enforceable at law. The laws also state that oral testimony to alter or vary the terms of such written agreements is not admissible as evidence in court.

Estates in real estate may also be classified according to (1) quantity or completeness of the interest, (2) time when interest is active and benefits are realized, and (3) number and relationship of the concerned parties.

In our discussion of interests, the terms tenancy and estate are often used interchangeably even though they technically do not mean the same thing. A *tenancy* is the manner of owning an estate, or interest in land, as, for example, a possessory right or interest. Stating ownership by tenancy gives more specific information about the interest held, as will be seen shortly. See Figure 4-2 for an overview of how estates and tenancies fit together.

COMPLETENESS OF OWNERSHIP

Fee Simple. *Fee, fee simple,* and *fee simple absolute* all mean the same thing; namely, complete or absolute ownership of realty subject only to certain limi-

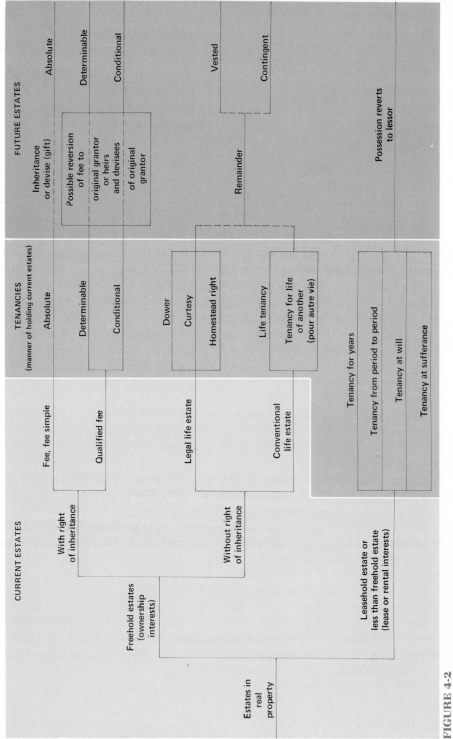

FIGURE 4-2
Real property estates and tenancies

tations imposed by the government. Fee simple is the most complete bundle of rights that anyone can acquire in the United States.

The fee simple owner of real property may use it or dispose of it in any legal way, including passing it on by will. Further, a fee owner may divide up the title in any of several ways. This is called fee splitting. Splitting up the fee is usually in terms of completeness, time, or number of owners. For example, three different people could be assigned the air rights, surface rights, and subsurface rights in a single parcel. Or title might be split between a present owner and a future owner. See Figure 4-3 for the alternative ways in which a fee interest may be split.

Most realty is held in fee simple, and the term "ownership" ordinarily means such a position. However, concurrent ownership (two or more owners) is often involved. All other estates are less than fee simple and, in fact, are some portion of it. All the lesser parts, if gathered again, would make the fee simple estate complete or whole again.

Qualified Fee. A qualified fee estate is a fee estate with a limitation imposed by the person creating the estate. Breaching the limitation may result in title being taken away from one owner and being placed in another. For example, Mr. Brown deeds land to a church "so long as" it is used for religious or educational purposes. If the land were used otherwise, as for a tavern or gambling house, the condition is violated. The grantor, or the heirs, might then exercise the power of termination and regain title. The interest is either determinable or conditional, depending on the limitation imposed.

TIME WHEN ACTIVE

An ownership interest limited to the life of a natural person is a *life estate.* Life estates split a fee according to time. The owner of a life estate is a life tenant. The interest may be measured by the life tenant's own life or by that of another person, termed *pour autre vie*. A life estate may be created by will, by deed, or by operation of

Fee Simple Ownership				
Quality: of fee	Time of Possession	Concurrent owners of undivided interests[a]	Physical or spatial	Rights to specified benefits
—Fee simple absolute —Qualified fee	—Life estate (present) —Remainder (future)	—T. by the entirety —Community property —Joint tenancy —T. in common —T. in partnership —Condomonium	—Air rights —Surface rights —Subsurface rights	—Water rights —Mineral rights —Oil and gas rights

[a]Ownership of corporations is personal property even though the business entity owns real property. Also, leases and cooperatives constitute personal property.

FIGURE 4-3
Alternative ways to "fee split" real property

the law. The ownership interest, for future possession, that becomes effective at the end of a life estate is known as a remainder. The person designated to receive the remainder interest is a remainderman.

A life tenant has certain rights and duties. A life tenant may sell, lease, encumber, or otherwise dispose of the interest. At the same time, the remainderman's interest must be kept in mind. Hence, while the tenant is entitled to the income and use of the land, he or she is also obliged to keep the property in fair repair and to pay the usual normal carrying charges, including taxes. The life tenant must also pay the interest on any mortgage. Any buildings erected on the land become the property of the remainderman. Because the rights cease at death, a life tenant is said to hold title without right of inheritance. Also, if the life tenant obtains a mortgage, the lien automatically expires at the end of the life estate.

Conventional Life Estates. A life estate created by a will or deed is termed a conventional life estate. For example, a husband wills land to his wife for as long as she lives and, then, upon her death, to his daughter. Upon his death, his wife becomes a life tenant and owns a life estate, the right to full use of the property for life. His daughter obtains a remainder position, which is the right to receive and use the property after the wife's death. Upon the wife's death, the fee is reunited in the daughter, who then becomes the owner of a fee simple interest.

Legal Life Estates. Life estates may also be created by law, which are termed legal life estates. Dower, curtesy, and homestead rights are legal life estates. Dower and curtesy were developed under English common law and are almost extinct now. In states where they are recognized, the division of property in a divorce terminates them.

An estate for life given by law to a wife in all property owned by a husband at any time during marriage is termed dower. Where dower still exists, the requirements are (1) a valid marriage, (2) ownership of real property by husband, and (3) his death. The interest attaches as soon as the property is acquired or the marriage takes place and cannot be cut off without the wife's consent. For this reason, she needs to sign the deed when she and her husband convey property by mutual consent. Upon his death she usually gets a one-third life estate in all the real property owned by her husband. Dower was intended to give her a means of support after his death. While the husband lives, the wife's rights are "inchoate" or inactive.

Curtesy is the interest given by law to a husband in real property owned by his wife. Requirements are (1) a valid marriage and birth of a child, (2) sole ownership of the property by the wife at her death, (3) her death, and (4) no disposition of the property by her will. This interest does not attach until the wife's death, and she may defeat it by deed in her lifetime or by her will, in either case without her husband's consent. If the curtesy right is created, it usually entitles the husband to all the net income as long as he lives.

A protection of residence that precludes its attachment or forced sale for nonpayment of debt, except for mortgage and tax liens, is a *homestead right.* This protection is statutory in origin; hence, its details vary from state to state. It usually has two purposes: (1) to exempt the home from general debts and (2) to provide a widow (sometimes a widower) with a home for life. In most states the value and area of the exempt homestead are limited. Usually, the dwelling must be occupied as the family home, and a written declaration of homestead must be filed. It is then free from general claims for debts except those that are a lien on the property, such as taxes and mortgages. Homesteads in a few states are exempt from taxes up to a certain assessed value, which is termed a homestead exemption. Homestead protection or rights should not be confused with this homestead exemption.

NUMBER AND RELATIONSHIP OF OWNERS

Real property may be owned by one or more persons. One person holding ownership gives sole title and is termed a *tenancy in severalty.* Two or more people holding title together are termed concurrent owners. In such circumstances, the owners frequently use or manage real property as a single unit without regard to the number of owners; that is, each holds an undivided interests.

Tenancy by the Entirety. A husband and wife, owning property as one person, is a *tenancy by the entirety.* The legal fiction of a husband and wife being one originated in English common law. As tenants by the entirety, neither can convey the property or force a partition during the marriage. If either dies, the entire property is owned by the survivor. A divorce converts the arrangement into a tenancy in common, unless the property is disposed of or awarded one party. A tenancy by the entirety is very useful in the purchase of a home by a husband and wife, since it makes certain that the survivor will continue to own the residence even though a will is drawn. Tenancy by the entirety is not recognized in community property states.

Community Property. Community property, of Spanish origin and applying only to property held by a married couple, is a recognized form of ownership in eight states: Washington, Idaho, Nevada, California, Arizona, New Mexico, Texas, and Louisiana. Thus, while community property is not designated as a tenancy, it has the same effect.

The community property system recognizes two kinds of property, community and separate, rather than personal and real. *Community property* means that any property acquired by a husband and wife during their marriage, individually or jointly, is held equally by each of them. The death of either gives full title to the survivor.

Separate property is property owned by either the husband or the wife before their marriage, or received by either after their marriage through gift or inheritance, which is specifically excluded from classification as community property. Separate property is free of any claim or interest by the other spouse. Each spouse, therefore, has full ownership and control of separate property and may sell, will, or give the property away or place a mortgage against it. Income or profit from separate property is also separate property. All property not classed as separate property is community property. Dower and curtesy are not recognized in community property states.

The rules are not uniform throughout the states that recognize community property. In most, the spouse is automatically entitled to one-half of the real and personal property, or income, of the other spouse. A divorce or mutual agreement dissolves the community ownership and divides the property between the two parties.

Our laws are continually challenged and modified. For example, "Do unmarried cohabitants, or *par vivants*, develop community property rights?" In one case,

Lee Marvin, the actor, lived with Michelle Triola for several years, though he did not marry her. She did not work outside the domicile during this time, and she legally changed her last name to Marvin. Subsequently, they parted. She sued for one-half of his income during the period they lived together. The court ruled that Lee Marvin must only pay $104,000 "for rehabilitation purposes" in that no contract was reached. Even this award was overturned, on appeal. Other cases indicate that where couples live together, share assets, and jointly invest, a property settlement is appropriate.

Joint Tenancy. Ownership of an undivided interest by two or more owners, not related by marriage and with right of survivorship, is *joint tenancy*. "Right of survivorship" means that if one owner dies, his or her interest passes to the remaining owners. The death of one of the owners is often referred to as the "grand incident" of this form of ownership. The right of survivorship has caused joint tenancy to sometimes be referred to as a "poor man's will." In fact, a will is not replaced because only one property is affected.

Joint tenancy is not favored by the courts between people not related by marriage. Many states have abolished joint tenancy, except that the right of survivorship may still be created if specified in the deed. For a joint tenancy to stand up in a court contest, it must be proved that the joint owners have the four unities required of a joint tenancy: (1) equal interests, (2) title acquired by a single deed, (3) title acquired at the same time, and (4) the same undivided possession of the entire property. A breach of any one of these unities in a conveyance means that a tenancy in common rather than a joint tenancy was created. Needless to say, owners in a joint tenancy share equally in the income and expenses of ownership.

Tenancy in Common. Ownership by two or more parties, without the right of survivorship, is called a *tenancy in common.* Thus, with the death of one of the owners, title to the deceased's share passes to his or her heirs or devisees. That is, the surviving owner or owners do not become owners of the interest of one who dies. Further, two or more heirs are presumed to receive and hold real property as tenants in common.

Tenants in common may have equal or unequal shares. They share in the income and are obligated to contribute to expenses according to their portion of ownership. They may all join to sell the property, or one may sell his or her interest, in which case the purchaser becomes a tenant in common with the others. If one wishes the property to be sold and the others do not, an action for partition may be brought, in which event the property is sold at an auction and each owner is paid his or her proportional share of the proceeds.

Tenancy in Partnership. A partnership is an organizational arrangement whereby two or more people join their expertise and resources to conduct business for profit. The partnership operates as a business entity, with its own name. At the same time, it is not a corporation or trust. Under the Uniform Partnership Act, articles of partnership are required to be drawn up and filed with a public official to form a partnership.

The Uniform Partnership Act provides that realty acquired in the name of a partnership, general or limited, is owned by the partners as a *tenancy in partnership.* Tenancy in partnership carries with it the right of survivorship, which is necessary for the entity to continue uninterrupted business operations. The estate of the deceased partner is entitled to an accounting and a pro rata share of the profits and net worth as of the time of death.

Two kinds of partnership interests are legally recognized: general and limited. The general partner (or partners) operates and manages the business and may be held liable for all losses and obligations of the entity not met by the other partners. A limited partner is exempt by law from liability in excess of his or her contribution. A limited partner, also termed a silent partner, may not participate in operations and management under penalty of losing the exempt or limited liability status. A limited partnership must have at least one general partner who conducts business for the entity.

CONDOMINIUM

Condominium ownership is holding a fractional interest in a larger property, part of which is separate and unique to each owner (the condominium unit) and part of which is held in general by all the owners (the common elements). Condominium ownership is similar to holding tenancy in common, except that a portion of the fractional share is held as a separate or divided interest. The larger property is, of course, the entire condominium development. An owner of a fractional share holds it in fee simple and may dispose of it without obligation to the other owner or owners.

Condominium co-ownership is most often used for multifamily residential properties. Each owner possesses an exclusive right to use, occupy, mortgage, and dispose of his or her particular dwelling, plus an undivided interest in the areas and fixtures that serve all owners in common. Each deed is subject to identical covenants and restrictions governing the repair and maintenance of the building. Owning an individual residential condominium offers tax advantages identical to those enjoyed by owners of detached single-family properties.

Condominium ownership dates back to ancient Rome. Legislation introducing condominium ownership into the United States was initially passed in the early 1960s. As a rule, the legislation requires the separate assessment and taxation of each space unit and its common interests. The legislation, therefore, stops the assessor from treating any part of the common elements of the property as a separate parcel for taxation purposes. As a rule, too, statutes bar the placement of mechanic's or other liens on the common elements of a property held jointly by two or more owners.

The condominium arrangement requires the formation of a central administrative body to act on behalf of all condominium owners for operation of the larger property as an integral whole. Thus, all co-owners must share the expenses of operation and maintenance, which are levied as monthly assessments to each according to his or her pro rata share. Owners, too, are bound to observe recorded rules and regulations governing use and occupancy of both individually owned premises and those held in common. An owner cannot ordinarily be ousted or dispossessed (as can a defaulting tenant) for infraction of bylaws or regulations but is subject to such court actions as necessary to compel compliance.

Condominium ownership is not limited to residential units. Business and industrial properties may also be subdivided into condominium units. Indeed, parking ramps have been subdivided into condominium parking spaces, and yacht clubs have been broken into condominium boat slips. Also, recreational housing is increasingly split into time-share condominiums; thus, a unit may have 50 different owners, each with the right of full use for 1 week per year.

NONFREEHOLD OR LEASEHOLD INTERESTS

Owners frequently give possession and use rights in real estate to other parties in exchange for rent by way of a contract termed a *lease.* A nonfreehold or leasehold estate, limited to right of occupancy and use only, is thereby created. The party to whom the property is rented is a lessee or tenant. The owner in a lease arrangement is termed a lessor or landlord. The owner's position is termed a leased fee. Leasing is discussed much more completely in the next chapter.

Owning Real Estate as Personal Property

A discussion of forms of ownership would not be complete without taking up corporations and trusts in their several forms. Even though they are personal property, they often own real estate as an estate in severalty. This means the owners of these entities control and get the benefits of real estate; they also get such penalties as double taxation when owning as as corporation. Thus, they serve as an alternative way to own real estate.

Figure 4-4 provides a comparison of the several forms of real estate ownership for investment purposes. Emphasis is on the extent of exposure to liability, to tax implications, to duration of the arrangement, to the ease of transferability of the interest, and to the form of management. Full flow through means that the income is not taxed at the initial level.

CORPORATION

A corporation is a legal entity with rights of doing business that are essentially the same as those of an individual. The entity is owned by stockholders, who can be many in number, and has continuous existence regardless of any changes in ownership. A corporation limits the liability of owners to the amount invested in the organization. A corporation ceases to exist only if dissolved according to proper legal process.

The major disadvantages of the corporate form for real estate ownership and investment purposes are that (1) costs of organizing and maintaining the corporation are relatively high, (2) the profits are subject to double taxation (taxation of the corporation and taxation of the shareholder upon distribution), and (3) corporations are subject to more governmental regulation, at all levels, than are most other forms of business organization.

A Subchapter S-corporation, a hybrid of the partnership and corporate forms of organization, is frequently used in holding real estate. A Subchapter S-corporation may have up to 35 shareholders, all of one class, who enjoy limited liability. Unlike a limited partnership, these shareholders may participate in centralized management decisions without jeopardizing their limited liability status. Further, shares are more

Ownership Form	Liability Exposure	Tax Status	Life Duration	Transfer-ability	Management Form
Individual (as condo or coop)	Unlimited	Full flow through, one level	Death terminates	Transferable	Personal
General partner-ship	Unlimited	Full flow through, one level	Terminated by death or with-drawal	Non-transferable	By mutual agree-ment, with equal say by each usually
Limited partner-ship	Limited for lim-ited partners	Full flow through, one level	As agreed in organizational contract	Restricted trans-ferability	Decisions by general part-ners, no say by limited partners
Corporation	Limited	No flow through, two levels	Perpetual	Easily transfer-able	Shareholder control, with board of direc-tors
S-Corporation	Limited	Full flow through, one level	Perpetual, if guidelines met	Easily transfer-able[a]	Shareholder control[a]
REIT	Limited	Substantial flow through, one level	Perpetual	Easily transfer-able[b]	Decisions by trustees

[a]Maximum number of stockholders is 35.
[b]Minimum number of shareholder-beneficiaries is 100.

FIGURE 4-4

Comparison of ownership forms for real estate investment purposes

easily transferred than are limited partner interests. At the same time, profits are exempt from corporate income taxes if distributed to shareholders immediately at the end of each accounting period. Operating losses may also be passed through to shareholders, with certain restrictions, to be used as tax deductions. Finally, a Sub-chapter S-corporation may have perpetual life, provided that certain guidelines are not violated.[1]

TRUST

A trust is a fiduciary arrangement whereby property is turned over to an individual or an institution, termed a trustee, to be held and administered for the profit and/or advantage of some person or organization, termed the beneficiary. The person set-ting up a trust is termed a trustor or creator. The trustee acts for the trust, which may hold property in its own name, just as an individual or a corporation does. The trustee is obligated to act solely for the benefit of the beneficiary. Two kinds of trust are mainly used in owning realty: a real estate investment trust and an express pri-vate trust.

A real estate investment trust (REIT) is much like a corporation. People buy shares (of beneficial interest) and, thereby, join for the ownership of real estate with

[1]Charles P. Edmonds, "Title of Work," unpublished manuscript. (Auburn, Ala.: Auburn University, 198x). Thomas L. Dickens, "The Appeal of Subchapters," *Tierra Grande*, vol. xx, no. 21, 19xx.

limited liability. At the same time, double taxation of profits may be avoided by meeting the requirements of the trust laws; that is, paying out earnings in the year earned.

An express private trust usually involves only a small number of beneficiaries, often a spouse and children. An express private trust may be created during one's lifetime (a living or *inter vivos* trust) or upon one's death (testamentary trust). The main advantages of a private trust are savings in estate taxes and extended protection for the beneficiary, who may not be familiar with business affairs.

COOPERATIVE

Ownership of shares in a cooperative venture, entitling the owner to occupy and use a specific space or unit, usually an apartment, under a proprietary lease is *cooperative* ownership. The cooperative form of mutual ownership differs from a condominium entity in that the ownership of the entire property (land and improvements) is acquired by a corporation or trust. As a rule the property is financed for up to 80 percent of its value with a mortgage loan; the balance is obtained from the sale of equity shares. Each buyer acquires a proprietary lease that is subordinate to financing taken on by the corporation.

A proprietary lease is an agreement, with the attributes of ownership, under which a tenant-shareholder in a cooperative occupies space designated according to the shares owned. The lease terms stipulate the payment of rent to the corporation to cover pro rata shares of the amounts necessary to meet mortgage debt service, maintenance expenditures, property taxes, and building-related expenditures, such as hazard insurance and sinking fund (replacement) reserves. Because of the priority of the financing, a default in payments by the corporation, owing to default in payments by some proprietary tenants, affects occupancy and title of all cooperative participants.

SYNDICATES AND JOINT VENTURES

Two other forms of organization often mentioned in regard to owning real estate are syndicates or joint ventures; neither is a distinct legal entity, in and of itself. A coming together of two or more people or firms for a single project is commonly termed a joint venture. A syndicate is the coming together of individuals, and sometimes of individuals and organizations, to conduct business and to make investments on a continuing basis. Either may take the form of a partnership, corporation, or trust. Personal and financial abilities are pooled because the members believe that as a group they will be able to accomplish ends that each could not undertake and complete by acting separately. The term, syndicate, is used because it connotes an organization that has limited goals, usually of an investment nature.

Encumbrances to Ownership

As was stated earlier, the value of fee ownership is decreased as each right is given up or as each encumbrance is placed against it. An *encumbrance* is a claim against clear title of or a limitation on use of a property. An encumbrance comes about as a result of a defect in line of ownership or of some action, or nonaction, of the owner. An encumbrance is often referred to as a "cloud on title."

Investor-owners need to know the causes and implications of encumbrances because losses caused by lack of knowledge can amount to thousands of dollars. An encumbrance of a slightly less serious nature may result in title being unmarketable, meaning that a buyer need not accept a clouded title to a property. Most encumbrances are created voluntarily, but some are created involuntarily by action of law as when an owner ignores someone's rights. In addition to defects of title, encumbrances take the form of liens, *deed restrictions*, leases, easements, and encroachments.

Figure 4-5 summarizes the many encumbrances that may accrue against property as well as the limitations to ownership imposed by public bodies. Figure 4-6 illustrates several of the encumbrances. Public limitations are discussed at length in Chapter 6. A written lease extending beyond the closing date in a sales transaction is an encumbrance. Other leases are not usually considered an encumbrance unless time of occupancy and use is of the essence to the buyer. Leases are discussed at length in the next chapter.

LIENS

A *lien* is a claim to have a debt or other obligation satisfied out of property belonging to another. Common examples are mortgage liens, mechanic's liens, property tax liens, and judgment liens. A lien generally signifies a debtor-creditor relationship between the property owner and the lienholder. The creditor, if not otherwise satisfied, may initiate an action at law to have the debtor's property sold to satisfy the claim. In most cases a lien results from a contract voluntarily entered into by an owner, but not always. Paying property taxes, for example, is certainly not done voluntarily, except by a great stretching of the imagination.

Note that a lien does not transfer title to the lienholder. Where more than one lien is filed against a property, the one recorded first has highest priority of claim.

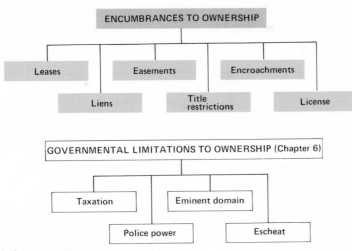

FIGURE 4-5
Limitations and encumbrances to fee ownership

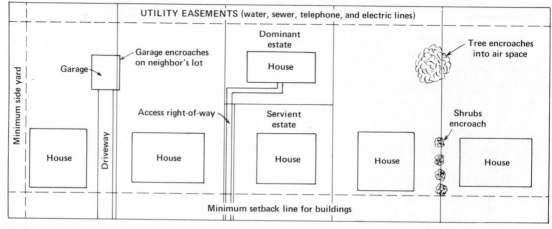

FIGURE 4-6
Typical encumbrances

The general rule is, "First in time is first in line." However, property tax liens, imposed by law, take priority over all other liens.

A mortgage lien is created when property is pledged as security for a loan, as from a financial institution. A mortgage lien is specific to the property pledged.

Anyone performing work or furnishing materials toward the improvement of realty expects to be paid, of course. In the event of nonpayment, the worker or material supplier has a specific, statutory claim for payment against the property, termed a mechanic's lien. The rationale is that the labor and materials enhance the property's value, and it would be a great injustice to let an owner avoid payment of a claim so closely connected to the property's value.

A tax lien is a claim against property caused by nonpayment of income, inheritance, or property taxes by an owner. A tax lien results from an implied contract in which the property owner owes tax payments to the government in return for protection, services, and other benefits received. The property tax lien is the most common and is property specific.

A judgment lien is a court declaration of an individual's indebtedness to another, including the amount. A judgment lien means that a claim in the amount of the

The High Cost of Ignoring Liens

In 1973 a law student in Sacramento, California, went to small claims court to recover a $50 cleaning deposit plus $200 in damages from a building owner. The owner refused to pay. In 1976 the owner's property, a 95-unit apartment complex valued at $1.5 million, was sold at auction to satisfy the claim. Only the student showed up at the auction, and in satisfaction of the default judgment, now put at $449, the student received a certificate of sale for the property. A 1-year-and-1-day statutory period allowed for redemption of publicly auctioned property passed, without the certificate's being redeemed, so the student became legal owner of the property.

In 1985 a court debt of $554 resulted in a prime piece of Florida Keys real estate, valued at $301,675, being auctioned off for $1.00. The only and winning bid at the auction was made by none other than the instigator of the auction, appropriately named Richard Fast.

court declaration is placed against all property owned by the debtor. Thus, a judgment lien is a general, or nonspecific, lien.

EASEMENT

An *easement* is a right or privilege to use the land of another for certain purposes, such as party driveways, ingress and egress, or drainage. An easement is a nonpossessory real property right, meaning that the holder of the easement does not have the right to occupy the property subject to the easement.

Easements are usually created by deed or by contract. For example, a rancher may sell off a section of land near a river but include in the sales contract and deed an easement to obtain and move water across the alienated land. Easements, except those for utilities and services, may be regarded as encumbrances to clear title in a sales transaction if detrimental to the use of the land. An investor should distinguish between the several types of easements and the implications of each.

Easement Appurtenant. An access right of way across an adjacent property, a joint driveway, or the right to use a party wall are examples of an appurtenant easement. A party wall is an exterior building wall that straddles the property line and is used jointly by the adjacent property owners. Title is held to the part of the wall on one's own property, and an easement is held in the remainder. A written party-wall agreement is best used to create and control the use of this easement. An easement appurtenant is considered part of the land and is said to "run with the land." Appurtenant means belonging to, or going with, another thing.

An easement appurtenant results in a slight gain or loss in real property rights (and values). The parcel benefited is known as the dominant tenement. The parcel subject to the easement is known as the servient tenement. The dominant parcel, of course, benefits and gains value, whereas the servient tenement becomes less desirable. Naturally enough, an easement resulting in a property's becoming a servient tenement is regarded as an encumbrance to clear or marketable title.

An easement appurtenant requires at least two parcels of realty owned by different parties. The parcels are usually but not necessarily adjacent. Although the parcels need not be adjacent, the dominant tenement must be at the beginning or end of the easement. For example, a road or right-of-way could cross several servient parcels (A, B, C, and D) to serve a dominant parcel (E).

Easement in Gross. An easement in gross is a personal right to use the property of another. Neither adjacent nor nearby property need be owned to possess the right. Examples of easements in gross are rights-of-way for pipelines, power lines, sewer lines, or roads used by public service companies.

Easement by Prescription. An easement by prescription is created by open, unauthorized, continuous use of a servient parcel for the prescriptive period. A prescriptive period is from 10 to 20 years in most states. The use must also have been under claim of right of use, without the approval of the owner of the encumbered parcel, and notorious to the point that the owner could learn of it.

Termination. Easements may be terminated by any one of several ways.

1. Consolidation or merger, as when the dominant and servient parcels are brought under one ownership

2. Agreement, as when the owner of the dominant tenement releases the right of easement to the servient owner, possibly for a price
3. Completion of purpose, as when the easement is no longer needed; a right-of-way easement of necessity ends if alternate access to the land-locked parcel is gained by its owner
4. Abandonment or lack of use

TITLE RESTRICTION

A title restriction is a covenant (promise) or condition entered into the public record to limit the nature or intensity of use of land. For example, a property may be limited by a title restriction to one-family residential use or to having no residence smaller than 1,500 square feet, or the requirement may be "not to keep goats, chickens, or pigs on the premises." Setback and sideyard standards may be imposed by title restriction (see Figure 4-6) as well as by a zoning ordinance.

Title restrictions were traditionally entered into the public record on a deed at the time of conveyance of title to another and were originally known as deed restrictions. The restrictions are now more commonly entered into the public record by subdividers and developers. In effect, rights are exchanged on all parcels to promote or enhance the value of the entire development. The purpose is to protect neighborhood quality and to preserve and enhance property value. Thus, the more appropriate term is title restrictions.

Enforcement is usually by proceedings at law or in equity against any person or persons violating or attempting to violate the covenants. In a subdivision or condominium development, the homeowner's association typically sees to enforcement.

Title restrictions that do not contain their own time limit (effective for 30 years from this date, for example) are terminated by the law of the state in which the property is located. A deed restriction may be, but need not be, an encumbrance to marketable title; it depends on the effect of the restriction on the use and value of the parcel.

ENCROACHMENT

An *encroachment* occurs when a building or other improvement, such as a fence or driveway, illegally intrudes on or into the property of another owner. Intrusion of a garage overhang or tree limbs are examples. The owner of the property intruded upon can require removal, and failure to do so may weaken his or her title. On the other side, a new owner of the encroaching property may be stuck with the unexpected expense of moving a building or cutting back a stately tree. See Figure 4-6.

An abstract of title or title insurance policy is not likely to evidence an encroachment unless it existed and was picked up in a previous transaction. That is, a physical inspection of a property, and sometimes a survey as well, is needed to ascertain that an encroachment exists. An encroachment is a title encumbrance and must be cleared up for marketable title to be conveyed to a buyer.

LICENSES

A *license* is the privilege to use or enter on the premises, granted by someone in legal possession of realty. The right to attend a ball game after purchase of a ticket or to hunt or fish on a farmer's land are examples. As a general rule, a license may be canceled at the will of an owner and is not usually considered an encumbrance to clear title.

Questions for Review and Discussion

1. Define and distinguish among the following:
   a. A freehold estate and a leasehold estate
   b. A conventional life estate and a legal life estate
   c. Estate and tenancy
2. Define and distinguish among the following:
   a. Tenancy in severalty
   b. Tenancy by the entirety
   c. Joint tenancy
   d. Tenancy in common
   e. Community property
3. List and explain briefly the four tenancies of leasehold estates.
4. Is government necessary for the existence of private property? Discuss.
5. Are there interests in real estate that do not involve ownership or possession? Discuss.
6. Does condominium ownership make sense in a rural setting? If so, are there some other forms of ownership that make more sense to accomplish the same purpose? Discuss.
7. Are the laws concerning ownership of real estate changing? In what ways? Give examples.
8. Distinguish between easement appurtenant and easement in gross. What is the usual purpose of each?
9. Identify and explain briefly two encumbrances, not caused by defect in title, in addition to liens, easements, and deed restrictions.
10. Giving tax liens priority, by law, is unfair to other lienholders. Discuss.
11. It has been proposed that a statute of limitations is needed to remove encumbrances as clouds on title; thus, liens, easements, and deed restrictions would become ineffective after some stipulated period, say 15 years. Discuss. What are the implications?
12. When is a deed restriction not an encumbrance? Discuss.

Case Problems

1. Able, owner of 160 acres of land along a river, sells half to Baker. An easement of access to the river for recreational purposes for Baker's benefit is written into the deed, though no right to use the frontage on the river is included. Baker later sells off five 10-acre parcels to others. Are these subsequent purchasers entitled to use the access easement across Able's land to the river? Discuss.

2. A, B, and C own land as joint tenants. C conveys her third to D and dies shortly after. A and B object, claiming that the conveyance is not valid without their approval. A and B further claim that the conveyance, if legal, makes D a joint tenant also. The case is taken to court. What is the result?

3. John Burgoyne is looking to acquire a home. One property interests him but upon investigation he determines the following. What effect does each have on value or John's probable offering price?
   a. Garage encroaches on neighbor's lot
   b. Deed restriction prohibits occupancy by minority races
   c. Easement appurtenant to cross neighbor's lot to next street
   d. Utility easement for 9 feet along rear lot line
   e. Occupant's written lease for another 6 months
   f. Ownership by two brothers as tenants in common

5

Leases and Leasing

The relationship of landlord and tenant is not an ideal one, but any relation on a social order will endure if there is infused . . . some of that spirit of human sympathy which qualifies life for immortality.

George Russell, an open letter in the *Dublin Times* during the 1913 general strike

An owner may exchange possession and use rights in real estate to another person for rent by way of a lease. A *leasehold estate,* meaning right of occupancy only, is thereby created. The owner's interest in a rented property is termed a *leased fee.*

The person to whom the property is rented is a lessee or tenant. One of the important advantages of leasing space is that no capital investment is required of the tenant. Each of us is likely to be a lessor or landlord and a lessee or tenant during our lifetime. Students become tenants when signing a lease for a dorm room, an apartment, or a house. Whether an owner or a tenant, we must know and understand leasing to make intelligent decisions in negotiating a rental agreement. Therefore, this chapter covers the basic terminology of, the kinds of, the typical covenants or clauses of, and the ways of terminating leases. Emphasis is on residential property, though key points regarding commercial or industrial property are included. Brief attention is also given to the relative negotiating positions of the parties and to some of the broader issues involved in negotiation, mainly tenant unions.

Important Topics or Decision Areas Covered in this Chapter

Creating a Valid Lease
Essential Elements of a Lease
Basic Terminology

Kinds of Leases
Classification by Rental Payment Agreement
Ground Lease
Sale and Leaseback

Key Concepts Introduced in this Chapter

Abandonment
Assignment
Eviction, actual
Eviction, constructive
Gross lease
Ground lease
Index lease
Lease option
Leased fee
Leasehold estate
*Lessee/tenant
*Lessor/landlord

Net lease
Percentage lease
Quiet enjoyment
Retaliatory eviction
Sale and leaseback
Sublessee
Sublessor
Sublet
Subordination clause
Tenancy for years
Tenancy from period to
    period

Creating a Valid Lease

A lease may be a verbal agreement under which the property is rented for a short term or a lengthy document containing many special provisions and covenants. Most state fraud statutes require a lease for more than 1 year to be in writing; it follows that a lease for less than 1 year may be oral. Written or oral, a leasehold interest is legally personal property.

A lease may be an encumbrance to clear title. Leases for 3 years or more are recordable in most states. However, in that possession gives actual notice of a tenant's claim in a property, recording may not be a crucial issue. Some leases are not recorded because the parties wish to avoid revealing rents, terms, and other contents of the agreement.

ESSENTIAL ELEMENTS OF A LEASE

No particular wording or form of agreement is required by statute to create a valid lease. It is sufficient in law, if the intention is expressed, to transfer from one to another possession of certain real property for a determinate length of time. Substance, not form, is what counts.

A long-term lease must contain the essential elements of a valid contract to be enforceable. These are (1) that the parties be legally competent, (2) that the objective be legal, (3) that there be a mutual agreement or meeting of the minds, and (4) that consideration be given. Additional elements necessary to make the contract a lease include (1) a named lessor and lessee; (2) adequate description of premises; (3) an agreement to let and take, or conveyance of the premises from the lessor to the lessee; (4) starting time and length of the arrangement; (5) agreed rental; and (6) a writing with signatures.

BASIC TERMINOLOGY

The party selling the right of occupancy and use in a lease is the *lessor* or *landlord*. The party buying is the *lessee* or *tenant*.

Four distinct tenancies are possible in leasing property: (1) tenancy for years, (2) tenancy from period to period or periodic tenancy, (3) tenancy at will, and (4) tenancy at sufferance. The rights of the lessee become weaker as the lessee goes from a tenancy for years to a tenancy at sufferance. The emphasis here is on tenancy for years and periodic tenancy. Tenancy, again, means the manner or conditions under which a property is held.

Tenancy for Years. A leasing agreement for a specific or definite period of time is a *tenancy for years.* Such an agreement is usually for more than 1 year and is usually written. The time may actually be for 1 month, 6 months, 1 year, or more than 1 year. A written lease for 9 months creates an estate or tenancy for years just as a lease for 99 years does. In both cases, the time of occupancy and use is definite. The tenant is required to vacate the property and return possession to the landlord at the end of a tenancy for years without notice being required of the landlord. A tenant continuing in possession beyond the end of the lease is a holdover. In a holdover situation, the landlord may evict the tenant or elect to hold the tenant for a further period of 1 year. By mutual agreement of the parties, the lease agreement may be converted from a tenancy for years to a tenancy from period to period.

Tenancy from Period to Period. A tenancy of uncertain duration, for example, month to month or year to year, is termed a *tenancy from period to period* or a periodic tenancy. The tenancy is usually from month to month for apartments in urban areas and continues until the landlord or tenant gives notice of termination. The rental period usually determines the length of notice required. That is, a week's notice is required to end a week-to-week tenancy. Only a month's notice is likely to be required to terminate a year-to-year tenancy, however. A lessee holding over from a tenancy for years, where rental payments are made monthly, is likely to create a month-to-month tenancy.

Other Tenancies. A lessee allowed to holdover with the consent of the landlord, subject to eviction at the will of the lessor, creates a tenancy at will. Note that the option to hold over is exclusive to the landlord. Holding over without any justification other than the implied consent of the lessor creates a tenancy at sufferance, which is the weakest possible estate in realty. The tenant must vacate the premises in such a situation at the will of the landlord.

Kinds of Leases

Broadly speaking, leases are classified as either short or long term. This division is rather arbitrary and has no particular legal significance. Generally, however, commercial or industrial leases extending over 10 or more years may appropriately be referred to as long-term leases. These leases are typically lengthy documents containing many special provisions and landlord-tenant covenants. At the same time, a 3-year term would be considered a long-term lease for residential use. A ground lease, defined later in this section, would be considered long term only if it exceeded 21 years.

The most usual lease classification system is by rental payment method. Ground leases and sale and leaseback arrangements are also classifications of leases. Note that these classifications may overlap and therefore are not mutually exclusive. For example, a sale and leaseback arrangement might actually be a ground lease calling for a net rental.

CLASSIFICATION BY RENTAL PAYMENT AGREEMENT

Beginning with the most common, classification by rental payment agreement is as follows.

Percentage Lease. An agreement whereby rent is a specified proportion of sales or income generated through tenant use of a property is called a *percentage lease.* A "floor" or minimum rent may be included to assure the owner of some basic income from the property.

The percentage of gross sales lease has gained steadily in popularity for commercial properties. Generally, such a lease provides for a minimum rental ranging from 40 to 80 percent of amounts considered fair in relation to property value. Percentage rentals may range from as low as 2 percent of gross sales for department stores or supermarkets to as high as 75 percent for parking lot operations.

In that the landlord's income is directly related to the success of the tenant's operations, lease clauses are generally included to ensure continuous and effective store operation. Agreement on methods of accounting and on a periodic audit is also generally included. The landlord, in turn, is expected to promise to maintain the property in prime operating condition and to exclude competitors from other nearby owned properties.

Index Lease. Index leases have come into vogue in recent years as a result of high and continuous inflation. An *index lease* either provides for rental adjustment in direct proportion to increases in taxes, insurance, and operating costs or provides for rental increments in proportion to changes in cost-of-living or wholesale price indexes. Index leases are more likely to be used where property value is going up but no easy measure of the value increase is available. Examples are warehouses, factories, and office buildings.

Net Lease. A rental agreement requiring the tenant to pay all maintenance costs, insurance premiums, and property taxes is a ***net lease.*** Net leases generally run for 10 years or more. A net lease assures an owner of a certain rate of return from an investment while shifting the burden of meeting increasing operating costs and taxes to the tenant. Net leases are deemed suitable for large office, commercial, and industrial properties. Net leases are preferred by investment trusts and insurance companies that acquire real estate under purchase and leaseback agreements.

Gross Lease. An arrangement calling for a fixed rental to be paid periodically throughout its entire life is a flat lease; it may also be called a straight or fixed rental lease. This arrangement, which at one time enjoyed wide use and popularity, has come into gradual disuse for long-term leases because of inflation. When rents are fixed in amount over a long period, a declining dollar value deprives the landlord (owner) of a competitive return in proportion to the value of the property. A flat lease requiring the lessor to pay all property carrying charges such as taxes, insurance, and maintenance is called a ***gross lease.***

Graduated Lease. A graduated lease, calling for periodic increases in the rental, is intended to give the tenant lighter operating expenses during the early, formative years of a business enterprise. In turn, the landlord shares in business growth through successively higher rental payments. This lease arrangement may result in excessive rents when growth fails to occur and cause business failure. This arrangement is also termed a step-up lease. Conceivably, "step down" rentals might be used for an older property.

Reappraisal Lease. A reappraisal lease calls for a property's value and rental amount to be reestablished at agreed intervals, usually 3–5 years. Reappraisal leases are rarely used today because reappraisals are expensive and time consuming. Also, they often involve lengthy litigation owing to conflicting value estimates between landlords and tenants.

GROUND LEASE

A ***ground lease*** provides use and occupancy of a vacant site in return for rental payments. The agreement usually contains a provision that a building is to be erected by the tenant. Frequently, the agreement contains a further provision that, at the end of the lease term, the building becomes the property of the landlord. The lease may provide that the landlord, at the expiration of the term, will pay the tenant all or part of the cost or appraised value of the building. The term of the lease, including renewal privileges, must therefore be long enough to allow the tenant to amortize the cost of the building during occupancy.

Ground rent is often a certain percentage of the value of the land. The tenant pays all taxes and other charges, the landlord's rent being net. No set rules govern ground leases. Each bargain is specifically negotiated. The provisions mentioned here merely suggest what might be agreed on.

SALE AND LEASEBACK

The transfer of title of a property for consideration (sale) with the simultaneous renting back to the seller (leaseback) on specified terms is a *sale and leaseback* arrangement. From the buyer's viewpoint, the arrangement is a purchase and leaseback. Businesses, such as Sears or Safeway, find it profitable to sell their real estate holdings and thus free additional capital for expansion of their operations, while leasing back the properties thus sold under custom-designed long-term agreements. Institutional investors, mainly nationally known insurance companies, have found that real estate occupied on a long-term basis by reliable tenants with high credit ratings is an excellent and secure investment.

In arranging a sale and leaseback, the parties exchange instruments. The seller, generally a corporation, deeds the realty to the buyer, an insurance company, or like investor, and the buyer in turn leases the property to the seller under previously agreed upon terms.

The leases extend for 20–30 years with options to renew for like periods. The rent is usually net to the new owner, the seller-lessee being required to pay all operating expenses, including taxes, maintenance, and insurance. Thus, the risk of a lower than expected rate of return to the buyer-lessor is reduced. The lessee-seller, in effect, obtains 100 percent financing. Further, the seller-lessee now enjoys significant income tax advantages since the entire rent paid becomes tax deductible as a cost of business operations. Such deductions are considerably larger than would be the owners' deductions otherwise allowable for interest on mortgage debt, real estate taxes, and permissible depreciation on older buildings and improvements.

Typical Lease Clauses

A number of clauses appear in most leases, for the benefit of the landlord or the tenant. See Figure 5-1, which shows a typical apartment lease.

LANDLORD RIGHTS AND OBLIGATIONS

Quiet enjoyment, meaning the right of possession and use without undue interference from others, is the primary covenant made by a landlord. There is an implied covenant of fitness for use. For example, if a landlord leases space in an apartment or office building, there is an implied covenant that the portions of the building used by all tenants are fit for the use for which they are intended. Many states have recently passed landlord-tenant laws requiring that the premises be kept in good repair. Failure to maintain may give the tenants the right to withhold rental payments or to apply the payments toward repair and maintenance.

The covenant of possession is that the tenant can hold possession against everyone, including the landlord. The lease usually allows the landlord to show the property to a prospective tenant or purchaser for a short period before expiration, with reasonable notice. Also, the lease usually gives the landlord the right to enter and make necessary repairs to comply with governmental requirements. Thus, the landlord gives the tenant possession, subject only to the conditions in the lease.

FORM No. 818
STEVENS-NESS LAW PUBLISHING CO., PORTLAND, OR. 97204
TO-BB

RENTAL AGREEMENT
(Dwelling Unit—Residence Oregon)

26-12

THIS AGREEMENT, entered into in duplicate this 10th *day of* September *, 19* 89 *, by and between* Everready Real Estate Management Co. *, lessor, and* Otto and Mary Mobile *, lessee;*

WITNESSETH: That for and in consideration of the payment of the rents and the performance of the terms of lessee's covenants herein contained, lessor does hereby demise and let unto the lessee and lessee hires from lessor for use as a residence those certain premises described as Unit 11, Douglas Manor
located at 2001 Century Drive, Urbandale, Anystate

☒ *on a month to month tenancy beginning* 16 September *, 19* 89 ⎰ *(Indicate*
☐ *for a term of* _____ *commencing* _____, 19 ____, *and ending* _____, 19 ____ ⎱ *which)*
at a rental of $ 520.00 *per month, payable monthly in advance on the* 1st *day of each and every month. Rents are payable at the following address:* Everready Management Co, 41 East Third, Urbandale, Anystate 00000

It is hereby agreed that if rent is unpaid after four (4) days following due date, the lessee shall pay a late charge of $1.00 per day computed to include the first day due and continuing until both rent and late charges are fully paid. Any dishonored check shall be treated as unpaid rent and shall be subject to the same late charge plus $5.00 as a special handling fee and must be made good by cash, money order or certified check within 24 hours of notification.

It is further mutually agreed between the parties as follows:

1. *Said aforementioned premises shall be occupied by no more than* two *adults and* two *children;*
2. *Lessee shall not violate any city ordinance or state law in or about said premises;*
3. *Lessee shall not sub-let the demised premises, or any part thereof, or assign this lease without the lessor's written consent;*
4. *If lessee fails to pay rent or other charges promptly when due, or to comply with any other term or condition hereof, lessor at lessor's option, and after proper written notice, may terminate this tenancy;*
5. *Lessee shall maintain the premises in a clean and sanitary condition at all times, and upon the termination of the tenancy shall surrender same to lessor in as good condition as when received, ordinary wear and tear and damage by the elements excepted; a fee is herewith paid, no part of which is refundable, for cleaning up and restoring the premises in the amount of $* 200.00
6. *There shall be working locks on all outside doors; lessor shall provide lessee with keys for same;*
7. *Lessee* ☒ *, Lessor* ☐ *shall properly cultivate, care for and adequately water the lawn, shrubbery and grounds;*
8. *Lessor shall supply electric wiring, plumbing facilities capable of producing hot and cold running water and adequate heating facilities;*
9. *Lessee shall pay for all natural gas, electricity, and telephone service. All other services will be paid for by Lessor and Lessee as follows:*

	Lessee	Lessor		Lessee	Lessor
Water	☒	☐	Garbage Service	☐	☒
Sewer	☐	☒	Cable tv	☒	☐

10. *Lessee agrees to assume all liability for, and to hold lessor harmless from, all damages and all costs and fees in the defense thereof, caused by the negligence or willful act of lessee or lessee's invitees or guests, in or upon any part of the demised premises, and to be responsible for any damage or breakage to lessee's equipment, fixtures or appliances therein or thereon, not caused by lessor's misconduct or willful neglect.*
11. *Nothing herein shall be construed as waiving any of the rights provided by law of either party hereto;*
12. *In the event any suit or action is brought to collect any of said rents or to enforce any provision of this agreement or to repossess said premises, reasonable attorney's fees may be awarded by the trial court to the prevailing party in such suit or action together with costs and necessary disbursements; and on appeal, if any, similar reasonable attorney's fees, costs and disbursements may be awarded by the appellate court to the party prevailing on such appeal;*
13. *If the lessee, or someone in the lessee's control, irreparably endangers the health or safety of the lessor or other tenants or irreparably damages or threatens immediate irreparable damage to the dwelling unit, the lessor, after 24 hours' written notice specifying the causes, may immediately terminate the rental agreement and take possession in the manner provided in ORS 105.105 to 105.160;*
14. *Lessee shall not allow any undriveable vehicle to remain on the premises for more than 24 hours. No car repairs are to be made on the premises, including minor maintenance such as an oil change;*
15. *Property of the tenant left on the premises after surrender or abandonment of the premises, or termination of this rental agreement by any means except court order, shall be deemed abandoned. Upon 15 days notice to tenant, in writing, landlord shall have the right to store, sell or otherwise dispose of any such property as provided by law, unless within said 15-day period tenant removes the property. Failure to remove the property within 15 days will be conclusive evidence of abandonment.*

16. *The owner (or* agent for service*) is* Everready Real Estate Mgt. Co.
Address 41 East Third
Urbandale, Anystate 00000 *Phone* 345-4330
The manager is H. "Handy" Overseer
Address 41 East Third
Urbandale, Anystate *Phone* 345-4331

17. *Any holding over by the lessee after the expiration of the term of this rental agreement or any extension thereof, shall be as a tenancy from month to month and not otherwise;*
18. *If this is a month-to-month tenancy only, then, except as otherwise provided by statute, this agreement may be terminated by either party giving the other at anytime not less than 30 days' notice in writing* *prior to the date designated in the tenancy termination notice, whereupon the tenancy shall terminate on the date designated.*
19. *Lessor acknowledges receipt of the sum of $* 400.00 *as a security deposit, of which the lessor may claim all or part thereof reasonably necessary to remedy lessee's defaults in the performance of this rental agreement (including nonpayment of past-due rent) and to repair damage to the premises caused by lessee, not including ordinary wear and tear. To claim all or part of said deposit, lessor shall give lessee, within thirty (30) days after termination of the tenancy, a written accounting which states specifically the basis or bases of the claim, and the portion not so claimed shall be returned to lessee within said thirty days. Lessor may recover damages in excess of said deposit to which lessor may be entitled. Lessor also acknowledges receipt of the sum of $* N.A. *to insure the return of keys to said dwelling unit; said sum to be refunded upon the return of all such keys;*
20. *Pets are allowed* ☒ *, not allowed* ☐ *(indicate which). If allowed to consist of* one cat
Lessee will be held responsible for all damage caused by pets and pay an additional non-refundable fee of $ 100.00 *prior to bringing a pet onto the leased premises.*
21. *Lessee further agrees that failure by the lessor at any time to require performance by the lessee of any provision hereof shall in no way affect lessor's right hereunder to enforce the same, nor shall any waiver by said lessor of any breach of any provision hereof be held to be a waiver of any succeeding breach of any provision, or as a waiver of the provision itself.*
22. *The following personal property is included and to be left upon the premises when tenancy is terminated* range, refrigerator electric globes, carpeting, drapes, fire alarm.

23. *Additional provisions:*
Door to kitchen cabinet to be repaired

Lessee ⎰ 1. *That he has personally inspected the premises and finds them satisfactory at the time of execution of this agreement;*
Further ⎱ 2. *That he has read this agreement and all the stipulations contained in the lease agreement.*
Agrees 3. *That no promises have been made to him except as contained in this agreement and lease, except the following:* None

IN WITNESS WHEREOF, the parties hereto have executed this agreement in duplicate the day and year first above written and lessee, by affixing his signature hereto, acknowledges receipt of one copy of the executed documents.

/s/Handy Overseer

/s/Otto Mobile

Lessor Lessee

for Everready Real Estate Management Co. /s/Mary Mobile
The words lessee and lessor shall include the plural as well as the singular. *See S-N Form Nos. 829, 971, 972, 973.

FIGURE 5-1

Typical Apartment Lease

TENANT RIGHTS AND OBLIGATIONS

Certain rights and obligations go to the tenant in making a lease. Some rights are automatic unless otherwise agreed to in the lease as follows: (1) use of the premises in any legal manner, (2) security deposit not required, (3) able to sublet, (4) able to assign, (5) able to mortgage, and (6) redemption.

Use of Premises. Unless restricted by agreement or zoning, a tenant may use the premises in any legal manner. Other occupants of other parts of the property may not be interfered with, however. The purpose for which the premises are to be used is often stated in the lease as, for example, "private dwelling," "boarding house," or "retail drugstore." The lease may contain a clause that the premises may not be used for any purpose that is extra hazardous, objectionable, detrimental to the local neighborhood, or similarly undesirable. Also, the tenant may vacate or give up use of the property, termed *abandonment,* before the lease expires; however, the tenant continues to be liable for rental payments.

Security Deposits. A landlord may properly require a security deposit to ensure performance of the lease terms. This deposit may be cash, negotiable securities, or a bond executed by a surety company. A transfer of the property to another owner by the lessor does not, of itself, include the security deposit. That is, the lessor's covenant to return the deposit to the lessee is personal.

Right to Sublet. A re-renting of a portion of the tenant's rights held under a lease is a *sublet* or sublease. The original tenant becomes a *sublessor;* the party to occupy the space is a *sublessee.* A landlord may include a clause against subletting to maintain control of occupancy.

Assignment of Lease. A tenant may also assign rights held under a lease unless otherwise agreed. An *assignment* is a transfer of all of a tenant's rights in a lease. A landlord, depending on the financial worthiness of the tenant, may include a clause against assignment. Even so, given a stable alternate tenant, a landlord may waive the clause and agree to a proposed assignment. A lease, once assigned, is generally considered freely assignable. In such event, the usual rule is that the original tenant-lessee can be held liable for rents under a lease even though it has been assigned and reassigned.

Mortgaging the Leasehold. A leasehold may be mortgaged unless the lease says otherwise. Unless otherwise agreed, the mortgage lien would not have any greater claim on the property than that held by the tenant under the lease.

Right of Redemption. A lessee has a right of redemption in some states. That is, if dispossessed when more than 5 years of the lease are unexpired, the tenant has a right to pay up all arrears and again obtain possession of the property. In a negotiated lease the tenant usually waives this right of redemption.

JOINTLY NEGOTIATED COVENANTS

The following clauses are not standard to most leases.

Lease Purchase Option. A provision giving the tenant the right to purchase the premises at a certain price during the lease is called a *lease option* or lease-purchase option. Frequently, the rental for the first year applies to the purchase price if the option is exercised within the first year. A lease option is used when an owner wants to sell to a tenant, who is undecided about purchasing or who does not have an adequate down payment. A lease option has priority over any other prospective purchaser's right to purchase.

Right of Renewal. A right of one or more renewals may be included in a lease, with rents adjusted from the initial lease payments. Renewal certainty gives the tenant a more stable basis for planning operations and the owner more stability of income value.

Subordination. Date of occupancy or recording establishes the priority of a tenant's claim to occupancy. Other liens and claims of record when the lease is made are superior to the rights of the tenant. A mortgage made after the lease, would, therefore, be subordinate to the lease.

But a lease may contain a clause stating that it will be subordinate or have lower priority than later mortgages, up to a certain amount. This *subordination clause* permits the landlord to increase existing mortgages up to the agreed amount. On the other hand, a vacant site may be leased on which the tenant proposes to build substantial improvements. The lessee may negotiate a clause with the owner-landlord to subordinate the fee ownership position to the proposed mortgage, up to an agreed amount.

In any event, an owner, a tenant, and a tentative lender should be aware of the significance of a subordinated position. There is a case on record in which a bank loaned $82,000 on a piece of property and ignored the rights of the people in possession. The mortgage was afterward foreclosed. It was then found that the property was occupied by tenants under a 10-year lease, with the option of a further 13-year renewal, at an annual rent of $6,000, an amount entirely inadequate to service a loan of $82,000.

Liability After Reentry. A lease may include a provision that if a tenant is dispossessed by summary proceedings or if the tenant abandons the property, the landlord must sublease the premises as an agent of the tenant. If the landlord relets the premises, the tenant must be credited with any monies collected from the sublessee.

Improvements and Repairs. A lease usually provides that no alterations to the building may be made without prior consent of the landlord. If made, improvements become the property of the landlord, unless otherwise agreed. It is proper in some cases to provide that some or all improvements may be removed at, or prior to, the expiration of the lease. Thus, trade fixtures and machinery installed by the tenant are usually considered personal property and are removable when the tenant vacates.

The general rule is that neither party to a lease is required to make repairs, but the tenant is required to surrender the premises at the expiration of the lease in as good a condition as they were at the beginning, reasonable wear and tear and damage by the elements excepted. In a multi-tenant property, there is no legal requirement that the landlord make the ordinary repairs for the upkeep of the property except that the building must be kept tenable. Failure to do so may allow the tenants to move out on the grounds of having been constructively evicted.

Liens. The tenant may make repairs, alterations, or improvements to the premises with the consent of the landlord. Such consent may result in the tenant's neglecting to pay for work performed and the consequent filing of mechanic's liens by those who did the work. Mechanics and materialpeople, under such circumstances, may enforce their liens against the landlord's property. At the same time, the tenant may be held personally liable.

The landlord may demand further protection from liens by requiring that the tenant deposit cash or file a bond as a guarantee that the cost of the repair or construction work will be paid. This requirement is very important in leases that require the tenant to make extensive repairs, alterations, or improvements.

Damage Claims. Agreement is desirable in a lease as to which party (landlord or tenant) is liable for claims developing from ownership, occupation, or use of the property. These claims may be by people injured on the property, or they may be by people damaged away from the property, as when a fire spreads from the property. With liability clarified, the party bearing the risk may obtain protection through insurance.

A landlord or tenant is not responsible for an accident unless it was caused by the negligence of one of them. Neither is liable for an injury caused by a negligent condition, unless either actually knew or should have known of the condition.

Damage/Destruction of Premises. Unless otherwise agreed, a lessee of a site must continue to pay rent even if the building thereon or other improvements are destroyed by fire, flood, wind, or other acts of nature. This rule does not apply to a lease of an apartment, office, or some other portion of a building, because such an arrangement is not a lease of land.

In the event that partial destruction makes a building untenantable or unusable, the landlord must make repairs in a "reasonable" time. If the premises are damaged and made unsuitable for occupancy before the tenant takes possession, the tenant may end the lease without liability to the landlord. A damage clause in a lease would, of course, enable the parties clearly to define their relationship and to protect themselves accordingly.

Compliance with Governmental Regulations. A clause concerning responsibility for compliance with such governmental regulations may be included in a lease.

Termination of Leases

TERM EXPIRATION

Written leases end on the last day of their term, without notice. Tenancies from period to period and at will continue, or are self-renewing, until notice of termination is given.

MUTUAL AGREEMENT

A tenant and landlord may end a lease by a mutual agreement of surrender and acceptance, which may be by expressed or implied agreement as well as by oral or written agreement. With a recorded lease the parties are advised to write, sign, and record any agreement to surrender.

DISPOSSESS/EVICTION

A breach of conditions, followed by dispossess proceedings, may terminate a lease. The conditions may be divided into two classes, those for which the landlord dispossesses the tenant by summary proceedings and those for which summary proceedings may not be brought. Summary (brief) dispossess proceedings may be used to terminate a lease for the following reasons:

1. Nonpayment of rent
2. Holding over at the end of the term
3. Unlawful use of the premises
4. Nonpayment of taxes, assignments, or other charges when, under the terms of the lease, the tenant undertook to pay them
5. The tenant in certain cases takes the benefit of an insolvent act or is adjudged a bankrupt

A landlord has the right to recover possession from a tenant through a summary proceeding known as dispossess or eviction. An eviction may be either actual or constructive. An *actual eviction* occurs if the tenant is ousted from the premise in whole or in part, by an act of the landlord or paramount title. *Constructive eviction* occurs when the physical condition of the leased premises has changed, owing to some act or failure to act of the landlord, so that the tenant is unable to occupy the premises for the purposes intended. No claim of constructive eviction will be allowed unless the tenant actually removes from the premises while the conditions exists. If the tenant removes and can prove a valid case, the lease is terminated. The tenant may also be able to recover damages for the landlord's breach of contract.

EMINENT DOMAIN

When leased property is taken for public purposes under the right of eminent domain, leases on it terminate. The tenant is given an opportunity to prove the value of the unexpired term of the lease in the proceeding under which the property is taken and may receive an award for it.

MORTGAGE FORECLOSURE

The foreclosure of a mortgage or other lien terminates a leasehold estate, provided that the lease is subordinate to the lien being foreclosed. The lessee must be made a party in the foreclosure suit for this to occur. Also, a lease may provide for termination upon bankruptcy of the tenant or lessee.

Tenant Unions

Tenants and landlords need each other. Landlords have space to sell. Tenants need places to live or to do business. Both benefit when the right tenant gets the right space. The tenant gets greater satisfaction or does more business. The landlord gets higher rent and, in turn, greater property value.

At the same time, the interests of the tenants and landlords are in direct conflict in a sense comparable to that of mortgagor and mortgagee. The negotiation between them goes on continuously, in one form or another. An important development of this negotiation/competition—tenant unions—is outside the traditional landlord-tenant relationship as discussed earlier. Even so, a brief look at the nature and implications of tenant unions seems warranted.

Tenant unions came into being because of abusive practices by some landlords. In apartment house operation, particularly, the landlord is generally both more knowledgeable and stronger financially than is any individual tenant. The situation is similar to that of a large employer with many individual employees. Organizing into unions increases the bargaining power of the tenants.

Tenant unions usually seek to negotiate (1) better leases and conditions for tenants and (2) a grievance procedure for dissatisfied tenants. Tenant unions have also been instrumental in getting landlord-tenant statutes passed in many states; these statutes put tenants on a more even footing with owners.

Tenant unions have successfully called rent strikes, meaning withholding rent payments to enforce their demands. The occasion of a rent strike might involve lack of security against criminal acts on the premises, wrongful eviction of tenants, or building code violations as when a serious hazard exists.

Courts have held that if rents are paid into escrow in such strikes, retaliatory evictions are illegal. A *retaliatory eviction* is removing a tenant from a property as punishment for the tenant's asserting his or her rights. Thus, landlords may not get even with tenants for joining tenant unions, for reporting violations of building codes or other local regulations, or for legally withholding rents. The movement toward tenant unions, perhaps, seems healthy for responsible landlords and for society as a whole as well as for tenants.

Questions for Review and Discussion

1. Explain clearly the distinction between tenancy for years and tenancy from year to year.
2. What are the advantages and disadvantages of a written tenancy for years relative to a periodic tenancy from the viewpoint of the tenant?
3. Explain these rental payment plan arrangements:
    a. Percentage
    b. Flat
    c. Net
    d. Graduated
    e. Index
    f. Reappraisal
4. Explain the following concepts of clauses as they relate to leasing:
    a. Use of premises
    b. Right to sublet
    c. Right to assign

    d. Right to mortgage

    e. Lease option

    f. Subordination

5. List and explain at least four ways for ending a lease.

6. A property is under lease on a long-term, step-up lease. The neighborhood deteriorates, and the property's value declines. Who benefits, if anyone? Explain.

7. Compare the advantages of leasing with the advantages of buying a business property. Is there a time when either is clearly more appropriate?

8. Is there a landlord-tenant code in your state? If so, what are its main provisions? If not, where are the major laws pertaining to landlord and tenant rights found?

Case Problems

1. Norman occupied a cabin on Henry's farm, without any provision for rent or duration. Both recognized that either could terminate the arrangement at any time. Norman died. Henry cleaned up the cabin, locked the door, and placed Norman's belongings on the porch. William, Norman's executor, now claims the right to occupy the cabin as a continuation of the lease arrangement. Does William have this right? Explain.

2. John Burgoyne rented a luxury apartment in Tudor Towers for $1,000 per month on a 2-year lease on December 10. Shortly after, he received a job offer he could not refuse in another city. He re-rented the apartment to Edward for $1,200 per month for the remainder of the lease. Nothing is said in the original lease about assignment or subleasing of rights. Now the owner of Tudor Towers objects to the re-renting and threatens to sue John. What are John's rights in this situation?

3. Gerald and Nancy Investor rent a building from Wendy Welloff to establish a restaurant and tavern on a 1-year lease. They add a storage room in the rear and arrange for the installation of a bar, kitchen equipment, booths, and miscellaneous other items, all of which are attached to the building. The business is unusually successful, and the Investors decide to move to larger quarters at the end of the year. Upon moving, they start to remove the improvements. Wendy objects and threatens to sue, saying that all improvements become property of the landlord unless otherwise agreed. No such "other" agreement was reached. What is the result?

4. Ellen was instrumental in organizing a tenant union. As a result of the union, many tenants, including Ellen, paid their rent into an escrow account until certain improvements were made to the property. When Ellen's lease ended, the landlord refused to renew. Ellen feels that she is being punished for her actions. What rights does she have? Can she be evicted under these circumstances?

6

Governmental Limitations to Ownership

Society in every state is a blessing, but government, even in its best state is but a necessary evil; in its worst state, an intolerable one.

Thomas Paine, *Common Sense*, 1776

The system of property ownership in the United States is a mix of the feudal and allodial systems of ownership brought over from Europe. Under the English feudal system, a king or sovereign owned all the land, with subjects obtaining use of the land in return for services and allegiance. On the other hand, the allodial system, initiated in France in 1789 following the French Revolution, recognized private ownership only; that is, no rights were reserved by a sovereign authority. The mix of systems gives private ownership to the individual, with the state reserving rights of police power, eminent domain, taxation, and escheat. The reservation of these four rights remains the same regardless of how the fee estate is split up.

Escheat is the reversion or automatic conveyance of realty to the state, upon an owner's death, when no will, heirs, or other legal claimants to title can be found. Escheat is seldom exercised in fact because someone almost always has a title claim. Also, for all practical purposes, escheat is not a restriction on ownership; escheat simply serves to keep property owned and productive or "in the system." Real estate is too valuable to society to go unused.

Regulation, condemnation, and taxation make up a substantial portion of the rules of the game for real estate; hence, an understanding of this chapter is crucial for investors and practitioners. These powers are reserved by governments to look after the public health, welfare, and safety, to facilitate growth and adjustment of communities to changing social and economic needs, and to financially maintain themselves. We look at these three reservations of powers to see how they constrain a rational investor in the development and use of land. Overall, these restrictions are considered to yield positive results for society.

Important Topics or Decision Areas Covered in this Chapter

Police Power
Nuisance Law
Planning
Zoning
Subdivision Regulations
Building Regulations
Rent Controls
Miscellaneous Controls

Eminent Domain
Need
Just Compensation

Taxation and Special Assessments
Uniformity
Tax Exemptions
Special Assessments

Questions for Review and Discussion

Case Problems

Key Concepts Introduced in this Chapter

Ad valorem
Assessed value
Certificate of occupancy
Contract zoning
~~Density zoning~~
Development charge
~~Down zoning~~
Eminent domain
Environmental-impact
    study
Escheat
Exclusionary zoning
Externality

Floor area ratio zoning
Just compensation
Land-use control
Master plan
Nonconforming use
Nuisance
Performance zoning
~~Rent control~~
Special assessment
Transferable development
    rights
~~Zoning~~
Zoning variance

Police Power

Police power means governmental regulation through due process of law to protect public health, welfare, safety, and morals. Villages, cities, and counties all have rights of police power based on state enabling acts, meaning the granting of express authority to carry out needed regulatory activities. The enabling legislation provides the basis for planning, zoning ordinances, subdivision regulations, building and housing codes, rent controls, and other land use regulations. Generally, compensation need not be paid for lowered property values resulting from the use of police power. Let us look briefly at how this power to regulate came into being.

NUISANCE LAW

A private *nuisance* is the interference with a neighbor's use and quiet enjoyment of land, other than by trespass or direct physical invasion. In English common law, if Able cut a tree from Baker's land, it is trespass, for which Baker can bring a civil action at law, sue, and get compensation or redress. But if Able remained on his own land and operated a pig farm, a chemical plant, a blasting operation, or a naughty house, no trespass occurred, even though the stench, chemical fumes, falling dirt and debris, and offending of the public moral senses substantially interfered with Baker's use of his land. Eventually, even though there was no trespass, common law come to recognize that these conditions constituted a moral wrong, a private nuisance for which the originator could be held liable. In modern times, particles of energy, light, dust, or gas from a neighboring property, storage of explosives or radioactive materials, noise from an airport, and even failure to drain mosquito breeding waters are considered a nuisance or "trespass." Other examples are acid rain and street litter.

In modern economics, nuisances as discussed are called externalities, indirect costs, or spillover effects. Thus, an *externality* is when my behavior indirectly affects others, positively or negatively, without their concurrence or agreement. These externalities result in a market not allocating resources efficiently, which failure keeps an economy from realizing its full potential.

Private efforts have been and are made to control externalities mainly through deed or title restrictions. But title restrictions have two major drawbacks. First, they are limited in geographic area; a developer cannot control land uses outside a subdivision. Second, an overt effort by the developer or owners within the subdivision is required for enforcement.

Thus, where negative externalities exist, the only truly socially satisfactory solution is almost certainly collective (government) regulation, such as planning or zoning. Other possibilities exist as an effluent or pollution tax or a subsidy to the pollutor to cease or control the activity. But our concern is with the various uses of police power.

PLANNING

Planning is a systematic process involving data collection, classification, and analysis aimed at developing a master plan. A *master plan* is a comprehensive scheme setting forth ways and means by which a community can adjust its physical makeup to social and economic changes. Almost every community, be it a city, county, village, or metropolitan area, has a master plan. Planning itself is not a solution to externalities, but it does provide an underlying rationale for the many other forms of regulation.

Growth in population, commerce, manufacturing, and other activities necessitates development and improvement of a community's infrastructure: roads, sewers, water systems, schools, hospitals, and other public facilities. Depreciation and evolving technology also make changes necessary in these facilities. Designing and building such facilities requires large amounts of money. One major purpose of planning is to create and maintain a high-quality environment, one aspect of which is stabilized property values. A second major purpose is to avoid wasteful mistakes in developing the infrastructure that result from poor coordination, duplication, and overbuilding.

A master plan really consists of several lesser coordinated plans for land use, transportation, schools, and other public facilities. It must at the very least be based on studies of (1) population, (2) economic base, (3) land use, and (4) transportation of the area or community. In turn, the master plan provides the underlying rationale for a community's zoning ordinance, subdivision regulations, and construction and building codes, our most often employed land use controls. A *land use control* is a public or private device used to regulate and guide use of realty, with deed restrictions often used by private parties.

Experience shows that for a plan to effectively meet a community's needs, it must be

1. In scale with the population and economic outlook of the community
2. In scale with the current and future financial resources of the community
3. Balanced and attractive in design relative to the environment to be created and maintained
4. In keeping with community sentiments on an attractive environment
5. Flexible and easily updated to accommodate changing conditions and projections

ZONING

Zoning is easily the most significant legal technique used to regulate externalities. *Zoning* is community regulation of land use, population density, and building size and appearance. It involves dividing the community into districts for regulation of land use by type (residential, commercial), by intensity (one-family, multifamily), and by height, bulk, and appearance. A zoning ordinance must undergo public review before being enacted into law.

Increasingly, uses are organized by performance classes rather than by district; using performance standards to define classes is called *performance zoning*. Performance, as used here, means to meet the requirements of standards of the class. That is, performance zoning is establishing districts that allow or accept uses, regardless of type, if they meet certain standards relative to such things as density, appearance, traffic generation, and pollution origination. Thus, uses that do not adversely affect each other, and may, in fact, complement each other, may be placed in the same class or "district."

Discontinuance of a Nuisance through Zoning

Hadacheck v. Los Angeles
U.S. Supreme Court; 239 U.S. 394 (1915)

Hadacheck v. LOS ANGELES is a landmark case in that it tied together nuisance law and a justification for zoning.

The Hadacheck Company bought 8 acres in 1902; the land contained valuable deposits of clay suitable for making bricks. Subsequently, kilns, buildings, and machinery for the manufacture of brick were assembled on the site, and the manufacture of brick was begun. The operation generated considerable smoke and dust, which interfered with the residential properties that developed in the surrounding area.

The entire area was later annexed to Los Angeles. A 3-square-mile district around the plant was given a zoning classification that made it "unlawful for any person to establish or operate a brick yard or brick kiln, or any establishment, factory or place for the manufacture or burning of brick ...." Extensive litigation followed. The case was taken to the California Supreme Court and eventually to the U.S. Supreme Court. The residential neighbors gave extensive evidence of the interference with their rights owing to the brick manufacturing operations.

The final judgment closed down the brick-making operation, with no damages being payable, though the court recognized "that the value of investments made in the business prior to any legislative action will be greatly diminished." The court also refused to recognize Hadacheck's claim of a preemptive right to carry on its business because it had been "in that locality for a long period." The company was not enjoined from removing the clay for manufacture into bricks at another location.

Zoning Ordinance Content. A zoning ordinance usually includes a zoning map in addition to written regulations along the following lines.

1. The community is divided into districts in which the land uses are specified as residential, commercial, industrial, and agricultural.
2. Standards limiting the height and bulk of buildings are set for each district.
3. Standards regulating the proportion of a lot that can be built on, including detailed front yard, side yard, and backyard requirements, are set for each district.
4. Limits are set on population density in the various districts by regulation of the foregoing factors; the procedure is called *density zoning.*

A zoning map is not the land use plan itself but, rather, just one way of implementing the land use plan.

A properly drawn zoning ordinance is not legally concerned with the following points:

1. Specifying building materials and construction methods (governed by construction or building codes)
2. Setting minimum construction costs (not legal by public ordinance but may be set by private deed restrictions)
3. Regulation of street design and installation of utilities or reservation of land for park or school sites (governed primarily by subdivision regulations, along with street or public works department, the park department, and the school board)

Height, Bulk, and Area Regulations. Building height and bulk restrictions prevent the taking over of air, ventilation, and sunlight by one parcel at the unreasonable expense of another parcel. The restrictions also limit fire risks, popula-

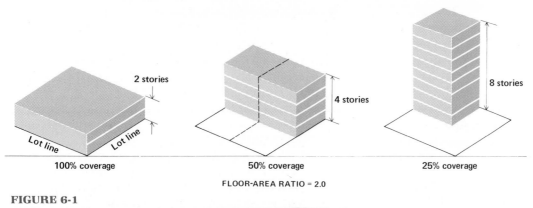

FLOOR-AREA RATIO = 2.0

FIGURE 6-1
Floor area ratio zoning, an example of performance zoning

tion density, and street congestion. Building heights are generally limited to a certain number of stories (i.e., one and a half, two, two and a half, 10).

Floor area ratio zoning, a form of performance zoning, is widely used to make possible greater design flexibility in a district while limiting population and development density. Floor area ratio (FAR) zoning is the relationship of building coverage to site area. For example, an FAR of 2.0 means that an owner is permitted to construct a two-story building over the entire lot or a four-story building over one-half of the lot or an eight-story building over one-fourth of the lot. Any combination of fraction-of-lot coverage times the number of stories therefore may not exceed the allowed FAR of 2.0. See Figure 6-1.

Solar energy requires that adequate sunlight be available on a continuing basis. Thus, "right-to-light" zoning might modify FAR zoning, as shown in Figure 6-2.

Multiple-Use Zoning. Allowing several compatible, but different, uses in a district is called multiple-use zoning. Thus, offices and small stores may be allowed in the same district as apartments or condominiums, an arrangement that may work to the benefit of all concerned. In fact, these uses may be combined into one project, termed a planned unit development (PUD), as a result of a transfer of development rights. A planned unit development means that improvements are added to realty at the same overall density as in conventional development, but the improvements may

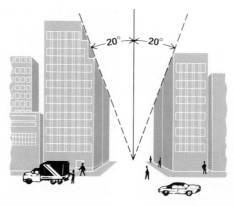

FIGURE 6-2
"Right-to-light" performance zoning

be clustered, resulting in more open, common areas. For example, assume a 10-acre parcel zoned for four dwelling units per acre. A developer is limited to 40 one-family houses by conventional zoning. With PUD, the developer might construct four closely clustered 10-unit buildings, leaving the balance of the acreage for open space. PUD may be used in residential, commercial, or industrial development. PUD zoning is also termed cluster zoning and is a form of density zoning.

Transferable development rights (TDR) means that one parcel may be developed more intensely if another parcel is developed less intensely. TDR therefore means that rights may be sold by one owner to another, thereby adding flexibility and variety to an area without increasing its overall density. In the PUD example, if commercial development rights were acquired by the investor in developing the PUD, stores could be included in the project while some other project would go without stores. This, of course, would be an extension of the multiple-use zoning concept.

Zoning Challenge and/or Negotiation. An owner, or potential owner, may petition for changes in, or relief from, a zoning ordinance by either of the following ways, or a direct challenge is possible.

A *zoning variance* is a deviation from zoning ordinance granted because strict enforcement would result in undue hardship on a property owner. The usual rules are simply set aside, as where a lot is so steep that front yard setback requirements cannot be met with reasonable expense. A variance must not violate the intent or spirit of the ordinance.

A technique known as contract zoning is sometimes used to fine tune a zoning ordinance. *Contract zoning* refers to an owner, who, by title restriction or side agreement, limits a property's use in return for a new zoning classification. For example, a parcel is rezoned as commercial, and at the same time the owner records a title restriction limiting use to one-story professional offices. Contract zoning is not a recognized legal concept.

An owner may try to circumvent the zoning board of appeals by going through the courts and challenging the zoning ordinance itself. The legal requirements of a valid ordinance are as follows:

1. Use districts must be provided for by enabling legislation, and applicable regulations must be uniform for each classification and kind of building. A reasonable rationale for classifying districts differently must exist.
2. An entire jurisdiction (such as a city) and not just small, isolated areas must be zoned.
3. Parcels must not be zoned for uses that they cannot physically accommodate.

A challenge on any of these points would argue that the ordinance is not based on a well-conceived land use or master plan. Also, a challenge might be based on the idea that an ordinance is arbitrary, unreasonable, destructive, or confiscatory in application.

Finally, zoning may not be used to discriminate against minorities or low-income people: this discrimination is termed *exclusionary zoning.* For example, a high-income residential district, by setting unreasonably large minimum lot sizes, floor-area requirements, or high construction quality standards, makes it improbable that low- and moderately low-income groups can afford to settle in the district.

Inconsistent Uses. Existing uses or structures, inconsistent with the applicable zoning, are termed *nonconforming uses*, which may be legal or illegal. If they existed prior to the original adoption of the ordinance, they are legal, nonconforming uses, and are allowed to continue, subject to several provisions. To require their removal would inflict severe and unreasonable financial hardship on owners. Generally, the provisions regulating a nonconforming use prohibit the following:

1. Enlargement
2. Rebuilding, or reconstruction after a specified percentage of damage or destruction, usually 50 percent
3. Changing to another nonconforming use
4. Resumption after a stated period of discontinuance, usually a year

New uses and structures must conform to current zoning. To introduce a use or to build a structure inconsistent with the ordinance is to create an illegal nonconforming use, which would be subject to immediate removal without compensation.

A parcel or small area may not be rezoned for a use or structure that is inconsistent with the rationale of the overall plan or ordinance, which is called spot zoning and is illegal. Therefore, an owner adversely affected by a proposed rezoning of a nearby parcel may successfully challenge the proposed rezoning in court as "spot zoning" if the circumstances are right.

Zoning and Value. On a community-wide basis, zoning does not create value in real estate. Market demand for a use is the basis of value, whether it involves an office building, a shopping center, or an apartment building. At the same time a well-conceived master plan along with appropriate zoning must prevail for the greatest value potential of all land in the community to be realized. If demand for a use is not present, commercial, industrial, or multifamily zoning will not enhance a property's value, except perhaps in the mind of the owner.

Zoning does channel values, however. Thus, obtaining a rezoning to commercial for a parcel where market demand exists will enhance the value of the parcel. But, rezoning all land in the community to commercial would not increase the total value of all commercially zoned parcels. In fact, inappropriate zoning, such as commercial when multi-family residential would be more appropriate, may distort or alter the use to which a parcel can be put, thereby limiting it to less than its highest and best use and its greatest value potential.

Occasionally, communities, in updating a master plan and zoning ordinance, will reclassify a property from a "high-value" use as commercial or industrial to a "low-value" use as single-family residential; this is *down zoning.* An owner must be constantly aware of possible down zoning. If demand for the high-value use exists, this would mean a substantial loss to the owner. On the other hand, such a rezoning may simply be a recognition of reality.

Zoning is intended to stabilize values, but it will not prevent value declines. For example, zoning cannot prevent the aging and depreciation of structures, factors that are likely to lower values.

SUBDIVISION REGULATIONS

Locally adopted laws governing the conversion of raw land into building sites are called subdivision regulations. The regulations work primarily through plat approval procedures. That is, a subdivider or developer is not permitted to split up land until the planning commission has approved a plat of the proposed project, based on its compliance with standards and requirements set forth in the regulations.

In almost all states a comprehensive plan, a major street plan, or an official map must have been adopted prior to subdivision regulations to provide a legal basis for their implementation. Either plan serves as evidence that the regulations are not arbitrary or discriminatory; that is, either plan coordinates the layout of a particular subdivision with others in the area and also ensures provision for rights of way for major thoroughfares, easements for utility lines, and school and park locations.

Elements controlled by most subdivision regulations are as follows:

1. Rights of way for streets, alleys, cul-de-sacs, highways, and walkways: location, alignment, width, grade, surfacing material, and possible dedication to community
2. Lots and blocks: minimum dimensions and building setback lines
3. Utilities: easements for sewer, water, and power; assurance of pure water and ability to dispose of wastes without health problems
4. Reserved areas for schools, parks, open space, and other public uses

Development charges appear to be increasingly incorporated into subdivision ordinances. A *development charge* is a fee imposed against a subdivider or developer by the community to pay the proportional costs of new waste-disposal facilities, roads, water storage tanks, and the like, necessitated by the new subdivision. The intent is that the owners of the developed parcels pay the marginal costs of new facilities rather than the citizenry in general.

Environmental impact studies are required for large development projects. An *environmental impact study* (EIS) is an investigation and analysis to determine the long-run physical effects of a proposed land use on its surroundings and the long-run economic and social effects on other people. The purpose of an EIS is to bring together in one report the likely costs and benefits of a project before the project is approved for development. For example, the EIS for a proposed shopping center would document the expected effects on automobile traffic, air quality, the waste-disposal system, energy demand, employment, and vegetation. If costs are too substantial, the proposal might require modification to obtain approval.

BUILDING REGULATIONS

Building codes take up where subdivision regulations leave off; that is, they apply mainly to improvements to the land. The objective is public safety and protecting against negative externalities. The method is preventive so that the effects of a hazard on one parcel do not result in loss of life and are not allowed to spill over to neighboring parcels. Thus, focus is on fireproof construction, means of emergency exit, windows, load and stress, size and location of rooms, adequacy of ventilation, sanitation facilities, electrical wirings and equipment, mechanical equipment, and the lighting of exits. Several separate codes such as the electrical, plumbing, and fire codes may make up the "building code."

The codes are particularly stringent for buildings likely to be occupied by large numbers of people, such as apartment buildings, schools, churches, hospitals, and office buildings. Special provisions also usually apply to potentially hazardous structures such as amusement parks, canopies, roof signs, grandstands, grain elevators, or cleaning plants.

Enforcement begins with the requirement that a building permit be obtained for new construction or alterations. Both the zoning ordinance and the building codes must be complied with. Also, blueprints must pass examination before a building permit is issued. Construction is inspected as it progresses. With full compliance, a required certificate of occupancy is obtained for the new or rehabilitated building. A *certificate of occupancy* is an official notice that all code inspections were passed and that the structure is fit for use.

RENT CONTROLS

Rent control is a governmental limitation on the amount that may be charged for apartments or other space units. Rent controls are often sought by tenant unions on the argument that housing is a unique good that is required by everyone and for which there is no real substitute. The same is not true of other goods. Many substitutes exist for foodstuffs, like pork, apples, and bread, or clothing, like pants, shirts, and shoes. Consumers can always shift to less expensive food or shop elsewhere for clothing items. Housing also tends to be unique in that supply cannot be expanded quickly in response to increased demand. Thus, tenants have little choice but to pay increased rents when demand outruns supply.

What are the implications of rent control? Assuming inflation, the immediate effect is to squeeze profits from a landlord, which leads to neglect of property maintenance. Property values also drop owing to limited rents. Property taxes to local government drop, resulting in tighter budgets and reduced services. Owners seek relief through efforts to convert to condominiums or to demolish and rebuild in a use that is not subject to controls. If their efforts are unsuccessful and all profits are squeezed out of ownership, properties are abandoned. Thus, severe blight and slums result. But the problems continue. Investors restrict the development of new housing projects to communities without controls. Lenders avoid making loans on properties in rent control areas. More blight and urban deterioration is the result. In the end, even the people intended to receive the benefits of rent controls lose out.

Rent controls are intended to benefit those with low incomes, though those who actually benefit are not necessarily low income. Further, the costs of controls to society as a whole appear to outweigh the benefits. On this, both liberal and conservative economists agree. The effect is to transfer wealth from landlords to tenants. But providing relief for these people should fall on the whole of society rather than on property owners.

Frederick Hayek, a conservative, Nobel Prize–winning economist, had this to say about rent controls: "If this account seems to boil down to a catalogue of inequities to be laid at the door of rent control, that is no mere coincidence, but inevitable. . . . I doubt very much whether theoretical research into the same problem carried out by someone of a different political-economic persuasion than myself could lead to a different conclusion."[1] And he was right. Gunnar Myrdal, a liberal economist, who also won a Nobel Prize, had this view. "Rent control has in certain

---

[1] A. F. Hayek, "The Repercussion of Rent Restrictions," in *Rent Control, A Popular Paradox, Evidence on the Economic Effect of Rent Control* (Vancouver, B.C.: The Fraser Institute, 1975), p. 80.

Western countries constituted, maybe, the worst example of poor planning by governments lacking courage and vision."[2]

MISCELLANEOUS CONTROLS

As a rule, fire and sanitation departments are empowered to make periodic inspections and to order compliance with directives to ensure safe and sanitary use and occupancy of buildings. Proper enforcement of fire control and sanitation ordinances may go a long way toward retarding housing blight and eventual elimination of unsightly and unsafe city slums. In almost all states, there are health regulations for wells, septic tanks, and other waste-disposal installations.

Eminent Domain

Eminent domain is the right of a governmental or quasi-governmental agency to take private property for public uses or purposes. Eminent domain literally means "highest authority or dominion." The right is based on the premise that an owner should sometimes be required to give up property, for just compensation, so that the common good or welfare may be advanced. Land for streets, parks, schools, and other public buildings, and for public or social purposes, is commonly acquired through eminent domain as a last resort. Most organizations seek to acquire desired properties by negotiation before exercising their right of eminent domain. The taking is without the consent of the owner and requires payment of reasonable or just compensation. This is sometimes called condemnation, or the right of expropriation. Semipublic organizations such as railroads, public utility companies, and universities may exercise eminent domain for limited purposes.

NEED

The right of eminent domain is needed because our society and economy changes continually. For example, in the 1930s, sociologists predicted that the U.S. population would mature and stabilize at 150 million by 1950. Nearly half the population lived in rural areas at the time. Automobiles were still a relatively new mode of transportation. Air travel was only for the wealthy. Most intercity passenger and freight transportation was provided by the railroads. Now, in the 1980s, the U.S. population exceeds 225 million people, about three-fourths of whom live in urban areas. Almost everyone drives a car, and air travel is much more common than is travel by rail. Trucks haul a large share of intercity freight.

In a more specific sense, the power of eminent domain is exercised to acquire property for highway construction, public building sites, flood control projects, and

[2] As quoted by Sven Oydenfelt in "The Rise and Fall of Swedish Rent Control," in *Rent Control, A Popular Paradox, Evidence on the Economic Effect of Rent Control* (Vancouver, B.C.: The Fraser Institute, 1975), p. 169.

airport expansion. The power has been legally exercised to acquire land for public parking lots to be operated by private concessionaires. The U.S. Supreme Court has even declared legal the acquisition of land in urban renewal areas for later resale and redevelopment by profit-seeking individuals and corporations. Thus, the emphasis is on public purposes and is not limited to public need and use.

JUST COMPENSATION

Just compensation is payment for property taken and is almost universally defined as the fair market value of the property. Many states provide for payment of severance damages to the owner if only part of the property is taken, but the value of the remainder is lowered as a result of the taking. That is, fair market value is paid for the portion of the property taken, and additional payment is made for any injury or reduction in value to the remainder.

Compensation is not usually paid for certain damages suffered by an owner. Examples are (1) loss of business profits or goodwill; (2) moving costs (although the federal government and some states do pay these in some situations, independent of the court's decision); (3) additional costs of securing replacement housing or facilities; and (4) adverse effects of having the proposed improvements as a new neighbor, such as an airport or a sewage treatment plant.

Taxation and Special Assessments

Governments cannot function without the power to levy and collect taxes. The U.S. Supreme Court has noted, "The power to tax is the one great power upon which the whole national fabric is based. It is as necessary to the existence and prosperity of the nation as the air he breathes is to the natural man. It is not only the power to destroy but also the power to keep alive."[3]

Local governments rely heavily on property tax revenues to finance their operation. The taxes are levied on an *ad valorem* basis, meaning the tax is levied on each property according to its value, usually its market value. Thus, each parcel must be periodically appraised and an assessed value placed on it. *Assessed value* means the amount in dollars assigned to a parcel by the tax administrator. Assessed value may equal or be a proportion of market value, and it varies directly with market value.

Property taxes typically run about 2 percent of market value each year, which to most owners is a lot of money. Thus, concerns of fairness in levying the tax and of efficiency in use of the monies become important. The taxes, if used wisely, may greatly benefit an owner in that they help to provide police and fire protection, schools, parks, and a road system, all of which, if of reasonable quality, enhance the value of a property.

From the viewpoint of the community, the property tax is efficient in its ability to raise a large amount of revenue, quickly and at relatively low cost. Sources of this efficiency are several. Most property in a community is subject to the tax, which

[3]Nichol v. Ames; 173 U.S. 509 (1899).

makes for a large tax base. Parcels are fixed in location, which means values can be established and the taxes levied and collected without undue effort. If not paid, liens may be recorded and enforced. Further, the federal government is precluded from taxing real property by the wording of the constitution. Finally, property values tend to keep up with inflation, meaning tax revenues tend to rise with inflation. The main limitation is property maintenance and new construction are inhibited because the tax is levied according to value.

UNIFORMITY

Equity or fairness of treatment is a major concern of owners, which means that properties of comparable value should pay comparable taxes. This occurs if all property is assessed at the same proportion of market value. Thus, a store that sold for $100,000 and is assessed at $60,000 would be treated the same as a residence that sold for $40,000 and is assessed at $24,000. Each is assessed at 60 percent of its market price. The store stands to pay 2.5 times more in property taxes, regardless of the rate at which taxes are levied, because its value is 2.5 times greater. If the store and the house were both assessed at $24,000, the store owner would not be paying taxes at comparable rates, which would clearly be unfair.

TAX EXEMPTIONS

Tax-exempt properties are a second equity issue of concern to owners. Property owned by government and nonprofit institutions such as churches, hospitals, and private schools are usually exempt. Such properties do require and get services such as fire and police protection whether taxes are paid or not. Also, military bases may house families who use local schools and public recreational facilities. Payments in lieu of taxes are often made from one level of government to another in recognition of the extra burden placed on local facilities in situations like this. However, an indirect burden also exists. Publicly owned properties mean that streets and sewer, water, and power lines must extend greater distances to tie privately owned properties together, thereby constituting an extra cost to the private owners.

An exemption may benefit an owner. For example, in some states, such as Florida, homeowners are given a homestead exemption from assessed value by statute. An exemption of $25,000 is typical and is doubled for owners who are 65 and over. Each $10,000 of exemption means $300 less per year in taxes, assuming a 3 percent tax rate.

SPECIAL ASSESSMENTS

Special assessments are charges upon real property to pay all or part of the cost of a local improvement that benefits the property. The charges do not recur regularly, as taxes do, and are not always apportioned according to the value of the property affected. For example, all lots fronting on a certain street are benefited by the paving of the street and are equally assessed for it, even though the corner lots may have a greater value than inside lots. Buildings are not considered in apportioning a special assessment, because it is assumed that the land receives all the benefit. Sometimes special assessments are spread over a large area, the property nearest to the improvement being charged with a greater proportion of it than the property more remote, the rate decreasing with the distance from the improvement.

Only where local governments are beneficial—that is, where they increase the value of the affected properties—will courts sanction the levying of special assessments. In a court case, property owners in Miami Beach, Florida, challenged the right of the municipality to levy assessments for the widening of Indian Creek Drive in Miami Beach, Florida. The property owners contended that the widening of the drive from 25 to 40 feet was initiated to relieve congested traffic on another street. They also contended that, as a result of the widening, their own street had turned into a noisy, heavily traversed thoroughfare for the use of the public generally and that the effect was to lessen the value and desirability of their homes. The state supreme court in a 4-to-3 decision held for the property owners, reversing an earlier decision by the Dade County circuit court. In the opinion, Justice Glen Terrell said, "Before the days of the automobile and creation of zoning ordinances, paving and widening of streets invariably conferred additional benefits to the abutting property. But this may be far from true at present. Commercial property is increased in value by widening and paving of streets . . . but who ever heard of making a traffic count to locate a home!"

Special assessments become liens when they are definitely known and fixed. They may be divided into installments payable over a period of five to ten years or more, with interest charged on the deferred installments.

Questions for Review and Discussion

1. Briefly identify and explain the nature of the three main governmental limitations to private ownership of real estate.
2. Explain the need for land use controls. Name and briefly explain four controls. Does an owner have any rights relative to these controls? Explain.
3. Indicate and discuss the purpose or purposes of urban planning. Do you agree with them?
4. Does zoning create value? Might zoning destroy value? Discuss.
5. Explain the need for eminent domain. What are an owner's rights relative to eminent domain?
6. Explain the need for taxation. Does an owner have any rights relative to taxation? Explain.
7. What is a special assessment? Is it related to land value in any way?
8. Is the real property tax system efficient? Equitable and fair? Discuss.
9. A ceiling on property taxes, as a percentage of market value, is frequently proposed. What would be the effects of such a ceiling? Would a 2 percent ceiling affect your community? A 1 percent ceiling?
10. What are the trends in the use of police power? Eminent domain? Taxation? Discuss.

Case Problems

1. John Burgoyne owns a 12,000 square foot lot zoned "residential 6,000," meaning that one dwelling unit may be built for each 6,000 square feet of area. Sales of similar lots show that lots sell for $8,000 per dwelling unit. John applies for a rezoning to "residential 2,000."
   a. Assuming that John gets the rezoning, how much increase in value does he stand to realize, assuming that the sale price per dwelling unit remains the same?
   b. What factors might make this value increment larger or smaller?
2. The Investors' own a 12,000 square foot lot next to John's. Their lot is also re-zoned to "residential 2,000." However, it has a deed restriction limiting its development to a one-family residence. What impact on value is likely as a result of the zoning change?
3. Wendy Welloff has owned a condominium unit on the twelfth floor of Lakeview Towers for 12 years. James Town, a developer, is building a 20-story building across the street, which the zoning allows, thereby spoiling her view. Wendy sues to have construction stopped, claiming that she has a scenic easement based on her continuous use of the view for more than 10 years, the time required to acquire an easement by prescription according to state law. What is the result? Discuss.

7

Property Productivity: The Source of Benefits

We shape our dwellings, and afterwards our dwellings shape us.
Winston Churchill

Our attention has, thus far, been mainly on defining ownership rights and the many possible claims and limitations to those rights. At some point the following key question becomes apparent: What exactly are the benefits associated with the ownership of a specific property? Answering this question is our immediate concern. In later chapters we take up the following questions: How might these rights be measured and evaluated? What is their value?

Someone has to use and operate a property for its benefits or services to be realized. User benefits center on the services provided, which take the form of housing for a family, of fertile land for a farmer, or of a well located place of business for a jeweler, a service station operator, or a manufacturer. A tentative user, seeking to find the "right property," must know his or her needs and preferences as to location, site size and quality, and improvements.

Taking the perspective of a tenant-user is extremely helpful in identifying the benefits connected with a specific property. After all, the user, as a leasee, pays rent to obtain these benefits. It is a fair assumption that such a tenant-user would shop around to get the benefits at the lowest possible rent. In turn, this rental income provides an excellent point to begin to determine the value of the entire property.

Important Topics or Decision Areas Covered in this Chapter

Property Productivity

Locational Analysis
Convenience
Environment or Exposure
Locational Dynamics
Protection from Externalities

Site Analysis
Size and Shape
Topography and Geology
Roads and Public Utilities
Legal Limitations on Use

Improvements Analysis
Structures
Physical Deterioration
Functional Obsolescense
Depreciation
Miscellaneous Improvements

Questions for Review and Discussion

Case Problem

Key Concepts Introduced in this Chapter

Accessibility
Convenience of location
Costs of friction
Depreciation
Effective demand
Exposure
Functional efficiency

Functional obsolescence
Linkage
Locational obsolescence
Plottage value
Productivity
Utility

Property Productivity

Productivity is the ability of the property to provide a flow of services or benefits to an owner. Productivity is the net result of a property's site, improvement, legal, and locational characteristics. Measuring productivity is the first step toward determining a property's rental worth to a user and, in turn, market and investment value to an owner.

Utility is the basis of value. An ability to render services to satisfy demand means that a property has utility. *Utility* is the ability of something to satisfy a human desire or need, which represents potential demand for the service. If the potential demand is backed up by purchasing power, it becomes *effective demand.* If people are willing to pay money to satisfy a desire or need, the utility, whether obtained for instance, from real property, diamonds, wine, gasoline, medical service, or shelter, has value in the marketplace. Thus, to say that real estate has utility is to say that it has value.

Owners expect to realize the benefits of property productivity in any of three ways.

1. *Ownership for cash flow*. Apartment houses, warehouses, office buildings, or shopping centers are bought as investments to be rented out in return for cash flow. Thus, the amount and certainty of the rental payments provide the utility to the investor. The return is generally to supplement occupational income and to reinvest for building an estate.

2. *Ownership for self-use.* Properties may be acquired for self-use as, for instance, a house is bought by a family for shelter or a store is built and occupied by a jeweler as a place of business. Additional reasons for self-use of real estate include greater security, greater flexibility, avoidance of rent payments, or controlling an advantageous location.

3. *Ownership for appreciation.* Raw land, vacant lots, timberlands, and other properties are often purchased entirely for expected value increases. It is hoped that during the waiting period the property will earn enough to cover carrying costs, although this will not necessarily happen. The plan might call for the raw land to be subdivided at some future time.

Ownership for cash flow requires knowing the many benefits a property might render to a renter-user. The rental a property is worth requires a judgment of the quality, quantity, and duration of services to be realized for the user's purposes. Of course, location is of major importance for most users. But the productivity of a property for a user also depends on the physical and functional capability of the site improvements, which will be taken up later in our discussion of improvements analysis. These very characteristics must be converted into dollar terms for most real estate decisions and transactions.

Locational Analysis

The three most important value characteristics of real estate are "location, location, and location," according to a popular saying, which contains considerable truth. Our discussion of finding the property with the greatest productivity for a specific purpose or use therefore begins with locational analysis.

Location is the result of fixity and concerns relationships external to a property. Location has two distinct dimensions. One, termed convenience, or accessibility, concerns the relative costs of getting to and from the site. The second, called exposure, or environment, concerns what is around the parcel.

CONVENIENCE

A social or economic activity takes place on a site as only one of many possible uses to which the parcel could be put. For example, a given site might be used for a residence, a professional office building, a gasoline service station, a dry-cleaning pickup station, or a tavern. What determines which use will win out in the competition among them?

If all possibilities are open, convenience or location is usually the dominant consideration in the competition among the alternative uses. *Convenience of location* or *accessibility* means that a property is easy to get to or that the relative costs in time and money of getting to and from it tend to be minimal.

Location determines whether demand exists for the services that a property, at a fixed site, is capable of rendering. Fixity is the principal reason that market studies are made before developing a site. Location also affects the costs of rendering services. A hotel in the desert may be physically capable of rendering services, but, if no demand exists, productivity cannot exist. If the demand is present, the costs of getting workers, foods, water, and the like may be much higher than if the hotel were located near an urban community.

Linkages. Social and economic activities are interdependent. Families in residences tend to be tied to schools, stores, churches, work centers, and friends in other dwelling units. Lawyers are typically in frequent contact with court proceedings and records, clients, abstracting and title companies, and financial institutions. A drive-in restaurant attracts customers, takes deliveries of food and drink, and is the daily workplace of its employees. Each of these relationships is termed a *linkage*, or a relationship between two land use activities that generates movement of people or goods between them.

A child going to school reflects a linkage. So does a parent going to the office or to the store for ice cream. A car getting gas at a service station constitutes a linkage, as does wheat going from the farm to the flour mill. The movement of cars from a factory in Detroit to a distributor in Denver is a linkage. All involve movement of people or goods.

A residence is considered to have an "outward orientation" in its linkages; each trip originates at the dwelling unit. See Figure 7-1. On the other hand, a shopping center, a factory, or an office complex has an "inward orientation"; most trips are initiated elsewhere and come to the activity. See Figure 7-2.

Costs of Friction. Moving people or goods between linked activities involves four types of costs, termed *costs of friction.* Costs of friction are measured in time and energy as well as in dollars. Some costs of friction cannot be easily estimated in dollar terms.

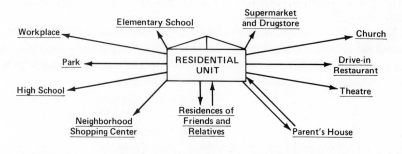

FIGURE 7-1
Linkages of a residential unit (outward orientation)

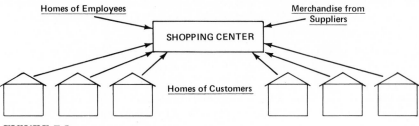

FIGURE 7-2
Shopping center linkages (inward orientation)

1. *Transportation costs.* The out-of-pocket costs of movement are measured as fares on public transit or operating expenses for privately owned vehicles.

2. *Time costs of travel.* Time is required for a person or good to move from one site to another, from one economic activity to another. The speed of alternative transportation modes, traffic controls, congestion, and the efficiency of the street and road system all affect time costs of travel. The dollar cost of a trip can be calculated based on the time required for the trip and the value of the traveler's time. For goods, estimating the dollar cost is much more difficult. It is a function of lost business because of the goods not being on hand, of spoilage owing to delays in transit, or of lost personnel or work time because of interrupted schedules.

3. *Terminal costs.* Many types of linkage involve expenses at one or both ends. Terminal costs include dollars spent for loading docks as well as for moving goods onto and from a truck or train. Storing an automobile during a downtown interview involves paying a parking fee, which is a terminal cost. Shopping centers absorb or internalize terminal costs to improve accessibility and reduce aggravation costs.

4. *Aggravation costs.* Traveler irritation and annoyances caused by delay, congestion, bumping and shoving, and heat or cold are costs of travel that, on a personal level, enter into the costs of friction. Aggravation costs are very difficult to measure in dollar terms.

In measuring the costs of friction connected with an economic activity, those associated with accessibility are considered first. Thus, the total cost of accessibility is estimated. The costs are measured as disutilities, whether dollars, time, or aggravations. For each linkage the cost of friction equals the product of the costs of each trip multiplied by the frequency of the trips. Subjective judgment is sometimes required for this calculation. The site with the lowest total costs of friction provides, by definition, the greatest convenience or accessibility for a use.

Example of Convenience. The importance of convenience can best be shown with an example. Retail trade activity sharply shifted from central business districts (CBDs) to shopping centers following World War II. The prices charged in the shopping centers were not any lower and were possibly a little higher. The out-of-pocket costs to reach the centers were in some cases greater than were those required to reach the downtown area. Yet it was not unusual for shoppers to go around a CBD to reach a center on the other side of town. Why? The centers provided free parking as against metered parking. The centers could be reached easily by car with congestion and delays minimized when compared with reaching the

CBD; thus, travel time and aggravation costs tended to be less. Overall, the centers were much more convenient. In turn, the centers captured most of the dollar growth in retail sales, while CBDs' dollars sales held steady.

A second example of the interrelationship between location and productivity is the revival of Atlantic City, New Jersey. In 1976, Atlantic City's economy was faltering, and its famed hotels were in severe disrepair. In late 1976, casino gambling was legalized for Atlantic City. Subsequently, construction and building renovation activities boomed. The nearness of the population centers of the East enables Atlantic City to tap the demand for gambling that formerly had been satisfied through illegal local means or by the casinos of Nevada.

ENVIRONMENT OR EXPOSURE

Exposure involves externalities, as discussed in the previous chapter. A good view, pleasant breezes, or nearness to centers of prestige and fashion provide a favorable environment for properties, thereby making them more desirable and more valuable. On the other hand, a property subject to loud or untimely noises, to foul-smelling odors and smoke, to unduly high property taxes, or to a distressing view is said to have an unfavorable environment or a negative exposure. Exposure affects the senses of people and is realized or experienced without moving from the site. Considerations, such as the social mix of a neighborhood, may be considered favorable or unfavorable, depending on the user's perspective. *Exposure* is the environment around a property as experienced by a user of the property.

Favorable Exposure. The primary benefits of exposure are aesthetic satisfactions and prestige, as tree-lined residential streets or a Wall Street address for a financial house. High ground tends to possess these attributes to a greater extent than do low-lying areas. These factors coupled with the ability to outbid low-income families are the reasons upper-income areas tend to dominate the hills in most urban areas.

Social and business prestige are important determinants of location also. In Washington, D.C., Georgetown or Chevy Chase addresses carry high social acceptance. The same is true of the Gold Coast north of the Chicago Loop. Likewise, a Madison Avenue address in New York City is important for acceptance in the world of advertising. Every large metropolitan area has several premium areas. As might be expected, these are usually associated with desirable aesthetic qualities.

Unfavorable Exposure. A social or economic activity prefers to avoid conditions that are distasteful, inharmonious, or objectionable. More than one slaughterhouse has been banned from a business district because it produced noxious odors. Slum areas are not inviting for high-income housing developments. Factories emitting excessive smoke cause residential areas downwind to become blighted. Polluted lakes and streams, trash dumps, open sewers, and sewerage-disposal plants are all undesirable neighbors for most land use activities. The result of unfavorable exposure is lower property values.

Locational Obsolescence. Properties suffer loss in value, depreciation, because other locations offer greater convenience or more favorable exposure; this is termed *locational obsolescence.* In other words, off-site factors may diminish the ability of a property to render services in the land use activity of interest.

LOCATIONAL DYNAMICS

The elements of location are constantly changing. Four types of change should be taken into account by a user in selecting a site. Failure to take account of them is likely to result in locational obsolescence.

Changes in Linked Activities. Tendencies and trends of linked activities to relocate are important. For example, Sears developed a policy of relocating at the edge of downtown areas or in the new shopping centers, following World War II. Montgomery Ward chose to be conservative and stay downtown. For over 3 decades, Sears far outstripped Montgomery Ward in growth, although the two firms started out approximately even.

Changes in Channels of Movement. New modes of movement or new channels of movement mean new travel patterns. Thousands of motels, truck stops, and gasoline service stations were hurt by the construction of the interstate highway system. If higher energy costs cause a shift toward greater use of mass transit, central or downtown locations for restaurants and motels would increase in demand. On the other hand, drive-in restaurants would probably be seriously hurt by the shift.

Changes in Nonlinked Establishments. The development, removal, or relocation of unrelated activities may have widespread effects on nonlinked land uses. The development of a civic center may break up a retail shopping pattern. A large new office building may touch off a whole series of moves by attorneys, engineers, realty brokers, and business services, leaving numerous vacancies in the process. Lower rents in the older buildings tend to allow a shift in the makeup of local office users to such types of business as bill collectors, insurance adjustors, printing agencies, and cheap photography studios. An "innocent" newsstand owner may find that the clientele has largely left, forcing either a move or a change in operational methods.

Changes in Nature of an Activity. Changes in technology and in ways of conducting business affect the ability of a property to perform the desired functions for the use involved. For example, supermarkets replaced the corner grocery because of a change in distribution methods that came about because supermarkets can serve larger areas at lower costs, even though they must be located on or near major traffic arteries.

PROTECTION FROM NEGATIVE EXTERNALITIES

Protection from undesirable externalities may be gained by a user searching for a location in several ways:

1. Select a site or area because of the protective planning, zoning, or deed restrictions that go with it.
2. If possible, select a location with a physical buffer against impending blight, as provided by freeways, a line of hills, or a river.
3. Promptly request or initiate enforcement of the land use controls when violations occur. If nearby land use activities are unregulated and generate

smog, dust, or unpleasant odors, initiate legal action to curtail or close them down as nuisance activities.

Site Analysis

A complete listing of all factors affecting site productivity for a user is probably impossible. Some factors are physical, some are legal, some are economic. The following categories of factors account for those considered most important. Physical factors in site analysis tend to be less important if the property has been developed and is in use; they no longer determine the size and type of improvements to be added to the site. However, physical factors may be the primary determinant of the highest and best use to which a vacant site might be developed. Off-site improvements necessary to make the site productive, such as road improvements and public utilities, are included as a part of site analysis.

SIZE AND SHAPE

Size and shape are of prime importance to productivity, particularly in urban areas. Lots that are small or of odd or irregular shape are difficult to develop and can accommodate only a limited number of uses. As a consequence, their worth per unit of area is generally lower than is that for parcels of standard size and shape.

For example, a lot that is triangular in shape does not lend itself to the siting of a rectangular building. As a result, either land is wasted or a triangular building is erected with higher construction costs and inefficient interior space arrangements. Long narrow lots are not desirable either; a lot 10 feet by 600 feet would not be practical as a site for a single-family residence even though it contained 6,000 square feet, a typical size lot in many communities.

Generally, land value per unit of area declines as the size of parcels increases and the method of measuring area changes. In rural areas, land values are lower, and size is stated in terms of acres or sections rather than square feet.

Sometimes, a value increment, called plottage, or plottage value, can be realized by bringing two or more smaller parcels of land under one ownership. *Plottage value* means that the value of the several parcels, when combined, is greater than the sums of values of the parcels taken individually under separate owners. Plottage comes about because the larger unit of land can be used more intensively or with lower costs than would be possible with the smaller parcels treated independently. Thus, combining two triangular business lots could provide a site able to accommodate a rectangular building. The benefit, as against two triangular-shaped buildings, would be lower construction costs and more efficient space arrangements. Another example of plottage would be the combining of two single-family lots to make a larger site on which a four-unit apartment building might be built, when allowed by the zoning ordinance.

TOPOGRAPHY AND GEOLOGY

Topography and geology determine the suitability of a site for support of buildings, for cultivation, or for other user purposes. Topography and geology must work together to produce desirable sites. The contours of the land affect water flow and drainage. Subsoil conditions also affect drainage. Fertile soil eases landscaping problems. In developing a site, test boring helps to foretell excavation and foundation needs. Rocks, gullies, quicksand, cliffs, or bog underlayment present special problems.

Topography, the contours and slopes of the surface, must generally not be unduly rough for business, industrial, or agricultural uses. Rough terrain increases the costs of putting in roads and streets, installing utilities, and landscaping, in addition to increasing building costs. On the other hand, improved amenities—view and relative privacy—frequently result in builders of upper-income housing seeking hilly terrain even though the costs are greater.

Topography also has an important bearing on the drainage and susceptibility to erosion. This applies to adjoining land as well as to the subject site. The possibility of flooding is always an important item. Stagnant or polluted waters can be a ready source of mosquitoes or disease and, therefore, a hazard to health.

Soil and subsoil conditions bear directly on the income-producing ability of sites. In urban areas, marshy conditions or subsurface rock usually mean much greater difficulty, and expense, in development. Soil fertility tends to be of less importance. In urban fringe areas, if not served by city sewer lines, soils must be relatively permeable to adequately absorb septic tank effluent.

ROADS AND PUBLIC UTILITIES

Access to the street and road system is essential for each privately owned parcel of land in a community. The system facilitates movement between and among all sites and thus serves them all. Without ready accessibility, transportation costs might become so great that most uses could not absorb them. Thus, a farm on a good road, or an industrial plant on a railroad and an interstate highway, tend to be prime property. The value of a farm or plant that is inaccessible except by foot is almost certain to be extremely low in comparison. A completely inaccessible site, as in the snowbound Antarctic or the jungles of Brazil, has no value for all practical purposes.

Public utilities are important to most sites as well. Telephone, gas, and electrical services are needed for rapid communication and for power. Sewer and water mains are necessary if septic tanks and wells cannot be accommodated. In many areas, storm water sewers must be installed to prevent periodic flooding.

The value of a site is likely to be reduced where these various services are not immediately available. That is, a site without water is worth less than is a site with water. That means that the value or price of a site is generally on an "as is" basis. The penalty should reflect the loss in benefits suffered because of the absence of the service. If improvements and services are in but not paid for, the value of the site is reduced by the amount of the unpaid costs or assessments.

LEGAL LIMITATIONS ON USE

The highest and best use of a site may be limited by zoning, deed restrictions, easements, leases, liens, or other clouds on title as discussed in earlier chapters. In the absence of limits on use, highest and best use is determined by supply and demand considerations only.

If several legal limits apply, the most limiting takes precedence. Thus, a site may be suitable by demand for a high-rise apartment building, zoned for a two-story apartment building, and limited by deed restriction to development as a single-family residence. The single-family use governs. If the deed restriction were removed, the zoning would control. Thus, restrictive zoning, an easement, or an awkward lease can reduce the productivity and therefore the value of a site just as surely as can poor drainage, lack of access, or inconvenient size or shape. The cause is less tangible, but the effect on use and value is just as real.

Lack of clear title or other title problems can also limit use and productivity. For example, three siblings may inherit a property as tenants in common. Unless all the siblings agree to the terms necessary for development, efforts by an investor to develop it would be fruitless. Another example of an encumbrance limiting use and productivity is a power-line easement across a site. Assume that the easement limits construction to 32 feet in height. Even though demand justifies a seven-story building, which would be allowed by zoning, the use would be limited to a three-story building.

Improvements Analysis

Improvements include the main structure plus necessary complements such as garages, utility buildings, and landscaping. Improvements must be compatible with the site and with one another for the highest and best use to be realized. Once built, improvements usually determine how a property will be used. For example, an office building is constructed on a site. For all practical purposes, this precludes the property's use as a motel, a warehouse, or an apartment building. A new use is feasible only if it is so profitable that it can absorb the cost of conversion of the existing improvements to its needs.

STRUCTURES

Structures are the main on-site improvements for most real estate and generally account for more than half the cost or value of a property. The primary purpose of structures is to provide shelter from the elements (wind, rain, sun, cold). Many modern buildings even provide year-round climate control for their inhabitants. They also provide privacy. They provide space for storage and for carrying on economic activities under controlled conditions.

Structures are increasingly designed to accommodate specific activities. Thus, a plant for the production of baby foods will differ greatly from a foundry. An insurance office building will differ from a warehouse. An additional purpose of some structures is to project an image of prestige, as with a bank or luxury hotel.

The primary concern in structural analysis is to weigh the value-generating characteristics of a building relative to its ability to provide services and benefits in its intended use. Locational capability has already been discussed because it applies to an entire property. Physical capability and functional efficiency are now taken up because they apply mainly to the improvement on a site.

PHYSICAL CAPABILITY AND DURABILITY

Physical capability refers primarily to the quantity of services that a property can render. The size or extent of the improvements, and the length of time services can be rendered, directly determine the quantity of services to be realized. That is, a 20,000 square foot, run-down building will not yield anywhere near the quantity of services that a new 200,000 square foot building will in satisfying the needs of an insurance company as a home office.

A building suffers physical deterioration in three ways:

1. Poor initial construction that later results in faults such as a cracked foundation or a sagging superstructure
2. Wear and tear from use, such as trim getting nicked, a stair railing torn loose, or a ball going through a window
3. Deterioration from time and action of the elements; examples are the need for repainting or for replacement of a roof, damage owing to storms, extreme temperatures, war, fire, explosion, or neglect

Although the cause is physical, the effect of deterioration is economic. Physical deterioration is generally not a major cause of ending the useful life of a building.

FUNCTIONAL OBSOLESCENCE

Obsolete buildings are frequently removed to clear a site for a new structure that can perform more effectively and efficiently. Hence, a well-known saying is, "More buildings are torn down than fall down."

A major concern of a potential tenant or user is therefore the functional capability of the property for the specific use being considered. To function means to work or operate. Functional capability reflects the functional efficiency of a property and refers to the quality of services it can render. *Functional efficiency* is a measure of how well a property is suited to its actual or intended use relative to a new property specifically designed for that use. Thus, a supermarket is tested against current needs for storage, displays, checkout stations, and customer parking. A property that measures up well relative to a new property is said to have a high functional efficiency.

Any inability to measure up to the new property is termed functional obsolescence. That is, *functional obsolecence* represents the decreased ability of a property to provide the benefit or service relative to the new property designed for the use. Functional obsolescence results in unduly high costs of operation and maintenance, in reduced ability to generate revenues, or in lowered amenities. Functional obsolescence may be due to deficiencies of a location, of site characteristics, or of structural characteristics. Thus, an old gasoline service station converted into a drive-in restaurant is likely to be functionally obsolete relative to a new drive-in restaurant.

New technology and methods of organization result in the continuing functional obsolescence of buildings. Currently, increased electrical requirements for air conditioning and computer operations are making many office buildings obsolete. Ability to build taller and larger buildings is leading to new and different architectural forms, including atriums that sometimes affect several stories of new hotels. At the same time it should be recognized that older buildings are increasingly gutted and renovated to retain their individuality.

Evaluation of a structure's ability to provide a useful service requires an analysis of the amount of functional utility it contains in its intended use. A dwelling unit is therefore tested against the needs and demands of family living and possibly for prestigious location. Thus, a five-bedroom house with only one bath is functionally obsolete. Outdated electrical writing or plumbing also means functional obsolescence, as does an inadequate floor plan necessitating that all traffic between bedrooms go through a living room.

The relation of a structure to its site also needs to be taken into account. A four-bedroom house on a small lot cannot have a yard large enough for the outdoor living demands of today; the house is too large for its site and is an overimprovement; too small a structure is an underimprovement. Thus, many older shopping centers provide too little parking space relative to sales space and are, therefore, relatively obsolete when compared with newer centers. An industrial plant with too little parking space for employees is in the same category. In all these cases, some loss in value from the optimum occurs.

Functional utility is optimal when the site, structure, and equipment are combined in proper proportion with no distracting features. Even building appearance is a consideration in functional utility. An older apartment house of forbidding appearance that deters tenants is functionally obsolete.

DEPRECIATION

The diminished utility and lowering in value from physical deterioration, functional obsolescence, or locational obsolescence is collectively referred to as *depreciation.* Depreciation may be curable or incurable. Curable depreciation is when the cost to correct the deficiency is less than the market value added because of the correction. Incurable depreciation, on the other hand, occurs when the cost to correct exceeds the increment of market value added by correction. Locational obsolescence is almost always outside the control of an owner to remedy and is, therefore, almost always incurable.

MISCELLANEOUS IMPROVEMENTS

Lesser site improvements may contribute to or detract from the productivity of a property. Examples include: (1) walks and driveways; (2) accessory buildings such as garages; (3) landscaping, including lawn, trees, shrubbery, and gardens; (4) fences and terraces; and (5) retaining walls.

Questions for Review and Discussion

1. What is property productivity? What is it based on? How is it realized? Explain.
2. Define the following concepts briefly, and then explain how each relates to the productivity of structures. Give examples where possible.

a. Physical capability, physical deterioration
   b. Functional efficiency, functional obsolescence
   c. Locational convenience, locational obsolescence
3. Four "costs of friction" are incurred in moving people or goods between linked activities. Identify and briefly explain the nature of each.
4. Explain briefly how each of the following site characteristics relates to property productivity.
   a. Size and shape
   b. Topography and geology
   c. Street improvements and public utilities
   d. Zoning
   e. Title encumbrances
5. What does "exposure" mean to a property in a locational sense? Give at least one example of positive and negative exposure.
6. Is all property productive? Does all property have value? Discuss.
7. Is a property's productivity related to economic and social activity on a regional basis? On a local basis? Discuss.
8. Is there a relationship between the energy crunch and the location of real estate? Explain or discuss.

Case Problem

1. Classify the following items of depreciation as physical, functional, or locational. Also indicate whether the deficiency is likely to be curable or incurable.
   a. Small rooms
   b. Paint blistered and cracked
   c. Rotting wall studs
   d. Cracked foundation
   e. Rough flooring
   f. One-car garage in two-car garage neighborhood
   g. Ultra-high ceilings
   h. Commercial development intruding into a residential neighborhood
   i. Leaky roof
   j. Industrial odors in residential neighborhood

8

The Investor · Broker Relationship

Let us begin anew—remembering on both sides that civility is not a sign of weakness, and sincerity is always subject to proof. Let us never negotiate out of fear. But let us never fear to negotiate.

John F. Kennedy, former U.S. president

A real estate broker is anyone engaged to negotiate the sale, purchase, lease, or exchange of realty, or arrange financing of realty, for a fee or commission. Brokerage specialization has now reached the stage where individuals—and entire organizations—limit operations to a single area, such as investments, commercial, industrial, land, or lease brokerage. Some organizations, however, do continue to provide a wide variety of functions and services, including appraising, brokerage, counseling, construction and development, financing, and insurance.

In looking at the investor-broker relationship, our concern is primarily with the legal and service relationship between an investor and a broker as it occurs in a buy-sell transaction. In the transaction, the broker is a negotiator and takes neither title nor possession of the realty. At the same time, the actions and success of the broker are of vital importance to the investor.

Important Topics or Decision Areas Covered in this Chapter

The Law of Agency
Duties, Liabilities, and Rights of a Principal
Duties, Liabilities, and Rights of an Agent

Listing Agreements
Open Listing
Exclusive Agency Listing
Exclusive Right-to-Sell Listing
Multiple Listing
Net Listing

Critical Issues in the Listing Arrangement
Asking Price
Reservation of Right to Sell
Broker Compensation
Duration/Termination of the Agreement
Broker Proof of Performance

More on Commissions
General Rules on Earning Commissions
Who Pays
Commission on an Installment Sale
Commissions on Exchanges, Loans, and Leases

Selecting a Broker

Questions for Review and Discussion

Case Problems

Key Concepts Introduced in this Chapter

Accountability

Agency

Agent

Disclosed principal

Dual/divided agency

Fiduciary relationship

Independent contractor

Listing agreement

Loyalty

Middleman

Principal

Procuring cause

Ready, willing, and able buyer

Third party

Tort

Undisclosed principal

The Law of Agency

Agency is the relationship created when one person is given the right to act on behalf of, or under the control of, another. In financial matters such as buying, selling, or leasing of property, the agency is considered a *fiduciary relationship,* in that trust and faith between the parties are expected and necessary.

The law of agency concerns the legal rights, duties, and liabilities of the principal, agent, and third parties based on contracts and/or relationships between them. The law of agency involves aspects of the law of contract and the law of torts. A *tort* is a wrongful or damaging act committed against another, for which a civil action may be brought. Causing personal injury to another, damaging another's property, fraud, and misrepresentation are examples of torts.

A person acting for or representing another, with the latter's authority, is an *agent.* Thus, a broker is an agent in selling property for an owner under a listing agreement. The person for whom an agent acts is a *principal.* An owner, therefore, becomes a principal when he or she signs a listing agreement with a broker.

Agency in real estate traditionally involves three parties: a principal (P), an agent (A), and a third party (T). A potential buyer, such as an investor negotiating to purchase a property, is a *third party* in the typical real estate sales transaction. See Figure 8-1. The broker, and agents of the broker, usually do not represent the buyer in this situation. Further, they have no obligation to the third party beyond what is given here.

A principal known or identified to a third party is a *disclosed principal.* A partially disclosed principal is one not known or identified to the third party, although the agent acknowledges that a principal is involved. Finally, an *undisclosed principal* is one who is secretly represented by an agent who appears to be acting in self-interest.

DUTIES, LIABILITIES, AND RIGHTS OF A PRINCIPAL

A principal's main duties to an agent are to compensate in accordance with the contract of employment. Thus, with the typical listing agreement, the owner must pay a commission to the broker when a "ready, willing, and able" buyer has been found. An owner also has a duty to give the broker-agent complete and accurate information when listing a property to be sold, leased, or exchanged.

A principal is liable on all agreements or contracts made by an agent within the authority given the agent. Unauthorized agreements also become a principal's liability, if subsequently affirmed or ratified by a principal with full knowledge of the pertinent facts. Unauthorized agreements are agreements outside or beyond the authority given the agent. Most listing agreements clearly spell out the authority given a broker, and usually that authority does not include signing or accepting an offer to purchase the subject property.

In the matter of torts, agents and independent contractors are personally liable for their own acts. At the same time, agents and independent contractors are not liable for torts committed by their principals. A principal may become jointly liable for torts committed by an agent. Thus, a tort committed by an agent within the scope

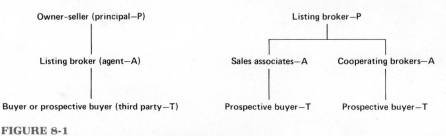

FIGURE 8-1
Traditional real estate agency relationships

of the employment agreement or under the direction of the principal becomes a liability of the principal.

Note, however, that a principal is not generally liable for acts of an independent contractor. An *independent contractor* is a person retaining personal control over work details while performing a service or task for an employer. A broker engaged to sell a property for an owner is almost certainly an independent contractor. A salesperson, engaged by a broker, may or may not be an independent contractor; the work relationship would be the primary determinant of whether the salesperson were an independent contractor. The greater the control exercised by the broker, the less the likelihood that the salesperson is an independent contractor.

A disclosed principal may enforce any contract made with a third party by an authorized agent for the principal's benefit. A real estate broker ordinarily does not enter contracts for a principal, but such is possible.

DUTIES, LIABILITIES, AND RIGHTS OF AN AGENT

An agent's duties to a principal are to (1) use reasonable care, (2) obey reasonable instructions, (3) give accountability, (4) be loyal, and (5) give notice. Using reasonable care means that the agent must be diligent and must act in good faith in representing the principal. The agent is expected to follow or obey all reasonable instructions of a principal, assuming that the instructions pertain to the purpose of the principal–agent relationship. Following instructions includes keeping within the authority given by the principal. Instructions creating a tort or criminal situation would not be reasonable. An agent also has a legal duty of *accountability*, which is to account for all money or property to the principal, including keeping adequate records concerning such money or property. In addition, it is illegal for a broker to comingle or mix personal funds and funds of a principal.

Loyalty means that the agent must not benefit from the relationship except through compensation from the principal unless otherwise agreed. Faithful performance is another term for loyalty. A broker, therefore, may not represent both parties in a buy–sell transaction without the knowledge and consent of both. Representing two principals is called *dual* or *divided agency.* Contracts involving agent disloyalty are voidable at the option of the principal, in that the broker cannot get the highest possible price for the seller and at the same time get the lowest possible price for the buyer. It follows that a broker cannot collect a commission for arranging a voided contract. If a broker acts for both buyer and seller, with the full knowledge of both, the double agency rule does not apply. In this situation the broker is termed a *middleman.*

"Giving notice" to a principal means that any information given the agent must be communicated immediately to the principal. Any knowledge given the agent legally binds the principal. Therefore, it follows that the agent is bound to keep the principal informed of any important facts concerning the object of the agency arrangement.

An agent is not personally liable for contracts entered into for the benefit of the principal. However, an agent exceeding his or her authority does incur personal liability, unless such an act is affirmed or ratified by the principal. A broker is usually engaged only to find a buyer and not to make a sales contract for the owner. Therefore, a broker's operations usually do not provide a situation where the authority of the agency agreement might be exceeded. However, if a principal lacks legal competence to make a valid agency contract (because of insanity or being underage), the agent incurs personal liability for any resulting contract.

An agent has a right to enforce a contract of a principal against a third party in which an interest is held. Thus, a broker may enforce a sales contract of an owner with a buyer because of an anticipated commission. Finally, a broker derives authority from an owner through the listing agreement. To enforce the collection of a commission, a broker must have the agreement in writing. Ordinarily, the broker is authorized only to negotiate for the principal under a listing agreement. Most listing agreements provide that a broker may engage salespersons to help conduct the negotiations. The salespersons also operate under the law of agency, with the broker as the principal.

Listing Agreements

After successfully completing a buy-sell or leasing transaction, the broker must show that a listing agreement was made with the owner, or the owner's agent, to enforce his or her right to the commission. A *listing agreement* is an oral or written contract of employment of a broker by a principal to buy, sell, or lease real estate. A listing agreement creates the traditional principal-agent relationship discussed earlier. Note, however, a broker may contract with a buyer and thereby become an agent of a buyer.

The listing agreement is the foundation of the broker's business. Out of it arise the broker's relation or trust and confidence with his or her principal and the broker's rights for compensation. It is highly important, therefore, that any person engaging in the real estate business fully understand the rights and obligations underlying each of the listing contracts.

Strictly speaking, the typical "listing" is not a contract. At most, it may be classified as a unilateral contract that becomes an actual or bilateral contract upon performance by the broker. However, a listing agreement containing promises by a broker to make a diligent effort and by an owner to pay some minimum monetary consideration and a commission becomes a bilateral contract. Lacking consideration—until performance—a unilateral contract is revocable by either party at any time prior to performance, even though a definite time is stipulated in the listing agreement.

Five listing agreements are in general use: (1) open, (2) exclusive agency, (3) exclusive right to sell, (4) multiple, and (5) net. Open and net listing agreements may be reached orally in some states. However, to enforce a claim for the collection of a commission, better brokers prefer written listings. In fact, most brokers refuse to handle or promote a property without a written listing.

OPEN LISTING

An open listing occurs when an owner-principal offers several brokers an equal chance to sell realty. The broker who actually arranges a sale receives compensation. The owner must remain neutral in the competition between the brokers to avoid obligation for a commission to more than one broker. The owner may reserve the right personally to sell the realty without becoming liable for a commission, and usually does so.

The sale of the property terminates the open listing. Usually, the owner need not notify the agents, since under the law effective in almost all states the sale cancels all outstanding listings. This safeguards the owner against paying more than one commission.

EXCLUSIVE AGENCY LISTING

An exclusive agency listing is the engaging of only one broker to sell realty for a commission, with a right retained by the owner to sell or rent the property without obligation for a commission. An exclusive agency listing contains the words "exclusive agency." Under this form of list agreement, the commission is payable to the broker named in the contract. The purpose of the exclusive agency listing is to give the broker holding the listing an opportunity to apply "best efforts" without interference or competition from other brokers. In nearly every state, the exclusive agency listing binds the owner to pay a commission to the listing broker in the event of a sale by the listing broker or any other broker.

An exclusive agency listing does not entitle the broker to compensation when the property is sold by the owner to a prospect not procured by the broker. This listing is also revocable, unless a consideration was made. Further, the listing may be terminated if the broker has not performed, in which case the owner's liability is limited to the value of any services actually performed by the broker.

EXCLUSIVE RIGHT-TO-SELL LISTING

An exclusive right-to-sell listing is the engagement of one broker to sell realty, with a commission to be paid the broker regardless of who sells the property, owner included. That is, the owner gives the rights personally to sell the realty and avoid paying a commission. An exclusive right-to-sell listing contains the words "exclusive right." This listing is similar in all respects to the exclusive agency listing except that under it a commission is due the broker named whether the property is sold by the listing broker, any other broker, or even the owner, within the time limit specified in the listing contract. An owner may reserve the right to sell to certain parties, who are or have been negotiating with the owner for the property, by including their names as exceptions in the contract. Figure 8-2 shows an exclusive right-to-sell listing contract that may also serve as a multiple-listing agreement.

MULTIPLE LISTING

Brokers commonly form into groups, called multiple-listing services, in which each member agrees to share any listings in his or her office with others in the group. Members of the group, in turn, use a multiple-listing service (MLS) listing agreement that is actually a special version of the exclusive right-to-sell listing agreement; it provides that any member of the MLS group may automatically sell the realty and share in the commission as a cooperating broker. An MLS listing arrangement is advantageous to an owner in that the property gets wider exposure, which tends to mean a

No. 678 © Rev. TT
Stevens-Ness L.P.Co.
Portland, Ore. 97204

REAL ESTATE BROKER'S EMPLOYMENT CONTRACT
(involving lease and lessee's interest only; Use Form 676)

APARTMENT, HOTEL, ROOMING HOUSE, MOTEL

Name of property **Douglas Manor**

Location **2001 Century Drive, Urbandale, Anystate, 00000** Tel Legal Description **Lots 16 & 17,**
Edgewood South Subdivision

(If said property is incorrectly described, owner hereby expressly authorizes broker subsequently to write in hereon or attach hereto, the correct legal description thereof.)

City **Urbandale** County **Rustic** State and Zip **Anystate 00000** For better description see owner's title deed on record, now made a part hereof.

No. of apts **16** No. of rms. **72** 4 rm. apts **8** No. of 5 rm. apts. **8** No. of rm. apts Does structure need remodeling or renovating? Yes ☐ No ☒

Selling price, free of encumbrances $ **680,000** Terms **Cash**

Is personal property included in this listing? Yes ☐ No ☐ If so, is signed inventory attached? Yes ☐ No ☐ to be attached? Yes ☐ No ☐

To **Ivan M. Everready, Realtor** Broker, City **Urbandale** State **Anystate** **September 1st 80**

FOR VALUE RECEIVED, you hereby are employed to sell or exchange the property described hereon at the selling price and on the terms noted. You hereby are authorized to accept a deposit on the purchase price. You may, if desired, secure the cooperation of any other broker, or group of brokers, in procuring a sale of said property. In the event that you, or any other brokers cooperating with you, shall find a buyer ready and willing to enter into a deal for said price and terms, or such other terms and price as I may accept, or that during your employment you supply me with the name of or place me in contact with a buyer to or through whom, any time within 90 days after the termination hereof **6% on 1st $100,000; 4% on excess of $100,000 (see below** or convey said property, I hereby agree to pay you in cash for your services a commission equal in amount to of the above stated selling price. I agree to convey said real estate to the purchaser by a good and sufficient deed, to assign the outstanding lease(s), if any, to transfer and deliver said personal property, if any, by good and sufficient bill of sale and to furnish title insurance in an amount equal to the selling price insuring marketable title to said real estate and good right to convey. I hereby warrant that the information shown hereon below is true, that I am the owner of said property, that my title thereto is a good and marketable title, that the same is free of encumbrances except as shown hereunder under "Financial Details," and except taxes levied on said property for the current tax year which are to be pro rated between the seller and buyer. In case of an exchange, I have no objection to your representing and accepting compensation from the other party to the exchange as well as myself. I hereby authorize you and your customers to enter any part of said property at any reasonable time to show same. Also, I authorize you, at any time, to fill in and complete all or any part of the "Information Data" below, except financial details. The following items are to be left upon the premises as part of the property purchased. All irrigation, plumbing, ventilation, cooling and heating fixtures and equipment (including stoker and oil tanks but excluding fire place fixtures and equipment), water heaters, attached electric light and bathroom fixtures, light bulbs and fluorescent lamps, venetian blinds, wall-to-wall carpeting, awnings, window and door screens, storm doors and windows, attached floor coverings, attached television antenna, all plants, shrubs and trees and all fixtures except **stove and refrigerators to be regarded as fixtures also.**

The following personal property is also included as a part of the property to be offered for sale for said price **none**

(or see signed inventory, if any attached). This agreement expires at midnight on **December 31** 19 **80** but I further allow you a reasonable time thereafter to close any deal on which earnest money has been deposited. In case of suit or action on this contract, it is agreed between us that the court, whether trial or appellate, may allow the prevailing party therein that party's reasonable attorney's fees. It is further agreed that my signature affixed to the renewal clause below shall have the effect of renewing and extending your employment to a new date to be fixed by me on the same terms and all with the same effect as if the said new date had been fixed above as the expiration of your employment. Disposition of forfeited Earnest Money, if any, to be negotiated and set forth in the Earnest Money Receipt (Oregon only, delete if inapplicable). *THIS LISTING IS AN EXCLUSIVE LISTING and you hereby are granted the absolute, sole and exclusive right to sell or exchange the said described property. In the event of any sale by me or any other person, or of exchange or conveyance of said property, or any part thereof, during the term of your exclusive employment, or in case I withdraw the authority hereby given prior to said expiration date, I agree to pay you the said commission just the same as if a sale had actually been consummated by you. I HEREBY CERTIFY THAT I HAVE READ AND RECEIVED A CARBON COPY OF THIS CONTRACT.

Accepted **September 1st** 19 **80** Owner

Ivan M. Everready, Realtor Broker **/s/ Wendy Welloff** Owner

Owner's Address **Unit 77, Condominium Towers, Urbandale** State **Anystate** Zip **00000** Phone **345-2020**

FOR VALUE RECEIVED, the above broker's employment hereby is renewed and extended to and including 19

Accepted 19 Owner

Broker Owner

-------FOLD ON DOTTED LINE FOR INSERTION IN RING BINDER-------

| FINANCIAL DETAILS | APARTMENT ☒ HOTEL ☐ ROOMING HOUSE ☐ MOTEL ☐ | | | |

APARTMENT ☒ **HOTEL** ☐ **ROOMING HOUSE** ☐ **MOTEL** ☐ ☐

(REAL ESTATE INVOLVED - WITH OR WITHOUT OUTSTANDING LEASE) **INFORMATIVE DATA** Office Listing No.

FINANCIAL DETAILS

Selling price (free of encumbrances)
$ **680,000** Terms **cash**
Mortgage not assumable

Payments include: Prin **X** Int **X** Taxes **X** Ins **X**
(Check items to be included in payments)
Interest on deferred payments $ **none** %

Fire ins. $ Ann'l prem $

Taxes last fiscal year $

ENCUMBRANCES **PAYABLE**
1st mtg. $ **481,647** Int **9** % **mo**
2nd mtg. $ **—** Int **—** %
Contr. bal. $ **—** Int **—** %
Delinquent taxes $ **none**
Municipal liens $ **none**

OPERATION
Gross annual income $ **106,667**
Gross annual outgo $ **34,000**
Net annual income $ **72,667**

CHATTELS
What included in this sale (check items involved)
Outstanding lease Furniture
Fixtures **X** Equipment
Goodwill Assumed Name
For details as to chattels included in sale:
See above See signed inventory
Are chattels fully paid for Are chattels mtg'd
Possession may be had **at closing.**

Name of property **Douglas Manor**
Location **2001 Century Drive, Urbandale, Anystate 00000**
Name of owner **Wendy Welloff** Tel **345-2020**
Owner has: Abstract Title Insurance Cert. of Title Contract Deed
Type of construction:

LEASE		HOW MANY		UTILITIES - METERS		DISTANCES	
Is lease outstanding? Yes No		Total No. of units **16**		Water **1** Gen Pvt. **16**		City center **2-1/2 mis**	
Name of lessor			Furn Un-F	Elect **1** Gen Pvt. **16**		Shopping center **1 mi**	
Name of lessee		1 bedrm. apt		Gas **1** Gen Pvt. **16**		Bus stop **in front**	
Date of lease 19		2 bedrm. apt	**8**			Grade school **6 blks**	
Expiration date 19		**3 bedrm. apt**	**8**	Phone Pub **1** Pvt Pay **X**		High School **8 blks**	
Monthly rent $		Rooms		Sewer **yes**		**University-1 mi**	
Are rents paid to date? Yes No				Heating **forced air**		**waterfront-6 blk**	
Any option to renew? Yes No		Baths	Pvt **16** Pub	Type **gas**			
If so, for how long		Showers	**24**	Refrigerators **yes**			
If so, for what rent $		Toilets	**24**	How Many **16**			
Rent paid in advance? Yes No		Elevator **yes**		Type **various**			
If so, how much $		Type **Otis-auto**		Ranges **yes**		**EMPLOYEES**	
Is lease otherwise secured?		Garage **Under-ade-**		How Many **16**		Operating help	
If so, how secured		**quate for 28 cars**		Type **various**		Maids	
				Garb Dis **16**		Janitors	
Can lessee assign without lessor's				Laundry Fac **Coin op**		Other	
consent? Yes No				**4 washers**			
				2 dryers			

Remarks **commission 6% on 1st 100,000; 4% in excess of $100,000, payable only on closing**

Listed by **H. Ardent**
Signs permitted **yes**
Will consider exchange for **much larger property** Inspected by

BROKER'S COPY

7711

*TO MAKE NON EXCLUSIVE Strike complete paragraph following asterisk in Employment Contract and have owner initial deletion

FIGURE 8-2
Real estate broker's employment contract

higher price and a shorter selling time. Commissions from cooperative sales are shared between the listing and selling broker, with a small percentage going to the MLS organization. In a typical MLS sale, the commission is shared as follows:

1. From 5 to 10 percent of the gross commission goes to the listing service to cover operating expenses and general overhead.
2. From 50 to 60 percent of the remainder goes to the selling broker.
3. From 40 to 50 percent (i.e., the balance) goes to the listing broker.

Assume a $1,000 commission with 5 percent going to the MLS organization and a 50–50 distribution of the remainder. The proceeds would be distributed as follows: $50 (5 percent of $1,000) to the listing bureau, $475 (50 percent of $950) to the broker effecting the sale, and $475 (50 percent of $950) to the broker who initiated the listing.

NET LISTING

A net listing is an agreement whereby an owner engages a broker to sell realty at a fixed or minimum price, with any excess to be considered as the broker's commission. A net listing is, therefore, a contract to obtain a minimum price for the owner. The broker usually adds the commission to the quoted net price. In some states the broker cannot lawfully obtain a compensation greater than the usual customary rate of compensation without the specific knowledge and consent of the owner. Because of the uncertainty of the agreed selling price, a net listing may give rise to a charge of fraud against the broker. This possibility is less with an experienced investor-owner than with a typical layperson homeowner.

Critical Issues in the Listing Agreement

As was mentioned, a listing contract must generally be in writing for a broker to collect a commission. Several additional critical issues must be resolved to create a fully satisfactory listing agreement.

ASKING PRICE

In self-interest, an owner wants the highest possible sale price and therefore prefers a high asking price. A broker ordinarily prefers to list a property at a price low enough to make a quick sale likely. A broker, however, as an agent in a fiduciary relationship, has a duty of keeping the principal informed of all material facts affecting the subject matter of the agency relationship. This duty includes providing knowledge of the market value of the property. In fact, the broker, as a real estate practitioner, has an obligation to document that any suggested listing price is not too low. Information from sales of comparable properties is one generally accepted way of documenting value. An owner is generally advised to list at a price above indicated market value, to take account of possible inflation in values and to retain room for bargaining. A property that sells too quickly may very well have been listed at too low a price.

RESERVATION OF RIGHT TO SELL

In an open listing, any broker selling the property is entitled to a commission; of course, the owner may personally sell the property and pay no commission. In an exclusive right-to-sell agreement, the listing broker is entitled to a commission if the property is sold by anyone, including the owner. An owner may retain a right to sell without a commission being required, however, in entering an exclusive right-to-sell agreement. The owner simply writes the names of the parties with whom negotiations have been or are being conducted into the contract as exceptions, along with a reservation of the right to sell to one of them without liability for a commission.

BROKER COMPENSATION

To an owner, the crucial number is the net sale price realized after payment of a sales commission. The most usual arrangement is for a broker to get some percentage of the selling price for a commission. Commission rates are largely set by local area custom. However, brokers are prohibited from collusion in setting commission rates, according to the Sherman and Clayton Antitrust Acts, which prohibit monopoly and agreements in restraint of trade. The anticollusion law means that brokers may charge what the traffic will bear, and owners are free to negotiate the amount of commission to be paid with the broker. Brokers may not, in turn, cite local agreement or custom as reasons for not cutting a commission.

The amount of commission, or method of determining the amount of commission, is best included in the listing agreement. It follows that flat and percentage commissions are possible, individually or in combination. Also, a net listing may be used.

Flat Commission. Some costs are almost certain to be incurred in selling any property. These costs include advertising, office expenses, broker's time, and overhead in general. Thus some flat amount, say, $1,000, might be justified, whether a small lot or a large house is sold. An owner may quickly determine the net amount to be realized from a sale when a flat commission is to be paid. For example,

Sale price	$100,000
Less brokerage commission	−6,000
Seller's net	$ 94,000

Percentage Commission. Brokers typically get 5–7 percent of the sale price as commission. Thus, a sale for $100,000 with a 6 percent commission would net a seller $94,000.

Sale price	$100,000
Less broker's "flat" commission	−1,000
Seller's net	$ 99,000

If a seller wants to net $100,000 from the property, the $100,000 would be 94 percent of the necessary gross sale price. To calculate the necessary sale price, the net amount would be divided by 0.94.

$$\frac{\$100,000}{0.94} = \$106,383$$

Six percent of $106,383 equals $6,383, when rounded to the nearest dollar.

Split Commission. A brokerage fee might also be negotiated on larger properties that would give a higher rate of commission up to a certain base amount, with a lower rate for any amount of sale price above the base amount. A flat fee plus a percentage might also be negotiated. For example, a commission of 6 percent on the first $100,000 plus 4 percent of any price in excess of $100,000 might be agreed to in listing a property. A sale for $640,000 would result in a commission of $27,600 under this arrangement:

Sale price			$640,000
Commission on first $100,000		$ 6,000	
Commission on price in excess of	$100,000		
Sale price	$640,000		
Less: Base	100,000		
Excess	$540,000		
At 4% gives commission of	× 4%	$21,600	
Total commission		$27,600	$ 27,600
Seller's net			$612,400

Assuming that the owner wants to net $640,000 from a property, the desired selling price would be calculated as follows:

Net + commission on base $100,000 = $94,000 + $6,000 = $100,000

$640,000 − $94,000 = $546,000

Incremental sale price to net additional $546,000		
at 4% rate = $546,000/0.96 = $568,750		568,750
Gross required sale price		$668,750

Proof		
Gross sale price		$668,750
Commission on first $100,000 @ 6%	$ 6,000	
$568,750 × 4%	22,750	
Minus total commission	$28,750	−28,750
Equals net sale price desired		$640,000

Net Listing/Residual Commission. A net listing means that the broker gets anything above the asking price stipulated by an owner. Net listings are illegal in some states because they invite fraud. Thus, a sale of a property for $750,000 for which the owner expected $640,000 would be almost prima facia evidence of disloyalty by the broker. The duties of loyalty and of keeping a principal informed would require the broker to make an owner aware that $640,000 was too low an asking price. An owner would have a strong case for avoiding the payment of $110,000 commission on a $750,000 sale, which calculates to 14.7 percent commission rate, far above the more usual 5–7 percent rates.

DURATION/TERMINATION OF THE AGREEMENT

A listing agreement may be terminated by action of the parties or by operation of the law. Actions of the parties that end the agreement include (1) mutual consent of the parties, (2) completion of the contract by sale, (3) time expiration or running out, (4) revocation by the principal, and (5) revocation or abandonment by the agent. Operation of the law ends the agreement upon (1) destruction of the property, as by fire, (2) death of the principal or agent, (3) legal insanity of principal or agent, and (4) bankruptcy of the principal or agent. If no time limit is specified, a listing agreement expires after a "reasonable time." A reasonable time might be 3 months for a one-family residence and from 6 months to 1 year for a large office building. An owner may terminate any time up to the start of performance by the broker if there were no consideration made by the broker.

An agreement for a fixed period expires at the end of the period unless an extension is arranged. Some agreements contain a clause for automatic renewal or extension, meaning that the listing continues unless terminated by written notice. Automatic extensions are generally deemed to be unfair to an owner and are actually illegal in some states.

BROKER PROOF OF PERFORMANCE

A broker must also perform according to the listing agreement to earn a commission. Generally, the broker's obligation is to produce a *ready, willing, and able buyer.* A purchaser acceptable to the seller or capable of meeting the seller's terms is such a buyer. The owner is not obligated to accept the offer of a third party even though the property is listed for sale. However, failure to complete a sale through fault of the owner does not cancel a commission. Such failure might result because of title defects, refusal of a spouse to sign a deed, fraud, inability to deliver possession within a reasonable time, owner change of mind, buyer–seller agreement to cancel, or owner insisting on terms not included in the listing agreement. In all these situations, a broker is entitled to a commission, whether or not the owner completes the sale to the aspiring purchaser.

An owner may include a "no-closing, no-commission" clause on a listing agreement. Such a clause means that, unless the transaction results in a conveyance of title, no commission need be paid. Also, courts are increasingly saying that a broker is better able to judge the ability of a buyer to obtain financing than is an owner. Therefore, a buyer is not "ready, willing and able," until adequate financing has been obtained.

GENERAL RULES ON EARNING COMMISSIONS

To recover commissions, the broker must (1) show an agreement or contract of employment, (2) be the *procuring cause* in the sale, (3) bring about the deal on the terms of his or her employer, (4) act in good faith, (5) produce an available purchaser who under the general rule is ready and willing to purchase and also legally able to do so, and (6) bring about a completed transaction. We have already seen that double employment or secret sharing in profits violates the requirement that the broker acts in good faith. The purchaser obtained by the broker must meet all the terms as stated by the seller, unless the seller is willing to modify them. The broker must successfully complete the agreement. He or she cannot abandon the negotiations and expect that if the parties, later and in good faith, get together and make a deal, a commission can be claimed. The employer must give the broker a fair chance to complete the transaction once it is commenced. But having done so, the owner may refuse to negotiate further through the broker and may take up the matter directly or through another broker. Mere introduction of the parties by a broker or initiation of negotiations does not commit the owner to deal forever with the aspiring purchaser through the broker.

WHO PAYS

An employer is liable for a commission in every case where performance has occurred. A broker's employer is usually the owner or the owner's representative. Buyers sometimes employ brokers to procure properties for them. With double employment, as was already noted, both principals may be liable for a commission. It is no violation of this rule for a potential purchaser to use a broker to locate a property with the understanding that any commission the broker is to receive shall be paid by the seller; of course, this means the broker acts as the owner's agent only.

Persons not owning the property, or those acting in a representative capacity, are personally liable for a commission if they employ a broker toward buying a property. It sometimes happens that such a purchaser assumes, in the contract, the seller's obligation to pay the broker's commission. Also, subagents, as salespersons, look to their principal, as a broker, as their employer, for their commissions.

COMMISSION ON AN INSTALLMENT SALE

Owners use installment sales to spread payments for a property over time to keep tax payments low. Brokers, as a condition of employment, may agree to accept commissions in proportion to principal cash payments received by a seller or his or her agent. Thus, the installment sales agreement might call for a 25 percent cash payment at closing with the balance to be paid in equal installments over a 3-year period. The balance would be secured by a purchase money mortgage loan. The broker under the listing agreement would receive only 25 percent of the total commission at closing and the balance in installments over the ensuing 3 years. Deferred commission payments are still the exception rather than the rule and, when agreed upon, rarely extend beyond a contract period of 5 years.

COMMISSIONS ON EXCHANGES, LOANS, AND LEASES

It is customary for all parties to an exchange to pay a commission based on the value or price of their respective properties. A statement in the exchange contract that each party shall pay the broker is sufficient notice to each for the broker to receive a double commission.

A broker is usually entitled to a commission for procuring a mortgage loan only if the loan is actually made. The commission may be earned if the broker procured a loan but it failed to close through a defect in the title to the property or through a fault of the borrower.

The rule on making commissions on leases is similar to that for procuring loans. The broker is not entitled to compensation unless a lease or a complete agreement on its terms is obtained. The broker would probably be entitled to a commission if the owner tried to impose new and unreasonable terms upon a prospective tenant and the lease was not made for that reason. Once a lease is made, the broker is entitled to a full commission, regardless of subsequent default by the tenant, unless, of course, the owner-broker agreement contains a clause to the contrary.

Commissions on percentage leases with a minimum rent required are usually paid as follows. An initial commission is paid when the lease is signed, based on the minimum rental. Further commissions are then payable at the end of each year, based on the percentage.

Selecting a Broker

Experienced real estate investors often buy through one broker and sell through another. In buying, these investors know that some brokers bargain/counsel owners down rather than negotiate buyers up, which is likely to result in lower purchase prices; hence, better buys may be made through them. Other brokers work very hard to get the highest possible prices for their principals and, hence, provide a strong advantage to owners in selling. The higher price may more than pay the broker's commission. Care in selecting a broker is therefore prudent. The decision is too important to leave it to chance, as by casually listing with a friend or relative.

Important considerations in selecting a broker are (1) office and agent specialization, (2) office location and procedures, (3) firm's attitude and reputation, and (4) a track record evidenced by satisfied clients. Names of promising firms and agents may be obtained from fellow property owners. Also, names of firms specializing in the types of property of concern may be obtained from classified ads and multiple-listing service listing books. Given several firm names, a survey to collect information necessary to making an informed selection is suggested. The first phase of the survey may be made by telephone. Later phases require personal contact.

1. Does your firm specialize in any particular property type? If so, what type?
2. Does your firm specialize in any particular areas or locations? If so, which locations?
3. What properties of _____ type were sold by your firm in the last 12 months?
4. I'd like to contact some of the former owners of properties sold through your office. Would you give me the names of several?
5. How long has your office/firm been in operation?
6. During what hours does your office/firm operate?
7. Are your phones covered during off hours? If so, how?
8. What are your commission rates? Are they open to negotiation?
9. What listings do you currently have in _____ type of properties? What is their age? For how long are they?
10. Is your office affiliated with the Multiple Listing Service?
11. Where does your office rank in its sales of _____ type properties relative to other firms/offices in this area/community? (Firm preferably is among the leaders.)
12. Do you personally own any properties of _____ type? If so, which are they?
13. Does your firm have a continuing agreement with any financial institutions that might facilitate obtaining loans in times of tight money? If so, what institutions? With whom might I talk at these institutions?
14. Who are your leading salespersons for _____ type properties? Does anyone clearly stand out above the others?
15. Is there anything else about your firm that you would like me to know?

FIGURE 8-3

Investor survey: questions for brokers or sales managers of firms

Much background knowledge may be obtained in making a survey, which is useful in the immediate selection as well as for long-term purposes. Thus, while the investor may have one type of property in mind at the moment, another type may be of concern later on. Also, once a survey has been made, the broker selection process may be short-circuited in later situations.

Figures 8-3 and 8-4 provide useful questions to ask in making such a survey. The sequence goes from the general to the specific, from the firm to the individual.

1. Do you specialize in any particular type of property?
2. If so, in what type? In what locations?
3. How long have you specialized in these types of property?
4. What properties of this type have you sold in the past 12 months?
5. What are the names of the former owners of these sold properties? I'd like to contact them for reference purposes.
6. Are you full time in real estate sales?
7. How long have you been licensed?
8. To what real estate organizations do you belong?
9. What real estate courses have you taken in the last 4 years?
10. Do you have any real estate designations? If so, what are they?
11. What real estate publications do you usually read?
12. Where do you rank in sales in your company? In sales of this type of property in the area?
13. What listings of property do you currently have?
14. Do you own any investment property? If so, of what type?
15. Do you have any other comments or information that I should be aware of about yourself or your firm?

FIGURE 8-4

Investor survey: questions for sales agents

At some point during an investor's survey it becomes apparent that the choice is really between two, three, or four firms. At this point the investor's concern should shift to selecting an agent, with an emphasis on specialization and performance. Suggested questions for a salesperson are given in Figure 8-4. Again, using a phone helps conserve time.

Eventually, the point is reached where the references of firms and agents still under consideration must be checked out. Visits to the firm's offices for interviews with agents and sales managers become necessary. Agents best measuring up to the "ideal agent" concept may be invited to the property. Each agent under consideration may then be asked to research the market as to the value of the property, how long a sale is likely to take, and so on. In responding to this situation, an agent is likely to reveal a great deal about his or her professional competence.

The responses may be compared as to probable sales value, consistency, and depth of analysis. Sales of comparable properties may be inspected as indicators of value. Conditions of sale may also be indicated by the agent, along with a marketing and advertising program. At some point, an owner-investor should be able to make an informed decision as to which agent-broker combination to select.

Questions for Review and Discussion

1. What is the law of agency?
2. What is a fiduciary relationship?
3. What duties does a principal owe an agent?
4. What duties does an agent owe a principal?
5. Identify and discuss at least four critical issues in listing a property from an owner's point of view.
6. List and discuss from an owner's point of view at least four important considerations in selecting a broker.
7. Identify and describe briefly at least four types of listing agreements; explain the use of each.
8. Outline and discuss the process suggested in this chapter for the selection of a broker.
9. Selecting and using the "right" broker in selling real estate may result in a benefit greater than the amount of a commission. Do you agree? Discuss.
10. Are there any advantages, from an investor's point of view, in using a broker as a buyer's agent in acquiring property, even though a commission would be required? Explain.

Case Problems

1. A property sells for $320,000. Calculate the commission
   a. At 5 percent
   b. At a split rate of 6 percent on the first $100,000 and 4 percent on anything in excess of $100,000

2. An owner wants to net $85,000 from the sale of a residence. What selling price would apply, assuming that the brokerage personnel were to realize a 7 percent commission?

3. Baker, a broker, was hired by way of a listing agreement to sell Angus's house. Baker showed the property to Marlboro. However, before a sale could be arranged, the following instances occurred.

    a. Angus died. The executor later sold the house to Marlboro directly, and refused to pay Baker a commission. Baker sued to collect a commission. What is the result?

    b. The house burned to the ground. Angus sold the lot and foundation to Marlboro shortly thereafter and refused to pay Baker a commission. Baker sued. What was the result?

    c. The listing expired. The next week, Angus sold the property to Marlboro and refused to pay a commission. Baker sued. What was the result?

    d. Angus rented the house to Marlboro during the last month of the listing agreement. The listing expired. Baker sued Angus for a commission, claiming to be the "procuring cause" for the lease. What resulted?

4. Victor contacted a real estate broker, Alfredo, to sell his ranch. No written listing agreement was made. Shortly thereafter, Alfredo mentioned Victor's interest in selling to Ivan, another broker but not a business associate of Alfredo. Ivan arranged a sale of the ranch. Alfredo now claims that Victor owes him a commission, because he was the "procuring cause" of the sale. Is a commission owed? Why or why not?

9

Brokerage Operations and Practices

Nature magically suits a man to his fortunes, by making them the fruit of his character.

Ralph Waldo Emerson, *Conduct of Life: Fate*

Brokerage is the marketing part of the real estate business. Brokerage personnel provide a critical service as catalysts or lubricants in the real estate market. Successful brokerage requires mastering "on the job" skills such as listing, selling, and self-management or "putting it all together," as discussed herein.

The approach taken in this chapter is to provide an overview of the work performed by brokers and the function they fulfill. Subsequently, subfunctions—listing, sales, and advertising—are taken up.

Important Topics or Decision Areas Covered in this Chapter

Key Concepts Introduced in this Chapter

AIDA	**Name advertising**
Canvassing	**Prospecting**
Closing	**Puffing**
Institutional advertising	**Specific advertising**

The Brokerage Function

Brokerage is the bringing together of buyers and sellers in return for a commission. See Figure 9-1. A brokerage office typically engages several sales agents. Thus, there is the need for a broker to be both a manager and a negotiator to successfully market real estate on a continuing basis.

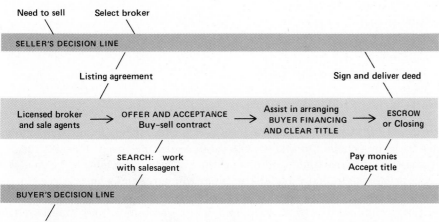

FIGURE 9-1
Brokerage and the Real Estate Transaction

WHY BROKERAGE?

People do not pay large brokerage commissions without reasons. This raises the question: Why is brokerage so widely used in real estate rather than other methods of marketing? The reasons go back to the nature of real estate as an asset.

1. *High value.* A parcel of real estate generally has high value. It is just not feasible for someone to maintain an inventory of properties waiting for buyers, as is done with cars, refrigerators, and other commodities; the cost would be too great.
2. *Fixed, unique asset.* Each parcel is unique because of its location and generally because of its improvements. A potential buyer would have to visit many properties to find the one that fits his or her specific need. Stated another way, sellers would have to show each property many times until the right buyer came along. Brokers, as specialists in information, simplify a complex and difficult search problem for buyers and sellers, thereby making the market more efficient.
3. *Financing needed.* Third-party lenders are usually needed to finance the purchase of real estate, because of its high value. Brokers frequently assist buyers in arranging such financing.

THE BROKER AS A MANAGER

A broker must first organize his or her own time. In addition, a broker with a large operation and many personnel must set up and establish organizational procedures. Attending to the details involved requires considerable managerial ability, attention to office procedures, and decision-making ability.

The Real Estate Office. Real estate offices are of many kinds and sizes. A few specialize in distinct lines of work, but many of them attempt to transact all kinds of business. Larger, well-rounded offices, with separate departments, each composed of an executive and various subordinates, are often found in major cities. Larger firms often provide several, or all, of the following functions:

1. Appraising
2. Brokerage (property, mortgage, and exchange)
3. Counseling
4. Development and construction
5. Insurance
6. Management and leasing

The Real Estate Organization. Each department has its own functions, but all are basically engaged in selling ownership equity, or space. The small office usually consists of the "manager" and one or more sales personnel. The large office expands this organization. Naturally, the ambition of many sales agents is to work up to an executive position and possibly to establish his or her own office. The broker-manager must obtain business, retain and train personnel, and maintain the organization.

Following Through. The broker is the originator or source of drive in almost every organization. Sales and other office personnel attend to details, but the broker, through his or her organizational ability, must see that the details are taken care of for each transaction of the business. The broker's skill and persistence in following through on matters of listing, finance, insurance, accounting, property management, and closings provide the key to customer satisfaction and to success.

THE BROKER AS A NEGOTIATOR

The basic function in brokerage is negotiation between buyers and sellers. In day-to-day operations, listing a property at a reasonable asking price is as great a challenge as selling the property. The objective in either case is to persuade another person, or other persons, to make a major decision about value and property ownership. Working arrangements must be negotiated with office personnel on a continuing basis as well as with other offices.

Basic qualifications for negotiations include being clean and neat in appearance, being reasonably well dressed, and conducting oneself with self-confidence. Tact, good judgement, and reasonable knowledge of property and laws are equally important qualifications. Important points of negotiating strategy that brokerage personnel should keep in mind as they seek to list or to sell property are shown in Figure 9-2.

---

1. Do not offer a property without having looked at it personally. You cannot sell what you do not know. You cannot know improved real estate without having inspected it thoroughly.
2. Analyze the property; know enough that you can answer almost any question about it. Get your thoughts down on paper because most read better than they listen.
3. Do not offer a property without clearly having thought out your presentation.
4. Talk to prospects in their own language. Never talk down to them.
5. Always try to please a prospect. A prospect does not have to deal with a broker or salesperson, and will not if irritated.
6. A prospect will not buy or sell unless he or she thinks it is personally advantageous. A prospect must be convinced that there is some good reason to act.
7. Do not lie or misstate. Almost all prospects are on the lookout for misstatements. You are finished the instant a prospect detects your making misstatements.
8. Never argue. You may be right, but you are still likely to lose the sale.
9. Get the prospect to the property as soon as possible. If more than one prospect, for instance, a husband and wife, get them there together; do not handle them separately.
10. Concentrate on a few prospects rather than working a little with many and closing none.
11. Speak with discretion, and give your client ample opportunity to ask questions. Know when to stop talking so as not to talk yourself out of a sale.
12. Use the telephone to save time and steps. But, bear in mind that if an issue is critical, a personal interview is better.
13. Never fail to submit an offer. It is not your function to turn down an offer for an owner. You cannot be absolutely sure of what a principal has in mind. Ridiculous offers are sometimes accepted.
14. Look for business at all times. Many listings are picked up while an agent is working on something else.
15. Most prospects are busy people. Do not waste their time.
16. Do not worry about competitors. You will get your share of business if you work intelligently and diligently.
17. Never assume anything. Overconfidence has lost many a sale.

FIGURE 9-2
Negotiations strategy for brokerage personnel

The Listing Process

A successful and continuing brokerage program must (1) obtain, (2) service, and (3) sell listings. The first two are discussed in this section; the third is discussed in the next.

Listings may be secured by brokers and sales personnel from many sources. The most usual sources are (1) repeat business or referrals from satisfied customers; (2) friends and acquaintances, for example, fellow members of clubs and organizations; (3) "for sale by owner" leads; (4) expiring listings of competing brokers, noted through a multiple listing pool; (5) leads based on births, deaths, marriages, promotions, or corporate transfers picked up from newspapers; (6) solicited office drop-ins of owners desiring to sell; and (7) *canvassing*, or contacting property owners by telephone or in person without a prior appointment. Leads to a possible listing opportunity must be followed up promptly.

OBTAINING THE LISTING

An owner must make at least the following four decisions in listing a property for sale:

1. The advantages of listing, using a broker, are worth the brokerage fee or commission to be paid upon sale of the property.
2. The advantages of listing with one particular broker, your firm, are greater than the advantages of listing with any other broker.
3. Setting the listing price.
4. The length of time to be allowed the broker to find a buyer.

Advantages of Listing. To an owner, the main advantage of listing a property for sale are (1) obtaining an objective negotiator, (2) professional assistance and service, (3) technical knowledge, and (4) broker cooperation.

A broker or sales agent can negotiate the sale without personal involvement. In any sale, and particularly in the sale of a home, a seller often has strong feelings about the property and its worth. These feelings make direct negotiations with a buyer very difficult. In addition, not all people are skilled negotiators. Many owners try to sell their own homes and fail because they are unable to negotiate effectively with potential buyers. Personal contact with owners often creates deep-rooted resistance in the prospect. Eventually, many owners give up and list their properties with brokers.

Owners also recognize that brokers render professional assistance and service in selling properties. Professional assistance includes items such as advice on preparing the property to get a higher price and quicker sale and on advertising. Service items include screening out unqualified prospects, showing the property to its best advantage, and being present when a prospect visits the listed property. Looking after a property if the owner is out of town or has moved to another community is also a service.

Brokerage personnel generally have better technical knowledge than do owners. Brokers know the real estate market and financing better. A broker's knowledge of sources of mortgage money is particularly useful in times of tight money.

Another major reason that owners engage brokers is that they give greater market exposure through broker cooperation, which is especially true of brokers who belong to multiple-listing services. Increasing the number of brokers, and people, who know about the property increases the likely sale price and shortens the time required for sale.

Specific Broker Advantages. Owners must decide whether or not the advantages of listing with one specific broker outweigh the advantages of listing with other brokers. The advantages of listing with a specific broker may be greater knowledge, better service, or more effective promotion and sales ability. A broker's reputation for professional, competent handling of listings helps greatly in obtaining listings. The broker's, or sales agent's, task in obtaining a listing is to convince the owner that the broker's firm can do a better job of selling the property than anyone else can.

The Listing Price. It is important that a property be listed at a price not greatly in excess of its market value. Every owner wants to sell his or her property for as much as possible. At the same time, almost all owners recognize that they are limited by market competition as to how much they will actually realize from their property. Very few owners know the market value of their properties. Usually, if they do have a value in mind, it may be well above the property's market value. Prudent brokers will not spend much time or effort promoting a property that is listed at a price greatly in excess of its market value.

An experienced broker usually has a fair idea of the most probable selling price or market value of a property, even as the listing is obtained. Even so, professional brokers use the principles of valuation, explained in later chapters, to advise owners on reasonable listing prices for their properties. These brokers do not rely on the owner's statement, "Let's list at my price, and I can always come down." Rather, they make a strong effort to persuade the owner to list at a price at which a sale can be made, relying on the adage, "a property well listed is half sold."

The Listing Term. A listing agreement may be written to run from 1 day to 1 year or more. Brokers prefer that a single-family house listing run for a minimum of 3 or 4 months to allow time for a reasonable promotion and sales effort. Usually, the larger and more valuable the property, the longer is the desired listing time. Some multiple-listing boards have minimum listing periods.

Obtain Accurate Listing Information. All information likely to help sell a property should be obtained when the property is listed. The listing contract is a major contract, and leaving a good impression with an owner is important. Thorough inspection, accurate measurement, and full and complete disclosure of all important facts at the time of listing are excellent ways to impress an owner of professional competence. A listing form usually provides space for specific items, such as the following ones:

1. Lot dimensions (frontage and depth) and area
2. Building dimensions and area or volume

3. Number and sizes of rooms
4. Kind of construction
5. Age and condition of structures
6. Equipment data (heat, water, electricity)
7. Financing offered by owner
8. Neighborhood data
9. Zoning (very important for vacant land)
10. Tax data

Additional items should be noted if they pertain directly to the sale of the property.

SERVICING THE LISTING

Owners select brokers more on the basis of their sales results and of service offered than for any other reason. A reputation for sales and service performance must be earned. Clear communication at the following times greatly helps to establish such a reputation.

1. *Initial communication.* Owner-seller should be specifically informed as to what services are to be provided, who will provide each service, and why the services are necessary at time of listing.
2. *Continuing communication.* Owner-sellers should be advised as to what services are rendered and what results are to be expected. Personal contact (setting up showings of the listed property and explaining the results of a showing) are particularly important.
3. *Periodic review and recommendation.* A listed property not sold within a reasonable time requires a discussion between the owner and the broker. The history of the listing and selling prices of comparable properties or houses should be reviewed. The broker or sales agent should have recommendations in mind before the review. This review typically takes place just before the expiration of the listing. If initial and continuing communications have been clear, and if all services have been performed, the owner should be receptive to extending the listing and following other suggestions.

Selling the Listed Property

Successful selling of listed properties involves three essential steps: (1) prospecting, (2) presenting and negotiating, and (3) closing. A broker and any sales agent must continually sell themselves, and the property, throughout the sales process.

PROSPECTING

A broker's task is to sell properties once they have been listed. A sale cannot be made until someone is located who might be interested in the property. Locating potential buyers is called *prospecting.*

Several methods are used to located prospects, the most widely used of which is advertising the property. Advertising is so important to locating prospects that the last major section of this chapter is devoted to the classes, methods, and principles of advertising.

Other methods of locating prospects are used. For example, a well-run brokerage office maintains a file of properties wanted in addition to the listing of properties for sale. Every time an inquiry comes in for property that the office cannot supply, a memorandum of that fact and the details of the location, kind, etc. of the property desired should be noted. Whenever a listing of property for sale comes into the office, a check can be made in a short time.

A second most likely source of prospects for many properties is the tenants in a building. They usually do not want to move, and there is always the chance that the new owner may wish to occupy their unit. This is particularly true of business property. The broker or salesperson should therefore interview the tenant or tenants immediately upon listing a property. If none of the tenants wants to buy, neighborhood tenants should be canvassed. One of them may be persuaded to stop paying rent and become an owner.

Finally, personal contacts are important and helpful in finding prospects. Friends who know that a broker is capable are likely to refer prospects to him or her. The same is true of old customers if they know that a broker is reliable and industrious. Brokers and sales agents are therefore wise to promote their listings among friends and old customers.

PRESENTING AND NEGOTIATING

Prospecting leads to negotiations, which begin once the initial contact has been made. The contact may be the result of an advertisement and comes in the way of a telephone call or an office drop-in.

A prospect must be carefully studied to determine whether he or she is serious or merely a looker. An experienced salesperson can usually determine whether the prospect is serious or not early in the interview. Considerations such as urgency to move, newness to the community, or a recent birth in a family indicate serious intent. Time should not be wasted on a looker.

The broker must be a keen student of human nature. The first contact with a prospect is often brief; in many instances the first impressions and analysis must be made in a few minutes. Older and more experienced brokers sometimes seem to have a sixth sense. In reality, it is merely the ability to judge the prospect quickly and with a minimum of error.

Some prospects harbor an inner fear of brokers. This fear is an internal defense against the power of persuasion or selling ability that may lead the prospect to a premature decision or a disadvantageous position in the negotiations. This fear is generally no longer warranted, or justified, because of improved brokerage practices and ethics.

Almost all established brokers are conscious of the benefits that arise from satisfied customers and community good will. Thus, efforts are made to sell the customer what is needed and affordable. The broker is foolish to allow a customer to contract to purchase a home beyond the customer's means. If nothing more, it only results in the customer's failing to qualify for a mortgage loan; or, if the customer does get title, he or she later becomes unable to carry the property and loses it, creating ill will. A considerate philosophy of negotiating is beneficially reflected in the increasing number of services that the broker is called upon to render for the property owner. Negotiating, when carried forth in a spirit of service, not only wins friends but aids in building a professional reputation that is essential to sound business growth and continued success for the broker.

Having classified the prospect, the sales agent next shows the property or properties. The initial presentation is to a large extent oral, but it must always be borne in mind that most people learn more by seeing than by hearing. Ordinarily, the sales agent should tell his or her story simply and truthfully, without exaggeration.

Use of the prospect's language is important. Few prospects are familiar with real estate terms, and some may be buying for the first time. The prospect should be taken out to the property as soon as possible, with full explanation of its advantages and disadvantages. A thorough knowledge of the property inspires confidence in the prospect.

Sales personnel may legally engage in puffing. *Puffing* is making positive statements and opinions about a property without misrepresenting facts and without an intent to deceive. The intent, of course, is to induce a purchase. Misstating facts is misrepresentation and the basis of fraud. Also, making superficial or inaccurate statements may cost the sale and injure the reputation of the brokerage firm. A salesperson should go into detail, describing structural or property limitations or faults in their true perspective. Good points, especially those that fit the prospect's needs or wants, should be stressed, with similar honesty.

It is usually helpful to have something in writing to show a prospect; this often takes the form of a property brief, which may be simple or complicated. If the subject of the transaction is an apartment house or office building, the brief may take the form of a pamphlet of several pages, including a description of the property, diagrams of the lot and the building, floor plans, elevation, information on nearness of mass transit, and a detailed financial setup of operating expense and income. If it is a one-family house, the property brief should give a diagram of the lot and of the house, photographs of the building, and a financial statement showing the operating expense reduced to an average monthly carrying charge. Almost all realty boards have a special form for this purpose. Placing the brief in the hands of prospects during the interview gives them something to look at that will probably be absorbed more readily than the sales agent's words. Further, prospects can take the property brief with them to study before making a decision.

A professional sales agent fits the presentation to the temperament of the prospect. In addition, the sales agent should seek out important facts about the prospect's occupation or business as early as possible in the negotiations. For example, approximate family income, marital status, number and ages of children, if any, interests outside his or her business, where and how he or she has previously lived, and church and club connections, if any, are all important items of information. A sales agent who has these facts in mind can more readily appeal to the prospect's situation. For example, if children are involved, he or she could say, "This is a safe, healthy place in which to bring up children," adding, if the children are of school age and the prospect is in the average income group, "The public schools are convenient and very good, and the trip to and from the school is safe."

CLOSING

Closing is the stage in the negotiations at which the prospect is finally persuaded to purchase a property; that is, when negotiations are brought to a conclusion. Much has been written on this subject, but as far as the salesperson is concerned, there are no set rules. Experience will teach him or her when to bring the matter to a head.

Rarely does the psychological moment to close arrive during the first interview. But, the time may be right during a second visit to the property while the sales agent and the prospect are standing in the living room of the home that is of interest. More often, several interviews may be necessary; in any event, there comes a time when the sales agent must frankly and tactfully bring the prospect to a decision. The trend of negotiations will usually indicate when the time is ripe.

The sales agent can learn to judge when to try to close by noting when the prospect has made the following key buying determinations: (1) recognition of the need for a new dwelling unit; (2) recognition of the unit most likely to fill the need; (3) acceptance, based on analysis, that the price is manageable; and (4) recognition that the time to decide is now. The sales agent, in continuing conversation with the prospect, must determine when the first three decisions have been made. When they have been made, then the sales agent's task is to persuade the prospect to make an offer to purchase the property.

Advertising Real Estate

Real estate prospects are usually found through advertising, though direct personal sales effort is needed to close the sale. Occasionally, a sales representative carries through an entire transaction without aid, but even here advertising almost always preceded the effort. Advertising is therefore clearly an essential element to successful brokerage.

CLASSES OF ADVERTISING

Real estate advertising falls into three general classes: (1) name, (2) institutional, and (3) specific.

Name Advertising. General or name advertising places the broker's name and business before the public; the purpose is to establish identity and location in the minds of potential clients or other brokers. When these people need real estate services, they are likely to recall the broker who advertised. *Name advertising* is not intended to sell or lease a specific piece of property or to obtain a mortgage loan on a certain home.

Name advertising often takes the form of professional cards in local papers. Occasionally, general advertising is used to indicate a specific aspect of real estate in which a broker is engaged. Examples would be small box advertisements. Advertisements often appear in real estate trade journals. Sometimes, several offices advertise as having a common specialty. Their objective is largely to establish a name and an identity with other brokers. Some brokers advertise in national real estate magazines, seeking to alert brokers in other areas who have prospects that desire to reside or to purchase investment property in the first broker's community.

Institutional Advertising. Advertising to create good will and confidence in real estate organizations or groups is known as *institutional advertising*. Such advertising is carried out by the National Association of Realtors®, by local real estate boards, and by other groups seeking to inspire interest in district, city, or a specialized area of real estate transactions and to direct business to member firms. The general public is likely to have greater confidence in an individual or firm governed by, or holding to, a code of ethics and business rules designed to protect its clients.

Specific Advertising. *Specific advertising* pertains to the promotion of a particular property or arrangement, which generally takes the form of a classified advertisement, though it may take the form of a sign or display. A news release is another means to get such information published. In any event, the purpose of such an ad or release, whether large or small, no matter where placed or how arranged, is to sell a specific piece or real estate, to secure a mortgage loan on a definite property, or to lease a particular location. The greatest individual effort is expended in direct or specific advertising.

ADVERTISING MEDIA

Many different types of advertising media merit attention by anyone engaged in brokerage and sales work. However, for our discussion, only four general classes of advertising media are recognized.

1. Newspapers
2. Billboards, signs, and posters, mainly outdoor
3. Direct mail, including pamphlets and circular letters
4. Miscellaneous

A survey to determine the effectiveness of various advertisements and promotions toward motivating home buyers was conducted by the Association of Newspaper Classified Advertising Managers. It covered 10 cities in all parts of the country, and disclosed the following:

1. Seventy-three percent of home buyers were motivated by newspaper advertisements.
2. Over 51 percent initially consulted real estate brokers.
3. Eight percent found the house through friends and neighbors.
4. Nine percent were motivated by open house signs, billboards, and other advertising sources.

ADVERTISING PRINCIPLES

Advertising is absorbed primarily through the eye. Newspapers, billboards, signs, window displays, and direct mail circulars must all produce a reaction when they are seen. Television and movie advertising are absorbed through the ear as well, and, of course, radio ads rely on the listener's ears only. In either case, the purpose of advertising is to initiate a chain of intended effects: (1) attention, (2) interest, (3) desire, and (4) action, coded *AIDA*.

The first intended effect is to catch the eye or to get attention. No matter how good the property offered may be, no matter how much care may have been taken in preparing the copy, no matter how important the message, unless the attention of the prospect is caught, the advertising is ineffective.

Second, the ad must arouse interest; the prospect's emotions or curiosity must be stimulated enough so that the entire message is read or heard. The copy, letter, or other advertising vehicle must be interesting and human.

Third, the ad must arouse desire. The desire for the property or service must be strong enough to cause the prospect to take the fourth step, action, by way of initiating contact with a sales agent. Once contact has been brought about, sales ability must take over.

ADVERTISING AGENCIES

Many brokerage firms engage advertising agencies to handle their needs, particularly in connection with major campaigns, such as promoting a large development or the auction of valuable properties. However, the expense of an agency is far too great for the average property.

Brokerage Trends

Real estate brokerage is fast becoming a part of the developing financial services industry. That is, the industry is changing from one of many small local firms to one dominated by a few national, full service firms. This change is largely due to recent advances in information processing, communications, and transportation. In other words, wider use of computers, of phones and other electronic communications, and of air travel have made national brokerage operations possible.

Computers are increasingly used to store information on properties, such as listing data, as well as to perform necessary calculations for analysis and for completing everyday transactions. Branch office information is readily transmitted over phone lines to other branch offices and to a national headquarters. Thus, referrals are easily made when executives and others are transferred from one community to another. The branch office selling a property for an owner is likely to have the trust and confidence of the owner. The office merely notifies a branch office in the new community of the seller's needs; the trust carries over. Alternatively, the original office may provide the seller with a listing of homes for sale in the new community before the seller makes the trip to the new community.

In a comparable fashion, data banks of commercial and investment properties for sale in the entire country are now provided by some national brokerage firms. Thus, an investor may view available properties from a brokerage office in his or her home community.

Sales agents are likely to find it highly advantageous to affiliate with firms that have the latest computer and communications equipment and that also provide necessary training as a result of this trend.

Questions for Review and Discussion

1. Explain the broker's function as a manager and as a negotiator.
2. Identify at least three key decisions an owner must make in listing a property.
3. Explain the real estate sales process from the viewpoint of the salesperson.
4. What are the three main advertising media used by brokers?
5. What steps or decisions must be made in purchasing realty?
6. What does AIDA means?
7. Name and explain at least four motives for buying real estate.
8. An owner wants to list a service station with a broker for $330,000, which is about $80,000 more than its market value. Should the broker accept the listing? If not, how might the broker best proceed? What about an interested buyer?
9. What advantages does selling through a broker offer an owner? What disadvantages? Should an owner always sell through a broker? Discuss.

10

Contracts for the Purchase and Sale of Real Estate

A verbal contract isn't worth the paper it's written on.
Samuel Goldwyn, movie executive

A *contract* is a voluntary and legally binding agreement between competent parties calling for them to do or not to do some legal act. A contract is also said to be a mutual set of promises to perform or not to perform some legal act. In making a contract, the parties create for themselves a set of rights and duties that are interpreted and enforced according to the law of contracts. A contract is created when the parties indicate their intention by their words or actions.

An expressed or explicit contract is created if words, spoken or written, lead to the agreement. Thus, a lease reached by a student answering a landlord's advertisement offering an apartment for rent at $500 per month is an expressed contract. A contract for the purchase and sale of real estate is also an expressed contract.

An implied contract is reached when actions lead up to the agreement, as when we step into a cab. Our entering the cab implies that we wish a ride for which we will pay; by allowing us into the cab, the driver implies that he or she will take us where we wish to go.

This chapter begins with a review of the essential elements of a legal contract; these elements are what makes the agreement legally binding. The emphasis then shifts to contracts for the sale of real property, with secondary emphasis on listing contracts and escrow agreements.

Important Topics or Decision Areas Covered in this Chapter

Essentials of a Valid Real Estate Contract
Legally Competent Parties
Offer and Acceptance: Mutual Agreement
Consideration
Legal Object
Written and Signed
The Uniform Commercial Code

Types of Sales Contracts
Earnest Money Form Contract
Binder
Installment Land Contract
Option

Components of a Form Contract
Earnest Money Receipt
Agreement to Purchase
Interim Handling of Earnest Money
Agreement to Sell
Forfeited Earnest Money

Remedies for Nonperformance
Buyer Remedies
Seller Remedies

Escrow Arrangements

Questions for Review and Discussion

Case Problems

Key Concepts Introduced in this Chapter

Assignment

Binder

Competent party

Consideration

Contract

Earnest money

Escrow

Installment contract

Liquidated damages

Option

Rider

Secured transaction

Uniform Commercial Code

Void contract

Voidable contract

Essentials of a Valid Real Estate Contract

As was mentioned, real estate contracts are subject to the Statute of Frauds. Under the statute, a contract for the sale or exchange of real estate must meet five criteria:

1. Legally competent parties
2. Bona fide offer and acceptance
3. Consideration
4. Legal object (including accurate property description)
5. Written and signed (some listing agreements are exceptions)

LEGALLY COMPETENT PARTIES

A legally *competent party* is a person qualified to enter into a binding contract. To begin with, a party must be of legal age, 18 years in most states, to be considered competent. A contract with a minor, a person not of legal age, is a *voidable contract,* meaning that it may be enforced or declared invalid at the option of the party that is a minor. A party must not be under some mental handicap that makes for incompetency.

Competence is also important when executors, administrators, trustees, people acting under a power of attorney, agents, and corporate officers are transacting real estate business. The people must have legal authority to perform their duties. These people have such rights and privileges only as contained in the legal instrument appointing them. For example, a corporation about to sell real estate must authorize its president or other officer, by resolution or bylaw, to execute the sales contract.

OFFER AND ACCEPTANCE: MUTUAL AGREEMENT

The entire purpose of a real estate contract is to bind the buyer and seller to do something at a future time. Written contracts are not needed to buy personal property that we pay for and then immediately take with us. But a real estate transaction is different. The seller claims ownership of the property, with good and marketable title, subject only to certain liens and encumbrances. None of these can be verified by a quick and simple examination of the property. The buyer must have the title searched and does not want to go to this expense unless the deal is relatively certain. The seller does not wish to remove the property from the market without a deposit and a commitment that binds the purchaser.

A writing safeguards the interests of both parties. Each promises to do certain things in the future: the seller to give possession and title, the buyer to pay the price in accordance with specified terms.

A contract is not created unless there is a meeting of the minds. The offer and acceptance in a real estate contract must therefore relate to a specific property. A mutual mistake or misunderstanding voids the contract. A *void contract* means that the agreement is not binding on either of the parties; thus, no contract was ever created.

CONSIDERATION

Consideration is the promise made or price paid from each party to the other. Consideration is also what each party receives or gives up in the agreement. The amount paid for a property is consideration from a buyer. The conveying of title, evidenced by a deed, is consideration from a seller.

Consideration must be given by both parties for an agreement to be legally binding. In other words, the promise by one party must be offset by an undertaking of the other. Each must undertake an obligation. A promise, even if made in writing, is not binding on its maker if there is no offsetting consideration. For example, Able, seeing his good friend, Baker, says to him, "Baker, I will give you my car tomorrow." Baker cannot enforce the delivery of the car. But if Able offers Baker the car if Baker will cease to use tobacco for 1 week, and Baker accepts, there is mutual consideration. If Baker performs, delivery of the car can be enforced.

LEGAL OBJECT

An enforceable agreement must contemplate the attainment of an objective not expressly forbidden by law or contrary to public policy. An agreement for the sale of realty to be used expressly for an illegal purpose is therefore void and unenforceable. An agreement, by which Charlie, a confirmed bachelor, promises David a house upon David's promise never to marry, is unenforceable in that it discourages marriage and is therefore considered against public policy.

WRITTEN AND SIGNED

Real estate contracts are governed by the Statute of Frauds of the state in which the subject property is located. The purpose of the Statute of Frauds is to avoid possible perjured testimony and fraudulent proofs in transactions of consequence. Thus, oral testimony is not admitted into court to alter the terms of a written real estate agreement.

Real estate contracts, to be enforceable, must therefore include the following points:

1. Signature of buyer or buyers
2. Signature of any and all owners or sellers
3. Spouse's signature (necessary to release marital rights as dower, homestead, or community property)
4. Proper written authority, as power of attorney when an agent signs for a principal

The contract should cover all points of agreements between the parties so that the provisions may be carried out without difficulty. A carelessly written contract may well give rise to disagreements, extended legal action, and much loss of time to all parties.

A real estate contract may be written by the parties themselves or by their attorneys. But, according to the Statute of Frauds, it must be complete on its face. Blank printed-form contracts are available and are widely used because almost all transactions are similar in nature and standard provisions therefore apply. There are, however, three problems in using blank printed forms: (1) What goes in the blanks? (2) Which clauses or provisions are not applicable and should be crossed out? (3) Which clauses or provisions, termed *riders*, need to be added?

The parties (usually buyer and seller) or their attorneys may prepare any contract or fill in the blanks on any printed forms. A property owner may prepare other legal documents connected with the handling of personal affairs. If form contracts are used, the parties usually initial near any additions or deletions.

A broker or salesperson may assist in completing a form contract only to the extent allowed by state law. In most states, brokerage personnel are not allowed to prepare other legal documents, such as deeds and mortgages. Finally, they are forbidden by law to give legal advice.

Real Estate Sales Contract Checklist

Items to include or facts to check

1. Date of contract.
2. Name and address of seller.
3. Is seller a citizen, of legal age, and competent?
4. Name of seller's spouse and whether that person is of legal age.
5. Name and address of purchaser.
6. Is the property description adequate? (Legal description preferred.)
7. The purchase price:
   a. Amount to be paid on signing of contract.
   b. Amount to be paid on acceptance by seller.
   c. Amount to be paid on delivery of deed.
   d. Purchaser's money mortgage, if any, and details thereof, including who is to draw it and who is to pay the expense thereof.
8. What kind of deed is to be delivered: full warranty, bargain and sale, special warranty, or quitclaim?
9. What agreement has been made with reference to any specific personal property (i.e., gas ranges, heaters, machinery, partitions, fixtures, coal, oil, wood, window shades, screens, carpets, rugs, hangings, or fire place irons)?
10. Is purchaser to assume or to take the property subject to the mortgage loan?
11. Are any exceptions or reservations to be inserted?
12. Are any special clauses to be inserted?
13. Are there any stipulations and agreements relative to tenancies and rights of persons in possession?
14. Is there compliance with all governmental regulations such as a zoning ordinance, building codes, sanitation laws?
15. Stipulations and agreements, if needed relative to the facts a survey would show such as party walls, encroachments, easements, and so forth.
16. What items are to be adjusted for at closing of title?
17. What is the name of the broker who brought about the sale, his or her address, the amount of the commission and who is to pay it, and whether or not a clause covering the foregoing facts is to be included?
18. Are any alterations or changes being made, or have they been made, in street lines, name, or grade?
19. Are condemnation or assessment proceedings contemplated or pending, or has an award been made?
20. Are there any covenants, restrictions, or consents affecting the title?
21. What is the place and date for the closing of title?
22. Is time of the essence in the contract?
23. Are any alterations to be made in the premises between the date of the contract and the date of closing?
24. What is the amount of fire and hazard insurance, the payment of premium, and the rights and obligations of parties in case of fire or damage to the premises from other causes during the contract period?

THE UNIFORM COMMERCIAL CODE

Sellers, buyers, and brokers must decide about the applicability of the Uniform Commercial Code to the transaction. The *Uniform Commercial Code* (UCC) is a set of laws governing the sale, financing, and security of personal property in secured transactions. A *secured transaction* is one in which a borrower or buyer pledges personal property to a lender or seller as collateral for a loan, with title remaining in a seller or lender until the loan is repaid. A secured transaction is often evidenced by a financing statement that is filed in the public record as evidence of the lender's interest or claim. Thus, in a sale of realty, fixtures, growing crops, and standing timber have the possibility of being regarded as security for a personal loan and as part of the subject property in the transaction. A financing statement, if properly recorded, would take precedence over a purchase contract and any deed-conveying title. A clear statement in the sales contract would reduce uncertainty as to intent.

Types of Sales Contracts

The sales contract holds an agreement together while the details are worked out. Neither the buyer nor the seller has assurance that the other can perform when the contract is drawn up. Time is needed to verify ownership, conditions of title, and the accuracy of representations concerning the property. Also, time is needed to arrange financing and to work out the mechanics of closing. The buyer and seller want to avoid the effort and expense of preparing for a title closing without assurance that the other party is bound to the agreement.

A property transfer may be arranged without a formal contract. A deed, conveying title, could be exchanged directly for cash or other consideration. Direct property transfers are most uncommon in practice, however, and are subject to many pitfalls, particularly from the buyer's viewpoint. The quantity and quality of an owner's interest in a property cannot be ascertained without title search, which takes a certain minimum time. For example, Able conveys ownership of a house to Baker by warranty deed; in fact, Able is merely a tenant in the house. The only rights Baker gets are those of a tenant, because Baker cannot get any rights that are greater than those possessed by Able, which in this case are those of a lessee. Baker might sue Able for damages and recovery of the money, of course; that is, if Able can be found.

Real estate buy–sell contracts take the forms of (1) an earnest money receipt, offer, and acceptance (for short-term transaction); (2) binder; (3) installment or land contract (for long-term transaction); and (4) option. Of these, the first, calling for a relatively immediate transfer of title, is the most common and most important.

EARNEST MONEY FORM CONTRACT

An earnest money receipt, offer, and acceptance is a special-purpose form contract. A typical form contract is shown in Figure 10-3. Because of its wide use, the earnest money form contract is taken up at length in the next section of this chapter.

The form contract gets its name from the general requirement of a cash payment, termed earnest money, expected of buyers when an offer is made on real estate. *Earnest money* is an initial deposit of money, or other consideration, made to evidence good faith in entering the agreement. Failure to live up to the proposed contract means forfeiture of the deposit. Typically, from 5 to 10 percent of the offered price is put up as earnest money.

Earnest money paid a broker, in almost all states, must be held in a special trust, or escrow, account and not comingled with personal funds of the broker. A separate account is not needed for each earnest money deposit received, however; one account for all funds is sufficient. But complete and accurate accounting records for each deposit must be kept.

BINDER

Some sales transaction are very involved and not suited to a standard form contract. Also, one of the parties may insist that the contract be drawn up by an attorney so that particular provisions may be included. In either case, the deal is nearly ready for agreement, but time is needed to draw up a formal contract. The transaction must be held together until the detailed contract can be written up and agreed to by both buyer and seller. The solution is a binder.

A _**binder**_ is a brief written agreement to enter into a longer written contract for the sale of real estate. The essential terms of the transaction and a brief description of the property are included along with a statement about the intent of the parties. A binder is, therefore, a valid contract, meeting the requirements of the Statute of Frauds. It is prepared in duplicate, with the buyer and seller each getting a copy. An attorney may then be contacted to prepare the more involved contract. If a broker is involved, a small earnest money deposit may be made by the buyer, for which a receipt is given. Also, a statement concerning the amount of a commission and who pays is usually included.

INSTALLMENT LAND CONTRACT

An _**installment contract,**_ widely termed a land contract, is a written agreement for the purchase of real estate that calls for occupancy by the buyer, who makes payments over an extended time (2 or more years) but with title remaining with the seller until the terms of the arrangement are satisfied. An installment land contract is also known as a contract for deed or an agreement of sale.

An installment contract may be used when the purchaser does not have sufficient cash to make a down payment acceptable to the seller. If title is transferred on a thin down payment, followed by default, the cost to the seller of regaining clear title may exceed the initial down payment. If the buyer is willing to pay the price in installments, a contract is drawn up specifying the amount and time of periodic payments. A land contract may also be used where a seller wishes to delay payment of taxes on capital gains realized in the sale. A completed installment land contract is shown in Figure 10-1.

OPTION

An _**option**_ is created when an owner agrees to sell property at a stipulated price to a certain buyer within a specified time, without the buyer's having to purchase. The tentative buyer pays a fee or price or gives some other consideration to obtain this right of purchase. An option is sometimes included as part of a lease; this combination is called a lease option. An option contains all the terms of a sale. An option is shown in Figure 10-2.

An option is used when a buyer is uncertain about whether or not to buy but is willing to pay something to the owner for the right to buy. For example, the buyer may be trying to purchase two or three different properties to assemble a larger property. Each owner gets paid for holding his or her property off the market for the agreed time. If the last owner refuses to sell for a reasonable price, of course, the buyer may not want to purchase any of the optioned parcels. The buyer, in this instance, loses the cost of the options. Another common use of the option is to purchase a portion of a large tract for development, with the right to buy additional acreage if the development program on the first parcel goes well.

FORM No. 854—CONTRACT—REAL ESTATE—Partial Payments—Deed in Escrow. STEVENS-NESS LAW PUBLISHING CO., PORTLAND, OR 97204

TT

38

CONTRACT—REAL ESTATE

THIS CONTRACT, Made this 31st day of February , 19 89 , between
Wendy Welloff, Unit 77, Condomium Towers, Urbandale, Anystate

, hereinafter called the seller,
and Gerald & Nancy Investor, 3278 Exotic Drive, Urbandale, Anystate 00000
, hereinafter called the buyer,

WITNESSETH: That in consideration of the mutual covenants and agreements herein contained, the seller agrees to sell unto the buyer and the buyer agrees to purchase from the seller all of the following described lands and premises situated in Rustic County, State of Anystate , to-wit:

Douglas Manor, 2001 Century Drive, Urbandale
(Lots 16 & 17, Block 3, Edgewood South Subdivision)

for the sum of Six Hundred Forty Thousand and no/100 Dollars ($ 640,000) (hereinafter called the purchase price) on account of which thirty two thousand and no/100 Dollars ($ 32,000) is paid on the execution hereof (the receipt of which hereby is acknowledged by the seller), and the remainder to be paid at the times and in amounts as follows, to-wit:

Equal installments of $7,402.40 on the first day of each month for sixty (60) months, at the end of which the buyer is to arrange financing for the remaining balance of five hundred thousand dollars ($500,000) from another source, for which title will be conveyed.

All of said purchase price may be paid at any time; all deferred balances shall bear interest at the rate of one (1) per cent per month from
March 1st, 1989 until paid, interest to be paid monthly and * in addition to being included in the minimum regular payments above required. Taxes on said premises for the current tax year shall be prorated between the parties hereto as of this date.

The buyer warrants to and covenants with the seller that the real property described in this contract is (B)
ª(A) primarily for buyer's personal, family, household or agricultural purposes,
(B) for an organization or (even if buyer is a natural person) is for business or commercial purposes other than agricultural purposes.

The buyer shall be entitled to possession of said lands on 1 March , 19 89 , and may retain such possession so long as he is not in default under the terms of this contract. The buyer agrees that at all times he will keep the buildings on said premises, now or hereafter erected, in good condition and repair and will not suffer or permit any waste or strip thereof; that he will keep said premises free from mechanic's and all other liens and save the seller harmless therefrom and reimburse seller for all costs and attorney's fees incurred by him in defending against any such liens; that he will pay all taxes hereafter levied against said property, as well as all water rents, public charges and municipal liens which hereafter lawfully may be imposed upon said premises, all promptly before the same or any part thereof become past due; that at buyer's expense, he will insure and keep insured all buildings now or hereafter erected on said premises against loss or damage by fire (with extended coverage) in an amount not less than $ in a company or companies satisfactory to the seller, with loss payable first to the seller and then to the buyer as their respective interests may appear and all policies of insurance to be delivered as soon as insured to the escrow agent hereinafter named. Now if the buyer shall fail to pay any such liens, costs, water rents, taxes, or charges or to procure and pay for such insurance, the seller may do so and any payment so made shall be added to and become a part of the debt secured by this contract and shall bear interest at the rate aforesaid, without waiver, however, of any right arising to the seller for buyer's breach of contract.

The seller has exhibited unto the buyer a title insurance policy insuring marketable title in and to said premises in the seller; seller's title has been examined by the buyer and is accepted and approved by him.

Contemporaneously herewith, the seller has executed a good and sufficient deed (the form of which hereby is approved by the buyer) conveying the above described real estate in fee simple unto the buyer, his heirs and assigns, free and clear of incumbrances as of the date hereof, excepting the easements, building and other restrictions now of record, if any, and none other

and has placed said deed, together with an executed copy of this contract and the title insurance policy mentioned above, in escrow with Hifidelity Escrow Services, Urbandale , escrow agent, with instructions to deliver said deed, together with the fire and title insurance policies, to the order of the buyer ,his heirs and assigns, upon the payment of the purchase price and full compliance by the buyer with the terms of this agreement. The buyer agrees to pay the balance of said purchase price and the respective installments thereof, promptly at the times provided therefor, to the said escrow agent for the use and benefit of the seller. The escrow fee of the escrow agent shall be paid by the seller and buyer in equal shares; the collection charges of said agent shall be paid by the buyer

(Continued on reverse)

*IMPORTANT NOTICE: Delete, by lining out, whichever phrase and whichever warranty (A) or (B) is not applicable. If warranty (A) is applicable and if the seller is a creditor, as such word is defined in the Truth-in-Lending Act and Regulation Z, the seller MUST comply with the Act and Regulation by making required disclosures; for this purpose, use Stevens-Ness Form No. 1308 or similar unless the contract will become a first lien to finance the purchase of a dwelling in which event use Stevens-Ness Form No. 1307 or similar.

FIGURE 10-1
An installment land contract

OPTION

KNOW ALL MEN BY THESE PRESENTS, *That* Wendy Welloff, Unit 77, Condominum Towers, Urbandale, Anystate 00000 *hereinafter called owner, in consideration of* Dollars ($ 20,000.00) *to owner paid by* P. O. Tential , *hereinafter called the purchaser, has given and granted and does hereby give and grant unto the said purchaser, his executors, administrators and assigns, the sole, exclusive and irrevocable option to and including midnight on* 30th *day of* November *, 19* 89 *, to purchase the following described property in the* city of Urbandale *, County of* Rustic *, State of* Anystate *Zip* 00000 *, to-wit:*

Douglas Manor, 2001 Century Drive
(Lots 16 and 17, Block 3, Edgewood South Subdivision)

at and for a purchase price of Seven Hundred Thousand *Dollars ($* 700,000 *) payable at the following times, to-wit: $* 50,000 additional *at the time the purchaser elects to purchase said property, said sum to be paid not later than the date above fixed for the expiration of this option;* $ 30,000 *of said purchase price to be paid* by November 30th *, 19* 89 *, and the balance to be paid as follows, to-wit:* $600,000 at closing hich is to be held on or before December 31st, 1989.

Within five (5) days after the purchaser elects to exercise this option and makes the first payment above provided, owner agrees to furnish said purchaser title insurance prepared by a reputable title insurance company insuring in the amount of said purchase price good marketable title in the owner free and clear of all incumbrances whatsoever excepting only as hereinafter stated. The purchaser shall have .... days after the delivery of said title insurance in which to examine same, and owner is to have thirty (30) days after written notice of defects is delivered to owner to remedy same.

Upon the payment of said purchase price, owner agrees to convey the above described property to the said purchaser by a good and sufficient deed containing covenants of general warranty, said property to be conveyed free of all incumbrances of every nature and description except easements of record filed as part of the subdivision

Owner further covenants and agrees to and with the said purchaser and to and with his heirs and assigns, that the undersigned are the owners of said property and have a valid right to sell and convey the same and to contract so to do.

Time is of the essence of this contract, and should the said purchaser fail for any reason whatsoever to elect to purchase said property on or before the expiration of the time above stated, then this contract shall be absolutely null and void and of no further force or effect.

DATED July 4th *, 19* 89

/s/Wendy Welloff
_____ OWNER   _____ OWNER

_____ OWNER   _____ OWNER

STATE OF _____ *, County of* _____ *) ss.* _____ *, 19* _____

Personally appeared the within named _____

and acknowledged the foregoing instrument to be _____ *voluntary act and deed.*

Before me: _____

[SEAL]   *Notary Public for* _____ **My Commission Expires** _____

FIGURE 10-2
An option to purchase

Components of a Form Contract

Figure 10-3 shows a completed earnest money receipt, offer, and acceptance form contract explained throughout this section. The form is designed to go with the flow of a transaction as it develops and is divided into six parts, A–F, as follows:

A. Earnest money receipt
B. Agreement to purchase
C. Buyer's and seller's agreement regarding earnest money deposit
D. Agreement to sell
E. Acknowledgment by buyer of seller's acceptance
F. Seller's closing instruction and agreement with broker regarding earnest money if forfeited.

The form must meet the five essentials discussed earlier, of course, to become a legal contract. It also automatically provides for the receipt for earnest money put up by the buyer in making the offer, for a seller's agreement to pay a commission in accepting, plus the type of deed to be used, the arrangement of financing, and the closing date and place. The purpose here is to identify and explain these elements as they occur in the transaction.

EARNEST MONEY RECEIPT

Before paying earnest money, a buyer wants the terms of the offer spelled out. Hence, the amount of consideration offered, the property description, the type of deed to be used, and the conditions related to financing are all stipulated in part A of our form contract.

The first five lines include the purchaser's name, the amount of the deposit, and the description of the property. In this case, the purchasers are Gerald and Nancy Investor. The amount of the earnest money is $32,000. By signing at the bottom of part A, Harvey Hustle, a sales representative of the Everready Realty Co., acknowledges getting $32,000 from the Investors, as evidenced by the opening words, "Received from."

Financing. The source of monies to finance the purchase price follows the legal description. The price offered is $640,000. The earnest money deposit is $32,000. The minimum conditional loan is $500,000. This means that the Investors will have to come up with an additional $108,000 in equity funds to see the transaction through. The offer is conditional on getting the $500,000 loan at 10 percent interest or less, with a life of 25 years or more and with monthly debt service. If any one of these conditions is not met, the buyer may withdraw from the transaction without penalty. On the other hand, if the seller can arrange financing that meets these conditions, the buyer must continue with the transaction.

Title Evidence and Deed. The first three paragraphs of the form pertain to title assurance and deed requirements. Paragraph 1 calls for title assurance by a title

EARNEST MONEY RECEIPT

FORM No. 671
Stevens-Ness Law Publishing Co
Portland, Oregon   TT

City Urbandale   State Anystate   November 28, 19 89

A. RECEIVED FROM   Gerald and Nancy Investor, husband and wife
(hereinafter called "purchaser") the sum of   Thirty-two thousand   Dollars ($ 32,000.00)
in the form of   check   as earnest money and in part payment for the purchase of the following described real estate situated in the City of Urbandale ,
County of Rustic , State of Anystate , to-wit: Douglas Manor, 2001 Century Drive
(Lots 16 and 17, Block 3, Edgewood South, Rustic County, Anystate)

which we have this day sold to said purchaser for the sum of   Six hundred forty thousand   Dollars ($ 640,000.00)
on the following terms, to-wit: The sum, hereinabove receipted for, of   Thirty-two thousand   Dollars ($ 32,000.00)
{ on owner's acceptance. (Strike whichever not applicable)
{ on   19   , as additional earnest money, the sum of
Upon acceptance of title and delivery of { deed (Strike whichever not applicable)   One hundred eight thousand   Dollars ($ 108,000.00)
Balance of   Dollars ($)
payable as follows   conditional on obtaining
mortgage loan for Five hundred thousand dollars ($500,000) or more, at ten (10)
percent interest or less, with a life of twenty five (25) years or more, with
monthly debt service; and no more than two points required to obtain financing.
Also, conditional on closing in escrow, with escrow costs shared equally between
seller and buyer.

1) A title insurance policy from a reliable company insuring marketable title in seller is to be furnished purchaser in due course at seller's expense; preliminary to closing, seller may furnish a title insurance company's title report showing its willingness to issue title insurance, which shall be conclusive evidence as to seller's record title.
2) It is agreed that if seller does not approve this sale within the period allowed broker below in which to secure seller's acceptance, or if the title to the said premises is not insurable or marketable, or cannot be made so within thirty days after notice containing a written statement of defects is delivered to seller, the said earnest money shall be refunded. But if said sale is approved by seller and title to the said premises is insurable or marketable and purchaser neglects or refuses to comply with any of said conditions within ten days after the said evidence of title is furnished and to make payments promptly, as hereinabove set forth, then the earnest money herein receipted for (including said additional earnest money) shall be forfeited and disposed of as stated in Section F below and this contract thereupon shall be of no further binding effect.
3) The property is to be conveyed by good and sufficient deed free and clear of all liens and encumbrances except zoning ordinances, building and use restrictions, reservations in Federal patents, easements of record and   none other, Title is to be conveyed by general warranty deed.
4) All irrigation, plumbing and heating fixtures and equipment (including stoker and oil tanks but excluding fireplace fixtures and equipment), water heaters, electric light fixtures, light bulbs and fluorescent lamps, bathroom fixtures, venetian blinds, drapery and curtain rods, window and door screens, storm doors and windows, attached linoleum, attached television antenna, all shrubs and trees and all fixtures except   No exceptions; stoves and refrigerators, one in each unit,
to be considered as fixtures
are to be left upon the premises as part of the property purchased. The following personal property is also included as a part of the property for said purchase price:
(Any personal property to be conveyed by separate bill of sale.)
5) Seller and purchaser agree to pro rate the taxes which are due and payable for the current tax year. Rents, interest, premiums for existing insurance and other matters shall be pro rated on a calendar year basis. Adjustments are to be made as of the date of the consummation of said sale or delivery of possession, whichever first occurs. Encumbrances to be discharged by seller may be paid at his option out of purchase money at date of closing.
6) Possession of said premises is to be delivered to purchaser on or before   Dec. 31, 19 80 , or as soon thereafter as existing laws and regulations will permit removal of tenants, if any. Time is the essence of this contract. This contract is binding upon the heirs, executors, administrators, successors and assigns of buyer and seller. However, the purchaser's rights herein are not assignable without written consent of seller. In any suit or action brought on this contract, the losing party therein agrees to pay the prevailing party therein (1) the prevailing party's reasonable attorney fees in such suit or action, to be fixed by the trial court, and (2) on appeal, if any, similar fees in the appellate court, to be fixed by the appellate court.

Address 41 East Third, Urbandale, Anystate   Everready Realty Co   ☐ Cooperating Broker ☐ Listing Broker
Phone 345-4321   By /s/ Harvey Hustle, Sales Representative

B.
AGREEMENT TO PURCHASE
We hereby agree to purchase and pay the price of $ 640,000   3:00 pm, November 28, 19 89   to purchase the property herein described in its present condition, as set forth above and grant to said agent
a period of   two   days hereafter to secure seller's acceptance hereof, during which period my offer shall not be subject to revocation. Said deed or contract to be in the name
of   Gerald I and Nancy O. Investor, husband and wife
Address 3278 Exotic Drive, Urbandale   Purchaser /s/ Gerald I. Investor
Phone 686-3343   /s/ Nancy O. Investor

C.
BUYER'S AND SELLER'S AGREEMENT RE DEPOSIT OF EARNEST MONEY   November 29, 19 89
The Earnest Money deposit in this transaction of $ 32,000.00 in the form stated above shall be deposited in the Client's Trust Account of the broker indicated above until this offer is accepted, whereupon the parties agree and direct that such funds be deposited (or retained) in the Client's Trust Account of   Everready Realty Co. , the listing broker to be held pending closing of this transaction.
/s/ Gerald I. Investor   Buyer   /s/ Wendy Welloff   Seller
/s/ Nancy O. Investor   Buyer   Seller

D.
AGREEMENT TO SELL   8:30 pm, November 29, 19 89
I hereby approve and accept the above sale for said price and on said terms and conditions and agree to consummate the same as stated.
Seller's Address   Condominium Towers, Unit 7,   Seller /s/ Wendy Welloff (widow)
Urbandale, Anystate   Phone 345-2020

E. Deliver promptly to buyer, either manually or by registered mail, a copy hereof showing seller's acceptance.
Buyer acknowledges receipt of the foregoing instrument bearing his signature and that of the seller showing acceptance 9:45 am Buyer /s/ Nancy O. Investor
Date November 30, 1980 /s/ Gerald I. Investor
| Copy hereof showing seller's signed acceptance sent buyer by registered mail to buyer's above address (return receipt requested) on   , 19
| Return receipt card received and attached to broker's copy   , 19

F.
SELLER'S CLOSING INSTRUCTIONS AND AGREEMENT WITH BROKER RE FORFEITED EARNEST MONEY   November 29, 19 89
I, the seller whose signature appears below, agree to pay forthwith to said broker a commission amounting to $ 27,600.00 for services rendered in this transaction. In the event that the buyer's deposit is forfeited pursuant to sub-paragraph 2, above, said forfeited deposit be disposed of between broker and seller in the following manner:
One third (1/3) to broker   ($10,667) and Two-thirds (2/3) to seller ($21,333)

Seller acknowledges receipt of a copy of this contract bearing signatures of seller and buyer named above.
Ivan Everready, Everready Realty Co. Broker /s/ Wendy Welloff   Seller
By /s/ Harvey Hustle, salesperson   Seller

7710

NOTE: IF ANY BLANK SPACES ARE INSUFFICIENT, USE S-N No. 810 "HANDY PAD", TO BE SEPARATELY SIGNED BY BUYER AND SELLER.   BROKER'S COPY - FILE IN DEAL ENVELOPE

FIGURE 10-3
Earnest money receipt and real estate contract

insurance policy to be provided to the buyer at the seller's expense. Paragraph 2 says that the seller must provide marketable title within 30 days of written notice or the earnest money is to be refunded to the buyer. Also, if the seller does not accept the offer, the earnest money reverts to the buyer. If, however, the seller accepts, and the buyer defaults, paragraph 2 says that the earnest money is to be forfeited by the buyer. Paragraph 3 specifies type of deed and types of acceptable loans. Paragraph 4 defines items borderline to being fixtures.

Prorations, Possession, and Assignment. Prorations of taxes, rents, interest, and so forth are provided for in paragraph 5. Also, the condition in the offer (typed in) says that the transaction must be closed in escrow, with the costs shared equally between buyer and seller.

Paragraph 6 calls for possession by the buyer on or before December 31, 1990. Prompt performance in accordance with the contract is required of the seller because the paragraph also states, "Time is of the essence." Finally, assignment of buyer's rights is allowed only with written consent of the seller. *Assignment* is the transfer of one's rights in a contract to another.

AGREEMENT TO PURCHASE

Part B contains an agreement to purchase the property "in its present condition" or "as is" for the price and under the conditions stated. By signing the contract, the Investors make an offer to buy under the terms outlined in part A, which may contain stipulations and contingency clauses to protect the prospective buyer. The binding words are, "We hereby agree to purchase and pay the price of $640,000." The offer is made at 3:00 P.M. on November 28, 19xx. The two-day limitation means that an acceptance by the owner before 3:00 P.M. on November 30, would immediately create a binding contract. The offer may be withdrawn by the buyer without obligation any time before it is accepted. An acceptance after the expiration time would really be an offer by the owner to sell under the specified terms and conditions.

The buyer is entitled to a copy of the offer immediately, as a record of the transaction.

INTERIM HANDLING OF EARNEST MONEY

The earnest money check must be cashed to protect the seller's and the broker's interests. Once cashed, what happens to the money? In part C of the contract, both the buyer and the seller agree that the $32,000 earnest money is to be held in the broker's client trust account until the contract is fulfilled or otherwise terminated. If a buyer and seller enter into a contract without a broker, the contract is likely to require that the money be held by an escrow officer.

AGREEMENT TO SELL

Part D provides for the seller's acceptance of the offer to purchase at the price, terms, and conditions stipulated by the buyer. The seller may refuse to accept if the price and terms are not satisfactory, or the seller may make a counteroffer. If no major change from the initial offer is involved, the counteroffer may be written in on the same form. A major change would necessitate a completely new contract. In this example, Wendy Welloff, the owner, accepts the offer of the Investors at 8:30 P.M. on the day after the offer was initially made.

The contract is now complete and binding. The parties are competent. There is a bona fide offer and acceptance, with consideration by both. The object is legal, and both parties have signed. A copy is given to the seller as a record of the price and terms of the agreement. The buyer is entitled to a copy of the contract promptly after the seller signs it. Good brokerage practice requires that the buyer sign, acknowledging receipt of a copy of the contract, as shown in part E.

FORFEITED EARNEST MONEY

Part F shows the amount of the commission ($27,600) due the broker, Everready Realty, for negotiating the sale. However, if a forfeiture of earnest money occurs ($32,000), the split is to be one-third ($10,667) to the broker and two-thirds ($21,333) to the owner-seller. Forfeiture is prima facie evidence that the buyer is not ready, willing, and able to complete the transaction. The split gives the broker some relief for effort and expenses incurred in arranging the transaction. In turn, the owner-seller is entitled to compensation as the principal party in the transaction and also for holding the property off the market.

By signing part F, the parties make the contract complete on its face, even to the commission to be paid by the owner to the broker, and also to the split in case of forfeiture. This completeness eliminates the need to refer back to the listing agreement in closing the sale. This signing of part F takes place at the same time the agreement to sell, part D, is signed.

Remedies for Nonperformance

Failure of a buyer or a seller to perform on a contract is variously called breach of contract, nonperformance, or default. Remedies for failure to perform are available to the parties.

BUYER REMEDIES

A buyer has three alternative courses of action against a seller who is able but unwilling to fulfill a contract. First, the buyer may end the contract and recover the earnest money deposit plus any reasonable expense incurred, such as for examination of the title. Second, the buyer may sue for specific performance, which means that the seller is required to live up to the contract. Third, the buyer may sue the seller for damages. Damages would be the loss of the bargain or the difference between the market value of the property and the contract price. If a seller has acted in good faith, but is unable to perform, as by inability to convey clear title, the buyer's recovery in a suit for damages is likely to be minimal. Some contracts contain a liquidated damages clause to be invoked on nonperformance. *__Liquidated damages__* is the money to be paid (usually a dollar amount) for nonperformance as agreed by the parties when making up the contract.

SELLER REMEDIES

A seller has five alternative courses of action against a buyer who is able but unwilling to fulfill a contract. First, the seller may rescind or cancel the contract and return the earnest money deposit and all other payments received from the buyer. This, of course, is not very probable. Second, the seller may cancel the contract and keep the earnest money deposit and all payments received from the buyer. Third, the seller may tender a valid deed to the buyer, which, if refused, would provide the basis for a suit for the purchase price. The deed must be offered to the buyer first to force the buyer to live up to the contract or to default. Fourth and fifth, the seller may sue the buyer for specific performance or for damages. Again, liquidated damages may be stipulated in the contract.

Escrow Arrangement

__Escrow__ is the depositing of money, of legal documents (deeds, mortgages, options, and the like), of other valuables, and of instructions with a neutral third party to be held until acts or conditions of a contract are performed or satisfied. Any contract may be placed in escrow. The parties to the contract make up the escrow agreement (separate from the contract that contains instructions for the escrow agent). The escrow agreement also states the duties and obligations of the parties to the contract and the overall requirements for completing the transaction. The escrow agent must perform his or her duties in a neutral or impartial manner. That is, the escrow agent must not be a party to the contract and must not be in a position to benefit in any way from the main contract, except for the escrow fee. Escrows are commonly used in the closing or settlement of a sale, an exchange, an installment sale, or a lease.

In a sale, the escrow agreement states all the terms to be performed by the seller and the buyer. The escrow holder is usually a title institution, an attorney, or a bank. Sometimes, at the signing of the escrow agreement, the buyer's cash and the seller's deed and the various other papers that are to be delivered by each are all turned over to the escrow holder, who, when the title search has been completed, makes the adjustments, holds the title instruments, and remits the amount due to the seller. Other escrow agreements provide for initial payment of the deposit only and for the seller and buyer later to deliver the papers and monies needed to consummate the transaction. A completed escrow instructions form is shown in Figure 10-4.

Usual requirements of a buyer and seller in closing a sale of real estate in escrow are as follows.

The buyer provides

1. The balance of the cash needed to close the transaction
2. Mortgage papers if a new mortgage is taken out
3. Other papers or documents as needed to complete the transaction

FORM No. 936
687 Stevens-Ness Law Publishing Co., Portland, Ore.

ESCROW INSTRUCTIONS

To: Hifidelity Escrow Services   Date   December 1st, 1989

221 N. Main

Urbandale, Anystate 00000

Re: Wendy Welloff   Gerald & Nancy Investor
         Seller   Buyer

Gentlemen:

The following checked items are enclosed for your use in closing the above transaction:

1. (x) Earnest money receipt
2. ( ) Exchange agreement
3. (x) Deed showing subject property description
4. (x) Previous title insurance covering subject property
5. (x) Fire insurance policy covering subject property
6. ( ) List of personal property included in sale
7. ( ) Rental list
8. ( ) Earnest money note executed by buyer
9. (x) Our check in the amount of $ 32,000 ....earnest money paid
10. ( ) ....
11. ( ) ....
12. ( ) ....
13. ( ) ....
14. ( ) ....

You are directed to:

a. (x) Pay Multiple Listing Bureau __5__ % of the commission
b. ( ) Pay ....% of the commission to ....
c. ( ) Pay ....% of the commission to ....
d. (x) Pay all commission (less MLB, if any), to I.M. Everready, Realtor ....

....
e. ( ) Have ....prepare contract of sale
f. (x) Order title insurance from Hifidelity Title Co. ....
g. (x) Pro-rate taxes, fire insurance, if any, and make necessary adjustments as of __closing date__
        Start interest on contract/trust deed or mortgage as of ....
h. (x) split escrow fee evenly between buyer and seller. ....
i. (x) payoff existing 1st mortgage w/ 1st National Bank of Rustic Co. and record release.
j. (x) collect additional money from buyer as necessary to complete settlement. ....
k. (x) take account of and adjust other fees and charges as appropriate. ....

Please call undersigned and/or Harvey Hustle ....should you need further information.

Very truly yours,

/s/ Ivan Everready

Receipt of above mentioned items and
instructions acknowledged.

Everready Realty Co.
41 East Third
Urbandale, Anystate 00000

By: /s/ Tom Barry

Telephone   345-4321

Form designed by
RUTH E. BEUTELL
MARION-POLK COUNTY ESCROW CO.
Salem, Oregon

FIGURE 10-4

Escrow instructions

The seller provides

1. Evidence of clear title (abstract, title insurance policy, or Torrens certificate)
2. Deed conveying title to the buyer
3. Hazard insurance policies, as appropriate
4. Statement from the holder of the existing mortgage specifying the amount of money needed to clear the mortgage
5. Any other documents or instruments needed to clear title and to complete the transaction

Instructions to the escrow agent contain authority to record the deed and the mortgage or deed of trust. When all conditions of the escrow agreement have been satisfied and clear title shows in the buyer's name, the escrow agent may disburse monies as provided in the instructions.

Advantages of an escrow closing include the following ones:

1. Neither buyer nor seller need be present at the closing of title.
2. The seller receives no money until the title is searched, found marketable, and is in the name of the buyer.
3. The seller has assurance that, if the title is found marketable, the contract will be carried out and monies will be forthcoming.

Questions for Review and Discussion

1. List and briefly explain the five essentials of a real estate sales contract. Might additional items be important in making up the contract? If so, what are some?
2. List and explain briefly the four types of real estate sales contracts, including the functions of each. How does a binder differ from a form contract?
3. In what ways in the Uniform Commercial Code of importance in real estate sales contracts?
4. List and explain at least three alternative remedies for the buyer and the seller upon nonperformance by the other.
5. Explain the nature and advantages of closing in escrow.
6. It is legally possible to sell a property without a written contract?
7. May an owner and a buyer make up a valid real estate sales contract without a broker or an attorney?
8. Must fixtures be specifically mentioned in a sales contract? Is there any reason to do so?
9. Give at least four examples of people not legally competent to make valid and binding contracts.

Case Problems

1. Martin enters into a written agreement to sell a tract of land to Beverly. The boundaries are stated in the agreement. After the closing, with full payment to

Martin, Martin discovers that the tract conveyed contained 10 acres rather than 5. Martin sues, contending that he had no intention of selling 10 acres to Beverly, that there was no meeting of the minds, and therefore that no contract existed. Can Martin get his land back? Why or why not?

2. Rita paid Steven $6,000 for a 90-day written option to buy Steven's farm. Thirty days later, a major highway improvement project is announced that will make the farm a prime location for a shopping center; the value increases tenfold. Steven refuses to convey title, claiming the consideration was insufficient. Rita sues. What result?

3. Joan agrees to sell her house to Jorge for $110,000; a written contract is made up. Subsequently, Joan decides she wants to keep her house and offers to return Jorge's earnest money. Jorge asks you what remedies are open to him. Explain his alternatives.

4. If Joan were agreeable to performing, and Jorge were not, what remedies are open to Joan in question 3 above?

11

Title Assurance and Title Transfer

Property is necessary but it is not necessary that it should remain forever in the same hands.

Remy de Gourmont, *French critic and novelist*

Having title to property means holding the elements that make up legal ownership. A person about to pay substantial monies for real estate wants the best possible title, usually called marketable title. Without marketable title, it is very difficult to sell for market value at a later time. This desire for high quality title is true even if ownership is to be obtained through inheritance or gift. Also lenders and lessees demand that an owner has marketable title to assure their position.

Marketable title means an ownership interest that is readily salable to a reasonable, intelligent, prudent, and interested buyer at market value. Ultimately, it means title of adequate quality for courts to require its acceptance by a purchaser, following a buy–sell agreement. The desire, of course, is for minimum risk of loss during ownership because of superior claims.

In addition, a prudent buyer wants the deed through which title is received to include the best possible assurance of valid title from the *grantor,* the person conveying title. Finally, our buyer wants the public records to be as current and clear as possible so that mistakes in title search and analysis are avoided.

The purpose of this chapter is to explain the ways and means by which marketable title is assured and transferred, with attention focused on the following critical concerns:

1. The tentative grantor must actually have an ownership interest in the property that can be conveyed. This means that the chain or history of ownership must run to the grantor.

2. The legal description must be accurate and complete.
3. Encumbrances against the property must neither preclude its use for the desired purposes nor hinder its reconveyance later.
4. Documentary evidence from experienced, competent, professional people must be provided so that the preceding conditions are satisfied. Adequate public records are a substantial part of the means by which documentary evidence is obtained.
5. The deed by which title is received gives the greatest possible assurances and protection to the recipient or grantee.

Important Topics or Decision Areas Covered in This Chapter

Methods of Transferring Title
Public Grant
Private Grant
Actions of Law

Title Evidence
Opinion or Certificate of Title
Title Insurance Policy
Torrens Certificate

Deeds
General Warranty Deed
Limited Warranty Deeds
Quitclaim Deed
Deeds of Trust and of Release
Miscellaneous Deeds

Essentials of a Valid Deed
Grantor and Grantee
Consideration
Words of Conveyance: Granting clause
Unique Description
Proper Execution
Delivery and Acceptance

Questions for Review and Discussion

Case Problems

Key Concepts Introduced in this Chapter

Abstract of title
Acceptance
Acknowledgment
Adverse possession, title by
Bargain and sale deed
Chain of title
Deed
Delivery
Devise
Donor/donee
General warranty deed

Grantor/grantee
Legacy
Marketable title
Quitclaim deed
Reliction/dereliction
Special warranty deed
Testate
Title evidence
Title insurance
Torrens system

Methods of Transferring Title

Transfer of title to real estate takes place in one of three general ways. Transfer, as used here, means the manner in which a change of ownership is directed, controlled, or brought about. For example, a will is a transfer arrangement to become effective at an owner's death, while a gift by deed may be effective immediately. Acquisition by an investor, of course, is usually through purchase. Other means of transferring title are covered here to make the reader fully aware of the alternatives open to an owner in acquiring and disposing of real estate. The actual conveyance of ownership from one person to another is by a deed. The three general ways title is transferred are by (1) public grant; (2) private grant, as a voluntary act of an owner; and (3) action of law.

PUBLIC GRANT

The original public domain was transferred to states, corporations (primarily railroads), and individuals by public grants to open up the West. Railroads were granted ownership to every other section for 6 miles on either side of any new line built. Under homestead laws, title was granted individuals or families after several years of occupancy and the making of improvements.

The federal government used patents in making the original public grants of ownership. A patent meant a conveyance or grant of real estate from the U.S. government to a private citizen or corporation. Thus, most private ownership in the United States traces back to the granting of a patent. Subsequent conveyances of ownership by grantees must conform to the laws of the state in which the land is located. For all practical purposes, patents are no longer being issued.

PRIVATE GRANT

An owner may voluntarily transfer property by (1) sale or exchange for consideration, (2) gift, and (3) will. Technically, in some states, a mortgage is also a voluntary title transfer; however, the owner retains the rights of possession and use, and the transfer is effectively only a lien on the title.

Transfer for Consideration. An owner may sell or otherwise agree to transfer any real property interest to another for consideration. A deed is used to actually convey the interest.

Transfer by Gift. An owner may transfer title by gift. The owner making the gift is termed a *donor*; the recipient is the *donee*. The transfer is not void because of lack of consideration. A donee, however, cannot enforce any covenants against the donor because of the lack of consideration.

Transfer by Will. A will, legally termed "a last will and testament," is a written instrument directing the voluntary conveyance of property upon the death of its owner, and not before. An owner may write a will, or have one drawn up, at any time before death. After making a will, an owner is free to draw up a new will, to sell, or to give the property away. The owner who makes a will is a testator. An owner, having a will, who dies, is termed a "decedent" and is said to have died *testate.*

The law requires certain formalities for the execution or carrying out of the will. The testator must be of legal age and mentally competent. The will must be written and signed. The will cannot cut off rights of a surviving spouse. In many states, two witnesses who have no interest in the will must acknowledge the signing. Upon the testator's death, the will must be submitted to probate court for judicial determination that it is the last will and testament of the decedent. Probate means to prove or establish the validity of the will left by a decedent. A probate court is a court specializing in wills and, when necessary, administering estates. If no valid objection is raised, the will is accepted for probate and entered into the public record.

The person empowered to carry out the terms and provisions of the will is an executor, also called a "personal representative" in some states. If a will does not name an executor, the probate court will appoint one. The executor settles the affairs of the decedent, which may involve selling off real property to raise cash for paying debts of the decedent or conveying property to designated people, organizations, or causes. The giving of real property under a will is a *devise*, and the recipient is a devisee. The giving of personal property under a will is a bequest or *legacy*, and the recipient is a legatee. An executor's deed is used to convey title to real property in probating a will and settling an estate.

ACTIONS OF LAW

Transfer by Descent.   Transfer of ownership by descent comes about when an owner dies without a will, or *intestate.* Owned property passes to certain relatives, termed heirs or distributees, of the decedent according to specific state statutes of descent and distribution. The rights of the surviving spouse are always protected by dower, community property, or "intestate share" laws, as they apply. A surviving spouse usually gets the entire estate in the absence of other surviving blood relatives of the decedent. Offspring, or lineal descendents of the deceased, share along with the spouse. If no offspring exist, parents of the decedent are next in line to inherit. Subsequent to parents come brothers and sisters, termed collateral heirs. If no heirs exist, the property goes to the state, by escheat.

The affairs of a decedent who dies intestate are settled by an administrator (in some states, personal representative) who is appointed by a probate court. Generally, close relatives to the decedent are selected as administrators. The job of the administrator is essentially the same as that of an executor. Any real property sold is conveyed with an administrator's deed, which is exactly comparable to an executor's deed.

Transfer by Lien Enforcement.   Failure of an owner to meet the obligations of a lien gives the creditor the right to enforce the lien. Thus, properties are sold as a result of mortgage default, unpaid taxes, unpaid assessments, or not meeting other lien obligations.

Transfer by Adverse Possession.   Title may be seized or taken from an owner of record who fails to maintain possession and control of the premises under a process known as ***adverse possession.*** In a few states, this is called "title by prescription." Title by adverse possession is particularly important in boundary disputes. Conditions for gaining title by adverse occupancy are generally that the possession must be

1. Actual and open
2. Notorious
3. Exclusive of the true owner
4. Uninterrupted
5. Hostile to the interests of the true owner
6. Under written claim of title [or payment of taxes]
7. For a prescriptive period as required by law

Actual, open, and notorious means the land has been occupied and used just as a typical owner would use it. The true owner must not use the property at the same time; exclusiveness is lost if this is the case. The use must not serve the interests of the true owner in some way. The prescriptive period varies from state to state, but it generally runs from 10 to 20 years, which is long enough that an attentive owner has ample opportunity to defeat the developing claim; see Figure 11-1. When the posses-

STATE	Without color of title	With color of title	STATE	Without color of title	With color of title
Alabama	20	10	Montana	—[a]	5
Alaska	10	7	Nebraska	10	10
Arizona	10	3	Nevada	—[a]	5
Arkansas	15	7	New Hampshire	20	20
California	—[a]	5	New Jersey	60	30
Colorado	18	7	New Mexico	10	10
Connecticut	15	15	New York	10	10
Delaware	20	20	North Carolina	30	21
Florida	—[a]	7	North Dakota	20	10
Georgia	20	7	Ohio	21	21
Hawaii	20	20	Oklahoma	15	15
Idaho	5	5	Oregon	10	10
Illinois	20	7	Pennsylvania	21	21
Indiana	—[a]	10	Rhode Island	10	10
Iowa	10	10	South Carolina	20	10
Kansas	15	15	South Dakota	20	10
Kentucky	15	7	Tennessee	20	7
Louisiana	30	10	Texas	25	5
Maine	20	20	Utah	—[a]	7
Maryland	20	20	Vermont	15	15
Massachusetts	20	20	Virginia	15	15
Michigan	15	10	Washington	10	7
Minnesota	15	15	West Virginia	10	10
Mississippi	10	10	Wisconsin	20	10
Missouri	10	10	Wyoming	10	10

[a]In these states, title may not be gained by adverse possession except under color of title, which includes payment of property taxes. Note that in some states special circumstances may reduce the prescriptive period.

FIGURE 11-1

Time required to claim title by adverse possession, by state

sor pays taxes under "color of title," the prescriptive method may be as short as 5 years. Prescriptive, as used here, means according to legal precedent or established custom.

Prescriptive title may be converted into marketable title by an occupant able to prove that all these conditions have been met, which is called an action to quiet title. Considerable proof is required of the claimant.

Transfer by Condemnation. A governmental or quasi-governmental agency may acquire title to real estate, against the owner's will, for public uses or purposes under the right of eminent domain. Just compensation must be paid the owner.

Transfer by Confiscation. The taking of property by a government in time of war, without compensation, is confiscation. Traditionally, only property of enemies of the government is confiscated.

Transfer by Erosion. An owner gains title by erosion or accretion when additional soil is gradually brought to his or her property by natural causes, such as water or wind. The eroded soil must be deposited somewhere. However, the sudden breaking away of land from one owner and attachment to the land of another, as when a stream changes course, does not transfer ownership. Title may be gained by *reliction*, also termed dereliction, when waters gradually recede, leaving dry land; this, however, is not necessarily transfer of title.

Title Evidence

Documentary proof, termed *title evidence*, must be developed for prospective owners before title is considered marketable and acceptable. Title evidence takes three basic forms: (1) an attorney's opinion or certification, (2) a title insurance policy, and (3) a Torrens certificate. The first two are based on a proper legal description, a proper chain of title, and a search of the public records. A *chain of title* is the succession of all previous owners, back to some acceptable starting point. A deed by itself is not evidence of title; it contains no proof concerning the kind or the conditions of the grantor's title.

Some interpretation and judgment are often necessary even after evidence of title is provided by one of the three forms. For example, certain easements or deed restrictions may or may not be acceptable to a buyer; or, if an encroachment is suspected, a survey may have to be ordered. That is, an encroachment would not necessarily be brought to light by any of the three forms.

OPINION OR CERTIFICATE OF TITLE

A certification of title or an opinion that title is good is rendered by an attorney or other qualified person after examination of public records, an abstract of title, or other sources of information. Historically, the search and opinion were made by an attorney, who made up an informal abstract of title for personal use. But, in recent decades, other people, working for or through abstract companies, have qualified as abstractors and title analysts. If flaws or encumbrances stand in the way of clear title, they are listed as exceptions. An attorney's opinion of title is primarily used in rural areas of the United States. The trend is away from using attorneys' opinions, based on abstracts of title, as evidence of marketable title.

An abstract of title differs from chain of title. An **abstract of title** is a condensed, written history of all transactions and events affecting the ownership of a given property. A chain of title, on the other hand, is a theoretical construct of all previous holders of title; it is not written, and actions or claims of nonowners are not a part of it.

An abstract contains a listing of all documents bearing on quality of title and often includes summaries of important segments of the documents. Thus, such items as mortgages, wills, liens, deeds, foreclosure proceedings, tax sales, and other matters of record are noted. The information is arranged in chronological order, without any judgments made concerning the rights of the parties involved. A properly prepared abstract indicates the records examined, the period covered, and a certification that all matters of record are included and indexed against the owners in the chain of title.

Abstracts of title have largely replaced the traditional attorney's search of public records; that is, an attorney's opinion is increasingly based on the abstract only. Companies specialize in producing abstracts, based on records they maintain for the purpose. An abstract does not guarantee title. The attorney's interpretation is required for title to be certified as good or to point out significant flaws and/or encumbrances.

In practice, title and abstract companies, attorneys, and other title analysts assume that a title is good or marketable at some early date. An irritating and expensive duplication of work in successive title examinations is involved, nevertheless. Some meticulous attorneys want an examination carried back to an unreasonable date, as shown by the following example.

In a legal transaction involving transfer of property in New Orleans, La., a firm of New York lawyers retained a New Orleans attorney to search the title and to perform other related duties. The New Orleans attorney sent his findings, which traced title back to 1803. The New York lawyers examined his opinion and wrote again to the New Orleans lawyer, saying in effect that the opinion rendered by him was all very well, as far as it went, but that title prior to 1803 had not been satisfactorily documented.

The New Orleans attorney replied to the New York firm as follows:

> I acknowledge your letter inquiring as to the state of the title of the Canal Street property prior to 1803. Please be advised that in 1803 the United States of America acquired the territory of Louisiana from the Republic of France by purchase. The Republic of France acquired title from the Spanish Crown by conquest. The Spanish Crown had originally acquired title by virtue of the discoveries of one Christopher Columbus, sailor, who had been duly authorized to embark upon the voyage of discovery by Isabella, Queen of Spain. Isabella, before granting such authority, had obtained the sanction of His Holiness, the Pope; the Pope is the Vicar on Earth of Jesus Christ; Jesus Christ is the Son and Heir Apparent of God. God made Louisiana.

TITLE INSURANCE POLICY

Title insurance is protection against financial loss owing to flaws, encumbrances, and other defects in the title of realty that existed but were not known when the insurance policy was purchased. Therefore, title insurance is protection against events in the past rather than the future. The purchase of a policy simply shifts the risk of loss from a property owner or lender to the title insurance company. The premium or purchase price is only paid once, and the term is forever into the future. Title insurance, introduced in the late 1800s, currently provides ownership protection on more than half of all realty in the United States.

New owners and distant lenders increasingly prefer title insurance to an attorney's certification of title as evidence of marketable title for several reasons. To begin with, an attorney depends on an abstract, which may not disclose all possible defects of title. Further, an attorney's ability is uncertain. In either case, if a claim against the property is missed and subsequently proven, the purchaser or lender suffers rather than the attorney. For example, a forged deed does not wipe out a dower interest. Recovering damages from an attorney for an error or omission is extremely difficult and costly. Recovering losses from a previous owner is often impossible because of death or change in location. With title insurance, defects such as these are automatically insured against if not listed as exceptions in the title policy. Also, claims of loss are usually settled promptly. Remote lenders prefer title insurance because of the reputation and corporate integrity of title insurance companies, which, to the lenders, means quick, easy settlements.

The main limitation to title insurance, from an owner's point of view, is that the amount of coverage is fixed. Reimbursement is only to the face amount of the policy even though improvements were added or land values increased sharply after the policy was issued.

The Insurance Contract. Title insurance policies are usually made between the company and an owner (usually a new or purchasing owner), a lender, or a lessee. In return for the premium, the company contracts to reimburse or compensate against all losses caused by title defects other than those listed as exceptions in the policy. However, as is typical of all insurance contracts, a loss must be shown in order to collect. The insurance company also agrees to pay legal expenses necessary to protect an owner against a title lawsuit.

The main items insured against are as follows:

1. Flaws in the chain of title owing to forged documents, improper delivery of a deed, incompetence or lack of capacity of a grantor, or lack of signature of a spouse
2. Errors and omissions in the title search and examination owing to negligence or fraud by a company employee or owing to improper indexing of public records
3. Possible lack of acceptability of title to a subsequent intelligent, prudent buyer, who may be unwilling to accept some minor encumbrance not listed as an exception in the title insurance policy; for example, a shared driveway easement

Items that may not be covered, unless extended coverage is obtained at some additional cost, are as follows:

1. Defects disclosed by title examination and listed as exceptions to the policy
2. Defects that a survey or physical inspection of the property would disclose; examples are encroachments, rights of an adverse possessor, unrecorded

easements or leases, uncertain or incorrect boundary lines, and lack of access

3. Defects known to the insured though not listed as an exception. Examples are a recorded mortgage known to the insured but missed by the title analyst and a violation of a covenant or condition
4. Police power restrictions, which legally are not considered to make title unmarketable in any event
5. Mechanic's liens not on record at time of policy issue
6. Rights of parties in possession at time of title transfer

The coverage provided a mortgagee or lessee in a mortgagee's or lessee's policy is basically the same as the coverage provided an owner.

Obtaining Insurance. In a sales transaction, the seller or the broker usually arranges for the insurance that is to serve as evidence of clear title, from a title company. The title company frequently issues a preliminary title or informational report. The report lists the owner of record, unreleased liens, easements, restrictions of record, and other apparent encumbrances. The report indicates clouds that are likely to require removal. It is the seller's obligation to remove serious encumbrances or "clouds" on title that block marketable title, if any. After completing a reexamination of title, the title company issued a commitment to issue a title policy.

The commitment (1) names all parties involved, (2) gives the legal description of the property, (3) defines the interest or estate covered, and (4) lists terms and stipulations, including exceptions, of the policy. In a sale or refinancing, the policy is actually issued shortly after the closing when all pertinent documents have been recorded.

TORRENS CERTIFICATE

The *Torrens system* is a method of title registration in which clear title is established with a governmental agency, which later issues title certificates to owners as evidence of their claim. The Torrens system of title registration operates in a fashion very similar to that used by states for automobiles. Title is initially cleared and registered into the system on a voluntary basis, at which point a certificate of ownership is issued that serves as proof of title. Sales, mortgages, and other claims against the property must be registered to be effective; thus, the status of title may be determined at any time by checking with the registrar.

In theory, the Torrens system is ideal. But the high initial cost of registering a property in the system has worked against its wide acceptance. Also, some uncertainty about its operation exists because laws establishing Torren's registration vary from state to state. Hence, the Torrens system is not widely used.

Deeds

A *deed* is a legal instrument that, when properly executed and delivered, conveys title to, or ownership of, an interest in realty from a grantor to a grantee. By definition and in accordance with the Statute of Frauds, a deed must be written. Proper execution means being signed by the grantor (or grantors), attested to by a witness or by witnesses, in nearly every state, acknowledged by a notary public or other qualified officer, and, in some states, sealed. A seal is a particular sign or mark to indicate the formal execution and nature of the instrument.

The circumstances surrounding the conveyance of real property vary greatly from one transaction to another. Generally, a grantor prefers to minimize the quality of title conveyed, consistent with the transaction, to avoid future obligation or liability to the grantee. Consequently, deeds take many forms to reflect the kind and quality of conveyance intended.

Deeds are sometimes classed as statutory or nonstatutory. Statutory deeds are short forms of the deeds in which any covenants or warranties mentioned are stipulated by law, as though written out in full. Nonstatutory deeds are usually written for special purposes or situations; thus, only covenants, warranties, and terms included in the deed apply. The main statutory deeds are the general or full warranty, the limited warranty, and the quitclaim.

GENERAL WARRANTY DEED

A general warranty deed provides a grantee the most complete set of assurances of title possible from a grantor and is therefore most preferred by a grantee. The grantor covenants (or warrants) good title, free of encumbrances, except as noted, which the grantee should be able to enjoy quietly; and, if necessary, the grantor will protect the grantee against other claimants. A grantee may not receive a full warranty deed unless it is provided for in the sales agreement.

A *general warranty deed* commits the grantor to several covenants, which, though not stated in the deed, are binding on the grantor because of the deed's statutory basis. Thus, the grantor legally incurs a continuing future obligation by the covenants when certain words, stipulated by state law, appear in the deed. The statutes of each state must be examined to determine the exact stipulated words. Typical stipulated words indicating a warranty of deed are "warrant generally" or "convey and warrant." See Figure 11-2 for an illustration.

1. *Covenant of seizen.* The grantor claims and warrants that he or she holds, or is seized with, ownership of the subject property and the right to convey it. If this covenant is breached or broken, the grantee may recover from the grantor any losses or expense up to the consideration paid for the property.

2. *Covenant against encumbrances.* The grantor claims and warrants that the property title is free of encumbrances except as stated specifically in the deed. Thus, it is promised that there are no unmentioned liens, easements, or title restrictions. If an encumbrance does exist against the property, the grantee may recover any expenses incurred to remove it.

3. *Covenant of quiet enjoyment.* The grantor claims and warrants that the grantee will be able to quietly enjoy or not be disturbed in the use of the premises because the title conveyed is good and superior to that of any third person. If the grantee, or any subsequent grantee, is dispossessed by a superior title predating the conveyance, the grantor is legally liable for any damages or losses incurred. Threats and claims of superior title by outsiders do not constitute a breach of this covenant.

FORM No. 963—Stevens-Ness Law Publishing Co., Portland, Ore. 97204

TN

WARRANTY DEED—STATUTORY FORM
INDIVIDUAL GRANTOR

Wendy Welloff (widow)

....*Grantor,*

conveys and warrants to .... Gerald & Nancy Investor, husband and wife ....

....

....*Grantee, the following described real property free of encumbrances*

except as specifically set forth herein situated in .... Rustic ....*County, Oregon, to-wit:*

Lots 16 & 17, Edgewood South Subdivision

(IF SPACE INSUFFICIENT, CONTINUE DESCRIPTION ON REVERSE SIDE)

The said property is free from encumbrances except

easements of record in subdivision plot

The true consideration for this conveyance is $ ... 640,000 .... *(Here comply with the requirements of ORS 93.030)*

....

....

Dated this ...15th... *day of* December .... , 19 88 .

/s/Wendy Welloff

STATE OF OREGON, County of .. Rustic ....) ss. December 15 .... , 19 88

Personally appeared the above named .. Wendy Welloff ....

....*and acknowledged the foregoing instrument to be*..............*voluntary act and deed.*

Before me: /s/Alfred B. Culbertson

(OFFICIAL SEAL) *Notary Public for Oregon—My commission expires:* December 31, 1989

FIGURE 11-2
A general warranty deed (statutory form)

4. *Covenant of further assurance.* The grantor warrants that any other instrument needed to make the title good will be obtained and delivered to the grantee. Under this covenant, if a faulty legal description were given in the deed, the grantor would be obligated to prepare a new deed, containing the correct legal description, for the grantee. Enforcement of this covenant is under a suit for specific performance rather than for damages.

5. *Covenant of warranty of title.* The grantor warrants forever the title to the premises, with monetary compensation to the grantee for any fault in the title, in whole or in part. This covenant is an absolute guarantee to the grantee of title and possession of the premises.

The first two covenants relate to the past and apply only at the time of conveyance. The last three relate to the future and run with the land.

A warranty deed with covenants does not guarantee clear title. A grantor may be a complete fraud and plan to leave town immediately after collecting money from the sale, or valid claims against the title may be outstanding even though not pressed by legal action. Therefore, evidence of clear title, independent of a warranty deed, is desirable even with the use of a general warranty deed.

LIMITED WARRANTY DEEDS

A limited warranty deed is also known as a special warranty deed or a bargain and sale deed. The difference between the two is slight, from a layman's point of view.

A ***special warranty deed*** contains a single covenant that title has not been impaired, except as noted, by any acts of the grantor, which is a covenant against grantor's acts. This means that the grantor has liability only if the grantee is disturbed by a claim arising from or due to some act of the grantor during his or her ownership. A special warranty deed may be considered as a "quitclaim deed with a covenant." In turn, it gives a grantee much less protection than does a general warranty deed.

A ***bargain and sale deed*** gives slightly different assurances in that the grantor asserts ownership, by implication, of an interest in the property and makes no other covenants or claims, unless stated. The granting words are usually "grant, bargain, and sell," "grant and release," or simply "conveys." Thus, the grantee must demand or obtain good title evidence to be sure of receiving marketable title. Covenants against liens and other encumbrances may be inserted if agreeable to the grantor; the instrument is then called a bargain and sale deed, with covenants.

QUITCLAIM DEED

A ***quitclaim deed*** conveys the rights of the grantor, if any, without any warranty, claim, or assertion of title by the grantor. A quitclaim deed is the simplest form of deed and gives the grantor the least possible title protection. It conveys only an interest that a grantor may have when the deed is delivered. The operative words in a quitclaim deed are that (the grantor) "releases and quitclaims" (to the grantee). Title may be conveyed just as effectively and completely with a quitclaim deed as with a warranty deed, but without any warranties. The grantee has no recourse against the grantor, however, if no color of title is received.

Quitclaim deeds are widely used to clear up clouds on title. For example, a quitclaim deed is used whenever an heir might have a very weak title claim or whenever a long-ago common law wife might have a dower claim. For a small consideration, the heir, or "wife," gives up any claim held. A quitclaim deed to make right a legal description, names of parties, or some other error in a previously recorded deed is termed a deed of confirmation or a deed of correction. The obvious purpose is to clear up or correct the defect so that it does not become, or continue to be, a cloud on title. A quitclaim deed is shown in Figure 11-3.

DEEDS OF TRUST AND OF RELEASE

A deed conveying title to a third party (trustee) to be held as security for a debt owed a lender-beneficiary is know as a deed of trust, a trust deed, or a trust deed in the nature of a mortgage. A deed of trust is a nonstatutory deed. When the terms have been satisfied (the debt has been paid off), the trustee reconveys title to the former borrower on a deed of release or of reconveyance. In that a trust deed is used primarily to pledge property as security for a debt, further discussion of it is delayed to Chapter 15.

A deed of release is used to lift or remove a claim from a dower, remainder, reversionary interest, or mortgage lien.

FORM No. 969—Stevens-Ness Law Publishing Co., Portland, Ore. 97204

TN

QUITCLAIM DEED—STATUTORY FORM
INDIVIDUAL GRANTOR

Wendy Welloff (widow) .... Grantor,

releases and quitclaims to Gerald & Nancy Investor, husband & wife .... Grantee, all right, title and interest in and to the following described real property situated in Rustic County, Oregon, to-wit:

Lots 16 & 17, Edgewood South subdivision

(IF SPACE INSUFFICIENT, CONTINUE DESCRIPTION ON REVERSE SIDE)

The true consideration for this conveyance is $ 640,000 *(Here comply with the requirements of ORS 93.030)*

Dated this 15th *day of* December *, 19* 88.

/s/Wendy Welloff

STATE OF OREGON, County of Rustic) ss. December 15th , 19 88

Personally appeared the above named .... *and acknowledged the foregoing instrument to be* her *voluntary act and deed.*

Before me: /s/Alfred B. Culbertson

(OFFICIAL SEAL) *Notary Public for Oregon—My commission expires:* December 31, 1989

FIGURE 11-3
A quitclaim deed (statutory form)

MISCELLANEOUS DEEDS

Many other deeds are used for special purposes or situations, sometimes by court order. For the most part the name of the deed indicates the nature of the purpose or situation. As fiduciaries, administrators, trustees, executors, and corporate officers do not wish to assume any greater future obligation than necessary when using these special-purpose deeds. They, therefore, include a covenant against grantor's acts in deeds they execute by stating that they "have not done or suffered anything whereby the said premises have been encumbered in any way whatsoever." A quitclaim deed may serve as the vehicle for this covenant. In most cases, fiduciaries affect title only briefly and have no personal interest in the realty.

Administrator's Deed. An administrator's deed is a nonstatutory deed used to convey realty of a person who died intestate to an heir or to a purchaser. The administrator executes the deed, which should recite the proceeding under which the court authorizes the sale or conveyance.

Executor's Deed. An executor's deed is used to convey title to realty, left by the person who died leaving a will, to a devisee or to a purchaser if the property is sold. If more than one executor is designated in the will, all must sign the deed.

Deed of Cession. A deed of cession is a nonstatutory instrument to convey street rights of an abutting owner to a municipality. The purpose should be recited.

Committee's Deed. A committee's deed is a nonstatutory instrument to convey property of infants, mentally retarded persons, and other incompetents whose affairs are managed by a court-appointed committee. Authority from the court must precede any such conveyance.

Gift Deed. An instrument conveying title from a donor-grantor to a donee-grantee is a gift deed. The usual consideration is "love and affection." The grantee has no recourse against the grantor if title is defective, because no monetary consideration was given by the grantee.

Guardian's Deed. A guardian's deed is an instrument used by a legal guardian to convey the realty interest of an infant or ward, with court permission. Full consideration should be recited because the guardian is a long-term fiduciary.

Referee's Deed in Foreclosure. An instrument used by an officer of the court to convey a mortgagor's title, following a foreclosure sale, is called a referee's deed in foreclosure or, in some areas, a "sheriff's deed." The conditions surrounding the conveyance, including the price paid by the purchaser, should be cited in the deed.

Referee's Deed in Partition. Concurrent owners sometimes sue for partition or splitting up of jointly owned property. The instrument used following a partition judgment and sale is a referee's deed in partition. An officer of the court (the referee) conveys the interests of the former concurrent owners to purchasers with no other supporting covenants.

Deed of Surrender. A deed of surrender is a nonstatutory instrument to convey a life estate to a remainderman or a qualified fee estate to the holder of the reversionary interest.

Essentials of a Valid Deed

A deed containing the following items will be valid in every state. Some states do not require the last two or three items.

1. Name of grantor with legal capacity to execute the deed
2. Name and address of grantee, adequate for identification with reasonable certainty
3. Granting clause or words of conveyance

4. A description of the realty, and if less than a fee interest is involved, a statement of the interest being conveyed
5. Proper execution-signature of the grantor, notarized, with witnesses and seal when required
6. Voluntary delivery and acceptance
7. A statement of some consideration
8. Habendum clause

GRANTOR AND GRANTEE

The conveyance must be from a competent grantor to a grantee capable of holding title. The rules of contracts usually apply in determining whether a grantor is competent to convey title. The names of the grantor and the grantee should be followed by their addresses to aid in their identification. The status of the parties should also be clearly indicated, for example, "John Jones and Mary Jones, husband and wife" or "brother and sister."

A deed conveying corporation property should be supported by a resolution properly passed by the corporate board of directors. The deed can be signed only by a corporate officer deriving authority from the corporate board of directors by resolution. Finally, the corporate seal must be affixed to the deed.

CONSIDERATION

Consideration is anything of value given in a contractual agreement, such as money, services, or love and affection. In most states the consideration must be cited, which shifts the burden of proving lack of consideration to anyone attacking the conveyance. Dollar consideration is usually required except in a gift deed in which love and affection is sufficient. Full dollar consideration is frequently not cited except when the deed is executed by a fiduciary.

WORDS OF CONVEYANCE: GRANTING CLAUSE

The granting clause includes words of conveyance such as "convey and warrant," "grant and release," "grant, bargain, and sell," "releases and quitclaims," "gives," or "grants." The interest being conveyed, including appurtenances, should follow the granting clause. Only a present interest in realty can be conveyed; that is, a deed to convey at some future time, for example, at the grantor's death, is invalid.

The habendum, "to have and to hold," clause indicates the estate being conveyed. If a habendum clause is included, the description of the interest cited should agree with the description in the granting clause. Title restrictions and other encumbrances are usually stated in the habendum clause.

UNIQUE DESCRIPTION

A description must be used that identifies the property clearly and uniquely. Street addresses are often inadequate because ambiguity and uncertainty might result; thus, a legal description is preferred.

PROPER EXECUTION

Proper execution includes signatures, a seal, witnesses (in some states), and an acknowledgment of the signing before a public notary. Customarily, only the grantor or grantors sign a deed. If a mortgage is being assumed, the grantee must also sign, unless a collateral agreement is made. A grantor who is unable to write may sign with a mark in almost all states. A cross is usually used as a mark, with the grantor's name typed near the cross:

John   (X)   Brown (seal)
        his mark

The "cross" must be made by the grantor, with two persons witnessing.

The word "seal" printed or written behind a grantor's signature is required in some states to indicate the formal nature of the deed. The signature of an authorized officer, in conveyance of corporate realty, must be followed by the corporate seal. In some states the signatures of the witnesses to the signing are also required for proper execution.

An acknowledgment is a formal declaration, before a notary public or other authorized public official, by a person signing a legal document that the signing is a "free and voluntary act." A justice of the peace, a judge, or a commanding officer in one of the military services may also acknowledge a signature. An *acknowledgment* is required for recording in nearly every state. The public official is expected to require proper identification of parties involved in an acknowledgment. The purpose of the acknowledgment is to prevent the recording of forged instruments. A deed without an acknowledgment is not a satisfactory instrument for most conveyance purposes. Deeds should be recorded as soon as received to give notice to the world of grantee's rights in the property received.

DELIVERY AND ACCEPTANCE

The final requirement for a valid deed is delivery and acceptance. *Delivery* means that the grantor, by some act or statement, signifies intent for the deed to be effective. The grantor handing the deed to the grantee is the most obvious form of delivery. Similarly, the grantor's directing an attorney or an escrow officer to give a signed deed to the grantee also constitutes delivery. Delivery must take place while the grantor is alive. If several people share ownership of a property, for delivery to occur, all must sign and in some way indicate that the deed is to be effective.

Delivery is essential to the validity of a deed. A grantor handing a deed to a grantee is clearly delivery. But delivery takes other forms as well.

Example: Seller signs a deed naming Buyer as grantee. The deed is then handed to Buyer's attorney, with intent to immediately give ownership to Buyer. The attorney is an agent of the grantee; therefore, the delivery is valid. (However, note that a Seller handing a deed to his or her own lawyer with a request that it be looked over *is not delivery* in that the lawyer is the Seller-grantor's agent.)

Example: Seller signs a deed naming Buyer as grantee. The deed is then placed with the ABC Escrow Company along with directions to deliver the deed to Buyer when certain monies are paid the Escrow Company by the Buyer. This constitutes an escrow delivery, which is valid.

The grantee must accept the deed for title to pass. ***Acceptance*** is agreement to the terms of a deed. Since most people desire to own property, acceptance is ordinarily assumed. Thus, if a grantor records a deed conveying title to a grantee, the grantee must object and dissent immediately to avoid an acceptance.

Questions for Review and Discussion

1. Briefly explain and distinguish between the following methods of transferring title:
   a. Contract for consideration
   b. Gift
   c. Will
   d. Descent
   e. Adverse possession
   f. Lien enforcement
2. Explain the use of an attorney's opinion of title, including any advantages or disadvantages from a prospective owner's or lender's point of view.
3. What is an abstract of title? What is its use or purpose?
4. A property survey is sometimes required to validate title. What purpose does a survey serve?
5. Explain title insurance in detail, including any advantages or disadvantages from a potential owner's or lender's point of view.
6. Explain the nature of a general warranty deed, including five accompanying covenants or warranties.
7. What kind of deed would you prefer to use as a grantor of title? As a grantee? Why? How is the difference in attitude reconciled in practice?
8. Explain the nature and uses of the following deed:
   a. Special warranty
   b. Bargain and sale
   c. Quitclaim
   d. Trust
9. List and explain at least five essentials of a valid deed.
10. Are deeds necessary? If not, what might be used instead?
11. Would extension of the Torrens system eliminate the need for deeds to convey title? Should the Torrens system therefore be adopted nationwide? Discuss. What major obstacles would have to be overcome? What would be the probable effect on costs of title transfer?
12. Title may be gained by adverse possession by occupying and using land for 20 years or longer in almost all states. Does title by adverse possession therefore not invalidate most claims of title more than 20 years old in that most real estate is now held under color of title? Are laws needed to make this situation clear to everyone? Discuss.

1. John Doe recently bought an older property and accepted a quitclaim deed and title insurance with typical coverage as sufficient assurance of ownership and quiet possession. Subsequently, the following situations came up. Indicate in each case whether John is protected against loss by the insurance.
   a. The grantor is a minor and now wants to rescind the conveyance.
   b. A contractor files a mechanic's lien against the property for repairing its roof after a storm 3 months prior to the sale.
   c. The property is zoned single-family residential. John had believed it to be zoned two-family residential, meaning that he could divide the house into two dwelling units.
   d. John's garage, built 22 years ago, extends 2 feet onto his neighbor's lot.
2. Henry Ponda notices 40 acres of unused land adjacent to his farm. He fences and farms the land for more than 20 years. The county assessor, in turn, levies and collects taxes on the land from Henry. In actuality, the land is a portion of an 800 acre spread owned by Marilyn, an attorney, who lives in a neighboring state. Marilyn dies. Upon settling the estate, the executor discovers Henry's use of the 40 acres. The exeucutor sues for back rent. What is the result?
3. Helen brings an abstract of title up to date for a house that is being sold to Vincent. Carol, an attorney, examines the abstract and certifies the title as marketable. Title is conveyed to Vincent, and the transaction is closed.
   a. After the closing, a forgery of an earlier deed is discovered, meaning that Vincent does not have marketable title. Vincent sues Carol for negligence. What is the result?
   b. Vincent also sues Helen, the grantor. What is the likely result if a quitclaim deed were used to convey title? A special warranty deed? A general warranty deed?
   c. Does Vincent have a basis for a valid claim for damages against the abstract company?
4. William is negotiating with Nancy about the sale of a bookstore he owns. Nancy verbally offers him $225,000 and asks him to think it over.
   a. William, planning to accept, prepares and signs a deed and puts it in a drawer in his office desk. That evening he has a heart attack and dies. Is there delivery?
   b. If William had given the signed deed to an escrow agent, would there have been delivery?

12

Title Closing

Buy land. They ain't making any more of the stuff.

Will Rogers, American Humorist

Necessary documents, typical closing costs, including prorations for the settlement statement for a buy-sell transaction, and recordation are all taken up in this chapter. Knowledge of closing procedures and adjustments is advantageous to a prospective buyer for at least two reasons. With an understanding of closing, an investor will have a better idea of what's going on in negotiations. The need for certain documents or information becomes much more obvious. Further, knowledge of closing procedures is absolutely essential for an agent or broker in arranging financing or closing and even in holding a deal together.

The most common settlement is actually a double transaction: a title transfer and a financing. That is, the sale of a property and the financing by a new mortgage loan are both considered. In fact, the settlement statement for John Burgoyne's purchase of a duplex, from Chapter 2, is the focus of this chapter. In this type of closing, the costs and adjustments may be substantial for the buyer, totaling to between 3 and 8 percent of the property's value.

Other common title closings are (1) sale of property financed by an existing loan, (2) exchange of two or more properties, (3) refinancing of a property under a continuing owner, and (4) sale of a leasehold. These closings are similar and are, therefore, not discussed separately.

Important Topics or Decision Areas Covered in This Chapter

Preliminaries for Closings
Survey and Inspection
Title Search and Report

Encumbrances: Acceptance or Removal
Instruments to be Delivered

Key Concepts Introduced in This Chapter

Accrued expense   **Prepaid expense**
Credit   **Prorate**

2-3 Q's

Preliminaries for Closings

Many details must be attended to between the signing of a sales contract and an actual closing. If an escrow closing is required, these details must be cleared through the escrow agent. Some of the more common and important details are shown in Figure 12-1. Parties primarily concerned with each detail are indicated.

The entire escrow closing process, within which these items must be processed, is shown in Figure 12-2. Even if a closing is not in escrow, the same considerations or details must be handled by the broker, lender, or others to complete the transaction.

Report or Document	Prepared By	Responsible Party
Property survey	Surveyor	Buyer
Property inspection	Buyer/buyer's agent	Buyer
Abstract of title, including title search	Abstract company	Seller
Preliminary title report	Title company	Seller
Title insurance policy	Title company	Seller
Deed	Attorney	Seller
Mortgage satisfaction or deed of reconveyance for retired loan	Old lender	Seller
RESPA disclosure statement	Lender	Lender
Mortgage or trust deed	Lender	Lender
Promissory note	Lender	Lender

FIGURE 12-1
Reports/documents/responsible parties in preparing for a title closing

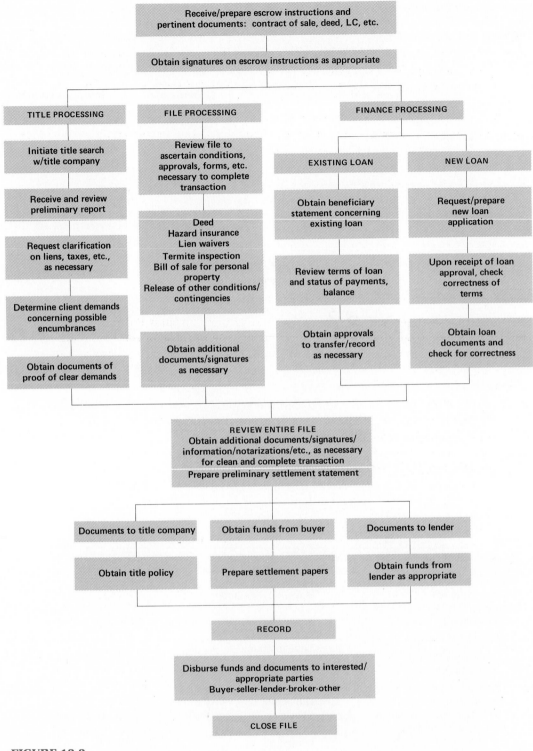

Receive/prepare escrow instructions and pertinent documents: contract of sale, deed, LC, etc.

Obtain signatures on escrow instructions as appropriate

TITLE PROCESSING

Initiate title search w/title company

Receive and review preliminary report

Request clarification on liens, taxes, etc., as necessary

Determine client demands concerning possible encumbrances

Obtain documents of proof of clear demands

FILE PROCESSING

Review file to ascertain conditions, approvals, forms, etc. necessary to complete transaction

Deed
Hazard insurance
Lien waivers
Termite inspection
Bill of sale for personal property
Release of other conditions/ contingencies

Obtain additional documents/signatures as necessary

FINANCE PROCESSING

EXISTING LOAN

Obtain beneficiary statement concerning existing loan

Review terms of loan and status of payments, balance

Obtain approvals to transfer/record as necessary

NEW LOAN

Request/prepare new loan application

Upon receipt of loan approval, check correctness of terms

Obtain loan documents and check for correctness

REVIEW ENTIRE FILE
Obtain additional documents/signatures/ information/notarizations/etc., as necessary for clean and complete transaction
Prepare preliminary settlement statement

Documents to title company

Obtain funds from buyer

Documents to lender

Obtain title policy

Prepare settlement papers

Obtain funds from lender as appropriate

RECORD

Disburse funds and documents to interested/ appropriate parties
Buyer-seller-lender-broker-other

CLOSE FILE

FIGURE 12-2
The escrow closing process

SURVEY AND INSPECTION

A survey specifically identifies the property and may bring to light encroachments onto or from the property. Lenders increasingly demand property surveys to ensure that the legal description of the property being financed applies to the subject property. Encroachments, if any, must be corrected by the seller before the closing can be completed.

If the property is an income property, a detailed property inspection is usually necessary prior to a closing to ascertain that conditions are as represented in the contract. The inspection is to verify such matters as names of tenants, rents, space occupied, lengths of leases, and amounts of security deposits. The inspection is also to make sure that no one in possession of any part of the premises has or claims any rights or ownership or other interest in the property. The law is clear that possession gives public notice of an interest just as strongly as does a recorded instrument. An inspection should be made shortly before the closing in conjunction with the title search and analyses.

TITLE SEARCH AND REPORT

Having the title searched and obtaining the title report are probably the most important requirements from the purchaser's viewpoint. The purpose of the search and report is for the purchaser to be sure that the seller's title is clear or at least meets contract requirements. The seller usually provides title evidence in the form of a current abstract of title and a commitment for title insurance. If an abstract of title is provided, the buyer must obtain an opinion of title from an attorney. The title insurance commitment or the title opinion sets forth liens, assessments, deed restrictions, and other encumbrances of record. The seller's title is subject to these limitations. The seller must remove any of these limitations that make the title unmarketable or otherwise do not meet the requirements of the sales contract.

ENCUMBRANCES: ACCEPTANCE OR REMOVAL

A marketable title must be delivered by the seller except for encumbrances specifically excepted in the sales contract. Customarily, the purchaser notifies the seller, shortly after receipt of the title report or opinion, of all encumbrances to be removed. The acceptability of encumbrances and other objections of title that show up on the title report or opinion must, therefore, be settled between the buyer and the seller prior to closing. If acceptable or waived by the buyer and the new lender, these limitations need not be removed or "cured."

Typical encumbrances to be removed are mortgage liens, tax liens, clouds on title because of improperly signed deeds, and unexpected easements, encroachments, or title restrictions. Title restrictions and setback lines placed against the property by the developer are typically exempt encumbrances.

A title report or opinion occasionally shows a title to be extremely unmarketable or clouded. After adequate opportunity has been given to the seller to remove the clouds and encumbrances, the buyer may reject such a title and rescind the sales contract. Upon rejection and rescission, the buyer is entitled to recover reasonable expenses incurred because of the seller's inability to perform according to the contract of sale.

INSTRUMENTS TO BE DELIVERED

The seller must sign and convey title either by a deed of the kind required by the sales contract or by one of higher quality. The new lender, in turn, provides a promissory note and a mortgage or trust deed to be signed by the buyer-borrower. If an existing loan is paid off as part of the closing, the old lender must sign and provide a mortgage satisfaction or deed of reconveyance. Finally, as was mentioned earlier, the seller is often asked to sign an affidavit of title. If the sales contract calls for an escrow closing, all these instruments must be delivered to the escrow agent, along with escrow instructions.

Elements of Closing Costs

The main classes or types of closing costs and adjustments include (1) title assurance charges and legal fees, (2) loan-related charges and fees, (3) brokerage commissions and miscellaneous fees, and (4) buyer-seller adjustments. Typical buyer closing costs range from 4 to 8 percent, not including adjustments for property taxes and special assessments. Tax adjustments and special assessments may double these percentages.

TITLE ASSURANCE CHARGES AND LEGAL FEES

Title assurance charges include costs for the search and examination of title and for title insurance. The cost of bringing the abstract of title up to date and of title insurance is usually paid for by the seller. A buyer may incur fees for legal counsel to examine the title evidence and to otherwise look after his or her interests throughout the transaction.

Buyers and lenders both want assurances that the title to the property of concern has no hidden claims or liens filed against it. Therefore, a detailed search of various documents in the public record must be made to assure that hidden claims and liens do not exist. Title assurance evidence most generally consists of an attorney's certification of title or of a title insurance policy.

Incidental charges connected with title assurance include deed recording fees and escrow fees. Unless otherwise agreed, escrow charges are usually split evenly between the buyer and the seller. A buyer must pay to have the deed recorded, to give public notice of the conveyance.

LOAN-RELATED CHARGES AND FEES

Fees likely to be incurred when loan financing is used are as follows.

Lender's Service Charge. Loan origination fees, also termed service charges, payable by a borrower typically amount to from 1 to 2 percent of the amount borrowed. In essence, the charge covers the expenses incurred in initiating a

Checklist for Closing a Real Estate Sale

(These items may be attended to by an escrow agent, rather then by the seller and purchaser on an individual basis.)

At title closing, the seller should have, or should do, the following items:

1. Seller's copy of the contract.
2. Latest receipts for payments of taxes, utilities, and assessments.
3. Latest meter readings of water, gas, and electric utilities.
4. Originals and certificates of all fire, liability, and other insurance policies.
5. Estoppel certificates from the holder of any mortgage loans that have been reduced, showing the loan balance, any amounts due, and the date to which interest is paid.
6. Receipts for latest payment of interest on mortgage loans.
7. Any subordination agreements called for in the contract.
8. Satisfaction pieces of mechanic's liens, chattel mortgages, judgments, and mortgage loans that are to be paid at or before closing.
9. Statement with names of tenants, dates when rents are due, amounts of rents paid and unpaid, and assignment of unpaid rents.
10. Assignment of leases.
11. Letters to tenants directing payment of subsequent rents to purchaser.
12. Seller's last deed.
13. Affadavit of title.
14. Authority to execute deed if seller is acting through an agent.
15. Bill of sale for personal property included in the contract.
16. Any unrecorded instruments that affect the title, including extension agreements.
17. Deed and other instruments that the seller is to deliver or prepare.

At title closing, the purchaser should have, or should do, the following items:

1. Purchaser's copy of the contract.
2. Up-to-date abstract of title.
3. Up-to-date title report.
4. Examine deed to see that it conforms to the contract.
5. Compare property description.
6. See that deed is properly executed.
7. Have sufficient cash or certified checks to make required payments at the closing.
8. See that all liens that were to be removed have been.
9. Obtain names and other details concerning tenants and rents.
10. Obtain assignment of unpaid rents and assignment of leases.
11. Obtain and examine estoppel certificates for mortgage loans that have been reduced and are being taken over.
12. Obtain letter(s) to tenant(s).
13. Obtain affidavit of title.
14. Obtain and examine (accept or reject) authority if the seller acts through an agent.
15. Obtain bill of sale for personal property included in the contract.
16. Examine survey.
17. Ascertain content and acceptibility of title report relative to covenants, restrictions, and consents affecting the title or use of the property.
18. Ascertain amounts due for unpaid utility and tax bills and assessments as of the closing date, including any accrued interest.
19. Arrange for adjustments as called for in the contract.
20. Examine purchase money mortgage loan documents and execute.
21. Have damage awards for public improvements, if any, assigned to the purchaser.
22. Obtain any unrecorded instruments affecting the title, including extension agreements.

mortgage loan with a lending firm. Also, a seller may be required to pay a penalty for prepaying a loan. Thus, a seller prepaying a loan balance of $200,000 might be penalized a 1.5 percent charge of $3,000.

Credit Report. A credit report showing a borrower's income, assets, outstanding debt, if any, and the borrower's credit history is required by almost all lending agencies. The charge is generally rather small.

Recording Fees. Recording fees for mortgages and loan assumption documents are customarily paid by the purchaser. The seller pays for recording a mortgage satisfaction to meet the requirement of delivering title free and clear of encumbrances. These fees vary with the length of the documents and local customs.

Appraisal Fee. An appraisal report is generally required when borrowed funds are used to purchase a property, with the cost paid by the purchaser.

Prepaid Interest. Prepaid interest is customarily charged from date of settlement to the end of the month, when a new loan is obtained. The first regular payment of debt service then begins at the end of the first full month of ownership. This prepayment makes it unnecessary to compute interest for periods of less than 1 month's time later on.

Hazard Insurance. At closing, lenders require the purchaser-mortgagor to provide hazard insurance on the property. This insurance protects the lender against loss by fire, windstorm, and other specified hazards. If new insurance is obtained, the buyer usually pays the premium in advance.

Property Survey. A property survey by a licensed land surveyor is often required by lenders, with the cost borne by the purchaser.

COMMISSIONS AND MISCELLANEOUS CHARGES

Brokerage commissions run from 4 to 7 percent of the sale price and are usually paid by the seller, in that a broker usually works as an agent of the seller. Of course, if the buyer employs the broker, the buyer pays the commission. Commissions on sales of lots and land may run up to 10 percent.

Other costs may be encountered in a title closing. Special handling costs, or mailing charges, incurred by the escrow agent will be assessed against the responsible party. Deed stamps, required by law in most states, are paid for by the seller. Some states require a documentary stamp on the promissory note, which is a tax on the intangible mortgage debt.

BUYER-SELLER ADJUSTMENTS

When an outstanding mortgage is assumed, an adjustment is made between the seller and the buyer, each bearing the interest costs for his or her time of ownership. Thus, an appropriate credit is given to the buyer for interest charges due up to and including the day of the settlement.

If the seller's insurance policy is taken over, an adjustment is necessary for prepaid premiums, representing the remaining term of the insurance being taken over. The buyer must also reimburse the seller for premiums in the reserve account if they are taken over.

Real property taxes, if unpaid, constitute a lien prior to the mortgage lien. Therefore, lenders frequently require a reserve account of a borrower to be sure the money for the tax payments is available when the payments are due. If a reserve account is required, the estimated real property tax for the year is prorated on a monthly basis. The pro rata amount is added to the payments due each month for loan interest, principal repayment, and hazard insurance. With a reserve account, the necessary adjustment must cover the amount the seller has in the account plus any other tax adjustments agreed to by the buyer and the seller.

In addition to these costs and settlement charges, adjustments are made for accrued or prepaid rentals if tenants are occupying the premises and for any security deposits held by the seller. Finally, fuel or supplies on hand, or other items transferred from seller to buyer, also call for appropriate adjustments.

Closing-Statement Entries and Prorations

A settlement statement is needed at a closing to satisfy all parties involved, particularly the buyer and the seller. The statement shows the amount of money the buyer must pay to get title and possession. The statement also tells how much the seller will net after paying the broker's commission and other expenses.

Prorations and adjustments are necessary in preparing a settlement statement. To *prorate* means to divide proportionately, as between a buyer and seller. The seller typically may have prepaid for property taxes and hazard insurance, and may own reserve deposits, all of which require adjustments. The buyer wants these and similar items cleared at or before the closing. Also, if an existing mortgage is taken over by the buyer, adjustments for accrued interest to date of the closing are necessary. These adjustments are representative of the many that may be necessary at the closing.

GENERAL RULES OF PRORATING

The rules or customs applicable to the prorations vary widely from state to state. In some states, closing rules and procedures have been established by the realty boards or bar associations. Rules most generally applicable are as follows:

1. The seller is generally responsible for the day of the closing, which means that prorations are made to and including the day of closing. In the few states where the buyer is responsible for the day of closing, adjustments are made as of the day preceding the closing.
2. A year is presumed to have 360 days, with twelve 30-day months, for prorations of mortgage interest, real estate taxes, and insurance premiums. The actual number of days in a month may be used in prorations if specified in the sales contract.
3. Accrued real estate taxes that are not yet payable are prorated at the closing. The amount of the last tax bill is used in prorating if current taxes cannot be ascertained.

4. Special assessment taxes are increasingly paid by the seller and are not pro-rated at the closing, unless the buyer agrees to a proration.

5. Rents are usually prorated over the actual number of days in the month of the closing. The buyer agrees in a separate statement to collect any unpaid rents for current and previous periods, if any, and to forward the pro rata share to the seller. (A buyer is advised against taking uncollected rents as an adjustment in the closing statement because the buyer should not accept the responsibility for rents that the seller cannot collect.)

6. Tenants' security deposits for the last month's rent or to cover possible damages to the property must be transferred to the buyer without any off-setting adjustment. The deposits belong to the tenants and not to the seller. As the new owner, the buyer will be responsible for refunding these deposits at a later time. Prior tenant consent to such transfers may be necessary.

7. If closing is between wage-payment dates, unpaid wages of employees working on the property are prorated, including amounts for social security and other fringe benefits.

8. Adjustment for chattels (personal property) is made according to local custom. No adjustment is required for fixtures. Unless otherwise stipulated in the sales contract, the following items are fixtures and are a part of the real property: plumbing, heating, built-in appliances, oil tanks, water heaters, light fixtures, bathroom fixtures, blinds, shades, draperies and curtain rods, window and door screens, storm doors and windows, wall-to-wall carpeting, shrubs, bulbs, plants, and trees. Hall carpets, refrigerators, stoves, and washers and dryers are also usually regarded as fixtures in apartment buildings.

CLOSING-STATEMENT ENTRIES

Several items on a closing statement are direct entries and do not require adjustments between the buyer and the seller. These items are commonly called credits. A *credit* is an entry in a person's favor, as, for example, the balance in a bank account is in the depositor's favor. We also speak of "giving credit to someone" for doing us a favor or showing honesty or otherwise being financially trustworthy. A credit, as used here, is recognition to the buyer or seller for a contribution made to the transaction. See Figure 12-3 for a summary of closing statement entries.

The obvious first entry on a closing statement is the sale price, which is credited to the seller. Crediting the seller with the sale price is recognition of the seller's contribution of the property to the transaction.

A direct credit at current market price is also given the seller for coal, oil, cleaning supplies, and other items on hand that are taken over by the buyer. These items are over and above the sale price of the real estate and represent additional seller contributions to the transaction. In a similar vein, the seller's reserve deposits that are being taken over by the buyer warrant a direct credit entry to the seller. Reserve deposits are commonly assumed by the buyer along with taking over an existing mortgage against the property.

A buyer is credited in the closing statement with any earnest money deposit or down payment made. In addition, if the buyer takes over an existing mortgage of the seller, a credit is due to the buyer, in that the buyer is taking over an obligation of the

Credits to Buyer	Credits to Seller
Direct entry, no proration necessary	
Earnest money and down payment	Sale price
Outstanding loan balance, if taken over by buyer	Fuel on hand (oil, gas, etc.) at current market price
New loans to finance purchase	Reserve deposits for taxes, and hazard
Tenant security deposits	insurance, when taken over by buyer
Proration necessary	
Accrued property taxes, seller's portion	Prepaid property taxes, buyer's portion
Accrued loan interest, seller's portion	Prepaid water and sewer charges, buyer's portion
Accrued employee wages, including vacation allowance, seller's portion	Prepaid hazard insurance, buyer's portion
Rents collected in advance by seller, buyer's portion	Uncollected rents, seller's portion

FIGURE 12-3
Settlement statement items

seller. A buyer's giving a purchase money mortgage to the seller as part of the sale price has a similar effect, in that it creates a new obligation from the buyer to the seller. A purchase money mortgage is a mortgage given to a seller by a buyer to cover all or a portion of the purchase price of the property.

Tenants' security deposits, if carried as an obligation of the property owner, must also be treated as a credit to the buyer. The buyer is relieving the seller of the obligation to repay the security deposits, which constitutes a contribution to the transaction. Alternatively, if the security deposits are carried in escrow accounts, the accounts may be transferred to the buyer's name, with no adjusting entry in the settlement statement.

PRO RATA CALCULATIONS

Some items must be prorated between the buyer and seller rather than directly credited to one or to the other. A proration is necessary when a charge or a payment covers a time period for which both the buyer and the seller are responsible. Real estate taxes, accrued interest, prepaid hazard insurance, and rents collected in advance are representative of items that must be prorated. Refer to Figure 12-4.

Three distinct steps are involved in prorating an item.

1. Identify the item to be prorated (taxes, insurance premiums, etc.)
2. Determine whether a prepaid or accrued expense is involved.
3. Calculate the amount of the proration.

Figure 12-3 lists settlement statement items and indicates whether the buyer or seller gets a credit entry on the closing statement. Figure 12-3 also tells whether an item is an accrued expense or a prepaid expense. An ***accrued expense*** means accumulated charges, such as interest and taxes, owed but not yet paid. A ***prepaid expense*** is a charge, such as hazard insurance, paid for in advance.

Item	Debits	Credits
Contract Sale Price	$100,000	
Title Assurance Entries		
Hifidelity Title Co.; lender's policy	110	
Recording fees: deed and mortgage	28	
Escrow fee (one half)	88	
Financing Entries		
New loan, Urbandale S&L		$ 90,000
New loan, interest to 4/30	450	
New loan, origination fee at 2%	1,800	
Attorney, Howard Light: prepare documents	40	
Credit report: Rustic County Credit Bureau	40	
Appraisal report, Allen Measure	240	
Earnest money		4,000
Buyer-Seller Adjustments		
Tenant security deposits		900
Property taxes, prepaid to 6/30	624	
Hazard insurance, prepaid to 8/15	205	
Rents, prepaid to 4/30		648
Accrued sewer and water charges		6
Subtotals	$103,625	$ 95,554
Check/cash required to balance		8,071
Totals (must balance)	$103,625	$103,625

FIGURE 12-4

Buyer's closing statement or summary of buyer's transaction

An accrued or prepaid expense, in turn, calls for a proration. For example, a hazard insurance premium prepaid by the seller means that the seller is due a credit for the portion of the premium that covers an ownership period of the buyer. Alternatively, accrued taxes of the seller, which the buyer eventually must pay, become a credit entry to the buyer on the closing statement.

Prepaid Expense Prorations. A typical adjustment of a prepaid expense involves the premium for hazard insurance. Hazard insurance premiums are usually prepaid for 1, 3, or 5 years. A buyer frequently takes over the insurance coverage of a seller, as a matter of convenience. A careful check to determine correctly the period for which a premium has been paid is necessary prior to any prorating calculations. The number of future years, months, and days for which the premium has been prepaid must then be calculated. Examples are given here to illustrate the usual method of prorating a prepaid insurance expense. It concerns a 1-year prepayment, which is part of the case problem. A second example is also given.

Assume a seller's policy with an annual premium of $600 ($50 per month) that runs to August 15, 1988. The closing is on April 12, 1988. The buyer agrees to take over the seller's policy. What is the amount of the adjustment?

	Years	Months	Days
Premium paid to 8/15/88	1988	8	15
Closing date 4/12/88	− 1988	− 4	− 12
Remaining coverage available	0	4	3

The end date of the prepaid periods is compared with the closing date. Then, beginning with the "Days" column, the closing date is subtracted from the end date. In this example, 4 months, 3 days of premium are prepaid as of the closing date. At $50 per month, this means a credit of $205 to the seller ($50/month × 4.1 months = $205.)

As a second, more complex example, assume a 3-year premium of $5,400 for a policy that ends on November 12, 1990. Closing is assumed to take place on September 15, 1988.

	Years	Months	Days
Premium paid to 11/12/90	1990	11	12
Closing date 9/15/88	− 1988	9	15
Future years, months, and days for which premium is prepaid	?	?	?

Again, begin with the "Days" column. When the days of the end time (12) are fewer than the days in the line for the closing date (15), a month must be borrowed from the "Months" column. This increases the days column by 30, to 42. The 15 days on the lower line may now be subtracted from the upper line to give 27 future days for which a premium has been paid. Next, move to the "Months" column. The months in the lower line in (9) may be directly subtracted from the months in the upper line (now 10 after 1 has been borrowed) to give one prepaid month. If the months in the upper line were less than the months in the lower line, 12 months (1 year) would have to be borrowed from the years column.

	Years	Months	Days
Premium paid to 11/12/90	1990	10 ~~11~~	42 ~~12~~
Closing date 9/15/88	− 1988	− 9	− 15
Future years, months, and days for which premium is prepaid	2	1	27

Finally, in the "Years" column, 1988 is subtracted from 1990 to give 2 future years for which the premium is paid. In total, the premium has been prepaid for 2 years, 1 month, 27 days.

The $5,400 premium breaks down to $1,800 per year or $150 per month. Two years multiplied by $1,800 equals $3,600. One month at $150 per month equals $150; and 27 days or 0.9 month (27 days/30 days) at $150 per month gives $135. The total credit due the seller for a prepaid insurance premium is $3,885.

Prepayment credit for 2 years	$3,600
Prepayment for 1 month	150
Prepayment for 27 days	135
Total prepayment credit due seller	$3,885

Accrued Expense Proration. Real property taxes, along with water and sewer charges, are typical accrued expenses. To illustrate the proration of an accrued expense, assume that the water and sewer charge on the duplex John Burgoyne is buying is payable at the end of each quarter. The quarterly charge is $45.00, or $.50 a day. The accrued portion is for the portion of the quarter from April 1 to the date of closing, April 12. Thus, 12 days of the 90 days in the quarter are chargeable to the seller. At $.50 a day, this totals to $6. With more involved numbers, the amount of the credit would be calculated as follows.

$$\$45.00 \times \frac{12}{90} = \underline{\underline{\$6.00}}$$

Accrued interest on an assumed loan is calculated in a similar fashion. To illustrate, assume a closing on April 12, with the seller paying off a $70,000 mortgage loan, plus accrued interest at 9 percent, compounded monthly. The accrued interest would be $210, calculated as follows:

$$9\%/12 = \tfrac{3}{4} \text{ percent (.0075) per month}$$
$$\$70,000 \times \tfrac{3}{4}\% \ (.0075) = \$525$$
$$\$525 \times \frac{12 \text{ days}}{30 \text{ days}} \ (2/5) = \$210$$

Escrow Closing

To illustrate escrow closing procedures and prorata calculations, the preparation of a settlement worksheet is used. Calculations for two adjustments in the example (hazard insurance and water and sewer charges) were shown earlier in this chapter. The closing is handled by Hifidelity Escrow Services. The data are intended to be representative. Some detail is omitted, and round numbers are used for greater clarity of illustration.

CASE PROBLEM

On March 7, 1988, John Burgoyne made an earnest money deposit of $4,000 toward the purchase of a duplex for $100,000. On March 8, the owner, Andrew Welsch, agreed to sell. The sale was negotiated by Harvey Hustle of Everready Realty Company. The parties subsequently agree to an April 12, 1988, closing date. Escrow closing costs are to be shared equally, as per contract. A 30-day month and a 360-day banker's year are customarily used for closing adjustments in the area.

The offer is conditional on John Burgoyne's obtaining a 30-year monthly payment loan for $90,000 or more at 10 percent interest or less. The Urbandale Savings and Loan agrees to make such a loan, with a 2 percent loan origination fee. Payments are to begin on June 1, so interest must be paid on the $90,000 to the end of April at the closing. The existing loan on the duplex is $70,000, with interest paid to the end of March 1988.

Details of the transaction requiring entries or buyer-seller adjustments are as follows:

A. Title Assurance Entries
1. Owner's title policy from the Hifidelity Title Company costs $360, which is payable by the seller. A lender title policy rider costs $110, payable by the buyer.
2. Escrow fee, by Hifidelity Escrow Services, is $176, to be shared equally by buyer and seller.
3. Recording fees are payable as follows: mortgage satisfaction, $4.00, by seller; deed, $4.00, by buyer; and new mortgage papers, $24.00, by buyer.
4. To prepare documents and to clear up some miscellaneous details, seller engaged Tangle & Webb, attorneys, who charged $120.

B. Financing Entries
1. Seller pays off existing loan of $70,000, along with accrued interest of $210.
2. Buyer gets new loan of $90,000 at 10 percent interest, compounded monthly, but must pay a 2 percent origination fee. Interest must be prepaid to the end of April at closing so that the first full payment will be due on June 1.
3. To obtain the financing, the buyer incurred the following charges: attorney fee for document preparation, $40.00; charge for credit report, $40.00; and appraisal fee, $240.

C. Miscellaneous Charges
1. Seller's brokerage commission at 6 percent is $6,000.
2. Seller lived in another state and shipped the deed and other materials for overnight delivery: charge is $14.00.

D. Buyer-Seller Adjustments
1. Sale price is $100,000; credit seller, debit buyer. Buyer made earnest money deposit with offer of $4,000.
2. Annual property taxes of $2,880 were prepaid to June 30 by seller.
3. Seller prepaid hazard insurance to August 15; policy is being taken over by buyer. Adjustment is $205, as calculated earlier.
4. Rents of $540 per unit prepaid to end of April.
5. Water and sewer charge accrued to April 12; quarterly charge is $45.00.

Summary Statements. Figures 12-4 and 12-5 summarize the necessary adjustments and prorations for the data presented. Figure 12-6 shows the Real Estate Settlement Procedures Act (RESPA) statement for the same data.

Title Conveyance

When all necessary payments are made, title is conveyed by delivery of a deed. In an escrow closing, title passes upon performance of all conditions in the escrow agreement upon recording and delivery of the deed.

A grantor must be legally competent at the time of deed execution to convey title. Competency includes being of legal age and acting voluntarily and intentionally,

Item	Debits	Credits
Contract Sale Price		$100,000
Title Assurance Entries		
Hifidelity Title Co.; owner's policy	$ 360	
Mortgage satisfaction recording fee	4	
Escrow fee (one half)	88	
Attorneys: Tangle & Webb	120	
Financing Entries		
Existing loan, pay off	70,000	
Existing loan, accrued interest	210	
Miscellaneous		
Commission: Everready Realty	6,000	
Federal Express: overnight delivery	14	
Buyer-Seller Adjustments		
Tenant security deposits	900	
Property taxes, prepaid to 6/30		624
Hazard insurance, prepaid to 8/15		205
Rents, prepaid to 4/30	648	
Accrued sewer and water charges	6	
Subtotals	$ 78,350	$100,829
Check/cash required to balance	22,479	
Totals (must balance)	$100,829	$100,829

FIGURE 12-5
Seller's closing statement or summary of seller's transaction

with understanding. All rights of the grantor cease upon delivery of the deed. The settlement statement becomes the buyer's and seller's permanent record of the transaction.

Real Estate Settlement Procedures Act

Figure 12-6 shows a completed Real Estate Settlement Procedures Act (RESPA) form for the Burgoyne-Welsch transaction just discussed.

RESPA was designed as consumer protection legislation to shield home buyers from unnecessarily high closing costs. Implementation has two ends: (1) ensure that borrowers purchasing one- to four-unit residential properties are fully informed of costs of closing and (2) preserve to borrowers the right to select the parties providing services to the transaction, as attorneys, appraisers, and title companies. Included is the financing (and closing) of individual condominium and cooperative units and of mobile homes. The Act requires one settlement form to be used nationwide and, therefore, standardizes closing practices across the United States.

The act extends to lenders investing more than $1 million per year in one- to four-family residential loans and to all federally related first mortgage loans. Therefore, lenders are at the heart of implementation. The Federal Reserve System directs implementation under Regulation X. Note that RESPA does not regulate or limit fees and does not pertain to disclosure of the loan terms of the transaction. Disclosure is provided for in the Truth in Lending Act.

| A. | U.S. DEPARTMENT OF HOUSING AND URBAN DEVELOPMENT
SETTLEMENT STATEMENT | B. | | T Y P E | O F | L O A N |

B.	T Y P E	O F	L O A N
1. ☐ FHA	2. ☐ FMHA	3. ☒ CONV. UNINS.	
4. ☐ VA	5. ☐ CONV. INS.		
6. FILE NUMBER:		7. LOAN NUMBER:	
8. MORTGAGE INS. CASE NO.:			

C. NOTE: *This form is furnished to give you a statement of actual settlement costs. Amounts paid to and by the settlement agent are shown. Items marked "(p.o.c.)" were paid outside the closing; they are shown here for informational purposes and are not included in the totals.*

D. NAME OF BORROWER: John Burgoyne
   ADDRESS OF BORROWER: 3278 Exotic Drive, Urbandale   00000

E. NAME OF SELLER: Andrew Welsch
   ADDRESS OF SELLER: Condominium Towers, Unit 77; Urbandale   00000

F. NAME OF LENDER: Urbandale Savings & Loan Association
   ADDRESS OF LENDER:

G. PROPERTY
   LOCATION: 2001 Zigzag Avenue, Urbandale   00000

H. SETTLEMENT AGENT: Hifidelity Escrow Services: Tom Barren
   PLACE OF SETTLEMENT: 221 N. Main; Urbandale   00000

I. SETTLEMENT DATE: April 12, 1988 (seller's day)

J. SUMMARY OF BORROWER'S TRANSACTION		K. SUMMARY OF SELLER'S TRANSACTION	
100. GROSS AMOUNT DUE FROM BORROWER:		**400. GROSS AMOUNT DUE TO SELLER:**	
101. Contract sales price	100,000	401. Contract sales price	100,000
102. Personal property		402. Personal property	
103. Settlement charges to borrower: *(from line 1400)*	2,796	403.	
104.		404.	
105.		405.	
ADJUSTMENTS FOR ITEMS PAID BY SELLER IN ADVANCE:		ADJUSTMENTS FOR ITEMS PAID BY SELLER IN ADVANCE:	
106. City/town taxes to		406. City/town taxes to	
107. County taxes to		407. County taxes to	
108. Assessments to		408. Assessments to	
109. Property taxes to 6/30	624	409. Property taxes to 6/30	624
110. H. Insurance 8/15	205	410. H. Insurance 8/15	205
111.		411.	
112.	103,625	412.	100,829
120. GROSS AMOUNT DUE FROM BORROWER: ▶		**420. GROSS AMOUNT DUE TO SELLER:** ▶	
200. AMOUNTS PAID BY OR IN BEHALF OF BORROWER:		**500. REDUCTIONS IN AMOUNT DUE TO SELLER:**	
201. Deposit or earnest money	4,000	501. Excess deposit *(see instructions)*	
202. Principal amount of new loan(s)	90,000	502. Settlement charges to seller *(line 1400)*	6,586
203. Existing loan(s) taken subject to		503. Existing loan(s) taken subject to	
204.		504. Payoff of first mortgage loan	70,000
205.		505. Payoff of second mortgage loan	
206.		506. Acc'd interest on loan	210
207.		507.	
208.		508.	
209.		509.	
ADJUSTMENTS FOR ITEMS UNPAID BY SELLER:		ADJUSTMENTS FOR ITEMS UNPAID BY SELLER:	
210. City/town taxes to		510. City/town taxes to	
211. County taxes to		511. County taxes to	
212. Assessments to		512. Assessments to	
213. Rents prepaid to 4/30	648	513. Rents prepaid to 4/30	648
214. Acc'd sewers&water charge	6	514. Acc'd sewer&water charge	6
215. Tenant security deposits	900	515. Tenant security deposits	900
216.		516.	
217.		517.	
218.		518.	
219.		519.	
220. TOTAL PAID BY/FOR BORROWER: ▶	95,554	**520. TOTAL REDUCTIONS IN AMOUNT DUE SELLER:** ▶	78,350
300. CASH AT SETTLEMENT FROM/TO BORROWER:		**600. CASH AT SETTLEMENT TO/FROM SELLER:**	
301. Gross amount due from borrower *(line 120)*	103,625	601. Gross amount due to seller *(line 420)*	100,829
302. Less amount paid by/for borrower *(line 220)*	(95,554)	602. Less total reductions in amount due seller *(line 520)*	(78,350)
303. CASH (☒ FROM) (☐ TO) BORROWER: ▶	8,071	**603. CASH (☒ TO) (☐ FROM) SELLER:** ▶	22,479

Previous Edition Is Obsolete
Form No. 1581
5/87

LENDER'S COPY

SB-4-3538-000-1
HUD-1 (3-86)
RESPA, HB 4305.2

To Reorder Call: Great Lakes Business Forms, Inc
Nationally **1-800-253-0209** Michigan **1-800-358-2643**

FIGURE 12-6
Completed RESPA form for the Burgoyne-Welsch transaction.

L.   **S E T T L E M E N T   C H A R G E S**

		PAID FROM BORROWER'S FUNDS AT SETTLEMENT	PAID FROM SELLER'S FUNDS AT SETTLEMENT
700. TOTAL SALES/BROKER'S COMMISSION: BASED ON PRICE $ 100,000 @ 6 % = 6,000			
DIVISION OF COMMISSION (LINE 700) AS FOLLOWS:			
701. $ 6,000 to Everybody Realty Co.			
702. $ to			
703. Commission paid at settlement			
704.			$6,000
800. ITEMS PAYABLE IN CONNECTION WITH LOAN:			
801. Loan Origination fee @ 2 % $90,000		1,800	
802. Loan Discount %			
803. Appraisal Fee to: Allen Measure		240	
804. Credit Report to: Rustic County Credit Bureau		40	
805. Lender's Inspection fee			
806. Mortgage Insurance application fee to			
807. Assumption fee			
808. Record Mortgage Satisfaction			4
809.			
810.			
811.			
900. ITEMS REQUIRED BY LENDER TO BE PAID IN ADVANCE:			
901. Interest from 4/12 to 4/30 @ $ /day		450	
902. Mortgage insurance premium for mo. to			
903. Hazard insurance premium for yrs. to			
904. Flood Insurance Premium for yrs. to			
905.			
1000. RESERVES DEPOSITED WITH LENDER:			
1001. Hazard insurance months @ $ per month			
1002. Mortgage insurance months @ $ per month			
1003. City property taxes months @ $ per month			
1004. County property taxes months @ $ per month			
1005. Annual assessments months @ $ per month			
1006. Flood Insurance months @ $ per month			
1007. months @ $ per month			
1008. months @ $ per month			
1100. TITLE CHARGES			
1101. Settlement or closing fee to Hifidelity Escrow Services		88	88
1102. Abstract or title search to			
1103. Title examination to			
1104. Title insurance binder to			
1105. Document preparation to Howard Light,Atty/Tange & Webb, Attys		40	120
1106. Notary fees to			
1107. Attorney's fees to			
(includes above items Numbers:)			
1108. Title insurance to Hifidelity Title Co.		110	360
(includes above items Numbers:)			
1109. Lender's coverage $ 110			
1110. Owner's coverage $ 360			
1111. Federal Express; overnight document delivered			14
1112.			
1113.			
1200. GOVERNMENT RECORDING AND TRANSFER CHARGES:			
1201. Recording fees: Deed $; Mortgage $; Releases $		28	
1202. City/county tax/stamps: Deed $; Mortgage $			
1203. State tax/stamps: Deed $; Mortgage $			
1204.			
1205.			
1300. ADDITIONAL SETTLEMENT CHARGES:			
1301. Survey to			
1302. Pest inspection to			
1303.			
1304.			
1305.			
1306.			
1307.			
1400. TOTAL SETTLEMENT CHARGES (Enter on line 103, Section J – and – line 502, Section K) ▶		2,796	6,586

I have carefully reviewed the HUD-1 Settlement Statement and to the best of my knowledge and belief, it is a true and accurate statement of all receipts and disbursements made on my account or by me in this transaction. I further certify that I have recieved a copy of HUD-1 Settlement Statement.

Borrowers _____   Sellers _____

The HUD-1 Settlement Statement which I have prepared is a true and accurate account of this transaction. I have caused or will cause the funds to be disbursed in accordance with this statement.

Settlement Agent _____   Date _____

WARNING: It is a crime to knowingly make false statements to the United States on this or any other similar form. Penalties upon conviction can include a fine or imprisonment. For details see: Title 18 U.S. Code Section 1001 and Section 1010.

Form No. 1582   SB-4-3538-000-1   **PAGE 2**

LENDER'S COPY

FIGURE 12-6
Continued

Under RESPA a lender has the following obligations to borrowers.

1. Supply an information booklet, *Settlement Costs and You: A HUD Guide for Homebuyers,* to anyone making a written loan application. The booklet explains the basics of settlement procedures, home financing, and the functions of the various parties in the sales transaction.
2. Supply a "good faith estimate" of the costs for settlement services likely to be incurred in a closing. The intent is to indicate the approximate amount of cash likely to be needed by the buyer at closing.
3. Supply specific costs to the buyer "at or before" actual settlement. Buyer may waive this requirement. At the same time, the buyer is entitled to see the settlement charges that have definitely been determined upon request within 1 business day of closing.

Questions for Review and Discussion

1. Explain the nature and importance of the following points in the title closing process:
   a. Survey and inspection
   b. Title search and report
   c. The acceptance or removal of encumbrances
2. List and briefly explain four classes of costs and adjustments in a title closing.
3. List and explain four rules of prorating.
4. Identify two buyer and two seller closing statement entries that do not involve proration.
5. Name two buyer and two seller closing statement entries that involve proration, and discuss the nature of each briefly.
6. All closings should be in escrow, by law. Discuss.
7. An escrow agent is apparently an agent of both the buyer and the seller. What are the implications of such a role? Discuss.
8. Discuss the advantages of a closing's being handled by each of the following people, from a buyer's point of view and from a seller's:
   a. Attorney
   b. Lender
   c. Broker
   d. Escrow agent

Case Problems

1. Property taxes of $19,200 are payable for the current year. Closing is to be on November 10. Calculate the amount of the adjustment, and indicate whether the buyer or seller gets the credit.

2. A 1-year hazard insurance premium of $660 provides coverage to April 15 of next year. Calculate the amount of the adjustment for a November 10 closing, and indicate whether the buyer or the seller gets the credit.

3. Todd Smith, a building contractor, listed a four-unit apartment building that he was about to complete for sale on October 15, 1988, with the Red Hot Realty Company for $160,000. A commission rate of 5 percent on the first $100,000 and 3 percent on anything in excess of $100,000 was agreed on in the listing contract. Dr. and Ms. I. M. Rich agreed to purchase the property for $150,000, with a stipulation for an escrow closing as of April 30, 1989. Their offer was conditional upon their getting a new first mortgage for $120,000 at an interest rate of 12 percent, or less, compounded monthly, with amortization over 30 years. A loan at exactly these terms was obtained from the Ace Savings and Loan Association. A 10 percent earnest money deposit was submitted with their offer to purchase.

   Mr. U. R. Wise contracted to act as escrow agent for the closing. Adjustments required of Mr. Wise are as follows.

   (1) Premium for title insurance, $300.
   (2) Mr. Smith's construction loan was for $100,000, at 12 percent, with interest payments of $1,000 being required on the last day of each month. His last payment was made on March 31, 1989.
   (3) Taxes for 1989 are expected to be $3,000, a figure agreed to by both parties. Being new, the property was not taxed as a fully completed property in 1988.
   (4) All four units are rented as follows.
       (a) Lower 1: $400 per month paid April 7, 1989, for April
       (b) Lower 2: $400 per month unpaid for April
       (c) Upper 3: $450 per month unpaid for April
       (d) Upper 4: $450 per month paid April 2, 1989, for April
   (5) Escrow fee is one-half of 1 percent, all payable by the buyers because they insisted on an escrow closing.
   (6) Some yard improvements are to be made later in the spring. All parties agree that $2,200, left in escrow, would ensure completion.
   (7) Fuel oil of 840 gallons is on hand at $.90 per gallon.
   (8) Hazard insurance was prepaid for 3 years, with $1,080 premium paid to run from September 21, 1988.
   (9) A part-time custodian cares for the property for $8.00 per day. She has not been paid for April.
   (10) A mortgage satisfaction recording fee of $8.00 must be paid.
   (11) Legal fee for drawing up deed to convey title is $50.00.
   (12) Cleaning supplies on hand, to be taken over by buyer, are valued at $210.

   a. Prepare a buyer's closing statement. (Additional amount to be paid by Dr. and Ms. Rich, including escrow fee, is $17,186.)
   b. Prepare a seller's closing statement. (Amount to be paid to Todd Smith upon closing, after paying commission, is $42,618.)

13

Real Estate Credit and Our Financial System

Bankers are just like anybody else, except richer.

Ogden Nash, American Poet

Money or credit is the lifeblood of real estate construction and sales activity. Money also constitutes a very strong and a very direct link between national economic conditions and real estate market activity. With adequate money, termed *easy money*, interest rates fall or remain low, and, in turn, construction and sales activity tend to be brisk. With a scarcity of money, termed *tight money*, interest rates go up or remain up. Loans for building properties and refinancing old ones become difficult to obtain. In turn, investment opportunities are scarce, sales and construction activity lags, and incomes of builders, brokers, and salespeople fall.

Money comes to real estate mainly through mortgage and trust deed arrangements. To simplify discussion, mortgages is used here to mean both kinds of loans. In addition to knowing the importance of money, a borrower needs to know how to obtain a loan locally and to be aware of the federal laws that apply to obtaining a loan. A sound knowledge of financial institutions and governmental agencies that make up mortgage markets is also helpful. These topics and others are covered in this and the next three chapters. We begin with discussion of money in the national economy and work down to the individual borrower.

Important Topics or Decision Areas Covered in This Chapter

Monetary Policy and Interest Rates
Costs and Availability of Mortgage Money
The Lender's Viewpoint
Shifting Interest Rates

Financial Markets and Money Flows

Primary Lenders
Savings and Loan Associations
Commercial Banks
Mutual Savings Banks
Life Insurance Companies
Mortgage Companies

Secondary Lenders
Federal Home Loan Bank System
Federal Home Loan Mortgage Corporation
Federal National Mortgage Association
Government National Mortgage Association
Private Mortgage Corporations

Lender Risks
Borrower Risks
Property Risks
Portfolio Risks

Lender Procedures and Commitments

Questions for Review and Discussion

Case Problems

Key Concepts Introduced in this Chapter

IMPORTANT
CHAPTER

df.

Borrower risk
Capital markets
~~Collateralized mortgage obligation (CMO)~~
Disintermediation
Easy money
Fannie Mae
Financial markets
Freddie Mac
Ginnie Mae
Housing affordability index
Intermediation
Liquidity

Loan commitment
Money market
Mortgage banker
Open market operations
Portfolio risk
Primary lender
Property risk
Risk
Secondary lender
Secondary mortgage market
Tight money

Monetary Policy and Interest Rates

The president of the United States, the Treasury Department, and the Federal Reserve Banking System all contribute to achieving our national economic goals. The main goals are full employment, economic growth, and price stability. The traditional way to achieve full employment and economic growth is to have an adequate supply of money in the economic system. Too much money puts more purchasing power (demand) in the system than can be satisfied by the available goods and services (supply) at existing price levels. The excess purchasing power competes for the available goods and services, driving prices upward. This increase in prices is not consistent with the third goal, price stability. Too little money in our economic system results in a series of adjustments in the opposite direction. Too little money causes interest rates to go up, discourages economic activity, and may result in a recession. Adjustments in the money supply, termed monetary policy, are made by our governmental officials to maintain an acceptable interest rate and an acceptable balance in our economic goals.

Monetary policy is usually implemented through the Federal Reserve Banking System. The Federal Reserve Banking System, often called the Fed, is the most dominant financial institution in the United States. The Fed, in managing the nation's money supply, directly affects most private financial institutions such as commercial banks, savings and loan associations, and mutual savings banks.

These institutions are also called financial intermediaries. Intermediary means to act as a go-between. Thus, a financial intermediary is a go-between in money matters, taking deposits from savers and lending to borrowers for investment. The process is called *intermediation*. Intermediaries also serve to channel funds from capital surplus areas, such as the central city, to capital deficit areas, such as the suburbs. Sometimes, savers withdraw monies from financial intermediaries and lend the monies directly to investors; this is called *disintermediation.*

In addition to private financial institutions, a number of public and semi-public agencies exist to buy and sell mortgages and to promote housing policies of the federal government. Taken altogether, these institutions and agencies financially tie construction and real estate activity to the national economy. Therefore, it is very much in the interest of the investor, builder, developer, finance officer, and broker to watch these public institutions and agencies.

COSTS AND AVAILABILITY OF MORTGAGE MONEY

The availability of money and the level of interest rates directly affect lending terms. As money gets tighter, lenders raise interest rates; they may also shorten the term of life of loans made. The result may be a substantial increase in debt service required of borrowers. For example, tighter money conditions may cause a lender to raise the interest rate from 9 to 12 percent and to lower the loan duration or life from 30 to 25 years. On a $100,000 mortgage, these changes would increase annual debt service from $9,734 to $12,750 or by more than 30 percent. See Figure 13-1. What does a 30 percent increase in borrowing costs mean?

Effect on Home Buyer. Lenders know from experience that a family can only afford to spend 25 percent of its income for PITI (principal interest, taxes, and insurance) payments. Of this 25 percent, 20 percent goes to loan debt service, principal and interest, with the remaining 5 percent going to taxes and insurance. A 30 percent increase in borrowing costs also means a 30 percent increase in the annual income needed to qualify to borrow $100,000, from $48,670 to $63,750. The increase would greatly reduce the number who could qualify, the demand for and the value of houses, and, in turn, the amount of construction and sales activity.

Duration	Interest Rate				
(Years)	6.00%	9.00%	12.00%	15.00%	18.00%
10	$13,587	$15,582	$17,698	$19,925	$22,251
15	10,296	12,406	14,682	17,102	19,640
20	8,718	10,955	13,388	15,976	18,682
25	7,823	10,181	12,750	15,470	18,292
30	7,265	9,734	12,414	15,230	18,126
35	6,897	9,464	12,232	15,113	18,055
40	6,646	9,296	12,130	15,056	18,024

FIGURE 13-1
Annual debt service varies directly with the interest rate and inversely with duration, with principal held constant at $100,000

The relationship between income and the sale prices of housing is so important that a housing affordability index is widely used to monitor it. The *housing affordability index* equals median family income divided by income needed to qualify for the purchase of the median priced existing single-family home. An index of 100.0 would mean that the family with a typical income would just qualify to buy the typically priced existing home. Interest rates are an important consideration in determining qualifying income and can cause wide fluctuations in the index. By using changes in this index, brokers, lenders, builders, and others can tell when housing is becoming more or less affordable and, in turn, anticipate increases or decreases in business activity.

A simple example shows how the index works. Mortgage interest rates were extremely high in 1981, averaging about 15.1%. In 1981, also, the median sale price of an existing home was $66,400; median family income was $22,388, and the income required to qualify for the purchase was $32,485. The affordability index stood at 68.9 ($22,388/$32,485). See Figure 13-2a. By 1986, interest rates had decreased to 10.25%. The median sale price had increased to $80,300, median family income to $29,200, and the qualifying income to $27,631. Even so, the index rose to 105.7, meaning that over half of the families could afford the median priced home. Needless to say, construction and sales activity picked up considerably from 1981 to 1986.

Year	Median Price of Existing Home	Median Family Income	Qualifying Income	Affordability Index	Interest Rate, %
1981	$66,400	$22,388	$32,485	68.9	15.12
1982	67,800	23,433	33,713	69.5	15.38
1983	70,300	24,580	29,546	83.2	12.85
1984	72,400	26,433	29,650	89.2	12.49
1985	75,500	27,735	29,243	94.8	11.74
1986	80,300	29,200	27,631	105.7	10.25
1987e	84,000	30,400	26,640	114.1	9.35

SOURCE: National Association of Realtors®: 1987: estimates by authors.

FIGURE 13-2A
Housing affordability index, 1981–1985

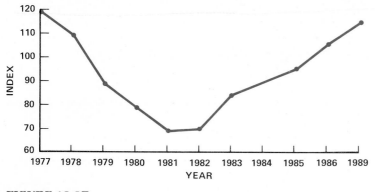

FIGURE 13-2B
Housing affordability index, 1977–1985

Effect on Investor. For income properties, debt service often runs to 80 percent of net operating income, or more. If cost of borrowed money goes up, an equity investor wants a proportionately higher rate of return because of being in a greater risk position. Net operating income must, therefore, go up by 30 percent to maintain values, meaning rents to tenants must be raised accordingly. Alternatively, if demand for space is weak, property values fall with very negative impact on existing owners. Obviously, an interest rate increase sharply reduces the number of potential equity investors at a given asking price.

THE LENDER'S VIEWPOINT

Financial institutions, as intermediaries, need a 1.5–2.0 percent spread between the interest rate they pay on savings deposited with them and the interest rate they charge on mortgage loans to be profitable. Mortgage loans have traditionally been long-term commitments with fixed terms. Interest rates are paid on all deposits, however, and go up with increasing interest rates in the economy. The result is a squeeze on profits.

To illustrate the squeeze, assume an institution with its assets invested as follows: 30 percent in mortgage loans made over 10 years ago at an average of 8 percent, 30 percent in loans made from 5 to 10 years ago, at an average of 10 percent, and 30 percent in loans made in the last 5 years, at an average of 12 percent. The balance of the firm's assets are held as cash, buildings, or equipment, and, hence, earn no income. The average interest rate paid by the institution on savings is expected to increase from 7.5 to 8.0 percent because of tightening money market conditions. What effect on profits?

$$30\% \times 8\% = 2.4\%$$
$$30\% \times 10\% = 3.0\%$$
$$30\% \times 12\% = 3.6\%$$
$$\underline{10\% \times 0\% = 0.0\%}$$

Weighted rate of return = 9.0%

The margin or differential equals 1.5 percent currently (9.0%–7.5%). The expected increase in the rate paid on savings deposits will drop the differential to 1.0%, not enough to cover operating costs and allow a profit. This type of squeeze caused financial institutions to turn to more flexible financing arrangements, such as ARM, RRM, and GPM loans in the early 1980s.

With an ARM, adjustable rate mortgage, the interest rate may vary. When made, an interest rate is agreed upon, with increases or decreases in accordance with fluctuations in an index beyond the control of the lender, such as the interest rates paid on U.S. Treasury securities. Typically, the terms provide that rate changes can be made only twice a year, at a maximum of 0.5 percent per change. The change may fluctuate a maximum of 5 percent, in most cases, above or below the original loan rate. If the interest rate increases, the term increases while the debt service is held constant. If too large an increase occurs, an increase in debt service might become necessary.

The benefit of an ARM loan to the lender is, of course, that an acceptable differential is more likely to be maintained between the interest rate paid on savings deposits and the interest rate earned on mortgage loans. Also, with adjustable terms, lenders may make loans more readily in a time of rising interest rates because they avoid running the risk of being locked into a long-term fixed interest rate mortgage that is below the current market rate.

SHIFTING INTEREST RATES

The two main methods used by the Fed in implementing monetary policy are (1) *open market operations* and (2) changing reserve requirements of member banks. Secondary methods are (1) changing the discount rate, (2) imposing selective controls when authorized by Congress, and (3) engaging in moral suasion. The process and effects of tightening or easing the money supply are summarized in Figure 13-3.

Open Market Operations. Government bonds and notes may be bought and sold in the open market by the Fed through its open market committee. Offering and selling large numbers of bonds drive bond prices down, because the supply exceeds demand. Individuals, banks, insurance companies, and other investors buy the bonds and pay by checks drawn on commercial banks, which reduces the number of dollars in the banks for loan purposes. This process makes money tight or scarce. Bankers ration out the scarce money by being more selective in making loans and by raising the interest rates charged on the loans. If the bankers cannot make sound loans at reasonable rates, they buy government bonds that are risk free and involve very low handling costs. Thus, the interest rate is pushed up and held up by the Fed's selling bonds on the open market. The Fed may buy bonds on the open market and lower the interest rate if easy monetary policy is the goal.

Changing Reserve Requirements. The Fed has the authority, within limits set by Congress, to raise or lower the reserve requirements of member banks. Reserve requirements are increased to make money tight or scarce. Since increasing requirements means that banks have less money to lend, the banks raise interest rates and credit requirements in making loans. For easy money, requirements are lowered so that banks have more money to lend. The banks, in turn, lower interest rates and act less selectively in making loans. Monetary policy is usually not implemented by changing reserve requirements of banks because a small change in re-

TO TIGHTEN MONEY SUPPLY	TO EASE MONEY SUPPLY
1. Federal Reserve System raises reserve requirements of member banks or sells bonds in open market to cause relative decrease in money supply.	1. Federal Reserve System lowers reserve requirements of member banks or buys bonds in open market to increase money supply.
2. Reserves of member banks are decreased. Money for new loans becomes limited.	2. Reserves of member banks are increased on relative basis. The reserves earn interest and produce profit only if put to work.
3. Member banks sell bonds and short-term notes to obtain money to meet demand of customers for new loans.	3. Member banks extend loans to customers more readily and buy bonds and notes with excess reserves.
4. As supply of bonds and notes offered for sale exceeds demand, prices drop; rate of return to buyers therefore increases.	4. As more bonds are purchased, demand exceeds supply offered for sale, and prices go up; rate of return to buyers decreases.
5. As rate of return increases, money is withdrawn from time and savings deposits to buy the bonds and notes. Also, bonds and notes are bought by savers in preference to putting new savings into time and savings accounts, which is *disintermediation*. Thus money is lost by banks and savings and loan associations.	5. As rate of return on bonds falls, more money is deposited in time and savings accounts in preference to more bond purchases. Therefore, *intermediation* increases as banks and savings and loan associations get more money to invest.
6. With less money to lend, banks and savings and loan associations raise lending standards and interest rates. Marginal borrowers are therefore unable to obtain credit.	6. With more money to lend, banks and savings and loan associations lower lending standards and interest rates. Marginal borrowers are therefore able to obtain credit.
7. Prepayment of mortgage loans and other low-interest debt drops off.	7. Prepayment of mortgage loans and other debt picks up as costs of refinancing drop.
8. Refinancing and new financing activity are slow because of higher interest rates and credit standards. Investment opportunities decline. Net result is reduced financial activity until money gets easier. Economy is slowed down, and inflation is hopefully brought under control.	8. Refinancing and new financing activity is brisk because of lower interest rates and credit standards. More investment opportunities become possible. Net result is increased financial activity as long as economy remains healthy and inflation remains under control.

FIGURE 13-3

Effects of changes in the money supply

quirements results in a large change in the money supply. Changing reserve requirements is too crude a tool for day-to-day monetary policy purposes.

Secondary Tools of the Fed. Members of banks may borrow from a federal reserve bank by pledging customers' promissory notes as collateral. The interest
rate the banks pay when borrowing is termed the discount rate. By raising the rate
of interest that member banks are charged for borrowing, the Fed can signal a desire
for tighter money. Lowering the interest rate signals easy money. Banks usually do
not borrow heavily from the Fed. Consequently, changing the discount rate does not
greatly affect the interest rate that banks charge their customers.

Selective financial controls are sometimes authorized by Congress and administered by the Fed. Selective controls, in the past, have been used only in times of
emergency, as when the Fed was authorized to raise down-payment requirements
on houses during the Korean emergency. Federal officials also sometimes use "moral
suasion" in an effort to convince banks to tighten or ease credit without any direct
regulation.

Financial Markets and Money Flows

Mortgage lending represents only a portion of the total money flows in our economy. Before looking closely at mortgage markets, let us take a brief look at overall flows of money in our economy, often referred to as "flow of funds" by economists.

In the overall scheme of economics, payments must be made by our business sector to the factors of production in generating the gross national product (GNP). The factors of production are land, labor, capital, and management. We earlier defined gross national product as the total value of all goods and services produced by our economy, valued at market prices. GNP is made up of all goods and services produced plus gross domestic private investment.

At the same time, the consuming sector of our economy, made up of the owner-managers of the factors of production, use the goods and services produced. These owner-managers get rents from land or realty, wages from labor, interest from money, and profits from ownership and management of business. The monies received go mostly to pay for the goods and services consumed. But some excess, or saving, is also realized by the consuming sector. This excess goes to the financial markets for investment. *Financial markets* are the places or the processes whereby those with funds lend to those wishing to borrow; money is exchanged for financial claims, such as bonds, bills, or mortgages. In financial markets, a distinction is usually made between money markets and capital markets. See Figure 13-4.

Money markets involve the exchange of money for short-term money instruments and the subsequent buying and selling of these short-term instruments. Examples are notes and Treasury bills. Short term means that the instruments have 1 year or less to maturity. Financial institutions, and others, continually create and trade short-term instruments to adjust and maintain liquidity positions.

Capital markets refer to the creation and exchange of long-term debt instruments (bonds and mortgage loans) and stocks for money. It follows that long term means that the instruments have maturity of longer than 1 year. Using 1 year as a dividing line is arbitrary but useful. Of course, stocks generally have no maturity date at all. The mortgage market is basically a capital or long-term market.

Competition for funds is implicit in a financial market. The function of the market is to channel the nation's savings to their highest and best use, usually meaning that use most able and willing to pay the highest rate of return. The competition for

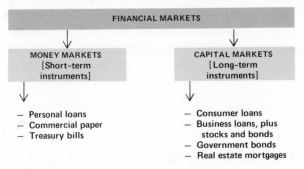

FIGURE 13-4

Allocation of funds through financial markets

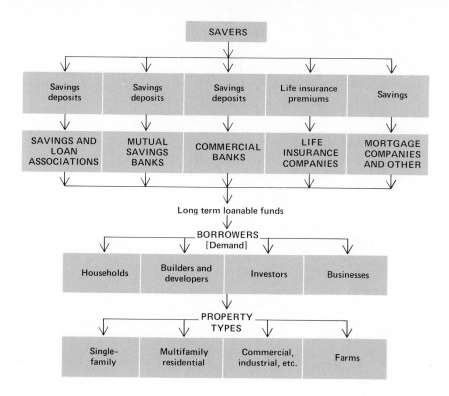

FIGURE 13-5
The flow of funds into the mortgage market through primary lenders

funds is between and among financial institutions as well as investment alternatives. The main institutions of concern are commercial banks (CBs), savings and loans (S&Ls), mutual savings banks (MSBs), and life insurance companies (LICs). The basic alternatives open to lenders are consumer loans, business loans, corporate stocks and bonds, government bonds, and mortgage loans. See Figure 13-4.

Broadly speaking, mortgage market participants may be divided into primary and secondary lenders. These lenders frequently buy and sell existing mortgages and mortgage-backed securities among themselves; this activity is called the *secondary mortgage market*. See Figure 13-5.

[handwritten: KNOW MAIN PRIMARY LENDERS "WHICH ONE ISN'T" Q SECONDARY "]

Primary Lenders

Primary lenders originate loans or supply funds directly to borrowers. Savings and loan associations, mutual savings banks, commercial banks, mortgage bankers, and life insurance companies make up the bulk of primary lenders. See Figure 13-5. *Secondary lenders* buy loans from, or originate loans through, someone else. Federally supported agencies, pension funds, and some life insurance companies are the major secondary lenders. Figure 13-6 shows the holders of outstanding mortgage debt in 1985, by both primary and secondary lenders; these main primary lending

Holder	Amounts	Percent of Total
Commercial banks	$ 426,103	18.88
Mutual savings banks	177,278	7.86
Savings and loan associations	586,085	25.97
Life insurance companies	170,460	7.55
Finance companies	30,402	1.35
Total: Selected Financial Institutions	$1,390,328	61.61
Government National Mortgage Association, GNMA	$ 1,473	.07
Farmers Home Administration, FmHA	733	.03
Federal Housing and Veterans Administration, FHA and VA	4,920	.22
Federal National Mortgage Association, FNMA	98,282	4.35
Federal Land Banks	47,548	2.11
Federal Home Loan Mortgage Corporation, FHLMC	14,022	.62
Total: Federal and Related Agencies	$ 166,978	7.40
GNMA pools	212,145	9.40
FHLMC pools	100,387	4.45
FNMA pools	54,987	2.44
FmHA pools	47,523	2.11
Total: Mortgage pools	$ 415,042	18.39
Individuals and Others	$ 284,430	12.60
Total, All Holders	$2,256,778	100.00

SOURCE: *Federal Reserve Bulletin*; percentages by authors.

FIGURE 13-6
Mortgage debt outstanding, 1985 (millions of dollars)

institutions held over 60 percent of outstanding mortgage debt in this year. Some financial organizations act as both primary and as secondary lenders. Primary lending institutions originate nearly seven-eighths of all mortgage debt. The laws and regulations governing them are taken up here in the order of their relative importance.

SAVINGS AND LOAN ASSOCIATIONS

There are approximately 4,000 savings and loan associations (S&Ls) in the United States. These associations account for more than one-third of all mortgage loans outstanding, in dollar terms, and nearly one-half of all home mortgages loans.

S&Ls have been active mortgage lenders for over 100 years. Yet, regulation of their activities on a national scale did not begin until 1932 when Congress created the Federal Home Loan Bank (FHLB) System. All federally chartered S&Ls are regulated by the FHLB System. Also, almost all savings and loan associations, if qualified, belong to the Federal Savings and Loan Insurance Corporation (FSLIC), which was created by Congress in 1934. FSLIC insures public deposits with member institutions for up to $100,000 per account. Depositor confidence in S&Ls is high because of this FSLIC insurance and because of FSLIC's uniform lending policy and accounting supervision.

S&Ls may make conventional installment loans for up to 95 percent of either the purchase price or appraised market value of any home offered as security, whichever is less. The loans must be amortized on a monthly basis and have a maximum life of 40 years. Almost all high loan-to-value ratios are made on an insured or guaranteed basis. FHA and VA loans may be made up to any loan-to-value limits acceptable to the Federal Housing Administration (FHA) or the Veterans Administration (VA). First mortgage loans may also be made on business and income properties, churches, and other improved properties up to a maximum loan-to-value ratio of 75 percent. S&Ls may also make loans for property improvement, alteration, repair, and equipment. Finally, mobile homes may be financed by S&Ls.

COMMERCIAL BANKS

Commercial banks (CBs) are required by law to maintain relatively greater liquidity in their assets than are other financial institutions because they are more subject to immediate withdrawal of deposits by the nature of their operation. Thus, although some 14,000 commercial banks control approximately one-half of the U.S. savings, their role in mortgage lending continues to be, for them, a secondary activity. Even so, CBs account for almost one-fifth of all mortgage loans outstanding. Making short-term commercial loans to local business firms is their primary lending activity. Short-term loans enable the banks to meet their liquidity requirements and at the same time to maximize their profits.

Commercial banks may make uninsured conventional loans on homes for up to 80 percent of the lesser of purchase price or appraised market value. The loans may be made, if fully amortized, for up to 30 years. Insured conventional loans may be made for up to 95 percent loan-to-value ratio. FHA-insured and VA-guaranteed loans may be made to any loan-to-value limits and terms allowed by the federal government. Commercial banks may also make construction loans for up to 24 months.

Commercial banks generally increase their mortgage lending activity when demand for local business is slow. They decrease mortgage lending activity when business loan demand is strong. That is, they tend to invest in real estate loans only when funds on hand exceed local business need. Recent improvements in secondary mortgage market operation has lessened the pressure on commercial banks to avoid mortgage lending activity. With an active secondary mortgage market, mortgages may be sold off at almost any time by a bank to increase cash on hand. Thus, mortgage loans are increasingly more liquid as assets.

MUTUAL SAVINGS BANKS

Mutual Savings Banks (MSBs) account for approximately one-eighth of all savings in the United States, of which about three-fourths is invested in mortgage loans. Thus, MSBs account for approximately 10 percent of all mortgage loans outstanding.

All of the approximately 450 mutual savings banks in the United States are state chartered. Most of them are located in the middle Atlantic states and in New England, with nearly seven-eighths in the states of New York, Massachusetts, Connecticut, Pennsylvania, and New Jersey. Mutual savings banks tend to be strong when savings and loan associations are weak, and vice versa. From the viewpoint of mortgage borrowers, the difference between S&Ls and MSBs is slight.

In almost all states, MSBs may make insured conventional loans up to 95 percent of value with a life of up to 30 years. Conventional, uninsured loans may generally be made up to 80 percent of value, also with an amortization period of up to 30 years. In a few states, uninsured conventional loans may be made up to 90 percent of value. FHA and VA loans may be made up to any loan-to-value ratios acceptable to the federal government.

LIFE INSURANCE COMPANIES

Life insurance companies (LICs) concentrate their mortgage lending efforts in multi-family and commercial properties. Larger loans and higher interest rates on loans for these properties make lending on them more profitable. Also, a share of the equity action, including participation in the income generated by these properties, is frequently arranged. Mortgage lending is particularly advantageous to LICs because of the long-term nature of their insurance policy obligations. Actuaries are able to forecast dollar requirements of their policy obligations and match them up with mortgages of appropriate terms.

Larger insurance companies make mortgages on a national scale. Some loans are made through branch offices, but many are made through mortgage bankers and brokers. Extremely large loans are usually arranged from the home office. LICs have considerable flexibility in their mortgage lending, but they generally limit loans to two-thirds of appraised value with amortization periods up to 30 years. FHA-insured and VA-guaranteed loans are purchased in secondary mortgage markets from time to time when excess reserves pile up and investment opportunities are limited.

MORTGAGE COMPANIES

Mortgage bankers and mortgage brokers hold little long-term mortgage debt. Instead, they service secondary lenders, such as life insurance companies and government agencies, that wish to invest in mortgages. *Mortgage bankers* originate and service loans for these secondary lenders for a fee. Mortgage brokers originate loans for the fee but do not provide any servicing. The secondary lenders must then arrange for servicing elsewhere, often through mortgage bankers. Mortgage bankers sometimes originate loans first and look for a buyer later if the loan presents a profit opportunity.

Eastern and midwestern banks and savings and loan associations sometimes become secondary lenders when they accumulate surplus funds that cannot otherwise be placed profitably; they use the surplus funds to buy loans, secured by properties in other regions, through mortgage bankers and brokers. The operations of mortgage firms become large in capital-scarce areas of the south and west where dependence on out-of-state funds is great.

Mortgage bankers generally charge three-eighths of 1 percent of outstanding loan balances per year as a servicing fee. Thus, an outstanding loan balance of $10,000 yields $37.50 per year to a mortgage banker. This $37.50 must cover the cost of accounting, filing, making monthly statements, correspondence, and office overhead. This effectively means that the mortgage banker must service a high volume of loans to have a profitable operation.

If left to themselves, primary lenders would soon run out of money for loans in periods of tight money. The federal government has worked to develop secondary mortgage institutions such as the Home Loan Bank Systems, FNMA, GNMA, and the Home Loan Mortgage Corporation to add liquidity to mortgage markets. See Figure 13-7. These agencies either advance monies to primary lenders or buy mortgages from them. In both events, monies of primary lenders are released to make more mortgages.

The main secondary lenders are agencies of the federal government and life insurance companies. Banks and S&Ls also sometimes act as secondary lenders if profit opportunities elsewhere exceed those locally. Pension funds also increasingly invest in mortgages. The combined activities of all these lenders link the nation's capital and mortgage markets.

In addition, primary lenders frequently buy and sell mortgages among themselves. For example, a New York MSB with excess funds may buy mortgages from an S&L in Colorado where funds are scarce, or life insurance companies may buy loans from mortgage bankers in several states. FHA-insured and VA-guaranteed loans facilitate this buying and selling of mortgages because of their standardized terms. Privately insured conventional loans on uniform FNMA/FHLMC instruments also give lenders protection and standardized terms. The result of this buying and selling activity among lenders is higher liquidity for mortgages and a broadening of the mortgage market. In addition, with commercial banks and life insurance companies being active in mortgage markets, mortgages must be directly competitive with other investments—stocks and bonds—in competing for excess funds. This competition means that mortgages and home construction are increasingly tied to the supply and demands for money in our entire economy.

A number of organizations promote loan safety, thus facilitating the purchase and sale of loans in the secondary mortgage market. These organizations offering

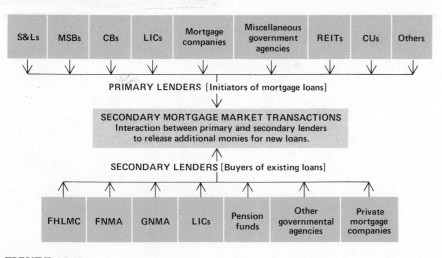

FIGURE 13-7
The Secondary Mortgage Market

protection to holders of mortgage loans include private insurance corporations, the Federal Housing Administration, the Veterans Administration, and the Farmers Home Administration.

FEDERAL HOME LOAN BANK SYSTEM

The Federal Home Loan Bank (FHLB) System was created by Congress during the financial crisis of the 1930s. The purpose was to establish a source of central credit for the nation's home financing institutions. This initial purpose has expanded into five functions as follows:

1. To link mortgage lenders to the nation's capital markets
2. To serve as a source of secondary credit for member institutions during periods of heavy withdrawal demand
3. To smooth out seasonal differences between savings flows and loan changes
4. To smooth flow of funds from capital surplus areas to capital deficit areas
5. To stabilize generally residential construction and financing

The FHLB advances funds to members in need, consistent with the foregoing functions. The system does not operate as a secondary mortgage market facility per se.

The Federal Home Loan Bank System is made up of 12 regional banks and member institutions. Membership is open to savings and loan associations, mutual savings banks, and life insurance companies. By law, all federally chartered savings and loan associations must belong. The system is governed by a three member board appointed by the president of the United States.

FEDERAL HOME LOAN MORTGAGE CORPORATION

The Federal Home Loan Mortgage Corporation (FHLMC) was created by Congress in 1970. The nickname for FHLMC is Freddie Mac. *Freddie Mac* functions as a secondary mortgage market facility under the supervision of the FHLB, and buys and sells conventional, FHA-insured, and VA-guaranteed mortgages. In recent years, FHLMC has promoted the development of mortgage-backed securities such as the *collateralized mortgage obligation* (CMO). Mortgage-backed securities generally pass through principal and interest, as received, to holders on a pro rata basis. The CMO provides a unique repayment structure to appeal to a wide variety of investors. CMOs are divided into three classes: short, intermediate, and long term. All holders receive semiannual payment of interest at the certificate rate. Holders of first class, short-term certificates receive all payments of principal from the collateralized loans until they are fully repaid. Next, holders of intermediate certificates receive all payments of principal. Of course, long-term holders are repaid their principal last. This unique repayment schedule reduces the uncertainty of holders as to the length of their investment. Pension funds have found the intermediate and long-term certificates particularly attractive.

The declared goal of the FHLMC is to make mortgages as liquid and attractive as other securities; in the past, mortgages have been considered a relatively illiquid investment. *Liquidity* refers to the ease or quickness with which an investment can be converted into cash and to the cash-to-value ratio realized. The easier the conversion into cash and the higher the cash-to-value ratio, the more liquid the investment.

The FHLMC seeks to accomplish its goal in several ways:

1. Development, in conjunction with the Federal National Mortgage Association (FNMA), of uniform mortgage instruments with standardized terms to facilitate the ready buying and selling of conventional mortgages in secondary mortgage markets.
2. Purchase and sale of conventional mortgage loans on a whole and a participation basis. Participation means that two or more investors or lenders share in the ownership of the loan.
3. Purchase and sale of FHA-insured and VA-guaranteed loans on a continuing basis.

FEDERAL NATIONAL MORTGAGE ASSOCIATION

The Federal National Mortgage Association (FNMA) was created by Congress in 1938. FNMA carries the nickname of Fannie Mae. *Fannie Mae* is a government-sponsored corporation, but its stock is privately owned. This unique combination of interests makes FNMA a private corporation with a public purpose.

The basic purpose of FNMA is to provide a secondary market for residential loans. FNMA buys, services, and sells loans to fulfill this purpose. It deals in conventional, FHA-insured, and VA-guaranteed loans. Operationally, FNMA buys mortgages when loanable funds are in short supply and sells them when funds are plentiful. FNMA and FHLMC jointly developed uniform instruments for conventional mortgage loans to facilitate their use in the secondary mortgage market.

* residential loans

GOVERNMENT NATIONAL MORTGAGE ASSOCIATION

The Government National Mortgage Association (GNMA) was created by Congress in 1968. GNMA is referred to in the trade as Ginnie Mae. *Ginnie Mae* is entirely owned by the federal government, and its financial activities are supported by borrowings from the federal government. In fact, Ginnie Mae is an agency of the Department of Housing and Urban Development and has its operating policies set by the HUD secretary. The GNMA has three main functions: (1) special assistance for disadvantaged residential borrowers; (2) raising additional funds for residential lending, and (3) mortgage portfolio management and liquidation.

The special assistance function involves providing funds for low-cost housing and for residential mortgages in underdeveloped, capital-scarce areas. The fund-raising function is to stabilize mortgage lending and home construction activities. The primary technique used to accomplish these two functions is government-guaranteed securities.

GNMA guarantees mortgage backed securities secured by government-insured or government-guaranteed loans, namely, FHA and VA loans. The loans underlying the guarantee are pooled, a covering security is issued, and repayments from the pool are used to pay off the security. Two basic types of securities are issued: the passthrough and the bond. The passthrough provides for monthly payments to the security holder. The bond provides for semiannual payments of principal and interest. Debt service from the pool of mortgages is used to make payments on the securities. The funds raised from sale of the security are used to purchase additional mortgages.

These programs, of course, result in GNMA's carrying a very large portfolio of mortgages, which requires continuing management. GNMA may buy, service, and sell mortgages in an orderly manner that will have a minimum adverse effect on the residential mortgage market and result in minimum loss to the federal government.

PRIVATE MORTGAGE CORPORATIONS

Some private mortgage insurance corporations organize subsidiary mortgage corporations to invest reserves in mortgages. Prepayments and monthly debt service on the mortgages are used to pay claims on insured mortgages on which lenders lost money. These companies constitute a private, secondary mortgage lender or investor. The largest of these firms is the MGIC Mortgage Corporation. The trade nickname for the MGIC Mortgage Corporation is Maggy Mae.

Lender Risks

Real estate credit can almost always be obtained if one is willing to pay the price by way of interest rate and other terms of borrowing. A sophisticated investor makes it a point to know the procedures of borrowing and to borrow at the most opportune time and at the most advantageous terms. Advantageous borrowing begins by understanding money market conditions. For example, the inverse relationship between money market supply and interest rates is an economic fact of life. The time required for a change in monetary conditions to be reflected in a changed level of residential construction is uncertain and depends on several complex factors. Nevertheless, the basic relationship continues; when plenty of money is available, interest rates drop, and vice versa.

A further consideration for the potential borrower is approaching the right institutions for the kind of loan desired. Savings and loan associations and mutual savings banks lend much more readily on one-family houses than do life insurance companies or commercial banks. Commercial banks and life insurance companies, however, are more likely to make loans on farms and commercial properties. Of course, individual lenders must be approached for purchased money mortgages and land contracts, as on undeveloped land.

A third major consideration is lender's risks, of which a potential borrower must be aware. Lenders continually balance opportunities for profits against *risk,* or the chances of loss of profit and principal. Lenders operate on the principle that as risk increases, profits should also increase. Mortgage lenders have three major sources of risk: (1) borrower, (2) property, and (3) portfolio.

BORROWER RISK

A lender's analysis of risk in making a loan begins with the borrower. This is called *borrower risk.* The categories of concern are (1) credit rating, (2) assets and net worth, (3) earning capacity or income, and (4) motivation. A lender is likely to have accept-reject guidelines for each category.

A credit rating may be obtained simply by ordering a credit report on the prospective borrower. The borrower's credit experience and reputation must show an acceptably stable performance, including job and income patterns and family life. Second, the credit report and the borrower's application also provide information on assets owned or net worth, including savings and checking account balances.

Third, the borrower's monthly or annual income must show a capability of making the principal, interest, taxes, and insurance (PITI) payments for the desired loan. For a homeowner's loan, the usual rule is that the PITI must not exceed one-fourth or 25 percent of the borrower's gross monthly income. The lender looks more to the property for security in making a loan on investment property.

Borrower's motivation is the final and perhaps the most important of the four categories. Motivation means that the borrower has sufficient incentive and desire to meet the requirements of the loan. A young family wishing to own their own home is usually considered highly motivated. Motivation may be judged in several ways. A strong credit report, a steady accumulation of assets, and rising income all indicate strong motivation.

PROPERTY RISKS

In analyzing *property risks*, three categories of concern must be addressed: (1) on-site characteristics, (2) location, and (3) marketability. Borrower risks are generally more important than are property risks for owner-occupied dwellings because the borrower is the primary source of money to meet the loan payments. But for investment properties, where the value may be many, many times the borrower's income, the property must be looked to more strongly for security. Property risks are largely evaluated in investment analysis, which is taken up in detail in Chapter 24.

The size, shape, and topography of a site are the first considerations in judging on-site characteristics. These characteristics must be complementary to the improvements and the use. Next, the size, condition, functional capability, mechanical equipment, and appearance of any improvements are taken into account.

Location means relative ease of accessibility, as discussed in Chapter 7. The exposure or environment of a property is also an important locational consideration.

Marketability risks pertain largely to market value and the economic makeup of the community. A growing community with diversified industries provides greater marketability, for example, than does a community with one industry that is declining. Also, stable employment and economic patterns are preferable to cyclical patterns.

PORTFOLIO RISKS

A portfolio, in finance, is all the securities, or investments, owned or managed. Undertaking the ownership and management of a large number of investments includes many risks, termed *portfolio risks*. For a mortgage lender, these risks may be categorized as (1) administrative, (2) investment, and (3) mix and turnover, or diversification, perils.

Administrative risks are perils inherent in making and servicing loans that might lead to losses. The chance of error in the property file and in keeping records of payments is ever present. Other administrative risks include overlooking some item in required periodic inspections to ensure upkeep and maintenance.

Investment risks are chances that an adequate rate of return will not be realized on loans. A loan may go sour for two reasons. First, the borrower might not be able to keep up with increasing costs of operation, in which event abandonment or foreclosure would result. Second, the property's value may decline faster than the loan is amortized. Thus, in a foreclosure, the unamortized principal plus foreclosure expenses might exceed the disposition value of the property.

Diversification in a portfolio is advantageous if the risks tend to offset each other or are not likely to occur at the same time. Thus, if all properties in the portfolio are not influenced in the same way at the same time, some risk is avoided. Examples would be that not all loans are made in the same community, not all borrowers are employed in the same industry, and not all borrowers have the same occupation.

Lender Procedures and Commitments

Making an application is the first step in obtaining a loan. Information required by lenders includes (1) the amount of the loan desired, (2) identification of the property to be pledged as security, and (3) annual income, kind of employment, and other financial information on the applicant. If the property and the applicant look acceptable to the lender, a loan commitment is given the borrower.

A **_loan commitment_** is a written pledge, promise, or letter of agreement to lend or advance money under specified terms and conditions. The amount, the interest rate, and the life of the loan are stated along with any other terms demanded by the lender. In most cases, the applicant has the right to shop with other lenders if the amount and terms of the commitment are unacceptable. At the same time, the lender is usually likely to include a termination date on the commitment, after which the offer to make the loan is withdrawn.

The four commonly used loan commitments are (1) firm, (2) conditional, (3) takeout, and (4) standby. The first two commitments, firm and conditional, are most applicable to consumer loans on residential properties. Takeout and standby commitments are important to builder-lender transactions as well as to transactions between lending agencies themselves.

A firm commitment is a definite offer to make a loan at stated terms and conditions. For all practical purposes, the borrower-applicant need only accept the offer and prepare for the loan closing. Nearly all commitments to homebuyers and small investors are firm commitments.

An agreement to make a loan, subject to certain limitations or provisions, is a conditional commitment. The provision may be completion of construction or development of a property. The Federal Housing Administration commonly issues conditional commitments for loan insurance to builders that depend on the builder's finding an acceptable buyer-borrower for the speculative house. The builder, therefore, accepts the risk of finding an acceptable buyer. Because the property is already approved, the conditional commitment facilitates the sale of the house.

A takeout commitment is an agreement by one lender to make a permanent loan to "take" another lender out of a temporary loan, such as a construction loan. A takeout commitment is also a firm agreement to buy a loan for an originating lender at a definite price. A takeout commitment is commonly used between financial institutions and government agencies. For example, a takeout commitment may be given by a governmental agency, such as the Government National Mortgage Association, to a local lender, such as a bank. The government agency agrees to buy and take over a mortgage loan from a local lender as soon as the loan is closed and all contingencies surrounding the loan are satisfied. The local lender is usually considered contractually bound to sell the loan at the stipulated price. The price to be paid for the loan is included in the written commitment. Takeout commitments usually involve properties under construction or development.

A standby commitment is the promise to buy a loan from a second lender, without the initial lender's being obligated to sell the loan. That is, standby commitment gives the owner of a loan the option to sell or not to sell the loan at the stipulated price. A standby commitment is usually issued by a large institutional lender, such as a life insurance company, to a local bank or mortgage banker.

Questions for Review and Discussion

1. Identify U.S. national economic goals. Explain how monetary policy helps to achieve these goals. How is monetary policy carried out?
2. Define or explain intermediation and disintermediation. When are these two concepts important?
3. What is the relationship of monetary policy and conditions to real estate construction and sales activity? What does this mean to a sophisticated investor?
4. Is the mortgage market a money or capital market? Why? What happens in capital markets?
5. What is the secondary mortgage market?
6. Identify and explain the three major sources of lender risk.
7. What is a primary lender? What financial institutions are most likely to be primary lenders?
8. What is a secondary lender? What institutions make up the bulk of secondary lenders?
9. Distinguish among conditional, takeout, and standby loan commitments.
10. Does real estate get its fair share of public savings? Explain how our various financial institutions affect the allocation of monies to real estate. What other considerations influence the portion of public savings channeled into real estate?
11. Real estate construction and sales activity are causes rather than effects of changing monetary conditions. Discuss.

Case Problems

1. The Ace Saving and Loan Association's assets earn at the following rates of return, based upon when the loans were made or what function the assets serve:
   20% earns at 8% rate

40% earns at 11% rate

30% earns at 13% rate

10% earns at   0% rate (operating cash, buildings, etc.)

What is Ace's weighted rate of return on its assets?

2. Ace pays the following rates for its monies:

Passbook	40% at $5\frac{1}{4}$%
Money certificates	50% at 11%
Owner's equity opportunity costs	10% at 15%

What is Ace's weighted cost of capital?

3. What spread does Ace realize between its earnings rate and its cost of capital? Is this spread adequate?

4. What actions can Ace take to improve its chances of maintaining an acceptable spread?

5. What type of risks does Ace S&L incur when doing the following:

a. Makes loans that require borrower to devote 30 percent of annual stabilized income (ASI) to housing expenses?

b. Restricts its loans to employees of the Uplift Fork Truck Manufacturing Corporation.

c. Consistently lends at 90 percent loan-to-value ratio (LVR) without requiring mortgage insurance?

d. Concentrates its loans on residences in the west side of the city?

14

Financing Alternatives

If you want to know the value of money, go and try to borrow some.

Benjamin Franklin

To borrow or not to borrow, that is the question faced by most people when buying real estate. Actually, most must borrow. The main financing choices for anyone not able or willing to put up 100 percent equity financing to control real estate are (1) leasing, (2) contracting for title, and (3) borrowing by way of a mortgage or trust deed. An option to purchase may be viewed as a financing device as well, but only for the short term.

We begin this chapter with a brief review of legal forms of ownership as they relate to equity financing. Reasons to borrow and loan terminology are taken up next because the concepts apply in most aspects of real estate finance. Lease and land contract financing are then discussed as the main alternatives to borrowing from established financial institutions; discussing these two at this point allows the entire next chapter to be devoted to mortgage and trust deed financing.

Owners financing an entire property with personal monies is known as 100 percent equity financing. *Equity,* therefore, is another way of referring to an owner's interest in a property. Alternatively, an owner may pledge the property as security for a loan, as with a mortgage. Taking out a loan to finance a property is termed *debt financing.* A lender making loans to help finance properties is said to be providing *credit financing.* Finally, for someone without any money or not wishing to make an equity investment, a property may be rented. Thus, from an owner's point of view, the choices range from 100 percent to zero percent financing. In any event, the total value of a parcel of real estate is financed by someone at all times.

Important Topics or Decision Areas Covered in This Chapter

Equity Financing
Individual Equity Financing
Group Equity Financing

Debt Financing
Necessity
Financial Leverage
Loan Terminology

Land Contract Financing
Example
Use
Default

Lease Financing
Lease Financing of Business Properties: Major
 Concerns
Sale-Leaseback Arrangement
Ground Lease with a Mortgaged Leasehold
Default

Questions for Review and Discussion

Case Problems

Key Concepts Introduced in this Chapter

Amortization
Credit financing
Debt financing
Debt service
Duration of a loan
Equity
Interest

Interest rate
Land contract
Leverage, financial
Loan-to-value ratio
Principal of a loan
Sale-leaseback
Subordination clause

Bank - credit financing
Buyer - debt financing

Equity Financing

An equity position may be owned by one individual or by two or more individuals and/or business organizations working together as a group. The legal concepts of ownership, explained in Chapter 4, are directly related to the equity positions described in this chapter, and a brief review to tie the concepts together seems appropriate.

The source of equity funds is mainly from the personal resources of individuals or monies accumulated by institutional investors. Some aspiring homeowners develop equity by providing work in kind: painting, labor, and so forth, in new construction, which is termed "sweat equity."

Financial institutions, such as insurance companies, banks, pension funds, business corporations, trusts, and savings and loan associations, may be equity investors or lenders. For an institution, acquiring an equity position is not lending money to the venture; it expects to share in the profits and the risks of property operations the same as other equity investors. Thus, an institutional investor is in a significantly different position relative to the property than an institutional lender.

INDIVIDUAL EQUITY FINANCING

Typically, an individual uses personal savings as equity funds to gain undivided ownership of a property, which is termed "sole ownership" or "an estate in severalty." Debt financing (e.g., a mortgage loan) may be used by the sole owner to help in acquiring and holding the property. A condominium interest in real property is also owned by an individual as an estate in severalty, even though debt financing is used to acquire the interest.

GROUP EQUITY FINANCING

An equity interest in real property may be owned and financed by a group, through a tenancy or a business organizational arrangement. Under either arrangement, individual members supply or provide the equity funds based on an agreement between the parties.

A major distinction between the arrangements is real property versus personal property. If property is held by a group as tenants, the laws of real property apply between and among the members of the group. If the property is held under a business organizational arrangement, the laws of personal property apply.

By Tenancy Arrangement. A husband and wife each own an undivided interest in the entire property under tenancy by the entirety and community property. The couple is considered as jointly putting up the equity funds to finance the property under either form of tenancy, except when the property is received as a gift or is inherited. At the same time, the couple usually borrows against the property as individuals.

Two or more persons may acquire and finance equal equity interests under a joint tenancy arrangement in some states. Partnerships sometimes use joint tenancy arrangements to hold and finance property to ensure continuity of the enterprise should one of the partners die. That is, the right of survivorship passes ownership to the surviving partners instantaneously. In return, life insurance is usually carried on each partner and is paid for by the partnership, with the insurance benefits going to the deceased partner's spouse or estate. Again, debt financing may be used to help finance the purchase of the property.

The equity position may be split into equal or unequal shares under tenancy in common ownership. Each tenant owns an undivided interest in the property. Debt financing, if obtained, would require that all tenants in common sign the note and mortgage or other security agreement and be jointly and individually responsible for the debt.

Finally, a condominium arrangement may be used to own and finance a large, complex property. Each condominium unit must be financed by its individual owner, however. In turn, default by one condominium owner does not obligate other owners to pick up the payments to protect themselves. The unit in default simply goes through foreclosure proceedings the same as any other property owned in fee simple.

By Business Organizational Arrangement. The main business organizational arrangements for owning and financing an equity position in property are the corporation, the trust, and the cooperative. Property owned by partnership is usually held by the general partners as tenants in partnership. A syndicate may be a partnership, corporation, or trust, depending on which is most advantageous.

The financial structure of a corporation is usually made up of stocks and bonds. The stock represents equity ownership, while the bonds represent debt financing. The stockholders enjoy limited liability but are subject to double taxation on income earned by the corporation: once at the corporate level and once at the personal level when the dividends are received. The corporation may own an equity interest in real property against which a mortgage loan has been obtained.

A trust operates much in the manner of a corporation except that profits or proceeds go to specific beneficiaries rather than to stockholders. Cooperatives are either corporations or trust. The corporation or trust owns the real estate. Shareholders get a proprietary lease to a specified unit of space upon purchase of stock. The cooperative pays taxes and obtains needed debt financing on the property. If shareholder-proprietary tenants fail to pay their pro rata share of taxes and debt service, the burden of keeping the cooperative solvent falls on the remaining shareholder-tenants, who make up the group owning the equity interest in the property.

Debt Financing

Any decision to own or control real estate must take account of its high value, which, in turn, makes an understanding of debt financing extremely important. With this brief introduction, let us look at reasons for borrowing and understanding loan terminology in some detail.

NECESSITY

Families borrow to buy homes because houses typically cost two to three times the homebuyer's annual income. That is, the average family only has savings equal to approximately 10 to 20 percent of the purchase price of the desired house. Homebuyers usually prefer to buy and make payments on a loan rather than to pay rent. In a similar manner, most investors find that they must borrow to buy real estate.

FINANCIAL LEVERAGE

Leverage, in finance, is the controlling of a large investment with a relatively small equity investment. In science, leverage means the physical use of a lever or bar to gain a mechanical advantage in applying a force to an object. The longer the distance from the force being applied to a pivot point relative to the distance from the pivot

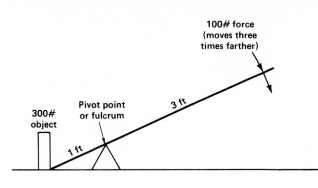

FIGURE 14-1
Physical leverage

point to the object, the greater the magnification of the force being applied. However, the force being applied must move a much greater distance as a compensation. The process works in reverse as well. Applying a force at the short end magnifies the distance moved by a point or an object at the long end. See Figure 14-1.

The concept of leverage carries over to economics and finance. An investor can control a high value property with a small equity investment by borrowing a major percentage of the value. In turn, the investor's gains or losses are magnified, which leads to positive and negative financial leverage. Positive financial leverage (PFL), occurs when borrowing magnifies or increases the rate of return earned on the equity portion of the investment. For this to happen, the property or investment must earn at a higher rate than the interest rate charged for the borrowed money. If the property earns at the same rate as the cost of the borrowed money, no leverage is realized. If the property earns at a lower rate, negative financial leverage (NFL) results. Financial leverage is also termed "trading on the equity," meaning exploiting or taking the best possible advantage of an equity position in an investment.

Financial leverage may be realized in two distinct ways, as illustrated by the following examples.

Leverage Through Value Increase. Assume that an investor owns a $1 million property with an $800,000 mortgage loan against it. The investor's equity in the property is $200,000. An increase of $200,000 in the market value of the property, to $1,200,000, accrues entirely to the owner-investor. This means that positive financial leverage is realized as the value of the equity position doubles from $200,000 to $400,000. Thus, there is a 100 percent increase in equity resulting from a 20 percent increase in the property's value, which means positive leverage of 5:1. The debt, $800,000, remains unchanged.

Interest in Property	Initial Financing	Financing after Increase in Property Value
Market value	$1,000,000	$1,200,000
Debt (fixed)	− 800,000	− 800,000
Owner's equity	$ 200,000	$ 400,000

Leverage Through Cash Flow. A second example shows leverage resulting from differences in cash flows. The facts are simplified to make the principle of leverage stand out. Assume that a commercial lot worth $1 million is under a long-term net lease for $100,000 per year; that is, the tenant pays all costs of operation. Without debt financing, the rate of return to the owner is 10 percent. But, suppose the owner obtains a long-term loan of $900,000 at 9 percent interest against the property, with no amortization required. That is, only interest payments of $81,000 need to be paid each year ($900,000 × 9% = $81,000). The difference in income of $19,000 ($100,000 − $81,000 = $19,000) goes entirely to the equity position, which now is $100,000 ($1,000,000 − $900,000 = $100,000). The rate of return has been leveraged up to 19 percent.

Total annual net income from lease	$100,000
Less interest on fixed debt ($900,000 × 9% = $81,000—	−81,000
Equals net cash flow to equity	$ 19,000
Divided by equity position's value ($1,000,000 − $900,000)	$100,000
Equals equity rate of return	19%

The advantages of leverage are not received without cost. The borrower incurs increased risk of loss of income or of the property if reality does not live up to expectations. Thus, in the first example, if the property value declined by $100,000, negative financial leverage at a 5:1 ratio would result because the equity position would be cut 50 percent by a 10 percent decrease in the property's value. In the second example, a net income decrease by $10,000, or 10 percent, would reduce the rate on return to equity to 9 percent, a decline of slightly more than 50 percent. Under worse circumstances, the equity position might become a liability, as a result of the more severe negative financial leverage. Use of leverage always increases the risk of loss to the equity position.

In using leverage it is important to distinguish between expected and unexpected events. Gain may be realized from using leverage with events developing as expected. Less gain, or losses, might result with slower rates of growth, foreseen as possibilities when the investment was made. Thus, investors used leverage with expectations of gains during the rapid period in growth in Houston, Texas, which was based both on the oil boom and NASA's flight schedule. The collapse of Houston's economy in the 1980s owing to conflicts in OPEC and the price of oil and to the loss of the space shuttle were certainly unexpected events for these investors. The result was a wave of foreclosures that wiped out many equity investors. But, many of these investors would probably have been wiped out, even if they had not tried to use leverage. In a parallel sense, unexpected gains might be realized, whether or not leverage were used. The sudden discovery of gold in Colorado would probably give Denver investors profits over and above anything they might have expected from using leverage.

LOAN TERMINOLOGY

Clear, well-defined terms are necessary in negotiating and arranging a loan to avoid incorrect calculations and confused communications. For the most part, the terms or concepts are the same, whether a mortgage, trust deed, land contract, or some other instrument is involved, because the terms relate to the financing arrangement, and not to the security instrument.

An $800,000 loan on a $1 million commercial property provides a convenient example to illustrate these loan terms and concepts.

Loan-to-Value Ratio. The proportion of a property's appraised market value borrowed is usually expressed as a percentage, called the *loan-to-value ratio* (LVR, sometimes LTV). Using the case example, the loan-to-value ratio is 80 percent.

$$\frac{\text{Loan}}{\text{Market value}} = \frac{\$800,000}{\$1,000,000} = 80\% = \text{LVR}$$

The higher the loan-to-value ratio, the higher is the risk to the borrower and to the lender. Therefore, maximum LVRs, for lending purposes, are set by law for most financial institutions. The LVR required of or used by a lender directly affects the amount of cash or equity down payment required of a borrower. If a lender is subject to a maximum LVR of 75 percent, a borrower with only $10,000 will not be able to bid for a property with a value in excess of $40,000. This is in contrast to a $100,000 property where a 90 percent LVR applies.

Loan Principal. The *principal of a loan* is the number of dollars actually borrowed or the remaining balance of the loan. Almost all homeowners derive their income from wages or salaries; typically, 25 percent of income goes for housing. The amount a homebuyer is able to borrow therefore depends directly on his or her income. In turn, the quality of housing that can be bought depends directly on how much can be borrowed.

Interest Rate. *Interest* is the rent or charge paid for the use of money. An *interest rate* is the amount paid to borrow money, calculated as a percentage of the amount borrowed. The higher the interest rate, the higher the interest charge. For example, at 6 percent, annual interest on $800,000 equals $48,000. At 9 percent, annual interest equals $72,000.

From a lender's point of view the interest rate charged to borrowers reflects several factors: (1) the lender's cost of money, (2) the interest rates of other lenders, (3) the risks in the loan based on the property's and the borrower's characteristics, and (4) the yields available on competitive investments such as Treasury bonds and consumer loans.

Loan Duration. The *duration of a loan* is the time given the borrower to repay the loan. The maximum acceptable duration is 40 years for loans to be bought and sold in the secondary mortgage market. However, most lenders have shorter loan periods based on management policy. A loan duration of from 20 to 30 years is typical for residential properties. The loan period for commercial loans is usually shorter, between 10 and 20 years.

Loan Amortization. *Amortization* means regular periodic repayment of the principal. The repayment is usually made at the same time interest payments are made. The longer the amortization period, the smaller the periodic installments to repay the principal. If amortization is not required, interest must usually be paid periodically, with repayment of the entire loan principal on the last day of the contract. A loan may be partially amortizing, meaning that periodic payments are made to reduce the principal balance, but at some date the entire remaining balance must be repaid in a single, lump-sum payment.

Debt Service. The periodic payment required on a loan for interest and, usually, principal reduction is termed *debt service.* If amortization is not called for (typical of construction loans), debt service is made up of interest only. Debt service reflects the principal amount, the interest rate, the duration, and the amortization schedule of a loan, already discussed. Understanding the interrelationships among these loan elements is extremely important in arranging terms suited to a property's income or the income of a homebuyer. See Figure 14-2 for a brief summary of these interrelationships.

Land Contract Financing

Several Q's

Buyers often lack adequate down payment to qualify for a loan from an established financial institution; or preserving an existing loan on the property being bought would be advantageous; or the property desired will not qualify for a mortgage loan, because of being vacant or being located in a run-down area. In all these situations, a land contract may well serve as a suitable financing alternative.

A *land contract* is a written agreement between a seller (vendor) and a buyer (vendee) for the sale of real property over an extended time, with the title remaining in the seller until the terms of the arrangement are met. The buyer usually takes possession when the contract is made. Payments are credited toward the purchase price in a manner parallel to that by which a mortgage loan is amortized. A land

---

Debt service is a function of the principal, interest rate, duration, and amortization schedule, as shown with the following $800,000 loan:

1. The larger the principal amount, the greater the required debt service. Thus, annual debt service on a $600,000, 12 percent, 25-year loan ($76,500) is less than that for an $800,000 loan on comparable terms ($102,000).
2. The higher the interest rate, the greater is the debt service. Increasing the interest rate on the $800,000 loan from 12 to 15 percent increases annual debt service from $102,000 to $123,760.
3. Duration has an inverse impact on debt service. The longer the duration, the smaller the debt service, although the relationship is not proportional. Thus, increasing the term of the $800,000 loan from 25 to 30 years only lowers debt service from $102,000 to $99,315.
4. The more frequent the payments (monthly versus annual, for example), the smaller the debt service. With annual payments, total annual debt service for our 12 percent, 25-year, $800,000 loan comes to $102,000. With monthly payments it decreases to $101,110 ($101,110 equals $8,425.79 times 12). The $890 lower amount comes about because principal repayment begins earlier with monthly payments. Thus, interest is paid on a slowly declining principal during the year.

FIGURE 14-2
Debt service in a nutshell

contract is also known as a contract for deed, an installment land contract, or a real estate contract. See Figure 10-1 for a sample land contract.

EXAMPLE

Assume that a 20-unit apartment building is being sold on a land contract for $1 million. The seller has an existing mortgage of $700,000 against the property at an interest rate of 8 percent. The owner's equity in the property is, therefore, $300,000.

Contract sale price	$1,000,000
Less the seller's mortgage at 8%	700,000
Equals owner's equity	$ 300,000

The buyer puts $50,000 down and agrees to make payments sufficient to cover interest and to reduce the balance due the seller from $950,000 to $800,000 by the end of 5 years. The buyer may refinance at any time and must refinance before the end of the sixth year. The interest rate on the unpaid land contract balance is a competitive 10 percent.

From a buyer's viewpoint a land contract is similar to a partially amortizing loan in that payments go for interest and principal reduction. However, the seller retains legal title and continues to pay debt service on the existing mortgage loan against the property. Thus, both parties may be in highly leveraged positions. The transaction now looks like this:

Item	Value Allocation	Interest/Return
Contract sale price	$1,000,000	
Less the buyer's down payment	– 50,000	
Equals amount of contract balance at 10%	$ 950,000	$95,000
Less the seller's mortgage loan at 8%	– 700,000	56,000
Equals owner-seller's equity	$ 250,000	$39,000

Amortization aside, the seller receives $95,000 in interest in the first year (10% × $950,000), while paying $56,000 interest on the mortgage loan (8% × $700,000). The difference is $39,000. At the same time, the owner-seller's equity amounts to only $250,000. This calculates to a rate of return to the owner-seller of 15.6 percent ($39,000/$250,000). Thus, the buyer gets a 95 percent loan-to-value ratio loan, and the seller both disposes of the property and stands to earn over 15 percent on the $250,000 loan to the buyer.

USE

A land contract is at one time extremely useful and extremely risky. It serves as a sales, financing, and tax-avoidance instrument. The buyer makes only a nominal or "thin" down payment, which certainly helps in making the sale. At the same time, a transaction may be set up quickly, as in the sale of a subdivision lot, where delay in arranging financing might allow a hot prospect to cool off; this clearly is a plus for a seller. The buyer gets a high loan-to-value ratio loan, which calls for regular payments (usually monthly) over a number of years, at a competitive rate of interest. In receiving the sale price over several years, the seller pays taxes at a lower rate than if the full sale price were received all in 1 year. Further, the buyer agrees to pay the annual taxes and insurance premiums on the property and to maintain the property in a reasonable condition, which means the seller has few carrying costs for the investment. At the same time, some definite risks or concerns are involved.

Seller Considerations. Traditionally, land contracts have been written to protect the seller for a number of reasons. As was mentioned, the buyer may be making only a thin down payment, may have a weak credit rating, and the property may be marginal. In these situations the seller wants to be able to recover the property, in case of buyer default, with a minimum of time and expense. Hence, a contract for deed makes possible the sale and financing of properties that would be very difficult to arrange in other ways while fully protecting the seller.

The vendor is advised to coordinate any required balloon payment or any prepayment privileges in the contract with comparable privileges in a mortgage against the property. Failure to do so might mean that the vendee has the right to prepay the land contract even though the vendor would not be able to prepay the mortgage. In such a situation the vendor is open to a heavy prepayment penalty to the mortgagee or a breach of contract suit from the vendee for failure to perform.

Buyer Considerations. A land contract gives a buyer time to build up equity in the property, at which time more traditional financing becomes possible. At the same time, several cautions should be exercised by a buyer in using a land contract.

First, evidence of clear and marketable title should be required at the time the land contract is drawn up. Failure initially to assure clear title might mean that the buyer would make payments for several years only to find that the seller cannot deliver marketable title.

Second, the transaction should be handled in escrow. Failure to have a deed signed by the seller immediately and delivered into escrow might result in delay and added costs to the buyer, if the seller dies or becomes incapacitated later on. Also, it is usually advisable to have periodic payments paid into escrow to ensure that mortgage debt service payments are made on schedule.

Third, the land contract or notice of the land contract should be recorded immediately, particularly if the vendee does not move into possession, as with a vacant lot. Without recording or possession by the buyer, the seller could conceivably sell the lot several times and leave town. The several buyers would be left with a serious and expensive litigation problem in addition to being out some dollars.

Fourth, the seller should not be permitted to put vendee's equity up as collateral for a loan. A simple clause in the contract to this effect, along with recording, would accomplish this restraint. To illustrate the problem, let us return to our earlier land contract example.

Assume that it is 5 years later and that the balance of the land contract has been paid down to $800,000. Meanwhile, the value of the property increased to $1,300,000. The buyer's equity should, therefore, be $500,000. But suppose that the seller refinanced the property with a $1,100,000 mortgage 6 months ago and left the area for whereabouts unknown. The vendee's equity has been reduced to $200,000 ($1,300,000 less $1,100,000). Of course, the vendee also has a legal claim for $300,000 against the seller, assuming that the seller can be found.

DEFAULT   CAUTIONS

Several options are open to the vendor if a buyer defaults, including forfeiture, specific performance, foreclosure suit, or suit for damages.

The vendor may declare forfeiture of rights by the buyer and retain as damages any amounts paid or any improvements made by the vendee. Second, the vendor may require specific performance of the vendee. This option would probably be exercised if the unpaid balance of the land contract exceeds the value of the property and if the vendee if financially able. Third, the seller may file a foreclosure suit upon buyer default and seek to have the property sold. Finally, the seller may file suit for damages against the buyer if none of the foregoing options seems satisfactory.

Lease Financing

Controlling nonresidential real estate by long-term lease rather than by purchase is often done to avoid ownership problems and to gain major financial advantages. Insurance companies, pension funds, and universities are dominant among investors that own and finance leased business properties. Oil companies, motel chains, retail chains, supermarket chains, trucking companies, and public utilities all frequently lease rather than buy facilities to conserve working capital while rapidly expanding activities and services. Even the federal government frequently leases rather than buys post offices.

LEASE FINANCING OF BUSINESS PROPERTIES: MAJOR CONCERNS

The rent, in a business lease arrangement, must be adequate to give the owner a competitive rate of return on the investment and to cover expected depreciation of the leased property. The tenant usually pays property taxes, insurance, and operating and maintenance expenses, an arrangement that is termed a net lease and sometimes a net, net, net lease. The more "nets," the more the operating expenses presumably paid by the tenant. Definitions are not fully standardized in this area. Thus, in negotiating a lease, clear communication between the parties is essential.

Unless otherwise agreed, the tenant-lessee receives the rights to occupy and use the premises and to sell the leasehold. At the same time, the owner-lessor may sell or assign the rights to the rental payments.

Long-term commercial leases run from 10 to 99 years and sometimes longer. The length of the lease, and any renewal options, must be stated, including a means of setting rents for any extensions. In addition to renewal options, a lease may contain an option to purchase or, in a sale leaseback, to repurchase.

Mortgages enter into lease negotiations by way of subordination clauses. A *subordination clause* establishes the relative priority of claims on a property. For example, subordination of a lease to a mortgage means that in default, the lessee's right of occupancy might be completely wiped out by default and foreclosure. Lease subordination is often used by an owner to obtain better loan terms. In accepting subordination, the lessee should expect better rental terms and may even reserve the right to pay debt service directly to the mortgagee to prevent default.

SALE-LEASEBACK ARRANGEMENT

A *sale-leaseback* is the transfer of title for consideration (sale) with the simultaneous renting back to the seller (leaseback) for a specified time at an agreed upon rent. A sale-leaseback might come about in the following manner. A supermarket chain has owned a store with high sales production for some 14 years. The improvements have been largely written off, that is, depreciated for tax purposes. Also, the property has tripled in value. The chain wishes to raise more working capital and, at the same time, to retain the store because it is on an excellent site. A mortgage could be placed against the store for two-thirds of its value, but the loan would show up on the chain's balance sheet as a liability. A sale-leaseback may be a better alternative.

The store may, therefore, simultaneously sell to a private investor and rent back the property. The rent is set high enough to allow the investor a reasonable profit on the investment while writing off the improvements over the life of the lease. By treating the property as an income property and by taking out a mortgage against it, the investor uses financial leverage to gain a higher rate of profit.

What does the supermarket chain gain from the transaction? First, the equity in an older, existing property, on which the depreciation tax shelter has largely been used up, is converted into working capital. That is, the owner by selling the property gets cash equity out to use in the business. Further, leasing back the property for continued use allows the owner-seller to retain a profitable site. In addition, the rental payments are fully tax deductible. Continuing to own and operate the property would mean that the imputed rent would be fully taxable in that it is no longer sheltered by depreciating the property improvements.

Some business firms use buy-build-sell leases to get facilities designed and built specifically to the needs of the business but financed by someone else. The result is identical to that of the sale and leaseback arrangement. Thus, a restaurant chain may buy land in a desired location, build a structure, sell the improved property to an interested investor, and simultaneously lease it back. Once a working relationship is established, the investor may buy and improve the land for subsequent lease to the business firm, without the chain ever taking title. This allows the chain to expand very rapidly with only a limited amount of money invested in real estate.

GROUND LEASE WITH A MORTGAGED LEASEHOLD

Another major option of a business firm is to use leasing and mortgage financing in combination. A desired parcel of vacant land is rented on a long-term lease, which is termed a ground lease. Improvements are added and financed with a leasehold mortgage, which means that only the lessee's interest in the property is pledged to secure the loan. With this arrangement, a lessee may depreciate improvements completely for tax purposes over the life of the lease. Thus, depreciation is kept as a tax shelter rather than passed on to an investor. In addition, the rental payments for the land are tax deductible.

DEFAULT

A breach of rental terms, most likely nonpayment of rent, constitutes lease default. The owner-landlord then has a range of options that run from suing the tenant for specific performance to eviction and re-renting as discussed in Chapter 5.

Questions for Review and Discussion

1. Explain fully the relationship between equity financing and debt financing as they pertain to a property's market value.
2. When is a tenancy arrangement most likely to be used in equity financing among a group, where business or investment objectives are paramount? When might a business organizational arrangement (corporation, for example) be a better alternative?
3. Debt financing is used out of necessity or to gain financial leverage. Explain how financial leverage works. Is the use of leverage always advantageous?
4. Identify and explain or define briefly the six key financial terms to be negotiated in arranging debt financing.
5. How does a land contract work as a financing device? Give two key considerations in the use of a land contract by a buyer; a seller.
6. Is a land contract more a sales or a financing device? Discuss. What circumstances influence your answer?
7. Does the buyer or the seller have greater power in negotiating a land contract sale? Discuss. What considerations enter into your answer?
8. Should a land contract have provisions pertaining to the applicability of payments for taxes, insurance, interest, and principal reduction?
9. Discuss a long-term lease as a financing device, with emphasis on the sale and leaseback arrangement. When might such an arrangement be most advantageous?
10. Does the lessor or the lessee have the greater power in negotiating a long-term lease? Explain. Would it make any difference if a sale and leaseback were being negotiated?

Case Problems

1. Joe Baloney buys a vacant lot on a land contract, agreeing to pay $24,000, with $4,000 initial down payment. Shortly after, rezoning is requested and obtained, increasing the lot's value to $36,000.

a. What percentage increase in property value and in equity has taken place?

b. Is this positive leverage?

2. Buck Montana buys a vacant lot on land contract, agreeing to pay $20,000 and paying $10,000 down. Black Bart, the seller, owns the lot free and clear. Buck and his wife move a mobile home onto the property and go into possession immediately. Owing to the construction of a new bridge, the lot increases in value to $30,000. Black Bart subsequently mortgages the lot to a local bank to secure a $15,000 loan, based on the increased value, and leaves town. The bank files for foreclosure. What are the rights of the Montanas?

3. White leases a vacant lot from Green on a long-term net, net, net lease for $12,000 per year. Nothing is said about a subordination clause between White and Green. White immediately adds improvements, financed by a mortgage loan of $150,000 from the Ace Savings and Loan Association. Subsequently, Green borrows $80,000 against the land from the Third National Bank. White defaults. Ace S&L takes over the property and proposes to re-rent it to Blue. The Third National objects. What results between Ace and the Third National?

15

Mortgage and Trust Deed Financing

The house was more covered with mortgages than paint.

George Ade, American Humorist and Playwright

Many of us in buying a car pledge the vehicle to a financial institution to get enough money to make the purchase. Likewise, most of us, in buying real estate, pledge the property to a bank or savings and loan association as security for a mortgage or trust deed loan. In either case, an application and credit approval is required. Beyond this, the process of obtaining a real estate loan is much more involved.

Important Topics or Decision Areas Covered in This Chapter

Applying for a Loan

Loan Documents

The Debt Financing Process
Loan Initiation
Interim or Servicing Phase
Loan Termination

Provisions of Mortgages and Trust Deeds
Uniform Covenants
Nonuniform Covenants

Types of Loans
Construction Loan
Conventional Loan
FHA-Insured Loan
VA-Guaranteed Loan
Privately Insured Loan
Purchase Money Mortgage Loan
Second or Junior Loan
Miscellaneous Mortgage Types

Key Concepts Introduced in this Chapter

Acceleration clause

Adjustable rate mortgage

Alienation or "due on sale" clause

~~All inclusive trust deed~~

Assumption (assuming a loan)

Balloon payment

Conventional loan

Deed in lieu of foreclosure

Default

Default-in-the-prior- mortgage clause

Defeasance clause

Deficiency judgment

Equitable right of redemption

FHA mortgage

Fixed-rate mortgage

Foreclosure

~~Junior mortgage~~

Mortgage satisfaction

Novation

Power of sale

Promissory note

Purchase money mortgage

Renegotiable rate mortgage

Second mortgage

Severability clause

Statutory right of redemption

Taking subject to a mortgage

Usury

VA mortgage

~~Wraparound mortgage~~

Applying for a Loan

Exactly what is involved in obtaining a real estate loan? Lenders, for the most part, want to make loans on high quality properties to credit-worthy borrowers. On the other hand, borrowers want the lowest possible interest rates and, therefore, shop lenders and terms. A borrower may also negotiate to avoid interest rate adjustments and penalties for early repayment. The application process is where lenders and borrowers come together.

A brief overview of the mechanics of the loan application process seems appropriate before getting into legalities and negotiations. Initial information require-

RESIDENTIAL LOAN APPLICATION

MORTGAGE APPLIED FOR	☐ Conventional ☐ FHA ☐ VA	Amount $	Interest Rate %	No. of Months	Monthly Payment Principal & Interest $	Escrow/Impounds (to be collected monthly) ☐ Taxes ☐ Hazard Ins. ☐ Mtg. Ins. ☐

Prepayment Option

SUBJECT PROPERTY

Property Street Address	City	County	State	Zip	No. Units

Legal Description (Attach description if necessary)	Year Built

Purpose of Loan: ☐ Purchase ☐ Construction-Permanent ☐ Construction ☐ Refinance ☐ Other (Explain)

Complete this line if Construction-Permanent or Construction Loan	Lot Value Data	Original Cost	Present Value (a)	Cost of Imps. (b)	Total (a + b)	ENTER TOTAL AS PURCHASE PRICE IN DETAILS OF PURCHASE.
Year Acquired	$	$	$	$		

Complete this line if a Refinance Loan

Year Acquired	Original Cost	Amt. Existing Liens	Purpose of Refinance	Describe Improvements [ ] made [ ] to be made
	$	$		Cost: $

Title Will Be Held In What Name(s)	Manner In Which Title Will Be Held

Source of Down Payment and Settlement Charges

This application is designed to be completed by the borrower(s) with the lender's assistance. The Co-Borrower Section and all other Co-Borrower questions must be completed and the appropriate box(es) checked if ☐ another person will be jointly obligated with the Borrower on the loan, or ☐ the Borrower is relying on income from alimony, child support or separate maintenance or on the income or assets of another person as a basis for repayment of the loan, or ☐ the Borrower is married and resides, or the property is located, in a community property state.

BORROWER				CO-BORROWER			
Name		Age	School Yrs ___	Name		Age	School Yrs ___
Present Address	No. Years ___ ☐ Own ☐ Rent			Present Address	No. Years ___ ☐ Own ☐ Rent		
Street				Street			
City/State/Zip				City/State/Zip			
Former address if less than 2 years at present address				Former address if less than 2 years at present address			
Street				Street			
City/State/Zip				City/State/Zip			
Years at former address	☐ Own ☐ Rent			Years at former address	☐ Own ☐ Rent		

Marital Status	☐ Married ☐ Separated ☐ Unmarried (incl. single, divorced, widowed)	DEPENDENTS OTHER THAN LISTED BY CO BORROWER NO. AGES	Marital Status	☐ Married ☐ Separated ☐ Unmarried (incl. single, divorced, widowed)	DEPENDENTS OTHER THAN LISTED BY BORROWER NO. AGES

Name and Address of Employer	Years employed in this line of work or profession? ___ years	Name and Address of Employer	Years employed in this line of work or profession? ___ years
	Years on this job ___ ☐ Self Employed*		Years on this job ___ ☐ Self Employed*
Position/Title	Type of Business	Position/Title	Type of Business
Social Security Number***	Home Phone	Business Phone	Social Security Number***	Home Phone	Business Phone

GROSS MONTHLY INCOME				MONTHLY HOUSING EXPENSE**			DETAILS OF PURCHASE	
Item	Borrower	Co-Borrower	Total		PRESENT	PROPOSED	Do Not Complete If Refinance	
Base Empl. Income	$	$	$	Rent	$		a. Purchase Price	$
Overtime				First Mortgage (P&I)		$	b. Total Closing Costs (Est.)	
Bonuses				Other Financing (P&I)			c. Prepaid Escrows (Est.)	
Commissions				Hazard Insurance			d. Total (a + b + c)	$
Dividends/Interest				Real Estate Taxes			e. Amount This Mortgage	( )
Net Rental Income				Mortgage Insurance			f. Other Financing	( )
Other† (Before completing, see notice under Describe Other Income below.)				Homeowner Assn. Dues			g. Other Equity	( )
				Other:			h. Amount of Cash Deposit	( )
				Total Monthly Pmt.	$	$	i. Closing Costs Paid by Seller	( )
				Utilities			j. Cash Reqd. For Closing (Est.)	$
Total	$	$	$	Total	$	$		

DESCRIBE OTHER INCOME

▷ B—Borrower C—Co-Borrower

NOTICE:† Alimony, child support, or separate maintenance income need not be revealed if the Borrower or Co-Borrower does not choose to have it considered as a basis for repaying this loan.

	Monthly Amount
	$

IF EMPLOYED IN CURRENT POSITION FOR LESS THAN TWO YEARS COMPLETE THE FOLLOWING

B/C	Previous Employer/School	City/State	Type of Business	Position/Title	Dates From/To	Monthly Income
						$

THESE QUESTIONS APPLY TO BOTH BORROWER AND CO-BORROWER

If a "yes" answer is given to a question in this column, explain on an attached sheet.	Borrower Yes or No	Co Borrower Yes or No	If applicable, explain Other Financing or Other Equity (provide addendum if more space is needed).
Have you any outstanding judgments? In the last 7 years, have you been declared bankrupt?			
Have you had property foreclosed upon or given title or deed in lieu thereof?			
Are you a co-maker or endorser on a note?			
Are you a party in a law suit?			
Are you obligated to pay alimony, child support, or separate maintenance?			
Is any part of the down payment borrowed?			

*FHLMC/FNMA require business credit report, signed Federal Income Tax returns for last two years, and, if available, audited Profit and Loss Statements plus balance sheet for same period

**All Present Monthly Housing Expenses of Borrower and Co Borrower should be listed on a combined basis.

***Neither FHLMC nor FNMA requires this information.

FHLMC 65 Rev. 8/78   FNMA 1003 Rev. 8/78

FIGURE 15-1
FHLMC/FNMA loan application

This Statement and any applicable supporting schedules may be completed jointly by both married and unmarried co-borrowers if their assets and liabilities are sufficiently joined so that the Statement can be meaningfully and fairly presented on a combined basis; otherwise separate Statements and Schedules are required (FHLMC 65A/FNMA 1003A). If the co-borrower section was completed about a spouse, this statement and supporting schedules must be completed about that spouse also. ☐ Completed Jointly ☐ Not Completed Jointly

ASSETS		LIABILITIES AND PLEDGED ASSETS			
		Indicate by (*) those liabilities or pledged assets which will be satisfied upon sale of real estate owned or upon refinancing of subject property			
Description	Cash or Market Value	Creditors' Name, Address and Account Number	Acct. Name If Not Borrower's	Mo. Pmt. and Mos. left to pay	Unpaid Balance
Cash Deposit Toward Purchase Held By	$	Installment Debts (include "revolving" charge accts)		$ Pmt./Mos. /	$
Checking and Savings Accounts (Show Names of Institutions/Acct. Nos.)				/	
				/	
				/	
Stocks and Bonds (No./Description)				/	
				/	
Life Insurance Net Cash Value Face Amount ($)		Other Debts Including Stock Pledges			
SUBTOTAL LIQUID ASSETS	$			/	
Real Estate Owned (Enter Market Value from Schedule of Real Estate Owned)		Real Estate Loans		✕	
Vested Interest in Retirement Fund					
Net Worth of Business Owned (ATTACH FINANCIAL STATEMENT)					
Automobiles (Make and Year)		Automobile Loans			
Furniture and Personal Property		Alimony, Child Support and Separate Maintenance Payments Owed To		✕	
Other Assets (Itemize)				/	
		TOTAL MONTHLY PAYMENTS		$	✕
TOTAL ASSETS	A $	NET WORTH (A minus B) $		TOTAL LIABILITIES	B $

SCHEDULE OF REAL ESTATE OWNED (If Additional Properties Owned Attach Separate Schedule)								
Address of Property (Indicate S if Sold, PS if Pending Sale or R if Rental being held for income)	◇	Type of Property	Present Market Value	Amount of Mortgages & Liens	Gross Rental Income	Mortgage Payments	Taxes, Ins. Maintenance and Misc.	Net Rental Income
			$	$	$	$	$	$
		TOTALS →	$	$	$	$	$	$

LIST PREVIOUS CREDIT REFERENCES						
◇ B–Borrower C–Co-Borrower	Creditor's Name and Address		Account Number	Purpose	Highest Balance	Date Paid
					$	

List any additional names under which credit has previously been received _____

AGREEMENT: The undersigned applies for the loan indicated in this application to be secured by a first mortgage or deed of trust on the property described herein, and represents that the property will not be used for any illegal or restricted purpose, and that all statements made in this application are true and are made for the purpose of obtaining the loan. Verification may be obtained from any source named in this application. The original or a copy of this application will be retained by the lender, even if the loan is not granted. The undersigned ☐ intend or ☐ do not intend to occupy the property as their primary residence.

I/we fully understand that it is a federal crime punishable by fine or imprisonment, or both, to knowingly make any false statements concerning any of the above facts as applicable under the provisions of Title 18, United States Code, Section 1014.

_____ Date _____   _____ Date _____
Borrower's Signature   Co-Borrower's Signature

INFORMATION FOR GOVERNMENT MONITORING PURPOSES

Instructions: Lenders must insert in this space, or on an attached addendum, a provision for furnishing the monitoring information required or requested under present Federal and/or present state law or regulation. For most lenders, the inserts provided in FHLMC Form 65-B/FNMA Form 1003-B can be used.

FOR LENDER'S USE ONLY

(FNMA REQUIREMENT ONLY) This application was taken by ☐ face to face interview ☐ by mail ☐ by telephone

_____   _____
(Interviewer)   Name of Employer of Interviewer

FHLMC 65 Rev. 8/78   REVERSE   FNMA 1003 Rev. 8/78

FIGURE 15-1 (continued)

ments are well illustrated by the Federal Home Loan Mortgage Corporation/Federal National Mortgage Association (FHLMC/FNMA) loan application form shown in Figure 15-1. The entire application procedure involves several basic steps:

1. Prospective borrower shops to obtain financial terms and repayment patterns required by alternative lenders.
2. Prospective borrower completes and submits loan application form to lender of choice.
3. Lender provides a "good faith estimate of closing costs" to borrower.
4. Lender obtains credit report on applicant.
5. Lender obtains "verification of employment" form on applicant, if a residential loan is requested. If borrower is self employed, or an investor, lender is likely to ask to see borrower's income tax returns for at least the 2 immediately prior years.
6. Lender obtains a "verification of deposit" form to assure the existence and availability of equity funds.
7. Lender obtains a market value appraisal on subject property to assure that its value represents adequate security for the requested loan; that is, that an acceptable LVR is present.
8. Approval for loan insurance or guarantee obtained from FHA, private mortgage insurance company, or VA.
9. Loan committee of lender reviews all information and makes "go" "no go" decision. If "go," loan is made. If "no go," applicant is notified, and file is closed.
10. Lender obtains evidence of marketable title (through title insurance or attorney's opinion), which also serves to detect presence of other claims that may exist against the subject property.

Borrower pays all costs, as for a credit report, an appraisal, a title report, attorneys, and recording. Some additional information and documentation would be required if FHA, VA, or private mortgage insurance is involved.

Loan Documents

Two separate and distinct legal instruments are executed in documenting a loan on real estate. The first is either a mortgage or a trust deed. The second is a promissory note or, in some states, a personal bond. A **_promissory note_** is a written commitment to repay a debt, and it serves as evidence of the debt. A personal bond is an interest-bearing certificate containing a promise to pay a certain sum on a specified date and thus is similar to a note. Usually only the mortgage or trust deed is recorded. Figure 15-2 summarizes the purposes and legal requirements for loan documentation.

Even though mortgages and trust deeds are commonly referred to as "mortgages," as in the secondary mortgage market, they are distinct instruments, with very different consequences if default occurs. In fact, a mortgage or trust deed only becomes meaningful if default occurs. **_Default_** means failure of the borrower to meet the terms of the contract.

Document	Purpose or Effect	Legal Requirements
Mortgage	Creates and pledges a property interest for the protection of the mortgagee-lender	1. In writing 2. Adequately identify property 3. Identify borrower, lender (and trustee)
Trust deed	Creates a property interest to be held by the trustee for the lender-beneficiary	4. Proper words to pledge 5. Signature of mortgagor-borrower 6. Voluntary delivery and acceptance
Promissory note or bond	Creates a personal obligation of borrower to repay debt according to agreed terms or schedule	1. A written instrument 2. A borrower (obligee) with contractual capacity 3. A lender (obligor) with contractual capacity 4. A promise or covenant by borrower to pay a specific sum 5. Terms of payment 6. A default clause, including reference to the mortgage or trust deed 7. Proper execution 8. Voluntary delivery and acceptance

FIGURE 15-2
Overview of loan documentation

Both pledge real property as security for a debt or other obligation until cleared or satisfied. The borrower in the contract is called the mortgagor; the lender is the mortgagee. Although fee ownership of realty is usually pledged as security, any real property interest may be pledged. Thus a leasehold, a life estate, rights of a remainderman, or improvements apart from the land all provide a legal basis for a security pledge.

The mortgage and promissory note used as illustrations later in this chapter were developed jointly by the Federal National Mortgage Association (FNMA) and the Federal Home Loan Mortgage Corporation (FHLMC). These instruments are as uniform as possible from state to state to facilitate their being bought and sold in the secondary mortgage market. In turn, the liquidity of the loan portfolios of lenders is greatly enhanced. With standardized wording, buyers of loans in the secondary mortgage market do not have to study each document in detail before acceptance. (Incidentally, these instruments are personal property, ownership of which may be sold or transferred by what is termed an assignment.) Approval of the borrower is not required in an assignment, nor are the nature and enforceability of the note or pledging instrument affected. Assignment is a critical feature for mortgages to be bought and sold in the secondary mortgage market.

The Mortgage Arrangement. A mortgage pledges property as security (collateral) for a debt. The arrangement gives the lender the legal right to have the property sold to satisfy the debt if it is not repaid on schedule; this process is called

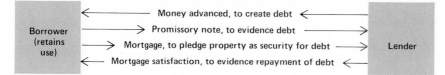

FIGURE 15-3
The structure of the mortgage arrangement

foreclosure. At the same time the borrower gets the right to occupy and use the property, as long as payments are made. The promissory note, a separate agreement, evidences the debt. The technical name for this is hypothecation, meaning the borrower retains the right of occupancy and use of the property while it serves as collateral for a loan. A mortgage is a two-party transaction, as shown in Figure 15-3.

Trust Deed Arrangement. A trust deed is often used in place of a mortgage for reasons of time and convenience to the lender if default occurs. A trust deed, instead of being merely a claim or lien, actually conveys title to the pledged property to a third party (trustee) to be held as security for the debt owed the lender, who is also the beneficiary of the arrangement. A promissory note still evidences the debt.

Note that a trust deed creates a three-party arrangement, as shown in Figure 15-4. The owner-borrower-trustor receives money and, at the same time, conveys title to the trustee and gives a promissory note to the lender-beneficiary. The trustee holds title to the property as security for the lender in case of default by the borrower.

If default occurs, the trustee usually has automatic power of sale. *Power of sale* means the right to sell without court proceedings, which considerably shortens the time required to get satisfaction by the lender. Thus, after three or four payments are missed, the lender may request sale, with satisfaction often realized in from 6 to 12 months. A trust deed is also referred to as a deed of trust or a trust deed in the nature of a mortgage.

The Promissory Note. A promissory note evidences the debt, makes it the personal obligation of the borrower, and gives life to a mortgage or trust deed. The note also contains the financial terms surrounding the debt. If the debt is unenforceable for any reason, the mortgage or trust deed is also unenforceable. See Figure 15-5.

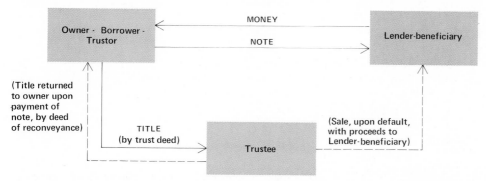

FIGURE 15-4
The structure of the trust deed arrangement

NOTE

(Multifamily)

US $ ....500,000..   ....Urbandale.., **Texas**

City

January 15 ...., 19 89

1. For Value Received, the undersigned promise to pay ......Urbandale Savings and Loan Association ...., or order, the principal sum of ....Five Hundred Thousand ....and no/100 ($500,000.00).. Dollars, with interest on the unpaid principal balance from the date of this Note, until paid, at the rate of ...10.... percent per annum. The principal and interest shall be payable at ....Urbandale Savings and Loan Association, 300 North Main, Urbandale .... in consecutive monthly installments of ....Four Thousand Five Hundred Forty Three and fifty/100 .... Dollars (US $....4,543.50.... ....1st........) on the ....1st........ day of each month beginning ....March 1st........, 19 89, (herein "amortization commencement date"), until the entire indebtedness evidenced hereby is fully paid, except that any remaining indebtedness, if not sooner paid, shall be due and payable on the ...1st.... day of ....February........................, 2006 ..... .

2. If the amortization commencement date is more than ...30... calendar days from the date of this Note, the undersigned shall pay the holder hereof interest only on the outstanding principal balance of this Note at the rate of ...10.... percent per annum in ....one........ installments beginning ....15 January........ 19..89.. and on ..no other.. thereafter until the amortization commencement date, at which time any remaining interest payable pursuant to this paragraph (and not paid as a part of the first monthly installment of principal and interest) shall be paid.

3. If any installment under this Note is not paid when due, the unpaid principal balance of this Note shall bear interest during the period of delinquency at a rate of ...10.... percent per annum, or, if such increased rate of interest may not be collected from the undersigned under applicable law, then at the maximum increased rate of interest, if any, which may be collected from the undersigned under applicable law; and, at the option of the holder hereof, the entire principal amount outstanding hereunder and accrued interest thereon shall at once become due and payable. Failure to exercise such option shall not constitute a waiver of the right to exercise such option if the undersigned is in default hereunder. In the event of any default in the payment of this Note, and if the same is referred to an attorney at law for collection or suit is brought hereon, the undersigned shall pay the holder hereof, in either case, all expenses and costs of collection, including, but not limited to, attorney's fees.

4. The undersigned shall pay to the holder hereof on demand a late charge of ...2.... percent of any installment not received by the holder hereof within ....15.... calendar days after the day the installment is due.

5. The undersigned shall have the right to prepay the principal amount outstanding hereunder in whole or in part at any time after the amortization commencement date, provided that the holder hereof may require that any partial prepayments shall be made on the date monthly installments are due and shall be in the amount of that part of one or more monthly installments which would be applicable to principal and further provided that the undersigned has given the holder hereof written notice of the amount intended to be prepaid at least ..five (5)............. days prior to such prepayment. The undersigned shall pay the holder hereof together with any prepayments (including prepayments occurring as a result of the acceleration by the holder hereof of the principal amount of this Note, but excluding prepayments occurring because of the application by the holder hereof of insurance or condemnation awards or proceeds pursuant to a Deed of Trust securing this Note) a percentage of the amount prepaid in excess of any amount upon which a charge is not permitted by applicable law as follows: ....4...... percent of the sums prepaid in the first year from the amortization commencement date, the percentage payable declining by the number one (1) each year thereafter until the percentage payable is ....0.... percent, which percentage shall be payable for the remaining term of the Note. Prepayments shall be applied against the outstanding principal balance of this Note and shall not extend or postpone the due date of any subsequent monthly installments or change the amount of such installments, unless the holder hereof shall otherwise agree in writing.

6. From time to time, without affecting the obligation of the undersigned or the successors or assigns of the undersigned to pay the outstanding principal balance of this Note and observe the covenants of the undersigned contained herein, without affecting the guaranty of any person, corporation, partnership or other entity for payment of the outstanding principal balance of this Note, without giving notice to or obtaining the consent of the undersigned, the successors or assigns of the undersigned or guarantors, and without liability on the part of the holder hereof, the holder hereof may, at the option of the holder hereof, extend the time for payment of said outstanding principal balance or any part thereof, reduce the payments thereon, release anyone liable on any of said outstanding principal balance, accept a renewal of this Note, modify the terms and time of payment of said outstanding principal balance or join in any extension or subordination agreement, and agree in writing with the undersigned to modify the rate of interest or period of amortization of this Note or change the amount of the monthly installments payable hereunder.

7. Presentment, notice of dishonor, and protest are hereby waived by all makers, sureties, guarantors and endorsers hereof. This Note shall be the joint and several obligation of all makers, sureties, guarantors and endorsers, and shall be binding upon them and their heirs, personal representatives, successors and assigns.

8. The indebtedness evidenced by this Note is secured by a Deed of Trust, dated of even date herewith, and reference is made thereto for rights as to acceleration of the indebtedness evidenced by this Note.

Douglas Manor
2001 Century Drive
Urbandale, Texas 00000
  (property address)

/s/Gerald I. Investor

/s/Nancy O. Investor

TEXAS—FHLMC—2/71—Over Four Families

FIGURE 15-5

Promissory note

The note's being a personal obligation of the borrower expands the lender's rights in case of default. If only a mortgage or trust deed were used, the borrower might abandon the property, move elsewhere, and have no further personal obligation or liability regarding the loan. The note or bond, as a personal obligation, is enforceable wherever the borrower might take up residence.

In the note shown, the amount and date appear in the heading, followed by numbered, specific clauses.

1. *Mortgage and terms.* Mortgagee is identified, along with the interest rate, maturity date, monthly debt service, and place of payment. Payments are to be made on the first day of each month at the Urbandale Savings and Loan.
2. *Adjustment of payment date.* Interest only is to be paid for first partial month so payments may be scheduled on first of month.
3. *Default and acceleration.* Noteholder has right to accelerate or call for immediate payment of the entire outstanding principal plus accrued interest if the contract is breached, such as by late payments. Acceleration is first step in foreclosure.
4. *Late charge.* If payment is over 15 days late, penalty is specified.
5. *Prepayment provisions.* Borrower may prepay, but only under stated conditions. Prepayment penalty as negotiated when the loan was taken out is included as part of the agreement.
6. *Negotiability.* The security and negotiability of the note is protected by stating that any modification to the terms shall not affect the obligation of the borrowers to abide by the terms and to repay the principal of the note.
7. *Joint and several.* Makers, endorsers, and others waive the right to protest or to deny the note as their obligation, individually or jointly.
8. *Reference to security instrument.* The security instrument of even date is identified and attached relative to acceleration rights in the note.

The Debt Financing Process

The debt financing process, for purposes of discussion, breaks down into three basic phases: (1) initiation, (2) interim or servicing, and (3) termination. These phases apply, regardless of the type of loan involved. See Figure 15-6.

Initiation Phase _____ > ___ [Time Line} > _____ :	Interim or Servicing Phase _____ > :	Termination Phase _____
Loan processing: —Application —Borrower analysis —Property analysis —Financial analysis —Letter of commitment —Loan closing	Debt service payments made on schedule Possible change of ownership with —Assumption of loan —Taking subject to	Mutual agreement Pay on schedule Default and —voluntary sale —deed in lieu of foreclosure —foreclosure and sale

FIGURE 15-6
Decisions or actions required in the debt financing process

LOAN INITIATION

A lender must make several basic decisions in making the loan. The applicant must be judged to have an acceptable credit rating and adequate income as evidence of being financially responsible. Also, the relative size of the loan must be determined. A residential loan is not likely to be initiated in excess of 90–95 percent of the market value of the pledged property. Assuming that all the lender's criteria are met, the loan application is approved. The borrower signs the mortgage and note and meets other settlement requirements, and the loan contract is made.

INTERIM OR SERVICING PHASE

As long as all terms of the contract are met, the agreement is continued without interruption. The borrower must make scheduled payments of principal and interest to the lender and maintain the property in reasonable condition.

A borrower may, unless prohibited by an *alienation* or *"due on sale" clause,* sell the pledged property without paying off the loan. The life of the loan is thereby continued even though ownership of the property has changed. The buyer, in these circumstances, may take title "subject to" the mortgage or the buyer may take title and "assume and promise to pay" the mortgage. The distinction between the two alternatives is substantial. Increasingly, lenders are including due on sale clauses in new loan agreements to prohibit the sale of the pledged property and continuation of the loan without prior consent from the lender.

Taking Subject to a Mortgage. A buyer, *taking title subject to a mortgage,* does not take over legal responsibility for the repayment of the debt. However, the buyer continues to make payments on the loan because it is in his or her self interest. If unable to meet required debt service payments, the buyer may simply walk away from the property without further obligation to the lender. That is, in case of default, the lender has no recourse or basis for action for debt satisfaction against the buyer.

Even so, it is usually in the buyer-owner's interest to continue making payment of debt service as long as the buyer-owner has an equity interest in the property. However, if market value drops below the loan's balance, the new owner may be rational in walking away because a negative equity has developed. For example,

At Time of Purchase		Two Years Later	
Purchase price	$100,000	Market value	$86,000
Initial loan	− 90,000	Loan balance	− 89,500
Cash equity	$ 10,000	Equity value	($ 3,500)

The original seller-borrower continues to be liable for the debt if the buyer defaults in making the payments.

Assuming and Promising to Pay a Loan. Agreement by a grantee (usually a buyer) to accept responsibility for repayment of an existing loan against a property is termed *assumption.* The buyer agrees to pay debt service and to pay any deficiency should a default occur. Unless released, the seller continues to be liable to the lender for payment of the loan as well. The release of a seller-borrower in an assumption is termed ***novation,*** which means that a new contractual obligation has been substituted for an old one by mutual agreement of all parties concerned.

LOAN TERMINATION

Termination by Satisfying the Contract. A borrower is, upon meeting all requirements of a mortgage loan contract, released from the obligation and is entitled to a receipt acknowledging payment, variously known as a ***mortgage satisfaction,*** release, or discharge. Recording a release ends the lien or claim against the pledged property. Under trust deed financing, the trustee provides a deed of release to clear the record.

Termination by Mutual Agreement. A borrower may refinance or recast a loan prior to complete repayment, provided that the lender or the contract so permits. Refinancing means obtaining a new and larger loan, usually at new terms. Recasting means keeping the same size loan but changing the interest rate and/or the amortization period, usually to reduce required debt service. Finally, the loan may be prepaid, as when a property is sold and the buyer obtains new financing.

What happens if a lender refuses to give the release? Almost all mortgages and trust deeds contain a defeasance clause to protect the borrower upon complete repayment of the loan. A ***defeasance clause*** states that if the loan and interest are paid in full, the rights and interests of the lender in the property cease. Thus, without a debt, the mortgage or trust deed is not enforceable.

Finally, even when a loan is in default, the parties may work out ways to avoid foreclosure. The owner-borrower may voluntarily sell the property rather than go into foreclosure, if the value exceeds the loan balance or the parties may "voluntarily" agree to a ***"deed in lieu of foreclosure"*** instead. Such a compromise is often reached when the owner's equity in the property is less than the expected costs of foreclosure and yet the property has enough value that the lender will not get seriously hurt. Effectively, the lender agrees to take the property in satisfaction of the debt if the borrower signs it over promptly. Both save time and money. Of course, the lender must then manage and dispose of the property.

Termination by Foreclosure. A lender must follow default with a foreclosure suit to get at the pledged security. The importance of the suit, and the time required for satisfaction, depends on the state in which the property is located. That is, mortgage law in each state is based on the principles of either title theory or lien theory. Some legal scholars say that there are also intermediate theory states, which use a blend of the other two. For brevity and clarity, the lien and title theories are emphasized here.

In early times, when real estate was used as security for a mortgage loan, the borrower deeded the property outright to the lender, who became its legal owner. The borrower usually retained possession, but upon default, the lender immediately took possession. Today, in title theory states, a limited form of legal title is still conveyed to the lender when a property is mortgaged. On default, the lender has the right of possession, which is not usually exercised for residences. For commercial and investment properties, the right is usually exercised through the collection of rents by the lender or the lender's representative. Even so, foreclosure proceedings must be initiated and completed by the mortgagee to clear the title.

In lien theory states, title remains with the borrower, who remains in possession, even after default. The mortgagee must initiate and complete foreclosure proceedings to get satisfaction from the pledged property. In intermediate states, title remains with the borrower until default, at which point it passes to the lender.

Over the years the distinction between title theory and lien theory states has blurred. The main difference is that rents from and possession of income properties are more readily realized by a lender in title theory states. In both classes of states, foreclosure means eventually selling the pledged property and paying off the debt with the proceeds.

Lenders recognize that borrowers miss payments occasionally and that most borrowers live up to their obligations if given an opportunity. In extended default, however, a lender must eventually file a foreclosure suit. The suit demands immediate payment of the debt and invokes the acceleration clause found in nearly every mortgage. An *acceleration clause,* upon default, gives the lender the right to declare all remaining debt service payments of the loan due and payable immediately. Without an acceleration clause, a lender must sue for each payment as it becomes due. If not paid, the mortgage says that the property may be disposed of at a judicial or foreclosure sale to raise money to pay the debt. Figure 15-7 summarizes the mortgage foreclosure process.

A borrower may recover the property under an *equitable right of redemption,* up until the foreclosure sale; this right is also called the equity of redemption. In exercising the equitable right of redemption, the borrower must make up all back payments and pay any costs of foreclosure incurred by the lender. The equitable right of redemption cannot be waived or cut off except by a foreclosure sale.

Some states give the borrower a statutory right of redemption after the foreclosure sale. A *statutory right of redemption* allows a borrower to recover foreclosed property for a limited time after the judicial sale by payment of the sale price plus foreclosure costs plus any other costs or losses incurred by the lender. For example, a foreclosed borrower might well arrange another loan to redeem a property rapidly increasing in value, or suddenly coming into a large inheritance might give a foreclosed borrower the means to recover a favorite property.

Any surplus in a judicial sale goes to the borrower. In some states, if the price is less than the debt plus interest plus foreclosure costs, a lender may obtain a deficiency judgment against the borrower. A *deficiency judgment* is a judicial decree in favor of a lender for that portion of the mortgage debt and foreclosure costs that remains unsatisfied from the proceeds of the judicial sale. The judgment attaches to real and personal property of the mortgagor.

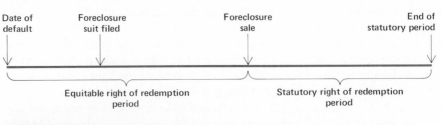

| Date of default | Foreclosure suit filed | Foreclosure sale | End of statutory period |

Equitable right of redemption period | Statutory right of redemption period

FIGURE 15-7
The mortgage foreclosure process

Trust Deed Foreclosure. Upon default, the trustee has authority, under the power of sale, in almost every state to promptly sell the pledged property. Many of the time-consuming requirements of mortgage foreclosure are therefore avoided. Further, the borrower is usually not entitled to any redemption rights after the trustee's sale. At the same time, a deficiency judgment is usually not recognized when the power of sale is exercised.

Provisions of Mortgages and Trust Deeds

Mortgages and deeds of trust, as mentioned, are very similar except in foreclosure. Each clearly establishes that the realty is to secure the debt. Each refers to a promissory note as evidence of the debt. Each identifies the borrower and the lender. Each contains an accurate legal description of the pledged property. Each must be signed by all parties with an interest in the realty, although the lender may sign neither.

The following points are generally considered the more important borrower obligations and, hence, are consistently provided for in a mortgage or trust deed.

1. Make debt-service payments in accordance with the note.
2. Pay all real estate taxes as they are levied.
3. Provide adequate hazard insurance to protect the lender against loss if the property is damaged or destroyed by fire, wind, or other peril.
4. Maintain the property in good repair at all times.
5. Obtain authorization from the lender before substantially altering the property.

In addition, the following points are usually, but not always, provided for in a mortgage or trust deed:

1. Reserve right of lender or noteholder to inspect and protect the property.
2. Stipulate that debt-service payments apply to taxes first, insurance second, interest third, and principal reduction fourth.
3. Stipulate that proceeds from insurance or condemnation go to the lender first, with any excess going to the borrower.
4. Reserve right of lender to approve transfer of ownership of secured property and assumption of the loan, including renegotiation of the interest rate (alienation or due on sale clause).

A prospective borrower needs to know and understand the specific clauses of the pledging document. The FNMA/FHLMC uniform instrument, discussed here, contains all these provisions, and more, with its 26 clauses or covenants. Much lender experience went into the development of this pledging document so that it would have wide acceptability. Thus, most provisions of a mortgage or trust deed are not usually negotiable to a borrower. Violation of any of the provisions constitutes default and sets the stage for possible foreclosure.

Each clause is discussed here only briefly as to purpose or content. They are taken up in the same order as they appear in the document in Figure 15-8. The reader may wish to study closely the specific wording of each covenant.

Uniform Covenants. Borrower and Lender covenant and agree as follows:

1. PAYMENT OF PRINCIPAL AND INTEREST. Borrower shall promptly pay when due the principal of and interest on the indebtedness evidenced by the Note, any prepayment and late charges provided in the Note and all other sums secured by this Instrument.

2. FUNDS FOR TAXES, INSURANCE AND OTHER CHARGES. Subject to applicable law or to a written waiver by Lender, Borrower shall pay to Lender on the day monthly installments of principal or interest are payable under the Note (or on another day designated in writing by Lender), until the Note is paid in full, a sum (herein "Funds") equal to one-twelfth of (a) the yearly water and sewer rates and taxes and assessments which may be levied on the Property, (b) the yearly ground rents, if any, (c) the yearly premium installments for fire and other hazard insurance, rent loss insurance and such other insurance covering the Property as Lender may require pursuant to paragraph 5 hereof, (d) the yearly premium installments for mortgage insurance, if any, and (e) if this Instrument is on a leasehold, the yearly fixed rents, if any, under the ground lease, all as reasonably estimated initially and from time to time by Lender on the basis of assessments and bills and reasonable estimates thereof. Any waiver by Lender of a requirement that Borrower pay such Funds may be revoked by Lender, in Lender's sole discretion, at any time upon notice in writing to Borrower. Lender may require Borrower to pay to Lender, in advance, such other Funds for other taxes, charges, premiums, assessments and impositions in connection with Borrower or the Property which Lender shall reasonably deem necessary to protect Lender's interests (herein "Other Impositions"). Unless otherwise provided by applicable law, Lender may require Funds for Other Impositions to be paid by Borrower in a lump sum or in periodic installments, at Lender's option.

The Funds shall be held in an institution(s) the deposits or accounts of which are insured or guaranteed by a Federal or state agency (including Lender if Lender is such an institution). Lender shall apply the Funds to pay said rates, rents, taxes, assessments, insurance premiums and Other Impositions so long as Borrower is not in breach of any covenant or agreement of Borrower in this Instrument. Lender shall make no charge for so holding and applying the Funds, analyzing said account or for verifying and compiling said assessments and bills, unless Lender pays Borrower interest, earnings or profits on the Funds and applicable law permits Lender to make such a charge. Borrower and Lender may agree in writing at the time of execution of this Instrument that interest on the Funds shall be paid to Borrower, and unless such agreement is made or applicable law requires interest, earnings or profits to be paid, Lender shall not be required to pay Borrower any interest, earnings or profits on the Funds. Lender shall give to Borrower, without charge, an annual accounting of the Funds in Lender's normal format showing credits and debits to the Funds and the purpose for which each debit to the Funds was made. The Funds are pledged as additional security for the sums secured by this Instrument.

If the amount of the Funds held by Lender at the time of the annual accounting thereof shall exceed the amount deemed necessary by Lender to provide for the payment of water and sewer rates, taxes, assessments, insurance premiums, rents and Other Impositions, as they fall due, such excess shall be credited to Borrower on the next monthly installment or installments of Funds due. If at any time the amount of the Funds held by Lender shall be less than the amount deemed necessary by Lender to pay water and sewer rates, taxes, assessments, insurance premiums, rents and Other Impositions, as they fall due, Borrower shall pay to Lender any amount necessary to make up the deficiency within thirty days after notice from Lender to Borrower requesting payment thereof.

Upon Borrower's breach of any covenant or agreement of Borrower in this Instrument, Lender may apply, in any amount and in any order as Lender shall determine in Lender's sole discretion, any Funds held by Lender at the time of application (i) to pay rates, rents, taxes, assessments, insurance premiums and Other Impositions which are now or will hereafter become due, or (ii) as a credit against sums secured by this Instrument. Upon payment in full of all sums secured by this Instrument, Lender shall promptly refund to Borrower any Funds held by Lender.

3. APPLICATION OF PAYMENTS. Unless applicable law provides otherwise, all payments received by Lender from Borrower under the Note or this Instrument shall be applied by Lender in the following order of priority: (i) amounts payable to Lender by Borrower under paragraph 2 hereof; (ii) interest payable on the Note; (iii) principal of the Note; (iv) interest payable on advances made pursuant to paragraph 8 hereof; (v) principal of advances made pursuant to paragraph 8 hereof; (vi) interest payable on any Future Advance, provided that if more than one Future Advance is outstanding, Lender may apply payments received among the amounts of interest payable on the Future Advances in such order as Lender, in Lender's sole discretion, may determine; (vii) principal of any Future Advance, provided that if more than one Future Advance is outstanding, Lender may apply payments received among the principal balances of the Future Advances in such order as Lender, in Lender's sole discretion, may determine; and (viii) any other sums secured by this Instrument in such order as Lender, at Lender's option, may determine; provided, however, that Lender may, at Lender's option, apply any sums payable pursuant to paragraph 8 hereof prior to interest on and principal of the Note, but such application shall not otherwise affect the order of priority of application specified in this paragraph 3.

4. CHARGES; LIENS. Borrower shall pay all water and sewer rates, rents, taxes, assessments, premiums, and Other Impositions attributable to the Property at Lender's option in the manner provided under paragraph 2 hereof or, if not paid in such manner, by Borrower making payment, when due, directly to the payee thereof, or in such other manner as Lender may designate in writing. Borrower shall promptly furnish to Lender all notices of amounts due under this paragraph 4, and in the event Borrower shall make payment directly, Borrower shall promptly furnish to Lender receipts evidencing such payments. Borrower shall promptly discharge any lien which has, or may have, priority over or equality with, the lien of this Instrument, and Borrower shall pay, when due, the claims of all persons supplying labor or materials to or in connection with the Property. Without Lender's prior written permission, Borrower shall not allow any lien inferior to this Instrument to be perfected against the Property.

5. HAZARD INSURANCE. Borrower shall keep the improvements now existing or hereafter erected on the Property insured by carriers at all times satisfactory to Lender against loss by fire, hazards included within the term "extended coverage", rent loss and such other hazards, casualties, liabilities and contingencies as Lender (and, if this Instrument is on a leasehold, the ground lease) shall require and in such amounts and for such periods as Lender shall require. All premiums on insurance policies shall be paid, at Lender's option, in the manner provided under paragraph 2 hereof, or by Borrower making payment, when due, directly to the carrier, or in such other manner as Lender may designate in writing.

All insurance policies and renewals thereof shall be in a form acceptable to Lender and shall include a standard mortgage clause in favor of and in form acceptable to Lender. Lender shall have the right to hold the policies, and Borrower shall promptly furnish to Lender all renewal notices and all receipts of paid premiums. At least thirty days prior to the expiration date of a policy, Borrower shall deliver to Lender a renewal policy in form satisfactory to Lender. If this Instrument is on a leasehold, Borrower shall furnish Lender a duplicate of all policies, renewal notices, renewal policies and receipts of paid premiums if, by virtue of the ground lease, the originals thereof may not be supplied by Borrower to Lender.

In the event of loss, Borrower shall give immediate written notice to the insurance carrier and to Lender. Borrower hereby authorizes and empowers Lender as attorney-in-fact for Borrower to make proof of loss, to adjust and compromise any claim under insurance policies, to appear in and prosecute any action arising from such insurance policies, to collect and receive insurance proceeds, and to deduct therefrom Lender's expenses incurred in the collection of such proceeds; provided however, that nothing contained in this paragraph 5 shall require Lender to incur any expense or take any action hereunder. Borrower further authorizes Lender, at Lender's option, (a) to hold the balance of such proceeds to be used to reimburse Borrower for the cost of reconstruction or repair of the Property or (b) to apply the balance of such proceeds to the payment of the sums secured by this Instrument, whether or not then due, in the order of application set forth in paragraph 3 hereof (subject, however, to the rights of the lessor under the ground lease if this Instrument is on a leasehold).

If the insurance proceeds are held by Lender to reimburse Borrower for the cost of restoration and repair of the Property, the Property shall be restored to the equivalent of its original condition or such other condition as Lender may approve in writing. Lender may, at Lender's option, condition disbursement of said proceeds on Lender's approval of such plans and specifications of an architect satisfactory to Lender, contractor's cost estimates, architect's certificates, waivers of liens, sworn statements of mechanics and materialmen and such other evidence of costs, percentage completion of construction, application of payments, and satisfaction of liens as Lender may reasonably require. If the insurance proceeds are applied to the payment of the sums secured by this Instrument, any such application of proceeds to principal shall not extend or postpone the due dates of the monthly installments referred to in paragraphs 1 and 2 hereof or change the amounts of such installments. If the Property is sold pursuant to paragraph 27 hereof or if Lender acquires title to the Property, Lender shall have all of the right, title and interest of Borrower in and to any insurance policies and unearned premiums thereon and in and to the proceeds resulting from any damage to the Property prior to such sale or acquisition.

6. PRESERVATION AND MAINTENANCE OF PROPERTY; LEASEHOLDS. Borrower (a) shall not commit waste or permit impairment or deterioration of the Property, (b) shall not abandon the Property, (c) shall restore or repair promptly and in a good and workmanlike manner all

Uniform Covenants—Multifamily—1/77—**FNMA/FHLMC Uniform Instrument** *(page 3 of 8 pages)*

FIGURE 15-8

FNMA/FHLMC uniform instrument

or any part of the Property to the equivalent of its original condition, or such other condition as Lender may approve in writing, in the event of any damage, injury or loss thereto, whether or not insurance proceeds are available to cover in whole or in part the costs of such restoration or repair, (d) shall keep the Property, including improvements, fixtures, equipment, machinery and appliances thereon in good repair and shall replace fixtures, equipment, machinery and appliances on the Property when necessary to keep such items in good repair, (e) shall comply with all laws, ordinances, regulations and requirements of any governmental body applicable to the Property, (f) shall provide for professional management of the Property by a residential rental property manager satisfactory to Lender pursuant to a contract approved by Lender in writing, unless such requirement shall be waived by Lender in writing, (g) shall generally operate and maintain the Property in a manner to ensure maximum rentals, and (h) shall give notice in writing to Lender of and, unless otherwise directed in writing by Lender, appear in and defend any action or proceeding purporting to affect the Property, the security of this Instrument or the rights or powers of Lender. Neither Borrower nor any tenant or other person shall remove, demolish or alter any improvement now existing or hereafter erected on the Property or any fixture, equipment, machinery or appliance in or on the Property except when incident to the replacement of fixtures, equipment, machinery and appliances with items of like kind.

If this Instrument is on a leasehold, Borrower (i) shall comply with the provisions of the ground lease, (ii) shall give immediate written notice to Lender of any default by lessor under the ground lease or of any notice received by Borrower from such lessor of any default under the ground lease by Borrower, (iii) shall exercise any option to renew or extend the ground lease and give written confirmation thereof to Lender within thirty days after such option becomes exercisable, (iv) shall give immediate written notice to Lender of the commencement of any remedial proceedings under the ground lease by any party thereto and, if required by Lender, shall permit Lender as Borrower's attorney-in-fact to control and act for Borrower in any such remedial proceedings and (v) shall within thirty days after request by Lender obtain from the lessor under the ground lease and deliver to Lender the lessor's estoppel certificate required thereunder, if any. Borrower hereby expressly transfers and assigns to Lender the benefit of all covenants contained in the ground lease, whether or not such covenants run with the land, but Lender shall have no liability with respect to such covenants nor any other covenants contained in the ground lease.

Borrower shall not surrender the leasehold estate and interests herein conveyed nor terminate or cancel the ground lease creating said estate and interests, and Borrower shall not, without the express written consent of Lender, alter or amend said ground lease. Borrower covenants and agrees that there shall not be a merger of the ground lease, or of the leasehold estate created thereby, with the fee estate covered by the ground lease by reason of said leasehold estate or said fee estate, or any part of either, coming into common ownership, unless Lender shall consent in writing to such merger; if Borrower shall acquire such fee estate, then this Instrument shall simultaneously and without further action be spread so as to become a lien on such fee estate.

7. USE OF PROPERTY. Unless required by applicable law or unless Lender has otherwise agreed in writing, Borrower shall not allow changes in the use for which all or any part of the Property was intended at the time this Instrument was executed. Borrower shall not initiate or acquiesce in a change in the zoning classification of the Property without Lender's prior written consent.

8. PROTECTION OF LENDER'S SECURITY. If Borrower fails to perform the covenants and agreements contained in this Instrument, or if any action or proceeding is commenced which affects the Property or title thereto or the interest of Lender therein, including, but not limited to, eminent domain, insolvency, code enforcement, or arrangements or proceedings involving a bankrupt or decedent, then Lender at Lender's option may make such appearances, disburse such sums and take such action as Lender deems necessary, in its sole discretion, to protect Lender's interest, including, but not limited to, (i) disbursement of attorney's fees, (ii) entry upon the Property to make repairs, (iii) procurement of satisfactory insurance as provided in paragraph 5 hereof, and (iv) if this Instrument is on a leasehold, exercise of any option to renew or extend the ground lease on behalf of Borrower and the curing of any default of Borrower in the terms and conditions of the ground lease.

Any amounts disbursed by Lender pursuant to this paragraph 8, with interest thereon, shall become additional indebtedness of Borrower secured by this Instrument. Unless Borrower and Lender agree to other terms of payment, such amounts shall be immediately due and payable and shall bear interest from the date of disbursement at the rate stated in the Note unless collection from Borrower of interest at such rate would be contrary to applicable law, in which event such amounts shall bear interest at the highest rate which may be collected from Borrower under applicable law. Borrower hereby covenants and agrees that Lender shall be subrogated to the lien of any mortgage or other lien discharged, in whole or in part, by the indebtedness secured hereby. Nothing contained in this paragraph 8 shall require Lender to incur any expense or take any action hereunder.

9. INSPECTION. Lender may make or cause to be made reasonable entries upon and inspections of the Property.

10. BOOKS AND RECORDS. Borrower shall keep and maintain at all times at Borrower's address stated below, or such other place as Lender may approve in writing, complete and accurate books of accounts and records adequate to reflect correctly the results of the operation of the Property and copies of all written contracts, leases and other instruments which affect the Property. Such books, records, contracts, leases and other instruments shall be subject to examination and inspection at any reasonable time by Lender. Upon Lender's request, Borrower shall furnish to Lender, within one hundred and twenty days after the end of each fiscal year of Borrower, a balance sheet, a statement of income and expenses of the Property and a statement of changes in financial position, each in reasonable detail and certified by Borrower and, if Lender shall require, by an independent certified public accountant. Borrower shall furnish, together with the foregoing financial statements and at any other time upon Lender's request, a rent schedule for the Property, certified by Borrower, showing the name of each tenant, and for each tenant, the space occupied, the lease expiration date, the rent payable and the rent paid.

11. CONDEMNATION. Borrower shall promptly notify Lender of any action or proceeding relating to any condemnation or other taking, whether direct or indirect, of the Property, or part thereof, and Borrower shall appear in and prosecute any such action or proceeding unless otherwise directed by Lender in writing. Borrower authorizes Lender, at Lender's option, as attorney-in-fact for Borrower, to commence, appear in and prosecute, in Lender's or Borrower's name, any action or proceeding relating to any condemnation or other taking of the Property, whether direct or indirect, and to settle or compromise any claim in connection with such condemnation or other taking. The proceeds of any award, payment or claim for damages, direct or consequential, in connection with any condemnation or other taking, whether direct or indirect, of the Property, or part thereof, or for conveyances in lieu of condemnation, are hereby assigned to and shall be paid to Lender subject, if this Instrument is on a leasehold, to the rights of lessor under the ground lease.

Borrower authorizes Lender to apply such awards, payments, proceeds or damages, after the deduction of Lender's expenses incurred in the collection of such amounts, at Lender's option, to restoration or repair of the Property or to payment of the sums secured by this Instrument, whether or not then due, in the order of application set forth in paragraph 3 hereof, with the balance, if any, to Borrower. Unless Borrower and Lender otherwise agree in writing, any application of proceeds to principal shall not extend or postpone the due date of the monthly installments referred to in paragraphs 1 and 2 hereof or change the amount of such installments. Borrower agrees to execute such further evidence of assignment of any awards, proceeds, damages or claims arising in connection with such condemnation or taking as Lender may require.

12. BORROWER AND LIEN NOT RELEASED. From time to time, Lender may, at Lender's option, without giving notice to or obtaining the consent of Borrower, Borrower's successors or assigns or of any junior lienholder or guarantors, without liability on Lender's part and notwithstanding Borrower's breach of any covenant or agreement of Borrower in this Instrument, extend the time for payment of said indebtedness or any part thereof, reduce the payments thereon, release anyone liable on any of said indebtedness, accept a renewal note or notes therefor, modify the terms and time of payment of said indebtedness, release from the lien of this Instrument any part of the Property, take or release other or additional security, reconvey any part of the Property, consent to any map or plan of the Property, consent to the granting of any easement, join in any extension or subordination agreement, and agree in writing with Borrower to modify the rate of interest or period of amortization of the Note or change the amount of the monthly installments payable thereunder. Any actions taken by Lender pursuant to the terms of this paragraph 12 shall not affect the obligation of Borrower or Borrower's successors or assigns to pay the sums secured by this Instrument and to observe the covenants of Borrower contained herein, shall not affect the guaranty of any person, corporation, partnership or other entity for payment of the indebtedness secured hereby, and shall not affect the lien or priority of lien hereof on the Property. Borrower shall pay Lender a reasonable service charge, together with such title insurance premiums and attorney's fees as may be incurred at Lender's option, for any such action if taken at Borrower's request.

13. FORBEARANCE BY LENDER NOT A WAIVER. Any forbearance by Lender in exercising any right or remedy hereunder, or otherwise afforded by applicable law, shall not be a waiver of or preclude the exercise of any right or remedy. The acceptance by Lender of payment of any sum secured by this Instrument after the due date of such payment shall not be a waiver of Lender's right to either require prompt payment when due of all other sums so secured or to declare a default for failure to make prompt payment. The procurement of insurance or the payment of taxes or other liens or charges by Lender shall not be a waiver of Lender's right to accelerate the maturity of the indebtedness secured by this Instrument, nor shall Lender's receipt of any awards, proceeds or damages under paragraphs 5 and 11 hereof operate to cure or waive Borrower's default in payment of sums secured by this Instrument.

(page 4 of 8 pages)

FIGURE 15-8 (continued)

14. ESTOPPEL CERTIFICATE. Borrower shall within ten days of a written request from Lender furnish Lender with a written statement, duly acknowledged, setting forth the sums secured by this Instrument and any right of set-off, counterclaim or other defense which exists against such sums and the obligations of this Instrument.

15. UNIFORM COMMERCIAL CODE SECURITY AGREEMENT. This Instrument is intended to be a security agreement pursuant to the Uniform Commercial Code for any of the items specified above as part of the Property which, under applicable law, may be subject to a security interest pursuant to the Uniform Commercial Code, and Borrower hereby grants Lender a security interest in said items. Borrower agrees that Lender may file this Instrument, or a reproduction thereof, in the real estate records or other appropriate index, as a financing statement for any of the items specified above as part of the Property. Any reproduction of this Instrument or of any other security agreement or financing statement shall be sufficient as a financing statement. In addition, Borrower agrees to execute and deliver to Lender, upon Lender's request, any financing statements, as well as extensions, renewals and amendments thereof, and reproductions of this Instrument in such form as Lender may require to perfect a security interest with respect to said items. Borrower shall pay all costs of filing such financing statements and any extensions, renewals, amendments and releases thereof, and shall pay all reasonable costs and expenses of any record searches for financing statements Lender may reasonably require. Without the prior written consent of Lender, Borrower shall not create or suffer to be created pursuant to the Uniform Commercial Code any other security interest in said items, including replacements and additions thereto. Upon Borrower's breach of any covenant or agreement of Borrower contained in this Instrument, including the covenants to pay when due all sums secured by this Instrument, Lender shall have the remedies of a secured party under the Uniform Commercial Code and, at Lender's option, may also invoke the remedies provided in paragraph 27 of this Instrument as to such items. In exercising any of said remedies, Lender may proceed against the items of real property and any items of personal property specified above as part of the Property separately or together and in any order whatsoever, without in any way affecting the availability of Lender's remedies under the Uniform Commercial Code or of the remedies provided in paragraph 27 of this Instrument.

16. LEASES OF THE PROPERTY. As used in this paragraph 16, the word "lease" shall mean "sublease" if this Instrument is on a leasehold. Borrower shall comply with and observe Borrower's obligations as landlord under all leases of the Property or any part thereof. Borrower will not lease any portion of the Property for non-residential use except with the prior written approval of Lender. Borrower, at Lender's request, shall furnish Lender with executed copies of all leases now existing or hereafter made of all or any part of the Property, and all leases now or hereafter entered into will be in form and substance subject to the approval of Lender. All leases of the Property shall specifically provide that such leases are subordinate to this Instrument; that the tenant attorns to Lender, such attornment to be effective upon Lender's acquisition of title to the Property; that the tenant agrees to execute such further evidences of attornment as Lender may from time to time request; that the attornment of the tenant shall not be terminated by foreclosure; and that Lender may, at Lender's option, accept or reject such attornments. Borrower shall not, without Lender's written consent, execute, modify, surrender or terminate, either orally or in writing, any lease now existing or hereafter made of all or any part of the Property providing for a term of three years or more, permit an assignment or sublease of such a lease without Lender's written consent, or request or consent to the subordination of any lease of all or any part of the Property to any lien subordinate to this Instrument. If Borrower becomes aware that any tenant proposes to do, or is doing, any act or thing which may give rise to any right of set-off against rent, Borrower shall (i) take such steps as shall be reasonably calculated to prevent the accrual of any right to a set-off against rent, (ii) notify Lender thereof and of the amount of said set-offs, and (iii) within ten days after such accrual, reimburse the tenant who shall have acquired such right to set-off or take such other steps as shall effectively discharge such set-off and as shall assure that rents thereafter due shall continue to be payable without set-off or deduction.

Upon Lender's request, Borrower shall assign to Lender, by written instrument satisfactory to Lender, all leases now existing or hereafter made of all or any part of the Property and all security deposits made by tenants in connection with such leases of the Property. Upon assignment by Borrower to Lender of any leases of the Property, Lender shall have all of the rights and powers possessed by Borrower prior to such assignment and Lender shall have the right to modify, extend or terminate such existing leases and to execute new leases, in Lender's sole discretion.

17. REMEDIES CUMULATIVE. Each remedy provided in this Instrument is distinct and cumulative to all other rights or remedies under this Instrument or afforded by law or equity, and may be exercised concurrently, independently, or successively, in any order whatsoever.

18. ACCELERATION IN CASE OF BORROWER'S INSOLVENCY. If Borrower shall voluntarily file a petition under the Federal Bankruptcy Act, as such Act may from time to time be amended, or under any similar or successor Federal statute relating to bankruptcy, insolvency, arrangements or reorganizations, or under any state bankruptcy or insolvency act, or file an answer in an involuntary proceeding admitting insolvency or inability to pay debts, or if Borrower shall fail to obtain a vacation or stay of involuntary proceedings brought for the reorganization, dissolution or liquidation of Borrower, or if Borrower shall be adjudged a bankrupt, or if a trustee or receiver shall be appointed for Borrower or Borrower's property, or if the Property shall become subject to the jurisdiction of a Federal bankruptcy court or similar state court, or if Borrower shall make an assignment for the benefit of Borrower's creditors, or if there is an attachment, execution or other judicial seizure of any portion of Borrower's assets and such seizure is not discharged within ten days, then Lender may, at Lender's option, declare all of the sums secured by this Instrument to be immediately due and payable without prior notice to Borrower, and Lender may invoke any remedies permitted by paragraph 27 of this Instrument. Any attorney's fees and other expenses incurred by Lender in connection with Borrower's bankruptcy or any of the other aforesaid events shall be additional indebtedness of Borrower secured by this Instrument pursuant to paragraph 8 hereof.

19. TRANSFERS OF THE PROPERTY OR BENEFICIAL INTERESTS IN BORROWER; ASSUMPTION. On sale or transfer of (i) all or any part of the Property, or any interest therein, or (ii) beneficial interests in Borrower (if Borrower is not a natural person or persons but is a corporation, partnership, trust or other legal entity), Lender may, at Lender's option, declare all of the sums secured by this Instrument to be immediately due and payable, and Lender may invoke any remedies permitted by paragraph 27 of this Instrument. This option shall not apply in case of

    (a) transfers by devise or descent or by operation of law upon the death of a joint tenant or a partner;

    (b) sales or transfers when the transferee's creditworthiness and management ability are satisfactory to Lender and the transferee has executed, prior to the sale or transfer, a written assumption agreement containing such terms as Lender may require, including, if required by Lender, an increase in the rate of interest payable under the Note;

    (c) the grant of a leasehold interest in a part of the Property of three years or less (or such longer lease term as Lender may permit by prior written approval) not containing an option to purchase (except any interest in the ground lease, if this Instrument is on a leasehold);

    (d) sales or transfers of beneficial interests in Borrower provided that such sales or transfers, together with any prior sales or transfers of beneficial interests in Borrower, but excluding sales or transfers under subparagraphs (a) and (b) above, do not result in more than 49% of the beneficial interests in Borrower having been sold or transferred since commencement of amortization of the Note; and

    (e) sales or transfers of fixtures or any personal property pursuant to the first paragraph of paragraph 6 hereof.

20. NOTICE. Except for any notice required under applicable law to be given in another manner, (a) any notice to Borrower provided for in this Instrument or in the Note shall be given by mailing such notice by certified mail addressed to Borrower at Borrower's address stated below or at such other address as Borrower may designate by notice to Lender as provided herein, and (b) any notice to Lender shall be given by certified mail, return receipt requested, to Lender's address stated herein or to such other address as Lender may designate by notice to Borrower as provided herein. Any notice provided for in this Instrument or in the Note shall be deemed to have been given to Borrower or Lender when given in the manner designated herein.

21. SUCCESSORS AND ASSIGNS BOUND; JOINT AND SEVERAL LIABILITY; AGENTS; CAPTIONS. The covenants and agreements herein contained shall bind, and the rights hereunder shall inure to, the respective successors and assigns of Lender and Borrower, subject to the provisions of paragraph 19 hereof. All covenants and agreements of Borrower shall be joint and several. In exercising any rights hereunder or taking any actions provided for herein, Lender may act through its employees, agents or independent contractors as authorized by Lender. The captions and headings of the paragraphs of this Instrument are for convenience only and are not to be used to interpret or define the provisions hereof.

22. UNIFORM MULTIFAMILY INSTRUMENT; GOVERNING LAW; SEVERABILITY. This form of multifamily instrument combines uniform covenants for national use and non-uniform covenants with limited variations by jurisdiction to constitute a uniform security instrument covering real property and related fixtures and personal property. This Instrument shall be governed by the law of the jurisdiction in which the Property is located. In the event that any provision of this Instrument or the Note conflicts with applicable law, such conflict shall not affect other provisions of this Instrument or the Note which can be given effect without the conflicting provisions, and to this end the provisions of this

(page 5 of 8 pages)

FIGURE 15-8 (continued)

Instrument and the Note are declared to be severable. In the event that any applicable law limiting the amount of interest or other charges permitted to be collected from Borrower is interpreted so that any charge provided for in this Instrument or in the Note, whether considered separately or together with other charges levied in connection with this Instrument and the Note, violates such law, and Borrower is entitled to the benefit of such law, such charge is hereby reduced to the extent necessary to eliminate such violation. The amounts, if any, previously paid to Lender in excess of the amounts payable to Lender pursuant to such charges as reduced shall be applied by Lender to reduce the principal of the indebtedness evidenced by the Note. For the purpose of determining whether any applicable law limiting the amount of interest or other charges permitted to be collected from Borrower has been violated, all indebtedness which is secured by this Instrument or evidenced by the Note and which constitutes interest, as well as all other charges levied in connection with such indebtedness which constitute interest, shall be deemed to be allocated and spread over the stated term of the Note. Unless otherwise required by applicable law, such allocation and spreading shall be effected in such a manner that the rate of interest computed thereby is uniform throughout the stated term of the Note.

23. WAIVER OF STATUTE OF LIMITATIONS. Borrower hereby waives the right to assert any statute of limitations as a bar to the enforcement of the lien of this Instrument or to any action brought to enforce the Note or any other obligation secured by this Instrument.

24. WAIVER OF MARSHALLING. Notwithstanding the existence of any other security interests in the Property held by Lender or by any other party, Lender shall have the right to determine the order in which any or all of the Property shall be subjected to the remedies provided herein. Lender shall have the right to determine the order in which any or all portions of the indebtedness secured hereby are satisfied from the proceeds realized upon the exercise of the remedies provided herein. Borrower, any party who consents to this Instrument and any party who now or hereafter acquires a security interest in the Property and who has actual or constructive notice hereof hereby waives any and all right to require the marshalling of assets in connection with the exercise of any of the remedies permitted by applicable law or provided herein.

25. CONSTRUCTION LOAN PROVISIONS. Borrower agrees to comply with the covenants and conditions of the Construction Loan Agreement, if any, which is hereby incorporated by reference in and made a part of this Instrument. All advances made by Lender pursuant to the Construction Loan Agreement shall be indebtedness of Borrower secured by this Instrument, and such advances may be obligatory as provided in the Construction Loan Agreement. All sums disbursed by Lender prior to completion of the improvements to protect the security of this Instrument up to the principal amount of the Note shall be treated as disbursements pursuant to the Construction Loan Agreement. All such sums shall bear interest from the date of disbursement at the rate stated in the Note, unless collection from Borrower of interest at such rate would be contrary to applicable law in which event such amounts shall bear interest at the highest rate which may be collected from Borrower under applicable law and shall be payable upon notice from Lender to Borrower requesting payment therefor.

From time to time as Lender deems necessary to protect Lender's interests, Borrower shall, upon request of Lender, execute and deliver to Lender, in such form as Lender shall direct, assignments of any and all rights or claims which relate to the construction of the Property and which Borrower may have against any party supplying or who has supplied labor, materials or services in connection with construction of the Property. In case of breach by Borrower of the covenants and conditions of the Construction Loan Agreement, Lender, at Lender's option, with or without entry upon the Property, (i) may invoke any of the rights or remedies provided in the Construction Loan Agreement, (ii) may accelerate the sums secured by this Instrument and invoke those remedies provided in paragraph 27 hereof, or (iii) may do both. If, after the commencement of amortization of the Note, the Note and this Instrument are sold by Lender, from and after such sale the Construction Loan Agreement shall cease to be a part of this Instrument and Borrower shall not assert any right of set-off, counterclaim or other claim or defense arising out of or in connection with the Construction Loan Agreement against the obligations of the Note and this Instrument.

26. ASSIGNMENT OF RENTS; APPOINTMENT OF RECEIVER; LENDER IN POSSESSION. As part of the consideration for the indebtedness evidenced by the Note, Borrower hereby absolutely and unconditionally assigns and transfers to Lender all the rents and revenues of the Property, including those now due, past due, or to become due by virtue of any lease or other agreement for the occupancy or use of all or any part of the Property, regardless of to whom the rents and revenues of the Property are payable. Borrower hereby authorizes Lender or Lender's agents to collect the aforesaid rents and revenues and hereby directs each tenant of the Property to pay such rents to Lender or Lender's agents; provided, however, that prior to written notice given by Lender to Borrower of the breach by Borrower of any covenant or agreement of Borrower in this Instrument, Borrower shall collect and receive all rents and revenues of the Property as trustee for the benefit of Lender and Borrower, to apply the rents and revenues so collected to the sums secured by this Instrument in the order provided in paragraph 3 hereof with the balance, so long as no such breach has occurred, to the account of Borrower, it being intended by Borrower and Lender that this assignment of rents constitutes an absolute assignment and not an assignment for additional security only. Upon delivery of written notice by Lender to Borrower of the breach by Borrower of any covenant or agreement of Borrower in this Instrument, and without the necessity of Lender entering upon and taking and maintaining full control of the Property in person, by agent or by a court-appointed receiver, Lender shall immediately be entitled to possession of all rents and revenues of the Property as specified in this paragraph 26 as the same become due and payable, including but not limited to rents then due and unpaid, and all such rents shall immediately upon delivery of such notice be held by Borrower as trustee for the benefit of Lender only; provided, however, that the written notice by Lender to Borrower of the breach by Borrower shall contain a statement that Lender exercises its rights to such rents. Borrower agrees that commencing upon delivery of such written notice of Borrower's breach by Lender to Borrower, each tenant of the Property shall make such rents payable to and pay such rents to Lender or Lender's agents on Lender's written demand to each tenant therefor, delivered to each tenant personally, by mail or by delivering such demand to each rental unit, without any liability on the part of said tenant to inquire further as to the existence of a default by Borrower.

Borrower hereby covenants that Borrower has not executed any prior assignment of said rents, that Borrower has not performed, and will not perform, any acts or has not executed, and will not execute, any instrument which would prevent Lender from exercising its rights under this paragraph 26, and that at the time of execution of this Instrument there has been no anticipation or prepayment of any of the rents of the Property for more than two months prior to the due dates of such rents. Borrower covenants that Borrower will not hereafter collect or accept payment of any rents of the Property more than two months prior to the due dates of such rents. Borrower further covenants that Borrower will execute and deliver to Lender such further assignments of rents and revenues of the Property as Lender may from time to time request.

Upon Borrower's breach of any covenant or agreement of Borrower in this Instrument, Lender may in person, by agent or by a court-appointed receiver, regardless of the adequacy of Lender's security, enter upon and take and maintain full control of the Property in order to perform all acts necessary and appropriate for the operation and maintenance thereof including, but not limited to, the execution, cancellation or modification of leases, the collection of all rents and revenues of the Property, the making of repairs to the Property and the execution or termination of contracts providing for the management or maintenance of the Property, all on such terms as are deemed best to protect the security of this Instrument. In the event Lender elects to seek the appointment of a receiver for the Property upon Borrower's breach of any covenant or agreement of Borrower in this Instrument, Borrower hereby expressly consents to the appointment of such receiver. Lender or the receiver shall be entitled to receive a reasonable fee for so managing the Property.

All rents and revenues collected subsequent to delivery of written notice by Lender to Borrower of the breach by Borrower of any covenant or agreement of Borrower in this Instrument shall be applied first to the costs, if any, of taking control of and managing the Property and collecting the rents, including, but not limited to, attorney's fees, receiver's fees, premiums on receiver's bonds, costs of repairs to the Property, premiums on insurance policies, taxes, assessments and other charges on the Property, and the costs of discharging any obligation or liability of Borrower as lessor or landlord of the Property and then to the sums secured by this Instrument. Lender or the receiver shall have access to the books and records used in the operation and maintenance of the Property and shall be liable to account only for those rents actually received. Lender shall not be liable to Borrower, anyone claiming under or through Borrower or anyone having an interest in the Property by reason of anything done or left undone by Lender under this paragraph 26.

If the rents of the Property are not sufficient to meet the costs, if any, of taking control of and managing the Property and collecting the rents, any funds expended by Lender for such purposes shall become indebtedness of Borrower to Lender secured by this Instrument pursuant to paragraph 8 hereof. Unless Lender and Borrower agree in writing to other terms of payment, such amounts shall be payable upon notice from Lender to Borrower requesting payment thereof and shall bear interest from the date of disbursement at the rate stated in the Note unless payment of interest at such rate would be contrary to applicable law, in which event such amounts shall bear interest at the highest rate which may be collected from Borrower under applicable law.

Any entering upon and taking and maintaining of control of the Property by Lender or the receiver and any application of rents as provided herein shall not cure or waive any default hereunder or invalidate any other right or remedy of Lender under applicable law or provided herein. This assignment of rents of the Property shall terminate at such time as this Instrument ceases to secure indebtedness held by Lender.

Uniform Covenants—Multifamily—1/77—FNMA/FHLMC Uniform Instrument   *(page 6 of 8 pages)*

FIGURE 15-8 (continued)

UNIFORM COVENANTS

1. *Payment of principal and interest.* Borrower agrees to make payments of debt service promptly and otherwise to live up to making payments as agreed, as, for example, for a late charge.

2. *Funds for taxes and insurance.* Borrower agrees to make monthly deposits with the lender for property taxes, hazard insurance, mortgage insurance, if any, water and sewer charges, if any, and rents or ground rents, if any. Lender is to make these annual payments when due.

3. *Application of payments.* Noteholder is awarded some discretion in applying payments to taxes, insurance, interest, and rents. (For one- to four-family residence, payments apply first to insurance and taxes as necessary, second to interest on the principal, and third to reduction of the principal.)

4. *Charges, liens.* Borrower agrees to pay any charges or liens against the property promptly. Also, the borrower agrees not to allow inferior or lower-priority liens to develop.

5. *Hazard insurance.* Borrower is required to keep the property insured against fire and other hazards up to the amount of the loan balance and against rent losses, with the insurance proceeds payable to the noteholder and any excess paid the borrower.

6. *Property preservation and maintenance.* Borrower agrees to maintain the property in good repair and not permit its waste or deterioration. Borrower further agrees that fixtures, buildings, equipment, and other improvements shall not be removed or demolished without prior written consent from the noteholder.

7. *Use of property.* Borrower agrees not to change the use of the property unless otherwise agreed to or required by law. Even a change in zoning is subject to review by the noteholder.

8. *Protection of lender's security.* Lender may protect the secured property by any actions necessary if the borrower fails to do so.

9. *Inspection.* Noteholder has reasonable entry to the property for inspections to assure its maintenance, safety, and proper operation.

10. *Books and records.* Lender is permitted reasonable access to the borrower's books and other financial records concerning the property.

11. *Condemnation.* Proceeds from condemnation shall first go to pay lender expenses and the debt, with any excess going to the owner.

12. *Borrower not released.* Lender does not release the lien or forgive any of the borrower's repayment obligation by extending time for payment or by failure to press for payment. That is, the lender loses no rights by being courteous and considerate in dealing with the borrower or debtor.

13. *Forbearance by lender not a waiver.* Noteholder forbearance—postponing action to a later time—does not waive or preclude exercise of a right or remedy. Thus, for example, in default, payment may be demanded immediately or at a later time, without damage to the noteholder.

14. *Estoppel certificate.* Borrower agrees to provide lender an estoppel certificate on demand. An estoppel certificate is a written statement that, when signed and given to another person, legally stops or prevents the signer from saying subsequently that the facts are different from those set forth. Such a certificate is usually used to verify the loan balance upon sale and assignment of the mortgage.

15. *UCC security agreement.* Borrower agrees to provide statements and to pay recording charges necessary to bring the mortgage into compliance with the Uniform Commercial Code.

16. *Leases of the property.* Borrower promises to provide lender with copies of leases and side agreements with tenants, on request.

17. *Remedies cumulative.* Lender remedies are distinct and cumulative and may therefore be exercised concurrently, independently, or successively.

18. *Acceleration upon borrower insolvency.* Lender may require immediate repayment of the debt upon the borrower's insolvency, as evidenced by filing for bankruptcy.

19. *Transfer of borrower's interests: Assumption.* On sale or transfer of ownership, lender may require immediate repayment or renegotiate and extend the loan, such as at a higher interest rate. This is often called the "due on sale" or alienation clause.

20. *Notice.* Certified mail must be used by the lender or borrower to give notice of changes of name or address, default and foreclosure, sale of the property, or damage or destruction to the property to the other.

21. *Successors and assigns bound.* People taking over the legal positions of the lender and/or borrower at a later time are equally bound by the contract provisions, jointly and severally.

22. *Governing law and severability.* Conflicts between the uniform instrument and local law are to be resolved according to the law of the jurisdiction in which the property is located. Any such conflict shall not invalidate the remaining provisions of the instrument. This provision, dividing the instrument into distinct, independent obligations or agreements any one of which may be removed without affecting the others, is termed the *severability clause.*

23. *Waiver of statute of limitations.* Borrower waives any statute of limitations rights to provisions in the mortgage.

24. *Waiver to marshalling of assets.* Right to the marshalling of assets (arranging in a certain order) in connection with default remedies in the contract is waived by the borrower, giving the lender greater freedom in pursuing remedies under the instrument.

25. *Construction loan provisions.* A construction loan may be made and tied into the instrument.

26. *Assignment of rents.* Upon breach of a condition, and with proper notice, rents are to be paid to a receiver, to protect the lender's interests better. A receiver is an officer of the court appointed to take possession and control of the property of concern in a suit.

NONUNIFORM COVENANTS

State statutes are specific and often vary substantially. Thus, the FNMA/FHLMC instruments provide for state specific covenants to comply with such statutes. For the instrument in Figure 15-5, these nonuniform covenants are as follows.

27. *Acceleration: Remedies.* Lender may declare all sums secured by the mortgage to be due and payable immediately. Lender shall also be allowed to collect all costs of remedies such as attorney's fees, abstracts, title reports, and other expenses.

28. *Release.* Lender will terminate this instrument upon payment of all sums due (desistance clause).
29. *Attorneys' fees.* Attorneys' fees shall include fees awarded by an appellate court.
30. *Future advances.* Lender, at borrower's request, may advance additional monies, which also will be secured by this mortgage (open-end provision).

Types of Loans

Mortgage and trust deed loans are named in many ways. The terms are not completely unique; some overlap often occurs from one to the other. The more commonly used terms are taken up first and their usage briefly explained. Terms based on repayment plans, provided for in the note, are taken up in a subsequent section.

CONSTRUCTION LOAN

A construction loan is made to finance the addition of improvements. A construction loan generally runs until the completion of the proposed improvements and possibly to the sale of the property.

A construction loan is distinct in that the total of the loan is not initially fully paid out to the borrower. Instead, funds are paid out in installments at agreed stages of construction. A lender representative usually inspects and certifies satisfactory progress prior to each payout. Lien waivers are commonly used with construction loans to prevent the development and curing of mechanic's liens, which might take priority over the construction loan itself.

CONVENTIONAL LOAN

A *conventional loan* is one not backed by government, as insured by the Federal Housing Administration (FHA) or guaranteed by the Veterans Administration (VA). The term developed historically. When FHA loans were first introduced in the 1930s, borrowers were given the choice of an "FHA-insured" or a "conventional" loan. Conventional loans, being contracts between private parties, are much less subject to government regulation than are FHA or VA loans. Further, conventional loans are traditionally made at lower loan-to-value ratios than are FHA or VA loans because the lenders have less protection in default and foreclosure. Private mortgage insurance is an option with conventional loans, however.

FHA-INSURED LOAN

The Federal Housing Administration insures lenders against loss in return for fees or premiums paid by borrowers by what are popularly referred to as *FHA mortgages*. The FHA, as an agency of the U.S. government, only insures loans made by approved lenders under regulated conditions and terms and does not, itself, lend money. The entire principal is insured.

VA-GUARANTEED LOAN

A loan partially guaranteed against loss by the US Veterans Administration is termed a _VA_ or "GI" _mortgage_. The VA sets no maximum amount for the loan although there is a maximum to the guarantee. Also, if no financial institution will make a loan to an eligible veteran, the VA will. The guaranteed loan must initially be made to a qualified veteran or the dependent of a qualified veteran, usually a surviving spouse, and requires a "certificate of eligibility" from the VA. The lending institution makes the loan from its own monies and gets the guarantee from the government. The loan may later be taken over by a nonveteran. A number of states sponsor loans to former service personnel, which are commonly referred to as "state VA" or "state GI" loans.

PRIVATELY INSURED LOAN

A conventional loan, on which the lender is partially protected against loss by a private mortgage insurance (PMI) company in return for a fee or premium, is termed a privately insured loan. The insurance companies, therefore, compete directly with the Federal Housing and Veterans administrations. Almost all states allow lenders to make loans up to 95% of value with PMI.

Private mortgage insurance for single-family residences began with the Mortgage Guarantee Insurance Company of Milwaukee, Wisconsin, in 1957. Spectacular growth followed because of lower costs and shorter turnaround times on applications for loan insurance as compared with the FHA and VA. Acceptance of PMI for secondary mortgage market purposes began with the Federal Home Loan Bank Board in 1971. PMI is now used for loans on apartment and office buildings, stores, warehouses, and leaseholds, though the rates are higher than for homes.

Private mortgage insurance covers only the top 20–25 percent of a loan, which is the portion most exposed to risk and loss. Thus, a lender can make a 90–95 percent loan, with PMI, with the same risk as an uninsured loan for 70–75 percent of value. With only 5–10 percent down, many more people can qualify for loans. Later, with the loan-to-value ratio lowered to 70–75 percent, the insurance may be discontinued. FHA, in contrast, insures the entire loan for its entire life. The cost of PMI is therefore much less than for FHA insurance.

PURCHASE MONEY MORTGAGE LOAN

A _purchase money mortgage_ is one given by a buyer to a seller that secures all, or a portion, of the purchase price of a property. Thus the seller is financing or partially financing the transaction. The loan becomes active at the exact time that title is passed, giving the seller's claim priority over any lien that might develop against the property caused by the purchaser's actions. The legal presumption is that since the property was pledged at the same time title passed, no other party could have developed a prior claim. The words "purchase money mortgage" are commonly included in the deed to give notice of its existence. Some states do not recognize a deficiency judgment on a purchase money mortgage, presuming that the seller-lender may recover the original property and thus be no worse off after foreclosure than if no sale had occurred and no mortgage were made.

SECOND OR JUNIOR LOAN

A mortgage with priority as a lien over all other mortgages against a property is a first mortgage. A mortgage subsequent in priority to a first mortgage is a *second mortgage*. A mortgage with two mortgages of higher priority is a third mortgage. Mortgages have been stacked six and seven deep as to priority. The collective name for mortgages lower in priority than the first mortgage is *junior mortgages*. It follows that the lower the priority of a mortgage, the greater the risk of loss to the lender involved.

A *default-in-the-prior-mortgage clause* in a junior mortgage is designed to protect the lender. The clause provides that, if the borrower fails to make payments on any prior mortgage, such payments may be paid by the junior mortgagee and added to the amount of the junior loan. In addition, the junior lender may immediately declare a default to the junior lien and legally foreclose.

A second provision often included, for the benefit of the borrower, is a subordination clause. At the time of origination, at least one lender had higher priority of claim than the junior lender. This means that the junior mortgage would automatically become a first lien upon full payment of the prior loan or loans. Such a situation would make it difficult for the owner to refinance to a reasonably high loan to value ratio at a later time. A subordination clause establishes the relative priority of a lien or claim so that the borrower would be able to easily obtain a new loan with higher priority than that of the junior loan at a later time. Subordination clauses are also used to establish relative priority of claims among mortgages, leases, and land contracts.

MISCELLANEOUS MORTGAGE TYPES

Some loan arrangements contain unique clauses for special situations or purposes, as follows.

Blanket Loan. One loan secured by two or more parcels of real estate is called a blanket mortgage. The most common use of a blanket loan is in subdividing, where an initial loan on raw acreage is continued after the land is split up into lots. Blanket mortgages usually include a partial release clause that provides for removal of parcels from the lender's claim in return for partial repayment of the loan.

Package Loan. A loan contract that includes fixutres and other building equipment (refrigerators, ranges, washing machines and dryers, and dishwashers) as collateral is termed a package mortgage. Package mortgages are often used in financing residences, hotels, motels, and apartment projects.

Open-End Loan. An open-end contract provides for later advances from a lender, up to but not exceeding the original amount of the loan. The interest rate may need to be renegotiated if the provision is exercised.

At one time, real estate was financed with straight-term loans that called for periodic payments of interest and a lump-sum repayment of the principal. Real estate loans are now made with a wide variety of repayment plans, each of which is designed to solve a particular problem. Needless to say, choosing between the alternative plans is a major decision for a borrower.

In the 1930s the FHA introduced the amortizing loan, a plan by which the periodic debt service pays interest and systematically repays the principal over the life of the agreement. Nearly all mortgages with an extended life now include an amortization provision. Home loans are usually amortized by monthly payments. Commercial loans, on the other hand, may call for monthly, quarterly, semiannual, or annual debt service.

In the 1970s, several new repayment plans were introduced in response to rapidly fluctuating interest rates; these were made technically possible by the increasing use of computers and calculators. A summary knowledge of the more widely used plans, and their advantages and limitations, is presented here.

FIXED-RATE MORTGAGE

A *fixed rate mortgage* (FRM) loan means that the interest rate remains unchanged and debt-service payments remain equal or uniform in size over its life. Debt-service payments during the early part of the life go mostly to interest with a small portion to principal reduction. As the loan ages, the portion going to principal reduction increases while the portion to interest decreases. See Figure 15-9.

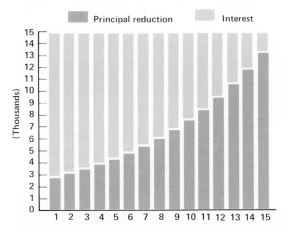

FIGURE 15-9A

Allocation of debt service to interest and principal reduction with a $100,000, 12%, fixed rate, 15 year amortizing loan

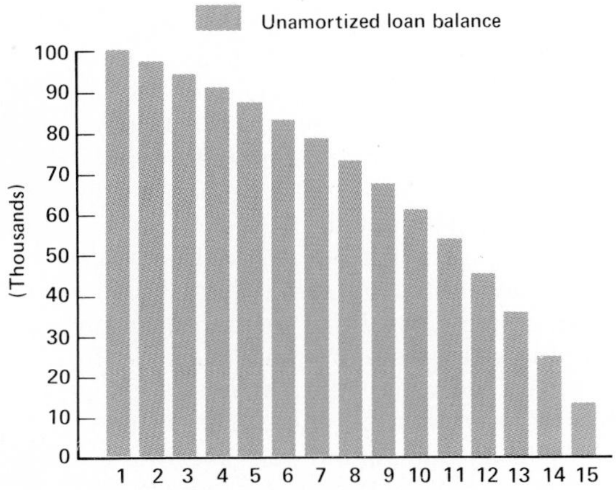

FIGURE 15-9B

Principal reduction with a $100,000, 12%, 15 year amortizing loan.

BALLOON LOAN

A loan contract calling for repayment of a portion of the original principal over its life and the balance in a single lump-sum payment at the end of the agreement is a partially amortizing mortgage. The lump-sum payment at the end of the agreement in commonly called a ***balloon payment***. An example is a loan set up with a 30-year amortization schedule while calling for a lump sum principal repayment at the end of the twelfth year.

Alternative Mortgage Instruments

The Federal Home Loan Bank Board, the Comptroller of the Currency, and the Federal National Mortgage Association originated several flexible mortgage instruments in the late 1970s to relieve the financial squeeze on lenders. These new instruments are known collectively as alternative mortgage instruments (AMIs). Several of these AMIs have gained considerable market acceptance.

Adjustable Rate Mortgage. A loan agreement allowing the interest rate to increase or decrease directly with the fluctuations in an index beyond the control of the lender is called a variable rate mortgage (VRM) or an *adjustable rate mortgage* (ARM). The VRM loan was introduced by the FHA in the mid-1970s, but the specifications were too tight for the wild interest rate gyrations that followed. Consequently, it did not gain wide acceptance. Subsequently, the Federal Home Loan Bank Board (FHLBB) and the Federal National Mortgage Association (FNMA) issued more flexible guidelines for ARM loans eligible for trading in the secondary mortgage market. In so doing, they made a due-on-sale clause mandatory in all ARM loans to enhance their negotiability in the secondary mortgage market.

ARM loans are amortizing with debt-service payments usually remaining level. Thus, if the interest rate increases, the life of the loan is simply extended, and vice versa. It is possible that the term remains fixed while debt service varies or that negative amortization can occur. A maximum interest rate adjustment per year (interest rate cap) and a maximum payment adjustment per year (debt-service cap) may be included. The fluctuating index may be any of eight suggested by FNMA that is acceptable to both the lender and the borrower. Interest rate increases are at the lender's option, but decreases are mandatory.

Allowing the interest rate to fluctuate shifts the risk of increasing interest rates to the borrower; at the same time, any decrease in interest rates benefits the borrower. The initial interest rate or cost of money on ARM and FRM loans depends on the interest rate outlook. When interest rates are low, ARM loans are likely to be made at slightly lower rates than are FRM loans, because the rate may go above the FRM rate during the life of the loan. The reverse may be true when interest rates are relatively high. A flexible rate allows lenders to continue making loans in the face of increasing interest rates without fear of being locked into a below-market fixed-rate loan. Hence, ARM lending helps to maintain a more even flow of funds into real estate. In turn, ARM loans have, at times, been the dominant lending arrangement.

Graduated Payment Mortgage. A graduated payment mortgage (GPM) loan provides for low initial debt-service payments with regular increases for several years until a level is reached where the payments will amortize the loan over its remaining term. Debt-service increases typically range from 2.5 to 7.5 percent per year. The interest rate may be fixed or variable. Sometimes payments in the early years will not cover all interest due on the loan, and the principal owed actually increases; this is termed "negative amortization." GPM loans are best suited to situations where the borrower expects steady increases in income at about the same rate as the scheduled increases in debt service. Thus, a GPM is sometimes called a young people's loan because it seems to suit best the needs of people who are just forming households and have increasing incomes. If the interest rate is adjustable, this becomes a graduated payment adjustable mortgage (GPAM) loan.

Growing Equity Mortgage. A growing equity mortgage (GEM) requires variable-sized payments that are tied to a borrower's ability to pay. However, the increase is not according to some fixed schedule, as is the GPM arrangement. A GEM loan is most likely to be made to a borrower with rising income expectations and, therefore, may be paid off well ahead of its maturity date. Increases in debt service above the original payment schedule go entirely to repay principal; hence, the borrower's equity builds up more quickly than with a more standard loan. The lender benefits from higher cash flow and greater liquidity. Payments are adjusted annually to reflect 75 percent of the rate of change in a national index of per capita disposable personal income.

Reverse Annuity Mortgage. The reverse annuity mortgage (RAM) loan was introduced by the FHLBB to enable elderly people to convert the equity in their homes into cash to meet living expenses. An elderly couple taking out a RAM loan would expect to live in their residence. Upon signing the loan agreement, the owner-borrower receives the money in one lump-sum payment or in periodic (monthly) payments. The loan is repayable, with interest, upon a specific event such as sale of the property or death of the owner, or at a specific date. The cash flows with a RAM loan are therefore the opposite of those under a traditional mortgage arrangement; hence the name. The interest rate on a RAM loan may be fixed or adjustable.

Renegotiable Rate Mortgage. Many lenders refused to renew the straight-term loans in the early 1930s because of the uncertain times; this refusal resulted in many foreclosures and only served to worsen the depression. In response, the FHA introduced the long-term, fixed-rate, fully amortizing loan. These long-term FRMs acted like a straitjacket on lenders when interest rates sharply increased in the mid- and late 1970s. That is, the lenders could not increase the rates on the loans to bring them in line with the suddenly much higher rates required to retain deposits.

Straight-term loans were reintroduced in Canada in the 1970s to give the lenders greater flexibility in adjusting their portfolios to changing economic conditions and were soon tabbed "Canadian rollovers." With wider acceptance by governmental agencies, rollover loans gradually became known as *renegotiable rate mortgages* (RRM), perhaps to gain initials comparable to those of other repayment plans. Under the FHLBB plan, an RRM is a series of short-term (3, 4, or 5 years) loans secured by a long-term mortgage; that is, the lender is required to renew the loan but at an interest rate adjusted to the market rate.

With an RRM, debt-service payments are smaller relative to amortizing plans, which enables borrowers to get higher cash flows in the early years of an investment and also to maintain a higher leverage ratio.

Shared Appreciation Mortgage. A loan in which any value increase in the subject property is split proportionately between the borrower and lender is termed a shared appreciation mortgage (SAM). In return for the right to share in appreciation, a SAM loan carries a below-market interest rate, which results in lower monthly debt service for the borrower. The lender's share of the value increase is expected to bring the actual rate of return on the loan to an effective yield greater than the market rate of interest.

The borrower makes a lump sum settlement if the property is sold or the loan is prepaid before the specified maturity date. If the loan runs its full term, the lender typically guarantees to refinance the entire property for the borrower, including the lender's share of the value appreciation.

A SAM loan involves risk for both the lender and borrower. For the lender, the higher rate of return may not be realized. For the borrower, a large value increase may require a much larger loan at a much higher and uncertain future market interest rate. Thus, the borrower may be unable to continue to afford the property.

Blended Mortgage. In refinancing a property or in a loan assumption in a sale, lenders and borrowers sometimes compromise on the interest rate. Thus, the new rate is somewhere between the low rate on the original older loan and the current market rate. In effect, there is a blending of the two rates; hence, the new loan is often termed a blended mortgage. It should be recognized that such a compromise is not really an alternative mortgage instrument. The compromise is an extremely practical way of solving a knotty problem for all parties involved, however.

WRAPAROUND LOAN

A *wraparound mortgage* (WAM) is created when a second mortgage loan is made with the new lender taking over the debt service payments on the first loan. The face amount of the wraparound loan equals the total of the first loan plus the amount of money advanced by the second lender; hence, the "wrapping." The amount of money actually advanced by the second lender equals the amount of the new loan less the amount of the existing first loan. The borrower pays debt service on the larger second loan only. Thus, the wraparound mortgage envelops existing mortgages though it is subordinate to them. This arrangement is termed an *all inclusive trust deed* if a deed of trust is the security instrument.

Federal Laws Affecting Lending

Federal laws increasingly extend into our lives so that what formerly was strictly private is now strictly regulated. Real estate financing is not exempt from this. Consumer protection is the most often cited motivation. The following brief summary is offered only to alert the reader to the many applicable regulations and their general content. The Real Estate Settlement Procedures Act (RESPA) was discussed in chapter 12, Title Closing.

EQUAL CREDIT OPPORTUNITY ACT

The Equal Credit Opportunity Act (ECOA), enacted in 1974, forbids discrimination by mortgage lenders because of race, color, religion, national origin, age, sex, or marital status or because all or part of an applicant's income is from a public assistance program. ECOA is implemented by the Federal Reserve System as Regulation B. People desiring credit must be informed of their rights under the act prior to completing an application. The reason for denial of credit must be given, upon request.

TRUTH IN LENDING ACT

The Truth in Lending (TIL) Act requires full disclosure of loan costs. TIL is, in truth, Title I of the Consumer Credit Protection Act and is implemented by the Federal Reserve System as Regulation Z. Under the act, a lender is required to provide advance disclosure of finance charges and loan terms, such as interest rate, origination fees, due date of payments, prepayment fees, and late payment fees so borrowers may shop for least cost or most advantageous credit terms. Note that the act does not regulate the cost of credit or set maximum allowable interest rates.

Coverage. To begin with, the TIL Act only applies to lenders who regularly extend or arrange credit. Further, in real estate, Regulation Z applies to loans for personal, household, or family residences if four or more payments are involved. A lease in which the lessee's obligation is less than $25,000 is also covered if the duration is greater than 4 months. A private party taking back a purchase money mortgage on the sale of a residence is exempt. Also, credit transactions on investment property are exempt.

Finance Charges and the APR. Finance charges are all costs associated with a loan that are directly or indirectly payable by a borrower and required by a lender as a precondition to making a loan. Examples are interest, origination fees, finder's fees, and service or carrying charges. Real estate purchase costs which would be incurred whether the loan were taken out or not are not included in the finance charge. Examples are costs of title insurance, recording fees, appraisal fees, and legal fees. These costs must be itemized and disclosed, however.

Disclosure of finance charges must be made in terms of an annual percentage rate (APR). Regulation Z specifies how the APR is to be calculated. The disclosure must be to within one-fourth of 1 percent, based on monies actually disbursed. The APR states in one number the cost of the loan, which facilitates comparison shopping.

Rescission. Although Regulation Z provides for a borrower's right to rescind certain loans during a 3-day waiting period, a borrower may not rescind or cancel a loan to purchase a personal residence that is secured by a lien on the residence.

USURY EXEMPTION LAWS

Usury is an unreasonably or unlawfully high interest rate. Prior to 1980, many states had usury laws setting a ceiling interest rate within their boundaries. FHA and VA loans were exempt from state usury laws by Congress in 1979. In 1980, Congress exempted conventional residential mortgage loans as well. However, each state could reenact a ceiling interest rate if it acted before April 1, 1983. The lifting of usury rates was intended to facilitate flows of funds.

Questions for Review and Discussion

1. Explain the mortgage financing process.
   a. What are the main legal documents involved?
   b. Who are the main parties involved?
   c. What is the legal process of foreclosure upon default?
2. How does the debt financing process differ when a trust deed is used to secure the debt?
3. What purpose is served by the promissory note in debt financing?
4. State at least four major provisions of the security instrument that are common to both mortgages and trust deeds.
5. List and explain "mortgages" by classification as follows:
   a. Five by general type
   b. Four by payment plan
   c. Three by special provision

6. What are the purposes or functions of the following?
   a. Satisfaction of mortgage
   b. Assignment of mortgage
   c. Subordination of mortgage
   d. Power of sale
   e. Deed in lieu of foreclosure
   f. Deed of reconveyance
7. Compare "assuming a mortgage" with "taking subject to a mortgage."
8. Distinguish between "equity of redemption" and a "statutory right of redemption."
9. Distinguish between a "deficiency judgment" and a "defeasance clause."
10. Does a prepayment privilege work to the advantage of the borrower or the lender?
11. First, second, and third mortgages are placed against a newly constructed apartment property. Which of these are senior mortgages? Which are junior claims? Explain.
12. Does the lender or the borrower have the greater power in debt-financing negotiations? Discuss.
13. Explain the significance of the uniform documents promoted by FNMA/FHLMC relative to the secondary mortgage market.

Case Problems

1. Evans mortgages his house to Thompson. Thompson does not record the instrument. To what extent is the mortgage valid between the parties? Relative to third parties?
2. Evans sells to Parker, who agrees to assume the mortgage. Parker defaults. Thompson forecloses, suing both Parker and Evans for damages suffered. Evans claims no liability. Is he right? Explain.
3. Linda Kuzzin obtains a loan from the Apex National Bank that is secured by an FNMA/FHLMC mortgage. Later, Linda loses her job and cannot make payments. Finally, after more than a year, Apex files a foreclosure suit. Linda claims that Apex is estopped from foreclosing because it failed to act within a year. Is this true? Explain.

16

Time Value of Money Mechanics

Seven percent has no rest, nor no religion; it works nights, and Sundays, and even wet days.

Josh Billings, American Humorist

We must almost always pay interest when borrowing money. The realty of interest rates in our economy gives a very pragmatic reason for understanding the time value of money (TVM). But, TVM goes far beyond interest rates. TVM is also important in choosing between alternative real estate investments and in other areas of finance. Value differences owing to varying times of receipt or payment of alternative cash flows provides the basis.

Money has time value for several reasons. Individuals prefer current consumption over future consumption and, therefore, must be compensated if they are to forego current consumption. Individuals, in addition, being rational, allocate money to alternative investment opportunities on the basis of comparative rates of return, the highest rates of return, risk adjusted, being preferred. Inflation causes people to demand a return on money lent out to maintain purchasing power. In short, a dollar in the hand is worth more than a dollar received tomorrow, next week, or next year.

The material presented here is introductory in nature and covers only the basic ideas and applications of time value of money. A few essential relationships are introduced. A reader interested in greater depth is referred to books on financial management and capital budgeting or the mathematics of finance. The problems discussed are difficult to work out by hand, using the TVM tables provided in the appendix. The reader is therefore encouraged to use a financial calculator to follow and verify the examples, for which some basic instruction is provided.

Important Topics or Decision Areas Covered in This Chapter

Time Value of Money Principles
Future Value or Compounding
Present Value or Discounting

TVM Factors
PV1 Factor
PVa Factor
PR Factor

Using Financial Calculators
Compounding/Discounting More than Once a Year

Interest Calculations

Mortgage Points: Discounts and Premiums
Sample Problems
Balloon Loan

NPV and IRR
Net Present Value
Internal Rate of Return

Questions for Review and Discussion

Case Problems

Key Concepts Introduced in this Chapter

2-3
Q's

Annuity	**Market interest rate**
Compounding	**Net present value**
Contract interest rate	**Percent discount**
Discounting	**Percent premium**
Discount rate	**Present value of 1 (PV1)**
Dollar discount	**factor**
Dollar premium	**Present value of an annuity**
Internal rate of return	**(PVa) factor**
Loan discount	**Principal recovery factor**
Loan premium	**Required rate of return**

Time Value of Money Principles

Time value of money (TVM) calculations involve either compounding or discounting. Before taking up compounding and discounting, a brief comment on the elements of TVM calculations is in order. Four elements are involved: (1) a cash payment or a series of uniform payments, (2) a percentage rate, (3) a time period, and (4) a calculated value. The time and percentage elements have traditionally been combined into TVM factors to speed calculations.

These four elements have fixed mechanical relationships, as expressed in the following equation.

$$\text{payment} \times \frac{\text{factor}}{(X\%, \ Y \text{ time})} = \text{value(s)}$$

In any application, if three of the elements are known, the fourth may be determined. It is this ability to determine unknown information that makes TVM techniques so useful in the financial analysis of real estate. We will return to this basic principle later in the chapter.

FUTURE VALUE OR COMPOUNDING

Money put into a savings account earning compound interest grows. In technical terms, it compounds. Why? What are the mechanics involved? According to the dictionary, *compounding* means to earn interest on principal and on accrued interest. That is, interest earned on a deposit in period one is added to the principal, and, in turn, in period two, interest is then earned on the original principal and on the accumulated interest.

Let us look at one example that illustrates the concept. Consider an individual depositing $100 into a savings account to earn 5 percent interest, compounded annually. What balance is in the account at the end of year one, EOY1? At EOY2? A simple calculation gives us an answer.

$$
\begin{aligned}
\text{EOY1 balance} &= \text{deposit (1 plus the interest } (i) \text{ rate)} \\
&= \text{deposit } (1 + i) \\
&= \$100 \ (1 + 0.05) \\
&= \$105
\end{aligned}
$$

Therefore, at EOY1, the account balance is $105. At the end of 2 years, the balance totals to $110.25. This means, in year two, interest at 5 percent is earned on the accumulated interest from year one; $5 is earned on the initial deposit of $100, and twenty-five cents is earned on the $5 interest earned in the first year.

$$
\begin{aligned}
\text{EOY2 balance} &= \text{deposit } (1 + i) \ (1 + i) \\
&= \text{deposit } (1 + i)^2 \\
&= \$100 \ (1 + 0.05)^2 \\
&= \$110.25
\end{aligned}
$$

Generalizing, the future value of a deposit at the end of n years may be calculated by the formula:

$$\text{EOY}n \text{ balance} = \text{deposit } (1 + i)^n$$

where n is the number of years and i equals the interest rate.

The compounding of interest on $100 for 10 years at 10 percent is shown in Figure 16-1. Interest being earned on interest shows up clearly in the interest earned column. Note that the balance grows much faster at 10 percent than in our earlier example using 5 percent. BOY means beginning of year.

Two basic principles of compounding follow from these calculations: (1) The higher the interest rate, the faster the balance increases, and (2) the greater the number of periods, the larger the future balance.

Year	Balance, BOY	Interest Earned	Balance, EOY
1	$100.00	$10.00	$110.00
2	110.00	11.00	121.00
3	121.00	12.10	133.10
4	133.10	13.31	146.41
5	146.41	14.64	161.05
6	161.05	16.11	177.16
7	177.16	17.72	194.87
8	194.87	19.49	214.36
9	214.36	21.44	235.79
10	235.79	23.58	259.37

NOTE: BOY, beginning of year; EOY, end of year.

FIGURE 16-1

Ten years of compound interest at 10 percent on a deposit of $100

PRESENT VALUE OR DISCOUNTING

We use the term "discounting" quite frequently. For example, we are sometimes told to discount a statement or rumor made by a commonly known gossip or liar, that is, to take the statement at less than face value. Merchants run sales at discounted prices, meaning reductions from regular or list price. Discounting, therefore, means to value a statement, an item, or a series of payments at less than its apparent worth; this concept carries over into time value of money.

A saver may want to know the deposit to be made now to have an account balance of a desired size in the future rather than the future balance in an account. The object is to find the deposit to be made now that will grow to the desired future balance. The process of finding the present value of a future payment or amount is called *discounting.*

The rate used in discounting is termed the discount rate. That is, a ***discount rate*** is the annual percentage rate that reflects the competitive rate of return on an investment.[1] Thus, if a mortgage loan were being evaluated, the discount rate would equal the interest rate on the loan. On the other hand, if an investment were being evaluated, it would equal be the rate of return required or desired by the investor.

For example, assume that you wish to have $1,000 on deposit at the end of 2 years. How much must you deposit now to have that balance? Again, assume an interest rate of 5 percent. Thus, the question is, "What deposit made today at 5 percent would grow to $1,000 2 years from now?"

To calculate the future value of a cash deposit made today (a present value), we multiplied the initial deposit by $(1 + i)^n$, where i equals the interest rate and n equals the number of periods. Here, we have a future balance and an interest rate. We can solve for the required initial deposit or present value by reversing the compounding process. Consequently, dividing the desired future value by $(1 + i)^n$ will give us our desired result. In our example, if the payment were to be received at the end of year 1, it would have a present value of $952.38

---

[1] Byrl N. Boyce, *Real Estate Appraisal Terminology*, rev. ed. (Cambridge, Mass.: Ballinger, 1981), p. 6.

$$\text{required deposit, BOY1} = \frac{\text{account balance, EOY1}}{(1 + i)^1}$$

$$= \frac{\$1,000}{1.05} = \$952.38$$

But, we are talking of 2 years. Repeating the calculation, we get the present value, or required deposit, for an account balance of $1,000 at EOY2 is $907.03.

$$\text{required deposit, BOY1} = \frac{\text{desired EOY2 balance}}{(1 + i)(1 + i)} = \frac{\text{desired EOY2 balance}}{(1 + i)^n}$$

$$= \frac{\$1,000}{1.05^2} = \frac{\$1,000}{1.1025} = \$907.03$$

The general formula for finding the present value of a future payment to be received at the end of year n, discounted at rate i, is, therefore,

$$\text{present value, BOY1} = \frac{\text{future payment, EOY}n}{(1 + i)^n}$$

Figure 16-2 shows the present value of $1,000, to be received at the end of years 1–10, and discounted at 10 percent. Note that the discounted values, required deposits, are less at 10 percent than at 5 percent.

Two basic principles of discounting follow from these calculations: (1) The higher the discount rate, the smaller the present value of a future payment; and (2) the greater the number of discounting periods, the smaller the present value.

TVM Factors

Tables of precalculated factors or multipliers have traditionally been used to speed TVM calculations. In making up TVM tables, $(1 + i)$ is termed the base. Thus, for a 5

Years Until $1,000 Received	Required Deposit
1	$909.09
2	826.45
3	751.31
4	683.01
5	620.92
6	564.47
7	513.16
8	466.51
9	424.10
10	385.54

FIGURE 16-2
Discounted value of $1,000 discounted at 10 percent, for years 1–10

percent table, 1.05 is the base. For a 10 percent table, 1.10 is the base. To illustrate the construction of a TVM table, let us develop three factors by using a discount rate of 10 percent.

PV1 FACTOR

Let us begin with three factors, which, multiplied by the $1,000 earlier, will quickly give us the first three discounted values of Figure 16-2. In TVM terminology, these are **present value of 1 (PV1) factors.** The general equation is

$$\text{factor} = \frac{1}{(1 + i)^n}$$

For year 1, $n = 1$, the factor is 0.909091, calculated as follows:

$$\text{factor} = \frac{1}{1.10^1} = 0.909091$$

For year 2, $n = 2$, the factor is 0.826446.

$$\text{factor} = \frac{1}{1.10^2} = \frac{1}{1.21} = 0.826446$$

For year 3, $n = 3$, the factor is 0.751315.

$$\text{factor} = \frac{1}{1.10^3} = \frac{1}{1.331} = 0.751315$$

The PV1 factors we have just calculated are shown in the PV1 column of the 10 percent annual TVM table in the appendix. The PV1 factor converts a single payment to be received in the future into a present, lump-sum value. See Figure 16-3.

The PV1 factor provides the means to calculate two other commonly used factors: the present value of an annuity (PVa) and the principal recovery factor (PR). An **annuity** is a series of equal or level payments made at regular intervals.

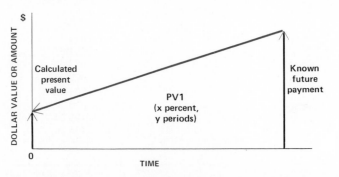

FIGURE 16-3
The PV1 factor converts a lump sum future payment to a present value

PVa FACTOR

Several PV1 factors may be used in a single problem, such as in determining the discounted value of an annuity. Suppose we are to receive an annuity of $20 at the end of each of the next 3 years. What is the present value of this series of payments by using a discount rate of 10 percent? By using PV1 factors, we obtain the answer of $49.74.

Time	Expected Payment		PV1 Factor		Present Value
EOY1	$20	×	0.909091	=	$18.18182
EOY2	20	×	0.826446	=	16.52892
EOY3	20	×	0.751315	=	15.02630
Total present value					$49.73704

Given a PV1 table, we might calculate the present value of any series of future cash flows in a similar manner. However, when the future cash flows are all equal, the procedure may be simplified, as with the preceding series of $20 payments. For one thing, we can add up the factors and have them precalculated in a table.

Time	PV1 Factor
EOY1	0.090901
EOY2	0.826446
EOY3	0.751315
Total of factors	2.486852

The total of the PV1 factors equals 2.486852. Multiplying 2.486852 by the $20 also gives us $49.74. Thus, totaling PV1 factors gives us a new, shortcut multiplier, termed the ***present value of an annuity (PVa) factor.*** The PVa factor, used as a multiplier, converts a series of equal or level payments into a single, lump-sum present value. See Figure 16-4.

A further example seems in order. Suppose that we wish to know the present value of a series of $20 payments to be received at the end of each of the next 4 years.

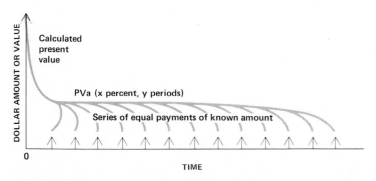

FIGURE 16-4
The PVa converts a level annuity into a present value

The discount rate is 12 percent. Looking in the PVa column of the 12 percent, annual, table in the appendix, we obtain the factor, 3.037349. The present value equals $60.75, rounded.

$$\text{payment} \times \underset{\text{(12\%, 4 years)}}{\text{PVa factor}} = \text{present value}$$

$$\$20 \qquad \times \quad 3.037349 \quad = \$60.75$$

PR FACTOR

In making a loan, a lender exchanges cash for a series of payments from the borrower. Of course, interest is charged on the loan. Is there a definite relationship between the amount of the loan and the amount of the payments? Is there an easy way to calculate the payment needed to amortize or pay off the loan over a specified time period? The answer to both questions is yes.

A ***principal recovery (PR) factor*** is a reciprocal of and acts in exactly the inverse way from the PVa factor. The PVa factor converts a series of equal cash flows into a present lump-sum value. The PR factor converts a present lump-sum amount, the loan, into a series of future cash flows, debt-service payments. In fact, the PR factor equals 1 divided by the PVa factor. See Figure 16-5.

For a concrete example, assume a lender makes a $4,000 fixed rate loan at 10 percent to be repaid by equal end-of-year payments over 4 years. How much is each payment?

$$\begin{array}{c}\text{present value} \\ \text{or loan principal}\end{array} \times \begin{array}{c}\text{PR factor} \\ \text{(10\%, 4 years)}\end{array} = \text{required payment}$$

$$\$4,000 \qquad \times \quad 0.315471 \quad = \$1,261.88$$

The PR factor allows us to quickly calculate the necessary payment of $1,261.88. A brief look at the amortization of the loan gives us assurance that the arithmetic works out. See Figure 16-6.

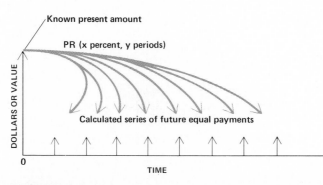

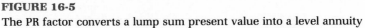

FIGURE 16-5

The PR factor converts a lump sum present value into a level annuity

Principal balance, BOY1		$4,000.00
Year 1 debt service	$1,261.88	
Less interest, 10% × $4,000	− 400.00	
Principal reduction	$ 861.88	− 861.88
Principal balance, EOY1, BOY2		$3,138.12
Year 2 debt service	$1,261.88	
Less interest, 10% × $3,138.12	− 313.81	
Principal reduction	$ 948.07	− 948.07
Principal balance, EOY2, BOY3		$2,190.05
Year 3 debt service	$1,261.88	
Less interest, 10% × $2,190.05	− 219.00	
Principal reduction	$1,042.88	− 1,042.88
Principal balance, EOY3, BOY4		$1,147.17
Year 4 debt service	$1,261.88	
Less interest, 10% × $1,147.17	− 114.72	
Principal reduction	$1,147.16	− 1,147.16
Principal balance, EOY4		$ 00.01[a]

[a]Difference owing to rounding in the calculation.

FIGURE 16-6
Amortization of a $4,000, 4-year, 10 percent loan with payments of $1,261.88

Using Financial Calculations

All the calculations in this chapter can be performed on financial calculators, a number of which can be bought for less than $50. Only four or five key strokes are required to solve simpler problems. Complex problems must be broken down into subproblems, each of which can be solved with four or five key strokes. Using financial calculators is faster and more accurate than using TVM tables. Also, interest rates not provided in the TVM tables are easily taken account of with calculators.

The basic approach is the same, whatever the calculator. However, the keystrokes required vary from calculator to calculator. To begin with, financial calculators have a row of five financial keys, as shown:

The inputs for the keys are

         = number of periods
         = periodic interest rate
         = periodic level payment, as in an annuity
         = present value (of a stream of payments or of a single future payment)
         = future value (of a stream of payments or of a single present value payment)

In most applications, known information for three variables must be fed in by pushing the appropriate keys. Each calculator has its own operating instructions and procedures, but generally pressing "2nd" or "CPT" (for compute) and the key representing the unknown information causes the desired answer to be displayed. These applications use problems previously solved so that the emphasis is on developing facility by using your calculator.

Calculating a Future Value. What is the end balance of $100 deposited in a savings account for 2 years and earning at 5 percent?

Calculating a Present Value. To have $1,000 in a savings account at EOY3, what deposit is required now, if the account earns at 10 percent per annum?

Calculating a PV1 Factor. What is the PV1 factor for 2 years with a 10 percent discount rate? Note that a 1 goes into the FV cell.

Calculating the Present Value of an Annuity. What is the discounted value of an annuity of $20 per year for 3 years at 10 percent? What present value if the annuity were for 4 years and the discount rate were 12 percent?

Calculating Debt Service. Calculate required debt service on a $4,000 loan made at 10 percent for 4 years.

Now for a few new problems. What debt service would be required on a $500,000 loan made at 12 percent for 25 years?

Calculating the Balloon Payment on a Loan. Assume that this loan was made and the borrower wanted to make a balloon payment of the balance at the end of year 15. What amount would be required of the borrower? At EOY15, there are 10 payments remaining. Debt service and the interest rate are unchanged:

Compounding/Discounting More Than Once a Year. The TVM elements must be modified when compounding or discounting takes place more than once a year. The necessary adjustments in the United States are as follows: (1) The interest rate must be divided by the number of periods per year to get the effective rate for the shorter period, and (2) the number of years must be multiplied by the number of periods per year to get the total number of periods. Thus, with monthly compounding, a 12 percent annual or nominal interest rate becomes a 1 percent per month effective interest rate.

12%/12 months = 1%/month

A 25-year loan becomes a 300 month loan (25 × 12). Finally, the monthly payments are approximately one-twelfth the size of the annual payment.

Thus, the debt service on the $4,000, 10 percent, 4-year loan just discussed earlier becomes $101.45 per month. In turn, total annual debt service is $1,217.40 (12 × $101.45) versus $1,261.88.

Mortgages frequently call for monthly payments. Therefore, let us consider one more illustration. Suppose that our $500,000 loan for 25 years is obtained at 12 percent interest but that monthly payments are called for. How much is monthly debt service?

Interest is usually calculated to the end of each payment period. In practice, debt-service payments are customarily due on the first day of the following period. The payment therefore includes accumulated interest for the previous period plus any principal reduction amount for the current period. Interest is deducted from each payment first, with the balance going to principal reduction. Interest is sometimes payable at the beginning of a payment period, which is termed interest due or interest due in advance. Interest paid is of considerable value to a borrower because it is a tax deductible expense for both home ownership and for real estate investments.

Interest calculations are shown here, using annual payments first, and then monthly. A $500,000, 12 percent, 25-year loan is used in our example.

Annual Payments. With annual payments, we earlier calculated debt service to be $63,749.98. Interest itself simply equals the beginning of year principal multiplied by the annual rate.

Loan balance, BOY1	$500,000
Times annual interest rate	× 12%
Equals interest for the year	$ 60,000

Principal reduction therefore equals $3,749.98 for the first year, ($63,749.98 − $60,000.00) leaving an EOY1, BOY2, loan balance of $496.250.02 ($500,000.00 − $3,749.98). Interest for year 2 would then equal $496,250.02 multiplied by 12 percent, or $59,550.

Total interest payable on a loan is easily calculated; it equals the total of all payments less the original principal. Thus, if our loan were paid off on schedule over its full 25-year life, the total amount of interest paid would be $1,093,749.62, more than twice the initial amount borrowed.

Annual debt service	$ 63,749.98
Multiplied by number of payments	× 25
Equals total of all payments	$1,593,749.62
Less initial principal	− 500,000.00
Equals total interest payable over entire life of loan	$1,093,749.62

Monthly Payments. For monthly payments, the calculation are somewhat more involved. Let us return to our 12 percent, 25-year loan of $500,000, but now with monthly payments of $5,266.12, as calculated earlier, or $63,193.45 per year. Two methods of calculating interest may be used with periodic debt service.

Period 1				
Method A			**Method B**	
Loan balance, BOM 1	$500,000	Interest rate		12%
Multiplied by annual interest rate	× 12%	Divided by months per year	÷	12%
Equals interest per year	$ 60,000	Equals monthly interest rate		1%
Divided by months per year	÷ 12	Multiplied by loan balance		$500,000
Equals interest for month 1	$ 5,000	Equals interest for month 1		$ 5,000

Monthly debt service of $5,266.12 less interest of $5,000 means a $266.12 principal reduction at the end of period 1. Thus, at the beginning of period 2, the balance is $499,733.88 ($500,000 less $266.12).

Period 2				
Method A		**Method B**		
Loan balance, EOM 1, BOM 2	$499,733.88	Loan balance		$499,733.88
Multiplied by annual interest rate	× 12%	Multiplied by monthly rate	×	1%
Equals interest per year	$ 59,968.07	Equals interest for month 2		$ 4,997.34
Divided by months per year	÷ 12			
Equals interest for month 2	$ 4,997.34			

Interest payable on a monthly pay loan, with no prepayment, is also easily calculated; it again equals the total of all payments less the original principal.

Monthly debt service	$ 5,266.12
Multiplied by number of payments, 25 × 12	× 300
Equals total of all payments	$1,579,836.21
Less original principal	− 500,000.00
Equals total interest payable over entire life of loan	$1,079,836.21

Note that yearly debt service is less with a monthly pay loan than with an annual pay loan, $63,193.45 versus $63,749.98. Also note that less interest is payable overall, $1,079,836.21 versus $1,093,749.62. The amounts are less on a monthly payment loan because the principal is reduced earlier, after the first month, rather then after the first year.

An important principle is inherent in this information; namely, the more frequent the compounding, other things being equal, the lower the yearly debt service and the less the interest paid in any given time.

Loan Amortization Schedule. A loan progress schedule to summarize the end-of-year principal balances and the interest paid during each year is necessary to determine tax deductible interest in any given year. The calculations are easily done with a calculator, as an extension of work done earlier. Our $500,000, 12 percent, 25-year loan is used to illustrate the process, the first 10 years of which are summarized in Figure 16-7. These numbers are used in a later chapter for investment analysis.

| Period Number | Balance Beginning of Period | Level Payment | | | Balance End of Period |
		Total Payment	Portion to Principal	Portion to Interest	
1	$500,000	$63,750	$3,750	$60,000	$496,250
2	496,250	63,750	4,200	59,550	492,050
3	492,050	63,750	4,704	59,046	487,346
4	487,346	63,750	5,268	58,482	482,078
5	482,078	63,750	5,901	57,849	476,177
6	476,177	63,750	6,609	57,141	469,568
7	469,568	63,750	7,402	56,348	462,166
8	462,166	63,750	8,290	55,460	453,876
9	453,876	63,750	9,825	54,465	444,592
10	444,592	63,750	10,399	53,351	434,193

FIGURE 16-7

First 10 years, annual loan amortization schedule for a $500,000, 12 percent, 25-year loan

Alternatively, these same numbers may be derived by using TVM factors, as follows. Two years of calculations are given.

At EOY1, the loan balance is $496,250.02, calculated as follows:

annual debt service $\times$ PVa factor   = loan balance, EOY1
(12%, 24 years)

$63,749.98 $\times$ 7.784316   = $496,250.02

At EOY2, the loan balance is $492,050.03, calculated as follows:

annual debt service $\times$ PVa factor   = loan balance, EOY2
(12%, 23 years)

$63,749.98 $\times$ 7.718434   = $492,050.03

With annual payments the amount of interest paid in any one year may be calculated directly. However, determining the interest paid in any one year when monthly payments are involved is a rather tedious process. By using the calculations just noted as a basis, the process of deriving the amount of interest paid in any one year, with monthly payments, is as follows, using year 1 as an example. The difference between the BOY and EOY loan balances is $3,749.98 ($500,000.00 − $496,250.02 = $3,749.98). Annual debt service is $63,749.98. Any excess over $3,749.98 went to interest, in this case $60,000 ($63,749.98 − $3,749.98 = $60,000.00). See Figure 16-7. This procedure must be done for each year for which the amount of interest paid is desired.

Mortgage Points: Discounts and Premiums

Earlier, it was noted that a discount is a reduction from face value. Therefore, it should be no surprise that a *loan discount* is an amount off, as of a mortgage loan.

A premium is the opposite of a discount; a premium means to buy or sell, or to offer to buy or sell, at a price above face value. Therefore, a *loan premium* is an amount in addition to the principal balance. A discount or premium is calculated on the balance when a loan is originated, when an offer is made to buy or sell a loan, or when a loan is sold.

Discounting a loan when it is originated is a way for a lender to cover costs of origination, as well as to increase the rate of return earned. Origination fees also provide negotiating flexibility in a market where interest rates fluctuate. That is, with interest rates fluctuating around a certain percent, say 12 percent, the origination fee, rather than the interest rate, can be raised or lowered to meet competition. Finally, lenders use origination fees to adjust for differences in risk between loans; thus, the higher the expected risk, the higher the origination fee.

In using an origination fee, debt service is based on the face amount of the loan rather than on the net amount disbursed. Thus, debt service on a $50,000, 25-year loan at 12 percent would be computed on the $50,000 face amount. However, with a 2 percent origination fee of $1,000, the net amount disbursed would be $49,000 ($50,000 − $1,000 = $49,000).

Loan discounts and premiums are expressed in terms of dollars and in terms of points or percentages. For example, a $10,000 loan that sells for $9,000 carries a dollar discount of $1,000 ($10,000 − $9,000). On the other hand, a sale price of $12,000 would mean a dollar premium of $2,000 ($12,000 − $10,000). A *percent discount* equals dollar discount divided by the loan balance. A dollar discount of $1,000 on a $10,000 loan is a 10 percent discount, or a discount of 10 points. A *dollar discount* is therefore a cash deduction from the face value of a loan because the market interest rate exceeds the contract rate.

$$\frac{\text{dollar discount}}{\substack{\text{face value} \\ \text{(unamortized balance)}}} = \frac{\$1,000}{\$10,000} = 10\% \text{ (or a 10-point discount)}$$

A dollar premium of $2,000 on the same loan is also a 20 *percent premium.* A *dollar premium* is therefore a cash addition to the face value of a loan because the market interest rate is less than the contract rate.

Mortgage discounts and premiums come about on existing loans because the market interest rate of a loan differs from the contract or face rate. The *market interest rate* is the rate currently being charged by lenders. The *contract interest rate* is the rate in a specific note, which was agreed to when the loan was made. When a loan is made, the two rates are equal or contain a difference reflecting an origination fee. Through time, market rates change, and differences develop. In this situation, a lender-investor has the option of making new loans at market rates or buying existing loans at prices that give an interest yield equal to the market rate.

The following rules apply when contract and market rates differ:

1. If the market rate is higher than the contract rate, the market value of an existing loan is always less than its face value or unamortized balance, and sales are at a discount.

2. If the market rate is lower, existing loans sell at premiums because the market value always exceeds face value.

Mortgage loans are historically prepaid in from 8 to 12 years. The futures market in Government National Mortgage loans (GNMA) loans assumes prepayment in 12 year.[2] Prepayment comes about because a borrower (1) sells to a buyer who obtains new financing; (2) refinances; (3) inherits money or otherwise suddenly becomes wealthy; or (4) defaults, followed by foreclosure. Sales and refinancing are less likely when interest rates are high or are going up.

SAMPLE PROBLEMS

The Urbandale Savings and Loan Association makes a $500,000, 12 percent loan for 25 years. Now, 3 years later, the association needs money and decides to sell the loan. At what price will it sell under varying market conditions? What dollar and percent discounts or premiums?

Discount, Without Prepayment. From previous work, Figure 16-8, we know that the yearly debt service is $63,749.98, rounded to $63,750, and the EOY3 loan balance is $487,346. Let us say that the market rate is 15 percent. Assuming no prepayment, a buyer of the loan stands to get $63,750 per year for the next 22 years. See Figure 16-8.

The market value of the loan equals the present value of $63,750 per year, discounted at 15 percent for 22 years (25 − 3), or $405,365.

yearly debt service × PVa = PV
(15%, 22 years)

$63,750 × 6.358663 = $405,365 (rounded)

Using a financial calculator, Keys: [N] [%i] [PMT] [PV] [FV]
Inputs: 22 15 63,750 ??? .....
Press: [2nd] or [CPT] and PV
Answer: $405,365

The dollar discount is, therefore, $81,981 ($487,346 − $405,365). The discount off face value is 16.82 percent:

$$\text{percentage discount} = \frac{\text{dollar discount}}{\text{loan balance (face value)}} = \frac{\$81,981}{\$487,346} = 16.82\%$$

[2]Chicago Board of Trade, *A Guide to Financial Futures at the Chicago Board of Trade* (1983), p. 30.

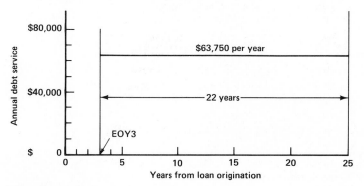

FIGURE 16-8
Cash flows of a 25-year, 12 percent loan discounted at end of year 3 in a 15 percent market, no prepayment expected, debt service equals $63,750 per year

Discount, With Prepayment. Let us now change the situation slightly and assume prepayment at the end of year 15 of the loan, or 12 years from the time of analysis. The prepayment equals the present value of the last 10 years of debt service at the 12 percent contract rate, or $360,202.

$$\text{prepayment} = \text{yearly debt service} \times \begin{array}{c}\text{PVa factor} \\ (12\%, \ 10 \text{ years})\end{array}$$

$$= \quad \$63,750 \quad \times \quad 5.650223$$

$$= \quad \$360,202$$

Therefore, at EOY3, a buyer would get the right to $63,750 per year for 12 years plus the right to a one-time payment of $360,202 at the end of year 15 of the contract. See Figure 16-9.

The present value of $63,750 per year for 12 years discounted at the market rate, 15 percent, is $345,564. The discounted value of the prepayment, $360,202, discounted 12 years at 15 percent, is $67,324. Thus, the market value of the loan is $412,889 ($345,564 + $67,324).

In turn, the dollar discount is $74,457 ($487,346 − $412,889). This calculates to a discount off face value of 15.28 percent ($74,457/$487,346).

The prepayment reduces the discount off face value. The reason is that the payments from EOY15 to EOY25 are discounted at a lower rate, making their EOY15 value larger. In turn, the market value of the loan is greater, meaning a smaller discount.

Premium, Without Prepayment. A market rate lower than the contract rate gives reason for a loan to have a market value in excess of face value. Remember, the lower the discount rate, the higher is the present value. Thus, with a 10 percent market rate, the last 22 years of debt service has a present (market) value of $559,186:

$$\text{PV} = \$63,750 \times 8.771540 = \$559,186$$

In turn, the premium is $71,840, or 14.89 percent.

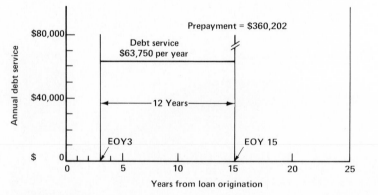

FIGURE 16-9
Cash flows of a 25-year, 12 percent loan discounted at end of year 3 in a 15 percent market, prepayment expected at end of year 15, debt service equals $63,750 per year

Premium, With Prepayment. Figure 16-9 applies whether the market interest rate is 15 or 10 percent. In either case, at EOY3 of the loan, a buyer would get the right to $63,750 per year for 12 years plus the right to a one-time payment of $360,202 at the end of year 15, or in 12 years. However, a 10 percent market interest rate means the cash flows would be discounted at 10 percent. The respective present values would total to $549,144 ($434,373 + $114,771), the market value of the loan in a 10 percent market.

PV of 12 years of yearly debt service = $63,750 × 6.813692 = $434,373

PV of EOY12 prepayment = $360,202 × .318631 = $114,771

The dollar premium is $61,798 ($549,144 − $487,346), which gives a percentage premium of 12.68 percent ($61,798/$487,346).

With prepayment, the premium is reduced because a portion of the cash flows are discounted at the higher contract rate. Thus, prepayment acts to lower a premium from that expected without prepayment.

BALLOON LOAN

Balloon loans are sometimes made to keep debt service down and leverage up for the benefit of the borrower; at the same time, a shortened maturity gives the lender greater liquidity in its portfolio. For example, the loan we have been working with could have been originated as a balloon loan. It would be described as a $500,000, 12 percent, compounded-annually loan, with debt service calculated on a 25-year amortization schedule, and a balloon payment called for at the end of year 15. Thus, the yearly debt service would be $63,750 per year, and the balloon payment at EOY15 would be $360,202.

NPV and IRR

Two additional TVM concepts are important in financial decision making in real estate. These are net present value (NPV) and internal rate of return (IRR). A simple example provides a basis to explain the concepts and how they are used in decision making. Both NPV and IRR are used in later chapters.

Assume an investor who has a *required rate of return* (RRR) of 12 percent, after-tax, of any investment. RRR is that rate required to compensate an investor for time and risk. An income property is offered, requiring $100,000 as an equity investment, which is expected to generate after-tax cash flows to the equity position over 4 years as follows. Should the investment be made?

Year	Amount
1	$ 12,000
2	13,000
3	14,000
4	125,000

NET PRESENT VALUE

Net present value is the present value of the cash flows from an investment minus the cost of the investment; or, stated another way, NPV is the difference between the cost of an investment and the present value of the cash flows from the investment, discounted at the investor's required rate of return.

For decision purposes, the rule is that NPV must be zero or positive for a "go" decision to invest. That is, a negative NPV means that the investment is not expected to earn the required rate of return. By using 12 percent TVM factors, we get a present value for the cash flows of $110,483. In turn, the net present value of the investment is $10,483 ($110,483 − $100,000). Therefore, the investment should be made.

Year	Cash Flow	12% PV1 Factor	Present Value
1	$ 12,000	0.892857	$ 10,714
2	13,000	0.797194	10,364
3	14,000	0.711780	9,965
4	125,000	0.635518	79,440
Sum of Present Values			$110,483

If the required rate of return were 20 percent, what would be the NPV? The present value of the cash flows would be $87,412, calculated as follows. This means a NPV of minus $12,588 ($87,412 − $100,000). In this case, the decision rule would say "do not invest."

Year	Cash Flow	20% PV1 Factor	Present Value
1	$ 12,000	0.833333	$10,000
2	13,000	0.694444	9,028
3	14,000	0.578704	8,102
4	125,000	0.482253	60,282
Sum of Present Values			$87,412

INTERNAL RATE OF RETURN

The internal rate of return is sometimes used as an alternative to NPV in making financial decisions. The *internal rate of return* (IRR) is that rate of return that discounts future cash flows to the exact amount of the investment. Stated another way, if used in NPV analysis, the IRR would result in a NPV of zero.

Let us calculate the IRR for the previous cash flows. We already have enough information to interpolate for the approximate IRR. The present value of the cash flows at 12 percent is $110,483, and at 20 percent it is $87,412. The investment cost $100,000; therefore, we know that the IRR is somewhere between 12 and 20 percent.

present value at 12% = $110,483

$110,483 - \$100,000 = \$10,483 =$ difference between 12% and X% present values

present value at X%, target rate $= \$100,000$

$110,483 - \$87,412 = \$23,071 =$ difference between 12% and 20% present values

present value at 20% $= \$87,412$

Therefore, by interpolation, the target rate, X%, equals 15.635 percent.

$X\% = 12\% + 8\% \times (\$10,483/\$23,071)$
$X\% = 12\% + 8\% \times 0.45438$
$X\% = 12\% + 3.635 = 15.635\% =$ approximate IRR

By calculator, the IRR is 15.316 + %. Using the PV1 factors at 15.316 + % of return gives a present value of $100,000. In turn, the NPV is zero, $100,000 − $100,000 = $0.

Year	Cash Flow	15.316 + % PV1 Factor	Present Value
1	$ 12,000	0.867180	$ 10,406
2	13,000	0.752001	9,776
3	14,000	0.652120	9,130
4	125,000	0.565505	70,688
Sum of Present Values			$100,000

The decision rule for IRR is that if the IRR is greater than the RRR, the investment should be made. The IRR of 15.32 percent exceeds 12 percent; therefore, the investment would be made.

Questions for Review and Discussion

1. What is the underlying concept of compound interest (and of time value of money calculations in general)? What is the importance of compound interest?
2. Explain the relation of compounding to discounting.
3. What is an annuity?
4. Explain the interrelation between the PR factor and the PV1/P factor. What makes this relationship hold true?
5. How might the amount of interest paid on a monthly payment loan be determined for any one year?
6. Distinguish between buying a loan at a 5-point discount and discounting debt service for a loan at 5 percent.
7. The market rate is less than the contract rate of a loan. If the loan were sold by the lender, would it sell at a discount or a premium? (Think through the logic on this; calculations should not be necessary.)

8. As an annuity lengthens, what happens to the present value of the most distant payment? What does this mean for the present value of a series of payments as the annuity goes to infinity?

9. An error is introduced in interpolating for present value with time value of money factors. What is the source of this error? Is the error likely to increase or decrease as the distance between known discount rates increases?

10. The amount, term, and interest rate for two loans are identical; however, one calls for monthly compounding, the other for annual. Will the annual debt service for the annual compounding loan be more than, equal to, or less than 12 times the monthly debt service? What is the source of the difference?

Case Problems

1. A $200,000 loan is arranged at 10 percent interest, compounded annually, and with 30-year amortization, but with a balloon payment due at EOY12.
   a. How much is debt service? ($21,215.85)
   b. What would be the amount of the EOY12 balloon payment? ($174,000)

2. Ann Cook obtains a 15 percent, $100,000 loan from the University Savings & Loan Association to be repaid over 25 years.
   a. What debt service with annual end-of-year payments? ($15,469.94)
   b. With monthly compounding and payments, what debt service is required? ($1,280.83)
   c. With annual compounding, how much interest would be paid in year 2 of the loan? ($14,930)
   d. With monthly compounding, how much interest would be paid in year 2 of the loan, assuming that all payments are made on schedule? ($14,910)

3. Joe Alum takes out a $100,000 loan from the Student Credit Union at a 12 percent rate with payments to be made over 25 years.
   a. What is the annual debt service? ($12,750)
   b. If there is a monthly debt service, how much? ($1,053.22)
   c. What is the amount of interest paid in year 3, assuming a monthly debt service? ($11,782)

4. The market interest rate goes up to 15 percent at EOY2, and the Student Credit Union decides to sell the Joe Alum loan. Assume annual payments.
   a. With no prepayment expected, what is the market value and what is the discount? ($81,585; $16,825; 17.10%)
   b. With prepayment expected at EOY10 of the loan, what is the market value and what is the discount? ($85,601; $12,809; 13.02%)

5. Suppose, instead, the market interest rate had dropped to 9 percent by EOY2 when the Student Credit Union decided to sell the Joe Alum loan.
   a. What market value should a potential buyer place on the loan, assuming no prepayment is expected? ($122,148)
   b. What percent premium does this represent? (24.12%)
   c. Assuming prepayment at EOY10 of the loan, what is the market value and what is the premium? ($114,150; 15.99%)

6. A 24-year loan is initiated for $50,000 at 9 percent with annual debt service called for.

a. Assume it is a RRM loan, with the interest rate subject to change at the end of every third year. At the EOY3, the market interest rate is 12 percent. What is the loan balance and debt service at the BOY4?

b. Assume it is an ARM loan, with a maximum change of 1 percent per year, all of which is to be reflected in higher or lower debt service. Shortly after initiation, the interest rate increased to 13 percent and remained there. What is the loan balance at the end of years 1, 2, and 3? What is the annual debt service in years 2, 3, and 4?

7. The Fifth National Bank of Clinton makes a 12 percent, 25-year, $40,000 mortgage loan with annual compounding to John L. Sullivan to finance a home he purchased. At EOY6, the bank needs money and wishes to sell the loan in a 10 percent market.

a. Assuming that all payments are made on schedule, what is the unamortized loan balance at EOY6? ($37,565)

b. Assuming no prepayment, at what price is the loan likely to sell? ($42,661)

c. Would the loan be selling for a discount or a premium? What percent? (13.57%)

d. Assuming prepayment at EOY12 and sale at EOY6, at what price is the loan likely to sell? ($40,704)

e. Diamond Jim Brady buys the loan at EOY6 for $40,000. Assuming that it *is not prepaid*, what yield, IRR, should he realize? (10.99)

f. If Diamond Jim Brady buys the loan at EOY6 for $40,000, assuming that it *will be prepaid* at EOY12, what yield, IRR, should he realize? (10.43)

8. Jose LaGuadia takes out a $200,000 mortgage loan from the Bears Credit Union. The terms are 15 years, 9 percent, and annual payments. The credit union decides to sell the loan at EOY4 in a 12 percent market.

a. What is the loan balance at EOY4? ($168,849)

b. What amount will the credit union realize, assuming no prepayment is expected on the loan? ($147,325)

c. What is the dollar and percent discount for the loan in part b? (12.75%)

d. Assuming prepayment at EOY10 and sale at EOY4, at what price is the loan likely to sell? ($150,906)

e. Isaac James buys the loan at EOY4 for $140,000. Assuming that it *is not prepaid*, what yield, IRR, should he realize? (13.18%)

f. If Isaac James buys the loan at EOY4 for $140,000, assuming that it *will be prepaid* at EOY10, what yield, IRR, should he realize? (14.09%)

17

Financing Home Ownership

The fellow who owns his own home is always just coming out of the hardware store.

Kim Hubbard, Bartlett's Unfamiliar Quotations

Homeownership has long been part of the Great American Dream that is slowly being realized. In 1900, 47 percent of all dwelling units were owner occupied; by 1950, 55 percent were. By the 1980s, about two-thirds of all residential units were owner occupied.

Choices between new housing types are also being made. Condominiums, cooperatives, and mobile homes are now widely accepted as alternatives to detached single-family residences. Changing life styles as well as higher costs account for this acceptance. The result is fewer people per occupied unit. From 1900 to 1980, the number of persons per occupied dwelling unit had dropped from 4.8 to 2.8. See Figure 17-1.

The purpose of this chapter is to discuss key decisions relative to owning one's own home. The two basic decisions are (1) how much can I afford to pay for housing and (2) should I rent or buy? Tax treatment of homeownership is also discussed.

Important Topics or Decision Areas Covered in This Chapter

Determining Housing Affordability
Annual Stabilized Income
Proportion for Housing
The 25 Percent Rule
The 33 Percent Rule

Federal Tax Laws and Homeownership
Relief on "Rollover"
Relief on Sale by Elderly
Conversion to Income Property

278

| | | | Occupied Units | | | | |
Year	Total Population	Total Number of Units	Owner Occupied Number	Owner Occupied Percent	Renter Occupied Number	Renter Occupied Percent	Population Per Unit
1900	76,212,168	15,964	7,455	46.7	8,509	53.3	4.8
1910	92,228,496	20,256	9,301	45.9	10,954	54.1	4.6
1920	106,021,537	24,352	11,114	45.6	13,238	54.4	4.4
1930	123,202,624	29,905	14,280	47.8	15,624	52.2	4.1
1940	132,164,569	34,855	15,196	43.6	19,659	56.4	3.8
1950	151,325,798	42,855	23,560	55.0	19,266	45.0	3.5
1960	179,323,175	53,024	32,797	61.9	20,227	38.1	3.4
1970	203,302,031	63,445	39,886	62.9	23,560	37.1	3.2
1980	226,545,805	80,390	51,795	64.4	28,595	35.6	2.8
1983E	233,700,000	83,175	54,342	65.3	28,833	34.7	2.8

SOURCE: *1986 Statistical Abstract of the United States*, p. 729, Table 1308 and U.S. Bureau of the Census Reports.

FIGURE 17-1

Tenure and population of occupied housing units, U.S. 1900 and 1980 (in thousands, except percent; Hawaii and Alaska excluded prior to 1960)

Rent or Buy?
Pros and Cons of Owning
Pros and Cons of Renting
Rent Capitalization
Net After-Tax Costs

Questions for Review and Discussion

Case Problems

Key Concepts Introduced in this Chapter

Adjusted sale price
Annual stabilized income
Date of sale
Housing expenses
Opportunity cost

Rent capitalization
"Rollover"
33 percent rule
25 percent rule

Determining Housing Affordability

The primary considerations of a lender in making a mortgage loan are an applicant's ability to pay and motivation to own. For most people, obtaining a loan is a necessary prerequisite to homeownership. So, over and above motivation, let us look at how a lender is likely to evaluate an applicant's ability to carry a loan, using Federal Home

Loan Mortgage Corporation (FHLMC) guidelines. We can then extend the analysis to determine how much housing one can afford.

ANNUAL STABILIZED INCOME

Ability to carry a loan depends on one's recognized earning capability, which, under the FHLMC guidelines, is called *annual stabilized income* (ASI). Annual stabilized income begins with a person's yearly wages or salary. To wage or salary is added income from overtime, commissions, bonuses, dividends, interest, alimony, welfare, and net rents. Payments for alimony and/or child support are deducted in arriving at ASI. Two years' "experience" on these additions and deductions is required for the figures to be fully accepted. Let us now assume John Burgoyne wants to buy a house, as a case example.

John, we have said, has an annual salary of $24,000. John and Marcia, a chemist, recently became engaged. They plan to marry in about a year. Marcia earns $18,000 a year. They have little additional income from investments. Together, they project, they should be earning $48,000, their annual stabilized income, at the time they want to buy a house.

PROPORTION FOR HOUSING

The FHLMC guidelines allow 25 percent of ASI for housing expenses. *Housing expenses* include loan interest, repayment of principal, hazard insurance premiums, and property taxes, frequently referred to as PIIT or PITI. Payments for mortgage insurance, homeowner association dues, and ground rental payments are also included, if the situation involves them. Utility charges are not included.

Alternatively, the guidelines allow up to 33 percent of ASI for housing expenses and other required periodic payments. Other payments include required outlays for utilities, installment debt, alimony, and child support. An additional 10 percent may be added to these limits, if justified by a large down payment, a substantial net worth, or a demonstrated ability and willingness to devote a larger portion of income for housing expense. Thus outside maximums of 28 and 36 percent of income may be devoted to housing. So, what does this all mean?

THE 25 PERCENT RULE

John and Marcia inquire of the loan officer at the Urbandale Savings and Loan Association as to current lending terms. The officer tells them that FRM (fixed rate mortgage) loans, for 80 percent of value, are now being made at 12 percent, with amortization calculated on a 30-year life. The loan officer also informs them that property taxes and mortgage insurance typically run about 3 percent of market value in Urbandale. John and Marcia recognize that these terms may not hold next year, but they do give a basis for making a judgment.

Under the *25 percent rule*, the amount John and Marcia would have available for housing is $12,000 per year ($48,000 × 25%). This amount must cover PITI only. On the basis of their conversation with the loan officer, they do not believe that they would qualify for a 10 percent bonus, to the absolute maximum, because of their short earnings record. The purchase price of affordable housing would be calculated as follows, based on their ASI. Purchase price translates into market value, when negotiating the purchase or the loan. Also, annual time value of money (TVM) factors are used here; in practice, monthly factors are used.

$$\begin{array}{ccc}
\text{amount} & \text{required debt service for} & \text{amount required for} \\
\text{available} = & \text{interest and principal} & + \;\; \text{property taxes and} \\
\text{yearly} & \text{repayment on loan} & \text{hazard insurance}
\end{array}$$

$12,000 = (80\%)(PP)(PR\ factor)(12\%,\ 30\ years) + (3\%)\ PP$

Inserting the principal recovery (PR) factor, we are in a position to solve for the purchase price (PP) of the home that is affordable by John and Marcia.

$12,000 = (0.80)(\text{purchase price})(0.124144) + (0.03)(\text{purchase price})$

$12,000 = (0.099315)(\text{purchase price}) + (0.03)(\text{purchase price})$

$12,000 = (0.129315)(\text{purchase price})$

$12,000/(0.129315) = \$92,796.66 = \text{purchase price}$

Thus, it appears that John and Marcia can afford to pay up to $92,800, rounded, for a home. Do the figures check out? The loan would be for 80 percent of $92,796.66 or $74,237.33. Payments total to $11,999.99; the difference of one cent is due to rounding.

Annual debt service on loan	($74,237.33 × 0.124144)	$ 9,216.09
Taxes and insurance at 3%	($92,796.66 × 0.03)	2,783.90
Total required for PITI		$11,999.99

Rounding to $92,800, John and Marcia must realize that a cash down payment of $18,560, or 20 percent of the purchase price, would be required of them. The amount may be realized by saving, an interest-free loan from their parents, via a gift letter, "sweat equity," or some other source. Even so, they have an initial indication of how much they can afford for housing. But they have a second way to determine the amount.

THE 33 PERCENT RULE

Under the **33 percent rule**, utilities and installment debt are taken into account. Thus, 33 percent of ASI must cover PITI plus utility costs and installment debt. Algebraically, the relationship is as follows:

$$\begin{array}{cccc}
\text{amount} & \text{debt service for} & \text{property taxes} & \text{utilities and} \\
\text{available} = & \text{loan interest} & + \;\;\; \text{and} \;\;\; & + \;\text{other installment} \\
\text{yearly} & \text{and repayment} & \text{hazard insurance} & \text{payments}
\end{array}$$

Next year, John and Marcia figure that they will still be paying $212 per month, or $2,544 per year, on a car. Also, inquiring of the loan officer and their parents, they determine that they can expect to pay an average of $95 per month, or $1,140 per year, for utilities if they buy a house. The amount available is $15,840 per year ($48,000 $\times$ 33%). Inserting known information into the equation gives

$$\$15,840 = (0.80)(PP)(0.124144) + (0.03)(PP) + (\$2,544 + \$1,140)$$

$$\$15,840 = (0.099315)(PP) + (0.03)(PP) + \$3,684$$

Transposing,

$$\$12,156 = (0.129315)(PP)$$

$$\$12,156/(0.129315) = \$94,003.02 = \text{affordable purchase price}$$

With a purchase price of $94,000, the loan amount would be $75,200, and the required down payment would be $18,800. Annual debt service would be $9,335.60. Property taxes and hazard insurance would total to $2,820, based on the 3 percent quotation. These amounts, plus $3,684 for installment payments, total to $15,839.60, just short of the $15,840 available each year.

After looking at available housing in the $85,000 to $95,000 range, John and Marcia decide to investigate whether they should rent or buy. Besides everything else, they would be stretched to come up with the down payment. Thus, they would like to compare the costs of renting versus owning. Before taking up the rent or buy decision, we need a look at federal tax aspects of owning a personal residence.

Federal Tax Laws and Homeownership

The owner-occupant of a personal residence does not get all the advantages of an owner-investor in other types of real estate. For one thing, an annual depreciation allowance may not be taken on a personal residence. Also, a personal residence is not "like kind" of real estate for business or investment property in a tax-deferred exchange.

On the other hand, interest on a mortgage loan and real property taxes can both be used as direct offsets against ordinary income to reduce taxes payable. Thus, a homeowner in the 28 percent tax bracket, with property tax payments of $1,500 and interest payments of $3,000 in a given year, pays $1,260 less income tax as a result ($4,500 $\times$ 28%). Renters get no such tax deduction. Interest and tax deductions, therefore, constitute a substantial advantage to homeownership as against renting.

RELIEF OF "ROLLOVER"

A U.S. Census Bureau survey indicates that one family in six moves each year, on average, because of job transfers or economic necessity.[1] The moves are, therefore, not made at a time of maximum advantage or by the choice of the taxpayer. Congress

---

[1] "When Did You Last Move?" *Wall Street Journal*, December 20, 1983.

therefore enacted special relief provisions to minimize the tax impact on sale and repurchase of a personal residence, and this is a *"rollover."*

Under the new legislation, a capital gain from the sale of a personal residence is "rolled over," that is, the tax is postponed, if a replacement residence is bought or built at a cost equal to or greater than the adjusted sale price of the old residence. The replacement residence must be purchased or built within the 48-month period beginning 24 months before and ending 24 months after the date of sale of the old residence. See Figure 17-2. *Date of sale* is when title passes; in an installment sale, date of sale is when buyer moves into possession and is clothed with all the benefits and burdens of ownership, even though delivery of a deed is delayed to a later time.

The *adjusted sale price* equals the full price or contract price less selling expense and less "fixing-up" expense. Selling expenses are primarily brokerage fees, prepayment penalties, and legal fees. Fixing-up expenses are noncapital outlays made to assist in the sale of the residence, such as painting, minor repairs, landscaping, and so on.

Example. Bob and Betty Able bought a Denver residence for $60,000 in 1982. In November 1986, Bob's company transferred him to Chicago. The old residence was promptly sold for $94,000, with title transferred in January 1987. Selling expenses of $8,000 were incurred in the sale. Bob and Betty realized a gain of $26,000:

Sale price	$94,000
Less: selling expenses	− 8,000
Adjusted sales price	$86,000
Less: purchase price (tax basis)	− 60,000
Equals long-term capital gain	$26,000

If Bob and Betty buy a home for $76,000 in Chicago, they would be taxed on $10,000 ($86,000 − $76,000), and their basis would remain at $60,000. Purchase of a new residence for $86,000 would mean no tax, and the basis would continue at $60,000. Purchase of a replacement residence for $100,000 would again mean no tax, but the basis would be increased to $74,000 ($100,000 − $26,000 unrecognized gain, or $60,000 + $14,000 additional input).

All cash proceeds from the sale need not be reinvested in the replacement residence. That is, a loan may be used to finance part of the purchase price of the new dwelling. But the new residence must be occupied within the period stipulated. Also, the replacement residence will not be considered a new residence if it is sold before

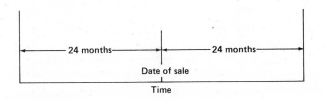

FIGURE 17-2
Tax exempt "Rollover" period for sale of personal residence

the disposition of the old or initial residence. Finally, a condominium or a cooperative unit qualifies as a replacement residence for a detached single-family house.

RELIEF ON SALE BY ELDERLY

Elderly citizens, 55 and over, are entitled to a once-in-a-lifetime capital gain exclusion of $125,000 on the sale of a personal residence. The property must have been used as the principal residence for 3 of the 5 years immediately preceding the sale. This exclusion recognizes that the value in a residence may be the basic source of retirement income of senior citizens. Also, elderly citizens often need and want less living space because of smaller family size and reduced income. Thus, this option may be taken even though the move is to a smaller dwelling unit, to a retirement home, or to the home of a son or daughter.

A married couple is treated as one taxpayer under this exclusion. Both spouses are treated as satisfying the requirements, if either is 55 at time of the sale and meets the 3- of 5-year holding provision. The "one-time exemption" means that if the exemption is used to avoid taxes on a gain of $80,000 on one sale, the taxpayer may not later claim a second exemption of up to $45,000.

Example. John and Jean, ages 56 and 57, sell their principal residence for $260,000. Their adjusted tax basis in the home is $100,000. Their fixing up and selling expenses amount to $20,000, making the adjusted sales price $240,000. Their taxable gain is $15,000, computed as follows.

Sale price	$260,000
Less: fixing up expenses	− 20,000
Equals adjusted sales price	$240,000
Less adjusted tax basis	− 100,000
Equals long-term capital gain	$140,000
Less: one-time exclusion	− 125,000
Equals taxable gain	$ 15,000

John and Jean would pay ordinary income taxes on the $15,000 at a 15 or 28 percent rate, depending on the amount of income they earned in this same year.

CONVERSION TO INCOME PROPERTY

The owner of a personal residence, upon moving, may convert it to an income property rather than sell it, to realize rental income, tax shelter, and capital appreciation as a result, while, at the same time, avoiding any selling expenses. But the property cannot be represented as an income property, and depreciation taken, while it stands vacant and up for sale. The intent must be to convert to an income property as evidenced by the owner's affirmative actions. The property need not actually be rented; however, reaching the status of income property, rental, is prima facie proof of the conversion.

Rent or Buy?

Renting is sometimes a better choice, financially speaking, than owning. Value is in the eye of the beholder, of course, particularly when choosing housing. But an economic comparison between renting and buying is worthwhile for anyone facing the rent or buy decision. At least the choice can then be made with full knowledge of the implications, based on one's value system. Opportunity costs must be taken into account here. An *opportunity cost* is the value of the best choice (opportunity) that is given up in selecting or deciding between several alternatives.

PROS AND CONS OF OWNING

Owning is usually perceived to offer many intangibles that renting does not, such as greater status, financial security, stability, ego satisfaction, privacy, and personal freedom. Ownership is also perceived as more desirable for a family with children. Explicit financial benefits include value appreciation, taxes on which can often be deferred or avoided, and deduction of interest and property taxes as expenses on income tax returns.

But owning has opportunity costs as well. The foregone return on equity invested in a home, including closing costs at purchase, is one of the most often overlooked opportunity costs of homeownership. This opportunity cost equals the rate of return that might be earned if the money were invested in stocks or bonds or some other investment media. Alternatively, the opportunity cost might be the cost of additional borrowing necessitated by the making of the down payment for the purchase. Thus, if additional consumer debt is incurred at an 18 percent annual percentage rate, the opportunity is 18 percent.

A second opportunity cost involves the activities forgone by the owner because of the need to repair and maintain the residence. Instead of repainting the house or repairing a faucet, the owner could be relaxing or doing whatever he or she wants.

Risk is a cost also. Dry rot or termites could necessitate major repairs, as could the foundation suddenly cracking or the roof developing serious leaks. Taking out a mortgage loan adds financial risk. Some risks can be covered by insurance, such as liability for injuries on the premises.

Transfer costs, financing costs, and administrative or maintenance costs must also be taken into account. Transfer costs include outlays for brokers, attorneys, title searches, surveys, recording deeds and mortgages, loan processing, and appraisals when the home is bought or sold. Transfer costs may run as high as 10 percent of value although 6–8 percent is more typical. Interest on borrowed money and mortgage insurance premiums are the main financing cost in owning. Administrative or maintenance costs include annual property taxes, hazard insurance premiums, and payments for repairs or replacements necessary to keep the property livable. Annual outlays for painting, yard work, equipment maintenance, and roof repair may average 2 percent of value over a long period. Property taxes and homeowners insurance typically amounts to 2–3 percent in urban areas and may sometimes be higher.

PROS AND CONS OF RENTING

Mobility, ease of moving, is a major advantage of renting. Thus, adjustment to changing family size, income levels, or job locations can be made easily. In some cases, location of rental units provides greater convenience and more amenities for living, such as for adult households. Also, time required to maintain the property is sharply reduced. If the roof springs a leak or another problem comes up, the risk and responsibility for correcting it is with the owner. Further, the money not used to buy a home may be invested in stocks, bonds, or money market certificates to enhance further the renter's income and wealth. Also, in a renter's market, as during an economic downturn, renting can be a major bargain. Finally, when a renter wants to move, it can generally be done on short notice, with perhaps the loss of a deposit. A renter need not worry about selling a property when interest rates are extremely high or times are economically difficult.

Renters get no direct tax benefits, but indirectly they get several benefits. Many housing expenses not deductible by a homeowner are deductible by an investor-owner on residential rental properties. Obviously, the owner-investor recovers these expenses from his or her rental income. Thus, in a sense, maintenance, supplies, property taxes, hazard insurance, and even tax depreciation are deductible housing expenses for the renter.

The costs obviously include rent payments. Also, premiums for renter insurance are a cost. A renter also has the opportunity cost of not realizing value appreciation of a home; on the other hand, the risk of value depreciation is avoided. Finally, deposits for last month's rent and for security or cleaning must be made; however, if the unit is properly maintained, these are eventually recovered.

RENT CAPITALIZATION

A rent or buy decision should obviously be based on more than a simple comparison of monthly rent versus monthly PITI payments on a mortgage loan. But information from mortgage lenders provides a quick basis for deciding whether renting is feasible. Consider this:

John and Marcia, in their investigation of alternatives, have located a very nice condominium offered for rent at $800 per month. "Is it a good deal?" They consider several other comparable condominiums up for sale and, by comparison, determine that the market value of the unit they are considering is about $100,000. They already know that mortgage loan interest rate is 12 percent, or 1% per month. Given this information, they might reason as follows.

If they buy the unit they would have to pay at least 12 percent per year in interest on a loan. Also, in that their equity position would involve more risk than that of the lender, they should expect at least a comparable rate of return on their equity. Thus, annual rental on the condominium should be at least $12,000 per year just to provide a reasonable return on the capital invested. Property taxes, insurance, and maintenance would only raise the cost of owning. Therefore, if they can rent the unit for less than $12,000 per year, or $1,000 per month, renting is clearly the better choice in the short run. In this case, $800 per month for rent looks like a good deal.

The approach might be used to determine a "break-even" market value of a rental unit as well; this process is sometimes called *rent capitalization*. Earlier, we determined that John and Marcia could afford $1,000 for housing expenses. Capitalizing $1,000 per month, or $12,000 per year, in perpetuity, by 12 percent works out to $100,000. Thus, if a unit worth more than $100,000 can be rented for $875, renting would appear to be the better choice. As market values dropped relative to the $875 per month, owning would improve as a choice, and further analysis would be warranted.

NET AFTER-TAX COSTS

Comparison of after-tax costs and benefits provides a much more accurate means of determining the alternative offering the greatest economic advantage. The analysis involves quantifying costs and benefits. Assumptions, calculations for a 3-year projection, and results of a 5-year analysis are shown in Figure 17-4. Figure 17-3 is a 10 year graphic presentation of results based on certain assumptions stated here and reflected in Figure 17-4.

The rent or buy decision under construction involves a dwelling offered for rent at 1 percent of its $100,000 market value. If bought, a 20 percent down payment would be required, with the balance financed by a 30 year, 12 percent loan. Closing costs are estimated to be 2 percent of the purchase price. The rental and market value, and other expenses are considered to increase by 5 percent per year. The owner's combined state and federal tax rate is 28 percent. Finally, if purchased, the owner is assumed to avoid any capital gains taxation upon disposition by rolling ownership over within 24 months.

Transaction costs are prorated, on a straight line basis, over the years of ownership. Thus, if the dwelling were only owned for 1 year, transaction costs of $9,000 (2 percent on purchase and 7 percent on sale) would be spread over the first year. If owned for 2 years, the average closing cost would drop to $1,000 ($2,000/2). If sold at the end of year 2, selling expenses of $7,350 ($105,000 $\times$ 7%) would be spread over 2 years at an average of $3,675. By similar calculations, average closing and selling costs for a 3-year holding period would be $667 and $2,573.

Rental payments are the major cost of a tenant, amounting to $12,000 in year 1. A major benefit to the renter is earning on money not used for a down payment or

Year	Net Cost To		Net Advantage to Owning
	Rent	Own	
1	($10,724)	($15,841)	($5,117)
2	(11,228)	(11,915)	(688)
3	(11,754)	(10,899)	855
4	(12,305)	(10,627)	1,678
5	(12,880)	(10,666)	2,214
6	(13,481)	(10,873)	2,608
7	(14,113)	(11,188)	2,926
8	(14,774)	(11.580)	3,194
9	(15,465)	(12,035)	3,430
10	(16,187)	(12,543)	3,645

SOURCE: Analysis, including assumptions, shown in Figure 17-4, extended to 10 years.

FIGURE 17-3
Growth rate: 5.00 percent. Net after-tax cost of owning versus renting with 1–10 years occupancy

Property and Owner			Financing						
(Market Value) Cost or Purchase Price	Buying Costs % of Market Value	Selling Costs % of Market Value	Annual Change Market Value Rent Expenses	Owner's Tax Bracket	Down Payment % of Market Value	Loan Term (Years)	Interest Rate (Nominal)	Loan To Value Ratio	Opportunity Cost of Capital
$100,000	2.00%	7.00%	5.00%	28%	20%	30	12.00%	80.00%	10%

NOTE: Homeowner assumed to avoid capital gains tax by buying another unit of equal or greater value within 24 months, using rollover.

Rental Data					Annual Expenses as Percent of Market Value		
Initial Monthly Rental	Required Security Deposit	Gross Rent Multiplier	Renter's Insurance (% of Market Value)	Renter's Capital Invested	Property Taxes	Hazard Insurance	Maintenance
$1,000	$1,500	100	0.20%	$20,500	2.00%	0.50%	1.00%

	Year 1	Year 2	Year 3	Year 4	Year 5
Beginning of year market value	$100,000	$105,000	$110,250	$115,763	$121,551
Monthly rental	$1,000	$1,050	$1,103	$1,158	$1,216
Gross rent multiplier	100	100	100	100	100

	Rent	Own	Rent	Own	Rent	Own	Rent	Own	Rent	Own
Costs										
Average buying expenses		$ 2,000		$ 1,000		$ 667		$ 500		$ 400
Interest on loan		$ 9,584		$ 9,548		$ 9,506		$ 9,459		$ 9,407
Property taxes, annual		$ 2,000		$ 2,100		$ 2,205		$ 2,315		$ 2,431
Hazard insurance		$ 500		$ 525		$ 551		$ 579		$ 608
Renter's insurance	$ 200		$ 210		$ 221		$ 232		$ 243	
Annual maintenance		$ 1,000		$ 1,050		$ 1,103		$ 1,158		$ 1,216
Equity opportunity cost		$ 2,000		$ 2,529		$ 3,087		$ 3,675		$ 4,295
Annual rent (12 × month)	$12,000		$12,600		$13,230		$13,892		$14,586	
Average selling expenses		$ 7,000		$ 3,675		$ 2,573		$ 2,026		$ 1,702
Total cost per year	$12,200	$24,084	$12,810	$20,427	$13,451	$19,691	$14,123	$19,712	$14,829	$20,058
Benefits										
Renter's return on money not invested in equity at rate of 10% minus taxes at 28%	$ 1,476		$ 1,582		$ 1,696		$ 1,818		$ 1,949	
Income tax savings										
For interest paid		$ 2,684		$ 2,673		$ 2,662		$ 2,649		$ 2,634
For property taxes paid		$ 560		$ 588		$ 617		$ 648		$ 681
Equity build-up- app'n		$ 5,000		$ 5,250		$ 5,513		$ 5,788		$ 6,078
Total benefits per year	$ 1,476	$ 8,244	$ 1,582	$ 8,511	$ 1,696	$ 8,792	$ 1,818	$ 9,085	$ 1,949	$ 9,392
Net cost per year	$10,724	$15,841	$11,228	$11,915	$11,754	$10,899	$12,305	$10,627	$12,880	$10,666
Net advantage to buying		($5,117)		($688)		$855		$1,678		$2,214

FIGURE 17-4

Net costs of owning versus renting for 1–5 years of occupancy

purchase closing costs. Thus, $22,000 less $1,500 for deposits is available for investment at 10 percent in our example earning $2,050 in year 1. This $2,050 is subject to tax at 28 percent, leaving a net benefit of $1,476. The investment in year 2 is presumed to be $21,976 ($20,500 + $1,476).

Results of the analysis show that renting is about $5,000 less costly in year 1, $10,724 versus $15,841. See Figure 17-4. In year 2, the difference narrows to $688. And from year 3 on, renting is more costly, approaching $4,000 by end of year 10. See Figure 17-3.

The example makes it quite clear that renting is almost certain to be less costly if occupancy is to be less than 2 years. Three years appears to be the break even period; this is consistent with conventional wisdom. But caution is advised; a slight change in assumptions quickly changes the result. A growth rate of 2 percent results in renting always having the lower net cost. A 10 percent per year value increase makes ownership break even with renting at the end of year 1.

Questions for Review and Discussion

1. Explain briefly, in your own words, the relationship of annual stabilized income to the affordability of housing.
2. What is the 25 percent rule of the FHLMC? The 33 percent rule?
3. Identify and explain two tax benefits an owner gets that a renter does not.
4. Are there any direct tax benefits a tenant gets that an owner does not? Are there any indirect benefits?
5. Explain the rollover of a personal residence in detail.
6. Does an owner realize any intangible benefits that a renter does not? If so, what are they?
7. What extra costs does an owner have that a tenant does not?
8. What does "home" mean? Does the wide use of "homeownership" mean that a "home" cannot be realized by one who rents a dwelling for personal use?

Case Problems

1. Tim and Terry Turner have annual stabilized income of $50,000 and can afford only a 10 percent down payment to buy a house. Local lenders are making 90 percent loans at 12 percent, compounded monthly, with amortization over 25 years. Hazard insurance and property taxes in their community generally run about 2 percent of a house's market value. By using the FHLMC guideline, with no overage, how much housing can they reasonable afford? (about $93,500)
2. Assume that Tim and Terry have monthly installment payments of $300. By using the FHLMC 33 percent guideline, how much housing can they expect to command? (about $96,500)
3. Walter and Hazel Nutt ask you how much housing they can afford. After working with them for a while, you determine that they have an ASI of $36,000. You know

that local lenders are making 90 percent, 30-year loans at nine percent, compounded monthly. Also, property taxes and hazard insurance come to 2.4 percent per year in your experience. The Nutts tell you they have long-term installment obligations of $240 per month.

    a. How much housing under the 25 percent rule?

    b. How much under the 33 percent rule?

    c. Check your answers by comparing the monthly payments on your answers in a and b with the amounts the Nutts can afford.

    d. How much down payment will be required of the Nutts?

4. Chech and Chung, both 55, sell their house, realizing a $75,000 long-term capital gain. They decide to take advantage of the $125,000 exemption allowed senior citizens and avoid taxes on the gain. They then buy a smaller house for $80,000, the value of which increases sharply. Six years later they sell the house for $125,000, net, after selling expenses. They take their situation to a certified public accountant, asking that their $45,000 gain be offset by the $50,000 of the senior citizen exemption they did not use earlier. What is the result?

5. Local lenders are making loans at 9 percent, compounded monthly. Richard and Lily figure they can afford $700 per month for housing. They have located a condominium, valued at $75,000, which can be rented for $700. On the basis of rent capitalization, would you advise them to rent it or consider buying? What is the result if the market interest rate were 12 percent? 15 percent?

6. Rocky and Angel were recently transferred to Cambridge by his company. They expect to be there 2 years, based on experience. They have located a house they like and can buy for $100,000. They can rent a similar house for $1,000 per month, which is the amount they can afford for housing. Housing values in the community are expected to increase 11 percent per year for the next few years. All other information is the same as in the case problem given in the chapter. They ask you, as a housing consultant, whether they should buy or rent. On the basis of a 2-year net, after tax, buy or rent comparison, what do you advise, economically speaking?

18

Spatial Economics, Urban Area Structure, and Highest and Best Use

The test of a civilization is the power of drawing the most benefits out of its cities.

Ralph Waldo Emerson, Journals

Fixity means that demand must come to each parcel of real estate. Fixity also means that the environment—the investment climate—around each parcel greatly influences its use and value. Physical, social, economic, and political forces taken altogether make up this investment climate. These forces determine where people live, play, work, and die because they push toward regional relocations and toward concentration or diffusion of human activity.

Most economic, social, and political forces are urbanizing in their effect; hence, the long-term trend toward larger and larger cities. An influence toward concentration of people, buildings, and machines is an *urbanizing force*. Manufacturing, trade, education, and government are prime examples of activities that are more advantageously carried on with people concentrated in one place. An influence toward scattering of people and activities is a *dispersing force*. Desire for isolation (e.g., a hermit) is an example.

Beyond this, at the local level, urbanizing forces interact with the immediate physical environment to create functional areas, which are the major components or building blocks of our urban areas. A *functional area* is a place where some specialized activity (e.g., manufacturing) is performed. Residential neighborhoods, commercial districts, and industrial districts are the most obvious examples of functional areas. Streets and other parts of our transportation system tie functional areas and specific land-use activities together by facilitating movement of people and/or goods between them. Land-use activities, functional areas, and the connecting transportation system, taken altogether, make up our urban areas.

The purpose of this chapter, in summary, is to look at self-interest as it creates urbanizing forces that push each owner to improve his or her specific parcel of real estate to its greatest value, which results in its being employed in its highest and best use, thereby structuring our urban areas; that is, physical, biological, economic, social, and political forces all influence property values and land-use decisions.

Important Topics or Decision Areas Covered in This Chapter

Three Categories of Forces
Physical and Biological Forces
Institutional Forces
Economic Forces

Urbanizing Forces
Components of Urbanizing Forces
Functional Basis of Urban Areas
Urban Location
The Urbanizing Process

Theories of Urban Growth
Concentric Circle
Direction of Least Resistance
Multiple Nuclei

Rent Theory and Urban Structure
Space Allocation in a Large Hotel
Rural Land Allocation
Space Allocation in Urban Areas
Rent Theory Restated

Determining Intensity of Improvement

Questions for Review and Discussion

Case Problems

Key Concepts Introduced in This Chapter

Comparative economic advantage principle
Concentric-circle theory
Direction of least resistance
Dispersing force
Economic capacity of the land
Economics
Extensive margin

External economies of scale
Functional area
Intensity of use
Intensive margin
Internal economies of scale
Multiple-nuclei theory
Opportunity cost
POSSLQ

Proportionality, principle of

Rent triangle

Submarginal land

Urban infrastructure

Urbanizing force

Three Categories of Forces

A force is an active influence that causes motion or change; it involves both energy and direction. An example, from science, is gravity, which pulls us toward the center of the earth with an energy equal to our weight.

As was discussed earlier, forces causing change in the use and value of real estate are traditionally classified as (1) physical and biological, (2) economic, and (3) institutional. An institutional force has social, political, religious, and legal components. These forces may complement or offset each other. The result of all these forces determines the direction and extent of change in our urban areas. Items making up these forces and their levels of influence are summarized in Figure 18-1.

National data are important in providing an overview for a real estate analyst or investor. But, at the national level, forces of change affect real estate in only a very general way. That is, while we have national population, resources, production, income, and traditions, these are seldom tied or linked directly to a specific parcel of land. Exceptions might be federal government decisions pertaining to dams, military bases, national parks, and the like. Thus, national data are probably best viewed as the aggregate of much local data, such as U.S. population, oil reserves, or miles of highway.

PHYSICAL AND BIOLOGICAL FORCES

Physical and biological forces include the natural environment in which we live, the nature and characteristics of the various resources with which we work, and living organisms, including humankind. Land provides the physical support, the site for the activities of humans and animals. The earth, land, and water provide the raw materials (minerals, fuels soil, climate, and so on) for our activities. The earth is, therefore, the physical setting or stage. Living organisms (humans, animals, plants, bacteria) are the players that interact on this stage.

How Many People? Population, the number of people, is the basic biological statistic at the national, regional, and local levels. The relative abundance and availability of natural resources constitute our major physical concern, which affect location for production or trade. Data on physical resources are extensive and ever changing. The distribution of population reflects the distribution and use of resources. Our discussion here is limited to population.

The U.S. population was 76.0 million in 1900, 151.7 million in 1950, and 226.5 million in 1980. By 2000 we are projected to have a population of about 260 million, with a gradual leveling off thereafter at about 310 million by 2050. See Figure 18-2, middle series.

A direct relationship exists between population trends and real estate values,

Category of Influence	Level of Influence		
	National and International	Regional	Local
Physical and biological	Population	Population (natural increase and migration)	Population (natural increase and migration); age-sex distribution
	Natural resources (minerals, soils, climate, water, topography)	Resource distribution	Specific natural resources (soils, minerals, terrain)
	World locations for trade and commerce	Location relative to raw materials and markets	Location relative to raw materials and markets; fabricated structures/constraints
Economic	Gross national product		
	Personal income		Personal income
	Employment and unemployment		Employment and unemployment
	Price levels (CPI)		Price levels (CPI)
	Money and credit (financial systems)		
Institutional Political	Federal powers and legislation	State powers and legislation	Local govermental powers and legislation
Religious Tradition, custom, and beliefs	Work ethic; attitude toward education		Attitude toward education; attitude toward architecture; chance

FIGURE 18-1

Forces influencing the development, use and value of real estate

assuming the population has buying power. An increasing population means increased demand for real estate services and, in turn, higher values, other things being equal. A declining population has the opposite effect. The population of the United States, by region and by state, for 1950 and 1980, with a projection to 2000 is shown in Figure 18-3.

Urbanization. In 1980, 73.7 percent of the U.S. population lived in urban areas according to the *1986 U.S. Statistical Abstract.* This is up sharply from 64.0 percent in 1950 and 39.7 percent in 1900. By way of comparison, 77.0 percent of the population of the United Kingdom and 76.0 percent of the population of West Germany are urbanized. Australia, a large country relative to its nearly 15.3 million population, is the most highly urbanized country at 86.0 percent. On the other hand, the Soviet Union is only 64.0 percent urbanized. China, with an estimated population of just over one billion people, is only 21.0 percent urbanized, while India, with an estimated 1980 population of 685 million people, is only 23.0 percent urbanized. Some differences in the definition of urban may be involved in these figures, but it is clear

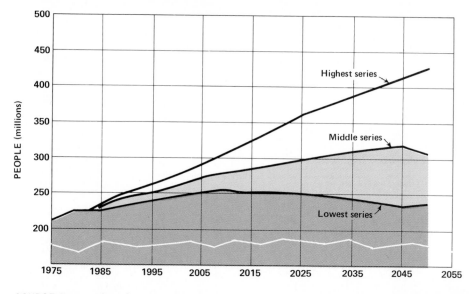

SOURCE: Bureau of the Cenusus, *Population Estimates and Projections*, Series p. 25, no. 922, October 1982
Table 1.

FIGURE 18-2
U.S. 1980 population, with projections to 2050

that high population concentration count does not directly translate into higher percentages of urbanization. Further, greater urbanization generally reflects advanced development of a country's economy.

The distribution of the U.S. population shows a steady shift toward the Pacific Ocean. See Figure 18-3. The western states grew at a much more rapid rate than did other areas, thereby gaining a much larger share of total U.S. population. A less obvious tendency has been for the south Atlantic states to grow at a steady rate. These shifts are the result of people following the sun for economic opportunity and for life style.

Number of Dwelling Units. With urban development comes more housing. As shown in Figure 18-4, the number of U.S. dwelling units increased from 16 million in 1900 to 88 million in 1980. U.S. population in 1980 was 226.5 million, meaning that the number of people per dwelling unit declined to 2.56. More people were living alone or in small households. In fact, from 1970 to 1980, the increase in dwelling units exceeded our population growth. Increasingly, dwelling units are classed as *POSSLQs* by the U.S. Census Bureau, that is, "persons of the opposite sex sharing living quarters."

INSTITUTIONAL FORCES

Our second category, institutional forces, includes our culture, social beliefs, religious beliefs, educational system, organizations, technology, and politics. Tradition, laws, governmental systems, and habitual ways of thinking are also included. In net, institutional forces reflect the collective conditioning and ways of acting, the value system, of people in a society. Thus, our use of land in the United States, with our emphasis on manufacturing and trade, on wide use of the automobile, and on living

Area	1940 Population (1,000)	1940 % of Total	1960 Population (1,000)	1960 % of Total	1980 Population (1,000)	1980 % of Total	2000: Projected Population (1,000)	2000: Projected % of Total
United States	132,165	100.00	179,323	100.00	226,546	100.00	267,462	100.00
New England	8,437	6.38	10,509	5.86	12,349	5.45	12,775	4.78
Maine	847	0.64	969	0.54	1,125	0.50	1,308	0.49
New Hampshire	492	0.37	607	0.34	921	0.41	1,364	0.51
Vermont	359	0.27	390	0.22	511	0.23	625	0.23
Massachusetts	4,317	3.27	5,149	2.87	5,737	2.53	5,490	2.05
Rhode Island	713	0.54	859	0.48	947	0.42	926	0.35
Connecticut	1,709	1.29	2,535	1.41	3,108	1.37	3,062	1.14
Middle Atlantic	27,539	20.84	34,168	19.05	36,787	16.24	33,626	12.57
New York	13,479	10.20	16,782	9.36	17,558	7.75	14,990	5.60
New Jersey	4,160	3.15	6,067	3.38	7,365	3.25	7,428	2.78
Pennsylvania	9,900	7.49	11,319	6.31	11,864	5.24	11,208	4.19
East North Central	26,627	20.15	36,224	20.20	41,683	18.40	41,648	15.57
Ohio	6,908	5.23	9,706	5.41	10,798	4.77	10,357	3.87
Indiana	3,428	2.59	4,662	2.60	5,490	2.42	5,679	2.12
Illinois	7,897	5.98	10,081	5.62	11,427	5.04	11,188	4.18
Michigan	5,256	3.98	7,823	4.36	9,262	4.09	9,208	3.44
Wisconsin	3,138	2.37	3,952	2.20	4,706	2.08	5,216	1.95
West North Central	13,517	10.23	15,395	8.59	17,185	7.59	18,067	6.75
Minnesota	2,792	2.11	3,414	1.90	4,076	1.80	4,489	1.68
Iowa	2,538	1.92	2,758	1.54	2,914	1.29	2,972	1.11
Missouri	3,785	2.86	4,320	2.41	4,917	2.17	5,080	1.90
North Dakota	642	0.49	632	0.35	653	0.29	682	0.25
South Dakota	643	0.49	681	0.38	691	0.31	688	0.26
Nebraska	1,316	1.00	1,411	0.79	1,570	0.69	1,662	0.62
Kansas	1,801	1.36	2,179	1.22	2,364	1.04	2,494	0.93
South Atlantic	17,824	13.49	25,972	14.48	36,959	16.31	48,974	18.31
Delaware	267	0.20	446	0.25	594	0.26	638	0.24
Maryland	1,821	1.38	3,101	1.73	4,217	1.86	4,582	1.71
District of Columbia	663	0.50	764	0.43	638	0.28	376	0.14
Virginia	2,678	2.03	3,967	2.21	5,347	2.36	6,389	2.39
West Virginia	1,902	1.44	1,860	1.04	1,950	0.86	2,068	0.77
North Carolina	3,572	2.70	4,556	2.54	5,882	2.60	6,868	2.57
South Carolina	1,900	1.44	2,383	1.33	3,122	1.38	3,907	1.46
Georgia	3,124	2.36	3,943	2.20	5,463	2.41	6,708	2.51
Florida	1,897	1.44	4,952	2.76	9,746	4.30	17,438	6.52
East South Central	10,779	8.16	12,050	6.72	14,667	6.47	17,174	6.42
Kentucky	2,846	2.15	3,038	1.69	3,661	1.62	4,400	1.65
Tennessee	2,916	2.21	3,567	1.99	4,591	2.03	5,420	2.03
Alabama	2,833	2.14	3,267	1.82	3,894	1.72	4,415	1.65
Mississippi	2,184	1.65	2,178	1.21	2,521	1.11	2,939	1.10
West South Central	13,064	9.88	16,951	9.45	23,746	10.48	32,678	12.22
Arkansas	1,949	1.47	1,786	1.00	2,286	1.01	2,835	1.06
Louisiana	2,364	1.79	3,257	1.82	4,206	1.86	5,160	1.93
Oklahoma	2,336	1.77	2,328	1.30	3,025	1.34	3,944	1.47
Texas	6,415	4.85	9,580	5.34	14,229	6.28	20,739	7.75
Mountain	4,149	3.14	6,855	3.82	11,373	5.02	20,139	7.53
Montana	559	0.42	675	0.38	787	0.35	963	0.36
Idaho	525	0.40	667	0.37	944	0.42	1,512	0.57
Wyoming	251	0.19	330	0.18	470	0.21	1,002	0.37
Colorado	1,123	0.85	1,754	0.98	2,890	1.28	4,657	1.74
New Mexico	532	0.40	951	0.53	1,303	0.58	1,727	0.65
Arizona	499	0.38	1,302	0.73	2,718	1.20	5,582	2.09
Utah	550	0.42	891	0.50	1,461	0.64	2,777	1.04
Nevada	110	0.08	285	0.16	800	0.35	1,919	0.72
Pacific	10,229	7.74	21,198	11.82	31,800	14.04	42,379	15.84
Washington	1,736	1.31	2,853	1.59	4,132	1.82	5,832	2.18
Oregon	1,090	0.82	1,769	0.99	2,633	1.16	4,025	1.50
California	6,907	5.23	15,717	8.76	23,668	10.45	30,613	11.45
Alaska	73	0.06	226	0.13	402	0.18	631	0.24
Hawaii	423	0.32	633	0.35	965	0.43	1,278	0.48

SOURCE: *Statistical Abstract of the United States 1986*, Tables 12 and 14.

FIGURE 18-3

U.S. population by state and region for 1940, 60 & 80 and projected to 2000

Year	Population (millions)	Dwelling Units (millions)	Population Per Dwelling Unit
1900	76.2	15.964	4.77
1910	92.2	20.256	4.55
1920	106.0	24.352	4.35
1930	123.2	29.905	4.12
1940	132.2	34.855	3.79
1950	151.3	42.826	3.53
1960	179.3	53.024	3.38
1970	203.2	63.450	3.20
1980	226.5	88.413	2.56
1983	233.5	93.519	2.50

SOURCE: U.S. Department of Commerce Bureau of the Census, Population Series Reports, 1960, 1970, and 1980; Census of Housing, 1980; *Statistical Abstract of the United States 1986*.

FIGURE 18-4
Population per dwelling unit in the U.S., selected years, 1900–1980

in single-family dwelling units differs appreciably from the use of land in India, Hong Kong, or Ethiopia.

Institutional forces cannot be quantified in the same way that population and income can. Even so, they exert considerable influence on real estate activities by way of the decisions made by individual investors.

ECONOMIC FORCES

Self-interest is the basic economic force that motivates people to achieve the highest possible standard of living. Self-interest is reflected in business decisions to maximize profits or wealth. In turn, *economics* is often defined as the allocation of limited resources to satisfy human needs and wants, which happens in a market-oriented society. The resources may be water, oil, minerals, or real estate.

Prices and a market system provide the signals for this allocation of resources. Price usually means money, dollars, paid or bid for an item, such as a house. Price also has a broader meaning in a market system, namely, opportunity cost. *Opportunity cost* is the value of what is given up in making a choice, as in choosing a one-family house in preference to a condominium. To maximize benefits, a decision maker minimizes opportunity costs.

Real estate prices and values, real estate sales activity, and construction and development activity are directly influenced by per capita personal income, which reflects economic opportunity at the local level. Per capita personal income for the United States in 1983 was $11,707. Figure 18-5 shows per capita income by state and region for selected years from 1970, providing a basis of comparison. Do the figures reflect what has been happening in your area? The data is from the U.S. Bureau of Economic Analysis.

A look at population and personal income trends tells much about what is likely to happen to real estate values in an area. That is, an area with sharp increases in population and personal income will have greatly increased effective demand for real estate and rising values.

For examples, Figures 18-3 and 18-5 show that California has been a growth

Area	1970		1980		1985	
	Current Dollars	% of U.S.	Current Dollars	% of U.S.	Current Dollars	% of U.S.
United States	$3,945	100	$ 9,494	100	$13,867	100
New England	4,306	109	10,029	106	15,914	115
Maine	3,303	84	7,751	82	11,887	86
New Hampshire	3,781	96	9,217	97	14,964	108
Vermont	3,530	89	7,970	84	12,117	87
Massachusetts	4,349	110	10,096	106	16,380	118
Rhode Island	3,924	99	9,200	97	13,906	100
Connecticut	4,913	125	11,559	122	18,089	130
Middle Atlantic	4,460	113	10,069	106	15,454	111
New York	4,695	119	10,242	108	16,050	116
New Jersey	4,737	120	10,811	114	17,211	124
Pennsylvania	3,928	100	9,352	99	13,437	97
East North Central	4,085	104	9,715	102	13,617	98
Ohio	3,971	101	9,401	99	13,226	95
Indiana	3,735	95	8,970	94	12,446	90
Illinois	4,515	114	10,448	110	14,738	106
Michigan	4,044	103	9,798	103	13,608	98
Wisconsin	3,774	96	9,361	99	13,154	95
West North Central	3,736	95	9,190	97	13,286	96
Minnesota	3,893	99	9,662	102	14,087	102
Iowa	3,792	96	9,211	97	12,594	91
Missouri	3,706	94	8,856	93	13,244	96
North Dakota	3,216	82	8,651	91	12,052	87
South Dakota	3,140	80	7,815	82	11,161	80
Nebraska	3,748	95	8,887	94	13,281	96
Kansas	3,777	96	9,799	103	13,775	99
South Atlantic	3,605	91	8,818	93	13,222	95
Delaware	4,505	114	9,949	105	14,272	103
Maryland	4,322	110	10,365	109	15,864	114
District of Columbia	4,775	121	12,210	129	18,168	131
Virginia	3,712	94	9,446	99	14,542	105
West Virginia	3,043	77	7,747	82	10,193	74
North Carolina	3,220	82	7,774	82	11,617	84
South Carolina	2,975	75	7,389	78	10,586	76
Georgia	3,323	84	8,041	85	12,543	90
Florida	3,779	96	9,245	97	13,742	99
East South Central	2,951	75	7,431	78	10,633	77
Kentucky	3,096	78	7,644	81	10,824	78
Tennessee	3,097	79	7,689	81	11,243	81
Alabama	2,903	74	7,454	79	10,673	77
Mississippi	2,556	65	6,614	70	9,187	66
West South Central	3,340	85	8,979	95	12,686	91
Arkansas	2,773	70	7,099	75	10,476	76
Louisiana	3,041	77	8,404	89	11,274	81
Oklahoma	3,337	85	9,029	95	12,232	88
Texas	3,536	90	9,439	99	13,483	97
Mountain	3,611	92	9,059	95	12,687	91
Montana	3,428	87	8,334	88	10,974	79
Idaho	3,315	84	8,100	85	11,120	80
Wyoming	3,686	93	11,009	116	13,223	95
Colorado	3,887	99	10,147	107	14,812	107
New Mexico	3,072	78	7,947	84	10,914	79
Arizona	3,688	93	8,855	93	12,795	92
Utah	3,220	82	7,679	81	10,493	76
Nevada	4,691	119	10,845	114	14,488	104
Pacific	4,394	111	10,777	114	15,490	112
Washington	4,046	103	10,248	108	13,876	100
Oregon	3,711	94	9,319	98	12,622	91
California	4,510	114	11,020	116	16,065	116
Alaska	4,726	120	13,007	137	18,187	131
Hawaii	4,674	118	10,129	107	13,814	100

SOURCE: *Statistical Abstract of the United States 1986*, Table 735, *Survey of Current Business*, August, 1986, Table 1.

FIGURE 18-5
U.S. per capita personal income by state and region, 1970, 1980, and 1985

state for many years. Conversely, New Mexico has had a stable population and lags behind the U.S. total in per capita personal income growth. Comparatively, it is a slow growth state. In turn, construction and real estate activity are not likely to be as strong, and values not as high, as in many other states. Even so, urbanization trends may make real estate investment very attractive in some communities in New Mexico.

Urbanizing Forces

At the local level, physical and biological, institutional, and economic forces become urbanizing forces. In that we are primarily interested in urban real estate, let us look at these urbanizing forces in greater depth.

COMPONENTS OF URBANIZING FORCES

History is filled with evidence of humankind's march toward urbanization. Manufacturing, trade, education, and government all benefit from a concentration of people and facilities.

Our early ancestors were hunters and nomads. They wandered about in response to the seasons, often with annual migrations. Gradually, they learned to harvest grains, berries, nuts, and other vegetation. With the shift to tilling the soil, they built permanent dwellings. Small villages developed as people banded together to share tools and benefit from mutual defense. Use of force to conquer and loot remained a way of life for many of the nomadic tribes.

Trade or exchange was eventually recognized as advantageous, based on territorial specialization. Some areas had gold or silver to trade; other areas had furs; and others yet had salt or grain. With trade, convenient transportation became advantageous. Settlements located near good harbors or on inland waterways tended to prosper most. Merchants found it more convenient to live near transport nodes, as did sailors. Inns or hotels and livery stables for traveling merchants prospered at these nodes. These strategic locations soon became important as military bases, particularly for the navy, and as political capitals.

Specialization of labor, in manufacturing as well as in trade, soon developed, so productivity greatly increased. Individual skills increased as did the variety of manufactured products.

With modern modes of transportation (trains, automobiles, and airplanes) urban concentration soon became advantageous at other points. In addition, advances in technology increased the use of, and need for, raw materials such as oil, copper, steel, coal, electricity, and rubber. Also, tractors replaced horses and oxen in agriculture, with a twofold benefit: tractors made greater production possible, and they did not require any part of the crop as feed. In turn, this change meant that a smaller proportion of the population had to remain on the land to grow food and fiber for those living in urban areas.

A number of urban analysts have studied these forces and broken them down into several components. One, W. F. Smith of the University of California, lists six components.[1] In brief, these are

1. Savings in costs of social interaction
2. Internal economies of scale to the firm
3. External economies of scale to the firm
4. Labor mobility or labor specialization
5. Greater consumer choice
6. Fostering of innovation

Savings in Costs of Social Interaction. Most of us like social interaction, preferably on a face-to-face basis. The closer we live together, and the better the transportation technology, the lower the cost of this interaction. Thus, cars, street-cars, buses, and bicycles, and the supporting road systems, enable us to see friends and relatives with a minimum of effort. In addition, we are able to join in more exchanges and get greater personal satisfaction by living close together.

Internal Economies of Scale. Using specialized labor and machinery that produces large numbers of units of output for one firm reduces the cost per unit; this is termed *internal economies of scale*. Lower costs per unit mean lower costs to users and consumers, and a larger market. Henry Ford capitalized on the idea of mass production or economies of scale in producing automobiles. A firm, using this principle, must concentrate large numbers of people in one place, and urbanization results.

External Economies of Scale. Firms realize lower costs by locating in a larger community where adequate support services and supplies are readily available from others at reasonable costs. The term for such action is *external economies of scale.* For example, large inventories are maintained by suppliers with several local customers, meaning that each firm can buy on a hand-to-mouth basis. Also, subcontractors are nearby to take over small jobs. In addition, law firms, accounting firms, machinery repair firms, and an adequate labor pool are readily available. Finally, users or consumers of the firm's product may be in the urban area, saving transportation costs to market for finished goods.

Jane Jacobs provides a vivid example of the importance of external economies of scale to a manufacturing effort:[2]

> The Rockefellers, early in the 1960s, decided to build a factory in India to produce plastic intrauterine loops for birth control. At the same time they were undertaking to combat the Indian birth rate, they also wanted to curb the migration of rural Indians to cities. A way to do this, they thought, was to set an example of village industry, placing new industry in small settlements instead of cities. The location they chose for the factory, then, was a small town named Etawah in highly rural Uttar state. It seemed plausible that the factory could as well be located one place in India as another. The machinery had to be imported anyway and the loops were to be exported throughout India. The factory was to be small for with modern machinery even a small factory could begin by turning out 14,000 loops a day. The work had been rationalized into

---

[1] W. F. Smith, *Urban Development* (Berkeley: University of California Press, 1975), chap. 2, pp. 21–47.

[2] Jane Jacobs, *The Economy of Cities* (New York: Random House, 1969), pp. 186–187.

simple, easily taught tasks; no pre-existing, trained labor pool was required. The problem of hooking up to electric power had been explored and judged feasible. Capital was sufficient, and the scheme enjoyed the cooperation of the government of Uttar.

But as soon as the project was started everything went wrong, culminating in what *The New York Times* called "a fiasco." No single problem seems to have been horrendous. Instead, endless small difficulties arose: delays in getting the right tools, in repairing things that broke, in correcting work that had not been done to specifications, in sending off for a bit of missing material. Hooking up to the power did not go as smoothly as expected, and when it was accomplished the power was insufficient. Worse, the difficulties did not diminish as the work progressed. New ones cropped up. It became clear that—even in the increasingly doubtful event the plant could get into operation—keeping it in operating condition thereafter would probably be impractical. So after most of a year and considerable money had been wasted, Etawah was abandoned and a new site was chosen at Kanpur, a city of some 1,200,000 persons, the largest in Uttar, where industry and commerce had, by Indian standards, been growing rapidly. Space in two unused rooms in an electroplating plant was quickly found. The machinery was installed, the workers hired, and the plant was producing within six weeks. Kanpur possessed not only the space and the electric power, but also repairmen, tools, electricians, bits of needed material, and relatively swift and direct transportation to other major Indian cities if what was required was not to be found in Kanpur.

Labor Specialization. The larger an urban area, the greater is the feasibility of labor specialization. As individuals, we seek the work we do best or the work from which we get the greatest satisfaction. At the same time, businesses want those workers who give greatest productivity or lowest costs per unit of output. An electrical engineer or a machinist has far fewer opportunities to specialize in a small town than in a large metropolitan area. Plus, in the event of a layoff, the chances of a specialist's finding a satisfactory job locally are much higher in a metropolitan area.

Greater Consumer Choice. Economies of scale and labor specialization are limited by the size of the market. For example, unless the market can absorb 1 million cases of beer a day, it does little good to amass the facilities and people to produce 1 million cases of beer a day. But, as a community grows larger, more and more firms find a market large enough for them to survive. Conversely, the greater the number of automobile dealers, restaurants, law firms, schools, hardware stores, and shoe stores, the greater the choices available to citizens of a community.

Fostering Innovation. An innovator or investor generally finds it easier to find needed equipment and services in a larger metropolitan area. This makes it easier to translate creative ideas into reality, though a determined innovator might succeed anywhere. The availability of supplies and services for an innovator is essentially an extension of the idea of external economies of scale, labor specialization, and wider consumer choice. Fostering innovation may be a small force relative to some of the earlier components of urbanizing forces, yet it does exert influence in the same direction.

Costs of Urbanization. In fairness, some costs are also associated with urbanization. Urban life increases our exposure to contacts that are involuntary and often undesirable. Panhandlers, drug pushers, gamblers, and high-pressure sales people are all more likely to be encountered in metropolitan areas. We are also more tied to the "system" in urban areas. Thus, a strike of garbage handlers, of transportation workers, or of teachers is more likely in a city and tends to have a greater debilitating effect than it would in a rural area. In a similar vein, we are committed to a greater support of things we may not use or believe in. For example, we pay taxes to support municipal parks, schools, and hospitals even though we may not use them. Air and water pollution, congestion, and costs of commuting tend to be higher in urban areas. Hence, these items decrease the quality of life in cities and act toward decentralization or dispersal. Finally, anonymity is sometimes considered a cost of urbanization, although many people consider it a benefit.

FUNCTIONAL BASIS OF URBAN AREAS

All urban areas exist for a reason. It follows that the investor or analyst who understands the forces that brought his or her community into existence is in a much stronger position to judge its future.

Cities, broadly speaking, may be classified as primary and secondary urban centers. A primary community is one that has its own economic base, that is, its existence is not dependent on the operations or well being of other communities within the state or metropolitan area. A secondary community, on the other hand, is a satellite whose size and strength of orbit depends on the principal city to which it owes its existence. These satellite communities are better known as "bedroom" towns and cities, where commuters (people who work where they would rather not live) reside. The economic strength of a satellite community depends entirely on the strength of its primary community.

Primary communities may be divided into classes, which in a general sense reflect their reason for existence, as follows:

Industrial cities	Detroit, Michigan; Pittsburgh, Pennsylvania
Commercial cities	Chicago, Illinois; San Francisco, California
Mining cities	Scranton, Pennsylvania; Wheeling, West Virginia; Butte, Montana
Resort cities	Miami, Florida; Atlantic City, New Jersey; Scottsdale, Arizona
Political cities	Tallahassee, Florida; Washington, D.C.; Springfield, Illinois; Salem, Oregon
Educational cities	Chapel Hill, North Carolina; Ann Arbor, Michigan; Champaign-Urbana, Illinois; Corvallis, Oregon

Many communities have a diverse economic base and may fall into two or more classifications. Thus, New York City is industrial and commercial in character as well as a tourist Mecca. Miami, Florida, which started as a resort city, is presently one of the most important commercial centers in the south, with one of the largest international airports in the country. Los Angeles, long known for movie making and citrus fruit, is important today as an international shipping center second only to New York in shipping tonnage.

URBAN LOCATION

Land is a resource necessary for almost all social and economic activities. But, characteristics of land vary from place to place. Both topography and soil characteristics are important for urban development, although soil fertility is generally not important per se. Beyond these basic observations, what can we say about the location and growth patterns of cities?

Initially, defense considerations were of primary importance in the location of cities, because invasion and conflict were common realities. Hence, Rome was founded on seven hills, Paris on an island, and London and Moscow in swamps. Walled cities were common in the Middle Ages.

As trade developed, those settlements with the greatest comparative advantage for transportation and communication between producers and their markets prospered most. The ***comparative economic advantage principle*** is that communities benefit most by specializing in producing goods or services providing the greatest advantage relative to other communities.

Locations of greatest advantage for trade were as follows:

1. At points on oceans or lakes with the greatest convenience between the hinterland and markets (e.g., San Francisco, California; Seattle, Washington; and Chicago, Illinois)

2. At or near mouths of rivers (e.g., New York City; New Orleans, Louisiana; Philadelphia, Pennsylvania; and Portland, Oregon)

3. At branches of rivers or near other inland water transportation (e.g., Pittsburgh, Pennsylvania; St. Louis, Missouri; Cincinnati, Ohio; Omaha, Nebraska; and Syracuse, New York)

4. At obstructions on the river requiring unloading and transshipment by another mode (e.g., St. Paul, Minnesota; and Albany, New York)

5. At river crossings (e.g., Rockford, Illinois, and Harrisburg, Pennsylvania)

6. At breaks in mountain chains or where mountain meets plain or intersections of land trade routes (e.g., Denver, Colorado; Salt Lake City, Utah; and Albuquerque, New Mexico)

7. At points where modes of transportation require servicing, even temporary (e.g., Atlanta, Georgia)

Note the importance of water transportation in the early development of the United States; large amounts of freight could be much more easily handled, at lower cost, by water than by any other means at that time.

The emphasis on urban location and prosperity shifted to other factors with the coming of the Industrial Revolution. Comparative advantage continues to be important relative to these factors. The most significant factors are availability of raw materials, skilled labor, adequate power, and suitable climate. Nearness to market also tends to be important, particularly when product weight gain or weight loss are involved. Some examples seem appropriate.

1. *Raw Materials.* (1) Relative availability of coal and iron ore were important in the development of Pittsburgh, Pennsylvania; Birmingham, Alabama; and Gary, Indiana. (2) Lumber mills were built near forests and at one time were prominent in the midwest. Tacoma, Washington, and Eugene, Oregon, are leading mill towns now. But, faster second growth of timber is causing the lumber industry to move to the southeast.

2. *Power.* Fall River, Massachusetts, Minneapolis, Minnesota, and Spokane, Washington, all owe much of their early growth to ready availability of low-cost water or hydroelectric power.

3. *Skilled labor.* The auto industry is concentrated largely in Ohio and Michigan because of the huge reservoir of skilled labor in these areas. Likewise, Seattle, Washington, and Los Angeles, California, have large reserves of skilled labor for airplane manufacture.

4. *Suitable climate.* Tucson, Arizona, Phoenix, Arizona, San Diego, California, and Miami, Florida, owe much of their growth to their pleasant climates. A general shift of economic activity to the Sun Belt is the current trend.

5. *Weight gain and weight loss.* A manufacturing process involving considerable weight gain is best located near the market for the product because the manufacturer avoids paying transportation costs on weight gain. Examples are soda pop, beer, and bread. Bulk, fragility, and perishability also increase market orientation. With considerable weight loss, the manufacturer avoids unnecessary transportation costs by processing near the raw materials. Examples are copper mining and processing and lumber manufacture. Some products, such as grains, may be processed anywhere between producer and market, because little weight is gained or lost.

THE URBANIZING PROCESS

Most urban real estate is manufactured space, created in response to physical, social and economic, and political forces, in what may best be described as the urbanizing process.

Initially, an urban area is raw land. Natural resources, such as oil, minerals, fertile soil, abundant snow (for skiing), or advantageous location may provide reason for a settlement. A community develops based on the beliefs, laws, political and financial systems, and other institutional considerations. Buildings and other improvements are added to the land, based on demand. These improvements constitute the supply of urban real estate. Opportunities for businesses, employment, or pleasure create the demand. Credit is usually needed to help create the supply as well as to help buyers in financing acquired realty. As time moves on, people buy and sell the existing supply of real estate, and new space may be built.

The combined activites of these buyers, sellers, and builders make up the real estate market. Their investment and development activity results in the cities we see today. And, with each passing year, the existing supply of space tends to become more dominant relative to new space added during the year. New construction typically adds only 2 or 3 percent to a community's supply of space in any one year. The market tends to be stable and predictable as a result. But what determines the structure and layout of the urban area?

Theories of Urban Growth

Cities or urban areas are established and grow in response to needs of people; they are not gifts of nature. The place of origin may be by design or by historical accident.

But, to fill the need, the area grows in spite of rugged topography and unfriendly climate. Problems of water supply, waste disposal, transport, and schools are overcome as the occasion demands. Again, are there any theories to explain the growth and location of activities in urban areas? Yes, many theories have been proposed, of which three have considerable applicability. These are (1) concentric circle, (2) direction of least resistance, and (3) multiple nuclei.

CONCENTRIC CIRCLE

Johann Heinrich von Thunen, an owner of a German estate, wrote *Der Isalierte staat (The Isolated State)*, in 1826, to explain the allocation of land to various activities. Von Thunen began by assuming a walled city or village in the middle of a level, productive, and isolated field or plain. Climate, soils, topography, and transportation and other factors were all held constant so as not to influence or distort the analysis. Automobiles and railroads were not yet known, so goods to be moved had to be hauled by wagons, hand carried, or driven, in the case of livestock. Differences in the use of land could, therefore, be attributed entirely to differences in transportation costs or location. See Figure 18-6. Also, see Raleigh Barlowe's *Land Resource Economics* for a technical explanation of von Thunen's theory.[3]

[3] Raleigh Barlowe, *Land Resource Economics*, 4th ed. (Englewood Cliffs, NJ: Prentice Hall, 1986), pp. 225–239.

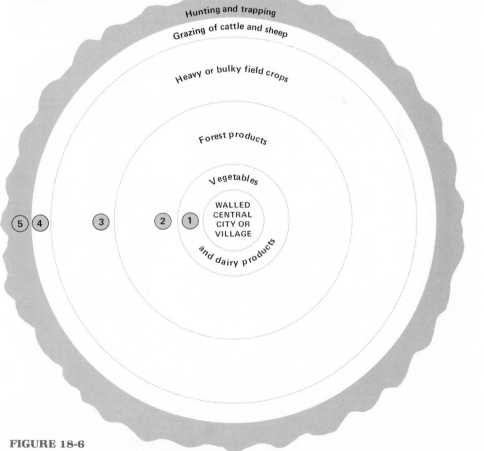

FIGURE 18-6
Concentric circle allocation of space in an isolated state

Von Thunen identified five zones or *concentric circles* outside the village or central city. Zone 1, immediately outside the walls of the city, would be used primarily for growing vegetables, milk cattle, and egg-laying hens. These activites are intensive, involving many trips from the village, with the products often hand carried into the city. Forest products production turned out to be the best use for zone 2. Forest products are both bulky and heavy and were used for fuel and construction in Von Thunen's day. Hence, production near the city saved considerable time and energy. Production of heavy or bulky field crops—potatoes, grain, hay—would be the main use in zone 3. Grazing of cattle and sheep was the appropriate use for zone 4, in that the livestock could be driven to zone 1 for slaughter or milking. The surrounding wilderness, zone 5, was appropriate for hunting and trapping.

Von Thunen's allocation of space was based on the net value of the product from the land after delivery in the city. Thus, both production and transportation costs were taken into account. Also, it was based entirely on the operation of an open market. Government control or intervention was not considered. The concern was only with rural land uses. And, it was a steady state rather than a dynamic society.

Adjusting the assumptions in von Thunen's model results in somewhat different outcomes as to the location of activities. Assuming a navigable stream flowing through the "isolated state" makes possible low-cost water transportation and would result in an elongated settlement pattern as shown in Figure 18-7b. While zone 1, vegetable and dairy products, would remain relatively unchanged, zone 2, forestry activities, could be located at a greater distance from the center, if upstream. Assuming improved land transportation routes would lead to a star-shaped settlement pattern, as shown in Figure 18-7c. Relaxing or changing other von Thunen assumptions, such as soil fertility, topography, or number of city markets, would create additional outcomes.

About a hundred years after von Thunen, in the 1920s, Ernest W. Burgess updated the concentric-circle theory to fit urban areas. According to Burgess, urban

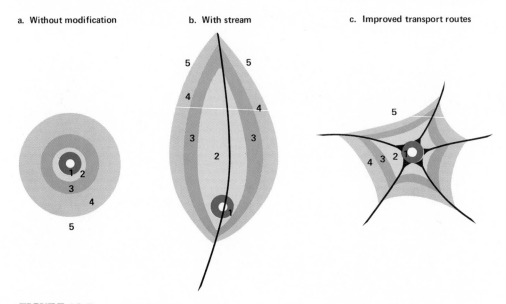

a. Without modification   b. With stream   c. Improved transport routes

FIGURE 18-7
Settlement patterns resulting from modified Von Thunen assumptions

areas expand outward from the central business district of retail stores, office buildings, and factories. The next circle out was a zone of transition containing low-income people and light-manufacturing plants. Zone 3 housed workers for zones 1 and 2. High-income residences were in zone 4. Zone 5 consisted of suburbs or semirural-type properties. At the time Burgess was writing, planning and zoning were relatively unknown, and automobiles and airplanes were just being introduced. Thus, their impact was not yet evident.

DIRECTION OF LEAST RESISTANCE

Richard M. Hurd, a mortgage banker, compiled information on the expansion and growth of more than 50 U.S. cities. In 1903, Hurd wrote that cities grow in the *direction of least resistance* or greatest attraction, or their resultants.[4] Direction of least resistance is really an extension or modification of von Thunen's concentric circle theory applied to urban areas with some modifications of the assumptions relative to barriers to growth.

> The point of contact differs according to the methods of transportation, whether by water, by turnpike, or by railroad. The forces of attractions and resistance include topography, the underlying material on which city builders work; external influences, projected into the city by trade routes; internal influences derived from located utilities; and finally the reactions and readjustments due to the continual harmonizing of conflicting elements. The influence of modern topography, all-powerful when cities start, is constantly modified by human labor, hills being cut down, waterfronts extended, and swamps, creeks and lowlands filled in, this, however, not taking place until the new building sites are worth more than the cost of filling and cutting. The measure of resistance to the city's growth is here changed from terms of land elevation or depression, and hence income cost, to terms of investment or capital cost. The most direct results of topography come from its control of transportation, the waterfronts locating exchange points for water commerce and the water grade normally determining the location of the railroads entering the city.
>
> Growth in cities consists of movement away from the point of origin in all directions, except as topographically hindered, this movement being due both to aggregation at the edges and pressure from the centre. Central growth takes place both from the heart of the city and from each subcenter of attraction, and axial growth pushes into outlying territory by means of railroads, turnpikes and street railroads. All cities are built up from these two influences, which vary in quantity, intensity and quality, the resulting districts overlapping, interpenetrating, neutralizing and harmonizing as the pressure of the city's growth brings them into contact with each other. The fact of vital interest is that, despite confusion from intermingling of utilities, the order of dependence of each definite district on the other is always the same. Residences are early driven to the circumference, while business remains at the centre, and as residences divide into various social grades, retail shops of corresponding grades follow them, and wholesale shops in turn follow the retailers, while institutions and various mixed utilities irregularly fill in the intermediate zone, and the banking and office section remains at the main business centre. Complicating this broad outward movement of zones, axes of traffic project shops through residence areas, create business subcentres, where

[4] Richard M. Hurd, *Principles of City Land Values* (New York: The Record and the Guide, 1903, 1924), pp. 13–15.

they intersect, and change circular cities into star-shaped cities. Central growth, due to proximity, and axial growth, due to accessibility, are summed up in the static power of established sections and the dynamic power of their chief lines of intercommunication.

Considerable research and writing have been done since Hurd made his statement. Yet no simpler, clearer, or more comprehensive statement about urban growth dynamics has since been made.

MULTIPLE NUCLEI

In the 1930s, Homer Hoyt developed the sector theory, based on wedge-shaped neighborhoods surrounding the central business district. New, high-income residential areas were seen as developing along highways and next to other fast transportation facilities. In this sense, the theory is not too different from the route, or axial, theory suggested by a number of scholars. The axial theory says that an urban area tends to grow along its lines of transportation, owing to the economic advantage of convenience, made possible by the easy, low-cost movement. Both theories appear to be restatements of Hurd's line-of-least-resistance theory, and the power of these theories to explain urban growth and change, over and above Hurd's theory, seems limited.

Frederick Babcock, an appraiser, studying urban growth and change in the 1930s, focused on how urban change comes about. He characterized urban areas as sliding, jumping, and bursting in their growth.[5] One district expands by gradually encroaching or moving into neighboring districts in a sliding manner. Jumping means that a district will sometimes leap over a barrier, such as another well-established district, in it expansion. Thus, an expanding business district will jump a river, a civic center, or a university. Bursting means the scattering of a district to several new subdistricts. Thus, the pre–World War II central business district of large metropolitan areas burst, and the suburban shopping center resulted. In like fashion, manufacturing areas scattered from the central city to the suburbs, taking the form of industrial parks and districts.

Ullman and Harris advanced the idea of **multiple nuclei,** or clusters of development in 1945.[6] Essentially, their theory is an extension of Babcock's bursting explanation, with physical, economic, and social considerations taken into account. It is also an extension of the ideas that cities are functional areas. Four reasons suggested by Harris and Ullman for the development of clusters or nuclei are

1. Some activities require specialized facilities.
2. Like activities tend to group together because they mutually benefit from cohesion.
3. Unlike activities are sometimes adverse or detrimental to each other.
4. Some activities can afford the high rents of the most desirable sites; others cannot and must take less desirable sites.

The multiple nuclei theory of land-use arrangements is based strongly on the rent-paying ability of the various uses. The use able to pay the highest rent gets the

[5]Fredric Babock, *The Valuation of Real Estate* (New York: McGraw-Hill, 1932), p. 59.
[6]Chauncy D. Harris and Edward L. Ullman, "The Nature of Cities," in *Building the Future City, Annals of the American Academy of Political and Social Sciences*, November 1945, pp. 7–17.

most desirable site for its purposes. The worth of a specific site or location depends on transportation and communication possibilities and the surrounding environment. Thus, business and industrial centers developed outside the central business district. Currently, these nuclei take the form of shopping centers, industrial parks, convention centers (often near major airports), and resort communities (functional areas). See Figure 18-8.

It should be noted that major changes occurred in transport as these theories developed. Until about 1900, trains, street cars, and buggies or wagons were the

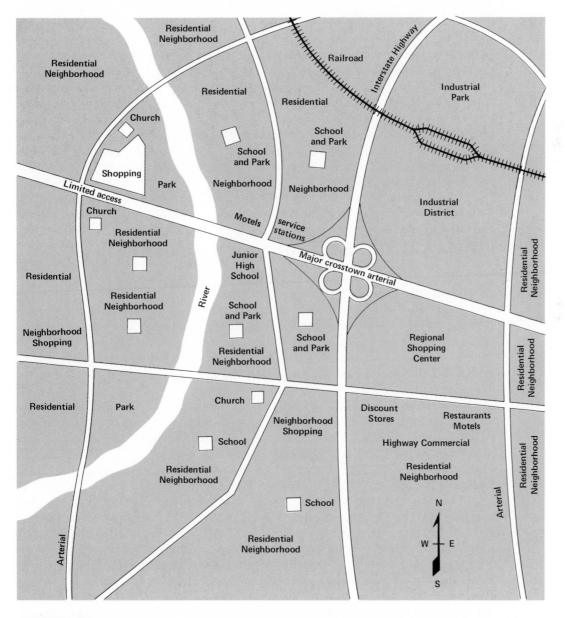

FIGURE 18-8
Functional activities (multiple nuclei) in a modern community

main modes of transport. The automobile gave everyone faster and greater flexibility of movement. It seems unlikely that central cities would have declined so sharply in the absence of widespread use of cars. But with increasing costs of energy, central cities seem to be getting new life, perhaps because they once again constitute the most accessible, least-cost locations.

Rent Theory and Urban Structure

Urban growth theory may be restated as rent theory to reflect the many decisions by individual owners about the use of their properties. In fact, it is the decisions by the individual owner-investors that make up urban growth theory. Also, rent theory, or value theory, is the means by which local economic activity is related to real estate. The key for rent theory is maximization of self-interest, expressed in monetary terms. Note that we are not discussing maximizing revenues or minimizing costs but rather of maximizing net profits, rents, satisfactions, benefits, or, in some cases, minimizing net losses. In the immediate context, we are discussing maximizing net benefits from land and buildings.

Our discussion of rent theory begins by looking at the allocation of space in a large hotel, which concepts extend to allocation of land to alternative uses in rural and urban areas. We conclude our discussion with a general statement of rent theory.

SPACE ALLOCATION IN A LARGE HOTEL

Which of all the uses in a large hotel gets its choice of location? Remember that owners and operators of hotels are rational and want to maximize the profitability and value of the space under their control. In effect, once the hotel use has been decided on and approvals obtained, there are few limits on the use of space within the structure.

In most tall structures, the premium location is the top floor, followed by space at the street level. Brief reflection or observation shows that a bar or cocktail lounge is usually found in both these locations. Very large hotels often have four or five bars in the most accessible or desirable locations. Restaurants follow closely behind bars in this respect. From experience, owners know that these two uses are the most profitable and are able to pay the highest rents.

Other common uses in slightly less advantageous locations are typically barber and beauty shops, drugstores, liquor stores, and newsstands. High-fashion clothing stores may also be included. The second to fourth floors are often devoted to ballrooms, meeting rooms, swimming pools, and health facilities. Automobile parking is typically below ground or on the side of the building away from the main thoroughfare. Guest rooms occupy the space from about the fifth floor to just under the top floor. One must look carefully to find the lobby and registration desk in our newer hotels. The owners know that the guests will not be turned away by a slight delay in finding the registration desk.

This hierarchy of uses is illustrated by rent triangles in Figure 18-9. A *rent*

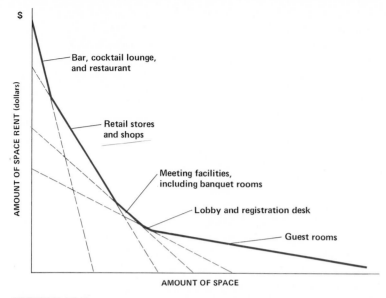

FIGURE 18-9
Hierarchy of space uses in a large hotel, based on rent-paying ability

triangle is a schedule showing the amount of rent a use or business activity can pay as an increasing amount of space is devoted to the use.

Thus, the cocktail bar in the Top of the Mark in the Mark Hopkins Hotel in San Francisco, California, may be able to pay a rent of $300 per square foot each year. But, as more space is allocated to serving liquor (more bars and restaurants are opened in the building), the rent-paying ability per square foot decreases. At some point, other uses—drug stores, newsstands, guest rooms—offer a higher rate of return and therefore command the space. Each type of use has its own triangle or schedule of payments it can afford. The use paying the highest rent gets it choice of space.

An important exception to this hierarchy occurs in hotels where gambling is legal. The exception reinforces rent theory as a basis for space allocation. In Las Vegas, Nevada, hotels devote much of their prime space at street level to gaming activities, such as slot machines, because this space is most easily accessible to potential gamblers.

RURAL LAND ALLOCATION

Fertile land in an area with a friendly climate is more productive than is land not so well endowed. That is, more bushels of corn, soybeans, wheat, and so on may be grown per acre on the productive land for a given amount of effort. In turn, each acre of the most productive land is more profitable and more valuable than is less productive lands, assuming that markets are available to use the crops grown.

An owner-operator of the more favorably endowed land would therefore use it to produce that crop giving the highest return per acre. A tenant-operator would also grow the crop or product giving the highest return. And, an owner-landlord would charge a rent based on the profitability of the crop giving the highest returns per acre. Thus, self-interest pushes the use of land to that use giving the greatest return or value or to the highest and best use. In the Midwest, known for its productive lands, owners concentrate on growing corn and soybeans. The two crops reinforce each other in maintaining soil productivity and are about equally profitable. Moving west, the lands of Kansas and North and South Dakota get less rain and are farther from the markets of the East. These areas concentrate on growing wheat rather than corn or soybeans. Grazing cattle and sheep is the most common use of lands in the drier areas of our western states.

Alternatively, rugged or inaccessible lands with abundant rainfall, as in the Southeast and the Northwest, are devoted to growing timber. Thus, we have lumber and wood products companies named Georgia Pacific and Boise Cascade. Finally, some lands (swamps, mountain tops, and deserts) yield no profit to human efforts and remain in their natural state; these are termed *submarginal lands*. Figure 18-10 depicts broad uses of agricultural land in the United States.

Almost every state has some land better suited to growing vegetables than to field crops, because of the nearness of markets. Also, climate in California, Hawaii, and Florida favors the growing of oranges, grapefruit, pineapple, grapes, nuts, and produce over corn, wheat, or soybeans. But, it turns out, these uses are able to pay higher rents and, therefore, give higher values to the land.

SPACE ALLOCATION IN URBAN AREAS

What land uses pay the highest rent or give the highest value to sites in urban areas? Location theory says that the most accessible site is likely to be the most productive or profitable. Unless rivers or hills intervene, the most central location is the most accessible in an urban area. What uses dominate in our central business districts?

Early in this century, large department stores and other retail outlets occupied the prime sites in our major cities. Office buildings, hotels, apartment buildings, and manufacturing plants were usually located nearby. Moving out from the central city, one-family homes became a dominant land use. Individual commercial and industrial districts sometimes developed along major arteries as wedges or sectors. Lot sizes increased as the edge of the city blended into the countryside. The hierarchy of land uses is diagramed in Figure 18-11.

With wide use of automobiles and trucks, industry moved to the suburbs after World War II. People and residential neighborhoods followed, pulling commercial

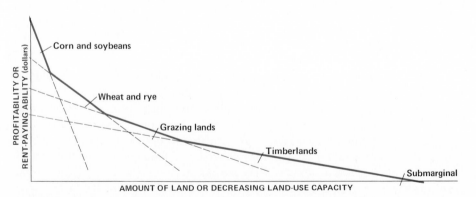

FIGURE 18-10
Allocation of land to alternative rural uses based on rent-paying ability

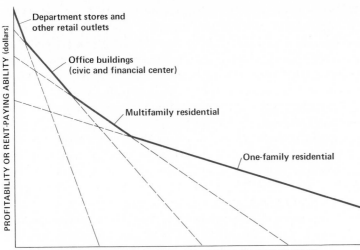

FIGURE 18-11
Hierarchy of urban land uses based on rent paying ability

districts with them. Satellite villages were often engulfed by the rapid urban expansion. Industrial parks, shopping centers, recreation centers, and residential neighborhoods combined to make up the community fabric. The land-use structure became a pattern of more or less distinct functional neighborhoods or districts superimposed on a network of street and highways. The typical value pattern that developed is shown, in cross section, in Figure 18-12. Thus, land-use patterns took on a structure that tended to minimize the costs of moving people and goods in the area and which is best described by the multiple nuclei concept, discussed earlier.

Rivers, lakes, marshes, and hills all act as barriers to the "normal" expansion of urban areas. In accordance with Hurd's direction-of-least-resistance principle, ex-

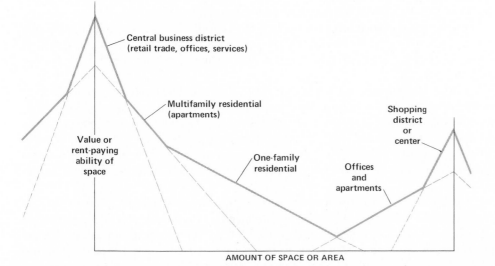

FIGURE 18-12
Schematic cross section of land uses and their rent-paying ability in a large metropolitan area

pansion takes place away from or around these barriers because the cost is less relative to the benefits realized. However, with time and growth, the time costs of travel to the urban fringe in other directions steadily increase. At some point it becomes feasible to incur the costs to bridge rivers and lakes, to fill in marshes, and to expand into hilly areas. The Golden Gate Bridge of San Francisco, California, the Lake Pontchartrain Bridge near New Orleans, Louisiana, and the recent filling in of the tidal marshes near Newark, New Jersey, for industrial development are examples of "delayed" development outward from an urban center.

Existing realty improvements tend to lag social and economic needs of a community. That is, several one-family houses or a church must often be moved or torn down to make way for a discount store. Likewise, the existing urban infrastructure acts to retard urban adjustment. *Urban infrastructure* is the basic installations and facilities of a community, such as schools, sewer and water systems, power and communications systems, and transportation systems, including streets, freeways, and subways. In either of these two situations, additional costs must be incurred for the immediate site or area to be used more intensely. At some point, the potential benefits may justify the additional costs.

RENT THEORY RESTATED

Let us now summarize our discussion and restate rent theory as an explanation of urban growth and change. First, land-use activities tend to locate at the point of greatest comparative advantage. If the site or location is not owned, it must be bought or rented. Land-use competition is based on rent-paying ability. Over a period of time, those uses able to pay the highest rents or prices get the choicest locations. In addition, a hierarchy of land uses develops. Department stores, office buildings, and apartment buildings, therefore, tend to get the choice or central urban sites. Moving out from the center, the hierarchy goes to one-family residences to field crops to grazing and forestry to submarginal deserts and mountaintops. Subcenters of value, for example, shopping centers and industrial parks, intervene into urban areas as business operators and other citizens strive to minimize transportation costs relative to benefits received in accepting a location.

At any given time an urban area may be expanding or contracting. Most of our experience is with growth and expansion. Growth usually begins with an expansion of the economic base of the community. An urban area may grow outward or upward.

Outward expansion, such as the urbanization and development of new lands, is growth at the extensive margin. The *extensive margin* is that point at which rents or values make it just barely financially feasible to convert land to urban uses and to add urban improvements. The extensive margin is symbolized by land subdivision and development at the urban fringe. The building of bridges and roads and the filling in of marshes are also activities associated with the extensive margin. See Figure 18-13.

Urban areas also expand upward or at the intensive margin. The *intensive margin* is that point at which rents or values make it just barely financially feasible to use urban land more intensely with the addition of more capital and labor. Replacing old houses with a discount store is an example. Alternatively, converting an old factory or cannery into a shopping center is another. See Figure 18-13.

Note that intensity of use and rent are related but not identical concepts. Rent is also the payment for the use of realty, in its more accepted meaning. *Intensity of*

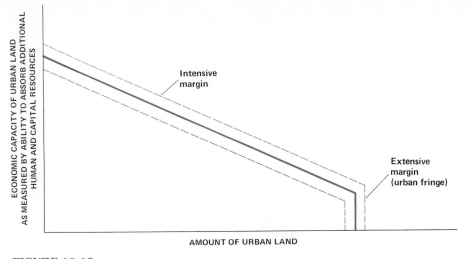

FIGURE 18-13
Intensive and extensive margins of urban land uses

use refers to the relative amount of human and capital resources added in the use of land. Generally, the higher the value of the site, the higher its rent and the greater its intensity of use. That is, there must be a proportionality between the value of a site and the number of improvements added to the land. Intensity of use, rent, and value are all closely related to highest and best uses of land.

Intensity of use is the key to understanding why urban areas grow upward as well as outward. Land, urban or rural, is not productive in and of itself. Corn, wheat, office space, or residential units all require labor, capital, and management in addition to land. These factors of production (land, labor, capital, and management) must be combined according to the principle of proportionality for each factor to get its greatest return. The *principle of proportionality* is that real estate reaches its maximum productivity, or highest and best use, when the factors of production are in balance with one another. This is also known as the principle of increasing and decreasing returns. The ability of a site to absorb human and capital resources, under the principle of proportionality, is the *economic capacity of the land*. Additional investment is added until the marginal profit no longer equals or exceeds the marginal cost or investment.

Stated another way, the factors of production must be used in optimum balance to achieve the highest and best use of realty. How is the optimum determined? In the construction or modification of a property, expenditures should be made for those items adding the most to value, as judged by the market. Thus, $2,000 might be used for a fireplace, a third bathroom, or a patio.

	Fireplace	Third Bathroom	Patio
Marginal contribution to market value of property	$4,000	$2,500	$3,000

Adding the fireplace gives $2.00 of market value for every dollar expended, the patio gives $1.50 of market value, while the third bathroom gives only $1.25 of market value. Clearly, the addition of a fireplace is the best choice. And, if another $2,000 were available, the addition of the patio would be second choice, with its $1.50 return for every dollar invested.

Obviously, the more money that is spent on improvements to the land, the more intensely the land is used. Intense development of land requires that high values (economic capacity) be justified. Urban uses are generally much more intense than are rural uses. Urban land values are generally higher than are rural. The highest and best use of a site is reached when no further value can be gained by the addition of resources. In fact, value may be decreased by more additions in accordance with the principle of increasing and decreasing returns. At the urban fringe or extensive margin, this point means that conversion of additional rural land to urban uses is just barely economically feasible. That is, a developer would earn either no profit at all or only a minimally acceptable one after paying costs of subdividing and construction. At the intensive margin, this point means that an owner of a developed property adding resources (to rehabilitate or convert to another use) realizes no value advantage or only a small increment of value in excess of costs incurred. In either case, any lower returns would result in a decision not to develop the land or rehabilitate the property.

Determining Intensity of Improvements

An owner of a vacant parcel, in attempting to maximize its value, must weigh many alternatives before deciding how to best use it. In the end, that use that is physically possible, financially feasible, and legally acceptable and gives the greatest "net present value" to the site is selected. Part of this selection process is the evaluation to determine how many improvements should be added to the land.

On the basis of principle of proportionality, improvements must be added to a vacant site to the point where a marginal dollar of input (cost) just produces a marginal dollar's worth of output (value) for highest and best use to be achieved. To illustrate, let us consider a vacant site to be improved with an office building.

An investor acquired a 10,000 square foot (s.f.) site for $600,000. Office space rents for $20/s.f. per year gross, which yields a net operating income per s.f. of $12. Net operating income (NOI) equals gross income less operating expenses. Planning and zoning regulations allow 100 percent land coverage for commercial uses, such as office space with no limit on height. The design of the building provides for 90 percent efficiency; that is, 90 percent of the building's area can be rented out. Finally, the ratio of annual net operating income to sale price for comparable properties approximates 10 percent. Building costs vary from $105/s.f. for the first story down to $90 for the fourth and fifth stories, after which they increase by $5.00 per story. How many stories should the investor add to the land?

Figure 18-14 illustrates the calculations by which an investor-developer might make this determination. To begin, a one-story office building covering the entire 10,000 s.f. site, with 90 percent efficiency, would provide 9,000 s.f. of rental area; see column 5 in Figure 18-14. At $12/s.f., an annual NOI of $108,000 would be realized.

Capitalized at 10 percent, the value realized would be $1,080,000 (column 10). However, the total cost for a one-story property would be $1,650,000 as shown in

ASSUMPTIONS:

$600,000	= site cost
10,000	= site area, square feet
90.00%	= building efficiency
$12.00	= net operating income (NOI) per square foot
10.00%	= overall capitalization rate (R)

	BUILDING				COSTS OF DEVELOPMENT					PROFIT ANALYSIS		
No. of Stories	Marginal Cost per Square Foot	Marginal Cost per Story	Total Accumulated Cost	Net Rentable Area (square feet)	Total Cost (land and building)	Average Cost per Square Foot of Rentable Area	Marginal Cost per Square Foot of Rentable Area	Net Operating Income (annual)	Total Value (NOI/.10)	Profit (total value minus total cost)	12 Average Profit per Square Foot of Rentable Area	13 Marginal Profit per Square Foot of Rentable Area
1	$ 105.00	$1,050,000	1,050,000	9,000	$1,650,000	$183.33	$183.33	$ 108,000	$ 1,080,000	($570,000)	($63.33)	($63.33)
2	100.00	1,000,000	2,050,000	18,000	2,650,000	147.22	90.00	216,000	2,160,000	(490,000)	(27.22)	8.89
3	95.00	950,000	3,000,000	27,000	3,600,000	133.33	85.50	324,000	3,240,000	(360,000)	(13.33)	14.44
4	90.00	900,000	3,900,000	36,000	4,500,000	125.00	81.00	432,000	4,320,000	(180,000)	(5.00)	20.00
5	90.00	900,000	4,800,000	45,000	5,400,000	120.00	81.00	540,000	5,400,000	0	0.00	20.00
6	95.00	950,000	5,750,000	54,000	6,350,000	117.59	85.50	648,000	6,480,000	130,000	2.41	14.44
7	100.00	1,000,000	6,750,000	63,000	7,350,000	116.67	90.00	756,000	7,560,000	210,000	3.33	8.89
8	105.00	1,050,000	7,800,000	72,000	8,400,000	116.67	94.50	864,000	8,640,000	240,000	3.33	3.33
9	110.00	1,100,000	8,900,000	81,000	9,500,000	117.28	99.00	972,000	9,720,000	220,000	2.72	(2.22)
10	115.00	1,150,000	10,050,000	90,000	10,650,000	118.33	103.50	1,080,000	10,800,000	150,000	1.67	(7.78)
11	120.00	1,200,000	11,250,000	99,000	11,850,000	119.70	108.00	1,188,000	11,880,000	30,000	0.30	(13.33)
12	125.00	1,250,000	12,500,000	108,000	13,100,000	121.30	112.50	1,296,000	12,960,000	(140,000)	(1.30)	(18.89)

FIGURE 18-14

Determining intensity of land improvement

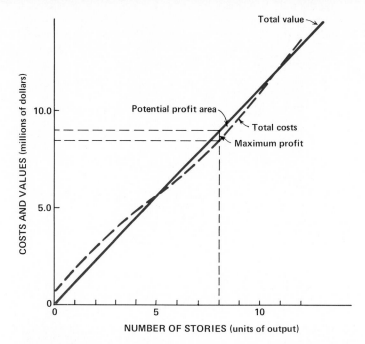

FIGURE 18-15
Total value and total cost curves for property improvement analysis

column 6; thus, the investor would suffer a loss of $570,000, column 11. Adding a second story lowers the loss to $490,000 while yielding a positive marginal profit per square foot of rentable area added.

The marginal cost of a square foot drops as floors are added. Footings and other supports only have to be strengthened, and one roof serves all floors. Offsetting these economies is the increasing costs to lift materials to ever higher levels, to install elevators, and to solve similar problems.

The marginal profit per square foot, at $20, is maximized at four and five floors. Yet, it is only at the fifth floor that value realized equals costs incurred. It is clear that the building must be built to at least five stories. Even so, it pays the developer to add more stories because marginal profit is positive and total profit is still increasing. See Figure 18-14 for a graphic summary, floor by floor, of the interaction of total costs and total value for this example.

The marginal cost of the eighth story, at $1,050,000, is just slightly exceeded by the marginal value realized of $1,080,000. The ninth floor would have a marginal cost of $1,100,000, $20,000 greater than the marginal value of the floor, meaning the point of diminishing returns had been reached and passed. Alternatively, it is in this area that marginal cost equals marginal revenue or profit, signaling that additional space produced will result in ever greater losses. Thus, the office building should only be built to eight stories. At eight stories, profit is maximized at $240,000.

Questions for Review and Discussion

1. Explain briefly four benefits and three costs of urbanization.
2. Concentric circle, direction of least resistance, and multiple nuclei are prominent

theories of urban growth and development. Are the theories related in any way? Explain.

3. Do any of the theories in question 2 fit your community? Discuss.
4. Illustrate and explain briefly with rent triangles the allocation of space in a large hotel toward maximizing rent or value. In a department store.
5. What is submarginal land? What are the intensive and extensive rent margins relative to use of urban land? Give one example of each.
6. Explain the interrelationships, if any, among intensity of use, rent levels, value, and highest and best use for a specific site.
7. Is anonymity a cost or a benefit of urbanization? Explain.
8. Explain in general terms the interrelationships among site value, construction costs, and rent levels as they concern highest and best use of a specific site.
9. What is the principle of increasing and decreasing returns? How does it apply in the development of real estate?

Case Problems

1. Survey your community. Note where development and redevelopment is taking place. Are there any bypassed hills or marshes that look ripe for development? Can you identify where development and redevelopment is most likely to take place in the next 5 years?
2. Refer to Figure 18-14. If the marginal cost per square foot of building started at $80 and increased $10 with each story added, what would be the optimal number of floors to be added to the site, all other assumptions remaining unchanged?

19

Real Estate Markets

Fortune is like the market, where many times, if you can stay a little, the price will fall.

Francis Bacon, English Philosopher, Statesman, and Jurist

A market is generally considered to be the coming together of people (buyers and sellers) who wish to exchange goods, services, and money. It is also the course of commercial activity by which the exchange of commodities within a market area is effected. While both definitions apply to real estate, there are differences as well.

The commodity of the real estate market is the elusive "property rights." Transactions are very diffused as to where they take place: they do not occur in a single public place. The real estate market is therefore more aptly described as a business activity in which an exchange of property rights is effected.

Important Topics or Decision Areas Covered in This Chapter

Market Types

Market Characteristics
Local in Character
Commodity Not Standardized
Market Diffused
Transactions Private in Nature
Absence of Short Selling
Poor Adjustment of Supply and Demand

Supply and Demand Forces
Population
Wage Levels and Income Stability
Personal Savings, Credit Availability, and Levels of
   Interest Rates
Rent and Vacancy Levels
Taxation and Land-Use Control
Costs of Land, Labor, and Building Materials
Construction Technology and Building Quality

Market Functions
Reallocation of Existing Space
Space Adjustment
Information Generation
Determination of Land Uses

Market Operation
Supply and Demand Dynamics
Short-Run Adjustments
Long-Run Adjustments
Cycles?

Perfectly Competitive?
Efficient Market?

Local Market Indicators
Demand Indicators
Supply-Demand Interaction
Finance Indicators
New Supply Indicators
Interrelatedness of Indicators

Questions for Review and Discussion

Key Concepts Introduced in This Chapter

Buyer's market	**Perfect market**
Cycle	**Potential demand**
Doubling up	**Prime rate**
Effective demand	**Seller's market**
Efficient market	**Short selling**

Market Types

In practice, real estate markets are typically classified according to type of property traded. Each property type may be further subdivided into smaller and more specialized market areas.

- Residential: (1) urban, (2) suburban, and (3) rural
- Commercial: (1) office buildings, (2) store properties, (3) lofts, (4) theaters, (5) garages, and (6) hotels and motels
- Industrial: (1) factories, (2) utilities, (3) mining, and (4) warehouses
- Agricultural: (1) timberland, (2) pasture land, (3) ranches, (4) orchards, and (5) open farmland (for produce, tobacco, cotton)
- Special purpose: (1) cemeteries, (2) churches, (3) clubs, (4) golf courses, (5) parks, and (6) public properties (buildings, highways, streets)

Real estate market may also be classified further as to rights of ownership or use. Thus, we may speak of (1) a rental market involving transfer of space and (2) an equity market involving transfer of ownership.

We might also recognize a buyer's market and seller's market. A *buyer's market* occurs when the supply of goods and services greatly exceeds demand, thereby enabling purchasers to bargain for lower prices and get them; thus, values fall. Conversely, a *seller's market* occurs when demand greatly exceeds supply, thereby enabling sellers to bargain for higher prices and get them, which results in rising values.

Market Characteristics

Product characteristics such as fixed location, situs, heterogeneity, indestructibility, and durability cause a real estate market to differ from other markets in several ways. Some of these characteristics were discussed in Chapter 2, so they will only be mentioned here.

LOCAL IN CHARACTER

Fixity causes the market for real estate to be local in character; demand must come to the parcel. An oversupply of land or land improvements in a midwestern state is of no avail to fill a market demand for like land or improvements in another region or metropolitan center. Real estate is, therefore, extremely vulnerable to shifts in local demand. Further, a real estate broker in Los Angeles, California, cannot well advise a business executive seeking a site in Atlanta, Georgia.

COMMODITY NOT STANDARDIZED

Real estate is heterogeneous; no two parcels of real estate are exactly alike. At the very least, each parcel has its own unique location. Even with two physically adjacent properties, situs and legal characteristics may cause a difference in their relative values. One may be zoned residential "A," the other "B," meaning different site uses; or one may be subject to deed restrictions limiting its use to high income residential, and the other may be free of any such limitations and thus open to any legal use.

MARKET DIFFUSED

Fixity and heterogeneity account for the wide fluctuations in value and number of transactions that characterize the real estate market. Such fluctuations occur from region to region as well as from state to state or community to community. The market for U.S. farmland, for instance, may be judged good (or "active") when based on number of sales and increases in overall values. But this "favorable" average may be a composite derived from the wheat, corn, tobacco, and cattle-raising regions, which more than offset unfavorable activity in the cotton-growing region. Likewise, Phoenix, Arizona, Los Angeles, California, and Miami Beach, Florida, may record sharp gains in sales while activity in Tacoma, Washington, and Dallas, Texas, drops through the floor.

TRANSACTIONS PRIVATE IN NATURE

Real estate transactions are very private. Buyers and sellers meet in confidence, often negotiating through brokers, and their bid and offering prices are rarely publicized. Also, deeds of record often do not specify the actual dollar amounts paid.

ABSENCE OF SHORT SELLING

Being heterogeneous, real estate is nonfungible; in turn, this leads to the legal right to specific performance. The right of specific performance discourages speculation and prevents the market stabilizing operation known as short selling. *Short selling* is selling a security or commodity not owned, when prices are high, with delivery promised at some future date. Anticipating a drop in prices, the speculator hopes to cover these short sales by purchasing at lower prices prior to the delivery date the quantities previously sold. Short selling can, however, only be done with articles or goods that are legally fungible or substitutable, such as grain, corn, or shares of stock. In the grain or security markets, short selling is both legally permissible and welcomed as a market-stabilizing influence. The speculator is "forced" to place a purchase order to fill short-selling positions, thereby shoring up demand when market activity might otherwise be low or even panicky.

POOR ADJUSTMENT OF SUPPLY AND DEMAND

Fixity prevents equalization of real estate supply and demand on an area, regional, or national level. Durability causes maladjustments in supply and demand on a local market level as well. Land itself is indestructible. Improvements, if properly maintained, may last a hundred years or more. Thus, where demand suddenly falls, inability to adjust (withdraw) supply causes real estate to become a drug on the market. An oversupply of space results in a buyer's market and lower values. In a similar sense, a sudden increase in demand creates a seller's market because additional space cannot be quickly built.

Supply and Demand Forces

A real estate market is sensitive to local changes in demographic, economic, political, and social forces. Among the more important local forces are the following:

1. Population: number, age-sex mix, and family composition
2. Employment and wage levels and stability of incomes
3. Personal savings, availability of mortgage funds, and levels of interest rates
4. Sales prices, rent levels, and vacancy percentage
5. Taxation rates and land-use controls, including rent controls
6. Availability and costs of land, labor, and building materials
7. Relative quality of existing structures and changes in construction technology

Population, employment, income, savings, and availability of credit combine to provide effective demand in contrast to *potential demand.* Population, by itself, represents raw or potential demand, in that the desire for land or space is without purchasing power. *Effective demand,* therefore, is desire armed with purchasing power.

POPULATION

Population is a prerequisite of demand for most types of real estate. An increase in numbers of people means increased potential demand. A decrease in population means declining demand. To become effective demand, the population must have wealth or income. For residential real estate, population is usually considered as number of households rather than as number of people.

Given population and purchasing power, demand then depends on characteristics of the population. For example, an elderly population means fewer children per household and, therefore, translates into demand for dwelling units with only one or two bedrooms. Alternatively, a community with many people under 18 years of age means strong demand for three- and four-bedroom, two-bath, dwelling units. More schools and playgrounds are also likely to be needed. A largely middle-aged population, most of whom work, is likely to translate into demand for two- and three-bedroom housing units of moderate to high value. With higher incomes, couples generally want larger and more attractive places in which to live.

WAGE LEVELS AND INCOME STABILITY

The real estate market is sensitive to changes in wage levels, employment opportunities, and stability of income. Rental payments and housing costs are closely geared to ability to pay. In fact, there are definite rules of thumb accepted by mortgage lenders and federal housing agencies under which total housing costs should not exceed 25–35 percent of the wage earner's income. Homes, too, are purchased on time-payment plans, like other consumer goods, and payments are made out of income on a monthly basis. But food, clothing, and transportation generally take priority over housing. Hence, income and employment outlook must be positive for residential space demand to be strong.

PERSONAL SAVINGS, CREDIT AVAILABILITY, AND LEVELS OF INTEREST RATES

Higher wage and salary payments are significantly reflected in the increase of total disposable personal income, which rose from $535 billion in 1960 to approximately $1,828.9 billion in 1980. During this time period, personal savings increased from $19.76 billion to $110.2 billion, more than five times. These personal savings, along with investments by financial institutions, provide a great reservoir of mortgage funds, which in turn influence mortgage credit availability and interest rate levels.

Mortgage credit availability and interest rates act as a barometer of residential real estate market activity. A tightening in the availability of money along with higher interest rates immediately and negatively influences home construction and existing home sales. Greater availability and lower interest rates have the opposite effect. Most homes are bought on credit. Terms, therefore, are an important part of a purchase transaction and often influence the transaction price. To many buyers with small equity down payments, price undoubtedly means size of monthly payments for principal, interest, insurance and taxes (PIIT).

RENT AND VACANCY LEVELS

The rental market is highly competitive. If rents are set too high in relation to servicing costs, tenants will economize on space, and vacancies will result. Housing supply cannot be withdrawn from the market, for all practical purposes. Competition to maintain full occupancy, therefore, forces prices into line. Vacancy rates exceeding 5–8 percent indicate either an oversupply or overpricing of rental space. In either case, construction cutbacks are likely until the market strengthens.

TAXATION AND LAND-USE CONTROLS

Taxation is sometimes used as a governmental tool to compel or deter real estate development or to direct employment of land for particular uses. For example, vacant land is sometimes overassessed and taxed to stimulate its improvement. Likewise, homestead laws shift municipal costs to owners of business and tenant-occupied properties. Such tax policy is directly designed to encourage homeownership and the use of land.

Land-use controls also affect real estate market operations. Tighter controls and permit requirements drive real estate prices upward and tend to discourage sales and construction.

COSTS OF LAND, LABOR, AND BUILDING MATERIALS

Availability of land and the cost of land, labor, and building materials affect real estate supply. Although physically abundant, land that is economically usable may be in short supply. Improvements in the form of access roads, drainage facilities, water, and other community utilities must ordinarily be added to "raw" land before it can be subdivided and offered for sale. Such improvements are costly and often can be successfully made only with community sanction and on a relatively large scale. Scarcity of building sites, in turn, causes upward pricing of existing properties and adversely affects market sales activity. On the other hand, speculative optimism may lead to an oversupply of improved land or space, resulting in a depressed market for months and even years.

CONSTRUCTION TECHNOLOGY AND BUILDING QUALITY

More buildings are torn down than fall down. This destruction of often physically sound structures is caused by changes in the methods of building and by building obsolescence. Rapid advances in building design and methods of construction have sparked the demand for modern homes that offer greater conveniences and, hence, greater amenities of living. Improvements in home heating, lighting, insulation, soundproofing, air conditioning, and interior design have brought about an active demand for home modernization and replacement that is likely to last for many years. Similar comments apply to commercial and industrial buildings.

Market Functions

By way of the price mechanism, the real estate market accomplishes its primary function, the exchange of space for money. Secondary functions are also performed.

1. Existing space is reallocated to alternative users based on their needs and relative ability to pay.
2. The quality and quantity of space is continually adjusted to meet changing conditions.
3. Land-use patterns are determined.
4. Price and value information is generated for the use of market participants in subsequent decisions.

The price mechanism serves to indicate values. The resulting pattern of land uses reflects the social and economic tastes and needs of the community.

REALLOCATION OF EXISTING SPACE

In a free market, property sales occur only when mutually advantageous to both buyer and seller. The buyer would rather have the property than the money. The seller prefers the money. The real estate market, therefore, reallocates property ownership and redistributes space according to the preferences of property users with financial capability.

Most sellers were buyers at one time, preferring property to the money. Through time, conditions changed to where the owner now prefers to give up ownership for money. The tax shelter provided by the property may have been largely used up. A related business may have gone bankrupt. A spouse may have died or children married and left home. Any one of these would be reason for owners to option for different space.

The reallocation function includes rentals and tax-deferred exchanges in addition to outright sales. Attention here is focused on the sales transaction because it is most common. The concerns of a renter are essentially the same as those of a buyer, except that the control of the property is gained by leasing rather than by purchase.

SPACE ADJUSTMENT

Owners change the use of properties in response to market pressures and opportunities. Remodeling and renovation may be necessary to adjust to the changing need of the market. For example, the value of a property in an office use may exceed the value of the property in its current use (residential) plus the cost of conversion. In this circumstance, a rational owner would convert the property to office space.

Likewise, if the demand for space exceeds the current supply, raw land must be subdivided and properties developed to increase the quantity of space. If, however, demand decreases and property values decline, little or no space adjustment (remodeling or new construction) is likely. Space adjustment is discussed much more fully in the next section on market operation.

INFORMATION GENERATION

Investors, lenders, managers, assessors, builders, developers, and brokers all want and use information about property sales for judgments and decisions that turn on value. An investor wishes to pay no more for a property than the amount for which a comparable property sold. On the other hand, an owner wishes to sell for no less. A lender does not want to make a loan on a property for more than it can be sold for. Managers need value information to set rent levels, assessors to establish assessed values. Builders and developers make value judgments on structures to be built or projects to be undertaken. Brokers need value information to show clients that transactions being proposed are sound. Price and value information are, therefore, important to the continuing operation and stability of the real estate market.

DETERMINATION OF LAND USES

Land-use activities differ in their profitability and, in turn, in their ability to pay for space. Location or situs greatly affect this ability to pay of various uses. Thus, uses compete for the best sites. The expectation is that the highest and best use for each site will win out in the competition. At any time, a definite pattern of land uses exists, which reflects the relative ability of users to pay for space.

Market Operation

Supply and demand interact constantly in the real estate market causing both short-run and long-run adjustments.

SUPPLY AND DEMAND DYNAMICS

The real estate market acts much like the market of economic theory in response to changes in supply and demand. Imperfections, such as lack of product standardization, long lead times for production of new supply, use of leverage, and tax shelters cause some deviations from the theory. Suggested guidelines to understand real estate market dynamics are as follows:

1. Units or types of real estate comparable in size and quality tend to sell at similar prices.
2. Prices tend to be stable if supply and demand are in balance.
3. If demand outruns existing supply, a seller's market is created, and prices advance. Higher prices cut back on the number of units demanded and, at the same time, stimulate construction of new units. Several weeks, and of-

ten several months, are required for new supply to be produced after the need is recognized. New construction will continue until supply and demand are again in balance and prices have stabilized.

4. If supply exceeds demand, as in a declining community or region, a buyer's market exists, and prices decline. Falling prices stimulate demand while discouraging new construction. Prices will continue to fall until supply and demand are again in balance.

5. Changing cost of credit has significant impact with lower interest rates stimulating demand.

SHORT-RUN ADJUSTMENTS

Space demand is much more dynamic than supply. If demand suddenly declines, the excess supply cannot be removed from the market area. On the other hand, if demand suddenly surges, additional supply cannot be provided on short notice.

For illustrative purposes, consider the housing market in a medium-sized community that is not tied to a large metropolitan area by commuters and is, therefore, independent of outside influences. An assumption of standardized housing units is made to simplify our discussion. This assumption is not too unrealistic in that any one housing unit can be substituted for another of nearly equal quality. With many market adjustments possible, no great distortion in the operation of the market needs to result. The short-run interaction among supply, demand, and price is shown in Figure 19-1.

In Figure 19-1, curve D_0 represents the original demand schedule for housing. Curve S represents the supply schedule. The vertical axis can represent either the rental or sale price of one housing unit. The horizontal axis indicates the number of housing units demanded or supplied.

The downward slope of the demand curve means that more units will be demanded at a lower price than at a higher price. The upward slope of the supply

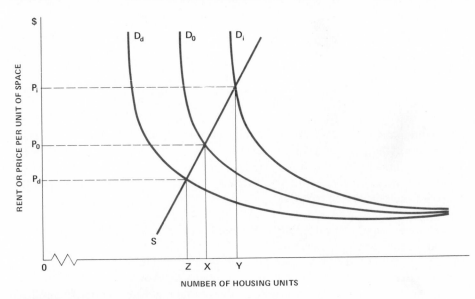

FIGURE 19-1
Short-run supply, demand, and price relationship

curve, on the other hand, says that at a high price, more housing units will be supplied than at a lower price.

Supply and demand forces are in balance at the point where curves D_0 and S intersect. The price at this point is P_0 at which level X units of housing are demanded. A sudden increase in population or income would shift the demand schedule to the right, curve D_i. Because new units cannot be readily produced, the price rises sharply to P_i. At this price, Y units are demanded and supplied. Alternatively, a decline in demand, curve D_d, would cause the price to drop to P_d, with fewer units, Z, being demanded.

A sudden increase in demand cannot greatly increase the number of housing units supplied in the short run. Several weeks would be required as a minimum to increase supply, even though the price had increase to P_i. The additional amount of supply equals Y — X. This would come about first by vacancies being absorbed. Purchase and rental prices would then increase as demand pressed on supply. Some people would use their living space more intensely by *doubling up*, that is, by crowding more people into their dwellings. The motives might be to earn more rent or to help out friends and relatives forced out of other units by higher prices. Low-income people would be forced to double up because they could not afford the higher prices. Some families would find housing in the country or in the surrounding villages, thus commuting greater distances to work. Trailers, mobile homes, and seasonal housing would also be brought in and occupied to increase the community's housing supply.

LONG-RUN ADJUSTMENTS

The cost of building new housing units enters into the long-run determination of a new equilibrium. Assume that several new industries move into our middle-sized community over a period of years. This is realistic, because many urban areas have steadily increased in population in recent decades. The successive increases in demand are represented by curves D_1 and D_2 in Figure 19-2. A long-run cost curve is also introduced in Figure 19-2 to recognize the cost of building an additional housing

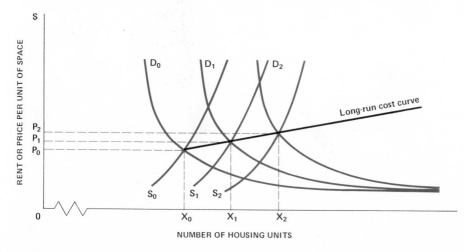

FIGURE 19-2
Long-run supply, demand, price, and cost relationships

unit. The supply curves are short run because of the long lead time needed to build additional units.

In Figure 19-2, an increase in demand, from curve D_0 to curve D_1, increases the short-run price above the marginal cost to produce an additional unit. This is represented by the intersection of curves S_0 and D_1. New housing units would be built (price exceeds cost), and eventually a new equilibrium is reached at the intersection of curves S_1 and D_1, at a price of P_1. Because the price at the intersection equals the cost of production, builders would not find it profitable to continue new construction beyond this point.

A second increase in demand, to curve D_2 (more new industry moving into town), would start the process again. With demand exceeding supply, prices again advance. Under conditions of steadily increasing demand, costs of land, labor, and building materials all tend to increase continually. That is, material suppliers and workers can bargain for higher prices and wages and almost always get the increase. Hence, the long-run cost curve slopes upward. Eventually, a new equilibrium is reached where the long-run cost curve and curves D_2 and S_2 all intersect. The new price level is P_2, whereas the number of housing units in the community has increased to X_2. The overall increase in housing units equals $X_2 - X_0$.

Little or no new construction would occur if demand decreased, that is, if the demand curve shifted to the left. The price would quickly drop below the cost curve, and no profit incentive would be present to justify starting construction of new housing units.

CYCLES?

Some analysts and authors assert that population, income, and the economy interact to produce *cycles,* or regular increases and declines in real estate sales and construction volume. Variations do occur in the level of these activities, as seasons and as economic conditions change. Seasonal changes or fluctuations are regular, with higher levels of activity usually occurring in the summer. But construction activity and real estate sales fluctuations have only limited regularity or rhythm in that they occur over periods of from 3 to 7 or more years. That is, each period of expansion and interaction seems to be unique.

Real estate construction and sales activity seem more closely related to the cost and availability of financing than to any regular cycle. For example, shortages of credit in 1966, 1969–1970, 1973–1974, and 1979–1982 pushed interest rates up, resulting in sharp cutbacks in housing starts across the United States. Thus, an investor or developer might better look to current and likely monetary policy than to regular cycles in deciding whether to take on a new project. On an overall basis, real estate construction and sales activities have been more stable in recent decades because of better fiscal and monetary policies by the federal government.

PERFECTLY COMPETITIVE?

Conditions necessary for a market to be perfectly competitive are:

1. *Freedom.* Market operates without external (government) regulation or controls.

2. *Knowledge.* All participants have complete or perfect knowledge about competing goods, prices, and future expectations.
3. *Number of participants.* Many buyers and sellers, none of which is large or powerful enough to influence the market's operation.
4. *Commodity.* Product is homogeneous, identical, or fungible, and is divisible into very small units for transactions.
5. *Mobility.* Product is readily transportable to satisfy excess demand conditions wherever and whenever they occur.

Markets range from perfect to imperfect in operation. As was indicated, a ***perfect market*** is one in which all information concerning future risks and benefits for each commodity is available to all participants. Real estate markets are generally considered to be imperfect in that full information is usually not readily available to all participants. For one thing, information costs considerable money, time, and effort to collect and analyze. Therefore, less wealthy investors find it relatively more expensive than wealthy investors to acquire information. This means that market participants have differing expectations of returns and risks from real estate and differing values for a given parcel of realty.

Several other factors act to keep real estate markets imperfect. Most properties are of large economic size with a long economic life, meaning that as a commodity, real estate is not readily divisible. Further, fixity of location of the physical property means that it is not readily transportable.

EFFICIENT MARKET?

Perfect or not, what is the efficiency of the real estate market? An ***efficient market*** is one in which changes in the information about the outlook for a given property are quickly reflected in the property's probable selling price or value. That is, favorable information about a parcel causes an immediate increase in its value, whereas negative or unfavorable information pushes its value down. In an inefficient market, participants with greater knowledge or skill can exploit other participants and thereby rapidly increase their wealth.

Research has not provided a clear answer to the question. One thing seems sure, information is generally captured and disseminated rather slowly in real estate markets. But once information is known, the value expectations of participants is influenced. This suggests relative inefficiency in that those able to gain the greatest knowledge are also able to gain the greatest advantage in the market. This conclusion provides an extremely strong reason to study and follow cause and effect market indicators in investment real estate.

Local Market Indicators

Market information is extremely important to an investor considering the development or purchase of a property. Levels of prices and values are uncertain and risky; they do not rise and fall in regular cycles. Uncertainty and risk may be reduced, however, by monitoring and interpreting local market indicators. Key market indicators for housing are discussed here. These same indicators may aid in interpreting change in other submarkets as well. The housing market is used as an example here because it is larger and more familiar and has more transactions.

Supply and demand and market theory, already discussed, must be understood to interpret these indicators. As buyers and sellers, most of us are opportunists, with a desire to buy low and sell high. Reading indicators enables us to follow this maximizing strategy better, insofar as it is possible. In short, market indicators help us identify "buyers'" and "sellers'" markets, possibly before they occur. But buyers must sometimes purchase in a sellers' market, and sellers must sometimes sell in a buyers' market. The result is that prices advance or decline according to the relative strengths of the supply and demand forces.

Four groups or categories of indicators are identified here. The basis of these groups are (1) demand, (2) supply-demand interaction, (3) financing, and (4) construction or new supply. (See Figure 19-3.) Supply indicators are conspicuous by their absence as a group, even though 95–97 percent of the space that influences market activity in any year already exists at the beginning of the year. Demand is the dynamic force in real estate markets. Trends, rates of change, and direction of change in these various indicators provide the most important information.

DEMAND INDICATORS

The four key demand indicators are (1) population, (2) employment, (3) unemployment, and (4) per capita personal income. Trends in these indicators tell a great deal about likely changes in effective demand.

CATEGORY AND ITEMS	SOURCES
1.Demand	
a. Population	Population center, Chamber of Commerce
b. Employment	Local U.S. Department of Labor office
c. Unemployment	Local U.S. Department of Labor office
d. Personal income per capita (wage levels)	Census data, local U.S. Department of Labor office
2.Supply-demand interaction	
a. Sales prices	Comparison of standard house with local sales prices
b. Rent levels	Comparison in market
c. Vacancy rate/utilization rate	Surveys, personal observation
d. Sales volume	Multiple listing service reports, want ads
3.Finance	
a. Relative availability of money	Survey of local lenders
b. Costs of money; interest rates	Survey of local lenders
c. Prime rate	News reports, local lenders
d. Foreclosure rates	Lenders, courthouse records
4.New supply	
a. Subdivision activity	Plat records, court house
b. Building permits	Local housing office/Dodge reports
c. Construction volume	Contractors, news reports
d. Construction costs	Contractors

FIGURE 19-3
Local real estate market indicators

Obviously, increases in population mean increased desire for housing. And an increase in employment, along with high levels of employment, indicates economic growth and is likely to result in immigration of additional workers and population. Per capita personal income tells how much purchasing power is available for housing. Declines in population and income obviously mean decreased effective demand.

Many states have population centers, usually at a major university, from which population data may be obtained. The U.S. Department of Labor provides employment, unemployment, and wage (income) information for most communities. Planning commissions and chambers of commerce often publish reports containing population and labor force information. And most newspapers periodically publish reviews and comments on the economic outlook for their area and region.

SUPPLY-DEMAND INTERACTION

Price levels, vacancy rates, sales volumes, and rent levels tell what is happening in regard to supply-demand interaction in local real estate. Information on these variables must generally be captured personally in that such data are not published on a regular basis.

Price-level information may be obtained by comparing prices for certain "standard" houses through time. That is, typical two-, three-, and four-bedroom houses might be priced on a comparative basis every few months. In like manner, rent levels for one-, two-, and three-bedroom apartments might be checked. The checking might concern asking prices or rents in want ads for dwelling units offered for sale or rent. Also, a summary of completed transactions published monthly by a multiple listing service could serve as a source of price information. Sales volume may also be estimated from this summary. A further indication of sales activity is the volume of deeds recorded by a county recorder. Again, trends and rates of change are vital information.

Vacancy rates tell what portion of the existing supply of space is not being used. Thus, the rate of property use in a community is the complement or flip side of the vacancy rate. Post office surveys are sometimes made to determine vacancy rates. Checks with property managers and monitoring want ads may also indicate vacancy levels. New, unsold houses must also be counted as vacancies. An increasing vacancy rate foretells a weakening in prices or rents, while a declining rate suggests that rents and prices are likely to advance.

FINANCE INDICATORS

Key finance indicators concern the relative availability of money, the prime rate, local mortgage interest rate quotations, and the mortgage foreclosure rate.

The *prime rate* is the rate that major commercial banks charge large, well-established, financially sound companies on business loans. The rate tends to be uniform across the country and, in a sense, ties all financial markets together. An increase in the prime rate indicates a tightening in the money markets, while a decrease indicates easier money. Changes in the prime rate are widely quoted in the financial news. A change in the prime rate usually precedes a comparable shift in mortgage interest rates.

Mortgage foreclosure rates tell of failures of borrowers to live up to their mortgage contracts. Deaths and divorces, two major causes, tend to be relatively stable through time in their incidence while unemployment fluctuates. Thus, a sudden increase in foreclosures is likely to be preceded by layoffs and declining economic conditions. Foreclosures translate into a decline in demand, at least in the short run.

NEW SUPPLY INDICATORS

Development and construction mean increases in the supply of real estate. Developers and builders generally add to supply only if they expect sales prices or market values to exceed costs. Starting construction of a new building means that an aspiring homeowner or investor has decided that value exceeds cost. In the short run, construction may continue as a builder strives to keep a crew going, in spite of discouraging market outlook. Key statistics in this area are subdivision activity, building permits, construction volume, and construction costs.

Subdivision requires several months to a year from plat approvals to market availability of sites. Housing construction may take only from 2 to 3 months. Construction does not always follow immediately after the taking out of a building permit. Thus, lags must be taken into account in interpreting development and construction indicators.

Building permits and dollar construction value tell of short-term increases in supply. These increases must be related to indicated effective demand. Subdivision activity indicates that the long-run outlook is more promising. Increasing costs of construction result in higher costs of space. In turn, the cost of new space is at the margin; any increases tend to spread over the entire existing supply, given time. Ever-higher costs means that less space is likely to be demanded and used.

INTERRELATEDNESS OF INDICATORS

Real estate supply and demand forces exert pressures in many directions. Increasing births or incomes translate into greater demand. At the same time, out-migration to better opportunities elsewhere decreases demand. Thus, supply and demand forces are interrelated in their effects. Market prices and sales volume are the result of these and many other conditions. Likewise, market indicators may not all point in the same direction. The investor-analyst must read and interpret the signs provided by indicators on a continuing basis.

Questions for Review and Discussion

1. Name at least two submarkets for each of the following market types of real estate: (a) residential, (b) commercial, (c) industrial, (d) agricultural, and (e) special purpose.
2. List and describe briefly at least four characteristics that make real estate markets relatively unique.

3. List and describe briefly four demand and four supply forces of local estate markets.

4. Describe briefly short-run and long-run adjustments in real estate markets. Illustrate with supply-demand diagrams.

5. Explain the need for market indicators.

6. Name and briefly discuss the nature of two market indicators in each of these four categories: (a) demand, (b) supply-demand interaction, (c) finance, and (d) new supply.

7. Identify and briefly describe three functions of real estate markets.

8. Would we need an urban real estate market if we did not have ownership rights in real property? Discuss.

9. Property owners sometimes oppose community growth even though values generally go up as a result of growth. Is this rational? Explain.

10. In earlier chapters we noted that real estate has characteristics of heterogeneity, durability, and interdependence. What implications do these characteristics have relative to stability in the real estate market? (Think hard, this is a tough one.)

20

Real Estate Market and Feasibility Analysis

He reads much; he is a great observer, and he looks quite through the deeds of men

William Shakespeare, Julius Caesar

An investor wants market and feasibility information before purchasing a large apartment complex to get assurance that the outlook for the property is sound as well as to have a basis for judging the amount to be bid for the property. A developer would use such a market study to judge whether a new shopping center is needed and where. Assuming justification, the study helps a lender to decide how large a loan may be made to finance its development. Further, tenants may be attracted to the center on the basis of the study conclusions. Finally, the study might be helpful in obtaining necessary approvals from planning officials or an owner might want such a market study to ascertain whether a property is being put to its highest and best use and merchandised to greatest advantage.

A real estate *market analysis* is a study to predict changes in the amount and types of real estate facilities needed in an area. The emphasis is usually on urban space needs, that is, on residential, retail trade, office, and industrial space needs. The time horizon used varies from 1 or 2 years to 10 years or more. The larger the probable need and size of investment, the longer the study horizon is likely to be. A market study is a management tool for decision making as well as for planning and budgeting.

Market and feasibility analysis is in its early stages of development; years will probably be required to refine the concepts, methodology, and applications. In the meantime, much judgment will be required of the analyst and the decision maker. The discussion here assumes that accurate, realistic information is desired and not a report to justify an action or development about which a decision has already been made.

Important Topics or Decision Areas Covered in This Chapter

Feasibility Analysis
Owner Looking for a Use
User Looking for a Site
Investor Looking for a Profit Opportunity

Urban Change and Market Analysis
Economic Change and Land Use
The Study Framework

Market Area Delineation

Economic Base Analysis
Identifying the Economic Base
Base Projections

Supply-Demand Analysis
Supply Factors
Demand Factors

Current Market Conditions
Unsold Inventory, Prices, and Construction Costs
Vacancies and Rent Levels
Mortgage Defaults and Foreclosures

Market Study Conclusions

Questions for Review and Discussion

Case Problem

Key Concepts Introduced in This Chapter

Base activity

Comparative economic advantage

Economic base

Feasibility analysis

Locational quotient

Market analysis

Service activity

Feasibility Analysis

An economic base and market study provide the foundation for a feasibility study and therefore must be completed prior to the making of a feasibility study. At the same time, property-specific information for investment and management decisions, as provided by a feasibility study, is generally the overall objective. That is, the decision about the property is what all the studies are about. Thus, the nature and content of a feasibility study is taken up first.

Feasibility analysis is the study of the practicality of a specific investment or development proposal and is an extension of the generality of the economic base and market analysis. Included is a study of the profit potential in a proposed project, with market, physical, locational, legal, social, governmental, and financial factors taken into account. A project is considered feasible only if expected value exceeds the cost or necessary cash investment.

A major purpose of a feasibility analysis is to enable a decision maker to minimize risks while getting the greatest possible benefits. Everyone involved in an investment situation expects to benefit. A property owner wants to realize as much profit or value increase as possible. A user, who may be the owner, wants a property in a location that best serves his or her needs. Any broker, architect, engineer, contractor, lender, or attorney involved expects to receive reasonable fees or commissions.

Feasibility analysis applies to three basic situations:

1. An owner of a site or property looking for a use
2. A user looking for a site or a property with improvements well suited to his or her needs
3. An investor or developer looking for the best profit opportunity available, with the pulling in of other equity investors or getting support from a mortgage lender a possibility

OWNER LOOKING FOR A USE

Costs must be incurred in developing a site or modifying an improved property to suit the needs of a proposed use. The problem is to find a use able to generate enough value or benefits from the completed project to justify the costs. An office building might be constructed on a site at a total cost of $8,400,000, for example. The present value of future rents or benefits must equal or exceed $8,400,000 for the project to be feasible. See the calculations in Chapter 18 on highest and best use.

Maybe a developer has an option to buy an old abandoned cannery for $1 million. The property is located near the waterfront, which is a major tourist attraction. The developer is considering converting the cannery into a tourist shopping center at an additional cost of $2 million. The value in the new use must equal or exceed $3 million to justify the project. Thus, cost must be bumped against expected value.

The process of feasibility analysis in the case of a site looking for a use begins with selection of the three or four or more most likely uses for the property. The total cost involved in preparing the site or property for each use is then determined. Categories of costs include

1. Cost of site, or market value if already owned
2. Site preparation costs: soil tests, grading, landscaping
3. Fees of architects, engineers, attorneys
4. Brokerage commissions
5. Construction costs of improvements
6. Financing charges
7. Developer's profit
8. All other costs incidental to the development of the project

The project is feasible if a reliable tenant can be found to pay a rent high enough to justify the costs. It is feasible also if the owner expects personally to use the property and considers the costs reasonable and within his or her financial capacity. If the project is to be rented to many tenants, the market analysis must show that sufficient effective demand exists. If conversion or rehabilitation is involved, the higher rents must be sufficient to justify the costs of modification.

A feasibility analysis of an owner looking for a use ends with the selection of the use giving the greatest value to the site, which use is, of course, its highest and best use. For example, alternative uses might indicate site values as follows: office building, $200,000; department store, $180,000; and hotel, $140,000. The owner, acting in self-interest, would almost certainly choose to construct the office building.

USER LOOKING FOR A SITE

A user values a property for the returns it will yield; the costs of renting or owning must be less than the present value of the benefits to be realized. For example, after analysis of his or her situation, a merchant decides that the highest rent he or she can pay for a certain store is $54,000 a year. The owner wants $60,000. The property is not a feasible alternative for the merchant. In a second example, a developer estimates that apartment rental levels justify a value of $40,000 per dwelling unit on a certain site. The site would cost $8,000 per unit, and improvement costs are estimated at $30,000 per unit. The $40,000 value exceeds the costs of $38,000; the project is feasible.

A user begins with the results of a market analysis and estimates the amount of unsatisfied demand available in the area. Several alternative sites are analyzed, based on their availability and suitability for the use under study. Street patterns and traffic flows, lot size, location, zoning, actual or potential building size and shape, and neighborhood quality would be important considerations in the analysis of the sites. On the basis of specific characteristics of each site, the amount of business to be conducted, gross sales to be realized, is estimated. From this, the amount of annual rental that can be paid for the property, or the capitalized value of the rents, is calculated. The site or property best serving the user's needs is selected, assuming the asking rent or price is less than that which the owner can afford to pay, based on the analysis.

An owner should be more concerned with highest and best use than a tenant. A user-renter may well take a better property and location than his or her purposes justifies if the asking rent is acceptable. Selection of the site that best meets the needs of the user ends the search.

INVESTOR LOOKING FOR A PROFIT OPPORTUNITY

An investor may use market and feasibility analyses to locate, and to choose between, profit opportunities. In the simplest situation, the investor may be trying to select the best of two or three investment properties available. The use and sites have already been joined into a going operation. The techniques for analysis and comparison in this situation are discussed in Chapters 24 and 25. The more investment value exceeds asking price, the greater is the profit opportunity.

In a more complex situation, an investor-developer may strive to join uses and sites for profits. Thus, the investors may determine from market analysis that demand for a supermarket exists in a neighborhood. Search produces the two or three best sites, which are tied up on options. The investor then approaches supermarket chains to induce one of them to locate a store on one of the sites under option. The effort ends when the store is built and put into operation, yielding a large commission or profit to the investor.

Urban Change and Market Analysis

Urban areas constantly change, usually expanding, though, in some cases, decline and contraction do set in. All sectors of expanding areas do not share equally in the growth. The important considerations are when, where, and what types of change will take place. Economic base and market studies are important in assessing such situations.

ECONOMIC CHANGE AND LAND USE

An urban area grows and expands because its economic base grows and expands. An *economic base* is made up of those activities that export goods and services outside the community in return for money or income. The economic base provides employment and income on which the remainder of the local economy depends. This remainder, often called service activity, expands and contracts in direct relation to changes in base activities.

A local economy that is expanding attracts additional workers and population. With increased economic activity and population, the space needs of the area or community also increase. Thus, the market function of space adjustment is called into play, which takes place in two major ways. One is essentially growth outward; the other is growth upward.

Land Development. In Chapter 18 we identified adding improvements to raw or vacant land as growth at the extensive margin. Vacant parcels, usually at the urban fringe, are constantly upgraded to productive urban sites. Examples are the construction of shopping centers, industrial plants, or stadiums in previously open fields. Subdivision of open land with subsequent construction of houses is a second example.

Land-Use Succession. Urban change, by way of land-use succession, also takes place at the intensive margin. Urban areas are dynamic; the use of land and the improvements to the land tend to be in a constant state of flux. The changes came about in one or more of the following ways:

1. *Change in type of use.* A large old house being converted into an office building represents a change in the type of use; so also is the tearing down of a gasoline service station to make way for an apartment house. A change in the type of use involves the modification of an existing structure or its replacement by new improvements. The new use must be able to absorb the cost of conversion or replacement to be profitable and feasible.

2. *Change in intensity of use.* Adding another story to increase display and sales area is an intensity of use change. Converting a large, old, single-family residence into several small apartment units is also. Although the type of use is not changed, the amount of economic or social activity on the site is modified. If the intensity is increased, the additional benefits must be great enough to justify the costs of necessary structural modifications.

3. *Change in quality of use.* The nature of the benefits of use of a property may be upgraded or downgraded. Creeping blight leads to the gradual deterioration in the benefits from a residential neighborhood or a commercial area. The rehabilitation of the Georgetown area in Washington, D.C., on the other hand, is an excellent example of improving the quality of use. Upgrading the quality of use depends on an explicit act of a manager or owner taking advantage of a favorable set of environmental conditions for the property.

As was discussed in Chapter 18, these changes tend to occur along the lines of least economic resistance or in the direction in which values realized exceed costs incurred by the greatest amount for the additional space gained. For an economist, this is another way of saying that marginal growth occurs where the marginal profit is greatest.

THE STUDY FRAMEWORK

Several distinct phases are involved in making a market study. A decision regarding the type of real estate of concern—office space, warehousing, or apartments—is presumed to have been made before entry into these steps. An awareness of the relation of the national and regional economy to the local economy is also taken as a given.

1. *Market-area delineation.* The market area is largely determined by the range of influence or competitiveness of the type of real estate under consideration. A housing study might cover one community, for example. On the other hand, a study for a regional shopping center might extend for 50–75 miles from a study site.

2. *Analysis of the area's economy.* Analysis of an area's basic resources, employment, income, population, and economic trends provides a setting for later detailed consideration of real estate needs. This is commonly called an economic base analysis.

3. *Supply and demand analysis.* Real estate supply and demand factors are identified, followed by data collection and evaluation. Supply factors ordinarily include an inventory of space, plus current new construction, conversion, and demolition activity. Common demand factors are age-sex distribution of the population, per capita disposable income levels, and family size.

4. *Analysis of current market conditions.* Current market conditions reflect the interaction of the supply and demand factors. Thus, such items as prices and construction costs, rent levels and vacancies, and the availability and costs of financing must be considered as they relate to the specific type of real estate under study.

5. *Projections and conclusions.* Conclusions about the relative strength of market demand currently and into the future must be reached. The types of

space needed at various prices or rent levels must be identified. Finally, a judgment on the share of the market that can be captured must be reached.

6. *Feasibility analysis.* A feasibility analysis makes a market study more specific, as was already discussed.

A market study is best conducted by an experienced analyst in that identifying and measuring significant variables is quite difficult. Even collecting existing data on important factors for a complete market and feasibility analysis is difficult, time consuming, and expensive. The decision maker's research budget is usually quite limited. Therefore, the intensity of emphasis given to each of the phases depends on the availability of data and on the size and type of decision to be made.

Market Area Delineation

The range of competition of the type of real estate under study determines the market area. Criteria for defining a market area include physical, social, legal, and economic elements. These change from one type of use to another. The importance given to each depends on the situation. Several brief examples illustrate the difficulty of the problem and how judgment must be used in delineating a study area.

Competition is communitywide for housing, except possibly in the largest metropolitan areas. People working in the central business district may live by themselves or with their families in a downtown apartment or a one-family suburban house. Workers in suburban factories, shopping centers, and offices are somewhat more likely to live near the urban fringe than in the central city. Therefore, the analysis of demand must be communitywide. The analyst can make some judgments about needs for apartments versus one-family homes and about needs for middle-income housing versus high-income housing to narrow the scope of the study. Even so, the market area continues to be communitywide.

By way of contrast, the market study area for a supermarket might be limited to a trade area or neighborhood. Groceries tend to be convenience goods; that is, people buy them on their way home from work, or, if they begin the shopping trip from their home, they usually go to one of the two or three nearest stores. Knowing this, the analyst can establish a trade area based on several considerations.

1. *Neighborhood boundaries.* Major streets and highways, freeways, railroad tracks, large parks, reservoirs, rivers, lakes, and steep hills may all to serve as boundaries between neighborhoods.
2. *Social and economic groupings.* Neighborhoods tend to be made up of people of similar tastes and income levels. Observation of people's dress, cars, and housing gives a clue as to the extent of the similarity. Similar information can be obtained from census tract data.
3. *Travel patterns.* Mode of travel affects where people buy food. Thus, street and traffic patterns for motor vehicles and public transit become important in delineating the trade area.

Another example would be the market area for a regional shopping center. People will drive a hundred miles, and sometimes farther, to shop. Hence, this is the trade area and the area of competition.

Finally, competition for office and industrial space occurs on a regional and national basis. In locating a new plant or relocating its main office, a major corporation may weigh relative merits of several cities like New York, Chicago, Houston, Los Angeles, and Atlanta.

Economic Base Analysis

Communities, areas, or regions tend to grow or decline in direct proportion to some particular economic advantage they possess relative to the rest of the country and world, which is termed their *comparative economic advantage*. The activities providing this advantage, which results in exports of goods and services in return for money, are collectively called the *economic base* of a community or area. The economic base is sometimes considered the product for which a community is famous, such as cars in Detroit.

Decision makers specialize in industries giving the greatest comparative advantage over time to maximize benefits or profits. This is the reason western Oregon and Washington excel in producing quality lumber, primarily Douglas fir, for export. Iowa farmers grow corn and soybeans rather than wheat or rice because the net returns per acre on the farm are greatest. Recreation and retirement have been built into major industries in Florida, Arizona, and southern California because their climate is preferred to that of most other states.

IDENTIFYING THE ECONOMIC BASE

Economic activity is generally identified and measured in terms of employment, income, or business earnings. If U.S. census data are used as a source, employment is most often used because it is more easily available and is more easily translated into population and demand for real estate. However, the Bureau of Economic Analysis of the U.S. Department of Commerce publishes reports that provide personal income, business earnings, and employment data, including projections. Data used in this chapter are from the U.S. Census Bureau.

In a base study, economic activity is divided into two categories: base and service or base and nonbase. *Base activity* produces goods or services that are exported to the outside world in return for money, which in turn is used to buy other goods and services from the outside world. The exchange enables the community or area to survive and to continue as an independent entity. Naturally enough, nonbasic or *service activity* produces goods or services for local consumption or use. That is, they are not exported. Base activity is also sometimes termed primary activity. In this event, service activity becomes secondary activity.

But how can base activity be identified? Frequently, people "know what the base is" and presumably can easily identify base activity. In fact, the problem is not so simple. For example, should a department store, a bakery, a service station, and a university be classified as base or service activities? The answer depends considerably on the size of the community or area being studied.

Almost all economic activity in the United States is service in that less than 5 percent of our production is exported. If the study unit is a relatively small city of 50,000 people, the answer is more difficult. To the extent that an activity satisfies the needs of a portion of the 50,000, it is a service. But to the extent that the department store draws farmers as customers or bakery goods are trucked to neighboring communities, the store and bakery are basic. Likewise, a service station, located on a highway and catering to through traffic, is basic. If a university draws students and funds from outside the city, it contributes to the economic base of the city.

A *locational quotient* (LQ) is commonly used to distinguish between base and service portions of economic activity. An LQ is the percentage of total local activity in an industry relative to the percentage of total national activity in the same industry. For example, using 1980 industry employment as the measure, the locational quotient of the Oregon lumber and wood products industry is calculated as follows.

$$\begin{array}{l} \text{Percentage of industry employment} \\ \text{for Oregon for the lumber and} \\ \text{wood products industry} \end{array} = \frac{74,308}{1,138,425} \times 100 = 6.53\%$$

$$\begin{array}{l} \text{Percentage of industry employment} \\ \text{for the United States for the} \\ \text{lumber and wood products industry} \end{array} = \frac{1,229,394}{97,639,355} \times 100 = 1.26\%$$

$$LQ = \frac{\begin{array}{c}\text{percentage of Oregon business employment}\\\text{from the lumber and wood products industry}\end{array}}{\begin{array}{c}\text{percentage of U.S. business employment}\\\text{from the lumber and wood products industry}\end{array}} = \frac{6.53\%}{1.26\%} = 5.18$$

An LQ of 1 would mean that Oregon provided employment in the lumber and wood products industry at the same rate as the entire U.S. industry, on average. Hence, the industry, on balance, would be service only. A locational quotient of less than 1 would mean that Oregon did not meet its needs from this industry and, hence, had to import lumber and wood products. In actuality, the LQ is 5.18, meaning that Oregon produces over five times its needs in lumber and wood products. Obviously, the industry is very important to the economic base of Oregon.

Other LQs are shown in Figure 20-1. Note the LQ of 8.9 for the Eugene-Springfield Standard Metropolitan Statistical Area (SMSA). At the other extreme, the very low LQ in mining says that Oregon does not produce its proportional share of oil and minerals. Finally, note that nonbase activities such as trade, transportation, public administration, and services all have LQs very near 1.

BASE PROJECTIONS

An analyst, working with employment data only, might project employment to 1990 based on trends and other information available.

The employment projection would then convert into population by dividing by the expected proportion of employment to population for the projection year. Typically, the proportion is about 42 percent and is slowly rising because of an increasing percentage of women working. Thus, a 1990 projection of 130,000 workers for a

MAJOR INDUSTRY GROUP	UNITED STATES		STATE OF OREGON			EUGENE-SPRINGFIELD SMSA		
	NUMBER EMPLOYED (000)	PERCENT DISTRI-BUTION	NUMBER EMPLOYED	PERCENT DISTRI-BUTION	INDUSTRY LOCATIONAL QUOTIENT	NUMBER EMPLOYED	PERCENT DISTRI-BUTION	INDUSTRY LOCATIONAL QUOTIENT
Agri., forestry, & fisheries	2,914	2.98%	52,302	4.59%	1.54	3,752	3.20%	1.07
Mining	1,028	1.05%	2,699	0.24%	0.23	239	0.20%	0.19
Construction	5,740	5.88%	73,250	6.43%	1.09	6,668	5.68%	0.97
Manufacturing	21,915	22.44%	222,017	19.50%	0.87	21,804	18.57%	0.83
Durable goods: total	13,479	13.81%	168,424	14.79%	1.07	17,513	14.91%	1.08
Lbr. & W. Prod.	1,229	1.26%	74,308	6.53%	5.18	13,155	11.20%	8.90
Primary Metal Industries								
Fabricated Metal Industries								
Machinery, except Electrical								
Electrical Machinery								
Motor vehicles & other trans. eq.								
Other durable goods								
Non-durable goods: total	8,436	8.64%	53,593	4.71%	0.54	4,291	3.65%	0.42
Food & Kindred products								
Textile mill & fabricated products								
Printing, publishing, & Allied								
Chemical & allied products								
Other non-durable goods								
Transport, comm., & pub. utilities	7,087	7.26%	81,621	7.17%	0.99	7,850	6.69%	0.92
Wholesale trade	4,217	4.32%	53,277 0	4.68%	1.08	5,127	4.37%	1.01
Retail trade	15,717	16.10%	203,220	17.85%	1.11	23,211	19.77%	1.23
Finance, ins. & real estate	5,898	6.04%	71,228	6.26%	1.04	6,465	5.51%	0.91
Services	27,976	28.65%	321,809	28.27%	0.99	37,129	31.62%	1.10
Public administration	5,147	5.27%	57,002	5.01%	0.95	5,176	4.41%	0.84
TOTAL	97,639	100.00%	1,138,425	100.00%		117,421	100.00%	

SOURCE: Employment data from U.S. census; calculations by authors.

FIGURE 20-1
Employment, employment distribution by industry, and location quotients for the U.S., the State of Oregon, and the Eugene-Springfield SMSA, 1980

community such as Eugene-Springfield would mean an expected population of about 310,000 people.

Many local planning commissions make economic base analysis studies and projections. Thus, unless an investor has a specific need and is willing to pay for information, the data sources mentioned may be used.

Supply-Demand Analysis

Each land use has its own unique determinants of supply and demand. Supply determinants are mainly physical and economic, whereas demand determinants tend to be more social and economic. Note that the supply and demand factors discussed here are those identified in Chapter 19.

SUPPLY FACTORS

The existing inventory of space for the use under study marks the point of beginning in considering determinants of supply. At best, new construction increases the total supply from 2 to 3 percent in any 1 year. With strong demand, the amount of space for a specific use, other than housing, can be doubled or tripled in 1 year, however, by the conversion of space from alternative uses in less demand.

An example will make the point clearer. In 1970, the United States had about 75 million dwelling units. The construction industry, operating at peak capacity, could add about 2.5 million units in 1 year. During the same year, about 300,000 units would be removed because of fire, flood, urban renewal, street and highway projects, and miscellaneous factors. The net added to the supply is, therefore, about 2.2 million units, just slightly less than a 3 percent increase.

To extend the example, assume that housing represents 50 percent of the total supply of space. Assume further that commercial office space represents 10 percent of the total supply of space. This means that supply of office space could be increased approximately five times faster than supply of housing, with the same input of resources. All housing construction activities would have to be redirected toward creating new office space. If the demand were strong enough, apartment buildings, houses, warehouses, and garages might be modified to increase the supply of office space. Although the example is highly unlikely, the net result might be to double the amount of office space in 1 year. Our example can be extended further by narrowing the use; that is, the supply of office space for public accountants could be increased several times with little effect on the supply of space for other needs.

In a similar sense, the supply of space in Madison, Wisconsin, can be increased sharply by shifting contractors, workers, and materials from surrounding communities. Milwaukee, Wisconsin, Chicago, Illinois, and Rockford, Illinois, the nearby communities, might grow at a slightly lower rate as a result.

The principal considerations in increasing space supply are as follows:

1. The availability and costs of land and utilities
2. The availability and costs of materials and labor

3. The availability and costs of financing
4. The availability and willingness of a developer to organize these factors toward manufacturing new space.

DEMAND FACTORS

The economic base is the primary determinant of space needs in a community. The essential variables are employment, population, and income. The function of the real estate market analysis is to relate the type and amount of economic activity to the specific type of space or use under study. The spending pattern of the population provides a means of relating population, income, and land use.

The recent spending pattern of the U.S. population, by product or service, is shown in Figure 20-2. Each of the items purchased represents some type of real estate improvement. Food, beverages, clothing, and furniture are distributed through stores, for example. Housing is purchased directly or rented. Medical and other services are dispensed through doctors' offices, clinics, and hospitals. By applying these percentages to a community's income, as determined in the base analysis, the amount of money available to each land use may be estimated.

Effective demand must be more specifically related to land use and location. For example, if the population is young and families are small, demand for living units in multifamily structures is likely to be relatively stronger. A few figures show the importance of age distribution in the population. In 1960, when family units usually included two or three children, only 22.8 percent of new housing starts were in multifamily structures. By 1970, the children were growing up and leaving the nest, and this proportion doubled to 45.2 percent. By 1980, the percentage had declined to 31.1 percent as the "baby boom" generation paired up to have families and children of their own.

	Current Dollars	Percent Distribution
Durable goods		
Motor vehicles and parts	$ 149.8	6.40
Furniture and household equipment	117.0	5.00
Other	52.0	2.22
Nondurable goods		
Food, beverages, including alcoholic, and tobacco	$ 474.4	20.26
Clothing, accessories, including jewelry	165.5	7.07
Gasoline and oil	91.4	3.90
Other	125.6	5.36
Services		
Housing	$ 397.9	16.99
Household operation	164.0	7.00
Transportation	78.3	3.34
Other	526.0	22.46
Total	$2,341.9	100.00

SOURCE: *Statistical Abstract of the U.S.*, Table 728, 1986

FIGURE 20-2
U.S. spending patterns, by category, 1984 (billions)

Current Market Conditions

Current market conditions are the result of the interaction of supply and demand in the past. The important indicators of current market conditions are unsold inventory and rental vacancies, prices and construction costs, and mortgage defaults and foreclosures. Many of these are the same as the market indicators identified and discussed in Chapter 19, but here we are concerned with their use in market analysis. With strong demand, unsold inventory, rental vacancies, and mortgage defaults should be down. Prices and construction costs are likely to be up or increasing. With weak demand, they are likely to point in the opposite direction.

UNSOLD INVENTORY, PRICES, AND CONSTRUCTION COSTS

Prices must exceed total construction costs for new construction to be justified. If new houses sell for $25 a square foot and costs are $23, a contractor will continue to build these units. However, if not all units sell, an inventory of unsold units develops. The increasing inventory should eventually drive prices down and signal the contractor to slow the rate of construction. Of course, units selling quickly and a very low inventory signal strong demand and the need for more construction. The shorter the time horizon of the study, the more important these signals become.

VACANCIES AND RENT LEVELS

Vacancies are the equivalent of unsold inventory. If the amount of vacant space builds up, rent levels should fall, and construction of new space should be slowed or stopped. Thus, for example, an office building developer might note an increase in the amount of unused office space and lower or not increase asking rental prices. On the other hand, an apartment house manager might note low vacancies and use the occasion to raise rents. Projected demand for an area must be reduced to the extent that vacancies exist because the vacant space is the equivalent of newly constructed space for market purposes.

MORTGAGE DEFAULTS AND FORECLOSURES

A small percentage of mortgages are constantly in default because of death, divorce, or other financial difficulty of mortgagors. But not all defaults end up in foreclosure. If conditions are not too severe, a borrower can usually find someone to take over the property, thus avoiding foreclosure. If current market conditions are extremely severe, lenders may have to take over a number of properties. The latter would be a strong signal that the market is down, and construction of new housing units should not be started until economic conditions improve.

A real estate market analysis should end with estimates of demand and competition for the use under study. The study may be extended to include a feasibility analysis. The report should be written in a clear and concise manner, with the data and the discussion logically leading the reader to the conclusions. Short- and long-run market outlooks should be blended into the discussion.

As we shall see in Chapters 21 to 25 on real estate valuation and investment, the market study conclusions provide the basis for projecting cash flows and the resale value of a property under study. If the market outlook is for decline or no growth, the productivity and income of the subject property is likely to hold fast or even to decline. Thus, market study conclusions are critical to the advisability and value levels of real estate investments.

Questions for Review and Discussion

1. Explain briefly the nature of a real estate market study and the uses of a study to a developer, an investor or owner, and a prospective tenant. In other words, why analyze the real estate market?
2. Explain why urban areas grow and change? Then, distinguish among changes in intensity of use, quality of use, and type of use relative to land use succession.
3. List the six phases of a market study in sequence, and explain each phase briefly.
4. What considerations enter into delineating a market area?
5. In economic base analysis, what is a locational quotient? Explain the use of an LQ in identifying the economic base of a community.
6. Identify and explain briefly at least three supply and three demand factors of supply and demand analysis.
7. Identify and explain briefly the three types of situations for which feasibility analysis is suited.
8. Does a market study remove all the risk from a project for a developer or an investor? Discuss.
9. Is there a relationship among a market study, a feasibility study, and the highest and best use of a property? Explain.
10. What special factors would warrant consideration in making a market analysis for an office building? A shopping center? A supermarket? A warehouse?

Case Problem

(Environmental and market considerations are combined in this case. Thus, elements of this and the previous three chapters are involved. National economic and political conditions at the time of discussion provide the broader setting for this case and should be taken into account.)

Your aunt recently died and willed you 31 acres of land on State Highway 33 connecting Sun City and Parkridge, two rapidly growing communities in the Sun Belt. The property has been in your aunt's family for over 110 years.

The 31 acres is actually made up of two parcels on opposite sides of Highway 33. The southern parcel contains 7 acres, has a cotton mill and an old pole-type warehouse on it, and is bordered on the east by Avion Way that comes off the highway and provides direct access to the airport. Avion Way is scheduled to be widened to four lanes with a center boulevard during the next year. Also, a railway line runs along the property's southern edge. It is doubtful that the improvements are consistent with today's highest and best use of the parcel. The larger parcel is vacant, except for an old farmhouse where your aunt lived, fronts on Highway 33 for .25 mile, and is bordered on both the eastern and western sides by public streets.

Highway 33 carries considerable traffic. The parcels along it generally range in size from .5 acre to 3 acres, with mostly mixed residential and highway commercial uses. Within 5 miles are many single family residences, apartment buildings, commercial and office buildings, medical buildings, two colleges and a state university, several churches, and a large county park. The metropolitan airport, recently expanded, is about 3 miles to the south, just beyond the East-West Interstate Highway.

The central business district of Sun City, population 210,000 and 8 miles to the east, is undergoing a major face lift as part of an urban renewal project. The Jackson County courthouse is in Sun City. Downtown Parkridge, population 80,000, is 4 miles to the west. Parkridge is the more rapidly growing of the two cities. The cities are growing toward each other, for the most part. Most industrial expansion of consequence in the last 2 decades has been south of the interstate highway and the airport in unincorporated areas. Several high-technology firms have built plants there in recent years. Thus, the location of the parcels appears to preclude their being developed for industrial purposes.

Taxes on the two parcels amount to about $30,000 per year, or $2,500 per month. The net income from operation of the mill has been sporadic; in fact, it is likely that the mill has been operating in the red since your aunt's death, 18 months ago. Having just entered the work force, your income is only about $1,600 per month, gross. Clearly, you must make some decisions.

All estate and probate problems have been resolved. Now, as the new owner, you are free to take whatever legal actions you deem necessary to preserve your position and to operate the properties at a profit. Major problems you now face are as follows.

1. Not being familiar with this real estate, you clearly need information and advice about it and how to operate it. How would you go about getting such information? Alternatives range from looking in the phone book and arranging an appointment with the broker with the biggest ad to engaging a marketing and planning consultant, probably at a minimum cost of several thousand dollars.
2. The mill is only operating at partial capacity and probably at a loss. Might an adjustment in property taxes be sought? Assume that the assessed value and taxes are one half on the land and one half on the improvements. How might you find out about this?
3. Assume that property taxes are $16,000 on the smaller parcel and $14,000

on the larger. For the smaller parcel, the taxes on the land are $9,000 per year, which represents about 2 percent of its market value. What is a rough estimate of the market value of the land? What limitations attach to estimating value by this method?

4. What steps might you take to develop some personal idea of the highest and best use of the properties?

5. Should the costs of demolition of the existing structures enter into your thinking and planning? What other alternatives are open to you regarding the improvements? Under what circumstances would you not demolish any structures?

6. Could and should the 7-acre parcel be developed independently of the larger parcel? What issues might be involved in making this decision?

7. In general, what effect are the following likely to have on the value of the land?
   a. Sun City downtown renovation?
   b. Industrial expansion to the south?
   c. The recently expanded airport?
   d. The mixed residential-commercial development along Highway 33?
   e. The railway line along the edge of the smaller parcel?
   f. The scheduled widening of Avion Way?

8. In your investigations, you uncover a rumor that Highway 33 is to be re-routed along the interstate highway. What probable influence on the value of your parcels, if true?

9. What, in your opinion, is the feasibility of preserving the buildings on the smaller parcel and converting it into a
   a. neighborhood shopping center?
   b. recreational center?
   c. retirement home?
   d. public market?
   e. office complex?
   f. research complex?
   What additional information might you want before making a decision on any of these?

10. What, in your opinion, is the feasibility of developing the larger parcel into:
   a. a subdivision for one-family residences?
   b. a shopping center?
   c. a medical office center?
   d. an apartment complex?
   e. a complex of four story office buildings?
   f. a race track?
   What additional information might you want before making a decision on any of these?

11. Would any combination of the foregoing uses make sense. Why?

12. Given that you now have a clearer idea of what your alternatives are, what are your next steps?

21

Appraising for Market Value: Single-Family Properties

Nothing can have value without being an objective of utility. If it is useless, the labor contained in it is useless, cannot be reckoned as labor, and cannot therefore create value.

Karl Marx, *Das Kapital*

An estimate or opinion of value of a property, or some interest therein, rendered by an impartial person skilled in the analysis and valuation of real estate, is termed an *appraisal;* the value most often sought is market value or the most probable selling price. An orderly, well-conceived set of procedures, termed the *appraisal process,* is used in making the estimate.

Market value is the focal point of almost any real estate decision. Whether buying, selling, investing, developing, lending, exchanging, renting, assessing, or acquiring property for public use, market value needs to be known for the decision and action to be sound. Therefore, anyone active in real estate transactions needs a working knowledge of market value appraisal principles and procedures.

The value estimate, along with any reservations or limiting conditions attached to it, are set forth in an appraisal report. A specific description of the property being evaluated and the date of the value estimate must be included, along with supporting data and analysis.

Obviously, all theoretical and practical knowledge necessary to become a professional appraiser cannot be condensed into one or two chapters. Therefore, the objective in this chapter is limited to defining terms and providing a basic explanation of the appraisal process as applied to single-family residential properties. Applications to income-producing properties are taken up in the next chapter.

Important Topics or Decision Areas Covered in this Chapter

The Need for Appraisals
Transfer of Ownership or Possession
Financing a Property Interest
Taxing Property Interests
Compensation for Property Loss or Damage
Property Utilization Program

The Nature of Value
Market Value
Market Value Versus Market Price
Market Value Versus Cost of Production
Value in Use Versus Value in Exchange

The Appraisal Process
Defining the Problem
Making a Survey and Plan
Collecting and Organizing Data

Principles of Appraising
Substitution
Change
Contribution or Marginal Productivity
Highest and Best Use

Direct Sales Comparison Approach to Value
The Basic Steps
Adjustments
An Example
Uses and Limitations

Cost Approach to Value
The Basic Steps
An Example
Use and Limitations

Income Approach: Gross Rent Multiplier
The Basic Steps
An Example
Uses and Limitations

Reconciliation

Questions for Review and Discussion

Case Problems

Key Concepts Introduced in this Chapter

Appraisal
Appraisal process
Cost approach to value
Cost of replacement
Cost of reproduction
Direct sales comparison approach
Gross rent multiplier

Market price
Market rent
Objective value
Reconciliation
Subject property
Subjective value
Value in exchange
Value in use

The Need for Appraisals

Situations in which a real estate decision must be made, an action taken, or a policy established usually turn on a market value estimate of the property of concern, the *subject property*; hence, the continuing need for appraisals and appraisers. Most real estate decisions or actions concern one of the following.

1. Transfer of ownership or possession (sell or rent)
2. Financing a property (mortgage loan)
3. Taxation of an interest
4. Compensation for loss of a property interest (eminent domain)
5. Making up a property utilization program

TRANSFER OF OWNERSHIP OR POSSESSION

Market value serves as a benchmark to both parties in buy-sell transactions. For example, assume that the market value or most likely selling price of a single-family residence is $100,000. A prudent buyer might well open negotiations at $80,000 and would not be willing to pay much in excess of $100,000. The owner certainly would not want to list the property at less than $100,000; most likely, the initial asking price would be $110,000 or maybe even $120,000. Further, the owner would be very unlikely to accept less than $100,000 unless under great pressure to sell. Knowing market value makes the negotiations much more uncertain for both parties.

Market value is also important in renting property, because rent is usually a percentage of market value. Value estimates are needed to establish a fair value basis for tax-deferred exchanges and for minimum bids in property auctions.

Market value estimates are helpful in group negotiations, such as in settling an estate in which several parcels were involved and in which several people are designated as heirs on a pro rata basis. In this situation, it is often preferable to assign properties to individual heirs rather than to sell the properties and distribute the proceeds to the heirs. Without objective value estimates, some of the heirs might believe that they received less than their fair share of the estate, and considerable bitterness and litigation could result. This is also true for a business reorganization, a corporate merger, the issuance of new or additional stock by a corporation or trust, or corporate bankruptcy.

FINANCING A PROPERTY INTEREST

A real estate lender's security is the property. Therefore, the lender wants assurance that the most probable selling price of the property is greater than the principal amount of the loan. To show the problem, suppose that a 90 percent loan were requested to finance the purchase of the $100,000 residence mentioned earlier, which sold at the owner's initial asking price of $120,000. A $108,000 loan is implied; this is $8,000 more than the $100,000 market value and $18,000 more than 90 percent of market value, $90,000. If a $108,000 loan were made, the lender would have little or no cushion if a foreclosure became necessary within a few years, meaning much greater risk than implied by the 90 percent loan-to-purchase-price ratio.

Of course, insurers of mortgage loans, such as the Federal Housing Administration (FHA), want assurance that the security exceeds the insured principal by an established percentage. Extending this line of reasoning, a prospective purchaser of mortgage bonds wants assurance that adequate security is provided by the pledged property.

TAXING PROPERTY INTERESTS

An error in estimating market value by an assessor directly affects the amount of property taxes levied against a property. In most areas, assessed value is some portion of market value. Assume that assessed value is supposed to equal 60 percent of market value. Assume that a residence with an actual market value of $100,000 is over appraised at $130,000. The $30,000 difference translates into an overassessment of $18,000, which, at a 3 percent tax levy, means extra annual taxes of $540.

Appraisals are used in state and federal tax situations as well. For income tax purposes, the allocation between the land and improvements may be in direct relation to the distribution made by the assessor, according to the U.S. Internal Revenue Service. The allocation determines the amount of annual deductible depreciation in an income tax return, and the larger the allowable deduction, the less the taxes to be paid. An investor may take exception with the assessor's distribution and hire an appraiser to make the determination. Either way, an appraisal is involved. Further, gift and inheritance taxes payable to federal and state governments depend directly on the market value of the property involved, of which a portion may be real property.

COMPENSATION FOR PROPERTY LOSS OR DAMAGE

Owners take out insurance to protect against risk of property loss or damage caused by natural disasters such as fire, wind, flood, lightning, and earthquake. In some cases, this insurance is for the cost of replacement or reproduction of the property rather than for market value. But, if the loss is realized, the insurance settlement depends on an appraisal.

Likewise, eminent domain actions constitute a continuing and major need for appraisals. If an entire property is condemned, the owner is entitled to just compensation equal to at least the market value of the property. If only part of the property were taken, the owner is usually entitled to compensation equal to the value of the part taken plus the amount of any damages to the remainder. Often, the taking authority and the owner will each have appraisals made as a basis for determining just compensation. If a settlement cannot be negotiated, the appraisers may have to testify at a court hearing.

PROPERTY UTILIZATION PROGRAM

Finally, determining the best way to use a property almost always involves an appraisal to determine highest and best use. All alternative ways to use the parcel must be considered to find the one that gives the greatest present value to the property. For all practical purposes, each alternative involves a market value appraisal. This analysis is closely akin to market and feasibility analysis that should precede any decision concerning development or redevelopment of realty.

The Nature of Value

Several attributes must be present for a parcel of real estate to have value. The first is utility, or the ability to satisfy human needs and desires, such as by providing shelter, privacy, or income. Second, effective demand must be present for the services or amenities that the property produces. The third attribute is relative scarcity; supply must be limited relative to demand. A fourth is transferability, meaning that rights of ownership or use can be conveyed from one person to another with relative ease. Finally, the property must be located in an environment of law and order so that people investing in real property will not suffer loss because of legal or political uncertainty.

MARKET VALUE

As was mentioned earlier, market value is easily the most basic value concept in real estate. A widely accepted definition of market value is most probable selling price, in cash, to the seller. Two other widely used definitions are (1) the amount in dollars, goods, or services for which a property may be exchanged and (2) the present worth of future rights to the income or amenities generated by a property.

Whatever definition is used, market value is estimated by methods shown later in this chapter. In applying the methods the following assumptions apply.[1]

1. Real estate buyers and sellers act with reasonable, but not perfect, knowledge. This is realistic because almost all market participants gather information about conditions before they act.
2. Buyers and sellers act competitively and rationally in their own best interests to maximize their income or satisfactions.
3. Buyers and sellers act independently of each other, that is, without collusion, fraud, or misrepresentation. If this were not the case, some transaction prices might be severely distorted.
4. Buyers and sellers are typically motivated; that is, they act without undue pressure. This means that properties placed on the market turn over or sell within a reasonable period. Thus, a forced sale or a sale occurring after the property has been exposed to the market for an extremely long time would not be considered typical.
5. Payment is made in cash in a manner consistent with the standards of the market; that is, the buyer uses financing terms generally available in the local market.

[1]See market value in *Real Estate Appraisal Terminology*, rev. ed., compiled and edited by Byrl N. Boyce under the joint sponsorship of the American Institute of Real Estate Appraisers and the Society of Real Estate Appraisers (Cambridge, Mass.: Ballinger, 1981).

MARKET VALUE VERSUS MARKET PRICE

Market value does not necessarily equal market price. In fact, market value for a property may be greater than, equal to, or less than its sale price in an actual market transaction. **Market price** is the amount negotiated between a buyer and a seller, who were not necessarily well informed, free from pressure, or acting independently. Market price is an historical fact. Market value, on the other hand, is an estimated price made by an objective, experienced, knowledgeable appraiser. The estimate is made after looking at and studying a number of actual transactions and other market data.

MARKET VALUE VERSUS COST OF PRODUCTION

Market value may also be greater than, equal to, or less than the cost of a property. As used here, cost means the capital outlay (including overhead and financing expenses) for land, labor, materials, supervision, and profit necessary to bring a useful property into existence. In appraisal analysis, cost means the cost of production. It does not mean the cost of acquisition (i.e., price).

A rational developer or investor creates sites and constructs new buildings on them only if the expected sale price (market value) equals or exceeds the cost of production. To subdivide or develop property or to remodel property otherwise would mean proceeding even though a loss were expected. Developing a major property without adequate market analysis ignores the simple reality that cost does not necessarily mean value.

VALUE IN USE VERSUS VALUE IN EXCHANGE

The worth of a property, based on its utility, to a specific user is its **value in use.** The utility may be from expected amenities, income, or value enhancement. Value in use depends on the unique judgments, standards, and demands of the user and is independent of identifiable market information. We also talk of **subjective value,** meaning dependent on the nature and mental attitude of the person making the judgment. In net, value in use is synonymous with subjective value. However, if the viewpoint of the typical person exchanging or evaluating a property is taken, the value in use estimate becomes basically consistent with the most probable selling price definition, or market value.

Recognition of this special case leads us to **value in exchange,** which is the amount of money or purchasing power (in goods and services) for which the property might most probably be traded. Such exchanges do take place and prices do result. In turn, appraisers and others can collect and analyze the prices, which are the result of observed or explicit actions of market participants. Effectively, by using price information, these analysts can make a neutral estimate of the value of properties, termed **objective value.** In net, value in exchange is roughly synonymous with objective value and market value.

A rational owner retains a property as long as value in use exceeds value in exchange. With time, however, depreciation is used up as a tax shelter, community change makes a location obsolete, or an owner decides to retire. Thus, for a variety or reasons, value in use drops down to and eventually below value in exchange. At this point, disposition becomes advantageous, and market activity results.

The Appraisal Process

In a specific assignment, several elements or steps that make up what professional appraisers call the "appraisal process" or "framework" must be developed. These elements, when taken up in the order presented, provide for systematic analysis of the facts that bear upon and determine the market value of a specific parcel. See Figure 21-1.

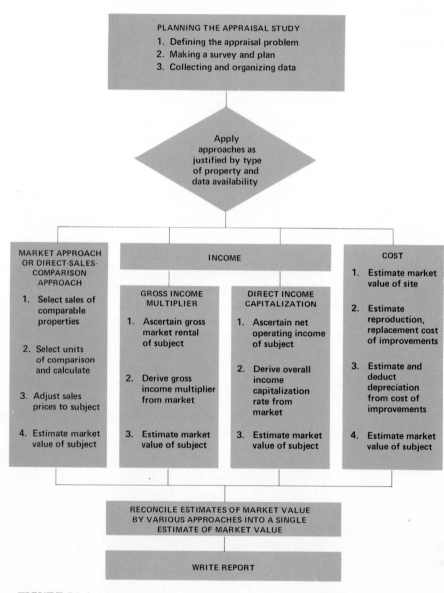

FIGURE 21-1

The appraisal process or framework: steps to estimating market value

DEFINING THE PROBLEM

The appraisal assignment must be agreed on jointly by the appraiser and by the owner or the owner's agent to ensure that the analysis and conclusions serve the decision or action to be made. In defining the problem, agreement is needed on each of the following points:

1. Specific identification of the subject property, preferably by both address and legal description
2. Specific identification of the legal rights to be valued, such as fee simple, leased fee, or lease hold
3. Specific purpose of the appraisal, such as for sale, financing, insurance, or condemnation
4. Specific date for which the value estimate is desired
5. Specific value to be estimated, such as market value, assessed value, condemnation damages; market value is the objective in most fee-appraisal assignments

MAKING A SURVEY AND PLAN

The scope, character, and amount of work involved must next be estimated. This determination constitutes the appraisal plan. In valuing a one-family residence, this is quite simple and routine. But, when a major property or when complex legal rights are involved, a check with data sources, such as brokers, lenders, or title companies, is often necessary. The highest and best use alternatives of the property must also be considered. Based on obtainable information, the appraiser must also decide which alternative approaches to value can be used, the effort likely to be involved, and the fee. If not already agreed on, the fee is usually cleared with the employer before further work is undertaken.

COLLECTING AND ORGANIZING DATA

National, regional, community, and neighborhood data are collected and analyzed on a continuing basis to provide background for the specific approaches to value. By way of example, the following considerations would be important in a residential appraisal.

1. *Physical and environmental data.* With an emphasis on topology and physical improvements, such as rolling or flat terrain; features of natural beauty; drainage facilities and quality of soil; condition and contour of roads; transportation and availability of essential public utilities; quality and housing design; and proximity to schools, stores, and recreational facilities
2. *Demographic and social data.* Nature and characteristics of population, such as living habits, care of homes, attitude toward government, homogeneity of cultural interests, and percentage of homeownership
3. *Economic data.* Personal income per capita, income stability, homogeneity of professional or business activities, frequency of turnover, housing market price levels and trends, assessment and tax levels and trends, building mortality, vacancies, and percentage of area development

An on-site inspection of the subject property must then be made, followed by a written description of it. With knowledge of the subject property, the appraiser is in a much better position to collect data on comparable properties. Once collected, the data are sorted according to the direct sales comparison, cost, and income approaches. From this point on, attention is focused on one approach at a time.

Principles of Appraising

Over the years, appraisers have developed the following principles of valuation. The principles treat real property interests as a commodity and are therefore applied economic theory.

1. *Supply and demand.* Market value is the result of supply and demand interaction.
2. *Change.* The forces of supply and demand are dynamic and change constantly, which results in price and value fluctuations. Thus, a market value estimate is only valid as of a given date.
3. *Competition.* Prices are kept in line, and market values are established through continuous rivalry and interaction of buyers, sellers, developers, and other market participants.
4. *Substitution.* A rational buyer will pay no more for a property than the cost of acquiring an equally desirable alternative property.
5. *Variable proportions.* Real estate reaches its point of maximum productivity, or highest and best use, when the factors of production (usually considered to be land, labor, capital, and management) are in balance with one another. This is the same as the principle of increasing and decreasing returns discussed in Chapter 18 relative to the determination of highest and best use; it is also known as the principle of proportionality.
6. *Contribution or marginal productivity.* The value of any factor of production, or component of a property, depends on how much its presence adds to the overall value of the property.
7. *Highest and best use.* For market valuation purposes, real estate should be appraised at its highest and best use so that maximum value is recognized.
8. *Conformity.* A property reaches its maximum value when it is located in an environment of physical, economic, and social homogeneity or of compatible and harmonious land uses.
9. *Anticipation.* Market value equals the present worth of future income or amenities generated by a property, as viewed by typical buyers and sellers.

The first four principles involve the real estate market. The next three apply primarily to the subject property itself. The eighth principle concerns the neighborhood or area around the property. The ninth principle looks at the property's productivity from the viewpoint of a typical buyer or seller.

The principles of substitution, change, contribution, and highest and best use are generally considered most important and, therefore, merit further explanation.

SUBSTITUTION

According to the principle of substitution, "A rational buyer will pay no more for a property than the cost of acquiring an equally desirable alternative property." An equally desirable alternative means one of equal utility or productivity, with time costs or delays taken into account. Therefore, a property of equal utility is one that provides satisfaction to people who use or own it equal to that which an alternative property would provide. The rational buyer is presumed to have the following three alternatives:

1. Buying an existing property with utility equal to the subject property: This alternative is the basis of the market or direct sales comparison approach to estimating market value.
2. Buying a site and adding improvements to produce a property with utility equal to the subject property: This alternative is the basis of the cost approach to estimating market value.
3. Buying a property that produces an income stream of the same size and with the same risk as that produced by the subject property: This alternative is the basis of the income approach to estimating market value.

A change of approach in applying the principle of substitution is necessary as one goes from income to nonincome properties. Nonincome properties include single-family homes, churches, vacant lots, and timberland, for which productivity is mainly realized through self-use. For income properties, annual rental income may be used as a basis of comparison in the income approach. With nonincome properties, annual rental data are not usually available. Therefore, greater reliance must be given the direct sales comparison and cost approaches with nonincome properties.

CHANGE

The principle of change is that "The forces of supply and demand are dynamic, thereby lending to price and value fluctuation." Because of this principle, a specific date must be attached to each value estimate. That is, physical, social, political, and economic conditions are in a continuing state of transition: buildings suffer wear and tear, people move, laws change, and industries expand and contract. The appraiser's task is to recognize cause and effect in these forces and to make a "snapshot" estimate of their effect on the market value of the subject property.

CONTRIBUTION OR MARGINAL PRODUCTIVITY

The principle of contribution is defined as "The value of any factor of production, or component of a property, depends on how much its presence adds to the overall value of the property." Alternatively, the value of the factor or component may be measured by how much its absence detracts from the overall value. That is, the absence of a garage or a second bath reduces the value of a residence by some incremental amount. This principle serves as the basis for making adjustments between properties in the direct sales comparison approach. It also provides the basis for estimating depreciation owing to property deficiencies in the cost approach.

HIGHEST AND BEST USE

Finally the principle of highest and best use states that "Real estate should be appraised at its highest and best use for market-valuation purposes." There is a simple logic behind this principle, namely, that a prudent owner will, in self-interest, put a property to that use that yields the greatest value or return. To do otherwise would not be rational. It is this value that is critical to any decision to be made about the property.

In applying this principle, it must be recognized that the value of an improved property in its highest and best use may not be as great as that of the site, if valued as vacant and available for an alternative highest and best use. This would be the case, for example, if a house were on a commercial site and not suited to its highest and best use. The value of the site exceeding the value of the total improved property would mean that the improvements made no contribution to value and should be removed. On the other hand, if the property value were greater, it would pay the owner to continue the use dictated by the improvements.

Direct Sales Comparison Approach to Value

substitution

The ***direct sales comparison approach,*** also termed the market approach, provides for the estimation of market value by referring to recent sale, listing, and offering prices of comparable properties. The underlying assumption is that a potential owner will pay no more for the subject property than would probably have to be paid for another property of equal productivity or utility.

THE BASIC STEPS

The direct sales comparison approach involves four basic steps. These are (1) collect data on sales of comparable properties, (2) select units of comparison and calculate, (3) adjust sales prices to subject property, and (4) estimate market value of subject. See Figures 21-1 and 21-2.

ADJUSTMENTS

The process begins with the obtaining of prices from recent sales of properties similar to, and competitive with, the subject property. Adjustments are made from the comparable to the subject for two reasons. First, it would be improper to adjust from the subject to the comparable in that the price or value of the subject is not known. Second, adjusting to the subject gives an indication of market value for the subject that may be compared because they all apply to the subject. Generally speaking, the greater the likeness between a comparable and the subject property, the fewer the necessary adjustments and the more reliable the resulting value estimate. Listing and offering prices are sometimes used if sufficient sales of comparable properties cannot be found.

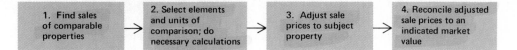

FIGURE 21-2
Steps in the direct sales comparison approach to market value

The ratio, sale price per square foot, is most frequently used in making adjustments from a comparable to the subject. In addition, sale price per living unit or per room is commonly used in comparing residences, motels, hotels, and apartments. Sale price per cubic foot is an important ratio of comparison for warehouses and storage facilities.

Differences that require adjustment between comparables and a subject property fall into four general categories: (1) terms and conditions of sale, (2) time of sale, (3) location, and (4) property characteristics.

Terms of Sale. The price for a comparable property should reflect an "arms-length" bargain. An adjustment to the price may be necessary otherwise. Differences in bargaining power between buyer and seller, undue pressure on either buyer or seller, or personal relationships within the transaction may all cause the price to be too high or too low. Price distortion might also result if an unusually high down payment were required or if one party knew more about market conditions than the other.

Time of Sale. An adjustment is made for time of sale if sale prices, market activity, or money availability have changed in general since the sale date and the date of the value estimate for the subject property. Thus, higher interest rates may have slowed sales activity and lowered prices paid since the sale of a comparable.

Location. Locational adjustments become necessary with differences in either convenience or environment. Time-distance differences between linked properties are the basis of convenience adjustments. That is, a comparable property may have better or worse accessibility, or situs, than the subject. Environmental differences also lead to locational adjustments. Thus, differences in housing quality, prevalence of deed restrictions, zoning, or neighborhood prestige between a comparable and a subject mean an environmental adjustment should be made. Thus, even differences in one-family houses between neighborhoods, such as age, style, size, and condition, imply an adjustment for location.

Property Characteristics. With single-family residential properties, characteristics provide a basis for adjustment between a comparable and a subject property. Thus, adjustments would be appropriate for differences in size, age, condition, number of rooms, number of baths, the presence or absence and size of a garage or carport, and the presence or absence of special features such as fireplaces, air conditioning, or a swimming pool.

AN EXAMPLE

Appraisers make adjustments in either dollar or percentage terms. To illustrate adjustments, in percentage terms, an appraiser's judgments of differences between comparables and a subject property are shown in Figure 21-3. The percentage adjustments that might apply are also given. Note that adjustments for differences in financing and physical characteristics are often made in dollar terms. In this example, the process of adjusting for comparables A and B is explained; the reader is asked to rationalize the adjustments for C.

All sales are considered to be arms length; thus, no adjustment is made for differences in terms of sale. As for a time adjustment, values are assumed to be going up at a rate of 6 percent per year. Thus, the price of comparable A, which sold 6 months ago, is adjusted upward by 3 percent.

The subject is considered to have an average location in the example, both as to situs and to environment. The convenience of comparable A is much better (+ +) than that of the subject; hence, a downward adjustment in this case of 4 percent.

Item of Comparison	Subject Property 175 Westwood	Comparable Sales		
		A 341 Westwood	B 122 Braeburn	C 55 Westwood
Sale price	—	$113,000	$95,000	$102,500
Unit size, s.f.	1,800	1,900	1,800	1,780
number of rooms	6	6	6	6
Lot size, s.f.	10,000	10,200	9,880	10,100
Sale price/s.f.		$59.47	$52.78	$57.58
Adjustments				
1. Terms of sale		Arms length	Arms length	Arms length
% adjustment		0.00%	0.00%	0.00%
2. Time of sale				
Months since sale		6	5	1
% adjustment		3.00%	2.50%	0.50%
3. Location				
Convenience/situs	Average	Average + +	Average −	Average +
% adjustment		− 4.00%	2.00%	− 2.00%
Environment	Average	Average +	Average	Average
% adjustment		− 2.00%	0.00%	0.00%
4. Physical characteristics				
Overall condition	Average +	Average +	Average	Average + +
% adjustment		0.00%	1.00%	− 2.00%
Number of baths	2.0	2.5	2.0	2.0
% adjustment		− 2.00%	0.00%	0.00%
Garage spaces	2.0	3.0	2.0	2.0
% adjustment		− 2.00%	0.00%	0.00%
Total % Adjustment		− 7.00%	5.50%	− 3.50%
Adjusted S.P./S.F.		$55.31	$55.68	$55.57
Indicated M.V. of Subject		$99,559	$100,225	$100,024

Note: s.f., square foot; s.p., selling price; m.v., market value.

FIGURE 21-3
Example: direct sales comparison adjustments for single-family residence

Comparable B is slightly below average (−); hence, an upward adjustment of 2 percent is needed to adjust the price to the subject. Also, comparable A is judged to have a superior environment (average +) relative to the subject; hence, the 2 percent downward adjustment.

Finally, adjustments are necessary for differences in physical characteristics. Comparable B has slightly worse overall condition than the subject, and an upward adjustment of 1 percent results. Finally, comparable A has more baths and more garage spaces than the subject, both of which require downward adjustments.

Total adjustments are −7 percent for A and 5.5 percent for B. Applying these percentages to the sale price per square foot makes adjustments for size differences in the structures automatic. The adjusted sale price per square foot is $55.31 for comparable A, $55.68 for B, and $55.57 for C. Multiplying these numbers by the area of the subject, 1,800 square feet, yields an indicated sale price for the subject based on the analysis for each comparable. The range is from $99,559 to $100,225. On the basis of these comparables, an indicated market value of $99,900 for the subject property seems justified.

USES AND LIMITATIONS

The direct sales comparison method is well suited to making an objective estimate of a property's market value. It depends entirely on market information. Including several comparable sales almost ensures that the thinking and behavior of typical buyers and sellers are taken into account in the resulting value estimate. Also, the approach takes into account varying financing terms, inflation, and other market elements that influence the typical purchaser. Consequently, courts place greater emphasis and reliance on this method than on any other.

The method is most applicable when the market is active and actual sales data are plentiful and readily available. This means the direct sales comparison method is most appropriate for a property type that is widely bought and sold, such as vacant lots, one-family houses, and condominium units.

Lack of adequate market data is the method's major limitation. By default, then, the method is not applicable to the kind of property that is infrequently bought and sold or is of a unique character, such as a church. Two other limitations are that (1) sales of truly comparable properties must be selected and that (2) the value estimate is based on historical data. An underlying assumption is that market trends of the past continue on to the date of the value estimate.

not good for churches

⭐ Cost Approach to Value 🏠

The **cost approach to value** provides for the estimation of market value based on the cost of acquiring a vacant site and constructing a building and other improvements to develop a property of equal utility. To go from a new property to the subject property may involve reductions in utility and value caused by accrued depreciation. The underlying assumption is that a rational potential owner will not pay more for a subject property than the cost of producing a substitute property with equal

deprn
contribution

utility and without any undue delay. Note that the cost involved is to the typical, rational, informed purchaser and not to a contractor or builder. This is also termed the summation approach.

THE BASIC STEPS

The basic approach to value involves the steps (1) estimate market value of subject site, (2) estimate reproduction cost of subject improvements, (3) estimate accrued depreciation and deduct from cost of improvements, and (4) add site value and depreciated costs of improvements together to get indicated market value of subject property, as shown in Figures 21-1 and 21-4.

Land value is best established by the direct sale comparison with similar sites that sold.

Two forms of cost new of buildings are recognized. The first, ***cost of replacement,*** involves determining the cost of producing a building or other improvement with utility equal to that of the subject property's improvement. Modern materials, design, and layout may be used, but the utility must be the same. ***Cost of reproduction,*** the second, involves determining the cost of an exact replica of the subject property's improvements, including materials, design, layout, in short, everything.

After deciding between replacement and reproduction cost new, an appraiser obtains current local construction cost per area or cubic content from builders or other sources. The total cost new is then calculated by multiplying the area or volume of the subject improvements by the current cost of construction per square foot or cubic foot.

Accrued depreciation, loss in value of a property owing to diminished utility, is deducted from cost new to arrive at an indicated market value. Three types of depreciation are recognized in appraising:

1. *Physical deterioration.* Loss in value brought about by the wear and tear of use, acts of nature, or actions of the elements

2. *Functional obsolescence.* Loss in value because of a subject property's relative inability to provide a service as compared with a new property properly designed for the same use; the cause may be poor layout and design or inefficient building equipment (in short, the improvements not up to current standards)

3. *External obsolescence.* Also termed economic, locational, or environmental obsolescence; loss in value of a site or property because of external or environmental factors that unfavorably affect the flow of income or benefits from the property, such as blight and declining demand

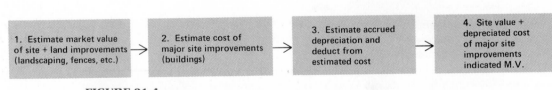

FIGURE 21-4

Steps in the cost less depreciation approach to market value

Type of depreciation	Explanation and examples
1. Physical deterioration *appliances* *parts of building*	Parts of building completely used up, worn out, or deteriorated: peeling paint, leaky roofing, heating, ventilating, air conditioning systems, appliances that will not work, storm damage; if deficiency involves foundation or structural mainframe, usually not curable
2. Functional obsolescence *outdated fixtures* *not up to day*	Aspects of building or property that work but are not up to current standards: outdated fixtures, lack of storage space, absence of a second bathroom, too few electrical outlets; if deficiency is due to architectural design, such as an inefficient floor plan, usually not curable
3. External obsolescence *things outside the home*	External or environmental factors that unfavorably affect the flow of benefits: neighborhood blight, noxious odors, unduly heavy traffic, nonconforming use nearby

FIGURE 21-5

Types of accrued depreciation, with explanation and examples

AN EXAMPLE

An example of the cost less depreciation approach to market value seems appropriate here. Assume that the depreciated cost of developing the subject property in its present condition is estimated at $101,400. Figure 21-6 gives a representative breakdown of calculations leading to this estimate; this value, in turn, becomes its indicated market value by the cost approach. But cost is not value. Only when depreciated cost is less than actual market value would a buyer or investor choose this alternative.

Land value (by direct sales comparison)	$ 14,000	
Plus: landscaping, walks, drive, etc.	7,000	
Total site value	$ 21,000	$ 21,000
Cost to construct new improvement		
Main structure: 1,800 square feet at $50/square foot	$ 90,000	
Garage area: 420 square feet at $12.00/square foot	5,040	
Miscellaneous (blinds, appliances, etc.)	7,600	
Total cost new	$102,640	
Less: accrued depreciation		
Physical deterioration	$ 4,470	
Functional obsolescence	5,770	
External obsolescence	13,000	
Total depreciation	$23,240	− 23,240
Depreciated value of improvements	$ 79,400	79,400
Indicated market value by cost approach		$101,400

FIGURE 21-6

Example: cost less depreciation approach to market value

USES AND LIMITATIONS

The cost approach to value has greatest application in estimating the value of unique or special-purpose properties that have little or no market, for example, churches, tank farms, or chemical plants. It is also well suited to new or nearly new properties where estimating depreciation is not too involved or difficult. The cost approach has long been used in assessing for property tax purposes, which involves mass appraising and, in the past, has demanded standardized methodology. Property insurance adjustors rely on the cost approach because improvements often are only partially damaged or destroyed and must be restored to their original design and layout or else completely torn down. Finally, the approach is very suitable in analysis to determine the highest and best use of a vacant site.

One major limitation of the cost approach is that depreciation is very difficult to measure for older properties. Another is the great difficulty in allowing for differences in quality of improvements that result from design and style, kind and quality of materials, and quality of workmanship. This limitation applies to both estimating cost new and estimating depreciation. Further, even getting an accurate estimate of costs new is difficult because costs often vary substantially from one builder to another. For these reasons, the cost approach is not as applicable as other approaches for older properties or properties that are frequently sold. Also, it is nearly impossible to find vacant lot sales to serve as comparables in determining site value in older, established neighborhoods.

Income Approach: Gross Rent Multiplier

The income approach uses a ratio, derived from the market, to convert income generated by a property into market value. By the principle of substitution, the underlying assumption is that a potential owner should pay no more for an income property than the cost of acquiring an alternative property capable of producing an income stream of the same size and with the same risk. Probably, the most basic version of the income approach is the *gross rent multiplier* (GRM) technique; it relates the total monthly income generated by a small residential property (one to four family) to its market value.

THE BASIC STEPS

The basic steps in the GRM technique are (1) ascertain the gross market rental of the subject property, (2) derive the GRM from the market, and (3) apply GRM to subject property to estimate its indicated market value, as set forth in Figures 21-1 and 21-7.

AN EXAMPLE

Ascertain Current Monthly Market Rental. Current monthly market rental of the subject property is obtained by comparison with similar properties that

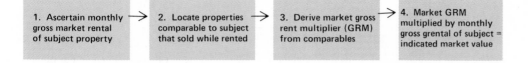

| 1. Ascertain monthly gross market rental of subject property | → | 2. Locate properties comparable to subject that sold while rented | → | 3. Derive market gross rent multiplier (GRM) from comparables | → | 4. Market GRM multiplied by monthly gross grental of subject = indicated market value |

FIGURE 21-7
Steps in the gross rent multiplier technique of estimating market value

are rented. *Market rent* is the amount that a property would command if exposed to the market for a reasonable time and rented by a reasonably knowledgable tenant. Market rental is analogous to market price.

Monthly rental is commonly used in comparisons of small, one- to four-family, residential properties. Adjustments are made for differences from the comparable property to the subject property in much the same way that a sales price is adjusted from the comparable to the subject in the market approach to value. Thus, if rental prices for three similar one family houses, after adjustment to the subject, equal $895, $915, and $925 per month, the subject may be considered to have a gross monthly market rental of $912 per month.

Derive the GRM. Dividing sales price by the gross monthly rental of comparable properties that recently sold gives a GRM. The calculations are as follows:

$$\text{GRM for a property} = \frac{\text{sale price}}{\text{monthly rent}}$$

$$\text{GRM, comparable D} = \frac{\$98,900}{\$895} = 110.5$$

$$\text{GRM, comparable E} = \frac{\$99,900}{\$915} = 109.2$$

$$\text{GRM comparable F} = \frac{\$102,800}{\$925} = 111.1$$

The average of the three is 110.3; an estimated market GRM of 110.0 therefore seems reasonable for single-family houses in this particular neighborhood at this time. A GRM may change through time with fluctuations in economic and financial conditions.

Apply the GRM. The indicated market value of the subject property may be calculated by multiplying its gross monthly income by the market-derived GRM. For the subject property, this comes to $100,320.

gross monthly rent × market GRM = indicated market value

$912 ×   110.0   = $100,320

USES AND LIMITATIONS

The multiplier technique is a quick, simple, and direct method of estimating value whenever properties are rented at the same time they are sold. Appraisers frequently use the technique early in the appraisal analysis to develop a quick idea of market value to aid their judgment in applying other techniques.

One limitation is that rental data for single family houses are not always available for deriving the multiplier. Another is that gross rents are used instead of net operating incomes; if the building to land ratios differ, or if the ages differ, the results may be distorted. In addition, the GRM is subject to some distortion because adverse zoning, lack of maintenance, or heavy property taxes will negatively influence sale price with little effect on rental levels. Thus, unless the comparables are similar in all respects to the subject, a distorted GRM may be derived from the market. This caution extends to the presence or absence of such extras as range, refrigerator, or furniture, which must be the same for the comparables as for the subject.

Reconciliation

Each approach yields a distinct indication of market value. For our subject property, value indications are as follows.

direct sales comparison	$ 99,900
depreciated cost approach	101,400
income approach: GRM	100,320

A reconciliation into a single estimate of market value is now expected. ***Reconciliation*** is the process of resolving differences in indications of value and of reaching a most probable sales price for the property being analyzed. Reconciliation involves weighing and comparing the indications according to the quality of the available data and the appropriateness of the approach for the kind of property and the value being sought. Reconciliation is a thought and judgment process: It is not the simple averaging of the value indications. In some situations, appraisers attach a range to the market value estimate, similar to the standard deviation from statistical analysis.

In our case study, therefore, a market value of $99,900 for the subject property seems reasonable and defensible. The direct sales comparison approach, when sufficient sales data are available, is generally regarded as giving the most reliable indication of market value. The GRM, on the other hand, is often regarded as a rule-of-thumb technique. The depreciated cost approach sets the upper limit on value in most situations. This example was designed for illustrative purposes; the reader should recognize that most appraisals do not work out with such a narrow range of value indications.

1. List and explain briefly three major reasons or needs for appraisals.
2. Distinguish among the following:
   a. market value
   b. value in exchange
   c. objective value
   d. reproduction cost
   e. market price
   f. value in use
   g. subjective value
   h. replacement cost
3. List and explain at least three principles of market value appraising, including the principle of substitution.
4. Give or briefly explain the following points concerning the direct sales comparison approach to value:
   a. The four basic steps
   b. Two appropriate applications
   c. Two major limitations
5. Relate the following points to the income approach to value:
   a. Three basic steps of GRM technique
   b. Two appropriate applications of each
   c. Two limitations of each
6. Explain the purpose and process of reconciliation.
7. Depreciation need not be considered in market value appraising because it is more than offset by inflation. Is this true? Discuss.
8. In what directions would the adjustments be for a comparable sale involving extremely low down payment and a first and second mortgage? Explain your reasoning.
9. Is depreciation taken into account in the GRM technique of the income approach to value? If so, how? Explain.
10. How do market values adjust or change in responses to changes in demand? How is the changing value incorporated into estimates of value by appraisers? Discuss.

Case Problems

1. You are appraising a vacant single-family residential lot that is in West Ridge, two blocks from Jefferson elementary school and three blocks from the Park Avenue neighborhood shopping center. Your client is contemplating buying the lot for personal use. The parcel is 80 feet × 120 feet in size, is located in the middle of the block, is level and on grade with the street, and has an excellent view. The asking price is $40,000. Three sales of comparable lots, all on grade with their street, occurred in the last year.

Comparable 1: 80 × 120 feet and directly across the street, sold for $37,500 2 months ago. It lacks a view.

Comparable 2: 70 × 120 feet and one block nearer the school and shopping center, sold 3 months ago for $36,500. It has an excellent view.

Comparable 3: 80 × 120 feet and located one block nearer Jefferson school and the neighborhood shopping center, sold 6 months ago for $40,000. It is very similar to the subject in all physical respects and has a comparable view.

Appropriate adjustments are as follows:

For time: values are increasing 1 percent per month.

For location: By way of convenience, being one block nearer the school and shopping center adds 5 percent to land value. Being across the street means being comparable to the subject. Having a high quality view adds 5 percent to the value relative to not having a view.

a. Set up a grid to adjust sale prices on a per square foot basis.

b. Make necessary adjustments, and estimate the market value of the subject site. [$40,400]

c. Is the proposed purchase at $40,000 a reasonable buy?

Income Property
Analysis and
Market Valuation

There are few sorrows, however poignant, in which a good income is of no avail.

Logan Pearsall Smith

Income-producing real estate is generally owned as an investment. In turn, the value of any income property is a direct result of the quality, quantity, and duration of the income it generates. That is, the higher the earning power of a property, the greater is its value.

Valuing income properties involves estimating both market value and investment value. *Investment value* is the value to a specific investor and is akin to subjective value or value in use. Market value, as discussed in Chapter 21, is most probable selling price and equivalent to objective value or value in exchange. Market value is based on impersonal and detached and market-oriented data and assumptions. Investment value depends on data and assumptions that are personal and subjective. Market and investment value may coincide if the data and assumptions of the specific investor are the same as those of the typical investor in the market.

Methods of determining the market value of income properties are discussed in this chapter. Methods of estimating investment value are discussed in subsequent chapters.

Important Topics or Decision Areas Covered in this Chapter

Income Property Productivity
Measuring Productivity
Analyzing Productivity

Income Approach: Direct Capitalization
The Basic Steps
An Application
Uses and Limitations

By Way of Review
Gross Income Multiplier Technique
Direct Sales Comparison Approach
Depreciated Cost Approach

Reconciliation

Case Problems

Key Concepts Introduced in this Chapter

Capitalization

Contract rent

Direct income capitalization

Effective gross income

Fixed costs

Gross income multiplier

Income ratio

Investment value

Net operating income

Operating expenses

Operating ratio

Overall capitalization rate

Vacancy and credit losses

Variable expenses

Income Property Productivity

Owners, users, lenders, and insurers all require some measure of a property's productivity, its ability to generate income, as a basis of value. The income generated must, first, be measured or determined and, second, be analyzed. This measurement and analysis is the same whether market value or investment value is sought.

MEASURING PRODUCTIVITY

The gross annual income a property earns serves as an initial index or measure of its productivity. For refined estimates of productivity, business executives, property managers, investors, and others use a pro forma annual operating statement. The statement shows both gross and net operating income, plus operating expenses.

The annual operating statement of Douglas Manor Apartments is representative as shown in Figure 22-1. The statement provides the starting point for a series of income and expenses projections, termed cash flow analyses, to be discussed in detail in later chapters. The statement should reflect actual market behavior because realistic estimates of income and expense must be used to obtain a useful estimate of productivity.

Gross Annual Scheduled Income, GI			$108,000
Less vacancy & credit losses @	4%		4,320
Effective Gross Income, EGI			$103,680
Less total operating expenses (TOE):			
Fixed			
Property taxes		$20,908	
Hazard insurance		1,460	
Licenses & permits		250	
		$22,618 $22,618	
Variable			
Gas, water, & electricity		$ 2,800	
Supplies		1,350	
Advertising		730	
Payroll, including payroll taxes		3,988	
Management, as percent of EGI	5%	5,184	
Miscellaneous services		1,160	
Property maintenance		1,850	
		17,062 17,062	
Total Operating Expenses		$39,680	39,680
Net operating income, NOI			$ 64,000

FIGURE 22-1

Pro forma annual operating statement, Douglas Manor Apartments

Gross Income. The total rents a property should earn in a year, based on market rents, constitute its gross scheduled income. The use of "should" here is important. Market rent rather than contract rent must be used in estimating gross income. *Contract rent* is the number of dollars to be paid in rent for a property based on a specific rental agreement. Contract rent is likely to equal market rent at the time a lease is negotiated. Later, contract rent may exceed or fall below market rent owing to changing economic conditions that are not accommodated in the lease. If the premises are leased for less than their market rental, then gross income is not an accurate reflection of the property's earning power. Too low an income might be reported because of a long-term lease or because of ignorance or incompetence on the part of an owner or manager.

Owners frequently rent subunits of space on a month-to-month basis, as with apartments. Office buildings, shopping centers, and even warehouses are also operated on this basis. By way of example, our sample property, Douglas Manor Apartments, contains 16 apartments: eight one-bedroom units and eight two-bedroom units. The rents are $525 and $600 per month, respectively. Gross scheduled income would be calculated as follows.

	One-Bedroom Units	Two-Bedroom Units
Monthly market rental per unit	$ 525	$ 600
Multiplied by number of months	× 12	× 12
Annual market rental per unit	$ 6,300	$ 7,200
Multiplied by number of units	× 8	× 8
Gross scheduled income from units	$50,400	$57,600

The total gross scheduled income equals $108,000 ($50,400 plus $57,600).

No income is earned if a subunit of space, such as an apartment, is not rented for a month or if it is rented but the tenant fails to pay. Therefore, gross scheduled income must be reduced by the amount of income not realized; this deduction is termed *vacancy and collection losses* (V&CL). In the sample operating statement, Douglas Manor Apartments is expected not to collect 4 percent of gross scheduled income because of vacancy and collection losses, based on experience in the area. A deduction of $4,320 is therefore made. The resulting figure, *effective gross income* (EGI), is the amount of money the manager or owner actually collects.

Operating Expenses. *Operating expenses* are out-of-pocket costs necessary to generate and maintain the income stream. These costs fall into two general categories: fixed expenses and variable expenses. A third general category, reserves for replacements, is sometimes used.

Property taxes and hazard insurance are the two main fixed costs. *Fixed costs* are outlays that remain at the same level, regardless of the intensity of use of the property. Property taxes, for example, are levied on an annual basis and do not increase if occupancy climbs to 100 percent, nor do they decrease if occupancy drops to 65 percent.

Variable expenses, on the other hand, fluctuate with occupancy; more gas, water, electricity, and supplies are used with full occupancy than with 75 percent occupancy. Management is usually calculated as a percentage of EGI rather than of gross income to give the manager an incentive to keep the property as fully rented as possible. Calculation in this way also causes the management fee to fluctuate with occupancy. Repairs and miscellaneous services also tend to rise and fall with the number of tenants.

Building parts and many items of equipment have lives longer than 1 year but much shorter than the expected life of the building. Stoves, refrigerators, elevators, roofs, boilers, washers, dryers, carpeting, and air conditioning are examples. Yet these items must be replaced, as periodic out-of-pocket expenses. Accountants used to believe that the annual deduction for replacement of equipment and building parts should be placed in a special account called reserves for replacements. But, until the expense is incurred, it is not recognized by the Internal Revenue Service.

Deductions may still be made on the operating statement under this heading, however. If deducted, the amounts must be added back in for calculating taxes. Also, the monies are not necessarily placed in a special account. Straight line depreciation, dividing the cost of an item by its expected useful life, is the usual method used in calculating this deduction. Thus, a roof with an expected life of 15 years and a cost of $9,000 is expensed at $600 per year, $9,000/15 years. Reserves for replacements are not taken account of as out of pocket property maintenance expense in Figure 22-1.

Net Operating Income. The amount left over after total operating expenses have been deducted is called *net operating income* (NOI). NOI is the bottom line amount a property earns in a year in competition with other properties that offer similar services. Average or typical management is assumed to avoid rewarding or penalizing the property for superior or inferior management. NOI directly reflects a property's productivity and, as such, is a basic input into techniques to find value.

NOI is preferred to gross income as a measure of productivity because it is a standardized concept. Differences in costs of operation or leasing terms are taken into account in reaching NOI. Thus, NOI allows comparison of the subject property's net productivity with that of other properties. A prestige office building that generates high rents but that also has extremely high operating costs can thus be more fairly compared to a more modest office building on a long-term net lease.

NOI is supposed to indicate what a property can do on its own. Thus, some items, often considered by an owner-investor in analyzing an income property, are not included in calculating NOI. Therefore, financing costs, owner's income taxes, depreciation, and corporation taxes are excluded. These items, though important to an investor, have no effect on a property's ability to generate net revenue.

Mortgaging does not increase or decrease a property's market rent. Likewise, the owner's income taxes on money earned from the property reflect the owner's tax situation and not the rent generating ability of the property. Corporate ownership is an aside, so corporate taxes do not constitute an operating expense. Other items to be excluded are outlays for capital improvements and personal property taxes of an owner.

Building depreciation is not deductible as an operating expense because it is really a recovery of capital; it does not affect productivity and is not necessary to produce gross income. Depreciation is simply a loss in value that may be taken as an income tax deduction.

ANALYZING PRODUCTIVITY

Calculation of important ratios and an income forecast are both necessary prerequisites to finding market value and investment value.

Productivity Ratios. The standardized accounting format of the pro forma operating statement provides an excellent basis for the calculation of useful operating ratios. The best operating data are available for apartment buildings, shopping centers, and hotels and motels. Thus, excellent norms for interpreting ratios for these property types are also available. Some caution is needed in interpreting the ratios, but still their potential usefulness is extremely great.

The Institute of Real Estate Management publishes *Apartment House Income-Expense Experience* annually. The Urban Land Institute publishes *Dollars and Cents of Shopping Centers* every third year. The Building Owner's and Manager's Association and specialized accounting firms periodically publish operating information on hotels and motels, office buildings, and other specialized property types.

Two of the more useful ratios for evaluating property productivity are the income ratio and the operating expense ratio. The **income ratio** is the proportion of gross scheduled income represented by net operating income.

$$\text{income ratio} = \frac{\text{net operating income}}{\text{gross scheduled income}}$$

For Douglas Manor Apartments, the income ratio equals 59.3 percent.

$$\text{income ratio} = \frac{\$64,000}{\$108,000} = 0.593 = 59.3\%$$

The higher the income ratio, the greater the productivity of the property. This might be the result of good management, keeping the property fully rented while keeping control of operating expense. It might also be the result of high-quality construction that minimizes costs of repairs and maintenance.

An alternative ratio emphasizing controls of expenses is necessary for cost-control purposes. An *operating expense ratio* reflects operating expenses as a percentage of gross scheduled income:

$$\text{operating expense ratio} = \frac{\text{total operating expenses}}{\text{gross scheduled income}}$$

$$= \frac{\$39,680}{\$108,000} = 0.367 = 36.7\%$$

OE = TOE / GSI

An operating expense ratio might be used as follows. New apartment buildings typically have an operating ratio between 35 and 40 percent. As the building ages, costs of repairs and maintenance go up. The ratio gradually increases toward 50 percent and eventually 60 percent. The ratio tells the experienced investor or lender if an operating statement is realistic. A ratio of 32 percent for a new apartment building would indicate that perhaps not all expenses were reported or that expenses have been understated. Operating ratios vary from property type to property type, that is, from apartment house to office building to hotel, and so on.

Note that the total of the income ratio (59.3 percent), the vacancy and credit losses ratio (4 percent), and the operating expense ratio (36.7 percent), total to 100%. Thus, the three ratios give a complete accounting of the gross scheduled income.

Forecasting Productivity. An investor's central task is to forecast and evaluate expected benefits before investing, because expected benefits are the basis of value. The forecast depends on the property's location, on its physical and functional capability, and on local market conditions.

Current revenues, expenses, and NOI provide a take off point of some certainty for forecasting. Unless secured by a lease with a strong tenant, a forecast is only a secular trend or tendency. Short-term influences will cause fluctuations above and below a projected trend. One can assume, however, that, over time, the up and down movements will offset each other, and the average will reflect the underlying long-term forces.

Income Approach: Direct Capitalization

Direct capitalization means dividing net operating income, taken from a pro forma operating statement, by a market-derived ratio to obtain an indicated market value, almost a one-step process. The approach is based on the premise that market value equals the present worth of future rights to income after operating expenses, as judged by the typical investor. This means that the market value of a subject property depends directly on its annual net operating income. The conversion of expected income payments into a lump-sum present value is termed *capitalization.*

Direct income capitalization is most meaningfully applied to investment properties (apartment buildings, office buildings, warehouses, stores). The idea of capitalization here is based on a ratio, rather than on time value of money (TVM), although TVM is implicit in the ratio.

THE BASIC STEPS

The basic steps in the direct income capitalization process are (1) ascertain net operating income of the subject property, (2) derive an overall capitalization rate from the market sales prices of comparable properties, and (3) apply derived rate to the net operating income of the subject property to estimate market value of subject property, as shown in Figure 22-2.

AN APPLICATION

*4,000

Ascertain NOI of Subject. Step 1 is obtaining the NOI for the Douglas Manor Apartments for the coming year. Gross market rental is first ascertained and deductions are then made for vacancy and credit losses and total operating expenses; this leaves NOI as was done in the previous section. For the Douglas Manor Apartments, NOI equals $64,000.

Deriving the Capitalization Rate. Step 2 centers on deriving a capitalization rate from the market. Assuming comparable properties are found, the only information required about each is its net operating income and its sale price. Dividing the sale price into the net operating income gives a ratio, called an *overall capitalization rate,* by convention designated as "R":

$$\text{capitalization rate, "R" for a property} = \frac{\text{net operating income}}{\text{sale price}}$$

With three comparables, the calculations might be as follows.

$$\text{for comparable D, R} = \frac{\$59,400}{\$600,000} = 0.0990 \text{ or } 9.9\%$$

$$\text{for comparable E, R} = \frac{\$74,800}{\$740,000} = 0.1011 \text{ or } 10.11\%$$

$$\text{for comparable F, R} = \frac{\$46,500}{\$468,000} = 0.09935 \text{ or } 9.94\%$$

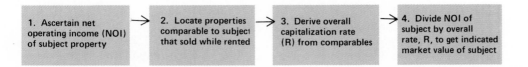

| 1. Ascertain net operating income (NOI) of subject property | → | 2. Locate properties comparable to subject that sold while rented | → | 3. Derive overall capitalization rate (R) from comparables | → | 4. Divide NOI of subject by overall rate, R, to get indicated market value of subject |

FIGURE 22-2
Steps in the direct capitalization technique of estimating market value

On the basis of these three ratios, an overall capitalization rate of 10 percent seems reasonable as a reflection of what the market is actually doing.

Applying the Capitalization Rate. In step 3, finding indicated market value, the NOI of the subject property is divided by the market-derived overall capitalization rate, R. This is really only a reversal of the process of deriving R. The relationship is

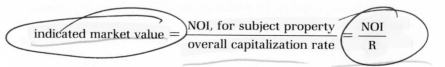

$$\text{indicated market value} = \frac{\text{NOI, for subject property}}{\text{overall capitalization rate}} = \frac{\text{NOI}}{\text{R}}$$

By using the $64,000 NOI from our Douglas Manor Apartments, we obtain an indicated market value of $640,000.

$$\text{indicated market value} = \frac{\$64,000}{10\%} = \$640,000$$

USES AND LIMITATIONS

The income approach obviously is applicable only to income properties, such as apartment buildings, office buildings, and rented warehouses and store buildings. In fact, it is best suited to larger income properties that have stable net operating incomes and are sold fairly frequently. Because of the manner in which the capitalization rate is derived, the approach yields value indications very similar to those generated by the market approach.

One major limitation of the direct capitalization technique is that sales of some income properties occur only infrequently; thus, the derivation of a capitalization rate must be based on limited information. In addition, obtaining or verifying the NOI of an income property that has been sold is often very difficult. Chance for error is introduced in calculating net operating income for the subject property because estimates of expense items are often based on judgment, and any error in estimating NOI is magnified several fold in the capitalization process. Further, the limitations that apply to deriving the gross income multiplier also largely apply to deriving R; for example, units, equipment, and so on must be comparable. Finally, the technique is not useful for properties that are unique or that generate income in the form of amenities.

By Way of Review

Several techniques or approaches to market value were discussed in chapter 21. A brief explanation of these methods, as they apply to income properties, seems appropriate here. The review will consist of a brief statement of the basic steps followed by an application.

GROSS INCOME MULTIPLIER TECHNIQUE

A *gross income multiplier* (GIM) relates total annual income to market value. It is the direct equivalent of the GRM technique discussed in the previous chapter, except the GIM applies to larger income properties. Also, the GIM technique focuses on total annual income rather than on monthly.

The basic steps of the GIM technique are set forth in Figure 21-1. By way of review, they are (1) ascertain the gross annual market income of the subject property, (2) derive a GIM from the market, and (3) apply the GIM to subject property to estimate its market value. Our application will be to the Douglas Manor Apartments.

The gross annual rental for the subject property, step 1, was ascertained as $108,000.

Derivation of the market GIM, step 2, is equivalent to extracting the market GRM (gross rent multiplier). That is, sales prices of comparable properties are divided by their respective gross annual incomes to get a range of GIMs. Sample calculations follow.

$$\text{gross income multiplier for a property} = \frac{\text{sale price}}{\text{gross annual income}} = \text{GIM}$$

$$\text{GIM, comparable K} = \frac{\$610,000}{\$101,400} = 6.02$$

$$\text{GIM, comparable L} = \frac{\$745,760}{\$124,500} = 5.99$$

$$\text{GIM, comparable M} = \frac{\$680,000}{\$113,200} = 6.01$$

On the basis of these calculations, a market GIM of 6.00 seems reasonable for apartment houses in this particular neighborhood at this time.

Step 3, applying the GIM to the gross income of the subject property gives an indicated market value of $648,000.

$$\begin{matrix} \text{Gross income} \\ \text{of subject} \end{matrix} \times \begin{matrix} \text{market-derived} \\ \text{GIM} \end{matrix} = \begin{matrix} \text{indicated market value} \\ \text{of subject} \end{matrix}$$

$$\$108,000 \times 6.00 = \$648,000$$

DIRECT SALES COMPARISON APPROACH

The direct sales comparison approach to market value was explained in the previous chapter, with an application to a single-family residence. The basic steps, again, are (1) collect data on sales of comparable properties, (2) select units of comparison and calculate, (3) adjust sales prices to subject property, and (4) estimate market value of subject.

Figure 22-3 assumes that data on comparable property sales have already been collected. It shows adjustments from the comparables to the subject property, the Douglas Manor Apartments. The three different adjusted sale prices per unit reflect comparison with each of the three respective comparable properties. The range is from $39,950 to $40,086. By using this information, an indicated market value of

Item of Comparison	Subject Property	Comparable Sales		
		730 Oakway	3320 Hilyard	1720 Park
Sale price	—	$610,000	$745,760	$680,000
Number of units	16	14	16	16
Sale price/unit		$ 43,571	$ 46,610	$ 42,500
Area/unit; square feet	1,102	1,145	1,088	1,092
Adjustments				
Terms of sale		Arms length	Arms length	Arms length
% adjustment		0.00	0.00	0.00
Time of sale				
Months since sale		0	3	4
% adjustment		0.00	3.00	4.00
Location				
Convenience ranking	6	6	9	6
% adjustment		0.00	− 10.00	0.00
Environment/view rank	8.0	8.0	8.0	8.0
% adjustment		0.00	0.00	0.00
Physical characteristics				
Overall condition	Rundown	Excellent	Fair	Excellent
% adjustment		− 10.00	− 5.00	− 10.00
Parking spaces/unit	$1\frac{1}{2}$	1	2	$1\frac{1}{2}$
% adjustment		2.00	− 2.00	0.00
Total % adjustment		− 8.00	− 14.00	− 6.00
Adjusted sales price/unit		$ 40,086	$ 40,085	$ 39,950
Indicated market value of subject based on this comparable		$641,371	$641,354	$639,200

FIGURE 22-3
Direct sales comparison analysis of the Douglas Manor Apartments

$40,000 per unit for the subject property would be justified. Figure 22-3 also shows the indicated market value of the Douglas Manor Apartments, based on each comparable; the range is from $639,200 to $641,371. On an overall basis, an indicated market value of $640,000 for the subject property seems reasonable.

16 units × $40,000/unit = $640,000

Again, analysis on a per unit basis allows comparisons between different sized properties. That is, a 14-unit property may be compared with a 20-unit property if other things are generally the same. Further, recognize that our purpose here is to again illustrate the concept and the process as applied to an income-producing property.

DEPRECIATED COST APPROACH

An application of the cost less depreciation to an income property is appropriate here. By way of review, the steps are (1) estimate market value of subject site, (2) estimate cost new of subject improvements, (3) estimate accrued depreciation and deduct from cost of improvements, and (4) add site value and depreciated costs of improvements together to get indicated market value of subject property.

The depreciated cost of the Douglas Manor apartments in their present condition is estimated at $641,600; see Figure 22-4. Thus, the indicated market value by

Land, market value (by direct sales comparison)		$ 88,000	
plus: landscaping, walks, drive, etc.		12,000	
Total site value		$100,000	$100,000
Reproduction cost new of improvements			
Main structure: 24,800 square feet at	$ 30.00	$744,000	
Garage area: 6,000 square feet at	$ 8.00	48,000	
Miscellaneous (blinds, storage areas, etc.)		43,200	
Total cost new		$835,200	
Less depreciation			
Physical deterioration	$106,000		
Functional obsolescence	86,000		
External obsolescence	101,600		
Total depreciation	$293,600	293,600	
		$541,600	541,600
			$641,600

FIGURE 22-4
Depreciated cost of Douglas Manor Apartments

the cost approach is $641,600. But cost is not value. Only if market value exceeds cost would an investor choose this alternative.

Reconciliation

Figure 22-5 summarizes the value indications for the Douglas Manor Apartments obtained in this chapter. They range from $640,000 to $648,000; the average or mean is $642,600.

The value indications are in a narrower range than is likely to be found in practice. The temptation is to take the average or mean as the final estimate of market value. However, an appraiser must rely on experience, logic, and judgment and assign weights to the alternative methods rather than simply averaging.

Approach or technique	Indicated market value	Analyst's weighting	Weighted indication
Income approach			
Direct capitalization	$640,000	45.00%	$288,000
Gross income multiplier	648,000	5.00	32,400
Direct sales comparison approach	640,000	50.00	320,000
Depreciated cost approach	641,600	0.00	0
Weighted estimated of market value			$640,400
Rounded estimate of market value			$640,000

FIGURE 22-5
Douglas Manor Apartments, summary and reconciliation of value indications

The value indications by the direct sales comparison and the direct capitalization approaches are considered most reliable when adequate data are available, as is presumed here. GIM analysis is generally thought of as giving an approximation of value that is not fully reliable. Finally, the cost approach has some serious limitations when accrued depreciation for older properties must be estimated. Thus, direct capitalization is given a weight of 45 percent, GIM analysis of 5 percent, and direct sales comparison of 50 percent. Given the adequacy of these three methods, the depreciated cost approach is weighted 0 percent. The final estimate of the most probable selling price of the Douglas Manor Apartments is therefore judged to be $640,000 at this time.

Case Problems

1. a. Organize the following items into a pro forma annual operating statement. All quantities are on an annual basis.

Gross income	$24,000	Mortgage debt	
Miscellaneous expenses	200	service	$6,400
Property taxes	2,000	Property maintenance	
Hazard insurance	600	expense	1,000
Salaries: maintenance		Owner's income taxes	4,600
and operating	2,000	Supplies	800
Management, as percent		V&CL as percent of	
of EGI	5%	gross income	5%
		(NOI = $15,060)	

   b. What is the income ratio?   (62.75%)
   c. What is the operating ratio?   (32.25%)

2. a. You obtain the following information about a property you are analyzing. All quantities are on an annual basis. Develop a pro forma annual operating statement based on this information.

Mortgage debt service	$72,000	Owner's income taxes	$12,800
Property taxes	10,200	Salaries: maintenance	
Property maintenance	4,000	and operating	4,800
Hazard insurance	1,200	Supplies	1,800
Security deposits	8,000	Utilities	3,000
Gross scheduled		Miscellaneous	600
income	96,000	Management as percent	
V&CL as percent of		of EGI	5%
gross income	4%	(NOI = $65,420)	

   b. What is the income ratio?
   c. What is the operating ratio?

3. A new zoning ordinance, allowing for less intense development of parcels, has just been initiated and makes the usual rules of thumb for valuing parcels obsolete. The following three sales of parcels, all zones for multi residential use, were made in the year just previous to the change. The subject site contains 18,000 square feet, but under the new zoning, it can only be developed with 36 dwelling units. Considering all factors, what is the probable value of the subject site? Explain any modifying circumstances, and their probable effect on value.

a. Price = $180,000, area = 12,000 square feet

Number of one- and two-bedroom apartments allowed = 30

b. Price = $221,400, area = 14,250 square feet

Number of dwelling units allowed = 36

c. Price = $166,000, area = 11,000 square feet

Number of dwelling units allowed = 28   ($6,250+/DU)

4. You are appraising a vacant downtown site, 1.5 blocks from the main business area of Park City. The owner is contemplating a long-term lease to a local parking lot operator. The subject parcel is 80 feet × 120 feet, is located in the middle of the block, is level and on grade with the street, and has a public rear alley. The offer is for $12,000 per year, net, to the owner. Three sales are available as comparables.

Comparable 1, 90 feet × 115 feet, is directly across the street and sold 2 years ago for $82,000. It is level and has a rear alley.

Comparable 2 is a corner parcel, 60 feet × 120 feet, one block south of the subject, that sold 2 months ago for $100,000. It also is level with a rear alley.

Comparable 3 is 80 feet × 120 feet, located in the middle of the next block south, sold 6 months ago for $105,000 and is very similar to subject.

Appropriate adjustments are as follows.

For time: Plus 10 percent per year.

For location: Subject area is considered to be 10 percent better than that one block to the north and 10 percent less desirable than that one block to the south. Site across the street is comparable to the subject. A corner site is 20 percent superior to a mid-block lot.

You are to analyze the property, with the following steps.

a. Diagram the locations of the vacant sites. Include some indication of relative desirability and values.

b. Set up a grid to adjust sale prices on a per square foot basis.

c. Estimate the market value of the subject site, and give recommendations for or against the proposed lease.   (M.V. = $96,000)

5. You are a loan officer. An owner approaches your lending institution for a $100,000 mortgage loan. The parcel is vacant, with a commercial zoning and an appraised market value of $50,000. The proposed improvements will cost $110,000, based on firm contractor estimates. No depreciation or diminished utility is expected because the structure would be well designed.

Your institution has an established policy of a 65 percent maximum loan-to-value ratio on commercial loans. The building is expected to have a 50-year economic life. The current interest rate is 12 percent. Expected gross annual income is $30,000, with V&CL plus total operating expenses coming to 40 percent of gross. Local gross income multipliers for this type property typically run about 5.2. Overall capitalization rates range from 11.1 to 11.3 percent in the area. No sales of comparable properties are available. Determine the following.

a. Indicated market value by the cost approach?

b. Indicated market value, using the GIM technique?

c. Indicated market value, using the overall cap rate?

d. Your estimate of market value, upon reconciling the several approaches?

e. Would the requested loan be within your company's guidelines?

f. Whether the property would be able to carry the debt service comfortably, assuming a 25-year term? A 15-year term?

23

Federal Taxes Affecting Real Estate

The art of taxation consists in so plucking the goose as to obtain the largest amount of feathers with the least amount of hissing.

Jean Baptiste Colbert

Taxes are what we pay for civilized society, according to a 1904 U.S. Supreme Court Ruling.[1] In 1947 Judge Learned Hand said,

> Over and over again, courts have said that there is nothing sinister in so arranging one's affairs as to keep taxes as low as possible. Everybody does so, rich or poor; and all do right, for nobody owes any public duty to pay more than the law demands: Taxes are enforced extractions, not voluntary contributions. To demand more in the name of morals is mere cant.[2]

Thus, no person is obliged to place himself or herself in the highest possible tax-paying position. Rather, the prudent person is expected to practice *tax avoidance,* which means to plan and conduct one's affairs and transactions to minimize the taxes paid. Such planning requires that the citizen be well informed on tax law. Tax evasion, on the other hand, is illegal and is punishable by fine, imprisonment, or both. Padding expense accounts, making false and fraudulent claims, and failing to submit a return are forms of *tax evasion.*

The basic purpose of U.S. tax law is to raise revenue to operate the federal

[1]Compania de Tobocas v. Collector, 275 US87, 100 (1904).
[2]Commissioner v. Newman, 159 F. 2nd 848 (2d. Cir. 1947).

government; it is hoped that this is done in an efficient and equitable manner. A second purpose is to promote and achieve socially and economically desirable ends.

The U.S. federal income tax law is administered and enforced by the Internal Revenue Service (IRS), which is a division of the U.S. Treasury Department.

Tax law is very complex and sticky. Because of this it is sometimes called a bramble bush, implying that everyone working with it gets stuck at one time or another. Many books and manuals have been written to explain the subject. Millions of dollars are spent in tax litigation each year. No last word is possible, because the law coming out of the tax courts changes almost on a daily basis. Decisions, therefore, should not be based solely on the material presented here; further checks should be made with competent accountants and attorneys and other reliable sources.

Important Topics or Decision Areas Covered in this Chapter

Tax Basics
Taxable Income
Tax Rates
Tax Shelters
Four Classes of Real Property

Administrative/Operations Phase
Depreciation or Cost Recovery
Tax Credits

Alienation or Disposition Phase
Ordinary Sale

Acquisition Phase
Tax Implications of Ownership Form
Tax Basis
Installment Sale
Tax-Deferred Exchange

Questions for Review and Discussion

Case Problems

Key Concepts Introduced in this Chapter

Adjusted cost basis
Book value
Boot
Capital gain income
Dealer
Installment sale
"Like kind" of property
Nonresidential property
Realized gain

Recognized gain
Residential rental property
Tax avoidance
Tax basis
Tax credit
Tax-deferred exchange
Tax depreciation
Tax evasion
Tax shelter

Tax Basics

Federal tax laws affect most real estate investment decisions as to income reported and taxes paid. Our discussion covers the federal tax regulations in generalized form, including recently enacted provisions of the Tax Reform Act (TRA) of 1986. Basic concepts are taken up first, to provide a framework, followed by applications in the three phases of the investment cycle. A generalized format for calculating income taxes due is shown in Figure 23-1.

```
Gross income (from wages, rents, interest, commissions, etc.)
 − adjustments (as payments to retirement plans, etc.)
 = adjusted gross income
 − deductions (operating expenses for real estate, depreciation, and mortgage interest payments)
 = taxable income
 × tax rate
 = tax on income
 − tax credits allowed
 = amount payable to IRS
```

FIGURE 23-1
Generalized calculation of federal income tax

TAXABLE INCOME

Taxable income has traditionally been divided into two classes: ordinary and capital gains, each with its own tax treatment. The 1986 TRA removed the difference in treatment; even so, there is a likelihood of distinct treatment again. So, each class is explained.

Ordinary Income. Wages, salaries, commissions, professional fees, and business income make up ordinary income. Dividends, interest, rental, and royalty income also fit into this class. Expenses incurred to generate this income and exemptions may be deducted to determine the ordinary income that is taxable.

Capital Gains Income. A *capital gain* is a profit realized when a capital asset, such as real estate, is sold for more than its book value or adjusted cost basis. *Book value,* for capital gains purposes, is value based on accounting calculations and events. It is also called the tax basis or adjusted cost basis. For example, an investor pays $300,000 for an apartment property, on which $90,000 in tax depreciation is taken during a 6-year ownership period. The investor then sells the property for $345,000. The realized capital gain or profit is $135,000, calculated as follows.

Sale price, end of year 6		$345,000
Purchase price	$300,000	
Less tax depreciation	− 90,000	
Book value of property	$210,000	− 210,000
Capital gain or profit		$135,000

The tax or bookkeeping depreciation accounts for $90,000 of the gain; market-value appreciation accounts for the other $45,000.

The rationale for distinct tax treatment of capital gains and losses is that the gain or loss takes place over an extended period. With a progressive income tax, the impact would be magnified if all the gain or loss were attributed to the year of sale or exchange. It is not practical to revalue each and every capital asset each year to determine possible gain or loss annually. So the tax code simply applied special rules to gains and losses realized from capital assets held for longer than a prescribed minimum period, such as 12 months, and termed long-term capital gains (LTCG) or losses.

A capital gain must be realized to be taxable. A *realized gain* means that cash or boot was obtained in the sale or exchange of the capital asset. *Boot* is cash or the value of personal property given or received to balance equities in the transaction. For example, an owner trades a hotel for an office building plus a 1988 Buick and $150,000 cash. The car and the cash are boot. A known increase in the value of a capital asset that is not realized as boot or cash is termed *recognized gain,* which is not taxable until it is realized. That is, a recognized gain may be transferred from one capital asset or property to another without being subjected to taxation in what is termed a tax-deferred exchange.

TAX RATES

Annual net taxable personal income is taxed at rates of either 15 or 28 percent; under special circumstances a top rate of 33 percent is possible. Corporate tax rates graduate from 15 up to 34 percent. See Figure 23-2.

TAX SHELTERS

A *tax shelter* is a means of reducing taxes on income, generally obtained by deferring realization of the income. Realization is deferred by using a bookkeeping loss, an expense not involving an expenditure of cash, to avoid paying taxes on income as it is received. Such expenses are termed "artificial losses."

Taxable Income	Tax Rate, %
Single	
Less than $17,850	15
Greater than $17,851	28
Married, filing jointly	
Less than $29,750	15
Greater than $29,751	28
Corporations	
$50,000 or less	15
$50,001 to $75,000	25
$75,000 and above	34

FIGURE 23-2
Marginal income tax rates under
1986 Tax Reform Act

Tax depreciation on buildings is an example of an artificial loss. The IRS recognizes buildings as wasting assets; therefore, an owner may take an annual depreciation allowance to recover an investment in a wasting asset even though the building does not decline in value as judged by the market. The allowance is deducted as an expense from the income generated by the property. Thus, the NOI of $64,000 for the Douglas Manor Apartments (see Chapter 22) may be reduced by $20,000 as a cost recovery or depreciation allowance; see Figure 23-3. In addition, interest on borrowed funds is deductible, e.g., $60,000 in year 1 on the Douglas Manor Apartments, obtained from Figure 16-7. This means that taxable income for the Douglas Manor Apartments in year 1 is a minus $16,000. Assuming a 28 percent tax rate, this means a tax saving of $4,480 ($16,000 multiplied by 28 percent) in year 1. See Figure 23-3 for the complete calculation.

The IRS does not consider land to be a wasting asset, and therefore no depreciation expense may be take against it. To benefit from tax depreciation, market value must not, in fact, decline; if it does, the depreciation allowance is really a recovery of the investment, and no advantage has been gained. In turn, no offsetting capital gain or profit will be realized upon sale of the property.

FOUR CLASSES OF REAL PROPERTY

We are now ready to take up the four classes of real property recognized in the federal tax code. These are (1) property held for sale; (2) property held for use in trade or business; (3) property held for investment; and (4) property held as for personal use. Tax treatment differs from class to class.

Property Held for Sale. The owner of property held for sale is termed a *dealer,* and such real estate is referred to as "dealer property." Dealer property is considered merchant inventory and not a capital asset. Lots being held by a subdivider or condominiums being held by a developer are examples. The purpose is sale for profit as opposed to generation of income from rents or investment appreciation for capital gains.

Calculation of Tax Payable		Calculation of CFAT	
Gross scheduled income	$108,000		
Less vacancy and credit (V&C) losses	− 4,320		
Effective gross income	$103,680		
Less operating expenses	− 39,680		
Net operating income	$ 64,000	Net operating income	$64,000
Less interest on loan	− 60,000	Less annual debt service	− 63,750
Less tax depreciation	− 20,000	Equal before tax cash flow	$ 250
Taxable income	($ 16,000)		
Multiplied by tax rate	× 28%		
Tax payable (saving)	($ 4,480)	Less tax payable (saving)	− (4,480)
		Equals cash flow after tax	$ 4,730

FIGURE 23-3

Douglas Manor Apartments: Calculation of tax payable and cash flow after tax, CFAT

Income or losses from dealer property receive the same tax treatment as income and losses on merchant inventory. To begin with, no tax depreciation is allowed. Further, all gains are treated as ordinary income and all losses as ordinary losses. Thus, houses held by a developer are the equivalent of cars held by an automobile dealer. Last, neither capital gains and losses nor a tax-deferred exchange is recognized.

Property Held for Use in Trade or Business. A service station owned by an oil company, an industrial plant owned by a manufacturer, or a store owned by a merchant are examples of property held for use in a trade or business. The real estate is considered a factor of production in much the same sense as equipment in a factory rather than as merchandise held for sale. Tax treatment is according to Section 1231 of the tax code; hence, trade or business property is often termed "1231 property."

Rental real estate qualifies as 1231 property, with the owner considered to be in the "rental business"; that is, in the business of owning and renting space, such as apartments or offices. Owners of apartment houses, stores, warehouses, shopping centers, and the like are therefore better off to take the 1231 classification. Key tax implications follow.

1. Tax depreciation may be taken on the wasting asset portion of the property, along with other expenses of operating and maintaining the property.
2. The property may be traded for like kind of real estate in a tax-deferred exchange, making possible deferral of capital gains taxes in relocating or in trading up in property size.
3. Gains and losses on sale may be used as direct additions or offsets to ordinary income or expenses.

Property Held for Investment. Investment property is held primarily for capital appreciation rather than the production of income; an investment motive must exist. Lots, unimproved land, or a condominium in a resort area fit into this class. Nominal income, such as that from rental for grazing or sign boards is not sufficient to move property from this class to that of trade or business property.

Owners of investment property face the following tax implications:

1. Interest payments may be "expensed" only up to the amount of "nominal" investment income earned by the owner or owners from this and other property. Interest payments beyond nominal income must be capitalized, that is, added to the tax basis. All interest expense may be capitalized if the investor wishes.
2. A depreciation allowance cannot be taken because the property is regarded as not producing income.
3. The property may be traded in a tax-deferred exchange for like kind of real estate.

Property Held for Personal Use. A single-family house or a condominium used as a personal dwelling are examples of property held for personal use. Tax treatment of personal residential property is looked at in detail in Chapter 17. Its tax treatment, in summary, is as follows.

1. Real property taxes and interest on a loan against the property may be taken as income tax deductions.

2. Depreciation may not be taken as an income tax deduction.
3. Sale or exchange results in a taxable gain but a loss that is nondeductible for tax purposes. That is, if sold for less than the purchase price, the loss may not be used as an offset against other income. A "rollover" privilege applies to the gain; that is, if a replacement residence of equal or greater value is acquired within 24 months before or after the sale data, no tax need be paid on the gain.
4. A personal residence does not qualify as "like kind" property in a tax-deferred exchange for other classes of real property.

Acquisition Phase

When acquiring income-producing real estate, the way ownership is held, ownership form, and depreciable tax basis are the two crucial decisions.

TAX IMPLICATIONS OF OWNERSHIP FORM

Selection of an appropriate ownership form (corporate, partnership, or sole) has definite implications for the amount of taxes payable on a real estate investment. Liability exposure and liquidity are also involved in selecting the form. These concerns must be balanced one against the other in selecting between ownership forms.

1. *Limit taxes payable.* Any taxes paid on income from an investment directly reduce the rate of return to be realized. Therefore, double taxation should be avoided; beyond this, opportunities to defer taxes are desirable.
2. *Limit liability.* Safety of principal is a primary concern of an investor; the less the chance of loss of principal, the better. Beyond this, for most investors, liability or chance of loss of more than the amount invested should be strictly avoided.
3. *Liquidity.* An investment that can readily be coverted to cash is preferable to one that lacks liquidity.

Alternative forms of ownership were discussed at length in Chapter 4. They include a sole or individual proprietorship, general and limited partnership, Regular or C-corporations, S-corporations, and real estate investment trusts, REITs. These forms are compared briefly in Figure 23-4 relative to how they meet the above criteria.

The 1986 Tax Reform Act effectively puts limited partnerships, S-corporations, and REITs on par in that each allows avoidance of personal liability and double taxation. Ownership of C-corporation shares offers limited liability but commits to double taxation. All four of these ownership forms are easier to sell or trade than equity positions, which gives them better liquidity than sole ownership or general partnership interests. Also, sole ownership and general partnership clearly have risks of loss and extended liability beyond the initial cash investment. Finally, REITs must pay out 90 percent of profits each year to maintain their status as a tax-free income conduit.

OWNERSHIP FORMS	Benefits or Pluses	Limitations or Minuses
Sole proprietorship or general partnership	Single taxation only Maximum tax benefits	Personal liability Liquidity is low
Limited partnership, S-corporations, and REIT	Single taxation only Limited personal liability Liquidity is high to moderate	Tax benefits not necessarily maximized
Regular or C-corporation	Limited personal liability Liquidity is high to moderate	Double taxation of income Tax benefits not necessarily maximized

FIGURE 23-4
Comparison of ownership forms for real estate investments

TAX BASIS

Tax basis is an expression of property value or cost for tax purposes that is determined at the time of acquisition. In an accounting sense, tax basis is book value. Basis is necessary to determine the amount of depreciation expense (tax shelter) that may be charged off for income tax purposes. Basis is also needed to determine the capital gain or loss on selling. Basis changes through time as a result of the taking of depreciation, the making of improvements, and exchanging. Modified tax basis is called adjusted tax basis or *adjusted cost basis* (ACB).

Acquisition of Tax Basis. The purchase price or cost of land plus improvements is the initial basis of a property. The use of credit to help finance the purchase has no influence on the basis acquired by the new owner. Thus, a property purchased for $640,000 has an initial basis of $640,000, even though a $500,000 mortgage loan were used to help finance the purchase. Special rules, not taken up here, determine the basis to a new owner when property is acquired by other means as gift, inheritance, or exchange.

Allocation of Tax Basis. Only the wasting-asset portion of a real asset may be depreciated for income tax purposes. Thus a new owner must allocate the purchase price or basis between the land and improvements. The ratio of this allocation must be based on the fair market value of the land and the improvements at time of acquisition, according to the IRS. Two methods of making this allocation are used most often:

1. The ratio of land value and improvement value to total property value as determined by the local tax assessor
2. An allocation of property value to land and improvements provided by a qualified fee appraiser

The allocation process is straightforward. For example, assume a property is purchased at its market value of $640,000. Its assessed value is $320,000, or 50 percent of market value. The assessor's records show an allocation of $45,000, or 14.06 percent, to the land and $275,000, or 85.94 percent, to the improvements. In turn, $550,000, or 85.94 percent, of the purchase price, may be depreciated by the new owner.

Changes in Tax Basis. Tax basis changes through time. Common ways of increasing basis are by making capital improvements, such as building an addition or installing an elevator. The purchase of adjacent property will increase the basis. Carrying expenses, property taxes, and loan interest may be capitalized to further increase basis for investment property. Taking depreciation, selling off a portion of a property, or an uninsured casualty loss (fire) decreases the basis.

An example may be helpful here. An investor buys two vacant lots for $40,000, adds $120,000 worth of improvements to one lot, and sells the other for $60,000. The investor takes $16,000 of depreciation. What is the current adjusted cost basis of the property still owned?

Action	Amount	Change in Basis	ACB
Purchase lots	$ 40,000	+ 40,000	$ 40,000
Add improvements	120,000	+ 120,000	160,000
Sell lot 2	60,000	− 20,000	140,000
Take depreciation	16,000	− 16,000	124,000

The adjusted cost basis is $124,000. Note that in selling lot 2, only the basis attributed to lot 2 is deducted in making the adjustment to basis. The $40,000 profit on lot 2 (sale prices less cost, or $60,000 less $20,000) is reported as a capital gain.

Administrative/Operations Phase

Important topics in the operations phase of owning an income property are use of depreciation as a tax shelter and of tax credits to directly reduce taxes payable.

DEPRECIATION OR COST RECOVERY

The federal tax laws allow the recovery of a wasting asset over its remaining useful life, which is consistent with economic principles. Prior to 1986, several methods of calculating depreciation or cost recovery were acceptable. The Tax Reform Act of 1986 reduced the methods to one—straight line depreciation—thereby greatly simplifying tax depreciation calculations. Either 27.5 or 40 years is the period allowed for depreciating residential rental real estate, and either 31.5 or 40 years are allowed for nonresidential real estate. The 27.5 year straight line schedule for the Douglas Manor Apartments is shown in Figure 23-5.

The distinction between residential and nonresidential real estate for depreciation purposes is to implement social policy. *Residential rental property* derives at

Time end of year	Tax basis of site	Adjusted basis of improvements	Tax basis of property
0	$90,000	$550,000	$640,000
1	90,000	530,000	620,000
2	90,000	510,000	600,000
3	90,000	490,000	580,000
4	90,000	470,000	560,000
5	90,000	450,000	540,000

Purchase price and initial tax basis of property	$ 640,000
Less site value	− 90,000
Initial tax basis of improvements	$ 550,000
Residential property depreciation term, years	27.5
Annual depreciation allowance: straight line	$ 20,000

FIGURE 23-5
Douglas Manor: First 5 years tax basis and depreciation schedule

least 80 percent of its income from rentals as dwelling units for long-term tenants; thus, motels and hotels are not classified as residential property. With shorter cost recovery times, real estate used for living units gets a faster write off, and, theoretically, rents for a given amount of space should be slightly lower for families and low-income people. It follows that *nonresidential property* is made up of commercial and industrial real estate, such as warehouses, stores, factories, office buildings, and motels and hotels.

TAX CREDITS

It is also social policy to encourage rehabilitation of older buildings, to encourage better insulation of buildings thereby promoting energy conservation, and to encourage the installation of pollution controls. Investment tax credits are used as incentives for these very worthy purposes. A *tax credit* is a dollar-for-dollar offset against taxes due and payable, which makes it a much more potent device than simply allowing costs incurred for these purposes to be expensed off in shorter periods.

Industrial, commercial, and other income-producing buildings (factories, office buildings, retail stores, hotels and motels) qualify for rehabilitation tax credits. However, residential rental structures do not qualify, except when certified historical structures. Costs of acquisition or enlargement of such properties are not recognized expenses. In addition, 75 percent of the existing exterior walls must be retained. The tax basis of the rehabilitated property is reduced by the amount of any such credit. The amount of the allowable tax credit varies with the age and use of the building, according to the following schedule.

Rehabilitation expenditures	investment credit percentage
30–39-year-old nonresidential structure	15
40-year-old nonresidential structure	20
Certified historical structure, residential or nonresidential	25

Example. Alfred Romero buys a 39-year-old office building for $100,000 and then waits 1 year before spending $120,000 renovating it. The property qualifies for a 20 percent investment tax credit, which amounts to $24,000 ($120,000 × 20%). What is the effect on Romero's taxes? What is Romero's tax basis in the property following renovation?

Effect on Romero's taxes:	
Tax liability prior to investment credit	$ 60,000
Less investment credit	− 24,000
Equals net taxes payable	$ 36,000
Tax basis of property following rehabilitation:	
Acquisition price	$ 100,000
Plus renovation costs	+ 120,000
Total invested	$ 220,000
Less investment tax credit	− 24,000
Equals adjusted tax basis	$ 196,000

An investment tax credit is subject to recapture upon early sale of the rehabilitated property, as follows.

Disposition	Recapture
1st year	100%
2nd year	80%
3rd year	60%
4th year	40%
5th year	20%

Thus, if Alfred sells the building in year 3, a $14,400 increase in tax liability is incurred ($24,000 × 60%) for the year.

Alienation or Disposition Phase

After several years an owner often finds it advantageous to dispose of or "get out of" a specific property, mainly because the depreciation tax shelter has largely been used up. This change may be accomplished by cash sale, installment sale, or a tax-deferred exchange. Advantages vary with each of these techniques but are generally considered to be greatest with the exchange. In looking at these alternatives, the owner is assumed to be in the 28 percent tax bracket.

ORDINARY SALE

Cash sale means the owner-seller gets all of his or her equity out in cash in the year of sale. Cash sale is desirable when a taxpayer wishes to change the makeup of his or her investment portfolio. Also, cash sale may be desirable if the taxpayer needs to release equity for personal reasons, such as to establish a retirement annuity.

Example. Ben Franklin sells a fourplex, that he owned for 4 years, for $150,000 in December. He used straight line depreciation since buying the property, and his present tax basis is $90,000. This means a profit of $60,000 and a potential tax of $16,800 on the sale.

Sale price	$150,000
Less adjusted tax basis	− 90,000
Equals profit or gain	$ 60,000
Multiplied by marginal tax rate	× 28%
Equals tax on gain	$ 16,800

With as large a tax bite as $16,800, deferring the tax as long as possible becomes important. Thus, installment sales and tax-deferred exchanges come into play in Ben's thinking.

INSTALLMENT SALE

An **installment sale** is when the buyer makes payments over more than 1 year. The seller pays taxes on gains as they are received. An installment land contract and a first or second purchase money mortgage are typical vehicles for deferring payments. To show the effect on Ben's taxes, let us restructure the previous cash sale to an installment sale.

Example. Assume Ben negotiates for equal payments of $30,000 per year for each of 5 years. The initial payment would occur in the year of sale. What is the impact on taxes payable by Ben?

First, a brief restatement of the situation.

Sale price (contract price)	$150,000
Less present tax basis (3/5 of contract price)	− 90,000
Equals long-term capital gain (2/5 of contract price)	$ 60,000

Ben will receive the full $150,000 over 5 years, of which $90,000 is a return of capital. The remaining $60,000 is the gain. Of every dollar received, 3/5 ($90,000/$150,000) is return of capital and 2/5 ($60,000/$150,000) is gain.

Thus, in the year of sale and in each of the next 4 years, Ben's situation would look like this:

Payment received (1/5 of contract price)	$30,000
Less basis (3/5 of installment)	− 18,000
Gain reported for year (2/5 of installment)	$12,000
Multiplied by Ben's tax rate	× 28%
Equals tax payable on installment	$ 3,360

Ben's tax payable in year of sale is $3,360, or one-fifth of his payment in a cash sale. The calculation of tax is identical with the cash sale, except for the proration by installment. Comparable calculations would be made as payments are received in subsequent years. Thus, total taxes paid remain the same, but the timing of payment is deferred. If, in later years, Ben were in a 15 percent tax bracket, the total tax bill could be greatly reduced. Also, Ben would expect to get interest on the unpaid balance with each installment received.

TAX-DEFERRED EXCHANGE

In an exchange for *"like kind" of property*, the gain, though realized in an economic sense, is not recognized for tax purposes. A transaction of this type is frequently referred as a "tax-free" exchange; a more accurate statement is that it is a *tax-deferred exchange.* In a well-structured exchange, little or no gain is realized for tax purposes, and, hence, little or no tax must be paid.

Tax basis, market value, mortgages, and equities must all be taken into account in arranging an exchange; the actual structuring of an exchange tends to be very complex. For this reason, other than to stipulate elements of an exchange, the subject will not be pursued further here. The elements that must be present in an exchange to qualify it for nonrecognition of gain or loss are as follows.

1. The transaction must be an exchange as distinguished from a sale and separate purchase.
2. The exchange must involve like kinds or similar properties. Business and investment properties may be exchanged for each other. Likewise, city real estate may be exchanged for country property. A warehouse may be traded for a supermarket. Like kind therefore refers to business or investment property that is exchanged for business or investment property.

On the other hand, a personal residence may not be exchanged for a business property, with taxes deferred. A tax-deferred exchange of real property for personal property is not recognized. Finally, "dealer" real estate may not be exchanged for investment real estate.

Considerable planning is required to properly structure a tax-deferred exchange. Usually, some unlike kinds of property (remember boot) must be added to balance the equities in the transaction. To the extent that boot is used and gain is recognized, taxes must be paid as a result of the transaction.

Questions for Review and Discussion

1. Distinguish between ordinary and capital gains income, and describe the methods of calculating tax payable on each.
2. What is a tax shelter? Give at least two examples or illustrations.
3. List four classes of real estate for tax purposes, and briefly explain the tax treatment applicable to each.

4. What is tax basis? How is it initially established? How does it change through time?
5. Explain briefly the calculation of depreciation by the straight-line methods.
6. Explain how investment and market values of real estate are influenced by tax factors.
7. Is tax depreciation different from market depreciation? If so, must there always be a difference? Discuss.

Case Problems

1. What is the marginal tax rate for an unmarried individual with a taxable income of $25,000? For a married couple with the same taxable income and filing a joint return?
2. For the taxpayers in problem 1, determine the value of an additional $2,000 of tax depreciation. Is the value higher for the unmarried individual or the married couple? Why? ($260 advantage to unmarried)
3. Jennie purchased a vacant lot for $100,000 and added a $600,000 building to create a residential income property. Rentals started as of January 1. Determine the cost recovery allowance, per year and total, by the 27.5- and 40-year straight-line methods for the first 4 years of ownership. Which period is normally preferred? Why?
4. Jennie sells the property of problem 3 above at end of year 4. The sale price is $900,000. What tax liability from the sale, assuming a 28 percent marginal tax bracket and use of 27.5-year straight-line depreciation? ($80,436)
5. If the property were an office building and 31.5-year depreciation were used, what tax liability for Jennie on sale at end of year 4? How much difference from the residential income property above? Is this a reason for using a longer-term depreciation schedule?
6. Jim sells a property for $300,000 on an installment sale with $50,000 down and the balance scheduled for equal payments over the next 5 years. His present tax basis is $200,000. What is the tax in the year of sale? What is the tax in subsequent years? ($4,667)

24

Investment Valuation: Overview and Strategy

Never follow the crowd.
Bernard Baruch, American financier and presidential advisor

We have already looked at the major components of the real estate decision-making cycle: (1) investor goals and constraints, (2) ownership rights, (3) financing, and (4) markets and the investment climate. Now, we look at how all these components fit together for anyone making an investment decision. Initially, we look at two broad considerations in real estate investing. These are the nature of real estate as an investment and the characteristics of property types as investments. Each involves general strategy rather than quantified analysis.

We conclude this chapter with an overview of discounted cash flow (DCF) methodology, including a look at key variables when using it to determine investment value. *Investment value,* for our purposes, is the total amount (loan + cash equity) that can be paid for a property with the expectation of realizing investment goals.

Important Topics or Decision Areas Covered in this Chapter

Nature of Real Estate as an Investment
Advantages
Disadvantages
Risk and Return
Comparing Investment Media

Characteristics of Property Types as Investments
Vacant or Raw Land
Apartments
Office Buildings

Warehouses
Small Shopping Centers
Hotels and Motels

Key Concepts Introduced in this Chapter

Business risk	**Management risk**
Financial risk	**Market risk**
Interest rate risk	**Purchasing power risk**
Investment value	**Pyramiding**
Legislative risk	**Required rate of return**
Liquidity	**Sensitivity analysis**
Liquidity risk	

Nature of Real Estate as an Investment

An investment is the act of putting money into property or a business to obtain profits. Real estate is like many other investments in its ability to provide profits in the forms of periodic income and/or value appreciation. But real estate also has its own unique advantages and limitations as an investment.

ADVANTAGES

Many of the advantages of real estate as an investment are in its surrounding traditions and institutions.

Leverage. As explained in Chapter 14, positive leverage is the use of borrowed monies to increase the rate of return earned from an equity investment. This presumes that the investment earns at a higher rate than is paid for the borrowed monies. Traditionally, real estate investors borrow from 60 to 90 percent of the value of any properties owned or acquired, which is a much higher ratio of leverage than is available on most other investments.

With positive leverage, the higher the ratio, the higher is the rate of return on equity. This often means a higher dollar cash flow per dollar of equity investment. Also, a high leverage ratio increases the likelihood that tax depreciation will shelter most of the cash flow.

Leverage also enables an investor to control more property with a given amount of money. By maintaining high leverage through slow repayment or frequent refinancing, an investor may pyramid investments more quickly. *Pyramiding* is controlling ever more property through reinvestment, refinancing, and exchanging, while keeping leverage at a maximum. The objective is to control the maximum value in property with given resources. Needless to say, pyramiding carries high risk of a total wipe-out during a recession.

Tax Shelter. Tax depreciation, long-term capital gains, tax credits, installment sales, and tax-deferred exchanges all enable a real estate investor to minimize or defer income taxes.

Purchasing Power Protection. Real estate offers unusual inflationary protection. This protection has been clearly evident in recent years. Whereas most capital assets have lost value in terms of purchasing power or constant dollars, adequately improved realty, especially apartments, shopping centers, and selected commercial properties, have gained value as measured in constant dollars. In the absence of rent and price controls, real property, like a ship upon ocean waters, floats above its purchasing power-constant dollar line irrespective of depth or rise in the level of prices. It is this purchasing power integrity that has, in recent years, popularized the demand for shares of real estate trusts and syndicates. For this real value holding power to be true of a specific parcel of income real estate, the property must be well located, have rentals that can be adjusted periodically, and not be subject to sudden sharp increases in operating costs.

Pride of Ownership. Many investors gain identity by being "in the game" of real estate or by being "shrewd operators." Some investors also realize great satisfaction from owning something tangible that can be touched, felt, and shown to friends and relatives.

Control. The immediate and direct control of an owner over realty enables the owner or an agent to make continuing decisions about the property as a financial asset and as a productive property. This control enables the investor to manage property to meet personal goals, whether they are to maintain the property as a showpiece for pride of ownership or to operate the property for maximum rate of return. Many owners experience a great sense of power and independence in this control.

Entrepreneurial Profit. A last important advantage is that profit may be realized by building or rehabilitating a property, and the profit is immediately invested in the property without being taxed. Thus, many investors also develop property. Other investors combine real estate investing with brokerage or property management.

DISADVANTAGES

A major disadvantage or limitation of real estate as an investment is that it requires continuing management and decision making. If an owner does not make the necessary decisions, or arrange for decisions to be made, nothing happens. The other major limitation or disadvantage involves risk, or the chance of loss, that is present with any investment. Most risks associated with real estate investment are either business or financial, but other risks do exist; see Figure 24-1.

Type	Example
Business	Income flows lowered as result of fluctuation in economic activity, such as local recession
Financial	Inability to meet debt service when borrowing to gain financial leverage
Market	Having to sell when values are at bottom of cycle
Liquidity	Selling at a loss owing to lack of marketability when cash is needed quickly
Management	Inability to adjust property to changing market conditions
Legislative	Changes in tax law; zoning, rent controls, and other governmental regulations
Purchasing power	Property income and value increases at slower rate than that of inflation
Interest rate	Value of property decreased because interest rates go up lowering present value of income flows

FIGURE 24-1

Types of risks in real estate investing, with examples

Business Risk. *Business risk* is the probability that projected or predicted levels of income will not be realized or will not be adequate to meet operating expenses. Income is dependent on a property's physical capability, function capability, and location. Each of these factors is subject to fluctuation and misinterpretation. Predicting income levels therefore involves uncertainty or risk. For example, a new freeway or bridge can destroy the locational advantage of a service station; likewise, a new shopping center can undercut a downtown department store or an unexpected decline in the economic base of a community can result in higher than expected vacancy rates for apartment houses. To the extent that events like these adversely influence the productivity of a property, business risk is involved.

In the analysis of business risk, the emphasis should be on the relative certainty of the prediction, not on the level or pattern of the prediction. Fluctuation in projected income should therefore not be confused with business risk. If the fluctuations are certain and predictable, an investor need only take the fluctuations into account. For example, in many university communities, occupancy levels in student housing drop below 50 percent in the summer months. An investor, by observation and analysis, can determine the nature and extent of fluctuations and thus remove uncertainty.

Financial Risk. *Financial risk* is the extra uncertainty created when money is borrowed to help finance a property. An investor who does not borrow has no financial risk. At the same time, no leverage is realized, and the rate of return to equity may be quite low. Financial risk might be rather slight for a wealthy owner with strong financial carrying capacity. Of course, the higher the loan-to-value ratio, the higher the risk. Note that a change in the financing for a property does not influence its net operating income (NOI), or productivity. This is because productivity and income are determined by the market; the financing pattern is the result of a decision by the specific owner.

Market and Purchasing Power Risk. Additional risks are involved in owning real estate: One is *market risk,* and another is *purchasing power risk.* Purchasing power risk is the chance of a drop in value, in real terms. We have already pointed out that real estate tends to ride with inflation; therefore, purchasing power risk is usually rather small for real estate.

Market values, however, do sometimes drop sharply such as when a major business closes a plant or when the local economy takes a nose dive because of changing economic conditions. Market risk is much more applicable to securities, however, because their values sometimes drop 20 to 30 percent in a matter of a few days.

Lack of Liquidity. Investment *liquidity* is judged by the ease with which an asset can be converted to cash and the ratio of the conversion. Any asset, of course, can be converted into cash if the price is low enough. An asset is considered to have high liquidity when it can readily be sold for cash at or near its market value. High-value real estate is generally considered to have low liquidity. *Liquidity risk* is the chance of having to convert the property to cash, incurring a loss in the process.

Lack of liquidity has traditionally been the economic Achilles heel of real estate despite the ready availability of syndicate and real estate investment trust shares on national stock exchanges. A well-informed capable investor, therefore, balances his or her investment portfolio so as to weather impending and generally short-range economic fluctuations. Thus, with a balanced portfolio approach, the relative nonliquidity of real estate need not be a serious handicap to garnering its long-term benefits of net return and capital safety. Also, in an urgent situation, such as an opportunity for an alternative investment, an investor has the option to raise cash by refinancing, giving a second mortgage or making a partial sale of the equity position, thereby entering into joint ownership.

Legislative Risk. Political risk, also known as *legislative risk,* tends to be area specific, but must still be recognized. That is, all properties in a jurisdiction may be affected by a single governmental action, such as when a city changes its zoning ordinance, initiates rent controls, or increases property taxes.

Management Risk. Management of real estate is a necessity. Part of the job is adjusting the property to changing economic conditions and environments. There is always the chance of a miscalculation when conditions change and a poor decision is made. *Management risk* is the chance of making a poor decision when adjusting a property to change.

Interest Rate Risk. Finally, interest rate risk affects real estate investing. *Interest rate risk* is the chance of lowered present values owing to rising interest rates. Interest rate risk may work for and against an investor. To the extent money is borrowed on a long-term mortgage loan at a low interest rate, it can work for the investor when interest rates go up. At the same time, when interest rates go up, the discounted value of cash flows to the equity position are decreased.

RISK AND RETURN

The equity rate of return expected by a specific investor should be, in part, a function of the risk involved in owning the property. That is, the greater the risk, the higher the rate of return to be expected.

A safe and sure return to a lender, such as in a riskless society, justifies a relatively low interest rate. However, even in a riskless society, people expect some minimum rate of return for saving money and lending it to someone else, as compensation for deferred consumption. At the same time, from a borrower's viewpoint, the maximum interest rate that could be paid for money would be a rate of return justified by the level of productivity in the economy. This is point A in Figure 24-2.

As risk and uncertainty increase, points B and C in Figure 24-2, the required rate of return should also increase. Real estate investors take on added risk, such as market, management, political, and purchasing power uncertainty, and should expect higher rates of return. Thus, an equity investor who borrows money to gain leverage takes on financial risk and should expect a higher rate of return than that realized by the lender. If a higher rate, to compensate for the higher risk, is not realized, the equity investor would be better off to lend money rather to borrow for financial leverage.

But, even when leverage is not used, some risk is involved. Increasing attention is now paid risk assessment. However, lest we expect too much of people in assessing risk, we might note some pitfalls facing decision makers as described by William Clark in recasting and updating the fable, "The Lady or the Tiger." The story applies equally to homebuyers or investors in high value, commercial properties.

> The young man could open either door as he pleased. If he opened the one, there came out of it a hungry tiger, the fiercest and most cruel that could be procured, which would immediately tear him to pieces. But, if he opened the other door, there came forth from it a lady, the most suitable to his years and station that His Majesty could select among his fair subjects. So, I leave it to you, which door to open?
>
> The first man (investor) refused to take the chance. He lived safe and died chaste.
>
> The second man hired risk assessment consultants. He collected all the available data on lady and tiger populations. He brought in sophisticated technology to listen for growling and detect the faintest whiff of perfume. He completed checklists. He developed a utility function and assessed his risk averseness. Finally, sensing that in a few more years he would be in no condition to enjoy the lady anyway, he opened the optimal door. And was eaten by a low probability tiger.
>
> The third man took a course in tiger taming. He opened a door at random and was eaten by the lady.[1]

[1]William Clark, "Witches, Floods, and Wonder Drugs: Historical Perspectives on Risk Management," in Richard C. Schwing and Walter A. Albers, Jr., eds. *Societal Risk Assessment—How Safe Is Safe Enough?* (New York: Plenum, 1980), p. 302.

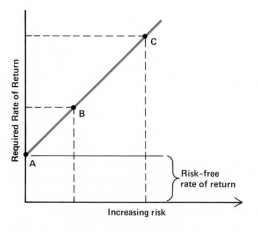

FIGURE 24-2

The basic risk-return relationship

COMPARING INVESTMENT MEDIA

Sound financial management is needed for a real estate investor to realize as many benefits and to avoid as many costs or disadvantages as possible. In fact, a prudent investor would compare the costs and benefits of all alternative investment media to determine that one or that combination that best serves his or her personal needs. Many subjective judgments would be involved in such a comparison. Let us look at some of these issues though we limit our attention to real estate.

The real estate investment cycle has three phases: (1) acquisition/development, (2) administration/operations, and (3) alienation. Considerable attention is paid to acquisition/development because most of the major decisions determining the success of an investment are made in this phase. It is much easier to finish correctly if you start correctly. Legal, financial, market, and tax factors must all be taken into account early for the optimal investment decision.

More than dollar costs are involved in real estate investing. Even so, some dollar costs are often overlooked and deserve brief attention here. Costs incurred in finding and administering real estate are usually not taken into account because they are not picked up as part of the transaction. Examples include investor payments for transportation, meals, lodging, telephone calls, and counselors while looking for, buying, and selling properties. These costs may be substantial and obviously deserve recognition when comparing investment media. Most of these expense are tax deductible; therefore, appropriate records should be kept by an investor.

More than money is involved in real estate investing. Considerable time for data collection and analysis, for negotiation, and for management is invested also. Aggravation costs are also sometimes incurred, such as when an owner is harassed by tenants and others. An owner is wise to log these costs also and fix a dollar value to them. Only then can a truly valid comparison of investment media be made.

Characteristics of Property Types as Investments

Differing property types offer distinct advantages to specific investors. Figure 24-3 summarizes these comments.

VACANT OR RAW LAND

Land is only one of several alternatives open to an investor. Supply is limited; demand is growing; therefore, investing in land is a sure thing. While generally valid, this argument is also limited.

Rate of return from land must be realized through value appreciation, which depends on supply and demand. The supply of land is limited. But the supply of urban land may be increased simply by extending roads, water and sewer lines, and electrical services. Demand for land depends on expansion of demand in the specific community. Location relative to local road and travel patterns goes far to determine the demand for a specific parcel of realty. Finally, planning, zoning, and probable highest and best use greatly determine chances for value enhancement.

Property Type	Main Value Determinants	Investment Characteristics	Principal Risks	Most Likely Investor Type
Vacant or raw land	Expansion of demand Convenient location Travel patterns Planning/zoning/ highest and best use	Passive Illiquid Limited leverage Rate of return by value appreciation No tax depreciation Capital gains taxation Expenses capitalized	Carrying costs: Must be fed, "alligator," distress sale possible Value appreciation uncertain ("Tax payer" may be used to help carry)	Speculator Developer Estate as store of value
Residential rentals (apartments)	Expanding population Rising incomes Location —convenience —favorable exposure Prestige, sometimes	Moderately active Moderately liquid High leverage, LVR R. of R. by periodic income and value appreciation Tax depreciation accelerated possible Ordinary and capital gains taxation	Start up when new Management (Probably necessary to hire professional for larger projects) Tenant harassment	High income benefiting from tax shelter Suitable for anyone but must be able to put up initial equity investment
Office Buildings	Expanding local economy Location linkages Prestige/status sometimes important Tenant-mix compatability	Active, unless leased to one firm Moderately liquid R. of R. by periodic income and value appreciation Tax depreciation Ordinary and capital gains taxation	Start up when new Management: high level of service required Competitive facilities Obsolescence Shift in location of business activity	High income–needing tax shelter Suitable for anyone if professional management hired and if able to put up initial equity investment
Warehouses	Commercial/industrial activity Location for ease of movement Structural design to endure change	Mostly passive— often on long-term lease Moderate liquidity Moderate leverage R. of R. mainly by periodic income Tax depreciation Ordinary and capital gain taxation	Obsolescence owing to changes in materials handling, equipment techniques, and equipment	Retired: desiring high cash flow and limited management Anyone desiring tax shelter with adequate initial equity capital
Neighborhood Shopping Centers	Community growth Effective demand —population —income Convenient location relative to competition Adequate parking Tenant mix relative to spending patterns and	Moderately active Liquidity limited Moderate leverage R. of R. by periodic income and value appreciation Tax depreciation Ordinary and capital gains taxation	Start up: getting proper tenant mix Management: provide adequate level of service Vacancies Competitive facilities Obsolescence	High value, large equity investment likely, therefore reasonably wealthy Anyone able to use tax shelter plus other benefits

(continued)

FIGURE 24-3
Generalized characteristics of real property investment types

Property Type	Main Value Determinants	Investment Characteristics	Principal Risks	Most Likely Investor Type
Hotels/motels	effective lease negotiation Location: linkages and convenience Demand: conference, tourist, resort, business Mix of facilities and services	Active Liquidity Moderate to poor leverage R. of R. by periodic income and value appreciation Tax depreciation Ordinary and capital gains taxation	Management: high tenant turnover (professional management almost a necessity) Competing facilities Larger than certain minimum size: economies of scale apply	Anyone able to use tax shelter and with adequate initial equity capital Smaller properties suitable for investors also willing to manage and maintain

NOTE: LVR, loan-to-value ratio; R. of R., rate of return.

FIGURE 24-3
Continued

Land is passive and illiquid as investment medium. Low loan-to-value ratios (LVR) make it difficult to leverage land highly. Owning land gives no tax depreciation, and carrying costs must be capitalized. In that land earns little or no income, an investor must pay carrying costs from other income. Such an investment is sometimes called an "alligator" because it has to be fed. If the owner suffers reduced income, a distress sale may be necessary. The rate and amount of value appreciation likely to occur over a period adds additional uncertainty to investment in land.

The most likely investors in land are speculators for short-term gains and developers for long-term operating needs. Estates and others seeking a store of value and an easily managed hedge against inflation are also likely investor types for land.

APARTMENTS

Number of households and income levels are the primary determinants of value for residential real estate. Some apartment buildings also realize value based on prestige considerations. Location, convenience, and environment also greatly influence value.

Apartments require moderately active attention as an investment. Apartments are more liquid than are most realty investments because investors are more knowledgeable in residential properties than in other types; that is, the market is broader. Also, high leverage is possible with up to 90 percent, and sometimes higher, loan-to-value ratios possible. Rate of return may be by both periodic income and value enhancement.

The major risks in apartment investment are during the start-up period of new properties and in obtaining or providing quality management on a continuing basis. For large complexes, professional management is almost a must because of the considerable "technical expertise" required and because of the need to avoid harassment from tenants and others. Smaller properties, roughly 12 units or less, may be managed and maintained by an owner with adequate time. Personal management gives the owner closer control in addition to "psychological payment" for the services rendered.

OFFICE BUILDINGS

The value of office buildings depends heavily on the business health of the area. Location or convenient linkages, a compatible tenant mix, and a prestigious image also add to value.

Office buildings generally require active participation of an owner unless leased to a single party, because tenant demands must be dealt with. Liquidity and leverage are generally moderate. Rate of return is by both periodic income and value appreciation.

The main risks with an office property are during start up, maintaining high-quality management, and obsolescence, most of which are within the control of the owner. Shifts in location of business activity and development of competitive facilities are risks outside the direct influence of the owner.

Likely owners of large office buildings are wealthy or high-income investors, who are likely to have the high initial equity investment required as implied by "moderate leverage." Syndicates are sometimes organized to own office buildings, thereby opening the investment opportunity to people of more moderate means.

WAREHOUSES

Warehouses obviously depend heavily on the level of commercial and industrial activity for value. To maintain value, warehouses must be designed and built to accommodate changes in methods of handling materials. Ceilings too low and aisles too narrow to accommodate forklift trucks caused many warehouses to become obsolete in the 1950s and 1960s, for example. Warehouse value also depends on a location that allows easy movement throughout a community.

A warehouse on long-term lease to one firm tends to be a passive investment. Leverage and liquidity are moderate. Cash flow tends to be somewhat higher as a proportion of value than with some other improved properties, because less value appreciation is expected. In turn, people desiring high cash flow and limited management requirements find warehouses an excellent investment. In most other respects, warehouses are similar to apartment and office buildings.

SMALL SHOPPING CENTERS

The value of shopping centers depends heavily on adequate purchasing power in their tributary area, meaning people and incomes. The location must be convenient for the population, and parking must be plentiful. Finally, the tenant mix must be suited to the demands of the population in the tributary area. Supermarkets, small variety and discount stores, restaurants, and gasoline stations are typical tenants.

Active management is required to establish and maintain a center. Effective lease negotiation is important. Liquidity is limited because few investors have the broad knowledge needed to manage a center; also, leverage is moderate. The tax treatment of shopping center investment is similar to that of other commercial properties. Vacancies and lease negotiation, obsolescence, and development of competitive facilities are the main risks of center ownership. Also, as with office buildings, a reasonably large equity investment is required. In other respects, any investor for periodic income and capital gain would find shopping center investment inviting.

HOTELS AND MOTELS

Hotels and motels depend primarily on tourist and business travelers for their demand. In recent years, it has been in vogue to hold business conferences in motels and hotels. Having a location and the facilities to satisfy this demand with ease is a large determinant of value.

Hotels and motels are active investments with limited liquidity and offer moderate-to-poor leverage. They receive tax treatment as business property.

Major risks in hotel/motel investment are maintaining adequate size and competent management. Economies of scale apply. High tenant turnover means that management must be effective. Obsolescence and the development of more adequate competing facilities are also major risks.

Large hotels and motels require considerable equity investment and are, therefore, limited to syndicates or wealthy investors. Smaller properties are suitable for less affluent investors who are also willing to personally manage and maintain the property.

Investment Strategy

Issues of ownership form and property type should generally be decided before concerns of investment value and market value for a specific property. So, now, it is appropriate to develop a general understanding of how discounted cash flow (DCF) analysis applies in developing an investment strategy.

DCF OVERVIEW

With DCF methodology, the two most critical items of information are certainly investment value and market value. The basic idea is to compare investment value and market value.

A "buy" decision is indicated with a positive net present value (NPV) based on the cash equity investment necessary to control the property. In other words, a buy decision is justified when the investment value of the subject property (justifiable loan plus justified equity investment at the required rate of return) equals or exceeds market value. It is at this point that an offer to purchase becomes a logical next step. This is summarized as follows.

investment value > market value: buy

investment value = market value: buy

In either of these circumstances, the investor's goals will be realized or exceeded.

But, if investment value is less than market value, and market value is paid, the buyer's goals will not be realized.

> investment value < market value: cannot realize goals with purchase at market value

At the same time, an offer at investment value may be made, and, if the owner accepts, the buying investor's goals will be realized. Of course, the owner is unlikely to sell.

The viewpoint of a specific investor must be used throughout the DCF analysis when determining investment value.

Analysis for investing is limited to one property in this and the next chapter for several reasons. To begin with, real estate is a "lumpy" investment; that is, a large cash equity investment is necessary to buy even one property. Most investors can, therefore, only afford to take on one new investment at any one time. Further, the methodology of analysis can more easily be emphasized when only one property is considered. Considerable effort and time is required to analyze even one property. In fact, a calculator with time value of money (TVM) capability is a minimum requirement to follow the analysis presented here. In addition, only a small portion of all investment properties is offered in a market at any one time. Finally, only one property is needed to make a decision when an investor operates on the basis of net present value with a required rate of return. *Required rate of return* (RRR) is that rate of return on invested capital adequate to compensate for time and risk involved in the investment; required rate of return is also known as the hurtle rate.

KEY VARIABLES

Austin Jaffe and David Walters independently conducted sensitivity analysis of real estate investment to determine the most significant variables involved.[2] *Sensitivity analysis* is the study of the impact of various elements in an investment decision on the rate of return to be earned from a property, that is, on the equity invested in the property. The elements are varied under controlled conditions to determine which exerts the most influence, which the second most influence, and so forth. The results help an investor to know and understand the most critical variables in an investment decision.

The research results of Jaffe and Walters are very similar. Each found the six most important variables to be (1) total operating expense (TOE), (2) loan-to-value ratio (LVR), (3) effective gross income (EGI), (4) property value growth rate, (5) mortgage loan interest rate, and (6) purchase price.

The significance of these variables is as follows. Property management is quite important to successful investment because operating costs must be kept under control and within certain industry bounds, whereas effective gross income, dollars actually collected, must be kept high. To keep EGI up, a manager must keep rents at market while keeping vacancy and collection losses low.

Financing showed up as important in two ways. A high loan to value ratio,

---

[2]Austin Jaffe, *Property Management in Real Estate Investment Decision Making* (Lexington, Mass.: D.C. Heath, 1979), Chaps. 5–7. David W. Walters, "Just How Important is Property Management?" *Journal of Property Management*, July–August, 1973.

along with keeping the interest rate low, combine to give high leverage and a substantial advantage. This means that great care should be exercised in arranging debt financing.

The last two variables, property value growth rate and cost or purchase price, effectively mean buy low and sell high. Buying low is the result of good analysis and shrewd negotiation. Selling high is the result of managing the property well during ownership and careful negotiations on disposition.

The importance of variables drops off sharply after these first six. Other variables considered include loan term, alternative tax depreciation schedules, investor's tax rate, expected holding period, and rate of return required by investor. Many were surprised that alternative tax depreciation schedules (straight line versus accelerated) do not show up as significant. However, it does not follow that tax depreciation is not significant to a successful investment; rather, the difference between straight line and accelerated depreciation is not very significant.

STRATEGY

In an earlier discussion we concluded that Nancy and Gerald Investor have the assets, the knowledge, and the capability to conduct a very successful investment program. Their main constraints are wanting to invest locally and not wanting to manage property personally any longer. By selling off their smaller properties and refinancing one other property, they would be able to generate enough cash equity for a larger property, Douglas Manor Apartments, at $640,000. They would thereby meet both constraints. Several smaller properties required considerable attention from them; one large property could be managed by a professional at an acceptable percentage fee.

With a larger property, the Investors expect to realize more stable cash flow. They would have to pay some extra taxes to make the transition but consider the cost acceptable. The purchase of the Douglas Manor Apartments would complete their transition to a concentrated investment, giving them more free time. Also, the transition will enable Gerald to attend more closely to financial management of investments rather than to the everyday details of property management.

The tax shelter aspect is expected to be especially beneficial as the Investors' income goes up. The size, 16 units, and high value, $640,000 or more, stretches the Investors slightly insofar as coming up with the initial cash equity is concerned. Fortunately, the age and condition of the property appear such that no unduly large expenditures or capital improvements are likely to be needed for several years.

Questions for Review and Discussion

1. List and explain briefly at least four advantages of real estate as compared with most other investment media.
2. What are the major disadvantages (not necessarily risks) of investing in real estate?
3. Define or explain the following risks involved in real estate investing. Give an example of each.

a. Interest rate
b. Liquidity
c. Business
d. Management
e. Legislative
f. Financial
g. Market
h. Purchasing power

4. Is there any necessary relationship between risk and return in investing? Explain.

5. In general terms, compare investing in stocks and bonds with investing in real estate. What similarities? What differences?

6. Compare vacant or raw land with an office building as an investment. On what bases or criteria should the comparison be made?

7. In real estate, only a small percentage of all properties are available for investment at any one time. Given this situation, is it possible to analyze only one property at a time and make an investment decision about it? Explain.

8. What are the six key variables in income-property investing, according to sensitivity analysis research?

9. Define or explain investment value. Market value? How are these two value concepts related when making an investment decision.

25

Investment Valuation: Discounted Cash-Flow Analysis

Rather than love, than money, than fame, give me truth.

Henry David Thoreau, *Walden*

The investment value (I.V.) of income real estate equals the mortgage lender's claim plus the equity investor's claim in the property.

I.V. = value of mortgage (Vm) loan + value of equity (Ve) investor's interest.

= Vm + Ve

The mortgage loan is the amount a financial institution would advance on the property within accepted lending guidelines. The value of the equity position equals the present value of after-tax cash flows from operations plus the present value of the after-tax equity reversion from a future sale of the property. The process of determining these amounts is discounted cash flow (DCF) analysis.

DCF methodology involves, first, estimating the amount of debt service that the projected net operating income (NOI) could handle within accepted lending guidelines, based on financial ratios. Second, it involves estimating after-tax cash flows from operations, and, third, estimating the net after-tax proceeds from sale or disposition. The final step is to discount the cash flows back to the present.

Rates used in discounting the cash flows back to the present are determined as follows. The current market mortgage interest rate is used in discounting debt service. Cash flows to equity are discounted at the investor's required rate of return.

The required rate of return (RRR) is the investor's hurtle rate, adjusted for the risk involved in the specific investment. In that the equity investor's position is more risky than a lender's, it follows that the RRR to the equity position should be greater than the interest rate paid for borrowed money.

The investment should be made if the net present value (NPV) of the equity position is equal to or greater than zero.

Important Topics or Decision Areas Covered in this Chapter

Financial Ratios
Vacancy and Credit Loss
Operating Expense
Debt-Service Coverage
Break-Even Occupancy
Return on Investment
Return on Equity
Loan to Value

Approaches to Investment Feasibility
Front Door Approach
Back Door Approach
Back Door Approach with DCF Analysis

Present Value of CFAT From Operations
Step One: Determining Tax Payable

Step Two: Determining CFAT
Step Three: Present Value of CFAT

Investment Value of the After-Tax Equity Reversion

Total Investment Value

Negotiation and Rate of Return
Realized Equity Rate of Return
Negotiating Strategy

Case Problems

Key Concepts Introduced in this Chapter

After tax equity reversion
Break-even occupancy
Cash flow after tax (to equity)
Debt-service coverage ratio

Equity rate of return
Investment value of the equity position

Financial Ratios

Investors calculate several financial ratios prior to actually discounting cash flows to determine the investment value of a property. They thereby know that the numbers used reflect realistic conditions, prior to "running the numbers" and doing extensive analysis. In turn, the investor knows that any proposal submitted for financing is likely to be within acceptable limits from a lender's point of view, because the lenders calculate and use the same ratios.

Names of the various ratios, their manner of calculation, and their meaning are provided in Figure 25-1. The ratios must be calculated in the sequence shown because they are interdependent; in particular, if either of the first two is seriously in error, all the remainder are also flawed.

Ratio	How Calculated	What Ratio Shows
V&CL $=$	$\dfrac{V\&CL}{GSI}$	Reflects supply-demand conditions; signals when new supply needed as well as when saturation or oversupply point has been reached. Highly sensitive to local economic conditions. Should have close relationship to vacancy rates reported by managers of similar type properties.
Operating expense $=$	$\dfrac{TOE}{GSI}$	Deviation from industry norms indicates that property is poorly managed or that expense items have been left out. Item-by-item comparison used to identify source of deviation. Important that this ratio be realistic before calculation of other financial ratios.
debt service coverage $=$	$\dfrac{NOI}{ADS}$	Indicates relative ability of property to generate income to adequately carry debt service on proposed loan.
breakeven occupancy (default point) $=$	$\dfrac{TOE + ADS}{GSI}$	Indicates level of occupancy necessary to adequately meet cash requirements for both operating expenses and debt service on proposed loan.
overall capitalization rate (also, return on investment) $=$	$\dfrac{NOI}{\text{total investment (cost, purchase price, or market value)}}$	R = ratio used in direct income capitalization for market value. Ratio also indicates rate of return on total investment, before debt service is taken out; used as a measure of property profitability. Unless a reasonable rate of return is earned, property management and/or maintenance may suffer.
Return on equity investment (also, cash on cash or equity dividend ratio) $=$	$\dfrac{\text{BTCF or ATCF, Year 1}}{\text{initial dollar equity investment}}$	Measures cash dividend expected on initial equity invested in the property. Inadequate rate of return may result in deferred maintenance.
LVR or LTV $=$	$\dfrac{\text{Debt}}{\text{total investment (cost, purchase price, or market value)}}$	Measure of lender's risk exposure; the higher the ratio, the greater the chance that the sale of the property, on default, will not generate enough cash to cover debt, such as in a down market.

NOTE: V&CL, vacancy and credit losses; GSI, gross scheduled income; TOE, total operating expenses; EGI, effective gross income; NOI, net operating income; ADS, annual debt service; BTCF, before tax cash flow, ATCF, after-tax cash flow; LVR or LTV, loan to value ratio.

FIGURE 25-1

Financial ratios for income property analysis

Gross Scheduled Income	$108,000
Less: vacancy and collection losses	– 4,320
Effective gross income	$103,680
Less: total operating expenses	– 39,680
Net Operating Income	$ 64,000

FIGURE 25-2

Douglas Manor Apartments: Summary pro forma operating statement

Several schedules are needed to calculate the ratios. The first is the summary pro forma operating statement, which is given in Figure 25-2 for the Douglas Manor Apartments. A 5-year loan amortization schedule is given in Figure 25-3. The calculated ratios are shown in Figure 25-4.

All the ratios must be considered in evaluating a property, whether looking at it as an investor or a lender.

Loan Balance	Principle Reduction during Year	Interest Paid during Year
$500,000	$5,084.04	$50,000.00
494,916	5,592.44	49,491.60
489,324	6,151.68	48,932.35
483,172	6,766.85	48,317.18
476,405	7,443.54	47,640.50
468,961	8,187.89	46,896.15

FIGURE 25-3

First 5-year loan amortization schedule: Douglas Manor Apartments Terms: $500,000; 10 percent; 25-year, with annual debt service of $55,084.04

Name of Ratio	Ratio	Comment
V&CL	V&CL/GSI = 4.00%	Low, but acceptable
Operating expense	TOE/GSI = 36.7%	Acceptable
DSC	NOI/DSC = 116.19	Within acceptable range
BO	(TOE + DSC)/GSI = 87.74%	Acceptable
ROI	NOI/TI = 10.00%	Acceptable
ROE	CFBT/$EQ = 6.37%	Low, but acceptable
LVR	debt/TI = 78.13%	Under 80%, okay

NOTE: V&CL, vacancy and credit loss; GSI, gross scheduled income; TOE, total operating expense; EGI, effective gross income; DSC, debt-service coverage; NOI, net operating income; BO, break-even occupancy; ROI, return on investment; TI, total income; ROE, return on equity; CFBT, cash flow before tax; $EQ, dollar equity; LVR, loan-to-value ratio.

FIGURE 25-4

Summary of financial ratios for Douglas Manor Apartments

VACANCY AND CREDIT LOSS

Vacancy and credit losses as a percentage of gross scheduled income must be the first ratio to be calculated. If the vacancy and credit loss (V&CL) ratio does not accurately reflect local economic conditions, all the remaining ratios will also fail to reflect reality. Therefore, the calculated ratio must bear a close relationship to vacancy rates reported by managers of similar type properties.

The ratio for the Douglas Manor Apartments is 4 percent ($4,320/$108,000). This is slightly on the low side, but acceptable. For residential properties, a typical or expected ratio is between 4 and 7 percent. A ratio less than 4 percent may be too optimistic; if justified, such a low ratio signals that additional supply is needed and that rents are likely to go up. A ratio in excess of 7 percent signals an oversupply of space and a likelihood of lower rents. Lenders monitor vacancy rates on a continuing basis as a way to limit their risk, that is, to guard against being "pulled in" by developers seeking to qualify for larger loans with dressed up operating statements.

OPERATING EXPENSE

An income property must incur operating expenses to earn rents and to maintain its earning capability. An operating ratio helps to determine if the net operating income reported for a property is realistic. By way of review, the operating expense ratio equals total annual operating expenses divided by gross annual scheduled income.

$$\text{Operating expense ratio} = \frac{\text{total annual operating expenses}}{\text{gross annual schedule income}}$$

The operating expense (OE) ratio was discussed in Chapter 22 and will only be touched on lightly here. For residential properties, a typical ratio is between 35 and 40 percent if recently built; this will climb toward 50 and 60 percent as the property ages. Too low a ratio indicates that some expenses may have been omitted; too high a ratio may indicate slipshod management. If there is substantial deviation from ratios reported for comparable properties, an item-by-item comparison may be made to determine the source of the difference. Effective gross income (EGI) is sometimes used as the denominator because it reflects money actually available to pay the expenses.

DEBT-SERVICE COVERAGE

Comparing NOI to annual debt service indicates whether adequate income is available to service a desired or proposed loan. Net operating income is what is left over after all operating expenses have been paid and is, therefore, the amount actually available for debt service. The **debt-service coverage ratio** equals NOI divided by the annual debt service required for principal and interest:

$$\text{debt-service coverage ratio} = \frac{\text{annual net operating income}}{\text{annual debt service}}$$

For the Douglas Manor Apartments, the ratio is 116.2, assuming a 10 percent, 25-year loan calling for annual payments. No hard and fast rule is possible, but a DSC ratio is expected to exceed 1.20 on a residential income property for a loan to be considered safe by a lender. A sound property, well located and with a proven track record, may get approval with a slightly lower ratio. This is the case for the Douglas Manor Apartments, because it is in a market with a 4 percent vacancy rate; that is, rents and NOI are likely to increase.

BREAK-EVEN OCCUPANCY

A second ratio used to measure the security offered a lender by a property is the *break-even occupancy (BO) ratio*. It identifies the level of occupancy at which a property's earnings exactly equals both operating expenses and required debt service. This is the default point.

$$\text{break-even occupancy ratio} = \frac{\text{total annual operating expenses}}{\text{plus annual debt service}}$$

$$= \frac{\$39,680 + \$55,084}{\$108,000} = 87.7\%$$

For the Douglas Manor Apartments, the break-even occupancy level is 87.7 percent; this means that the property could have a 12.3 percent vacancy level and still meet all its cash obligations. The industry standard for residential income properties is that a 10–15 percent vacancy must be allowed for. In a market at a 4 percent vacancy level, a BO ratio of 87.7 percent would seem acceptable.

RETURN ON INVESTMENT

Another ratio used by investors and lenders is the return on total investment (ROI), which we discussed in the appraisal chapter as the overall capitalization rate (R). For the Douglas Manor Apartments, ROI equals 10 percent.

$$\text{ROI} = \frac{\text{NOI}}{\text{total investment, as cost, purchase price, or market value}} = \frac{\$64,000}{\$640,000} = 10\%$$

ROI gives an indication of the profitability of the total investment in the property; however, the ratio is somewhat flawed in that value appreciation or depreciation is not taken into account in its calculation. In particular, in times of rapid inflation, a very low ROI is likely. Also, experience has shown that ROI varies through time as interest rates fluctuate. The thought behind the ratio is that if the ratio is too low, maintenance may not be adequate, and the property will waste through time.

RETURN ON EQUITY

Cash flow before tax equals NOI minus annual debt service. Cash flow after tax (CFAT) is the "cash throw off" to an investor in the first year of ownership; in this sense, it is a before tax dividend to the investor. For the Douglas Manor Apartments, the return on equity (ROE) ratio calculates to 6.37 percent, as follows.

$$ROE = \frac{\begin{array}{c} \text{cash flow before tax} \\ \text{(NOI} - \text{annual debt service)} \end{array}}{\begin{array}{c} \text{initial cash equity} \\ \text{(purchase price} - \text{loan)} \end{array}}$$

$$= \frac{\$64,000 - \$55,084}{\$640,000 - \$500,000} = \frac{\$8,916}{\$140,000} = 6.37\%$$

ROE measures the return earned by an investor on cash equity invested in the first year of ownership. The ratio is often referred to by investors and brokers as "cash on cash" or the equity dividend rate. ROE varies with economic conditions. As with a low return on total investment, a low return on equity is thought to lead to deferred maintenance. Some investors prefer to use the ratio on an after-tax basis, though the calculation is more involved.

LOAN TO VALUE

The loan-to-value ratio, discussed earlier, is used by lenders as a measure of risk; the higher the ratio, the greater the risk for the loan. The ratio equals the proposed loan divided by the total cost or purchase price of a property. For the Douglas Manor Apartments, the ratio equals 78 percent, which is in line with industry standards for residential properties.

So, all financial ratios considered, the Douglas Manor Apartments appears to be a viable investment. Therefore, continuing on with the discounted cash flow analysis is worthwhile.

Approaches to Investment Feasibility

The objective in income property analysis is to identify a situation where the total cost of an investment can be justified by rent levels below market rent levels or, taking the opposite perspective, a situation where market rent levels justify the required cost of the investment. In either approach, the financial ratios must be acceptable. James Graaskamp, of the University of Wisconsin, developed two distinct techniques of investment valuation, which he calls the "front door" and "back door" approaches to feasibility.[1]

The front door approach starts with the expected cost or most likely purchase price of the property, from which required cash flows necessary to justify the investment are calculated. These cash flows are then compared with those that may be realized in the market by the subject property. This approach is particularly useful in feasibility analysis for proposed development projects.

[1]James A. Graaskamp, *Fundamentals of Real Estate Development.* (Washington, D.C.: Urban Land Institute, 1981), pp. 14–22.

Several versions of the back door approach are possible. The basic approach starts with the scheduled gross income based on market rents, from which NOI is calculated. NOI provides the basis for determining investment value. The front door approach is only explained briefly here, while the back door approach is discussed at length.

FRONT DOOR APPROACH

The market value of the Douglas Manor Apartments was earlier determined to be $640,000. Let us say that the Investors believe they can buy it at this price. They want to know what rent levels would be necessary to justify this price for comparison with what is actually obtainable locally. So, they apply the front door approach to the expected cost of $640,000, which is summarized in Figure 25-5.

A $500,000, first mortgage loan at 10 percent, with repayment by annual debt service over 25 years, can be obtained on the Douglas Manor Apartments. The Investors have a required first-year pre-tax distribution rate of 6 percent; this is the same as the return on equity ratio developed earlier, which equals CFAT divided by the necessary equity investment. Is the purchase feasible within their decision criteria?

The required equity investment becomes $140,000 ($640,000 − $500,000). Cash flow before tax (CFBT) equals NOI minus annual debt service. By using time value of money (TVM) methodology, the annual debt service constant is .110168, and annual debt service would be $55,084. CFBT would have to be at least $8,400, obtained by multiplying $140,000 by 6 percent. In turn, required NOI would be $63,484 ($55,084 + $8,400). This is less than the $64,000 NOI determined earlier for the Douglas Manor Apartments, so the purchase appears feasible by the front door approach.

In practice, the front door approach would be extended to determine the maximum gross income required of a property. The gross would in turn be allocated to the various units of space for comparison with current market rents.

Capital Amounts	Cash Flow Amounts
Cost or purchase price: $640,000	
−	
Available loan: $500,000; 10%, 25 year	Required annual debt service = $55,084
=	
Cash equity required: $140,000	Required pre-tax cash distribution at 6% of equity = 8,400
	Required net operating income = $63,484

FIGURE 25-5
Front door investment analysis; cost or purchase price = $640,000

BACK DOOR APPROACH

The back door approach moves from market rents to meeting debt service of a loan and then on to the value of the equity position. Several versions are possible. A simplified version is used first to demonstrate the technique. A more complex version that relies on discounted cash flow (DCF) analysis quite heavily is demonstrated later.

We begin with the NOI of $64,000 for the Douglas Manor Apartments, which reflects current market rents. Again, we use a first-year return on cash equity invested rate of 6 percent. Again we use a 25-year, 10 percent, mortgage loan. However, local lenders require a minimum debt service coverage (DSC) ratio of 1.20. Given this information, what is the investment value of the Douglas Manor Apartments, the maximum justifiable price with these criteria? This back door approach is summarized in Figure 25-6.

A DSC ratio of 1.20 means a maximum debt service of $53,333.

$$\text{DSC ratio} = \text{NOI/DS} = \$64,000/\text{debt service} = 1.20$$

By algebra:

$$\text{DS} = \$64,000/1.20 = \$53,333$$

In turn, with loan terms of 25 years and 10 percent, annual debt service of $53,333 justifies a loan of $484,106.

Cash Flow Amounts	Capital Amounts
Cash available for debt service Minimum DSC ratio = NOI/DS 1.20 = $64,000/DS DS = $64,000/1.20 DS = $53,333	
	Justified mortgage loan at 10%, 25 year, DS = $53,333 loan = $484,106
	+
CFBT, cash available for pre-tax distribution, equity dividend NOI − DS = CFBT $64,000 − $53,333 = $10,667 CFBT = $10,667	
	Justified cash equity investment CFBT/equity dividend rate = equity $10,667/0.06 = $177,783 justified cash equity = $177,783
	=
	Total justified investment value I.V. = loan + equity value I.V. = $661,889 justified purchase price = $661,889

FIGURE 25-6

Douglas Manor: back door investment analysis, NOI = $64,000

First year CFBT would be $10,667 ($64,000 — $53,333). this means a cash equity investment of $177,783 required of the Investors.

Cash equity dividend rate = CFBT/0.06 = $10,667/0.06 = $177,783.

In turn, the total investment value of the Douglas Manor Apartments would be $661,889, the justified mortgage loan of $484,106 plus the justified equity investment of $177,783. In that the $661,889 exceeds the market value of $640,000, the purchase appears justified. In this case, both the front and back door approaches are considered preliminary, while indicating that further analysis is justified.

BACK DOOR APPROACH WITH DCF ANALYSIS

We now go a step further and introduce DCF into our analysis for investment value. In that investment value is the worth of property benefits to a specific individual or group, we must now use a required rate of return (RRR) specific to the individual or group. Personal assumptions or judgments of the investor about the projections are also used. In seeking market value, on the other hand, the assumptions of the "typical investor" for the type of property under consideration are used.

Our case property, Douglas Manor Apartments, will be used to illustrate the elements and techniques of DCF analysis, with cash flows on an after-tax basis. The viewpoint is that of Gerald and Nancy Investor.

The data or information needed to determine investment value have been discussed in earlier chapters. These data, plus any additional assumptions or inputs for Douglas Manor Apartments, are restated here in summary form for easy reference. Figure 25-7 provides a visual summary of projected cash flows and market value levels for the Douglas Manor Apartments. What follows is summary data:

1. Net operating income is $64,000, as presented in the pro forma operating statement, Figures 22-1 and 25-2.
2. Market value for Douglas Manor Apartments is taken at $640,000, as determined in Chapter 22 on appraising income properties. This $640,000 is also the assumed purchase price.
3. **Improvements are assumed to make up 85.9 percent of the $640,000 pur-**

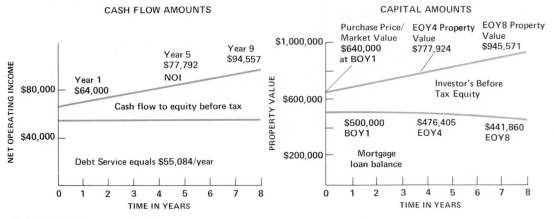

FIGURE 25-7
Projected cash flows and market value levels, **Douglas Manor Apartments**

chase price, or $550,000. Using a 27.5-year life, with straight-line cost recovery as required by the Tax Reform Act of 1986, gives $20,000 per year of tax depreciation. See Figure 23-5.

4. The property is to be financed with a 25-year, 10 percent mortgage loan of $500,000 requiring annual debt-service payments of $55,084. This gives a 78.1 percent loan-to-value ratio. Figure 25-3 shows the first 5 years of the loan amortization schedule.

5. The Investors are assumed to have a 28 percent marginal income tax rate, which applies to both operations and capital gains earnings.

6. The Investors have a minimum of 15 percent per year after-tax required rate of return (ATRRR) on any equity investment.

7. The property is assumed to be held for 4 years, during which time both its net operating income and its market value increase at 5 percent per year. The end of year (EOY) 4 market value, which is also disposition price, is therefore $777,924. Disposition or transaction costs at EOY 4 are taken at 7 percent of the sale price.

   A 4-year cash flow projection is used to make the analysis of Douglas Manor Apartments easy to follow. According to a study by Daniel E. Page, the most popular projection (holding) period is actually 10 years.[2]

8. Annual compounding or discounting is used for both loan and equity TVM calculations.

Figure 25-8 provides a visual summary or overview of the process by which investment value is determined. Investment value equals available credit financing (mortgage loan) plus the discounted value, at the 15 percent RRR, of after-tax cash flows to equity. To repeat, the value of the equity position is made up of two components: (1) the present value of after-tax cash flows from operations and (2) the present value of the net after-tax equity reversion on sale at the end of the holding period.

[2]Daniel E. Page, "Criteria for Investment Decision Making: An Empirical Study," *The Appraisal Journal,* October (1983), 505.

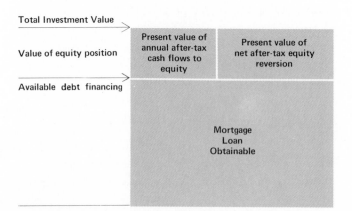

FIGURE 25-8
Investment value equals the present value of annual after-tax cash flows and after-tax equity reversion plus available credit financing

Present Value of CFAT from Operations

In Chapter 23 we calculated tax payable and the *cash flow after tax* (CFAT) from year 1 of operations of a property. Figure 25-9 shows the steps in outline form. The process is used heavily in after-tax discounted cash flow analysis.

STEP ONE: DETERMINING TAX PAYABLE

Taxable income from real estate equals net operating income less the depreciation allowance and less interest paid on money borrowed to finance the property. Multiplying the taxable income by the tax rate gives the tax payable on income from the property.

Figure 25-10 gives a detailed cash flow projection for the Douglas Manor Apartments, including the calculation of the income tax payable by an owner in a 28 percent tax bracket.

For year 1 in Figure 25-10, taxable income is actually a minus $6,000, because depreciation and interest exceed net operating income:

Net operating income	$64,000
Less: depreciation	− 20,000
Interest paid	− 50,000
Taxable income	($ 6,000)
Income tax rate	× 28%
Income tax payable (tax savings)	($ 1,680)

The minus income offsets $6,000 of income from other real estate investments, meaning a tax savings of $1,680 on this other income, which is therefore its value to the investor. The effects of depreciation to shelter income and interest paid to leverage the property lead to this result. By year 4, in Figure 25-10, NOI has increased and

Calculation of Tax Payable		Calculation of Cash Flow After Taxes	
Gross scheduled income	$		
Less vacancy and credit losses			
Effective gross income	$		
Less operating expenses			
Net operating income	$	Net operating income	$
Less interest on loan		Less annual debt service	
Less tax depreciation		Equals cash flow before taxes	$
Taxable income	$	Less tax payable	
Multiplied by tax rate	28%	Equals cash flow after taxes	$
Tax payable (saving)			

FIGURE 25-9
Process for calculating tax payable and cash flow after tax

	Year			
Accounting Item	1	2	3	4
NOI, Rate of change = 5.00%	$64,000	$67,200	$70,560	$74,088
− S/L tax depreciation	− 20,000	− 20,000	− 20,000	− 20,000
− Interest paid	− 50,000	− 49,492	− 48,932	− 48,317
= Taxable income	($6,000)	($2,292)	$1,628	$5,771
× Investor's tax rate	× 28.00%	× 28.00%	× 28.00%	× 28.00%
= Income tax payable	($1,680)	($642)	$456	$1,616

NOTE: NOI, net operating income; S/L, straight line.

FIGURE 25-10

Douglas Manor cash flow projection and calculation of annual tax on income to equity owner in 28 percent tax bracket

interest payments have declined so that the $1,680 tax savings on income from the Douglas Manor Apartments has now become a tax payable of $1,616.

STEP TWO: DETERMINING CFAT

The next step in DCF analysis is to determine the CFAT from the property for each year of ownership. Before-tax cash flows, CFBT, equal NOI less annual debt service. Subtracting the tax payable on income from operations yields the cash flow after-tax (CFAT) that can be pocketed. This second step is repeated for each year in Figure 25-11.

For year 1, the CFBT to equity equals the NOI of $64,000 less the annual mortgage debt service of $55,084, or $8,916. Deducting the minus income tax (tax savings of $1,680) from this $8,916 gives a CFAT of $10,596. By year 4, CFAT has increased to $17,388.

Net operating income	$64,000
Less: annual debt service	− 55,084
Before-tax cash flow to equity	$ 8,916
Less: income tax payable	− (1,680)
After-tax cash flow to equity	$10,596

	Year			
Accounting Item	1	2	3	4
Net Operating Income	$64,000	$67,200	$70,560	$74,088
− Annual Debt Service	− 55,084	− 55,084	− 55,084	− 55,084
= Cash Flow Before Tax	$8,916	$12,116	$15,476	$19,004
− Income Tax Payable	− (1,680)	− (642)	− 456	− 1,616
= Cash Flow After Tax	$10,596	$12,758	$15,020	$17,388

FIGURE 25-11

Douglas Manor Apartments: Calculation of the Present Value of Annual CFAT

Year	CFAT	PV1 Factor 15%	Present Value
1	$10,596	0.869565	$ 9,214
2	12,758	0.756144	9,647
3	15,020	0.657516	9,876
4	17,388	0.571753	9,942
Total (rounded)			$38,678

FIGURE 25-12
Calculating the present value of CFAT, Douglas Manor Apartments

STEP THREE: PRESENT VALUE OF CFAT

The final step in DCF analysis for cash flows from operations is to apply present value factors to the annual CFATs. By convention, each cash flow is assumed to be received at the end of the year and must be discounted with an annual TVM factor. Figure 25-12 shows the calculations for all 4 years, and the total present value of $38,678, rounded.

For year 1, the 15 percent present value for year 1 (PV1) factor is 0.8696; and the present value of the after-tax cash flow for year 1 is $9,214. For year 4, the present value of the CFAT is $9,942. The beginning of year (BOY) 1 value of all four after-tax cash flows to equity is $38,678 ($9,214 + $9,647 + $9,876 + $9,942). Projected annual increases in NOI are just being offset by decreasing tax savings and a decreasing PV1 factor. The $38,678 is the investment value of the equity position from operations.

Investment Value of the After-Tax Equity Reversion

DCF analysis also requires that the present value of the after-tax equity reversion from disposition be determined. Some of this reversion will, of course, be a return of the initial cash investment. To the extent that tax depreciation exceeded market depreciation, capital gains are recognized upon disposition. Also, to the extent that value appreciation occurred during the ownership period, capital gains are generated and taxed. Costs must also be incurred in disposing of the property. *After-tax equity reversion* equals sale price less disposition costs, less the amortized mortgage balance, and less capital gains taxes.

Let us look now at the projected disposition or sale of Douglas Manor Apartments. The calculations are summarized in Figure 25-13. Douglas Manor Apartments is projected to have increased in value by more than 20 percent, so that a disposition sale price of $777,924 is realized. This figure is arrived at by taking the expected NOI for year 5, $77,792.40, and dividing by the 10 percent overall capitalization rate we developed earlier.

At the end of 4 years, the mortgage balance has been reduced to $476,405. Disposition costs are estimated at $54,455 ($777,924 × 7%). The long-term capital

Sale price, EOY4		$777,924
Less transaction costs at 7.00%		− 54,455
Equals net disposition price		$723,469
Less adjusted tax basis		
Purchase price	$640,000	
− Accumulated S/L tax depreciation	− 80,000	560,000
at $20,000 per year		
Equals taxable capital gain		$163,469
× Investor's LTCG tax rate:		28.00%
Equals tax payable on LTCG		$ 45,771
Transaction summary and present value calculation		
Sale price, EOY4		$777,924
Less:		
Transaction costs	$ 54,455	
Loan balance, EOY	476,405	
LTCG taxes	45,771	
	$576,631	576,631
Net after-tax equity reversion		$201,293
Times annual PV1 factor:	15.00%	0.5718
BOY1 value of after-tax equity reversion		$115,090

NOTE: EOY, end of year; S/L, straight line; LTCG, long-term capital gains; PV1, present value for year 1; BOY, beginning of year.

FIGURE 25-13

Calculation of end of year 4 net after-tax equity reversion and of its beginning of year 1 present value for Douglas Manor Apartments

gain equals $163,469, all of which is subject to the tax rate applying of 28 percent. Thus, total taxes payable are $45,771. Total payments from the $777,924 sale price amount to $576,631, which leaves a net after tax equity reversion of $201,293.

The 4-year PV1 factor at 15 percent is 0.5718. Multiplying this factor by $201,293 gives a BOY1 present value of $115,090 to the net after-tax equity reversion. The following, taken from Figure 25-13, summarizes this calculation.

Disposition price		$777,924
Less: Transaction costs at 7%	$ 54,455	
Loan balance, EOY 4	− 476,405	
Capital gains taxes	− 45,711	
	$576,631	576,631
Net after-tax equity reversion, EOY 4		$201,293
Multiplied by annual PV1 factor (15%, 4 years)		×0.571753
Equals BOY1 value of the after tax equity reversion		$115,090

Total Investment Value

The *investment value of the equity position* equals the present value of the annual after-tax cash flows from operations and of the net after-tax equity reversion.

	Calculated	Rounded
Investment value of annual CFAT to equity	$ 38,678	
Investment value of net after tax equity revision	115,090	
Total investment value of equity position	$153,768	$153,800
Plus: available mortgage loan		500,000
Equals total investment value of Douglas Manor		$653,800

NOTE: CFAT, cash flow after tax.

FIGURE 25-14
Calculation of the investment value of Douglas Manor Apartments

Investment value of the property equals the combination of the investment value of the equity position plus the obtainable mortgage. Figure 25-14 summarizes the arithmetic, while Figure 25-15 provides a visual summary. The total investment value of Douglas Manor Apartments to Gerald and Nancy Investor therefore equals $653,800.

Therefore, the maximum that the Investors can pay for the property and still realize their objective of earning a RRR of 15 percent on equity invested is $653,800. Naturally, the Investors would prefer to purchase the property for less.

Negotiation and Rate of Return

An owner wants to sell for as much as possible and is not likely to accept less than market value. An interested investor wants to buy for as little as possible and is unlikely to agree to pay much more than market value, even though investment value is higher. Even so, undue pressure on a buyer or seller, differences in negotiating ability, lack of adequate information, and changing market conditions might result in an agreed price being above or below market value.

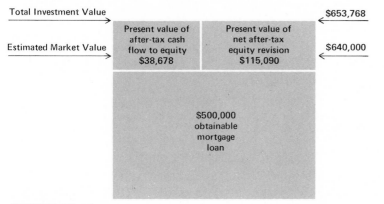

FIGURE 25-15
Components of investment value for Douglas Manor Apartments

The market value of Douglas Manor Apartments was estimated as $640,000. The investment value is $653,800. An investor needs both of these figures going into negotiations. If the property can be purchased for $640,000 rather than $653,800, the investor accomplishes several things. The cash equity invested is reduced to $140,000, and, in turn, the equity rate of return will be greater than 15 percent, if all other assumptions hold. Further, the investor has $13,800 left over, which might be invested in another property, possibly at 15 percent or more. Investing in more than one property also spreads out the investor's risk.

REALIZED EQUITY RATE OF RETURN

Assuming purchase of the property for $640,000, the equity rate of return can easily be calculated, assuming that no other factors vary. The *equity rate of return* is the internal rate of return on any monies invested by the owner.

To calculate, an equity rate of return high enough to give a total investment value less than $640,000 must be used to discount the cash flows to equity, including the net after-tax equity reversion. Remember, the higher the rate of discount, the lower the present value of a series of payments. A 20 percent rate is used here. After-tax cash flows calculated earlier and presented in Figure 25-16 are used in that they are not influenced by an increase in the RRR to 20 percent.

Now the equity rate of return may be calculated. The total investment value of Douglas Manor Apartments at alternative equity rates of return are as follows:

$$
\begin{array}{llll}
 & 15\% & \$653,800 & \\
 & & & \searrow \$13,800 \\
\text{unknown, target rate} = & X\% & \$640,000 & \\
 & & & \$22,000 \\
 & 20\% & \$631,800 & \\
\end{array}
$$

	CFAT	PV1 Factor 20%	Present Value
Year			
1	$ 10,596	0.83333	$ 8,830
2	12,758	0.69444	8,860
3	15,020	0.57870	8,692
4	17,388	0.48225	8,385
Reversion			
4	201,293	0.48225	97,074
Total investment value of equity			$131,841
Available mortgage loan			500,000
Total investment value of property			$631,841
Round to $631,800			

NOTE: CFAT, cash flow after taxes; PV1, present value for year 1.

FIGURE 25-16
Calculating the present value of cash flow after taxes at 20 percent, Douglas Manor Apartments

The investment values at 15 and 20 percent bracket the expected purchase price and market value of $640,000. Therefore, with purchase at $640,000, the expected equity rate of return, or internal rate of return, is between 15 and 20 percent. Remember, the internal rate of return is that rate of discount that makes future cash receipts equal to the initial cash investment. In fact, the internal rate of return (IRR) would be approximately $13,800/$22,000 of the way from 15 to 20 percent, which equals 18.14 percent, by interpolation.

$$X = 15\% + 5\% \left(\frac{\$13,800}{\$22,000} \right)$$

$$= 15\% + 5\% \, (0.6273)$$

$$= 15\% + 3.14\%$$

$$= 18.14\% = \text{internal rate of return to equity}$$

NEGOTIATING STRATEGY

According to the Jaffe and Walter studies mentioned earlier, purchase price and value appreciation are two of the most important items in a successful investment. Negotiation directly affects both of these figures, one when buying and the other when selling. What can an investor do to improve negotiating performance? Entire books have been written on negotiation, but, for our purposes, four items stand out.

1. An investor must understand his or her personal goals and negotiating style. What are the relative priorities of the goals? What negotiating style best suits achieving the goals?

2. The property must be understood. What is its highest investment value to me as a buyer-investor? What is the lowest price at which I will sell, as an owner (market value, unless in distress)? What influence will terms have on these prices?

3. Know the opponent and his or her goals. In buying, look in the public records to find out how much the seller paid for the property and how long it has been owned. Is the owner's tax depreciation about used up? Also, estimate owner's mortgage balance and terms, if not included in the listing. Are there other liens against the property? Under how much pressure to sell is the owner?

4. In negotiating, remain objective. Losing one's temper or getting highly emotional leads to mistakes and to failure to achieve goals. Have high expectations in the negotiations, be determined while pursuing them, but also be courteous. Recognize that no transaction occurs unless both parties expect to benefit. In buying, the property must have as high, or higher, a value in use to you than it does to the seller. The owner is selling because the value in exchange exceeds value in use. Once a bargain is struck, look for ways in which to improve it by modifying terms. Cooperative negotiations are better for both parties in the long run.

Questions for Review and Discussion

1. Explain in general terms the process of determining the investment value of an income property.
2. Explain in general terms the front door approach to determining rents required of an income property, given its purchase price or development cost.
3. Explain in general terms the back door approach to determining the investment value of an income property, given its gross scheduled income based on market rental levels.
4. Outline the accounting steps to calculate each of the following in DCF analysis.
   a. Tax payable on annual income from a property.
   b. CFAT from annual operations of property.
   c. Capital gain or loss from sale of property.
   d. Net after-tax equity reversion.
5. How might an investor best estimate the amount of a loan obtainable on a property? Discuss.
6. It has been said that a skilled negotiator can buy for 20 percent less than can a typical citizen. Does this apply to real estate? Discuss.

Case Problems

Ronald Wregan is considering the purchase of Lincoln Towers, an office building, for $620,000, of which $116,000 is attributable to the land. According to the Tax Reform Act of 1986, he expects to use a 31.5-year straight-line cost recovery schedule.

Academic Savings and Loan agrees to lend $520,000 to help finance Lincoln Towers, on a renegotiable rate mortgage (RRM) loan with a 30-year amortization period and with the interest rate at 10 percent, compounded annually.

1. What is the cost recovery allowance each year? ($16,000)
2. a. What is the annual debt service?
   b. What are the loan balances at the end of years 1, 2, and 3, assuming that all debt-service payments are made on schedule? ($516,839, $513,361, $509,536)
3. NOI is $64,000 in year 1, and $68,000 in year 2. At EOY 2, Wregan projects that he will sell for $720,000. Wregan has a 14 percent after-tax required rate of return on any real estate investments. Income from investments will be taxed at the 28 percent rate.
   a. What CFATs for the 2 years of ownership and operation? ($9,959; $12,750)
   b. What after tax equity reversion from disposition at EOY 2? ($169,679)
   c. What is the present value of CFAT from operations and of after-tax equity reversion?
   d. What is the maximum amount that Wregan can bid for Lincoln Towers and

still expect to realize his objective of a 14 percent after-tax rate of return? ($669,109)

   e. Should Wregan bid for Lincoln Towers?

4. If Wregan were to buy Lincoln Towers for $620,000 with the aid of the $520,000 loan, what internal rate of return to equity? (40.1%)

     You, a developer, just completed Case Center, an apartment complex. The land cost $2,000,000, and the improvements cost $8,000,000; therefore, total development costs are $10,000,000. You obtained 70 percent financing, $7 million, on a 30-year RRM loan with interest at 12 percent compounded monthly. You are in the 28 percent tax bracket. Also, you expect to take 27.5-year straight-line cost recovery. In year 1 of operations, NOI is $900,000 and in year 2, $1,200,000. At EOY 2, you receive an offer you cannot refuse and sell Case Center for $12 million, net after transaction costs.

5. Determine the CFAT for both years of the investment.
6. Determine tax payable upon disposition at EOY2.
7. Determine after tax equity reversion from sale at EOY2. ($4,331,116)
8. Assuming that you have a 15 percent after-tax required rate of return, what investment value of the equity position at BOY1?
9. Given the $10,000,000 total development cost, what after-tax internal rate of return (ATIRR) was earned on equity?

26

Property Development and Redevelopment

City building is just a privilege of citizenship.
Robert Thornton, Sr., former mayor of Dallas

An understanding of property development and redevelopment is important to an investor for at least two reasons. An alternative to buying an existing income property is to buy vacant land and add improvements. Then, after owning an improved property for several years, it may be necessary to modernize or redevelop it.

Whatever the situation, realty, whether vacant or improved, must produce a surplus, or profit, to warrant its improvement and use. That is, in development, a specific parcel of land is combined with other factors of production (labor, capital, and management) only if each factor stands to obtain a return sufficient to attract it to the project. Combining these factors in optimum proportions gives the highest value to the property, meaning that it has been developed to its highest and best use.

A parcel that does not promise an increment of profit is termed *submarginal land.* Submarginal lands are made up of deserts, jungles, arctic areas, marshes, and mountain tops.

A parcel may be submarginal in one use and yet promise a surplus in another. Thus, a parcel may have value as a site for a service station but not as a residential lot.

Competition to control and develop desirable properties is often very keen, making acquisition necessary long before a site is ripe for actual development. A *ripe property* is one that yields a maximum profit to a developer after all other factors of production have been satisfied. With advance acquisition, *carrying costs* (expenses and outlays of holding, such as taxes) must be met during the ripening period. Thus, downtown sites are often devoted to interim uses, known as *taxpayers* (parking lots and one-story fast-food outlets are common), to meet carrying costs.

An economic anomaly that applies more to real estate development than almost any other activity is worth noting at this time. Real estate developments, such as apartment houses, shopping centers, office buildings, and hotels, are often designed and built as "one-of-a-kind" projects. In turn, total cost also becomes average cost and marginal cost. The developer is working in a batch rather than a flow process. In turn, a developer must be extremely alert in undertaking any project because the costs of mistakes apply only to the project at hand; there are no second, third, or fourth projects over which the costs of mistakes may be spread.

Important Topics or Decision Areas Covered in this Chapter

History and Economics of Property Development
Subdividing Versus Developing
Changing Development Practices
Land-Use Succession: The Reason for Development

Site Selection and Analysis
Residential
Commercial
Industrial

Analysis for Property Development
Black Oaks Case Data
Backdoor Equity Analysis
Risk Analysis

The Property Development Process
Preliminary Planning Stage
Final Planning Stage
Construction/Disposition/Start-Up Stage

Analysis for Redevelopment/Modernization
Case Data
DCF Analysis
Marginal NPV and IRR

Case Problems

Key Concepts Introduced in this Chapter

Carrying costs
Developing
Land-use succession
Ripe property

Subdividing
Submarginal land
Taxpayer

History and Economics of Property Development

Property development and redevelopment are market responses to the changing social and economic needs of a community. In a new and growing area, the need is simply for space, meaning the extension of roads and utilities and the adding of structures to vacant sites. Later, the need is to adjust aging and functionally obsolete physical structures, with their long lives, to the changing space demands of a dynamic society.

SUBDIVIDING VERSUS DEVELOPING

Subdividing and developing, terms sometimes used interchangeably, actually have very distinct meanings. *Subdividing* means the breaking up of vacant lands into sites, such as for one-family houses, office buildings, or warehouses. In most communities, the subdividing must be done in accordance with the regulations of the city, village, or county in which the land is located. Also, to provide identification and an adequate legal description, the plat must be entered into the public records.

Developing is a broader concept, generally taken to mean combining land and improvements to produce a completed, operational property. Adding improvements to subdivided land is also considered development. Development is a much more complex undertaking, requiring the coordination of many people and activities.

CHANGING DEVELOPMENT PRACTICES

During the boom period following World War I, land speculators often took advantage of the naivete of people desiring homes and of the unconcern of community and governmental leaders. Planning, zoning, and subdivision regulations had not yet been initiated. Subdivisions sprang up at random, principally in remote suburban places and often miles away from connecting utility services such as electricity, water, and waste disposal. Often, too, imposing pillars were erected at the entrance to proposed subdivisions. Promotional schemes were then set in motion and supported by extravagant advertising campaigns. Municipal authorities, in turn, frequently jumped on the bandwagon and agreed to extend utilities, install paved roads, build schools, provide police and fire protection, and otherwise encourage the new development. Except in isolated cases, the mad rush to the suburbs failed to occur, and the cities found themselves heavily burdened with the long-term bonded debt floated to finance the ill-fated undertakings.

The Great Depression of the 1930s brought home to citizens everywhere the serious consequences of hasty faith by local officials in the overtures of fast talking real estate promoters. States and federal agencies increasingly acted to prevent a recurrence of runaway subdivisions and their attendant civic burdens.

Following World War II, most cities initiated strict subdivision controls. Now, when subdivisions are proposed, assurances must be given and often a performance bond posted that all costs, from the grading and paving of streets to the installation of municipal services, can and will be borne by the subdivider. Necessary land for schools and other civic facilities must immediately be dedicated to public use. Proof of demand for space, too, must often be provided before authority to subdivide is granted.

However, abuses continue to occur, primarily in interstate land sales. Typical examples, cited by the Comptroller General in the "Need for Improved Consumer Protection in Interstate Land Sales," make the point.[1]

---

[1] *Report to the Congress by the Controller General of the United States* (Washington, D.C.: U.S. General Accounting Office, 1973), pp. 31–33.

A purchaser of a lake front lot in Texas reported that there had never been any water in the manmade lake areas.

A purchaser of a lot in Arizona attempted to re-sell his property but was told by the developer that he could not sell the lot until the subdivision was completely developed. He was not informed of this restriction when he purchased the lot.

A purchaser of a lot in Florida reported that he was advised that monthly charges would be on the unpaid balance of the contract. He later learned that monthly interest was computed on the original balance due, without considering payments made.

A purchaser of a lot in California reported that a drainage easement on his property had rendered the land useless.

Notwithstanding the foregoing excesses, developers are much more responsible now than in the past. The public expects greater livability in its communities and buys from the developers offering the best values. Also, more land use controls (community plans, zoning ordinances, subdivision regulations, building inspections) are in effect now than in the past. Consequently, the quality of development continues to improve.

LAND-USE SUCCESSION: THE REASON FOR DEVELOPMENT

Land, and space, tends to go to that use paying the owner the highest return (rent) or giving the owner the greatest value, as was discussed in Chapter 18. Examples abound. Forest lands are cleared, or marshes are drained to make way for farms. Farmland, in turn, is converted into residential neighborhoods, shopping centers, and industrial parks. Older houses are remodeled and converted to office use. Old factories, mills, breweries, and canneries are rehabilitated for shopping centers and other commercial uses. Houses and stores are removed to make way for bridges and freeways.

Almost every change increases the intensity of use, productivity, and value of the land involved and adds to the general welfare at the time it is made. In effect, each parcel is continually seeking its highest and best use, whether urban and rural. The highest and best use will be realized unless prevented by institutional limitations (such as community plans and zoning ordinances) or lack of owner insight and initiative. Thus, each parcel is subject to continual development and redevelopment, a process termed *land-use succession.*

The reason for land-use succession may better be visualized with the aid of a graph. Effectively, each new or succeeding use must be so productive or profitable that it can absorb the old use. Figure 26-1 illustrates the process. In the figure, use B might be a high-rise office building replacing an old, obsolete apartment building. The value of the site in office use is, therefore, great enough to absorb the value of the site in residential use plus the value of the depreciated building. If remodeling is involved, the new use must absorb the value of the property in its old use plus the construction costs involved.

Our cities historically developed outward, or at the extensive margin, until recent years. The energy crunch of the early 1970s, and other factors, brought about a turning point toward more growth upward, or at the intensive margin. Higher costs of energy (gasoline) resulted in smaller cars and more compact urban areas. Construction costs have inflated so rapidly that it is now often more economical to rehabilitate older buildings than it is to build new ones. Rehabilitation is also advantageous because cities are optimally located for the most part and involve a substantial

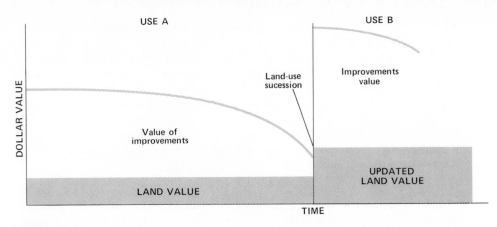

FIGURE 26-1

Land-use succession results when a new use is so profitable that it can absorb the value of the property in its older use

infrastructure of streets, utilities, and civic buildings. A centrally located older building is generally preferable to a new building at the urban fringe. Further, with zero population growth (ZPG) becoming a reality, high quality, well located space is in greater demand than is simply more space. Finally, tax incentives favor rehabilitation of existing buildings as against construction of new buildings for business uses.

Thus, our present communities, with their houses, apartments, schools, recreational, and cultural facilities, shopping centers, industrial districts, and churches all tied together by the transportation system, seem likely to endure for many years. In turn, it seems likely that rehabilitation of existing structures will become increasingly more important relative to construction of new buildings.

Site Selection and Analysis

Judging whether a site is ready for change is probably the most basic decision of a subdivider or developer. Most other decisions in the development process flow from the site-selection decision. In many cases, the site-selection decision is made twice. It is made first with the acquisition, or even the committing of resources to study the site and its potential for development. It is made a second time with the committing of resources to actually subdivide and/or develop the site. The second decision is of greater importance than the first, in that an acquired site may be sold or held vacant as well as developed.

Many elements are considered in site selection and analysis. Most were discussed in the early chapters.

1. Location or situs
2. Accessibility
3. Size and shape
4. Physical characteristics
5. Utilities and services
6. Applicable public regulations
7. Cost or value

These elements are considered here briefly as they apply to the major alternative uses, namely, residential, commercial, and industrial.

RESIDENTIAL

Location is essentially the relation of a site to other land uses. Showing a site on a vicinity map enables a developer to visualize its location relative to existing or future schools, churches, shopping centers, major roadways, and other urban facilities. Desirable residential location includes living amenities. Thus, adverse or conflicting land uses, such as air-polluting industrial plants, are best avoided. Location and accessibility are closely related. Accessibility, you will remember, is the relative ease or convenience of getting to and from a particular parcel. Most trips from homes are to schools, shopping facilities, places of work, and homes of friends or relatives. Thus, proximity to schools and shopping is important. Most wage earners are willing to commute up to an hour if the neighborhood and living environment are otherwise acceptable. Beyond proximity, immediate access to freeways and mass transit is important to good accessibility.

Each site is unique in its size, shape, and physical characteristics. The size and shape of a parcel must accommodate reasonable layout for residential use. Similarly, the topography, soils, hydrology, trees and bushes, and other physical characteristics of a site must be suitable to residential development. The most desirable topography is gently rolling hills that allow adequate drainage and facilitate the creation of an interesting living environment. Fertile soils that support vegetation are also advantageous.

Relative availability of utilities such as water, sanitary sewers, and storm sewers, is critical to most residential development. These may be provided through private or public systems, with public being much preferred to assure continuity of services at a reasonable cost. The installation of utilities and of streets is a major cost in development. On the other hand, electrical and telephone services are extended to most urban sites at time of development, without costs to the project. In many areas, gas is available on a no-cost basis also.

Public regulation of development increased dramatically in the 1960s and 1970s; the situation became so serious that in 1976, the Urban Land Institute published *The Permit Explosion* to emphasize the serious need for greater coordination in permitting procedures by public agencies. Permits add to development costs, directly in the charge made to obtain them and indirectly through the long delay in getting the many required approvals and inspections. Greater permit requirements also act to bar entry into development, making it easier for existing owners and developers to ask for and get higher prices.

Cost is a final major consideration in selecting a site for development. If the cost or asking price is so high that little profit is likely, the site is unacceptable. On the other hand, if the value of an owned site on the market is higher than a developer considers justified, the site may be sold rather than developed.

COMMERCIAL

A distinct trade area is the prime consideration in locating a convenient commercial district. Population size and income levels must be examined in the market analysis and must justify the development. Then the most accessible site to homes, one that cannot be readily cut off by competition, becomes important. Easy accessibility from several directions, without undue congestion and with easy entry onto the parcel itself, makes up a substantial part of this locational and accessibility need. High visibility to passing traffic is a location plus.

The size and shape must be suited to the type of development proposed, with consideration given to any necessary structure and also to easy and adequate parking for customers. Thus, while a 5- to 10-acre site may be adequate for a neighborhood shopping center, 80–100 acres or more are needed for a regional center. A large discount store might need 10 acres or more. Fast-food outlets and service stations increasingly need from 1 to 3 acres.

A level site, at or slightly above street level, is most desirable. That is, uneven terrain, or sites substantially above or below street level, discourage entry by potential customers and are therefore to be avoided. All urban utilities and services are necessary for most commercial development. Proper zoning and other public approvals must be obtained in developing a commercial center or district, as for other types of development. In addition, an environmental impact statement is required. Finally, the cost or value of the site must be consistent with the proposed use to allow the developer an acceptable profit.

INDUSTRIAL

Primary concerns in location and accessibility for industrial purposes are raw materials, labor, supplies and component parts, and the market for the finished product. Larger firms, such as metal and mineral processors, are tied to raw materials. Weight-gaining industries must locate near their markets. Most other manufacturers need only be sure of readily obtaining component parts, supplies, and services from suppliers. That makes proximity and access to a freeway or interstate highway highly important to them. Large plants may need railroad or water access in addition. Immediate airport access is becoming increasingly important. An adequate labor pool with appropriate skills is necessary for any plant. But except for the most specialized processes, labor may be readily obtained almost anywhere in the United States because of the high technical capability of the population.

An industrial park may occupy several hundred acres in a large metropolitan area. Of course, many parks and districts are much smaller. The size and shape of the parcel must accommodate a reasonable layout. That is, the parcel must not necessitate sites of odd and inefficient shape. The topography must be level for the most part, and the soil must have high load-bearing capability. That is, sites with soft ground, such as marshes, are best avoided because they may not be able to support large buildings and heavy machines.

All utilities are required in an industrial area. In many cases, the utilities may have to be oversized to handle the many wastes resulting from the processes. Likewise, gas and electrical services may have to be oversized.

Highly restrictive local air and water pollution regulations discourage industrial location. Some communities, in addition, have a "no-growth" posture, which results in reluctance to accommodate the needs of prospective industries. An environmental-impact statement is required in creating any industrial park or district. As with residential and commercial parcels, the cost or value of a site intended for industrial purposes must be in line with its profit potential.

The analysis for developing a real estate investment is quite similar to that required when buying an investment. The main difference is that the costs of land plus improvements are incurred instead of a purchase price. Also, the details of construction management must be handled, and the delay for construction must be taken into account. A specific example seems appropriate at this point.

BLACK OAKS CASE DATA

Wendy Welloff expects to net, after taxes, $300,000 from the sale of the Douglas Manor Apartments. She is considering reinvesting this money in a new apartment building, Black Oaks, to be developed. She has estimates for the cost of land plus improvements that round to $1,001,000; see Figure 26-2. Market and feasibility analysis, summarized in a pro forma annual operating schedule, indicate a first-year net operating income (NOI) of $97,134 for Black Oaks; see Figure 26-3.

In shopping financing, Wendy obtained a commitment for a $750,000 loan through ABC Mortgage Bankers. Debt service would be based on a 30-year amortization schedule, a 10 percent interest rate initially, with renegotiation every 5 years, and a balloon payment at the end of year 15. Annual debt service would therefore be $79,559.

If developed, Wendy expects the NOI and value to increase at least 5 percent per year. The Tax Reform Act of 1986 sets straight-line depreciation over 27.5 years. In that interest rates have dropped, Wendy decides an after-tax required rate of return of 13 percent would be reasonable on the venture. To determine feasibility, she considers a 4-year projection and analysis adequate. If feasible in 4 years, she considers that she would then have flexibility to sell or exchange as opportunities occur.

Annual interest payments on the loan in the first 4 years would be $75,000, $74,544, $74,043, and $73,491. Straight-line cost recovery on the $825,000 in land improvements would be $30,000 per year. Wendy's marginal tax rate is 28 percent.

Given this information, the question is, Is developing Black Oaks a worthwhile venture for Wendy?

Land (including road improvements and installation of utilities)	$ 176,000
Improvements	
Building costs, including architectural fees	586,395
Financing and legal costs	96,080
Contingencies	40,000
Developer fees and profit	102,500
Total	$1,000,975
Round to	$1,001,000

FIGURE 26-2
Black Oaks Apartments: project cost summary

Gross Scheduled Income			
1 BR units with $1\frac{1}{2}$ baths: 20 at $450 per month		$ 9,000	
2 BR units with $2\frac{1}{2}$ baths: 4 at 600		2,400	
3 BR units with $2\frac{1}{2}$ baths: 4 at 695		2,780	
Gross monthly income		$14,180	
Gross Annual Income (Gross monthly income multiplied by 12)			$170,160
Less: Vacancy and credit losses at 5.00%			− 8,508
Equals: Effective gross income			$161,652
Less: Total operating expenses			
Fixed			
Real estate taxes	$24,503		
Hazard insurance	1,702		
Licenses	200		
Variable			
Management at 5.0%	8,083		
Resident manager	6,000		
Custodian and gardener	8,000		
Workman's compensation and Social Security	1,555		
Advertising	1,020		
Utilities	1,455		
Elevator service	1,800		
Supplies	1,200		
Other (Pool, etc.)	2,400		
Repair and maintenance	6,600		
Total	$64,518		64,518
Equals: Net operating income			$ 97,134

FIGURE 26-3

Black Oaks Apartments: pro forma annual operating statement

Front Door Approach. Let us begin testing feasibility with the front door approach, as presented in the previous chapter.

Mortgage loan	$ 750,000,	10%, 30 years	Debt service = $79,559
Cash equity	251,000,	6% required dividend	CFBT = 15,060
Total cost	$1,001,000		Required NOI = $94,619

Required first-year NOI for a total development cost of $1,001,000 is therefore $94,619. Figure 26-3 shows the expected NOI is $97,134. Thus, by the front door approach, the project appears feasible.

Back Door Equity Analysis. By using the back door approach to feasibility with discounted cash flow (DCF) methods, Figures 26-4 and 26-5 provide cash flow projections for Black Oaks. The beginning of year 1 (BOY1) values of cash flow after taxes (CFAT) for years 1–4 are $17,502, $18,127, $18,489, and $18,632 when discounted at 13 percent; the total is $72,749. Figure 26-6 shows the calculations leading to the BOY1 value of the after-tax equity reversion, $183,668. Thus, the indicated value of the equity position at BOY1 is $256,417 ($72,749 + $183,668).

Figure 26-7 summarizes the analysis, showing that the investment value of the entire property is $1,006,417 ($256,417 + $750,000). Wendy Welloff's initial cash investment would actually be $251,000 (actual development cost of $1,001,000 less

	Year			
Accounting Item	1	2	3	4
NOI, Change/year = 5.00%	$97,134	$101,991	$107,090	$112,445
− S/L Depreciation: Years 27.5	30,000	30,000	30,000	30,000
− Interest paid	75,000	74,544	74,043	73,491
= Taxable income	($7,866)	($2,553)	$ 3,048	$ 8,954
× Investor's tax rate	28.00%	28.00%	28.00%	28.00%
= Income tax payable	($2,202)	($715)	$ 853	$ 2,507

NOTE: NOI, net operating income; S/L, straight line.

FIGURE 26-4

Black Oaks Apartments: cash flow projection and calculation of annual income tax to equity owner in 28 percent tax bracket

the available loan of $750,000). Thus, Black Oaks appears to be a viable investment for her.

Stated another way, the total investment value of Black Oaks is $1,006,417 (rounded to $1,006,000), some $5,000 greater than the total development cost. Thus, in that Wendy's investment value, based on her resources and criteria, exceeds cost, the development of Black Oaks is feasible.

Wendy would have to invest any proceeds in excess of $251,000 from the sale of the Douglas Manor Apartments elsewhere.

RISK ANALYSIS

A final step in the analysis is to again look at the applicable financial ratios to assess the risk involved. The ratios must meet the criteria of the lenders, the ABC Mortgage

	Year			
Accounting Item	1	2	3	4
Net operating income	$97,134	$101,991	$107,090	$112,445
− Annual debt service	79,559	79,559	79,559	79,559
= Cash flow before tax	$17,575	$ 22,431	$ 27,531	$ 32,885
− Income tax payable	(2,202)	(715)	853	2,507
= Cash flow after tax	$19,777	$ 23,146	$26,677	$ 30,378
× PV1 factor at 13.00%	0.8850	0.7831	0.6931	0.6133
= PV of annual CFAT	$17,502	$ 18,127	$ 18,489	$ 18,632
Accumulated PV of CFAT	$17,502	$ 35,629	$ 54,117	$ 72,749

NOTE: CFAT, cash flow after taxes; PV1, present value for year 1; PV, present value.

FIGURE 26-5

Black Oaks Apartments: Calculation of annual cash flow after taxes

Disposition Price, EOY	4		$1,216,722
Less transaction costs at	7.00%		− 85,171
Equals net disposition price			$1,131,551
Less adjusted tax basis			
Development cost		$1,001,000	
− S/L Cost Recovery		− 120,000	881,000
Equals LTCG			$ 250,551
Minus exclusion of	0.00%		0
Equals taxable portion of LTCG			$ 250,551
Times investor's LTCG tax rate			28.00%
Equals tax payable on LTCT			$ 70,154
Disposition price, EOY	4		$1,216,722
Less:			
Transaction costs		$ 85,171	
Loan balance		728,840	
LTCG taxes		70,154	
		$ 884,165	884,165
Net after-tax equity reversion			$ 332,557
Times annual PV1 factor	13.00%		0.552291
BOY1 value of after-tax equity reversion			$ 183,668

NOTE: EOY, end of year; S/L, straight line; LTCG, long-term capital gains; PV1, present value for year 1; BOY1, beginning of year 1.

FIGURE 26-6

Black Oaks Apartments: Beginning of year 1 value of after tax reversion from end of year 4

Banking Company, for the debt financing to actually be obtainable. The ratios for Black Oaks are shown in Figure 26-8.

The ratios appear acceptable. Briefly, the operating expense ratio at 37.92 percent is acceptable, in that a range of 38–40 percent is generally considered reasonable for new residential properties. The break-even occupancy (BO) ratio, at 84.67 percent, is a little on the low side. A BO ratio over 90 percent is generally considered a "no go." Effectively, Black Oaks could have a vacancy rate of slightly over 15 percent and still meet its obligations. The debt-service coverage (DSC) ratio, at 122.09, is

BOY1 Value of annual CFAT to equity	$ 72,749
Plus BOY1 value of after-tax equity reversion	183,668
Equals investment value of equity position	$ 256,417
Plus available mortgage loan	750,000
Equals total investment value of Black Oaks	$1,006,417

NOTE: BOY1, beginning of year 1; CFAT, cash flow after tax.

FIGURE 26-7

Black Oaks Apartments: Beginning of year 1 investment value of equity position and of total property, if developed

1. Operating ratio $= \dfrac{\text{TOE}}{\text{GI}}$	$= \dfrac{\$64{,}518}{\$170{,}160}$	$= 37.92\%$
2. BO ratio $= \dfrac{\text{TOE + ADS}}{\text{GI}}$	$= \dfrac{\$144{,}077}{\$170{,}160}$	$= 84.67\%$
3 DSC ratio $= \dfrac{\text{NOI}}{\text{ADS}}$	$= \dfrac{\$97{,}134}{\$79{,}559}$	$= 122.09\%$
4. LVR $= \dfrac{\text{Loan, BOY1}}{\text{market value}}$	$= \dfrac{\$750{,}000}{\$1{,}001{,}000}$	$= 74.93\%$

NOTE: TOE, total operating expenses; GI, gross income; BO, break-even occupancy; ADS, annual debt service; NOI, net operating expenses; LVR, loan-to-value ratio; BOY1, beginning of year 1.

FIGURE 26-8
Black Oaks Apartments: financial ratios

also quite safe; a ratio of over 1.20 is preferred by lenders. Finally, the loan-to-value ratio (LVR) at 74.93 percent, is well within acceptable limits for almost any lender. By using the calculated investment value of $1,006,000, the ratio would be slightly lower, 74.55 percent. With a growth expectation of 5 percent per year and Wendy's extensive experience, ABC should find all of these ratios within acceptable bounds and be willing to make the loan, subject to negotiation of details.

The Property Development Process

A property developer must judge that a project is feasible and coordinate the process, much like a music maestro, for success depends on a series of positive decisions by the many interests concerned with the project. The land owner, if not the developer, must be satisfied as to the price and terms for the land. Expected users must be satisfied that the space provided suits their needs at an acceptable price. Planners and other public officials must accept the project as meeting applicable zoning and subdivision regulations and as being in the public interest generally. Realtors, financiers, engineers, architects, and attorneys must also solve problem situations to make the project "go."

The development process only moves forward with positive decisions and actions by the players noted. One negative or "no-go" decision may shut down an entire project. Hence, the developer's ability to coordinate the many participants is critical to success. That is, all elements are interrelated, and a weakness or inadequacy in any one element may endanger the entire project. The many decisions necessary in property development may be classified into a physical, institutional, and economic framework, as shown in Figure 26-9.

Stage of Development	Type of Consideration				
	Physical	Institutional		Economic	
	Physical Design and Development	Governmental	Legal	Financial	Marketing and Promotion
Preliminary plans	Locate property if not already owned	Discuss possibilities with planning agency and others	Arrange for option to purchase land if not owned	Make estimate of cost and value of land	Market analysis
					Highest and best-use analysis
	Complete preliminary design	Tentative approvals		Locate financial backing	
Final plans	Details of final plat	Work with planning and other agencies to get final approvals of proposed development	Develop land-use controls	Feasibility analysis	Marketability study
				Make up initial capital and operating budgets and solvency statement	Develop marketing and promotional program based on market analysis
			Purchase land, if not owned		
		Approvals obtained		Verify backing	
				Make up final budgets	
Disposition or start up	Install utilities and streets, build houses, etc., if part of operation	Record plat and controls		Recheck profit picture	Initiate marketing program
			Transfer parcels as sold	Pay bills, watch money come in	Rent space if ownership to be retained

FIGURE 26-9
The property development process

Institutional considerations break down further into legal and governmental limitations and constraints. Zoning ordinances, subdivision regulations, and approvals by the planning commission are examples of governmental constraints. Legal constraints include options to purchase, obtaining clear title, and preparing privet plans and actions.

The process involves three stages: preliminary plans, final plans, and disposition or start up. The process, as presented here, is schematic only. In fact, it varies from one project to another.

PRELIMINARY PLANNING STAGE

Initially, a developer must own or search for a property suitable for improvement. Once a property is located, its development possibilities must be checked out with the planning commission and other governmental agencies. A market analysis is necessary to ascertain the probable demand, if the property were to be approved by local governmental agencies and the value, and probable cost, if the land were to be purchased. If the situation looks right, an option to purchase is arranged with the owner.

Assuming that these constraints or limitations are satisfied, the highest and best use of the property must be determined and financial backing located. A preliminary plan is drawn up and submitted to the planning commission and other agencies for tentative approval. Upon receipt of tentative approval, the financial planning stage is entered. No definite time limit applies in the preliminary planning stage, but several months to a couple of years is typical.

FINAL PLANNING STAGE

In the final planning stage, details of the plat to be recorded are worked out. This means removing or satisfying any reservations or conditions attached to the approval of the preliminary plan by governmental agencies.

Private land-use controls must be written. Capital and operating budgets must be worked out to determine if the project is feasible and likely to leave the developer solvent. On the basis of these accounting statements, financial backing must be arranged if not already in hand. Also, concurrently, a marketing and promotional program must be drawn up.

Toward the end of the final planning stage, governmental approvals must be in hand and final budgets firmed. If everything continues to appear feasible, the land is purchased if not already owned. One year is usually the maximum time allowed from preliminary plan approval to final plat approval, as stipulated in local regulations. If this time is exceeded, the developer is likely to have to begin all over again, which frequently involves having additional conditions attached to the project.

CONSTRUCTION/DISPOSITION/START-UP STAGE

Upon getting all necessary approvals, a developer suddenly gains considerable independence from outside influence except for the market. Of course, performance is still necessary. Utilities and streets must be installed or a performance bond put up, and deed restrictions recorded if appropriate. Also, a marketing program must be initiated. Finally, if improvements are to be added, arrangements must be made for architects, landscape architects, contractors, and others.

The adding of improvements and the rent up or disposition of the properties may take several years. If the project is an urban subdivision, model dwellings may be built as demonstration homes. On sale, clear title must be conveyed. If the project is an income property being developed for use as an investment, space must be leased and a management plan initiated. The disposition stage continues until all parcels are sold or all space is rented out.

Analysis for Redevelopment/Modernization

Modernization/redevelopment is necessary from time to time to keep a property productive and in its highest and best use. The question becomes, At what time is modernization/redevelopment suitable?

In simple terms, modernization is appropriate when the marginal value created exceeds the marginal costs. In financial management terms, when the present value of the marginal revenues, discounted at the required rate of return (RRR), exceeds the costs of modernization. The Douglas Manor Apartments, newly owned by Gerald and Nancy Investor, illustrates the methodology. Our DCF model will continue to serve as the analytical framework.

CASE DATA

Gerald Investor, after completing his analysis of the Douglas Manor Apartments, recognizes that some modification and modernization is needed, at an additional cost of $27,500. The lender agrees that the modernization is desirable and will lend an additional $20,000 toward it at the original terms: 25 years, 10 percent, with annual compounding.

Modernization will increase the annual NOI by $4,800 in year 1 to $68,800. Gerald considers that according to the Tax Reform Act of 1986 his tax bracket will remain at 28 percent. The $27,500 modernization cost would be amortized over 27.5 years, meaning an additional $1,000 per year in straight-line cost recovery. Thus, total allowable depreciation would be $21,000 per year. All other investment assumptions regarding the Douglas Manor Apartments, from Chapter 25, would hold as before, including a 5 percent growth rate.

DCF ANALYSIS

Figures 26-10 and 26-11 show the revised annual NOI projections for the Douglas Manor Apartments, including income taxes payable and the annual cash flow after

		Year		
Accounting Item	1	2	3	4
NOI, Rate of change = 5.00%	$68,800	$72,240	$75,852	$79,545
− S/L tax depreciation	21,000	21,000	21,000	21,000
− Interest paid	52,000	51,471	50,890	50,250
= Taxable income	($4,200)	($231)	$ 3,962	$ 8,395
× Investor's tax rate	28.00%	28.00%	28.00%	28.00%
= Income tax payable	($1,176)	($65)	$ 1,109	$ 2,351

NOTE: NOI, net operating income; S/L, straight line.

FIGURE 26-10
Douglas Manor Apartments modernized: annual income tax by owner in 28 percent tax bracket

Accounting Item	Year			
	1	2	3	4
Net operating income	$68,800	$72,240	$75,852	$79,645
− Annual debt service	57,287	57,287	57,287	57,287
= Cash flow before tax	$11,513	$14,953	$18,565	$22,357
− Income tax payable	(1,176)	(65)	1,109	2,351
= Cash flow after tax	$12,689	$15,017	$17,455	$20,007
× PV1 factor at 15.00%	0.8696	0.7561	0.6575	0.5718
= PV of annual CFAT	$11,034	$11,355	$11,477	$11,439
Accumulated PV of CFAT	$11,034	$22,389	$33,866	$45,305

NOTE: PV1, present value for year 1; CFAT, cash flow after taxes; PV, present value.

FIGURE 26-11
Douglas Manor Apartments modernized: Beginning of year 1 present values of annual cash flow after taxes from operations discounted at 15 percent

taxes (CFAT) from operations. The format is almost identical to that in Figures 25-8 and 25-9. CFAT from operations for years 1–4 is $12,689, $15,017, $17,455, and $20,007, respectively. The accumulated present value of these cash flows is $43,305.

Figure 26-12 shows the calculation of the net after-tax equity reversion for EOY4, assuming modernization; the amount is $226,764. The BOY1 present value,

Disposition Price, EOY	4		$836,268
Less transaction costs at	7.00%		58,539
Equals net disposition price			$777,730
Less adjusted tax basis			
Purchase price + improvements		$667,500	
− Accumulated S/L tax depreciation		88,000	579,500
Equals LTCG			$198,230
Minus exclusion of	0.00%		0
Equals taxable portion of LTCG			$198,230
× Investor's LTCG tax rate			28.00%
Equals tax payable on LTCG			$ 55,504
Disposition price, EOY	4		$836,268
Less:			
Transaction costs at	7.00%	$ 58,539	
Loan balance		495,461	
LTCG taxes		55,504	609,504
Net after-tax equity reversion			$226,764
Times annual PV1 factor	15.00%		0.571753
BOY1 value of after-tax equity reversion			$129,653

NOTE: EOY, end of year; S/L, straight line; LTCG, long-term capital gains; PV1, present value for year 1.

FIGURE 26-12
Douglas Manor Apartments modernized: beginning of year 1 value of end of year 4 after tax reversion, discounted at 15 percent

BOY1 Value of annual CFAT to equity	$ 45,305
Plus BOY1 value of after-tax equity reversion	129,653
Equals investment value of equity position	$174,958
Plus available mortgage loan	520,000
Equals total investment value of Douglas Manor	$694,958

NOTE: BOY1, beginning of year 1; CFAT, cash flow after tax.

FIGURE 26-13

Douglas Manor Apartments modernized: Investment value of equity position and of total property

discounted at 15 percent, is $129,653. Again, the calculations closely parallel the calculations of Chapter 25.

Figure 26-13 summarizes the foregoing calculations. Note that the total investment value of the Douglas Manor Apartments would be increased to $694,948 (rounded to $695,000) by the modernization.

MARGINAL NPV AND IRR

Annual CFAT, from both operations and disposition, before and after modernization, are shown in Figure 26-14, from which the increase in marginal revenues resulting from the modernization are derived. Note that, in the figure, after tax equity reversion from EOY4 is combined with CFAT from operations for year 4. The marginal equity investment for modernization is $7,500, and the marginal CFAT for each of the 4 years is $2,093, $2,260, $2,435, and $13,069, respectively. In accordance with the RRR of the Investor's, the marginal cash flows are discounted at 15 percent. Figure 26-14 shows that the accumulated present value of all marginal cash flows after taxes to the equity position is $12,602. In turn, the net present value (NPV) of the modernization investment is $5,102 ($12,602 − $7,500). Therefore, according to Gerald and Nancy Investor's criteria, the modernization should be undertaken.

		Year			
	0	**1**	**2**	**3**	**4**
CFAT, after modernization		$12,689	$15,017	$17,455	$246,771
CFAT, before modernization		$10,596	$12,758	$15,020	$233,701
Initial investment and marginal increase	($7,500)	$ 2,093	$ 2,260	$ 2,435	$ 13,069
× PV factor at	15.00%	0.869565	0.756144	0.657516	0.571753
PV of marginal increase in CFAT		$ 1,820	$ 1,709	$ 1,601	$ 7,473
Accumulated PV of modernization		$ 1,820	$ 3,528	$ 5,129	$ 12,602
ATIRR to marginal equity of $7,500 = 36.30%					

NOTE: CFAT, cash flow after taxes; PV, present value; ATIRR, after-tax internal rate of return.

FIGURE 26-14

Douglas Manor Apartments modernized: Marginal revenues, and the IRR to the marginal equity investment

Alternatively, the internal rate of return (IRR) of the marginal cash flows, based on a $7,500 initial investment, calculates to 36.30 percent. This easily exceeds the 15 percent RRR of the Investors, again indicating that the program should be initiated.

An analysis for a major redevelopment of the Douglas Manor Apartments, while more complex, would follow this same basic format. In summary, the marginal revenues must justify the cost of modernization or redevelopment to be financially feasible.

Questions for Review and Discussion

1. Define and explain the interrelationships among carrying costs, taxpayer, and a ripe property.
2. Distinguish between subdividing and developing.
3. Explain briefly how the economics of land-use succession leads to property development and redevelopment.
4. List five elements or considerations in site analysis and selection. Explain each as it applies to selecting a site for residential use.
5. State briefly the necessary relationship between costs and value for a property to be ripe for development.
6. Identify and discuss briefly the activities in each of the three stages of the property development process.
7. In property modernization, what is the necessary relationship between costs and value?
8. Do zoning and other land-use controls affect profits realized by a developer? If so, how? Discuss.
9. Is advance acquisition of land for development productive? Explain. Is it socially desirable?
10. Do we, as a society, need planning, zoning, subdivision regulations, and other land-use controls?
11. What major areas of your community are being developed from bare land now? What type of development is it: residential, commercial, or industrial? Is such development consistent with the economic and social outlook for your community?

Case Problems

1. Assume that NOI for Black Oaks were not expected to increase at all over the 4-year projection period but that Wendy Welloff wanted only a 12 percent after-tax rate of return. Would Black Oaks still be viable as an investment for Wendy?
2. Assume that modernizing the Douglas Manor Apartments were expected to cost $33,000, with the bank still only lending $20,000. Would modernization be worthwhile from the viewpoint of the Investors, based on the IRR to their equity requirement of $13,000? (Yes, ATIRR = 16.1%)

27

Property Administration

Labor can do nothing without capital, capital can do nothing without labor, and neither can do anything without the guiding genius of management; and management, however wise its genius may be, can do nothing without the privileges which the community affords.

W. L. MacKenzie King, former prime minister of Canada

Considerable administrative effort is needed to make real property productive on a continuing basis. An owner must personally provide or contract for the necessary effort and attention. Our intent is to provide an overview of necessary property ownership and management activities and decisions and not a detailed explanation of day-to-day routine. Our primary concern is with income properties; therefore, attention is not given to vacant land or owner-occupied residential properties.

The basic function of a manager, with income properties, is to balance periodic cash flow against preservation of value toward maximizing the rate of return on investment. An owner has a further concern, namely, deciding when to disinvest and reinvest in another property. In Chapter 24 we noted the six most important variables in income property investing; three of these are directly related to effective property administration: (1) maximizing the property's gross income, (2) controlling operating expenses, and (3) maintaining positive leverage. Our discussion centers on these variables, sometimes directly and sometimes indirectly.

Financial Management of Real Property
Continue without Change
Refinancing
To Sell or Not to Sell
Making the Choice

Managing Property as a Business
Merchandising Space
Maintaining Favorable Tenant Relations
Collecting Rents
Purchasing Supplies and Authorizing Wages
Maintaining Favorable Employee Relations
Maintaining the Property
Maintaining Records and Rendering Reports

Property Assessments and Taxes
The Property Taxation Process
Challenging the Assessed Value

Property Insurance
Manager's Insurance Responsibility
Buying Insurance
Loss Adjustments

Management Requirements by Property Type
Residential
Commercial
Industrial

Questions for Review and Discussion

Case Problems

Key Concepts Introduced in this Chapter

Assessed value
**Business interruption
    insurance**
Coinsurance

Escalation clause
Tax base
Tax capitalization
Tax levy

Financial Management of Real Property

Three major issues face an owner in administering a property to maximize its rate of return as a long-term investment.

The first is maintaining leverage and disinvesting. Analysis for possible refinancing or reinvestment should be undertaken periodically to assure that the owner is getting the best possible rate of return on equity, on a risk-adjusted, after-tax rate-of-return basis. The discounted cash flow (DCF) model is highly useful in this analysis. The chance for a higher rate of return from refinancing must be weighed against the higher financial risks to be incurred. The same DCF methodology allows determination of the appropriate time for disinvestment from one property and reinvestment in another. At such time as a higher rate of return might be earned by investing in and owning another property, a shift in investment is indicated. Such analysis must take account of both the difference in risk and the transaction costs involved.

The second is adapting to change. Periodically, a property's productivity relative to changing market and environmental conditions must also be looked at. The possibility of investing additional capital to change the use, such as modernizing the building or making an addition to the property, is always present. Analysis for modernization/modification is considered in Chapter 26. To keep our discussion clear, it is assumed here that Nancy and Gerald Investor did not modernize the Douglas Manor Apartments as discussed in the previous chapter.

The third is routine administration. An owner must arrange for a competent manager to maintain the property's cash flow and value. The objective is to have routine details attended to by the manager while having necessary financial decisions brought to the owner's attention at appropriate times, as through periodic reports. Administrative concerns are discussed here following financial management concerns, with an emphasis on property tax and hazard insurance considerations.

In summary, then, the basic alternatives to be looked at by the Investors are (1) to continue without change, (2) to refinance for continued or greater leverage, and (3) to sell and reinvest. A property manager or real estate consultant might do much of the analysis needed for these decisions. But, because of the major, long-term implications, any actual decision should be made by the owner or owners.

CONTINUE WITHOUT CHANGE

The obvious place for the Investors to begin is to gain knowledge of what would be likely to happen if they continued without change. Thus, let us review the situation of Gerald and Nancy Investor relative to the Douglas Manor Apartments.

Having owned the Douglas Manor Apartments for 4 years, they consider it time to evaluate their position. When the Douglas Manor Apartments was acquired for $640,000, their expectation was that both net operating income (NOI) and values would increase by 5 percent per year; in fact, the increases have only been 3 percent. Further, because of competition and a weak local economy, the Investors expect the 3 percent growth rate to continue. Figures 27-1a, 27-1b, and 27-2 summarize the historical DCF analysis for the Douglas Manor Apartments, plus their projection for years 5–8.

	Historical				Projection			
Accounting Item	1	2	3	4	5	6	7	8
NOI, annual growth = 3%	$64,000	$65,920	$67,898	$69,935	$72,033	$74,194	$76,419	$78,712
− S/L tax depreciation	− 20,000	− 20,000	− 20,000	− 20,000	− 20,000	− 20,000	− 20,000	− 20,000
− Interest paid	− 50,000	− 49,492	− 48,932	− 48,317	− 47,640	− 46,896	− 46,077	− 45,177
− Interest on second					0	0	0	0
= Taxable income	($6,000)	($3,572)	($1,035)	$1,617	$4,392	$7,297	$10,342	$13,535
× Investor's tax rate	×28.00%	×28.00%	×28.00%	×28.00%	×28.00%	×28.00%	×28.00%	×28.00%
= Income tax payable	($1,680)	($1,000)	($290)	$453	$1,230	$2,043	$2,896	$3,790

NOTE: NOI, net operating income; S/L, straight line.

FIGURE 27-1a

Douglas Manor Apartment: cash flow history (years 1–4) and projections (years 5–8) and calculation on annual income tax to equity owner in 28 percent tax bracket

	Year							
Accounting Item	1	2	3	4	5	6	7	8
NOI	$64,000	$65,920	$67,898	$69,935	$72,033	$74,194	$76,419	$78,712
− ADS	− 55,084	− 55,084	− 55,084	− 55,084	− 55,084	− 55,084	− 55,084	− 55,084
− ADS on second					0	0	0	0
= Cash flow before tax	$8,916	$10,836	$12,814	$14,850	$16,949	$19,110	$21,335	$23,628
− Income tax payable	− (1,680)	− (1,000)	− (290)	− 453	− 1,230	− 2,043	− 2,896	− 3,790
= Cash flow after tax	$10,596	$11,836	$13,103	$14,398	$15,719	$17,066	$18,440	$19,838

NOTE: NOI, net operating income; ADS, annual debt service.

FIGURE 27-1b
Douglas Manor Apartments: calculation of annual cash flow after taxes, years 1–8

The Investors' net after-tax equity at end of year 4 (EOY4) is $162,725, as shown in Figure 27-2. Note again that the modernization program discussed in Chapter 26 is assumed not to have been undertaken. They know that this current (EOY4) after-tax net equity is the appropriate base when making decisions about their alternatives.

		End of Year 4		End of Year 8
Disposition price		$720,326		$810,733
Less disposition costs at	7.00%	− 50,423		− 56,751
Equals net disposition price		$669,903		$753,982
Less adjusted tax basis				
BOY1 basis	$640,000		$640,000	
+ Improvements	0		0	
− S/L tax depreciation	80,000	− 560,000	160,000	− 480,000
Equals LTCG		$109,903		$273,982
Minus exclusion at	0.00%	− 0		− 0
Equals taxable portion of LTCG		$109,903		$273,982
Multiplied by investor's tax rate on				
LTCG income		×28.00%		×28.00%
Equals tax payable on LTCG		$30,773		$76,715
Disposition price, EOY	4	$720,326	8	$810,733
Less:				
Transaction costs	$50,423		$56,751	
Loan balance	$476,405		$441,860	
RRM second loan	0		0	
LTCG taxes	$30,773		$76,715	
	$557,601	− 557,601	$575,326	− 575,326
Net after-tax equity reversion		$162,725		$235,407

NOTE: BOY1, beginning of year 1; S/L, straight line; LTCG, long-term capital gains; EOY, end of year; RRM, renegotiable rate mortgage.

FIGURE 27-2
Douglas Manor Apartments: After-tax equity at end of year 4 and end of year 8

Cash flows for continuing "as is" for the next 4 years (years 5–8), are taken from Figures 27-1a and 27-1b; and net after-tax equity reversion at EOY8 is taken from Figure 27-2. The net present value (NPV) of the cash flows at the required rate of return (RRR) of 15 percent is $21,910, calculated as follows. (Note that PV denotes present value; CFAT, cash flow after taxes; and BOY5, beginning of year 5.)

	EOY	CFAT	15% PV Factor	PV of CFAT	EOY4/BOY5 Value
	5	$15,719	0.869565	$ 13,669	
	6	17,066	0.756144	12,904	
	7	18,440	0.657516	12,125	
	8	19,838	0.571753	11,342	
After tax equity	8	235,407	0.571753	134,595	
EOY4/BOY5 value of after tax cash flows				$184,635	$184,635
− after tax equity 4					− 162,725
Net present value, EOY 4					$ 21,910

These same figures provide an internal rate of return on EOY4, current, equity of 19.16 percent. Thus, refinancing or selling and reinvesting must offer a higher NPV than $21,910 or a higher after-tax equity rate of return than 19.16 percent to be a better alternative.

REFINANCING

The Investors' second alternative uses the same NOI projection for years 5–8, but with a second mortgage loan taken into account. After some searching they determine that they can get an interest only $80,000, RRM loan at 12 percent from the Latent Mortgage Corporation. The interest rate is to be renegotiated at the end of 5 years, with a balloon payment required at the end of 10 years. Annual interest (and debt service) would therefore come to $9,600 ($80,000 × 12%). Cash flow calculations are shown in Figures 27-3, 27-4, and 27-5.

	Years			
Accounting Item	5	6	7	8
NOI, annual growth = 3%	$72,033	$74,194	$76,419	$78,712
− S/L tax depreciation	20,000	20,000	20,000	20,000
− Interest paid	47,640	46,896	46,077	45,177
− Interest on second	9,600	9,600	9,600	9,600
= Taxable income	($5,208)	($2,303)	$742	$3,935
× Investor's tax rate	28.00%	28.00%	28.00%	28.00%
= Income tax payable	($1,458)	($645)	$208	$1,102

FIGURE 27-3
Douglas Manor Apartments refinanced: cash flow projections and tax payable, years 5–8

Accounting Item	Years			
	5	**6**	**7**	**8**
NOI	$72,033	$74,194	$76,419	$78,712
− ADS	55,084	55,084	55,084	55,084
− ADS on second	9,600	9,600	9,600	9,600
= Cash flow before tax	$7,349	$9,510	$11,735	$14,028
− Income tax payable	(1,458)	(645)	208	1,102
= Cash flow after tax	$8,807	$10,154	$11,528	$12,926

FIGURE 27-4
Douglas Manor Apartments refinanced: cash flow after taxes, years 5–8

The loan would reduce their EOY4 after-tax equity investment in the Douglas Manor Apartments to $82,725 ($162,725 − $80,000). After-tax cash flows for years 5–8, taken from Figures 27-3 and 27-4, would be as follows: (5) $8,807, (6) $10,154, (7) $11,528, and (8) $12,926. Their net after-tax equity reversion at EOY8 would be reduced to $155,407 ($235,407 − $80,000). See Figure 27-5.

		End of Year 4		End of Year 8
Disposition price		$720,326		$810,733
Less disposition costs at	7.00%	− 50,423		− 56,751
Equals net disposition price		$669,903		$753,982
Less adjusted tax basis				
BOY1 basis	$640,000		$640,000	
+ Improvements	0		0	
− S/L tax depreciation	80,000	− 560,000	160,000	− 480,000
Equals LTCG		$109,903		$273,982
Minus exclusion at	0.00%	− 0		− 0
Equals taxable portion of LTCG		$109,903		$273,982
Multiplied by investor's tax rate on				
LTCG income		×28.00%		×28.00%
Equals tax payable on LTCG		$30,773		$76,715
Disposition price, EOY		$720,326		$810,733
Less:				
Transaction costs	$50,423		$56,751	
Loan balance	$476,405		$441,860	
RRM second loan	$80,000		$80,000	
LTCG taxes	$30,773		$76,715	
	$637,601	− 637,601	$655,326	− 655,326
Net after-tax equity reversion		$82,725		$155,407

NOTE: BOY1, beginning of year 1; S/L, straight line; LTCG, long-term capital gain; EOY, end of year; RRM, renegotiable rate mortgage.

FIGURE 27-5
Douglas Manor Apartments refinanced: after-tax equity position at end of year 4 and end of year 8

The result of the refinancing would give a NPV of $36,436 for the 4-years from their investment in Douglas Manor. Also, the refinancing would give an ATIRR of 27.36 percent on their EOY4 after-tax equity investment of $82,725 left in the property.

In addition, they would have $80,000 released for another venture. Leverage has been increased, and the after-tax equity rate of return on equity has therefore been increased slightly. For refinancing to be a better alternative, the released $80,000 would have to give a high enough return that the overall benefits on the entire EOY4 equity, $162,725, exceeded those realized without the refinancing, namely, a NPV of $21,910 or an after-tax equity rate of return of 19.16 percent.

TO SELL OR NOT TO SELL

The third alternative open to the Investors is to sell the Douglas Manor Apartments and reinvest the proceeds, which at the EOY4, amounts to $162,725 based on our earlier analysis. The Swift Office Building can be purchased for $675,000 with a down payment of $125,000. The first year NOI is projected at $74,250. Value and NOI are expected to grow by 4 percent per year, owing to differences in property type and location, relative to the Douglas Manor Apartments. The loan would be for $550,000 at 11 percent with amortization by annual payments over 30 years. The interest rate would be renegotiable after 5 years. The land is valued at $108,000. This means the improvements of $567,000 would give a straight-line depreciation write off of $18,000 per year over the 31.5-year life set by the Internal Revenue Service. See Figures 27-6 and 27-7 for cash flows.

Sale of EOY4 of ownership of the Swift Office Building would result in a net after-tax equity reversion of $160,608; see Figure 27-8. The result would be a 4-year ATIRR of 17.43 percent, slightly above the 15 percent RRR of the Investors. Net present value for the equity investment of $125,000 comes to $9,549. Thus, the Swift Office Building is a viable alternative for the Investors.

However, in making the changeover, the Investors would have an additional $37,725 to invest; this amount is the EOY4 after-tax equity realized from selling the Douglas Manor Apartments, $162,725, less the $125,000 down payment for the Swift Office Building. The Investors would also incur risk in the changeover in that they

Accounting Item	Year			
	1	2	3	4
NOI, annual growth = 4%	$74,250	$77,220	$80,309	$83,521
− S/L tax depreciation	− 18,000	− 18,000	− 18,000	− 18,000
− Interest paid	− 60,500	− 60,196	− 59,859	− 59,484
= Taxable income	($4,250)	($976)	$2,450	$6,037
× Investor's tax rate	×28.00%	×28.00%	×28.00%	×28.00%
= Income tax payable	($1,190)	($273)	$686	$1,690

NOTE: NOI, net operating income; S/L, straight line.

FIGURE 27-6

Swift Office Building: cash flow projections and calculation of annual income tax to equity owner in 28 percent tax bracket

Accounting Item	Year			
	1	2	3	4
Net operating income	$74,250	$77,220	$80,309	$83,521
− Annual debt service	− 63,264	− 63,264	− 63,264	− 63,264
= Cash flow before tax	$10,986	$13,956	$17,045	$20,258
= income tax payable	− (1,190)	− (273)	− 686	− 1,690
= Cash flow after tax	$12,176)	$14,230	$16,359	$18,567

FIGURE 27-7

Swift Office Building: cash flow projection and calculation of the beginning of year 1 values of annual cash flow after taxes, discounted at 15 percent

would be switching from a residential-type property, with which they are familiar, to a business-type property. In addition, considerable stress would be involved.

MAKING THE CHOICE

The alternatives facing the Investors are summarized in Figure 27-9. Effectively, the choices are as follows.

1. Continuing to hold the Douglas Manor Apartments, as is, with an expected ATIRR of 19.16 percent and a NPV from the entire EOY4 equity of $21,910.

Disposition price		$789,655
Less disposition costs at	7.00%	− 55,276
Equals net disposition price		$734,379
Less adjusted tax basis		
BOY1 basis	$675,000	
+ improvements	0	
− S/L tax depreciation	72,000	− 603,000
Equals LTCG		$131,379
Minus exclusion at	0.00%	0
Equals taxable portion of LTCG		$131,379
Multiplied by investor's tax rate on LTCG income		×28.00%
Equals tax payable on LTCG		$36,786
Disposition price, EOY		$789,655
Less:		
Transaction costs	$55,276	
Loan balance	$536,985	
LTCG taxes	$36,786	
	$629,046	− 629,046
Net after-tax equity reversion		$160,608

NOTE: BOY1, beginning of year 1; LTCG, long-term capital gains; EOY, end of year.

FIGURE 27-8

Swift Office Building: after tax equity position at end of year 4

Alternative	After Tax Equity Investment	Net Present Value	ATIRR	Cash released for investment elsewhere
Continue without change	$162,725	$21,910	19.16%	None
Refinance Douglas Manor	82,725	36,436	27.36%	$80,000
Sell and reinvest in Swift Office Building	125,000	9,549	17.43%	37,725

FIGURE 27-9
Investment alternatives

2. Refinancing Douglas Manor Apartments by way of an additional $80,000 loan would result in a NPV of $36,436 and an ATIRR of 27.36 percent on the equity left in Douglas Manor Apartments. They would also have $80,000 to invest elsewhere, or to use for consumption purposes.

3. Selling Douglas Manor Apartments and buying the Swift Office Building would provide a NPV of $9,549 from the $125,000, which is the result of an ATIRR of 17.43 percent. The Investors would have an excess of $37,725 to invest elsewhere or to use for consumption purposes.

Would other considerations enter in? Possibly. But, in financial terms, a simple refinancing looks likes the most attractive alternative.

The financial returns would clearly be the greatest, though some additional financial risk would be incurred. Risks and concerns with selling and reinvesting in a different property type, an office building, would be avoided. The Investors are already well aware of the operating requirements of residential property, and of the Douglas Manor Apartments in a specific sense. The time and effort to make the change would also be avoided. Further, owning two properties, via the $80,000 loan, would help to spread the Investors' risk. Even so, each individual or group chooses a best alternative based on personal preferences, including desire to seek profit or to avoid risk.

Managing Property as a Business

Most owners of larger properties arrange for a property manager to handle the daily administrative routine. The property manager, if working for an owner, is an employee and acts as an agent of the owner. On the other hand, an individual managing properties for several owners is an independent contractor. In either case, the property manager's role is to satisfy both the owner and the tenants.

The property manager assumes all executive functions involved in the operation and physical care of the property, thereby relieving the owner of all labor and details associated with day-to-day operation of the property. The functions of a manager are several.

1. Merchandising space to secure suitable tenants at the best rents obtainable
2. Collecting rents

3. Maintaining favorable tenant relations
4. Purchasing operating supplies and equipment
5. Maintaining favorable employee relations
6. Maintaining property
7. Keeping proper accounts and rendering periodic reports
8. Looking after property assessment and taxation levels
9. Maintaining adequate insurance protection

The first seven of these functions are discussed briefly in this section. Property taxes and insurance are so important that a separate section is devoted to each. Each function obviously bears on the overall success of the property management effort.

MERCHANDISING SPACE

Merchandising space is more difficult than outright selling in some ways. After a sale, a broker can go on to seek other prospects or listings. After renting space, a manager must keep the tenant satisfied in preparation for extending the rental period or renewing the lease.

In merchandising space, rent levels must first be established on a market comparison basis because, in the short run, they are a result of supply and demand. That is, a manager must establish a rental schedule in line with market rentals for similar properties. On a longer-term basis, rent levels must be high enough to pay all property operating costs plus provide for a fair return on the investment in the property.

Advertising is usually necessary to fill vacant space. Tenants react, as a whole, to a congenial atmosphere and amenities for living, both of which are important to a feeling of belonging and a pride of occupancy. Efforts should be made to attract qualified tenants who are relatively homogeneous in their requirements. Thus, some building managers cater to young couples; others cater to older, retired people who cherish an atmosphere of quiet restfulness.

Experienced managers know the importance of selecting tenants with sound credit ratings. Such tenants tend to take better care of their space and are more likely to keep current in paying their rents.

MAINTAINING FAVORABLE TENANT RELATIONS

Clear communications and an open manner go far toward establishing and maintaining cordial tenant relations. Cordial relations with tenants go far toward obtaining tenant cooperation in general and, specifically, toward making rent collections easier while avoiding the organization of tenant unions. Prompt and courteous attention to tenant requests is important toward this end, though all requests may not be met. If a request cannot be met, the tenant should be immediately so informed.

COLLECTING RENTS

Tenants expect to pay rent, and most do so without coercion. However, some do not. Therefore, a firm and clear rent collection policy is needed, the existence of which is the mark of a good manager. Upon moving in, tenants should be impressed with the importance of making payments on time. A follow-up notice should be sent promptly when rents are past due. After a second notice, say, 10 days later, legal proceedings are best initiated to collect the unpaid rent or to obtain possession of the space. Prompt action in a few cases quickly teaches marginal tenants what is expected of them in the payment of their rents.

PURCHASING SUPPLIES AND AUTHORIZING WAGES

Costs must be incurred to operate and maintain a property. Many costs are recurring, and payment becomes routine, such as for employee wages and utility bills. On the other hand, in ordering or arranging for nonroutine services, such as repairs, remodeling, or pest control, close monitoring and inspection becomes necessary to ensure that value is received prior to any payment. A manager deals with these issues on a continuing basis; it is, therefore, likely that he or she will obtain the services at a much lower cost and with better quality than an individual owner might. It is in these matters that managers justify their fees.

MAINTAINING FAVORABLE EMPLOYEE RELATIONS

Much of a manager's success depends on arranging for technically competent people for specialized tasks. Thus, the selection and training of personnel is a major management function. Clear communication and fair treatment are also necessary for satisfactory long-term management-employee relations.

MAINTAINING THE PROPERTY

A thorough knowledge of property service and maintenance requirements is required to be a competent manager. Certainly, the premises should be kept clean and attractive at all times. Periodic inspections should be made to ascertain that halls are kept lighted, janitorial duties are being performed, elevators, heating, and other building systems are property functioning. Flaws and hazards should be checked for, and removed, from sidewalks, stairs, roofs, wiring, plumbing, or anywhere else they might cause an accident. In some leases, tenants contract to perform these functions; inspections are still necessary to ascertain compliance. Trust, but verify.

MAINTAINING RECORDS AND RENDERING REPORTS

A professional manager must keep an adequate system of accounts, because records are necessary for historical data on occupancy and as a basis for management policy. Managers are also usually charged with maintaining records and filing government reports, such as for tax withholding and social security purposes. Finally, monthly and annual statements for owners must be provided in a format similar to that shown in Figure 27-10.

Monthly Property Management Report						

Name of building . . . .
Location . . . .
Statement for the month of . . . . 19 . . . . .
And accounts receivable as of . . . . 19 . . . . .
Number of units rented . . . .
Number of units vacant . . . .

Rental Information and Receipts

Property	Name of Tenant	Rent per Month	Arrears	Amount Paid	Arrears at Close	Remarks

Disbursements and Distribution

Work Done or Article Bought Contractor or Vendor	Capital or Cost	Pay-roll	Fuel	Water Gas Elec-tricity	Gen-eral Sup-plies	Insur-ance & Taxes	Main-tenance & Repairs	Com-mis-sions	Total

Amount Collected $_____
Less: Amount Disbursed $_____
Net Amount Deposited $_____

FIGURE 27-10
Typical formats for a manager's report to an owner

Property Assessments and Taxes

Taxes, of from 1 to 8 percent of market value, for local government support are a continuing fixed cost against real property. The intent here is to explain real property taxes as they affect the economics of property ownership.

A property may pay more or less taxes than its market value justifies because of overassessment or underassessment or because of being located in high or low tax rate districts. A property's value may be influenced to the amount of the capitalized value of the overtaxation or undertaxation, which is termed tax capitalization. That is, *tax capitalization* is the present value of all future tax payments incurred (or avoided).

For example, assume that the assessed value of a property is higher by $10,000 than its market value justifies. In addition, annual taxes amount to 3 percent of the assessed value. Thus, the property pays $300 per year too much tax. If the condition persists, and the $300 per year is capitalized into perpetuity at 10 percent, the value is influenced by $3,000. If sold, the property should sell for $3,000 less than its market value, based on comparable properties that are taxed proportionately, because the owner expects to get $300 per year less than he or she should.

THE PROPERTY TAXATION PROCESS

The property taxation process breaks down into three phases for our purposes: (1) property assessment, (2) budget and tax levy, and (3) tax billing and collection.

In the valuation and assessment phase, all real estate in a tax jurisdiction (township, school district, park district, city, or county) is appraised at market value. Each parcel is then assigned an assessed value, which is typically a legally required proportion of market value. *Assessed value* is therefore the worth of a property for tax purposes. Nationally, the ratio of assessed value to market value averages about 40 percent, though in some states it is set at 100 percent. The assessed values of all properties in a tax district, when added together, make up the *tax base* of the district.

In the budget and tax levy phase, the tax district makes up a budget summarizing its financial needs for the coming fiscal year. The proportion of the budget financed by property taxes is then decided on, and the dollar amount is calculated. This amount is divided by the tax base for the district to arrive at the tax levy rate, or that amount of tax to be paid per $1,000 of assessed value. The *tax levy,* the actual amount in dollars payable by each property, is then determined by multiplying the assessed value of each property by the tax levy rate. Levying the tax on each property completes this phase.

A tax roll is then made up, listing taxes levied against properties, as a basis for easy determination of the claim against each property; at this point, the claim becomes a lien against each property. Owners are then billed for the taxes due. Failure to pay would eventually result in a tax foreclosure sale of the property.

Uniformity of assessment is important for the property tax to be fair. Too high or too low an assessment results in tax capitalization, which works against or for the owner. Too low an assessment means other owners must pay greater amounts to meet the budget requirements.

As a matter of social policy, exemptions from taxes are given in some states for homesteads, elderly persons, and veterans. Typically, the exemption serves to lower the taxable assessment value.

Each taxing district establishes its own levy rate, often stated in mills; a mill is one-one thousandth of a dollar. Several districts, such as the city, county, school district, park district, may then levy taxes against a given property. Typically, the assessor is also the tax collector.

Figure 27-11 gives an overview of the entire assessment and taxation process, which begins with an appraised property value of $112,000. In this state, the assessed value is set at 50 percent of market value, or $56,000. The owners qualify for homestead and elderly exemptions totaling $6,000. Thus, taxable assessed value is $50,000. The total millage or levy rate is $30.00 per $1,000 (3.00 percent) of taxable assessed value. The total tax levy on this property therefore calculates to $1,500 ($50,000 × 3.00%).

```
Determination of Taxable Assessed Value
Land value                                                            $20,000
Building value                                    $104,000
  less depreciation                              − 12,000
Depreciated building value                        $92,000            92,000

Total property value                                                 $112,000
Multiplied by assessed value percent of total value                 ×50.00%

Equals assessed value                                                 $56,000
Less exemptions:
  Homestead                     $5,000
  Elderly                        1,000
Total of exemptions             $6,000                                 $6,000

Taxable assessed value                                                $50,000    $50,000

Determination of Total Millage Rate (levy rate/$1,000)
County rate                                        5.40
City rate                                          8.60
School district rate                              14.20
Park district rate                                 1.80
Total millage rate (levy rate)                    30.00                           30.00

Total Property Tax Levy (taxable assessed value × levy rate) =                   $1,500
```

FIGURE 27-11
Determination of taxable assessed value and tax due on a residence

CHALLENGING THE ASSESSED VALUE

Each assessing district, usually a county, has a board of review to consider protests from any owner that considers his or her property to be assessed at too high a value. This board considers all information available and makes a decision. Owners frequently hire appraisers to present evidence of value. If relief is denied, an owner may then petition the court for a judicial review.

Property Insurance

The purpose of insurance is to substitute certainty for uncertainty by shifting th risk of a disastrous event to an insurance company. A fee, termed an insurance premium, must, of course, be paid the company for accepting the risk. A contract, an insurance policy, between the two parties stipulates the details of the arrangement, including amount and time of coverage. The overall effect is to spread the cost of a disastrous event, which otherwise would fall on one person, over many persons exposed to the same hazard.

MANAGER'S INSURANCE RESPONSIBILITY

The manager's responsibility is to arrange protection for the owner against all major insurable hazards, which is a part of the management arrangement. The manager's task then is to identify and evaluate the risks involved and to secure the best and most economical protection available in the insurance market. It follows that the manager should also keep accurate records regarding all insurance matters and renew coverage well in advance of expirations.

Insurance coverage to be considered include

1. *Standard fire insurance.* Protects against all direct losses or damages to real property by fire, except losses caused by perils or forces specifically excluded in the policy.
2. *Extended coverage.* Broader protection including risk compensation for losses caused by perils excluded from a standard fire insurance policy such as explosion, windstorm, hail, riot, civil disturbance, aircraft, vehicles, and other miscellaneous causes. Cost is usually low.
3. *General liability.* Insures against liability imposed by law for injuries or damages caused to persons or properties of others.
4. *Workmen's compensation.* Employee protection against on-the-job injuries; required in most states.
5. *Inland marine insurance.* Protection against personal property losses and, more generally, damage to property that is mobile in nature.
6. *Casualty insurance.* Protects against losses caused by theft, burglary, plateglass breakage, and the failure or breakdown of elevators, steam boilers, machinery, and other similar incidents. Policies may also be obtained to cover a variety of accident and health injuries.
7. *Rent insurance and consequential losses.* Compensates owner for consequential losses incident to damage or destruction of the property; also known as **business interruptions insurance.**

BUYING INSURANCE

Selecting a competent and cooperative agent is probably the first priority in buying insurance. An agent helps balance the costs against the choice of company and adequacy of coverage. Contracting with an insurance company that has a sound reputation and is financially capable is the next priority. Price considerations is third in priority. Assuming a capable agent and a strong company, let us look at price considerations.

Rates. Insurance is based on the law of averages. Disasterous events are very property specific, so what the owner will suffer in losses is impossible to predict. However, for a company insuring 10,000–20,000 similar type properties, the incidence of loss can be statistically predicted. Knowing the expected total amount of losses and the total value of all the buildings, the company can calculate a premium rate per thousand dollars of value required of any owner seeking protection. In practice, the rate is increased to take care of administrative expenses and profits for the company.

Coinsurance. From an owner's viewpoint, understanding the coinsurance requirement of an insurance contract is crucial. In figuring rates for various risks, the insurance company must take into consideration both the total premium revenues that it will get relatives to risks and the losses to be covered. From experience, insurers have found it necessary to use coinsurance. *Coinsurance* is a technique to keep insurance premiums collected related to losses paid to equalize the distribution of the cost of insurance among policyholders. A coinsurance or averaging clause is now included in policies to penalize policyholders that underinsure. The clauses generally call for 80, 90, or 100 percent averaging; of these, 80 percent is most popular.

An 80 percent clause does not mean that the insurance company will only pay 80 percent of any losses, as many people think. Nor does it mean that with a total loss, the owner would only be able to collect 80 percent of the face amount of the policy. Both ideas are wrong. The typical 80 percent clause reads, in part, "This company shall not be liable for a greater proportion of any loss or damage to a property described herein than the sum hereby insured bears to the eighty percent (80 percent) of the actual cash value of said property at the time such loss shall happen, nor for more than the proportion that this policy bears to the total insurance thereon."

An example will show why coinsurance is needed. Most fire losses are partial. Thus, owner A, knowing that most losses are partial, might decide to carry only a nominal amount of insurance, such as $20,000 worth on a building valued at $100,000; at a rate of $10.00 per thousand, this means a total premium of $200. A second owner, B, not knowing that most losses are partial, insures for the entire $100,000 at a total premium of $1,000.

Without coinsurance, in the event of a $20,000 loss, each would receive this amount as compensation, though owner B paid five times as much for coverage. It can be argued that owner B received a greater limit of protection. But, the chance of total loss is not as great as partial loss. Therefore, if the rate charged for the initial $20,000 of coverage were correct, it was excessive for the coverage beyond $20,000.

Let us reconsider the situations of owners A and B, with the coinsurance clause in effect, to see how insurance companies use the coinsurance requirement to correct for this imbalance. Figure 27-12 summarizes the discussion. Again the loss for each is $20,000.

Item	Owner A	Owner B
Situation		
Actual cash value of building	$100,000	$100,000
Required coverage to meet coinsurance clause		
80.00% of $100,000 =	$80,000	$80,000
Insurance coverage actually carried	$20,000	$80,000
Actual loss	$20,000	$20,000

Consequences for A
A required to carry $80,000 insurance and actually carried $20,000 of coverage.
Insurance company therefore pays $20,000 / $80,000 of the $20,000 loss, or $5,000
A must therefore suffer balance, $15,000, of the actual loss.

Consequences for B
B required to carry $80,000 insurance and actually carried $80,000 of coverage.
Insurance company therefore pays $80,000 / $80,000 of the $20,000 loss, or $20,000
B must therefore suffer balance, $0, of the actual loss.

FIGURE 27-12
Result of underinsuring, with coinsurance requirement of 80 percent

Owner A carried only $20,000 of the required $80,000 coverage and becomes a coinsurer with the insurance company. The insurance company is responsible for 25 percent of any losses ($20,000/$80,000 = 25%), while A is responsible for 75 percent of any losses (uncovered portion, $60,000, divided by required coverage, $80,000). As shown in Figure 27-12, the company therefore absorbs $5,000 of the loss and A absorbs the remaining $15,000.

Owner B, on the other hand, carried the required 80 percent insurance coverage and therefore received compensation for 100 percent of its loss. Thus, if coinsurance is carried up to the required percentage, the policy can be considered as written without any coinsurance clause and will pay losses, dollar for dollar, up to its face amount. A loss of $80,000 would thus be completely covered. A loss in excess of the $80,000 coverage (80 percent) would fall on the owner, however.

LOSS ADJUSTMENTS

The insurance company should be notified immediately if a loss occurs. Also, the insured should act to protect the property from further damage, even to the extent of making temporary repairs. Full restoration should not be undertaken until a settlement with the insurance company has been reached. Estimates of cost to repair might also be obtained, toward reaching an equitable settlement with the company.

Management Requirements by Property Type

Apartment buildings are the most commonly managed property types, so they serve as the standard in our society. Even so, each property type has management requirements unique to itself. Here, we seek only to highlight the differences. Professional management requires a much deeper look. Excellent sources of in-depth information on property management are the Institute for Real Estate Management (IREM), the Building Owners and Managers Association (BOMA), the Urban Land Institute (ULI), and the International Council of Shopping Centers (ICSC).

RESIDENTIAL

Apartments usually lease on a month-to-month basis, though 1–3 year leases are used. Awareness of changing environmental and market conditions is necessary, in any event. For example, in recent years, many apartment buildings have been converted to condominiums, because of the strong demand for ownership in multi-family structures.

What are the management requirements for residential properties? Whether apartments or condominiums, physical maintenance and security are necessary to retain value. A full set of accounting records must be maintained. In condominium properties, tenant-owners are served rather than absentee-owners, the main implications of which are that the interior of each unit must be maintained by its owner and the manager need not be concerned with maintaining full occupancy.

COMMERCIAL

Commercial space rents in units of size varying from a small cubicle for a newstand or an office up to a multistory building. Leases are usually complex and long term, and therefore require considerable negotiation; they often contain *escalation clauses,* which call for an automatic increase in rents as costs of taxes, insurance, and operating costs go up; the increase may be based on an index of costs. Appearance, cleanliness, and efficiency must be carefully monitored to maintain prestige, occupancy, and rent levels. Retail outlets, stores, shops, and shopping centers are likely to be rented on percentage leases. Administrative reports to owners are often more involved because of the wide variety of spaces rented and tenant occupants.

INDUSTRIAL

Industrial properties often require a large capital investment and tend to be special purpose, being built to user specifications. In turn, most are owner occupied. Value is therefore tied closely to the success and financial capability of the firm if not the industry. Thus, not a great many industrial properties require professional managers. Warehouses, an exception to this statement, tend to be rented out for several years at a time through contracts similar to commercial leases.

Questions for Review and Discussion

1. Identify and discuss briefly the three key issues in managing a property as a long-term investment.
2. In general terms, explain the process by which an owner optimizes in deciding about remaining with a present property, refinancing, remodeling, or selling and reinvesting in another property.
3. List and explain briefly five important but routine functions of a manager in operating a property as a business.
4. The property taxation process involves three distinct phases. What is the manager's (and owner's) concern about the process? What action, and when, is necessary by an owner pertinent in this process?
5. What is tax capitalization? How does it affect a property's value?
6. What issues are important in buying property insurance?
7. Explain coinsurance.
8. What criteria would be most important in hiring a property manager? Would the nature of the property make any difference?
9. How far should a property manager go in analyzing financial alternatives and recommending alternative decisions to an owner?
10. Is an owner's time well spent in seeking out and managing investment properties? Discuss.

Case Problems

Assume Ronald Wregan bought Lincoln Towers for $640,000 in case problems 1–4, Chapter 25. He is now at EOY2 and considering several alternatives. He seeks you out, as a real estate consultant, and asks you to help analyze the following alternatives. His projection period is 2 years.

1. Assume Wregan's EOY2 after-tax equity is $160,000. What after-tax rate of return on this equity will he receive if he does nothing? Assume NOI continues to go up by $4,000 per year, and the disposition price continues to go up by $40,000 per year. All other assumptions remain as in original problem.
2. Wregan might modernize Lincoln Towers at a cost of $63,000. Wregan forecasts the following points based on such a modernization effort.
   a. Academic S&L Association would advance $50,000 for the effort at the same terms as on the original mortgage, except the maturity date would remain unchanged.
   b. The additional outlay would be depreciated over 31.5 years by straight-line recovery, or $2,000 per year.
   c. NOI for the next 2 years would be increased $6,000 above that in case problem 1.
   d. Disposition price at the end of year 4 would be increased by $63,000.
      What rate of return on EOY2 after-tax equity if Wregan modernizes and holds Lincoln Towers 2 more years?
3. Academic S&L Association offers to refinance the entire property, at EOY2, with a $570,000 loan at 12 percent, with amortization scheduled over 30 years, but with a balloon payment required at EOY15 of the new loan. No other changes from case problem 1. What rate of return on EOY2 after-tax equity with this alternative?
4. Compare the likely results from the three alternatives, indicate which one you recommend, giving reasons for your choice.

Appendix

Time Value of Money Tables

These time value of money tables show annual and monthly factors at the following interest rates:

6.00%	11.00%	20.00%
7.00%	12.00%	25.00%
8.00%	13.00%	30.00%
9.00%	14.00%	40.00%
10.00%	15.00%	50.00%

SYMBOLS AND FORMULAS FOR THE FACTORS

	Annual interest rate $= i$	$m = 12$	Number of years $= n$	
	ANNUAL FACTORS		**MONTHLY FACTORS**	
	SYMBOL	*FORMULA*	*SYMBOL*	*FORMULA*
Future value of 1 factor	FV1	$(1 + i)^n$	MFV1	$(1 + i/m)^{n \times m}$
Future value of 1 per period factor	FV1/P	$(FV1 - 1)/i$	MFV1/P	$(MFV1 - 1)/(i/m)$
Sinking fund factor	SFF	$i/(FV1 - 1)$	MSFF	$(i/m)/(MFV1 - 1)$
Present value of 1 factor	PV1	$1/FV1$	MPV1	$1/MFV1$
Present value of 1 per period factor	PV1/P	$(1 - PV1)/i$	MPV1/P	$(1 - MPV1)/(i/m)$
Principal recovery factor	PRF	$i/(PV1/P)$	MPRF	$(i/m)/(MPV1/P)$

6.00% NOMINAL RATE

Annual Compounding

EFFECTIVE (ANNUAL) RATE = 6.00%

YEAR	Future Value of 1 — FV1	Future Value of 1 per Period — FV1/P	Sinking Fund Factor — SFF	Present Value of 1 — PV1	Present Value of 1 per Period — PV1/P	Principal Recovery Factor — PRF	YEAR
1	1.060000	1.000000	1.000000	0.943396	0.943396	1.060000	1
2	1.123600	2.060000	0.485437	0.889996	1.833393	0.545437	2
3	1.191016	3.183600	0.314110	0.839619	2.673012	0.374110	3
4	1.262477	4.374616	0.228591	0.792094	3.465106	0.288591	4
5	1.338226	5.637093	0.177396	0.747258	4.212364	0.237396	5
6	1.418519	6.975319	0.143363	0.704961	4.917324	0.203363	6
7	1.503630	8.393838	0.119135	0.665057	5.582381	0.179135	7
8	1.593848	9.897468	0.101036	0.627412	6.209794	0.161036	8
9	1.689479	11.491316	0.087022	0.591898	6.801692	0.147022	9
10	1.790848	13.180795	0.075868	0.558395	7.360087	0.135868	10
11	1.898299	14.971643	0.066793	0.526788	7.886875	0.126793	11
12	2.012196	16.869941	0.059277	0.496969	8.383844	0.119277	12
13	2.132928	18.882138	0.052960	0.468839	8.852683	0.112960	13
14	2.260904	21.015066	0.047585	0.442301	9.294984	0.107585	14
15	2.396558	23.275970	0.042963	0.417265	9.712249	0.102963	15
16	2.540352	25.672528	0.038952	0.393646	10.105895	0.098952	16
17	2.692773	28.212880	0.035445	0.371364	10.477260	0.095445	17
18	2.854339	30.905653	0.032357	0.350344	10.827603	0.092357	18
19	3.025600	33.759992	0.029621	0.330513	11.158116	0.089621	19
20	3.207135	36.785591	0.027185	0.311805	11.469921	0.087185	20

Monthly Compounding

EFFECTIVE (MONTHLY) RATE = 0.500000%

MONTH	MFV1	MFV1/P	MSSF	MPV1	MPV1/P	MPRf	MONTH
1	1.005000	1.000000	1.000000	0.995025	0.995025	1.005000	1
2	1.010025	2.005000	0.498753	0.990075	1.985099	0.503753	2
3	1.015075	3.015025	0.331672	0.985149	2.970248	0.336672	3
4	1.020151	4.030100	0.248133	0.980248	3.950496	0.253133	4
5	1.025251	5.050251	0.198010	0.975371	4.925866	0.203010	5
6	1.030378	6.075502	0.164595	0.970518	5.896384	0.169595	6
7	1.035529	7.105879	0.140729	0.965690	6.862074	0.145729	7

YEAR						
8	1.040707	8.141409	0.122829	0.960885	7.822959	0.127829
9	1.045911	9.182116	0.108907	0.956105	8.779064	0.113907
10	1.051140	10.228026	0.097771	0.951348	9.730412	0.102771
11	1.056396	11.279167	0.088659	0.946615	10.677027	0.093659

YEAR						
1	1.061678	12.335562	0.081066	0.941905	11.618932	0.086066
2	1.127160	25.431955	0.039321	0.887186	22.562866	0.044321
3	1.196681	39.336105	0.025422	0.835645	32.871016	0.030422
4	1.270498	54.097832	0.018485	0.787098	42.580318	0.023485
5	1.348850	69.770031	0.014333	0.741372	51.725561	0.019333
6	1.432044	86.408856	0.011573	0.698302	60.339514	0.016573
7	1.520370	104.073927	0.009609	0.657735	68.453042	0.014609
8	1.614143	122.828542	0.008141	0.619524	76.095218	0.013141
9	1.713699	142.739900	0.007006	0.583533	83.293424	0.012006
10	1.819397	163.879347	0.006102	0.549633	90.073453	0.011102
11	1.931613	186.322629	0.005367	0.517702	96.459599	0.010367
12	2.050751	210.150163	0.004759	0.487626	102.474743	0.009759
13	2.177237	235.447328	0.004247	0.459298	108.140440	0.009247
14	2.311524	262.304766	0.003812	0.432615	113.476990	0.008812
15	2.454094	290.818712	0.003439	0.407482	118.503515	0.008439
16	2.605457	321.091337	0.003114	0.383810	123.238025	0.008114
17	2.766156	353.231110	0.002831	0.361513	127.697486	0.007831
18	2.936766	387.353194	0.002582	0.340511	131.897876	0.007582
19	3.117899	423.579854	0.002361	0.320729	135.854246	0.007361
20	3.310204	462.040895	0.002164	0.302096	139.580772	0.007164
21	3.514371	502.874129	0.001989	0.284546	143.090806	0.006989
22	3.731129	546.225867	0.001831	0.268015	146.396927	0.006831
23	3.961257	592.251446	0.001688	0.252445	149.510979	0.006688
24	4.205579	641.115782	0.001560	0.237779	152.444121	0.006560
25	4.464970	692.993962	0.001443	0.223966	155.206864	0.006443
26	4.740359	748.071876	0.001337	0.210954	157.809106	0.006337
27	5.032734	806.546875	0.001240	0.198669	160.260172	0.006240
28	5.343142	868.628484	0.001151	0.187156	162.568844	0.006151
29	5.672696	934.539150	0.001070	0.176283	164.743394	0.006070
30	6.022575	1004.515042	0.000996	0.166042	166.791614	0.005996

7.00% NOMINAL RATE

Annual Compounding

EFFECTIVE (ANNUAL) RATE = 7.00%

YEAR	Future Value of 1 FV1	Future Value of 1 per Period FV1/P	Sinking Fund Factor SFF	Present Value of 1 PV1	Present Value of 1 per Period PV1/P	Principal Recovery Factor PRF	YEAR
1	1.070000	1.000000	1.000000	0.934579	0.934579	1.070000	1
2	1.144900	2.070000	0.483092	0.873439	1.808018	0.553092	2
3	1.225043	3.214900	0.311052	0.816298	2.624316	0.381052	3
4	1.310796	4.439943	0.225228	0.762895	3.387211	0.295228	4
5	1.402552	5.750539	0.173891	0.712986	4.100197	0.243891	5
6	1.500730	7.153291	0.139796	0.666342	4.766540	0.209796	6
7	1.605781	8.654021	0.115553	0.622750	5.389289	0.185553	7
8	1.718186	10.259803	0.097468	0.582009	5.971299	0.167468	8
9	1.838459	11.977989	0.083486	0.543934	6.515232	0.153486	9
10	1.967151	13.816448	0.072378	0.508349	7.023582	0.142378	10
11	2.104852	15.783599	0.063357	0.475093	7.498674	0.133357	11
12	2.252192	17.888451	0.055902	0.444012	7.942686	0.125902	12
13	2.409845	20.140643	0.049651	0.414964	8.357651	0.119651	13
14	2.578534	22.550488	0.044345	0.378817	8.745468	0.114345	14
15	2.759032	25.129022	0.039795	0.362446	9.107914	0.109795	15
16	2.952164	27.888054	0.035858	0.338735	9.446649	0.105858	16
17	3.158815	30.840217	0.032425	0.316223	9.763223	0.102425	17
18	3.379932	33.999033	0.029413	0.295864	10.059087	0.099413	18
19	3.616528	37.378965	0.026753	0.276508	10.335595	0.096753	19
20	3.869684	40.995492	0.024393	0.258419	10.594014	0.094393	20

Monthly Compounding

EFFECTIVE (MONTHLY) RATE = 0.583333%

MONTH	MFV1	MFV1/P	MSSF	MPV1	MPV1/P	MPRF	MONTH
1	1.005833	1.000000	1.000000	0.994200	0.994200	1.005833	1
2	1.011701	2.005833	0.498546	0.988435	1.982635	0.594379	2
3	1.017602	3.017534	0.331396	0.982702	2.965337	0.337230	3
4	1.023538	4.035136	0.247823	0.977003	3.942340	0.253656	4
5	1.029509	5.058675	0.197680	0.971337	4.913677	0.203514	5
6	1.035514	6.088184	0.164253	0.965704	5.879381	0.170086	6
7	1.041555	7.123698	0.140377	0.960103	6.839484	0.146210	7

YEAR							YEAR
8	1.047631	8.165253	0.122470	0.954535	7.794019	0.128304	8
9	1.053742	9.212883	0.108544	0.948999	8.743018	0.114377	9
10	1.059889	10.266625	0.097403	0.943495	9.686513	0.103236	10
11	1.066071	11.326514	0.088288	0.938024	10.624537	0.094122	11

YEAR							YEAR
1	1.072290	12.392585	0.080693	0.932583	11.557120	0.086527	1
2	1.149806	25.681032	0.038939	0.869712	22.335099	0.044773	2
3	1.232926	39.930101	0.025044	0.811079	32.386464	0.030877	3
4	1.322054	55.209236	0.018113	0.756399	41.760201	0.023946	4
5	1.417625	71.592902	0.013968	0.705405	50.501994	0.109801	5
6	1.520106	89.160944	0.011216	0.657849	58.654444	0.017049	6
7	1.629994	107.998981	0.009259	0.613499	66.257285	0.015093	7
8	1.747826	128.198821	0.007800	0.572139	73.347569	0.013634	8
9	1.874177	149.858909	0.006673	0.533568	79.959850	0.012506	9
10	2.009661	173.084807	0.005778	0.497596	86.126354	0.011611	10
11	2.154940	197.989707	0.005051	0.464050	91.877134	0.010884	11
12	2.310721	224.694985	0.004450	0.432765	97.240216	0.010284	12
13	2.477763	253.330789	0.003947	0.403590	102.241738	0.009781	13
14	2.656881	284.036677	0.003521	0.376381	106.906074	0.009354	14
15	2.848947	316.962297	0.003155	0.351007	111.255958	0.008988	15
16	3.054897	352.268112	0.002839	0.327343	115.312587	0.008672	16
17	3.275736	390.126188	0.002563	0.305275	119.095732	0.008397	17
18	3.512539	430.721027	0.002322	0.284694	122.623831	0.008155	18
19	3.766461	474.250470	0.002109	0.265501	125.914077	0.007942	19
20	4.038739	520.926660	0.001920	0.247602	128.982506	0.007753	20
21	4.330700	570.977075	0.001751	0.230910	131.844073	0.007585	21
22	4.643766	624.645640	0.001601	0.215342	134.512723	0.007434	22
23	4.979464	682.193909	0.001466	0.200825	137.001461	0.007299	23
24	5.339430	743.902347	0.001344	0.187285	139.322418	0.007178	24
25	5.725418	810.071693	0.001234	0.174660	141.486903	0.007068	25
26	6.139309	881.024427	0.001135	0.162885	143.505467	0.006968	26
27	6.583120	957.106339	0.001045	0.151904	145.387946	0.006878	27
28	7.059015	1038.688219	0.000963	0.141663	147.143515	0.006796	28
29	7.569311	1126.167659	0.000888	0.132112	148.780729	0.006721	29
30	8.116497	1219.970996	0.000820	0.123206	150.307568	0.006653	30

8.00% NOMINAL RATE

Annual Compounding

EFFECTIVE (ANNUAL) RATE = 8.00%

YEAR	Future Value of 1	Future Value of 1 per Period	Sinking Fund Factor	Present Value of 1	Present Value of 1 per Period	Principal Recovery Factor	YEAR
	FV1	FV1/P	SFF	PV1	PV1/P	PRF	
1	1.080000	1.000000	1.000000	0.925926	0.925926	1.080000	1
2	1.166400	2.080000	0.480769	0.857339	1.783265	0.560769	2
3	1.259712	3.246400	0.308034	0.793832	2.577097	0.388034	3
4	1.360489	4.506112	0.221921	0.735030	3.312127	0.301921	4
5	1.469328	5.866601	0.170456	0.680583	3.992710	0.250456	5
6	1.586874	7.335929	0.136315	0.630170	4.622880	0.216315	6
7	1.713824	8.922803	0.112072	0.583490	5.206370	0.192072	7
8	1.850930	10.636628	0.094015	0.540269	5.746639	0.174015	8
9	1.999005	12.487558	0.080080	0.500249	6.246888	0.160080	9
10	2.158925	14.486562	0.069029	0.463193	6.710081	0.149029	10
11	2.331639	16.645487	0.060076	0.428883	7.138964	0.140076	11
12	2.518170	18.977126	0.052695	0.397114	7.536078	0.132695	12
13	2.719624	21.495297	0.046522	0.367698	7.903776	0.126522	13
14	2.937194	24.214920	0.041297	0.340461	8.244237	0.121297	14
15	3.172169	27.152114	0.036830	0.315242	8.559479	0.116830	15
16	3.425943	30.324283	0.032977	0.291890	8.851369	0.112977	16
17	3.700018	33.750226	0.029629	0.270269	9.121638	0.109629	17
18	3.996019	37.450244	0.026702	0.250249	9.371887	0.106702	18
19	4.315701	41.446263	0.024128	0.231712	9.603599	0.104128	19
20	4.660957	45.761964	0.021852	0.214548	9.818147	0.101852	20

Monthly Compounding

EFFECTIVE (MONTHLY) RATE = 0.666667%

MONTH	MFV1	MFV1/P	MSSF	MPV1	MPV1/P	MPRF	MONTH
1	1.006667	1.000000	1.000000	0.993377	0.993377	1.006667	1
2	1.013378	2.006667	0.498339	0.986799	1.980176	0.505006	2
3	1.020134	3.020044	0.331121	0.980264	2.960440	0.337788	3
4	1.026935	4.040178	0.247514	0.973772	3.934212	0.254181	4
5	1.033781	5.067113	0.197351	0.967323	4.901535	0.204018	5
6	1.040673	6.100893	0.163910	0.960917	5.862452	0.170577	6
7	1.047610	7.141566	0.140025	0.954553	6.817005	0.146692	7

YEAR							YEAR
8	1.054595	8.189176	0.122112	0.948232	7.765237	0.128779	8
9	1.061625	9.243771	0.108181	0.941952	8.707189	0.114848	9
10	1.068703	10.305396	0.097037	0.935714	9.642903	0.103703	10
11	1.075827	11.374099	0.087919	0.929517	10.572420	0.094586	11
1	1.083000	12.449926	0.080322	0.923361	11.495782	0.086988	1
2	1.172888	25.933190	0.038561	0.852596	22.110544	0.045227	2
3	1.270237	40.535558	0.024670	0.787255	31.911806	0.031336	3
4	1.375666	56.349915	0.017746	0.726921	40.961913	0.024413	4
5	1.489846	73.476856	0.013610	0.671210	49.318433	0.020276	5
6	1.613502	92.025325	0.010867	0.619770	57.034522	0.017533	6
7	1.747422	112.113308	0.008920	0.572272	64.159261	0.015586	7
8	1.892457	133.868583	0.007470	0.528414	70.737970	0.014137	8
9	2.049530	157.429535	0.006352	0.487917	76.812497	0.013019	9
10	2.219640	182.946035	0.005466	0.450523	82.421481	0.012133	10
11	2.403869	210.580392	0.004749	0.415996	87.600600	0.011415	11
12	2.603389	240.508387	0.004158	0.384115	92.382800	0.010825	12
13	2.819469	272.920390	0.003664	0.354677	96.798498	0.010331	13
14	3.053484	308.022574	0.003247	0.327495	100.875784	0.009913	14
15	3.306921	346.038222	0.002890	0.302396	104.640592	0.009557	15
16	3.581394	387.209149	0.002583	0.279221	108.116871	0.009249	16
17	3.878648	431.797244	0.002316	0.257822	111.326733	0.008983	17
18	4.200574	480.086128	0.002083	0.238063	114.290596	0.008750	18
19	4.549220	532.382966	0.001878	0.219818	117.027313	0.008545	19
20	4.926803	589.020416	0.001698	0.202971	119.554292	0.008364	20
21	5.335725	650.358746	0.001538	0.187416	121.887606	0.008204	21
22	5.778588	716.788127	0.001395	0.173053	124.042099	0.008062	22
23	6.258207	788.731114	0.001268	0.159790	126.031475	0.007935	23
24	6.777636	866.645333	0.001154	0.147544	127.868388	0.007821	24
25	7.340176	951.026395	0.001051	0.136237	129.564523	0.007718	25
26	7.979407	1042.411042	0.000959	0.125796	131.130668	0.007626	26
27	8.609204	1141.380571	0.000876	0.116155	132.576786	0.007543	27
28	9.323763	1248.564521	0.000801	0.107253	133.912076	0.007468	28
29	10.097631	1364.644687	0.000733	0.099033	135.145031	0.007399	29
30	10.935730	1490.359449	0.000671	0.091443	136.283494	0.007338	30

9.00% NOMINAL RATE

Annual Compounding

EFFECTIVE (ANNUAL) RATE = 9.00%

YEAR	Future Value of 1 — FV1	Future Value of 1 per Period — FV1/P	Sinking Fund Factor — SFF	Present Value of 1 — PV1	Present Value of 1 per Period — PV1/P	Principal Recovery Factor — PRF	YEAR
1	1.090000	1.000000	1.000000	0.917431	0.917431	1.090000	1
2	1.188100	2.090000	0.478469	0.841680	1.759111	0.568469	2
3	1.295029	3.278100	0.305055	0.772183	2.531295	0.395055	3
4	1.411582	4.573129	0.218669	0.708425	3.239720	0.308669	4
5	1.538624	5.984711	0.167092	0.649931	3.889651	0.257092	5
6	1.677100	7.523335	0.132920	0.596267	4.485919	0.222920	6
7	1.828039	9.200435	0.108691	0.547034	5.032953	0.198691	7
8	1.992563	11.028474	0.090674	0.501866	5.534819	0.180674	8
9	2.171893	13.021036	0.076799	0.460428	5.995247	0.166799	9
10	2.367364	15.192930	0.065820	0.422411	6.417658	0.155820	10
11	2.580426	17.560293	0.056947	0.387533	6.805191	0.146947	11
12	2.812665	20.140720	0.049651	0.355535	7.160725	0.139651	12
13	3.065805	22.953385	0.043567	0.326179	7.486904	0.133567	13
14	3.341727	26.019189	0.038433	0.299246	7.786150	0.128433	14
15	3.642482	29.360916	0.034059	0.274538	8.060688	0.124059	15
16	3.970306	33.003399	0.030300	0.251870	8.312558	0.120300	16
17	4.327633	36.973705	0.027046	0.231073	8.543631	0.117046	17
18	4.717120	41.301338	0.024212	0.211994	8.755625	0.114212	18
19	5.141661	46.018458	0.021730	0.194490	8.950115	0.111730	19
20	5.604411	51.160120	0.019546	0.178431	9.128546	0.109546	20

Monthly Compounding

EFFECTIVE (MONTHLY) RATE = 0.750000%

MONTH	MFV1	MFV1/P	MSSF	MPV1	MPV1/P	MPRF	MONTH
1	1.007500	1.000000	1.000000	0.992556	0.992556	1.007500	1
2	1.015056	2.007500	0.498132	0.985167	1.977723	0.505632	2
3	1.022669	3.022556	0.330846	0.977833	2.955556	0.338346	3
4	1.030339	4.045225	0.247205	0.970554	3.926110	0.254705	4
5	1.038067	5.075565	0.197022	0.963329	4.889440	0.204522	5
6	1.045852	6.113631	0.163569	0.956158	5.845598	0.171069	6
7	1.053696	7.159484	0.139675	0.949040	6.794638	0.147175	7

YEAR						
8	0.129256	7.736613	0.941975	0.121756	8.213180	1.061599
9	0.115319	8.671576	0.934963	0.107819	9.274779	1.069561
10	0.104171	9.599580	0.928003	0.096671	10.344339	1.077583
11	0.095051	10.520675	0.921095	0.087551	11.421922	1.085664

YEAR						
1	0.087451	11.434913	0.914238	0.079951	12.507586	1.093807
2	0.045685	21.889146	0.835831	0.038185	26.188471	1.196414
3	0.031800	31.446805	0.764149	0.024300	41.152716	1.308645
4	0.024885	40.184782	0.698614	0.017385	57.520711	1.431405
5	0.020758	48.173374	0.638700	0.013258	75.424137	1.565681
6	0.018026	55.476849	0.583924	0.010526	95.007028	1.712553
7	0.016089	62.153965	0.533845	0.008589	116.426928	1.873202
8	0.014650	68.258439	0.488062	0.007150	139.856164	2.044921
9	0.013543	73.839382	0.446205	0.006043	165.438223	2.241124
10	0.012668	78.941693	0.407937	0.005168	193.514277	2.451357
11	0.011961	83.606420	0.372952	0.004461	224.174837	2.681311
12	0.011380	87.871092	0.340967	0.003880	257.711570	2.932837
13	0.010897	91.770018	0.311725	0.003397	294.394279	3.207957
14	0.010489	95.334564	0.284991	0.002989	334.518079	3.508886
15	0.010143	98.593409	0.260549	0.002643	378.405769	3.838043
16	0.009845	101.572769	0.238204	0.002345	426.410427	4.198078
17	0.009588	104.296613	0.217775	0.002088	478.918252	4.591887
18	0.009364	106.786856	0.199099	0.001864	536.351674	5.022638
19	0.009169	109.063531	0.182024	0.001669	599.172747	5.493796
20	0.008997	111.144954	0.166413	0.001497	667.886870	6.009152
21	0.008846	113.047870	0.152141	0.001346	743.046852	6.572851
22	0.008712	114.787589	0.139093	0.001212	825.257358	7.189430
23	0.008593	116.378106	0.127164	0.001093	915.179777	7.863848
24	0.008487	117.832218	0.116258	0.000987	1013.537539	8.601532
25	0.008392	119.161622	0.106288	0.000892	1121.121937	9.408415
26	0.008307	120.377014	0.097172	0.000807	1238.798495	10.290989
27	0.008231	121.488172	0.088839	0.000731	1367.513924	11.256354
28	0.008163	122.504035	0.081220	0.000663	1508.303750	12.312278
29	0.008102	123.432776	0.074254	0.000602	1662.300631	13.467255
30	0.008046	124.281866	0.067886	0.000546	1830.743483	14.730576

10.00% NOMINAL RATE

Annual Compounding

EFFECTIVE (ANNUAL) RATE = 10.00%

YEAR	Future Value of 1 FV1	Future Value of 1 per Period FV1/P	Sinking Fund Factor SFF	Present Value of 1 PV1	Present Value of 1 per Period PV1/P	Principal Recovery Factor PRF	YEAR
1	1.100000	1.000000	1.000000	0.909091	0.909091	1.100000	1
2	1.210000	2.100000	0.476190	0.826446	1.735537	0.576190	2
3	1.331000	3.310000	0.302115	0.751315	2.486852	0.402115	3
4	1.464100	4.641000	0.215471	0.683013	3.169865	0.315471	4
5	1.610510	6.105100	0.163797	0.620921	3.790787	0.263797	5
6	1.771561	7.715610	0.129607	0.564474	4.355261	0.229607	6
7	1.948717	9.487171	0.105405	0.513158	4.868419	0.205405	7
8	2.143589	11.435888	0.087444	0.466507	5.334926	0.187444	8
9	2.357948	13.579477	0.073641	0.424098	5.759024	0.173641	9
10	2.593742	15.937425	0.062745	0.385543	6.144567	0.162745	10
11	2.853117	18.531167	0.053963	0.350494	6.495061	0.153963	11
12	3.138428	21.384284	0.046763	0.318631	6.813692	0.146763	12
13	3.452271	24.522712	0.040779	0.289664	7.103356	0.140779	13
14	3.797498	27.974983	0.035746	0.263331	7.366687	0.135746	14
15	4.177248	31.772482	0.031474	0.239392	7.606080	0.131474	15
16	4.594973	35.949730	0.027817	0.217629	7.823709	0.127817	16
17	5.054470	40.544703	0.024664	0.197845	8.021553	0.124664	17
18	5.559917	45.599173	0.021930	0.179859	8.201412	0.121930	18
19	6.115909	51.159090	0.019547	0.163508	8.364920	0.119547	19
20	6.727500	57.274999	0.017460	0.148644	8.513564	0.117460	20

Monthly Compounding

EFFECTIVE (MONTHLY) RATE = 0.833333%

MONTH	MFV1	MFV1/P	MSSF	MPV1	MPV1/P	MPRF	MONTH
1	1.008333	1.000000	1.000000	0.991736	0.991736	1.008333	1
2	1.016736	2.008333	0.497925	0.983539	1.975275	0.506259	2
3	1.025209	3.025069	0.330571	0.975411	2.950686	0.338904	3
4	1.033752	4.050278	0.246897	0.967350	3.918036	0.255230	4
5	1.042367	5.084031	0.196694	0.959355	4.877391	0.205028	5
6	1.051053	6.126398	0.163228	0.951427	5.828817	0.171561	6

YEAR						
7	0.147659	6.772381	0.943563	0.139325	7.177451	1.059812
8	0.129733	7.708146	0.935765	0.121400	8.237263	1.068644
9	0.115792	8.636178	0.928032	0.107459	9.305907	1.077549
10	0.104640	9.556540	0.920362	0.096307	10.383456	1.086529
11	0.095517	10.469296	0.912756	0.087184	11.469985	1.095583

YEAR						
1	0.087916	11.374508	0.905212	0.079583	12.565568	1.104713
2	0.046145	21.670855	0.819410	0.037812	26.446915	1.220391
3	0.032267	30.991236	0.741740	0.023934	41.781821	1.348182
4	0.025363	39.428160	0.671432	0.017029	58.722492	1.489354
5	0.021247	47.065369	0.607789	0.012914	77.437072	1.645309
6	0.018526	53.978665	0.550178	0.010193	98.111314	1.817594
7	0.016601	60.236667	0.498028	0.008268	120.950418	2.007920
8	0.015174	65.901488	0.450821	0.006841	146.181076	2.218176
9	0.014079	71.029355	0.408089	0.005745	174.053713	2.450448
10	0.013215	75.671163	0.369407	0.004882	204.844979	2.707041
11	0.012520	79.872986	0.334392	0.004187	238.860493	2.990504
12	0.011951	83.676528	0.302696	0.003617	276.437876	3.303649
13	0.011478	87.119542	0.274004	0.003145	317.950102	3.649584
14	0.011082	90.236201	0.248032	0.002749	363.809201	4.031743
15	0.010746	93.057439	0.224521	0.002413	414.470346	4.453920
16	0.010459	95.611259	0.203240	0.002126	470.436376	4.920303
17	0.010212	97.923008	0.183975	0.001879	532.262780	5.435523
18	0.009998	100.015633	0.166536	0.001665	600.563216	6.004693
19	0.009813	101.909902	0.150751	0.001479	676.015601	6.633463
20	0.009650	103.624619	0.136462	0.001317	759.368836	7.328074
21	0.009508	105.176801	0.123527	0.001174	851.450244	8.095419
22	0.009382	106.581856	0.111818	0.001049	953.173779	8.943115
23	0.009272	107.853730	0.101219	0.000938	1065.549097	9.879576
24	0.009174	109.005054	0.091625	0.000841	1189.691580	10.914097
25	0.009087	110.047230	0.082940	0.000754	1326.833403	12.056945
26	0.009010	110.990629	0.075078	0.000676	1478.335767	13.319465
27	0.008941	111.844605	0.067962	0.000608	1645.702407	14.714187
28	0.008880	112.617635	0.061520	0.000546	1830.594523	16.254954
29	0.008825	113.317392	0.055688	0.000491	2034.847258	17.957060
30	0.008776	113.950820	0.050410	0.000442	2260.487925	19.837399

11.00% NOMINAL RATE

Annual Compounding

EFFECTIVE (ANNUAL) RATE = 11.00%

YEAR	Future Value of 1 — FV1	Future Value of 1 per Period — FV1/P	Sinking Fund Factor — SFF	Present Value of 1 — PV1	Present Value of 1 per Period — PV1/P	Principal Recovery Factor — PRF	YEAR
1	1.110000	1.000000	1.000000	0.900901	0.900901	1.110000	1
2	1.232100	2.110000	0.473934	0.811622	1.712523	0.583934	2
3	1.367631	3.342100	0.299213	0.731191	2.443715	0.409213	3
4	1.518070	4.709731	0.212326	0.658731	3.102446	0.322326	4
5	1.685058	6.227801	0.160570	0.593451	3.695897	0.270570	5
6	1.870415	7.912860	0.126377	0.534641	4.230538	0.236377	6
7	2.076160	9.783274	0.102215	0.481658	4.712196	0.212215	7
8	2.304538	11.859434	0.084321	0.433926	5.146123	0.194321	8
9	2.558037	14.163972	0.070602	0.390925	5.537048	0.180602	9
10	2.839421	16.722009	0.059801	0.352184	5.889232	0.169801	10
11	3.151757	19.561430	0.051121	0.317283	6.206515	0.161121	11
12	3.498451	22.713187	0.044027	0.285841	6.492356	0.154027	12
13	3.883280	26.211638	0.038151	0.257514	6.749870	0.148151	13
14	4.310441	30.094918	0.033228	0.231995	6.981865	0.143228	14
15	4.784589	34.405359	0.029065	0.209004	7.190870	0.139065	15
16	5.310894	39.189948	0.025517	0.188292	7.379162	0.135517	16
17	5.895093	44.500843	0.022471	0.169633	7.548794	0.132471	17
18	6.543553	50.395936	0.019843	0.152822	7.701617	0.129843	18
19	7.263344	56.939488	0.017563	0.137678	7.839294	0.127563	19
20	8.062312	64.202832	0.015576	0.124034	7.963328	0.125576	20

Monthly Compounding

EFFECTIVE (MONTHLY) RATE = 0.916667%

MONTH	MFV1	MFV1/P	MSSF	MPV1	MPV1/P	MPRF	MONTH
1	1.009167	1.000000	1.000000	0.990917	0.990917	1.009167	1
2	1.018417	2.009167	0.497719	0.981916	1.972832	0.506885	2
3	1.027753	3.027584	0.330296	0.972997	2.945829	0.339463	3
4	1.037174	4.055337	0.246589	0.964158	3.909987	0.255755	4
5	1.046681	5.092511	0.196367	0.955401	4.865388	0.205533	5
6	1.056276	6.139192	0.162888	0.946722	5.812110	0.172055	6
7	1.065958	7.195468	0.138976	0.938123	6.750233	0.148143	7

YEAR						
8	0.130211	7.679835	0.929602	0.121044	8.261427	1.075730
9	0.116266	8.600992	0.921158	0.107099	9.337156	1.085591
10	0.105111	9.513783	0.912790	0.095944	10.422747	1.095542
11	0.095985	10.418282	0.904499	0.086818	11.518289	1.105584

YEAR						
1	0.088382	11.314565	0.896283	0.079215	12.623873	1.115719
2	0.046608	21.455619	0.803323	0.037441	26.708566	1.244829
3	0.032739	30.544874	0.720005	0.023572	42.423123	1.388879
4	0.025846	38.691421	0.645329	0.016679	59.956151	1.549598
5	0.021742	45.993034	0.578397	0.012576	79.518080	1.728916
6	0.019034	52.537346	0.518408	0.009867	101.343692	1.928984
7	0.017122	58.402903	0.464640	0.007956	125.694940	2.152204
8	0.015708	63.660103	0.416449	0.006542	152.864085	2.401254
9	0.014626	68.372043	0.373256	0.005459	183.177212	2.679124
10	0.013775	72.595275	0.334543	0.004608	216.998139	2.989150
11	0.013092	76.380487	0.299846	0.003926	254.732784	3.335051
12	0.012536	79.773109	0.268747	0.003369	296.834038	3.720979
13	0.012075	82.813859	0.240873	0.002909	343.807200	4.151566
14	0.011691	85.539231	0.215890	0.002524	396.216042	4.631980
15	0.011366	87.981937	0.193499	0.002199	454.689575	5.167988
16	0.011090	90.171293	0.173430	0.001923	519.929596	5.766021
17	0.010854	92.133576	0.155442	0.001687	592.719117	6.433259
18	0.010650	93.892337	0.139320	0.001484	673.931757	7.177708
19	0.010475	95.468685	0.124870	0.001308	764.542228	8.008304
20	0.010322	96.881539	0.111919	0.001155	865.638038	8.935015
21	0.010189	98.147856	0.100311	0.001022	978.432537	9.968965
22	0.010072	99.282835	0.089907	0.000906	1104.279485	11.122562
23	0.009970	100.300098	0.080582	0.000803	1244.689295	12.409652
24	0.009880	101.211853	0.072225	0.000714	1401.347165	13.845682
25	0.009801	102.029044	0.064734	0.000634	1576.133301	15.447889
26	0.009731	102.761478	0.058020	0.000565	1771.145485	17.235500
27	0.009670	103.417947	0.052002	0.000503	1988.724252	19.229972
28	0.009615	104.006328	0.046609	0.000448	2231.480981	21.455242
29	0.009566	104.533685	0.041775	0.000400	2502.329236	23.938018
30	0.009523	105.006346	0.037442	0.000357	2804.519736	26.708098

12.00% NOMINAL RATE

to amortize P+I · 12%

Annual Compounding

EFFECTIVE (ANNUAL) RATE = 12.00%

YEAR	Future Value of 1 FV1	Future Value of 1 per Period FV1/P	Sinking Fund Factor SFF	Present Value of 1 PV1	Present Value of 1 per Period PV1/P	Principal Recovery Factor PRF	YEAR
1	1.120000	1.000000	1.000000	0.892857	0.892857	1.120000	1
2	1.254400	2.120000	0.471698	0.797194	1.690051	0.591698	2
3	1.404928	3.374400	0.296349	0.711780	2.401831	0.416349	3
4	1.573519	4.779328	0.209234	0.635518	3.037349	0.329234	4
5	1.762342	6.352847	0.157410	0.567427	3.604776	0.277410	5
6	1.973823	8.115189	0.123226	0.506631	4.111407	0.243226	6
7	2.210681	10.089012	0.099118	0.452349	4.563757	0.219118	7
8	2.475963	12.299693	0.081303	0.403883	4.967640	0.201303	8
9	2.773079	14.775656	0.067679	0.360610	5.328250	0.187679	9
10	3.105848	17.548735	0.056984	0.321973	5.650223	0.176984	10
11	3.478550	20.654583	0.048415	0.287476	5.937699	0.168415	11
12	3.895976	24.133133	0.041437	0.256675	6.194374	0.161437	12
13	4.363493	28.029109	0.035677	0.229174	6.423548	0.155677	13
14	4.887112	32.392602	0.030871	0.204620	6.628168	0.150871	14
15	5.473566	37.279715	0.026824	0.182696	6.810864	0.146824	15
16	6.130394	42.753280	0.023390	0.163122	6.973986	0.143390	16
17	6.866041	48.883674	0.020457	0.145644	7.119630	0.140457	17
18	7.689966	55.749715	0.017937	0.130040	7.249670	0.137937	18
19	8.612762	63.439681	0.015763	0.116107	7.365777	0.135763	19
20	9.646293	72.052442	0.013879	0.103667	7.469444	0.133879	20

Monthly Compounding

EFFECTIVE (MONTHLY) RATE = 1.000000%

MONTH	MFV1	MFV1/P	MSSF	MPV1	MPV1/P	MPRF	MONTH
1	1.010000	1.000000	1.000000	0.990099	0.990099	1.010000	1
2	1.020100	2.010000	0.497512	0.980296	1.970395	0.507512	2
3	1.030301	3.030100	0.330022	0.970590	2.940985	0.340022	3
4	1.040604	4.060401	0.246281	0.960980	3.901966	0.256281	4
5	1.051010	5.101005	0.196040	0.951466	4.853431	0.206040	5
6	1.061520	6.152015	0.162548	0.942045	5.795476	0.172548	6
7	1.072135	7.213535	0.138628	0.932718	6.728195	0.148628	7

YEAR						
8	1.082857	8.285671	0.120690	0.923483	7.651678	0.130690
9	1.093685	9.368527	0.106740	0.914340	8.566018	0.116740
10	1.104622	10.462213	0.095582	0.905287	9.471305	0.105582
11	1.115668	11.566835	0.086454	0.896324	10.367628	0.096454

YEAR						
1	1.126825	12.682503	0.078849	0.887449	11.255077	0.088849
2	1.269735	26.973465	0.037073	0.787566	21.243387	0.047073
3	1.430769	43.076878	0.023214	0.698925	30.107505	0.033214
4	1.612226	61.222608	0.016334	0.620260	37.973959	0.026334
5	1.816697	81.669670	0.012244	0.550450	44.955038	0.022244
6	2.047099	104.709931	0.009550	0.488496	51.150391	0.019550
7	2.306723	130.672274	0.007653	0.433515	56.648453	0.017653
8	2.599273	159.927293	0.006253	0.384723	61.527703	0.016252
9	2.928926	192.892579	0.005184	0.341422	65.857790	0.015184
10	3.300387	230.038689	0.004347	0.302995	69.700522	0.014347
11	3.718959	271.895856	0.003678	0.268892	73.110752	0.013678
12	4.190616	319.061559	0.003134	0.238628	76.137157	0.013134
13	4.722091	372.209054	0.002687	0.211771	78.822939	0.012687
14	5.320970	432.096982	0.002314	0.187936	81.206434	0.012314
15	5.995802	499.580198	0.002002	0.166783	83.321664	0.012002
16	6.756220	575.621974	0.001737	0.148012	85.198824	0.011737
17	7.613078	661.307751	0.001512	0.131353	86.864707	0.011512
18	8.578606	757.860630	0.001320	0.116569	88.343095	0.011320
19	9.666588	866.658830	0.001154	0.103449	89.655089	0.011154
20	10.892554	989.255365	0.001011	0.091806	90.819416	0.011011
21	12.274002	1127.400210	0.000887	0.081473	91.852698	0.010887
22	13.830653	1283.065279	0.000779	0.072303	92.769683	0.010779
23	15.584726	1458.472574	0.000686	0.064165	93.583461	0.010686
24	17.561259	1656.125905	0.000604	0.056944	94.305647	0.010604
25	19.788466	1878.846626	0.000532	0.050534	94.946551	0.010532
26	22.298139	2129.813909	0.000470	0.044847	95.515321	0.010470
27	25.126101	2412.610125	0.000414	0.039799	96.020075	0.010414
28	28.312720	2731.271980	0.000366	0.035320	96.468019	0.010366
29	31.903481	3090.348134	0.000324	0.031345	96.865546	0.010324
30	35.949641	3494.964133	0.000286	0.027817	97.218331	0.010286

13.00% NOMINAL RATE

Annual Compounding

EFFECTIVE (ANNUAL) RATE = 13.00%

YEAR	Future Value of 1 FV1	Future Value of 1 per Period FV1/P	Sinking Fund Factor SFF	Present Value of 1 PV1	Present Value of 1 per Period PV1/P	Principal Recovery Factor PRF	YEAR
1	1.130000	1.000000	1.000000	0.884956	0.884956	1.130000	1
2	1.276900	2.130000	0.469484	0.783147	1.668102	0.599484	2
3	1.442897	3.406900	0.293522	0.693050	2.361153	0.423522	3
4	1.630474	4.849797	0.206194	0.613319	2.974471	0.336194	4
5	1.842435	6.480271	0.154315	0.542760	3.517231	0.284315	5
6	2.081952	8.322706	0.120153	0.480319	3.997550	0.250153	6
7	2.352605	10.404658	0.096111	0.425061	4.422610	0.226111	7
8	2.658444	12.757263	0.078387	0.376160	4.798770	0.208387	8
9	3.004042	15.415707	0.064869	0.332885	5.131655	0.194869	9
10	3.394567	18.419749	0.054290	0.294588	5.426243	0.184290	10
11	3.835861	21.814317	0.045841	0.260698	5.686941	0.175841	11
12	4.334523	25.650178	0.038986	0.230706	5.917647	0.168986	12
13	4.898011	29.984701	0.033350	0.204165	6.121812	0.163350	13
14	5.534753	34.882712	0.028667	0.180677	6.302488	0.158667	14
15	6.254270	40.417464	0.024742	0.159891	6.462379	0.154742	15
16	7.067326	46.671735	0.021426	0.141496	6.603875	0.151426	16
17	7.986078	53.739060	0.018608	0.125218	6.729093	0.148608	17
18	9.024268	61.725138	0.016201	0.110812	6.839905	0.146201	18
19	10.197423	70.749406	0.014134	0.098064	6.937969	0.144134	19
20	11.523088	80.946829	0.012354	0.086782	7.024752	0.142354	20

Monthly Compounding

EFFECTIVE (MONTHLY RATE) = 1.083333%

MONTH	MFV1	MFV1/P	MSSF	MPV1	MPV1/P	MPRF	MONTH
1	1.010833	1.000000	1.000000	0.989283	0.989283	1.010833	1
2	1.021784	2.010833	0.497306	0.978680	1.967963	0.508140	2
3	1.032853	3.032617	0.329748	0.968192	2.936155	0.340581	3
4	1.044043	4.065471	0.245974	0.957815	3.893970	0.256807	4
5	1.055353	5.109513	0.195713	0.947550	4.841520	0.206547	5
6	1.066786	6.164866	0.162210	0.937395	5.778915	0.173043	6
7	1.078343	7.231652	0.138281	0.927349	6.706264	0.149114	7

YEAR						
8	1.090025	8.309995	0.120337	0.917410	7.623674	0.131170
9	1.101834	9.400020	0.106383	0.907578	8.531253	0.117216
10	1.113770	10.501854	0.095221	0.897851	9.429104	0.106055
11	1.125836	11.615624	0.086091	0.888229	10.317333	0.096924

YEAR						
1	1.138032	12.741460	0.078484	0.878710	11.196042	0.089317
2	1.295118	27.241655	0.036708	0.772130	21.034112	0.047542
3	1.473886	43.743348	0.022861	0.678478	29.678917	0.033694
4	1.677330	62.522811	0.015994	0.596185	37.275190	0.026827
5	1.908857	83.894449	0.011920	0.523874	43.950107	0.022753
6	2.172341	108.216068	0.009241	0.460333	49.815421	0.020074
7	2.472194	135.894861	0.007359	0.404499	54.969328	0.018192
8	2.813437	167.394225	0.005974	0.355437	59.498115	0.016807
9	3.201783	203.241525	0.004920	0.312326	63.477604	0.015754
10	3.643733	244.036917	0.004098	0.274444	66.974419	0.014931
11	4.146687	290.463399	0.003443	0.241156	70.047103	0.014276
12	4.719064	343.298242	0.002913	0.211906	72.747100	0.013746
13	5.370448	403.426010	0.002479	0.186204	75.119613	0.013312
14	6.111745	471.853363	0.002119	0.163619	77.204363	0.012953
15	6.955364	549.725914	0.001819	0.143774	79.036253	0.012652
16	7.915430	638.347406	0.001567	0.126336	80.645952	0.012400
17	9.008017	739.201542	0.001353	0.111012	82.060410	0.012186
18	10.251416	853.976825	0.001171	0.097548	83.303307	0.012004
19	11.666444	984.594826	0.001016	0.085716	84.395453	0.011849
20	13.276792	1133.242353	0.000882	0.075319	85.355132	0.011716
21	15.109421	1302.408067	0.000768	0.066184	86.198412	0.011601
22	17.195012	1494.924144	0.000669	0.058156	86.939409	0.011502
23	19.568482	1714.013694	0.000583	0.051103	87.590531	0.011417
24	22.269568	1963.344717	0.000509	0.044904	88.162677	0.011343
25	25.343491	2247.091520	0.000445	0.039458	88.665428	0.011278
26	28.841716	2570.004599	0.000389	0.034672	89.107200	0.011222
27	32.822810	2937.490172	0.000340	0.030467	89.495389	0.011174
28	37.353424	3355.700690	0.000298	0.026771	89.836495	0.011131
29	42.509410	3831.637843	0.000261	0.023524	90.136227	0.011094
30	48.377089	4373.269783	0.000229	0.020671	90.399605	0.011062

14.00% NOMINAL RATE

Annual Compounding

EFFECTIVE (ANNUAL) RATE = 14.00%

YEAR	Future Value of 1 FV1	Future Value of 1 per Period FV1/P	Sinking Fund Factor SFF	Present Value of 1 PV1	Present Value of 1 per Period PV1/P	Principal Recovery Factor PRF	YEAR
1	1.140000	1.000000	1.000000	0.877193	0.877193	1.140000	1
2	1.299600	2.140000	0.467290	0.769468	1.646661	0.607290	2
3	1.481544	3.439600	0.290731	0.674972	2.321632	0.430731	3
4	1.688960	4.921144	0.203205	0.592080	2.913712	0.343205	4
5	1.925415	6.610104	0.151284	0.519369	3.433081	0.291284	5
6	2.194973	8.535519	0.117157	0.455587	3.888668	0.257157	6
7	2.502269	10.730491	0.093192	0.399637	4.288305	0.233192	7
8	2.852586	13.232760	0.075570	0.350559	4.638864	0.215570	8
9	3.251949	16.085347	0.062168	0.307508	4.946372	0.202168	9
10	3.707221	19.337295	0.051714	0.269744	5.216116	0.191714	10
11	4.226232	23.044516	0.043394	0.236617	5.452733	0.183394	11
12	4.817905	27.270749	0.036669	0.207559	5.660292	0.176669	12
13	5.492411	32.088654	0.031164	0.182069	5.842362	0.171164	13
14	6.261349	37.581065	0.026609	0.159710	6.002072	0.166609	14
15	7.137938	43.842414	0.022809	0.140096	6.142168	0.162809	15
16	8.137249	50.980352	0.019615	0.122892	6.265060	0.159615	16
17	9.276464	59.117601	0.016915	0.107800	6.372859	0.156915	17
18	10.575169	68.394066	0.014621	0.094561	6.467420	0.154621	18
19	12.055693	78.969235	0.012663	0.082948	6.550369	0.152663	19
20	13.743490	91.024928	0.010986	0.072762	6.623131	0.150986	20

Monthly Compounding

EFFECTIVE (MONTHLY) RATE = 1.166667%

MONTH	MFV1	MFV1/P	MSSF	MPV1	MPV1/P	MPRF	MONTH
1	1.011667	1.000000	1.000000	0.988468	0.988468	1.011667	1
2	1.023469	2.011667	0.497100	0.977069	1.965537	0.508767	2
3	1.035410	3.035136	0.329475	0.965801	2.931338	0.341141	3
4	1.047490	4.070546	0.245667	0.954663	3.886001	0.257334	4
5	1.059710	5.118036	0.195387	0.943654	4.829655	0.207054	5
6	1.072074	6.177746	0.161871	0.932772	5.762427	0.173538	6
7	1.084581	7.249820	0.137934	0.922015	6.684442	0.149601	7

YEAR						
8	0.131651	7.595824	0.911382	0.119985	8.334401	1.097235
9	0.117693	8.496696	0.900872	0.106026	9.431636	1.110036
10	0.106528	9.387178	0.890483	0.094862	10.541672	1.122986
11	0.097396	10.267392	0.880214	0.085729	11.664658	1.136088

YEAR						
1	0.089787	11.137455	0.870063	0.078120	12.800745	1.149342
2	0.048013	20.827743	0.757010	0.036346	27.513180	1.320987
3	0.034178	29.258904	0.658646	0.022511	44.422800	1.518266
4	0.027326	36.594546	0.573064	0.015660	63.857736	1.745007
5	0.023268	42.977016	0.498601	0.011602	86.195125	2.005610
6	0.020606	48.530168	0.433815	0.008939	111.868425	2.305132
7	0.018740	53.361760	0.377446	0.007073	141.375828	2.649385
8	0.017372	57.565549	0.328402	0.005705	175.289927	3.045049
9	0.016334	61.223111	0.285730	0.004667	214.268826	3.499803
10	0.015527	64.405420	0.248603	0.003860	259.068912	4.022471
11	0.014887	67.174230	0.216301	0.003220	310.559534	4.623195
12	0.014371	69.583269	0.188195	0.002705	369.739871	5.313632
13	0.013951	71.679284	0.163742	0.002284	437.758319	6.107180
14	0.013605	73.502950	0.142466	0.001938	515.934780	7.019239
15	0.013317	75.089654	0.123954	0.001651	605.786272	8.067507
16	0.013077	76.470187	0.107848	0.001410	709.056369	9.272324
17	0.012875	77.671337	0.093834	0.001208	827.749031	10.657072
18	0.012704	78.716413	0.081642	0.001037	964.167496	12.248621
19	0.012559	79.625696	0.071034	0.000892	1120.958972	14.077855
20	0.012435	80.416829	0.061804	0.000769	1301.166005	16.180270
21	0.012330	81.105164	0.053773	0.000663	1508.285522	18.596664
22	0.012239	81.704060	0.046786	0.000573	1746.336688	21.373928
23	0.012162	82.225136	0.040707	0.000495	2019.938898	24.565954
24	0.012095	82.678506	0.035417	0.000428	2334.401417	28.234683
25	0.012038	83.072966	0.030815	0.000371	2695.826407	32.451308
26	0.011988	83.416171	0.026811	0.000321	3111.227338	37.297652
27	0.011945	83.714781	0.023328	0.000279	3588.665088	42.867759
28	0.011908	83.974591	0.020296	0.000242	4137.404359	49.269718
29	0.011876	84.200641	0.017659	0.000210	4768.093467	56.627757
30	0.011849	84.397320	0.015365	0.000182	5492.970967	65.084661

15.00% NOMINAL RATE

Annual Compounding

EFFECTIVE (ANNUAL) RATE = 15.00%

YEAR	Future Value of 1 FV1	Future Value of 1 per Period FV1/P	Sinking Fund Factor SFF	Present Value of 1 PV1	Present Value of 1 per Period PV1/P	Principal Recovery Factor PRF	YEAR
1	1.150000	1.000000	1.000000	0.869565	0.869565	1.150000	1
2	1.322500	2.150000	0.465116	0.756144	1.625709	0.615116	2
3	1.520875	3.472500	0.287977	0.657516	2.283225	0.437977	3
4	1.749006	4.993375	0.200265	0.571753	2.854978	0.350265	4
5	2.011357	6.742381	0.148316	0.497177	3.352155	0.298316	5
6	2.313061	8.753738	0.114237	0.432328	3.784483	0.264237	6
7	2.660020	11.066799	0.090360	0.375937	4.160420	0.240360	7
8	3.059023	13.726819	0.072850	0.326902	4.487322	0.222850	8
9	3.517876	16.785842	0.059574	0.284262	4.771584	0.209574	9
10	4.045558	20.303718	0.049252	0.247185	5.018769	0.199252	10
11	4.652391	24.349276	0.041069	0.214943	5.233712	0.191069	11
12	5.350250	29.001667	0.034481	0.186907	5.420619	0.184481	12
13	6.152788	34.351917	0.029110	0.162528	5.583147	0.179110	13
14	7.075706	40.504705	0.024688	0.141329	5.724476	0.174688	14
15	8.137062	47.580411	0.021017	0.122894	5.847370	0.171017	15
16	9.357621	55.717472	0.017948	0.106865	5.954235	0.167948	16
17	10.761264	65.075093	0.015367	0.092926	6.047161	0.165367	17
18	12.375454	75.836357	0.013186	0.080805	6.127966	0.163186	18
19	14.231772	88.211811	0.011336	0.070265	6.198231	0.161336	19
20	16.366537	102.443583	0.009761	0.061100	6.259331	0.159761	20

Monthly Compounding

EFFECTIVE (MONTHLY) RATE = 1.250000%

MONTH	MFV1	MFV1/P	MSSF	MPV1	MPV1/P	MPRF	MONTH
1	1.012500	1.000000	1.000000	0.987654	0.987654	1.012500	1
2	1.025156	2.012500	0.496894	0.975461	1.963115	0.509394	2
3	1.037971	3.037656	0.329201	0.963418	2.926534	0.341701	3
4	1.050945	4.075627	0.245361	0.951524	3.878058	0.257861	4
5	1.064082	5.126572	0.195062	0.939777	4.817835	0.207562	5
6	1.077383	6.190654	0.161534	0.928175	5.746010	0.174034	6
7	1.090850	7.268038	0.137589	0.916716	6.662726	0.150089	7

YEAR							YEAR
8	1.104486	8.358888	0.119633	0.905398	7.568124	0.132133	8
9	1.118292	9.463374	0.105671	0.894221	8.462345	0.118171	9
10	1.132271	10.581666	0.094503	0.883181	9.345526	0.107003	10
11	1.146424	11.713937	0.085368	0.872277	10.217803	0.097868	11

YEAR							YEAR
1	1.160755	12.860361	0.077758	0.861509	11.079312	0.090258	1
2	1.347351	27.788084	0.035987	0.742197	20.624235	0.048487	2
3	1.563944	45.115505	0.022165	0.639409	28.847267	0.034665	3
4	1.815355	65.228388	0.015331	0.550856	35.931481	0.027831	4
5	2.107181	88.574508	0.011290	0.474568	42.034592	0.023790	5
6	2.445920	115.673621	0.008645	0.408844	47.292474	0.021145	6
7	2.839113	147.129040	0.006797	0.352223	51.822185	0.019297	7
8	3.295513	183.641059	0.005445	0.303443	55.724570	0.017945	8
9	3.825282	226.022551	0.004424	0.261419	59.086509	0.016924	9
10	4.440213	275.217058	0.003633	0.225214	61.982847	0.016133	10
11	5.153998	332.319805	0.003009	0.194024	64.478068	0.015509	11
12	5.982526	398.602077	0.002509	0.167153	66.627722	0.015009	12
13	6.944244	475.539523	0.002103	0.144004	68.479668	0.014603	13
14	8.060563	564.845011	0.001770	0.124061	70.075134	0.014270	14
15	9.356334	668.506759	0.001496	0.106879	71.449643	0.013996	15
16	10.860408	788.832603	0.001268	0.092078	72.633794	0.013768	16
17	12.606267	928.501369	0.001077	0.079326	73.653950	0.013577	17
18	14.632781	1090.622520	0.000917	0.068340	74.532823	0.013417	18
19	16.985067	1278.805378	0.000782	0.058875	75.289980	0.013282	19
20	19.715494	1497.239481	0.000668	0.050722	75.942278	0.013168	20
21	22.884848	1750.787854	0.000571	0.043697	76.504237	0.013071	21
22	26.563691	2045.095272	0.000489	0.037645	76.988370	0.012989	22
23	30.833924	2386.713938	0.000419	0.032432	77.405455	0.012919	23
24	35.790617	2783.249347	0.000359	0.027940	77.764777	0.012859	24
25	41.544120	3243.529615	0.000308	0.024071	78.074336	0.012808	25
26	48.222525	3777.802015	0.000265	0.020737	78.341024	0.012765	26
27	55.974514	4397.961118	0.000227	0.017865	78.570778	0.012727	27
28	64.972670	5117.813598	0.000195	0.015391	78.768713	0.012695	28
29	75.417320	5953.385616	0.000168	0.013260	78.939236	0.012668	29
30	87.540995	6923.279611	0.000144	0.011423	79.086142	0.012644	30

20.00% NOMINAL RATE

Annual Compounding

EFFECTIVE (ANNUAL) RATE = 20.00%

YEAR	Future Value of 1 FV1	Future Value of 1 per Period FV1/P	Sinking Fund Factor SFF	Present Value of 1 PV1	Present Value of 1 per Period PV1/P	Principal Recovery Factor PRF	YEAR
1	1.200000	1.000000	1.000000	0.833333	0.833333	1.200000	1
2	1.440000	2.200000	0.454545	0.694444	1.527778	0.654545	2
3	1.728000	0.640000	0.274725	0.578704	2.106481	0.474725	3
4	2.073600	5.368000	0.186289	0.482253	2.588735	0.386289	4
5	2.488320	7.441600	0.134380	0.401878	2.990612	0.334380	5
6	2.985984	9.929920	0.100706	0.334898	3.325510	0.300706	6
7	3.583181	12.915904	0.077424	0.279082	3.604592	0.277424	7
8	4.299817	16.499085	0.060609	0.232568	3.837160	0.260609	8
9	5.159780	20.798902	0.048079	0.193807	4.030967	0.248079	9
10	6.191736	25.958682	0.038523	0.161506	4.192472	0.238523	10
11	7.430084	32.150419	0.031104	0.134588	4.327060	0.231104	11
12	8.916100	39.580502	0.025265	0.112157	4.439217	0.225265	12
13	10.699321	48.496603	0.020620	0.093464	4.532681	0.220620	13
14	12.839185	59.195923	0.016893	0.077887	4.610567	0.216893	14
15	15.407022	72.035108	0.013882	0.064905	4.675473	0.213882	15
16	18.488426	87.442129	0.011436	0.054088	4.729561	0.211436	16
17	22.186111	105.930555	0.009440	0.045073	4.774634	0.209440	17
18	26.623333	128.116666	0.007805	0.037561	4.812195	0.207805	18
19	31.948000	154.740000	0.006462	0.031301	4.843496	0.206462	19
20	38.337600	186.688000	0.005357	0.026084	4.869580	0.205357	20

Monthly Compounding

EFFECTIVE (MONTHLY) RATE = 1.666667%

MONTH	MFV1	MFV1/P	MSSF	MPV1	MPV1/P	MPRF	MONTH
1	1.016667	1.000000	1.000000	0.983607	0.983607	1.016667	1
2	1.033611	2.016667	0.495868	0.967482	1.951088	0.512534	2

YEAR						
3	1.050838	3.050278	0.327839	0.951622	2.902710	0.344506
4	1.068352	4.101116	0.243836	0.936021	3.838731	0.260503
5	1.086158	5.169468	0.193444	0.920677	4.759408	0.210110
6	1.104260	6.255625	0.159856	0.905583	5.664991	0.176523
7	1.122665	7.359886	0.135872	0.890738	6.555729	0.152538
8	1.141376	8.482551	0.117889	0.876136	7.431865	0.134556
9	1.160399	9.623926	0.103908	0.861773	8.293637	0.120574
10	1.179739	10.784325	0.092727	0.847645	9.141283	0.109394
11	1.199401	11.964064	0.083584	0.833749	9.975032	0.100250

YEAR						
1	1.219391	13.163465	0.075968	0.820081	10.795113	0.092635
2	1.486915	29.214877	0.034229	0.672534	19.647986	0.050896
3	1.813130	48.787826	0.020497	0.551532	26.908062	0.037164
4	2.210915	72.654905	0.013764	0.452301	32.861916	0.030430
5	2.695970	101.758208	0.009827	0.370924	37.744561	0.026494
6	3.287442	137.246517	0.007286	0.304188	41.748727	0.023953
7	4.008677	180.520645	0.005540	0.249459	45.032470	0.022206
8	4.888145	233.288730	0.004287	0.204577	47.725406	0.020953
9	5.960561	297.633662	0.003360	0.167769	49.933833	0.020027
10	7.268255	376.095300	0.002659	0.137585	51.744924	0.019326
11	8.862845	471.770720	0.002120	0.112831	53.230165	0.018786
12	10.807275	588.436476	0.001699	0.092530	54.448184	0.018366
13	13.178294	730.697658	0.001369	0.075882	55.447059	0.018035
14	16.069495	904.169675	0.001106	0.062230	56.266217	0.017773
15	19.594998	1115.699905	0.000896	0.051033	56.937994	0.017563
16	23.893966	1373.637983	0.000728	0.041852	57.488906	0.017395
17	29.136090	1688.165376	0.000592	0.034322	57.940698	0.017259
18	35.528288	2071.697274	0.000483	0.028147	58.311205	0.017149
19	43.322878	2539.372652	0.000394	0.023082	58.615050	0.017060
20	52.827531	3109.651838	0.000322	0.018930	58.864229	0.016988

25.00% NOMINAL RATE

Annual Compounding

EFFECTIVE (ANNUAL) RATE = 25.00%

YEAR	Future Value of 1 — FV1	Future Value of 1 per Period — FV1/P	Sinking Fund Factor — SFF	Present Value of 1 — PV1	Present Value of 1 per Period — PV1/P	Principal Recovery Factor — PRF	YEAR
1	0.250000	1.000000	1.000000	0.800000	0.800000	1.250000	1
2	1.562500	2.250000	0.444444	0.640000	1.440000	0.694444	2
3	1.953125	3.812500	0.262295	0.512000	1.952000	0.512295	3
4	2.441406	5.765625	0.173442	0.409600	2.361600	0.423442	4
5	3.051758	8.207031	0.121847	0.327680	2.689280	0.371847	5
6	3.814697	11.258789	0.088819	0.262144	2.951424	0.338819	6
7	4.768372	15.073486	0.066342	0.209715	3.161139	0.316342	7
8	5.960464	19.841858	0.050399	0.167772	3.328911	0.300399	8
9	7.450581	25.802322	0.038756	0.134218	3.463129	0.288756	9
10	9.313226	33.252903	0.030073	0.107374	3.570503	0.280073	10
11	11.641532	42.566129	0.023493	0.085899	3.656403	0.273493	11
12	14.551915	54.207661	0.018448	0.068719	3.725122	0.268448	12
13	18.189894	68.759576	0.014543	0.054976	3.780098	0.264543	13
14	22.737368	86.949470	0.011501	0.043980	3.824078	0.261501	14
15	28.421709	109.686838	0.009117	0.035184	3.859263	0.259117	15
16	35.527137	138.108547	0.007241	0.028147	3.887410	0.257241	16
17	44.408921	173.635684	0.005759	0.022518	3.909928	0.255759	17
18	55.511151	218.044605	0.004586	0.018014	3.927942	0.254586	18
19	69.388939	273.555756	0.003656	0.014412	3.942354	0.253656	19
20	86.736174	342.944695	0.002916	0.011529	3.953883	0.252916	20

Monthly Compounding

EFFECTIVE (MONTHLY) RATE = 2.083333%

MONTH	MFV1	MFV1/P	MSSF	MPV1	MPV1/P	MPRF	MONTH
1	1.020833	1.000000	1.000000	0.979592	0.979592	1.020833	1
2	1.042101	2.020833	0.494845	0.959600	1.939192	0.515679	2
3	1.063811	3.062934	0.326484	0.940016	2.879208	0.347318	3

YEAR						
4	1.085974	4.126745	0.242322	0.920832	3.800041	0.263155
5	1.108598	5.212719	0.191838	0.902040	4.702081	0.212672
6	1.131694	6.321317	0.158195	0.883631	5.585712	0.179028
7	1.155271	7.453011	0.134174	0.865598	6.451310	0.155007
8	1.179339	8.608283	0.116167	0.847932	7.299242	0.137001
9	1.203909	9.787622	0.102170	0.830628	8.129870	0.123003
10	1.228990	10.991531	0.090979	0.813676	8.943546	0.111812
11	1.254594	12.220521	0.081830	0.797070	9.740616	0.102663

YEAR						
1	1.280732	13.475115	0.074211	0.780804	10.521420	0.095044
2	1.640273	30.733120	0.032538	0.609654	18.736585	0.053372
3	2.100750	52.835991	0.018926	0.476021	25.151016	0.039760
4	2.690497	81.143837	0.012324	0.371679	30.159427	0.033157
5	3.445804	117.398588	0.008518	0.290208	34.070014	0.029351
6	4.413150	163.831191	0.006104	0.226596	37.123415	0.026937
7	5.652060	223.298892	0.004478	0.176927	39.507522	0.025312
8	7.238772	229.461053	0.003339	0.138145	41.369041	0.024173
9	9.270924	397.004337	0.002519	0.107864	42.822522	0.023352
10	11.873565	521.931099	0.001916	0.084221	43.957406	0.022749
11	15.206849	681.928746	0.001466	0.065760	44.843528	0.022300
12	19.475891	886.842783	0.001128	0.051346	45.535414	0.021961
13	24.943389	1149.282656	0.000870	0.040091	46.075642	0.021703
14	31.945785	1485.397684	0.000673	0.031303	46.497454	0.021507
15	40.913975	1915.870809	0.000522	0.024442	46.826807	0.021355
16	52.399819	2467.191327	0.000405	0.019084	47.083966	0.021239
17	67.110102	3173.284913	0.000315	0.014901	47.284757	0.021148
18	85.950026	4077.601254	0.000245	0.011635	47.441536	0.021079
19	110.078911	5235.787733	0.000191	0.009084	47.563949	0.021024
20	140.981536	6719.113709	0.000149	0.007093	47.659530	0.020982

30.00% NOMINAL RATE

Annual Compounding

EFFECTIVE (ANNUAL) RATE = 30.00%

YEAR	Future Value of 1 FV1	Future Value of 1 per Period FV1/P	Sinking Fund Factor SFF	Present Value of 1 PV1	Present Value of 1 per Period PV1/P	Principal Recovery Factor PRF	YEAR
1	1.300000	1.000000	1.000000	0.769231	0.769231	1.300000	1
2	1.690000	2.300000	0.434783	0.591716	1.360947	0.734783	2
3	2.197000	3.990000	0.250627	0.455166	1.816113	0.550627	3
4	2.856100	6.187000	0.161629	0.350128	2.16241	0.461629	4
5	3.712930	9.043100	0.110582	0.269329	2.435570	0.410582	5
6	4.826809	12.756030	0.078394	0.207176	2.642746	0.378394	6
7	6.274852	17.582839	0.056874	0.159366	2.802112	0.356874	7
8	8.157307	23.857691	0.041915	0.122589	2.924702	0.341915	8
9	10.604499	32.014998	0.031235	0.094300	3.019001	0.331235	9
10	13.785849	42.619497	0.023463	0.072538	3.091539	0.323463	10
11	17.921604	56.405346	0.017729	0.055799	3.147338	0.317729	11
12	23.298085	74.326950	0.013454	0.042922	3.180260	0.313454	12
13	30.287511	97.625036	0.010243	0.033017	3.223277	0.310243	13
14	39.373764	127.912546	0.007818	0.025398	3.248675	0.307818	14
15	51.185893	167.286310	0.005978	0.019537	3.268211	0.305978	15
16	66.541661	218.472203	0.004577	0.015028	3.283239	0.304577	16
17	86.504159	285.013864	0.003509	0.011560	3.294800	0.303509	17
18	112.455407	371.518023	0.002692	0.008892	3.303692	0.302692	18
19	146.192029	483.973430	0.002066	0.006840	3.310532	0.302066	19
20	190.049638	630.165459	0.001587	0.005262	3.315794	0.301587	20

Monthly Compounding

EFFECTIVE (MONTHLY) RATE = 2.500000%

MONTH	MFV1	MFV1/P	MSSF	MPV1	MPV1/P	MPRF	MONTH
1	1.025000	1.000000	1.000000	0.975610	0.975610	1.025000	1
2	1.050625	2.025000	0.493827	0.951814	1.927424	0.518827	2

YEAR						YEAR
3	1.076891	3.075625	0.325137	0.928599	2.856024	0.350137	3
4	1.103813	4.152516	0.240818	0.905951	3.761974	0.265818	4
5	1.131408	5.256329	0.190247	0.883854	4.645828	0.215247	5
6	1.159693	6.387737	0.156550	0.862297	5.508125	0.181550	6
7	1.188686	7.547430	0.132495	0.841265	6.349391	0.157495	7
8	1.218403	8.736116	0.114467	0.820747	7.170137	0.139467	8
9	1.248863	9.954519	0.100457	0.800728	7.970866	0.125457	9
10	1.280085	11.203382	0.089259	0.781198	8.752064	0.114259	10
11	1.312087	12.483466	0.080106	0.762145	9.514209	0.105106	11

YEAR						YEAR
1	1.344889	13.795553	0.072487	0.743556	10.257765	0.097487	1
2	1.808726	32.349038	0.030913	0.552875	17.884986	0.055913	2
3	2.432535	57.301413	0.017452	0.411094	23.556251	0.042452	3
4	3.271490	90.859582	0.011006	0.305671	27.773154	0.036006	4
5	4.399790	135.991590	0.007353	0.227284	30.908656	0.032353	5
6	5.917228	196.689122	0.005084	0.168998	33.240078	0.030084	6
7	7.958014	278.320556	0.003593	0.125659	34.973620	0.028593	7
8	10.702644	388.105758	0.002577	0.093435	36.262606	0.027577	8
9	14.393866	535.754649	0.001867	0.069474	37.221039	0.026867	9
10	19.358150	734.325993	0.001362	0.051658	37.933687	0.026362	10
11	26.034559	1001.382375	0.000999	0.038410	38.463581	0.025999	11
12	35.013588	1360.543518	0.000735	0.028560	38.857586	0.025735	12
13	47.089383	1843.575325	0.000542	0.021236	39.150552	0.025542	13
14	63.329985	2493.199404	0.000401	0.015790	39.368388	0.025401	14
15	85.171789	3366.871568	0.000297	0.011741	39.530361	0.025297	15
16	114.546587	4541.863497	0.000220	0.008730	39.650797	0.025220	16
17	154.052425	6122.097012	0.000163	0.006491	39.740348	0.025163	17
18	207.183385	8247.335405	0.000121	0.004827	39.806934	0.025121	18
19	278.638619	11105.544769	0.000090	0.003589	39.856445	0.025090	19
20	274.747965	14949.518599	0.000067	0.002669	39.893259	0.025067	20

40.00% NOMINAL RATE

Annual Compounding

EFFECTIVE (ANNUAL) RATE = 40.00%

YEAR	Future Value of 1 FV1	Future Value of 1 per Period FV1/P	Sinking Fund Factor SFF	Present Value of 1 PV1	Present Value of 1 per Period PV1/P	Principal Recovery Factor PRF	YEAR
1	1.400000	1.000000	1.000000	0.714286	0.714286	1.400000	1
2	1.960000	2.400000	0.416667	0.510204	1.224490	0.816667	2
3	2.744000	4.360000	0.229358	0.364431	1.588921	0.629358	3
4	3.841600	7.104000	0.140766	0.260308	1.849229	0.540766	4
5	5.378240	10.945600	0.091361	0.185934	2.035164	0.491361	5
6	7.529536	16.323840	0.061260	0.132810	2.167974	0.461260	6
7	10.541350	23.853376	0.041923	0.094865	2.262839	0.441923	7
8	14.757891	34.394726	0.029074	0.067760	2.330599	0.429074	8
9	20.661047	49.152617	0.020345	0.048400	2.378999	0.420345	9
10	28.925465	69.813664	0.014324	0.034572	2.413571	0.414324	10
11	40.495652	98.739129	0.010128	0.024694	2.438265	0.410128	11
12	56.693912	139.234781	0.007182	0.017639	2.455904	0.407182	12
13	79.371477	195.928693	0.005104	0.012599	2.468503	0.405104	13
14	111.120068	275.300171	0.003632	0.008999	2.477502	0.403632	14
15	155.568096	386.420239	0.002588	0.006428	2.483930	0.402588	15
16	217.795334	541.988334	0.001845	0.004591	2.488521	0.401845	16
17	304.913467	759.783668	0.001316	0.003280	2.491801	0.401316	17
18	426.878854	1064.697136	0.000939	0.002343	2.494144	0.400939	18
19	597.630396	1491.575990	0.000670	0.001673	2.495817	0.400670	19
20	836.682554	2089.206386	0.000479	0.001195	2.497012	0.400479	20

Monthly Compounding

EFFECTIVE (MONTHLY) RATE = 3.333333%

MONTH	MFV1	MFV1/P	MSSF	MPV1	MPV1/P	MPRF	MONTH
1	1.033333	1.000000	1.000000	0.967742	0.967742	1.033333	1
2	1.067778	2.033333	0.491803	0.936524	1.904266	0.525137	2

YEAR				
3	0.355798	2.810580	0.906314	0.322465
4	0.271175	3.687658	0.877078	0.237841
5	0.220437	4.536444	0.848785	0.187104
6	0.186642	5.357849	0.821405	0.153309
7	0.162529	6.152757	0.794908	0.129195
8	0.144466	6.922023	0.769266	0.111133
9	0.130438	7.666474	0.744451	0.097105
10	0.119233	8.386910	0.720436	0.085900
11	0.110082	9.084106	0.697196	0.076749
1	0.102471	9.758813	0.674706	0.069138
2	0.061188	16.343144	0.455229	0.027854
3	0.048110	20.785634	0.307146	0.014777
4	0.042047	23.783010	0.207233	0.008713
5	0.038752	25.805358	0.139821	0.005418
6	0.036806	27.169849	0.094338	0.003472
7	0.035599	28.090479	0.063651	0.002266
8	0.034829	28.711634	0.042946	0.001496
9	0.034328	29.130732	0.028976	0.000995
10	0.033998	29.413499	0.019550	0.000665
11	0.033779	29.604284	0.013191	0.000446
12	0.033633	29.733008	0.008900	0.000299
13	0.033535	29.819859	0.006005	0.000201
14	0.033469	29.878458	0.004051	0.000136
15	0.033425	29.917995	0.002734	0.000091
16	0.033395	29.944670	0.001844	0.000062
17	0.033375	29.962669	0.001244	0.000042
18	0.033361	29.974812	0.000840	0.000028
19	0.033352	29.983006	0.000566	0.000019
20	0.033346	29.988534	0.000382	0.000013

YEAR		
3	1.103370	3.101111
4	1.140149	4.204481
5	1.178154	5.344631
6	1.217426	6.522785
7	1.258007	7.740211
8	1.299941	8.998218
9	1.343272	10.298159
10	1.388048	11.641431
11	1.434316	13.029479
1	1.482126	14.463795
2	2.196699	35.900968
3	3.255786	67.673570
4	4.825486	114.764586
5	7.151981	184.559427
6	10.600140	288.004211
7	15.710749	441.322465
8	23.285317	668.559511
9	34.511785	1005.353555
10	51.150831	1504.524930
11	75.812002	2244.360048
12	112.362976	3340.889274
13	166.536143	4966.084287
14	246.827629	7374.828867
15	365.829767	10944.893015
16	542.205989	16236.179658
17	803.617859	24078.535757
18	1191.063316	35701.899472
19	1765.306491	52929.194733
20	2616.407513	78462.225385

50.00% NOMINAL RATE

Annual Compounding

EFFECTIVE (ANNUAL) RATE = 50.00%

YEAR	Future Value of 1 FV 1	Future Value of 1 per Period FV1/P	Sinking Fund Factor SFF	Present Value of 1 PV1	Present Value of 1 per Period PV1/P	Principal Recovery Factor PRF	YEAR
1	1.50000	1.00000	1.000000	0.666667	0.666667	1.500000	1
2	2.25000	2.50000	0.400000	0.444444	1.111111	0.900000	2
3	3.37500	4.75000	0.210526	0.296296	1.407407	0.710526	3
4	5.06250	8.12500	0.123077	0.197531	1.604938	0.623077	4
5	7.59375	13.18750	0.075829	0.131687	1.736626	0.575829	5
6	11.39063	20.78125	0.048120	0.087791	1.824417	0.548120	6
7	17.08594	32.17188	0.031083	0.058528	1.882945	0.531083	7
8	25.62891	49.25781	0.020301	0.039018	1.921963	0.520301	8
9	38.44336	74.88672	0.013354	0.026012	1.947975	0.513354	9
10	57.66504	113.33008	0.008824	0.017342	1.965317	0.508824	10
11	86.49756	170.99512	0.005848	0.011561	1.976878	0.505848	11
12	129.74634	257.49268	0.003884	0.007707	1.984585	0.503884	12
13	194.61951	387.23901	0.002582	0.005138	1.989724	0.502582	13
14	291.92926	581.85852	0.001719	0.003425	1.993149	0.501719	14
15	437.89389	873.78778	0.001144	0.002284	1.995433	0.501144	15
16	656.84084	1311.68167	0.000762	0.001522	1.996955	0.500762	16
17	985.26125	1968.52251	0.000508	0.001015	1.997970	0.500508	17
18	1417.89188	2953.78376	0.000339	0.000677	1.998647	0.500339	18
19	2216.83782	4431.67564	0.000226	0.000451	1.999098	0.500226	19
20	3325.25676	6648.51346	0.000150	0.000301	1.999399	0.500150	20

Monthly Compounding

EFFECTIVE (MONTHLY) RATE = 4.166667%

MONTH	MFV1	MFV1/P	MSSF	MPV 1	MPV1/P	MPRF	MONTH
1	1.04167	1.00000	1.000000	0.960000	0.960000	1.041667	1
2	1.08507	2.04167	0.489796	0.921600	1.881600	0.531463	2

YEAR						
3	0.361489	2.766336	0.884736	0.319822	3.12674	1.13028
4	0.276573	3.615683	0.849347	0.234906	4.25702	1.17738
5	0.225680	4.431055	0.815373	0.184013	5.43439	1.22643
6	0.191798	5.213813	0.782758	0.150132	6.66083	1.27753
7	0.167637	5.965261	0.751447	0.125971	7.93836	1.33076
8	0.149552	6.686650	0.721390	0.107885	9.26912	1.38621
9	0.135516	7.379184	0.692534	0.093850	10.65534	1.44397
10	0.124316	8.044017	0.664833	0.082649	12.09931	1.50414
11	0.115177	8.682256	0.638239	0.073511	13.60345	1.56681

YEAR						
1	0.107585	9.294966	0.612710	0.065918	15.17026	1.63209
2	0.066711	14.990082	0.375413	0.025044	39.92955	2.66373
3	0.054114	18.479535	0.230019	0.012447	80.33904	4.34746
4	0.048502	20.617557	0.140935	0.006836	146.29114	7.09546
5	0.045605	21.927544	0.086352	0.003938	253.93117	11.58047
6	0.043994	22.730186	0.052909	0.002328	429.60984	18.90041
7	0.043063	23.221973	0.032418	0.001396	716.33395	30.84725
8	0.042511	23.523295	0.019863	0.000844	1184.29470	50.34561
9	0.042180	23.707918	0.012170	0.000513	1948.05069	82.16878
10	0.041980	23.821039	0.007457	0.000313	3194.57236	134.10718
11	0.041858	23.890349	0.004569	0.000191	5229.01306	218.87554
12	0.041784	23.932816	0.002799	0.000117	8549.41179	357.22549
13	0.041738	23.958835	0.001715	0.000072	13968.61509	583.02563
14	0.041711	23.974778	0.001051	0.000044	22813.26498	951.55271
15	0.041694	23.984546	0.000644	0.000027	37248.56618	1553.02359
16	0.041683	23.990531	0.000395	0.000016	60808.33658	2534.68069
17	0.041677	23.994198	0.000242	0.000010	99260.09961	4136.83748
18	0.041673	23.996445	0.000148	0.000006	162016.99645	6751.70819
19	0.041670	23.997822	0.000091	0.000004	264442.15957	11019.42332
20	0.041669	23.998666	0.000056	0.000002	431609.66734	17984.73614

Glossary

Abandonment. Tenant vacates or gives up possession before a lease expires; tenant may continue to be liable for rental payments.

Abstract of title. A digest of all recorded documents pertaining to the title to a given parcel of real estate.

Acceleration clause. Provision allowing lender to require immediate repayment of entire loan upon borrower's default.

Acceptance. Agreement to all the terms of a contract, such as a deed.

Accessibility. Relative ease or difficulty of getting to and from a property; a property that is easy to get to has good accessibility or convenience of location.

Accountability. Responsibility for record keeping, money and property.

Accrued expense. A charge owed but not yet paid, such as property taxes or accrued interest.

Acknowledgment. A formal declaration that a contract was signed freely and voluntarily.

Acre. A unit of land measurement 43,560 square feet in area.

Actual notice. Knowledge of an interest in real property imputed to all the world because claimant was or is in actual possession of the property.

Ad valorem. According to value; real property is typically taxed proportionally according to its market value.

Adjustable rate mortgage. Loan arrangement in which the interest rate rises or falls in line with changes in prevailing market rates.

Adjusted cost basis. Book value in an accounting sense; also known as tax basis.

Adjusted sale price. Full sales contract price less selling expense and "fixing-up" expense.

Adverse possession, title by. Obtaining title to real estate by long-term, unauthorized occupancy, possibly under color of title.

After-tax equity reversion. Sale price less disposition costs, less amortized mortgage loan balance, and less capital gains taxes.

Agency. A legal relationship created when one party, as an agent-broker, is authorized to act as the representative of another, as an owner-principal.

Agent. A person who represents another, a principal, by the latter's authority, as a broker represents an owner.

AIDA. (1) Attention, (2) interest, (3) desire, and (4) action. The purpose of advertising is to initiate this chain of effects.

Alienation or "due on sale" clause. Provision in a mortgage loan giving the lender the right to require immediate repayment if the property is sold or otherwise conveyed.

All inclusive trust deed. A trust deed that envelops existing mortgage or trust deed claims against a property even though it is subordinate to them; equivalent to the wraparound mortgage.

Amortization. Systematic repayment of a loan with installments that include both interest and partial debt reduction.

Annual stabilized income, ASI. Income from salary or wages plus two years experience of income from bonuses, commissions, etc.

Annuity. A series of equal or level payments made at equal time intervals.

Appraisal. An estimate of the value of a property, or of some interest therein.

Appraisal process. An orderly, well conceived set of procedures used in making an appraisal.

Assessed value. Amount or worth assigned a property for property taxation purposes; sometimes set by statute as a percentage of market value.

Assignment. Transfer of one's rights in a contract to another party, as by a lessee.

Assumption (assuming a loan). Obligation of the purchaser to repay a loan in buying a property.

Balloon loan. A loan whose last payment is much larger than preceding payments of debt service.

Bargain and sale deed. A deed without convenants, except that it is implied that the grantor does have title.

Base activity. An industry that produces foods or services for export outside the area or region in return for money; also known as primary economic activity.

Base line. An imaginary east-west line, north and south of which are rows of townships, in the government rectangular survey system.

Bench mark. A permanent point of reference of known elevation used by land surveyors, as in establishing the floors and ceilings of condominium units.

Binder. A short buy-sell contract that is used to hold a transaction together until a more formal contract can be signed.

Blockbusting. Inducing owners to sell at depressed prices by introducing people of another race or class into a neighborhood, thereby playing on the fears and prejudices of current owners.

Book value. Adjusted cost basis; tax basis.

Boot. Cash, or the market value of personal property, given or received in a tax-deferred exchange to balance equities; unlike property.

Borrower risk. A type of lender risk due to the borrower's not being able to meet loan terms.

Breakeven Occupancy (BO) ratio. Total annual operating expenses plus annual debt service divided by gross annual scheduled income; the default point for a rental property in that the property can just meet its obligations.

Broker. A person licensed to negotiate the sale, purchase, lease, or exchange of realty, or to arrange the financing thereof, for a fee or commission.

Business interruption insurance. Protection to a business owner from loss of income due to fire, flood, or other peril.

Business risk. Chance that projected or predicted levels of income will not be realized, or will not be adequate to meet operating expenses.

Buyer's market. Market in which supply greatly exceeds demand, thereby enabling purchasers to bargain for and get lower prices; result is falling values.

Canvassing. Contacting owners by telephone or in person without a prior appointment to obtain listings.

Capital gain income. Profit from resale of a capital asset, such as real estate, that has been held longer than one year, when net proceeds exceed the tax basis.

Capital markets. Markets wherein intermediate- and long-term loans, bonds, and stocks are originated and traded.

Capitalization. Conversion of expected income payments into a lump-sum present value.

Carrying costs. Expenses and outlays to be met until a property is ripe for development or redevelopment.

Cash flow after tax, CFAT [to equity]. NOI less debt service and less the tax payable on income from operations.

Certificate of occupancy. Official statement that all required inspections have been made and passed, and that a structure is fit for use.

Chain of title. The succession of previous owners back to the original source of title.

Client. A principal, usually a property owner, who employs a broker as an agent.

Closing. The stage at which negotiations are brought to a conclusion.

Coinsurance. Provision in a fire insurance policy to encourage adequate coverage; if a required percent of value is not insured against loss, the owner shares the risk of loss with the insurance company.

Collateralized mortgage obligation (CMO). A mortgage pay-through bond.

Community property. Property acquired by a husband and wife during their marriage, with each owning a one-half interest.

Comparative economic advantage. Ability of an industry to earn greater profits in a specific area or region than elsewhere. Communities and regions specialize in those economic activities that provide the greatest relative advantage or least relative disadvantage to themselves.

Competent party. A person legally qualified to enter into binding contracts.

Compounding. Earning interest on principal and on accrued interest.

Concentric circle theory. von Thunen's proposal of community growth that says differences in land use may be attributed directly to differences in transportation costs or location around a central city.

Condominium. Individual ownership of a unit of space in developed real estate plus an undivided ownership of common areas.

Consideration. Something of value, such as money, an act, or a promise given or received as part of a contractual arrangement.

Constructive notice. Knowledge presumed of everyone, by law, as a result of properly entering documents and/or other information into the public record.

Contract. A legally binding agreement to take, or not to take, a specific action.

Contract interest rate. Rate agreed to in a specific mortgage note.

Contract rent. Agreed payments for the use of land or realty.

Contract zoning. Title restriction or side agreement that limits a property's use in return for a new zoning classification.

Convenience of location. Relative costs, in time and money, of getting to and from a property; lower costs means greater convenience or accessibility.

Conventional loan. A real estate loan that is not FHA-insured or VA-guaranteed.

Cooperative. Ownership of real property by a corporation or trust, with share holders occupying specific units of space under proprietary leases.

Cost approach to value. Method of valuing property based on site value plus current construction costs less accrued depreciation.

Costs of friction. Costs of moving goods or people between linked land use activities: money, time, terminal, and aggravation costs.

Credit. In bookkeeping, an entry in a person's favor.

Credit (debt) financing. Lending money to others (borrowing money from others) to help finance the purchase of real estate.

Customer. A buyer, or potential buyer, of property listed with a broker.

Cycle. Regular rise and fall in sales and construction volume.

Date of sale. Date that title passes, for purposes of determining capital gain or rollover right in homeownership.

Dealer. Owner of property held for sale, such as lots by a subdivider.

Debt service. Periodic installments of interest and partial repayment of a loan.

Debt service coverage (DSC) ratio. Annual net operating income/Annual debt service.

Decision-making cycle. The three broad phases regarding choices as an investor goes into and out of real estate ownership: (1) acquisition or purchase, (2) administration and management, and (3) alienation or disposition.

Deed. A written document that, when properly executed and delivered, conveys title to real estate.

Deed in lieu of foreclosure. Owner-borrower, in default, voluntarily conveys title to lender to avoid hassle and costs of foreclosure.

Deed restriction. A limitation on nature or intensity of use of real property entered in the public record; a.k.a. title restriction.

Default. Failure to fulfill or live up to an agreement, such as a mortgage contract.

Default in prior mortgage clause. Provision in a junior loan allowing a junior mortgagee to make payments on a prior mortgage, if not made by a borrower, with such amounts added to the balance of the junior loan.

Defeasance clause. Provision that defeats or voids any mortgage claim if secured debt is fully repaid on time.

Deficiency judgment. A judicial decree in favor of a lender for the portion of the mortgage debt and foreclosure costs that were unsatisfied from the proceeds of the foreclosure sale.

Delivery. An act by a grantor showing intent to make a deed effective.

Density zoning. Limits on population density in various districts established or implemented through a zoning ordinance.

Depreciation. Lowering in value due to a variety of causes that lead to diminished utility.

Developing. Process of combining land and improvements to produce a completed, operational property.

Development charge. Fee imposed to pay the proportional costs of new community infrastructures such as waste-disposal facilities, roads, water storage tanks, necessitated by the property being developed.

Devise. A transfer of real property ownership through a will.

Direct income capitalization. Division of net operating income by an overall capitalization rate, R, to arrive at market value.

Direct sales comparison approach. Method of valuing property based on recent sales prices of similar properties.

Direction of least resistance. Hurd's theory of community growth that says cities grow in the direction of least resistance or greatest attraction, or their resultants; really an extension or modification of von Thunen's concentric circle theory.

Disclosed principal. A principal known or identified to a third party by an agent.

Discount rate. The annual percentage rate that reflects the competitive rate of return on an investment.

Discounting. Process of converting a future cash payment into a present value.

Dispersing force. An influence toward the scattering of people and economic activities.

Dollar discount (premium). Amount subtracted from (added to) the face value of a loan because the market interest rate exceeds (is less than) the contract rate.

Dollar premium. Amount added to the face value of a loan because the market interest rate is less than the contract rate.

Donor/donee. Persons giving and receiving a gift.

Doubling up. Using living space more intensely; crowding more people into each dwelling unit.

Down zoning. Rezoning from a high-intensity to a low-intensity use; likely to lower the value of a parcel.

Dual/divided agency. An agent who represents two principals; illegal except with knowledge and consent of both.

Durability of fixity of investment. An economic characteristic of real estate; the length of time required to recover outlays for improving realty, such as for buildings.

Duration of loan. The life, or contract period, of a loan; also known as the term of a loan.

Earnest money. Money submitted with an offer to purchase as evidence of good faith.

Easement. Right to use the land of another for certain purposes, such as ingress and egress or drainage.

Easy money/(tight money). Money plentiful (scarce) enough that interest rates are low or falling (high or rising).

Economic base. Industries, with a comparative economic advantage, that export goods and services outside an area or region in return for money. Also, the product or products for which a community is famous, such as cars in Detroit.

Economic capacity of land. Ability of a site to profitably absorb human and capital resources under the principle of proportionality.

Economic person. A fictional person in economic theory motivated by self-interest to maximize economic returns; considered a prime mover in an economic society.

Economics. Science and study of the allocation of limited resources to satisfy human needs and wants.

Economies of scale. Producing ever larger output to reduce the cost per unit of output.

Effective demand. Desire, as for land or space, armed with purchasing power or ability to pay.

Effective gross income. Revenues actually collected in operating an income property; gross scheduled income less vacancy and collection losses.

Efficient market. Market wherein changes in information about the outlook for a given commodity, such as a property, are quickly reflected in its probable selling price and value.

Eminent domain. Right of a government to take private property for public uses or purposes, with payment of just compensation required.

Encroachment. Unauthorized intrusion of a building or other improvement onto the land or into the airspace of an adjoining property.

Encumbrance. Any impediment to clear title, such as a lien, lease, or easement.

Environmental impact study. Report concerning the long-run physical, economic, and social effects of a proposed development project.

Equity. Owner's interest in the property; the market or disposition value of the property less transaction costs of selling and less any liens and encumbrances against the property.

Equitable right of redemption. The right of a borrower, by paying amounts due on a delinquent loan prior to the foreclosure sale, to recover a mortgaged property; also known as equitable right of redemption.

Equity rate of return. Internal rate of return on monies invested by the owner.

Escalation clause. Provision in a contract to adjust, usually increase, payments based on some index or level of costs.

Escheat. Conveyance of realty to the state after an owner's death when no will, heirs, or other legal claimants to title can be found.

Escrow. The deposit of monies, documents such as mortgages and deeds, and other valuables with a neutral third party, under instructions that the items are to be held until all acts or conditions of a contract are met.

Estate. Extent and quality of one's interest in land or other property.

Eviction, actual. Removal of a tenant from premises through direct action of a landlord.

Eviction, constructive. Removal of a tenant from premises through indirect action of a landlord, as when physical conditions make continued occupancy hazardous or unsuitable for purposes intended, and landlord fails or refuses to correct situation.

Exclusionary zoning. Zoning intended to discriminate against a particular group, as extra large lot size would discriminate against low income families.

Exposure. Environmental influences experienced at a property.

Extensive margin. The point at which rents or values make it just financially feasible to add urban improvements and to convert farm land to urban uses; symbolized by land development at the urban fringe.

External economies of scale. Relocation of a firm to a larger community in order to obtain support services and supplies from others at lower costs than it could realize by providing these same service and supplies to itself.

Externality. Effect of acts of an individual or a firm on others without their consent; effects may be positive or negative on the allocation of resources. Examples are air or water pollution.

Extended coverage insurance. Protection from losses other than fire, as from wind, rain, hail, explosion, smoke, rust, etc.

Fair housing laws. Laws that ensure equality of treatment regardless of sex, race, color, religion, or national origin.

Fannie Mae. FNMA, Federal National Mortgage Association; a federal-government-sponsored secondary lender.

Feasibility analysis. Study of the practicality (value exceeds cost) of a specific investment or development proposal; extension of economic base and market analysis to a specific development or investment problem.

Fee, fee simple, fee simple absolute. The most complete bundle of rights one can own in land or real property.

FHA mortgage. Lender insured against loss on a loan by the Federal Housing Administration.

Fiduciary relationship. An arrangement calling for trust and confidence, such as that of principal-agent between a broker and an owner.

Financial markets. Market wherein money is created and financial claims, such as bonds, bills, and mortgage loans, are bought and sold.

Financial risk. Added uncertainty created when money is borrowed to help finance a property; chance of not meeting debt service, etc.

Fixed cost. Outlays that remain at the same level, regardless of the intensity of use of a property.

Fixed rate mortgage, FRM. A loan on which one interest rate applies over its entire life.

Fixture. Item of personal property attached to a piece of land or a building in such a manner as to be legally considered part of the real estate.

Floor Area Ratio (FAR) zoning. Ratio of building area to site area; a form of density zoning.

Foreclosure. A legal process to force sale of a pledged property to satisfy an unpaid debt.

Freddie Mac. FHLMC, Federal Home Loan Mortgage Corporation; an active participant in secondary mortgage markets.

Functional area. An area where some specialized activity is performed; residential neighborhoods and commercial and industrial districts are the most obvious examples of functional areas.

Functional efficiency. The relative ability of a property to render services, i.e., perform its function; also known as functional utility.

Functional obsolescence. Diminished ability of a property to render services relative to a new property as a result of improvements in technology, design or layout; results in a lowered value.

General Warranty Deed. A deed giving the greatest assurances to a grantee, including covenants of seizing, against encumbrances, of quiet enjoyment, of further assurance, and of title.

Ginnie Mae. GNMA, Government National Mortgage Association; a federal-government-sponsored corporation created for special assistance functions, such as to provide mortgage monies for low-income and elderly groups.

Grantor/grantee. A persons conveying and receiving property rights in a deed; *grantor* conveys ownership; *grantee* receives title or ownership.

Grantor-grantee index. Public records filing system used to locate ownership documents, primarily deeds.

Gross income multiplier, GIM. A ratio derived from the market; sale price/annual gross income = GIM.

Gross lease. Tenant pays a fixed rent and landlord pays all property expenses.

Gross rent multiplier, GRM. A ratio used in valuing property, which, when multiplied by a property's gross monthly rent, gives an indication of its market value.

Ground lease. Contract giving right of use of land or a vacant site.

Guide meridian. North-south survey lines used to correct for earth's curvature.

Heterogeneity. A physical characteristic of real estate, referring to dissimilarities from one property to another owing to differences in location, size, shape, and topography.

Highest and best use. The use of a parcel that gives it the greatest present value; must be legal, possible, and probable.

Homestead. Occupancy of a residence as a home; often given protection by state laws known as homestead exemptions.

Housing affordability index. Median family income divided by income needed to qualify for the purchase of the median-priced existing single family home.

Housing expenses. Payments for housing as debt service, hazard insurance, property taxes PITI, plus mortgage insurance, homeowner association dues, and ground rental payments; excludes utility charges.

Immobility. A physical characteristic of real estate that means a site is fixed with regard to location; also termed "fixity."

Income ratio. Net operating income divided by gross scheduled income; a measure of the efficiency of an income property.

Independent contractor. One who agrees to act or work for another, being responsible only for results using own methods.

Indestructibility. A physical characteristic of land or space, meaning it cannot be destroyed; it goes on forever.

Index lease. Agreement providing for rental adjustment based on changes in a neutral index, such as the consumer price index.

Infrastructure, urban. Basic service systems, such as sewer and water, schools, electricity, telephone, streets, freeways and subways, that make a parcel more useful.

Installment contract. An arrangement for purchasing and financing property in which the seller retains title while the buyer takes possession and makes payments over time; also called a land contract.

Installment sale. Sale of property for two or more payments.

Institution. An established organization, principle, law, belief, or custom.

Institutional advertising. Promotions to create good will and confidence in an organization or group.

Intensity of use. The relative amount of human and financial resources added to a site.

Intensive margin. The point at which rents or values make it just financially feasible to add more capital and labor so urban land can be used more intensely; an example would be replacing old houses with a new discount store.

Interdependence. An economic characteristic of real estate, meaning each parcel has an interaction of uses, improvements, and value that is shared with surrounding parcels.

Interest. The price paid to borrow money.

Interest rate. The price paid to borrow money stated as a percent per year of the loan balance.

Interest rate risk. Chance of lowered present values due to rising interest rates, which would reduce value of a portfolio of debt instruments.

Intermediation/(disintermediation). Action by a financial institution as a go-between in money matters, taking deposits from savers and lending to borrowers for investment (occurs when savers withdraw monies from financial institutions to lend them directly to investors).

Internal economies of scale. Use of specialized labor and machinery, within a firm, for greater output and reduced cost per unit, which, in turn, means lower prices to users and consumers and a larger market share.

Internal rate of return, IRR. Rate of return that discounts future cash flows from an investment to the exact amount of the investment.

Investment value. Total amount [justified loan + cash equity investment] that can be paid for a property with the expectation of realizing investment goals, mainly the required rate of return. Also, the worth of a property to a specific investor, based on available financing, desired rate of return, tax position, and other assumptions unique to the investor; equivalent to value in use or subjective value.

Investment value of the equity position. Present value of annual after-tax cash flows to equity position from operations and of after-tax equity reversion to equity position.

Joint tenancy. Undivided co-ownership of property that features the right of survivorship.

Junior mortgage. Generic name for any mortgage lower in priority than a first mortgage.

Just compensation. Required payment for property taken; almost universally defined as the market value of the property.

Land contract. A method of buying and financing a property whereby the purchaser gets occupancy but the seller retains title; also known as contract for deed.

Land use. The employment of land for productive purposes, as in agricultural, residential, industrial, or commercial activities. Thus, stores, factories, houses, and farms are all examples of land uses.

Land use control. Public or private legal restriction on how a parcel of land may be used.

Land use succession. Continuing process of land development and redevelopment, as owners adjust their properties to changing conditions.

Lease. An agreement giving possession and use rights to real estate to another person in exchange for rent.

Lease option. Provision giving a tenant the right to

purchase an occupied property at a specified price and within a stipulated time; a.k.a. a lease-purchase option.

Leased fee. Owner's interest or position in a leased property.

Leasehold estate. Tenant's interest or position in a property under lease.

Legacy. Personal property given or received under a will.

Legal description. An identification of a specific parcel of real property that is unique to the parcel.

Legislative risk. Probability of loss in property value due to a "change in the rules of the game" through governmental action; an example is a city changing its zoning ordinance, initiating rent controls, or increasing property taxes; also known as political risk.

Lessee/tenant. One who occupies a property in exchange for rental payments.

Lessor/landlord. One who gives up the right of occupancy and use of property in exchange for rent.

Leverage, financial. Use of borrowed money to finance a property; impact may be positive or negative; also known as trading on the equity.

License. Freedom to act, as to enter onto a property with the permission of the party in legal possession of the property.

Lien. A right or claim, secured by the property of another, to have a debt or other obligation satisfied.

Life estate. Ownership of right to use real estate during the lifetime of a specified person.

"Like kind" of property. A trade for similar property, which results in only a recognized gain rather than a taxable realized gain.

Linkage. A relationship between two land use activities that requires the movement of people or goods between them.

Liquid asset. Easy conversion of an asset to cash at a favorable ratio relative to market value.

Liquidated damages. A monetary penalty provided for in a contract as compensation if the arrangement is not satisfactorily completed.

Liquidity. Ease of converting an investment into cash, with account taken of the ratio of the cash realized relative to the market value of the investment.

Liquidity risk. Chance of loss in converting an asset into cash within a short time.

Listing agreement. A contract whereby a broker agrees to sell or lease property for an owner.

Loan commitment. A letter in which a lender states that a loan will be made at stipulated terms.

Loan discount. Amount subtracted from the face value of a loan when it is originated or sold; may be expressed as a dollar amount or a percentage.

Loan premium. Amount added to the face value of a loan when it is sold.

Loan-to-value ratio. The amount borrowed against a property divided by its market value, usually expressed as a percentage.

Locational obsolescence. Diminished utility of a site or property due to external factors of environment or location which unfavorably affect its ability to render services; results in a lowered value.

Locational quotient (LQ). A ratio used to identify economic base industries; equal to the percent of total local activity in an industry divided by the percent of total national activity in the same industry.

Loyalty. Legal requirement that an agent give priority to a principal's interest.

Management risk. Chance of making a poor decision when adjusting a property to new conditions, such as a changing population mix or road system.

Market analysis. Study to predict changes in the amount and types of real estate facilities needed in an area, with emphasis on urban space needs: residential, retail trade, office, and industrial.

Market interest rate. Rate currently being charged by lenders in making new loans.

Market price. Amount actually negotiated between a buyer and a seller for a property; a historical fact.

Market rent. Amount of rent a property would command if exposed to the market for a reasonable time and rented by a reasonably knowledgeable tenant; analogous to market value.

Market risk. Probability of loss in value due to changing economic conditions; an example is a major local business closing a plant.

Market value. The most probable selling price of a parcel of real estate; often equated to value in exchange. (More technical definitions are used by professional appraisers.)

Marketable title. Real property for which there is reasonable certainty as to who owner is; title likely to be accepted by an interested, reasonable, prudent, intelligent buyer at market value.

Master plan. A document to guide a community's future physical growth as it adjusts to social and economic change; also called comprehensive plan.

Metes and bounds. Description of real property by "measures" of distance and "boundaries" as markers or survey lines.

Middleman. A person bringing two parties together for a transaction.

Money markets. Markets wherein money is created and exchanged for short-term (less than one year) money instruments, such as bills or notes.

Monument. A point, such as an iron pipe, a large boulder, or a tree, used as a marker in describing real estate.

Mortgage banker. One who makes mortgage loans with the expectation of selling same to an institutional investor while retaining the servicing rights.

Mortgage satisfaction. Receipt or certificate from a lender stating that a loan has been repaid in full.

Multiple-nuclei theory. The Ulman and Harris proposal of clusters of development, which is an extension of the idea that cities are a collection of functional areas.

Name advertising. Promotion to establish identity and location for a brokerage office in the minds of potential clients or customers.

Net lease. Rental payments to an owner whereby the tenant agrees to pay the costs of hazard insurance, property taxes, and maintenance.

Net operating income. Earnings of an income property after operating expenses and maintenance have been deducted from effective gross income.

Net present value, NPV. Present value of the cash flows from an investment minus the cost of the investment.

Nonconforming use. An existing land use or structure that is inconsistent with current zoning.

Nonresidential property. Income property that derives less than 80 percent of its rents from letting of living units; examples are warehouses, stores, factories, office buildings, and motels and hotels.

Novation. Replacing an old contract with a new one.

Nuisance. Interference with a neighbor's use and quiet enjoyment of land other than by trespass or direct physical invasion, without consent.

Objective value. A "neutral" estimate of the value of properties based on market price information.

Open market operations. The buying and selling of money instruments by the Federal Reserve to regulate the money supply and influence interest rates.

Operating expenses. Expenses necessary to generate revenues on a sustained basis by an income property; examples are management, water, electricity, taxes, insurance, and maintenance.

Operating ratio. Operating expenses divided by effective gross income; a measure of a property's operating efficiency.

Opportunity cost. Value of best choice [opportunity] that is given up in selecting or deciding among several alternatives. To maximize benefits, a decision maker minimizes opportunity costs.

Option. The right to buy or lease a property at a stipulated price within a stated time.

Overall capitalization rate, "R." A ratio in property valuation; net operating income divided by sale price.

Percent discount (premium). Percent reduction from (addition to) the face value of a loan because the market interest rate exceeds (is less than) the contract rate.

Percentage lease. Rental payments by tenant are calculated as a proportion of sales or other income generated by the property.

Perfect market. Market in which all information concerning prices, risks, and benefits for each commodity is available to all participants, and the commodity is easily divisible and readily transportable.

Performance zoning. Zoning for a land use, the intensity or nature of which is defined in terms of standards to be met, as FAR zoning.

Personalty, personal property. Any property not realty, usually movable objects; ownership of movable objects as books, bikes, or bread.

Plat. A drawing or map that shows boundaries, shapes and sizes, and locations of individual parcels or real estate, as for a subdivision.

Plottage value. Incremental value realized by combining two or more sites; the value of the larger parcel is greater than the combined values of the individual parcels.

Portfolio risk. Chance that a lender will not realize an expected rate of return on an entire portfolio of loans.

POSSLQ. Persons of the opposite sex sharing living quarters.

Potential demand. Raw desire for land or space; population.

Power of sale. The right of a lender to hold a foreclosure sale without going to court.

Prepaid expense. A charge paid in advance, such as rent or an insurance premium.

Present value of 1 (PV1) factor. A TVM multiplier used to convert a single future payment into a lump-sum present value.

Present value of an annuity (PVa) factor. A TVM multiplier used to convert a series of equal future payments into a current lump-sum value.

Primary lender. A lender that initiates or originates new loans.

Prime rate. Interest rate that major commercial banks charge large, well-established, financially sound companies on business loans.

Principal. In law, a person who authorizes (employs) another to act for him or her in some undertaking, such as selling property. In finance, the unamortized balance of a loan; amount owing.

Principal meridian. A north-south survey line used as a reference in the government rectangular survey system.

Principal recovery factor. A TVM multiplier used to convert a current lump sum payment into a series of equal future values.

Procuring cause. The broker primarily responsible for bringing about a transaction, such as a sale.

Productivity. Ability of a property to provide valuable services or benefits, such as shelter, fertile soil, and advantageous location.

Promissory note. A written statement evidencing a debt and containing a commitment to repay the debt.

Property risk. A type of lender risk due to the property not having a value great enough to cover the loan amount plus any foreclosure costs.

Proportionality, principle of. When the factors of production are in balance with one another, real estate reaches its maximum productivity or highest and best use; also known as the principle of increasing and decreasing returns.

Prorate. To divide ongoing expense and income items into proportionate shares, as between a buyer and a seller in a closing statement.

Prospecting. Locating potential buyers for a property; might be done by advertising.

Puffing. Making exaggerated positive statements to induce a purchase.

Purchase money mortgage, PMM. A mortgage pledging a property as collateral for a loan to finance its purchase.

Purchasing power risk. Chance of a drop in value of an asset, in real terms, due to inflation.

Pyramiding. Controlling ever more property through reinvestment, refinance, and exchange, while keeping leverage at a maximum.

Quiet enjoyment. Right of possession and use of a property without undue disturbance or interference by others.

Quitclaim deed. A legal instrument whereby a grantor conveys any interests held, but makes no claims, covenants, or warranties of ownership.

Range. A column of townships east or west of a principal meridian in the government rectangular survey system.

Rational investor. A person acting in the most logical manner to maximize self-interest, within the limits of his or her knowledge and perceived risks or uncertainties.

Ready, willing, and able buyer. A purchaser meeting all of a seller's terms, including ability to finance the property.

Real estate, realty. Land, including oil, water, and minerals, and improvements to the land; often equated with real property.

Real property. Ownership right of use, control, and disposition of real estate.

Realized gain. A capital gain received as cash or boot, and therefore subject to taxation.

Realtor®. A broker or salesperson who is an active member of the National Association of Realtors®

Recognized gain. A capital gain not subject to taxation because it was received in an exchange of like property.

Reconciliation. Resolving differences between alternative approaches in estimating market value.

Rectangular survey system. Government grid arrangement for legally describing land; uses principal meridians and base lines as references.

Reliction/dereliction. Process of gradual increase in the area of an owner's land owing to lowering of water level.

Renegotiable rate mortgage, RRM. A loan on which the interest rate must be periodically adjusted to the current market rate.

Rent capitalization. Conversion of rent demanded (or payable) into the market value of dwelling unit that is to be provided (or that is affordable).

Rent control. Governmental limitation on the amount that an owner-landlord may charge.

Rent triangle. A schedule showing the rent a use or business activity can pay as an increasing amount of space is devoted to the use.

Replacement cost. Cost of producing a building with a given level of utility using modern materials, design, and layout.

Reproduction cost. Cost of producing an exact replica of a subject property's improvements, using identical materials, design, and layout.

Required rate of return. Yield necessary to compensate for time and risk of an investment; also known as hurtle rate.

Residential rental property. Income property that derives at least 80 percent of its income from rentals as dwelling units for long-term tenants.

Retaliatory eviction. Removal of a tenant from a property as punishment for the tenant's asserting his or her rights; generally illegal.

Rider. An addition to a document, such as a contract, that is made part of the document by reference only.

Riparian rights. The right of use and enjoyment of the waters of a stream or lake by the owner of land bordering the body of water.

Ripe property. A property with a potential use that would yield a profit sizable enough to justify development.

Risk. Chance of loss or injury, as from an investment.

"Rollover." Purchase or building of a replacement residence at a cost equal to or greater than the adjusted sale price of the previous residence, within a limited time [+ or − 24 months], to postpone any capital gains tax payable.

Sale and leaseback. Transfer of property ownership (sale) with the simultaneous renting back of the premises to the seller (leaseback).

Scarcity. An economic characteristic of real estate, referring to the relative inadequacy of the supply of realty in a given use or a desired location.

Second (or junior) mortgage. A mortgage immediately behind another mortgage (or other mortgages) in priority of claim.

Secondary lender. An investor that purchases existing loans or that originates loans through a primary lender.

Secondary mortgage market. That portion of the financial markets in which existing mortgage loans are bought and sold.

Section. A square unit of land in the rectangular survey system that measures one mile one each side and contains 640 acres.

Secured transaction. The pledging of personal property as additional collateral for a loan or purchase of a property.

Seller's market. Market in which demand greatly exceeds supply, thereby enabling sellers to bargain for and get higher prices; result in rising values.

Sensitivity analysis. Study of the impact of various elements on the rate of return to be earned on equity invested in a property.

Separate property. Property owned by a spouse that is excluded from community property status, because it was owned prior to marriage or was received through gift or inheritance after marriage.

Service activity. An industry that produces goods or services for local consumption or use, that is, not for export. Also known as secondary economic activity.

Severability clause. Provision that invalidation of one clause in a contract will not invalidate the other clauses.

Short selling. Selling a security or commodity not owned when the price is high, with delivery promised at some future date, by which time the price is expected to have fallen.

Situs. An economic characteristic of real estate that refers to the locational aspects of a property (accessibility, exposure, and personal preference) relative to other properties.

Special assessment. A charge on private property to pay all or part of the cost of a local improvement that may benefit the property.

Special warranty deed. Deed containing only one warranty, which is against title defects caused by acts of the grantor.

Specific advertising. Promotion of a particular property or article.

Specific performance. A legal remedy compelling a defendant to carry out or live up to the terms of an agreement; often necessary in real estate because no other remedy would be adequate or appropriate because of a unique situs or location.

Standard parallel. East-west survey lines at 24-mile intervals north or south of standard parallels in the rectangular survey system.

Statute of Frauds. Law requiring that certain contracts be written to be legally enforceable; includes any agreement creating or transferring an interest in real property.

Statutory redemption. Borrower's right to recover a property after a foreclosure sale by paying all accumulated charges on the defaulted loan; also known as statutory right of redemption.

Steering. Guiding a buyer to a specific property or area so as to create or avoid a blockbusting situation; illegal under fair housing laws.

Subdividing. The breaking up of a tract of land into smaller sites or plots; sites may be for homes, small offices, warehouses, etc.

Subject property. Property of concern or under study.

Subjective value. Dependence of worth on the nature and mental attitude of the person making the judgment.

Sublessee. A tenant who rents from a prior lessee.

Sublessor. A lessee who rerents to another lessee.

Sublet. Transfer of only a portion of a tenant's rights to another party.

Submarginal lands. Lands (swamps, mountaintops, and deserts) not able to yield a profit which would financially justify their development.

Subordination clause. A clause in a lien, lease, or other document that establishes relative priority of claim on the property.

Taking title subject to a mortgage. Taking title to a

property "subject to an existing loan" but without obligation to repay the loan.

Tax avoidance. Legal administration of one's affairs to minimize taxes to be paid.

Tax base. Total assessed values of all properties in a tax district.

Tax basis. Book value of property; *see* adjusted cost basis.

Tax capitalization. Present value of all future tax payments incurred (or avoided).

Tax credit. A dollar-for-dollar offset against taxes payable.

Tax-deferred exchange. Exchange for "like kind" property, with gain not recognized for tax purposes.

Tax depreciation. Annual cost recovery allowed by the IRS as return of the investment in a wasting asset, such as a building, even though there is no decline in value as judged by the market.

Tax evasion. Use of illegal means to avoid taxes; an example is padding an expense account.

Tax levy. Amount of property tax to be paid in a fiscal year, usually from 2 to 5 percent of value, depending on the jurisdiction.

Tax shelter. Use of a bookkeeping loss to avoid or defer paying taxes on income.

"Taxpayer." An interim use that enables an owner to pay real estate taxes and other carrying costs of a property until it is ripe for major development.

Tenancy by the entirety. Form of joint ownership of property by a husband and wife, with right of survivorship. Neither spouse can dispose of the interest without the consent of the other.

Tenancy for years. Rental of a property for a specified time, usually under a written lease agreement.

Tenancy from period to period. Rental of a property for a period of uncertain duration; a.k.a. a periodic tenancy.

Tenancy in common. Ownership of property by two or more person, *without* right of survivorship; shares need not be equal.

Tenancy in partnership. Ownership of firm assets by the general partners that carries with it the right of survivorship, which is necessary for the entity to continue uninterrupted business operations. Property may not be disposed of without consent of all partners.

Tenancy in severalty. Sole ownership of property by one person.

Tenure. Manner of owning something, such as an interest in land or real estate, which is known as a tenancy.

Testate/(intestate). To die with (without) a last will and testament.

Third party. A person negotiating or entering into an agreement with the agent of a principal.

33% rule. FHLMC guideline allowing up to 33% of ASI for housing expenses plus other required periodic payments such as outlays for utilities, installment debt, alimony, and child support.

Tier. A row of townships north or south of a base line in the government rectangular survey system.

Title. Ownership of property; sometimes involves necessary documentation to evidence legal ownership.

Title evidence. Documentary proof of real property ownership.

Title insurance. Insurance against financial loss due to defects not listed in a title report or abstract.

Torrens system. State registration of real property ownership.

Tort. A wrongful or damaging act against another for which legal action may be initiated.

Township. In the rectangular survey system, land units that are six miles square, [36 sections], defined by the intersections of tier and range lines.

Tract index. Public record filing system, listing documents affecting each parcel of land.

Transferable development rights (TDR). Allows the sale of the right to develop so that one parcel may be developed more intensely if another parcel is developed less intensely; permits greater flexibility and variety in zoning and development of an area without increasing its overall density.

25% rule. FHLMC guideline allowing 25% of ASI for housing expenses.

Undisclosed principal. An agent who appears to be acting in self-interest, with no awareness by a third party.

Uniform Commercial Code. Laws governing the sale, financing, and use as security of personal property in commercial transactions.

Urban infrastructure. Necessary facilities of an urban community, such as sewer, water, power, transportation, communications, and school systems.

Urbanizing force. An influence for the concentration of people, buildings, and machines.

Usury. A rate of interest higher than that permitted by law charged on a loan.

Utility. Ability to satisfy human needs and desires.

VA loan. A mortgage loan on which the lender is guaranteed against loss by the Veteran's Administration; also known as a GI loan.

Vacancy and collection losses, V&CL. Income not received either because space is not rented or, if it is rented, the tenant fails to pay.

Value in exchange. Price that a property would most probably bring if sold; synonymous with objective value or market value.

Value in use. Worth of a property based on its merits to a specific user; usually greater than market value.

Variable expenses. Operating costs that fluctuate with occupancy; for example, more gas, water, electricity, and supplies are used with full occupancy than with partial occupancy.

Void contract. A contract that is not legally binding or enforceable.

Voidable contract. A contract that binds one of the parties but gives the other party the right either to live up to the agreement or to withdraw.

Wraparound mortgage, WAM. A mortgage that envelops existing mortgage or trust deed claims against a property even though it is subordinate to them.

Zoning. Public regulation of the use of land that is parcel specific.

Zoning variance. A deviation from a zoning law granted to alleviate hardship.

Index